Philological and Historical Commentary
on Ammianus Marcellinus XX

Philological and Historical Commentary on Ammianus Marcellinus XX

by

J. den Boeft
D. den Hengst
H.C. Teitler

Groningen
Egbert Forsten
1987

© Copyright 1987 by Egbert Forsten Groningen, Netherlands.

All rights reserved. No part of this book may be reproduced or translated in any form, by print, photoprint, microfilm or any other means without written permission from the publisher.

This book was translated and printed with financial support from the Netherlands Organisation for the Advancement of Pure Research (Z.W.O.)

CIP-GEGEVENS KONINKLIJKE BIBLIOTHEEK, DEN HAAG

Boeft, J. den

A commentary on Ammianus Marcellinus "Res Gestae" book 20
/ J. den Boeft, D. den Hengst and H.C. Teitler. -
Groningen : Forsten
Voortz. van: Philological and historical commentary on
Ammianus Marcellinus / by P. de Jonge. - Bd. 1-8. -
Groningen, 1935-1982. - Met lit. opg.
ISBN 90 6980 012 8 geb.
SISO klas-1 851 UDC 871
Trefw.: Ammianus Marcellinus "Res Gestae".

Printed by Wolters-Noordhoff Grafische Bedrijven bv, Groningen

To P. de Jonge

Preface

This commentary on book 20 of Ammianus Marcellinus' *Res Gestae* continues the series of commentaries started by P. de Jonge in 1935. The last of these, which treated book 19, was published in 1982. In its preface the author announced his retirement from the project. Consultations with him and with the publisher made us decide to carry on the work after the example which had been set, viz. to write a detailed philological and historical interpretation of the text. If our decision already gave expression to our great respect for the scholarship of our predecessor, during the preparations for this book our admiration has continually grown. On numerous occasions we have referred to his notes on the preceding books. The cases where we could not share a particular insight and the alterations in emphasis, design and contents which we deemed necessary are due either to the progress made by the increasing scholarly attention to the *Res Gestae* and their author over the past decades or of course to our own idiosyncrasies. Because in writing our commentary we were always aware of the standards set by our predecessor, we found it natural to dedicate these primitiae of our labours to him.

Our commentary, the character of which apart from our own predilection is due to its being a continuation of an existing series, differs considerably from the valuable historical commentaries on books 20 and 21 by J. Szidat. Whereas the latter in accordance with the title of his work first and foremost dealt with the historical aspect of the *Res Gestae* and paid only restricted attention to philological, linguistic and literary matters, our purpose is to provide a commentary in which notes on contents and form are combined into an integrated whole. Apart from this difference in overall design we favoured another interpretation or a change of emphasis in a number of cases and we further had the possibility of introducing the results of more recent research. Consulting Szidat's two volumes has always been stimulating, as our references to his comments make clear.

We gladly express our gratitude for the help we received from others. Dr. De Jonge has read a draft of the whole commentary and his advice has resulted in many improvements. Professors Leeman and Pinkster deprived Cicero of some of their precious attention to look at parts of our work. Their criticism of certain sections of the text has also proved helpful to us in designing the rest of the commentary. The papers of our students Pia van de Wiel, Dick van de Vrie and Gabriel Bakkum on problems in ch. 4, 8 and 11 respectively were useful for our comments on these chapters. In correcting our English Hotze Mulder rendered us a much needed service.

Thanks are due to the Netherlands Organization for the Advancement of Pure Research (ZWO), which subsidized the correction and publication and also granted us a subsidy for a stay at the Fondation Hardt at Vandoeuvres

(CH), where we put the finishing touches to our manuscript. Finally we thank the publisher, Mr. E. Forsten, for his continuous devotion to Ammianus Marcellinus.

J. den Boeft
D. den Hengst
H.C. Teitler

Introduction

Neque multo post, cum Germaniciani exercitus a Galliarum praesidio tollerentur, consensu militum Iulianus factus Augustus est (Eutr. *Brev.* 10.15.1). This concisely worded information from another contemporary historian may serve as a short summary of the contents of Ammianus Marcellinus' *Res Gestae* book 20, which is dominated by Julian's unexpected and unpremeditated – that is the author's emphatically defended version – rise to Augustan dignity. All other facts are presented as either directly connected with the pronunciamento or given such a place in the overall composition of this book that they are relevant to the description of the central event. The book itself can be regarded as the hinge in the diptych formed by books 15-19 and 21-25 respectively. In these books the *Res Gestae* gradually turns into a *Res Gestae Divi Iuliani*, beginning with the brief snapshot of the prince in 15.2.7-8 and winding up with the elogium in 25.4. In the first half of the history, viz. books 15-19, much space is allotted to Julian's successful career as Caesar in the Western part of the empire, whilst in the second part, viz. books 21-25, Julian's actions and measures as Augustus in the Eastern provinces take first place. The cardinal function of book 20 comes out clearly in the flashbacks to and the anticipations of the first and second half respectively, especially in Julian's speech in ch. 5, sections 3-7, where the newly installed Augustus reminds his soldiers of the dangers and victories which they have shared in the past and briefly sketches the guidelines for his future administration.

In the composition of the book itself several examples of diptych structure can be detected, which testify to the author's wish to provide contrasting pictures of the two protagonists, Constantius and Julian. Two of these cases frame the book. At its beginning, the first chapter reports Julian's sound military insight in sending an experienced soldier to Britain, currently harried by Picts and Scots, whereas in the second chapter we are told how Constantius dismissed a general whose skill could have been of great use on the Eastern front. This clear contrast finds its counterpart at the end of the book in chapters 10 and 11 respectively. The first of these consists of a deliberately succinct report of Julian's successful campaign against the Franks, for which barely 100 words are used, although the expedition lasted three months, as Julian himself tells. In contrast Constantius' protracted and ultimately unsuccessful attempt to recapture Bezabde occupies almost ten times the space in ch. 11. Just as the first two chapters oppose Julian's correct handling of military matters to Constantius' irresponsible removal of a competent officer, the concluding pair emphasizes the contrast between Julian's swift success and Constantius' slow failure. Ammianus was not responsible for the chapter-divisions, but nonetheless the symmetry we note confirms their correctness.

A further diptych appears in the main part of the book, viz. ch. 4–9. In chapters 4 and 5, which contain the narrative of Julian's elevation to the purple, Ammianus sketches Julian's relationship with the soldiers, who, for all their rash and emotional behaviour, show a correct appreciation of their hero's worth. Chapters 8 and 9, on the other hand, are devoted to Julian's relations to Constantius, who through envy is unable to appreciate his cousin. Flashbacks and anticipations provide a link between both pairs of chapters, e.g. when Julian fails to persuade the soldiers to obey the orders of the legitimate emperor in ch. 4 sections 16 sqq. and when in ch. 9 section 7 Constantius' answer, which is being read before the assembly of soldiers, merely draws the cry '*Auguste Iuliane*' from them. A more general connection is created by the reminiscences of the narrative in ch. 4, to be found in the text of Julian's letter to Constantius in ch. 8.

Chapters 6 and 7, which occupy the center of the book, form the hinge of the diptych 4–5 and 8–9. In order to clarify this, it is necessary to look at possible alternative locations for Ammianus' narrative of the eastern events reported in these two chapters. A full report of the events of March-June 360 on a scale commensurate with his history was naturally required. Now Ammianus could have provided this after having given a continuous account of the pronunciamento and its immediate sequel, viz. the break-down of all negotiations with Constantius. A formula like *eodem tempore* or *haec dum geruntur*, which in fact appears at the beginning of ch. 6, would have marked quite aptly the return to a previous point in the chronological order. Ammianus, however, chose a different arrangement of the facts. Precisely in the middle of the narrative of Julian's rise and the subsequent fruitless negotiations with Constantius he places an extensive description of Sapor's siege and capture of Singara and Bezabde. The horizon against which the mounting conflict between the two adversaries stands out is suddenly darkened by the appearance of the dangerous and menacing Persian king (*truculentus rex ille Persarum*, 6.1), a circumstance which ought to have given Constantius all the more reason to agree to Julian's urgent proposal to cooperate. He did not and the reader will have no difficulty in drawing the right conclusions after studying the 20th book. At the beginning Constantius dismissed the only general who would have been capable of handling the Persian threat; in the middle he underestimates the menace when dealing with Julian's proposal; it comes as no surprise that at the end he suffers a major military reverse.

The fine symmetrical structure sketched above seems to lead to the inevitable conclusion that the astronomical material in ch. 3 is a 'Fremdkörper', isolated from the rest of the book. Although this view is not entirely impossible, it is unattractive and indeed unlikely, as will be pointed out in the introduction to ch. 3. Possibly the main subject of the chapter, the solar and lunar eclipses, which of course are short-lived by definition, point to the downfall of Ammianus' great favourite Ursicinus and the subsequent rise of another man whom he greatly revered, the emperor Julian.

As to the author's sources the last scholarly word has not been said, but it is perfectly clear that apart from any authors he may have used he relied first and foremost on personal experience and the testimony of eye-witnesses and that he did research on official documents. The first of these sources of information is irrelevant for the present book, an example of the second can be found in ch. 2, the contents of which, viz. Ursicinus' 'trial' and dismissal, in all probability are owed to the leading character in that tragic scene, whilst the third comes out tantalizingly in the section in ch. 8 in which Ammianus tells how he was refused permission to investigate the contents of a letter from Julian to Constantius (ch. 8 section 18).

Our examination of book 20 has not revealed any fresh clues concerning the author's sources, but it has shown that the interpretation of Ammianus' version can profit from a comparison with the other main sources for the episode. These are in chronological order Julian's *Letter to the Athenians* 281c sqq., some passages in Libanius' *Orations* 12, 13 and 18, Zosimus' *New History* 3.8.3–3.9.4 and Zonaras' *Epitome* 13.10.11–28. The commentary will often refer to these accounts and to the many similarities which, as could be expected, are to be found in them. It is worth noting that the closest parallels, at times even of a verbal nature, are presented by Zonaras, especially concerning Julian's letter to Constantius. The first three accounts mentioned testify to an evident pro-Julianic bias. Although Zonaras is by no means sympathetic to Julian, neither is he rabidly hostile. He even takes into consideration the possibility that Julian was pressed into his revolutionary action: perhaps he yielded unwillingly (τάχα καὶ ἄκων ... ὑπείξας) to the soldiers' pressure. Prejudice or partiality is felt more strongly in the other three reports, not only in the eulogies of Libanius or Julian's own apologetic account, but also in Zosimus' history. Ammianus without doubt is a supporter of Julian, but his report clearly distinguishes itself from the other three by a far more subtly devised survey of the events. The overall structure has already been dealt with above, but even in details some deft touches can be detected. Two examples may illustrate this. In sending the *magister equitum* Lupicinus to turbulent Britain Julian may well have intended to get rid of this potential nuisance. In ch. 1, however, Ammianus stresses that he found it politically unwise to leave France himself and that Lupicinus was a true military expert; near the end of ch. 4, in which the author has managed to interweave Julian's loyalty to Constantius and his reluctance to accept the demands of the soldiers into his own account of the pronunciamento proper, he casually drops the term *perterritus* to add the finishing touch to his portrait of Julian's conduct of the affair; perhaps the neatest example occurs in ch. 9, where we are told that, after the utter failure of his mission to Paris, Leonas returned home *incolumis*. By explicitly stating this self-evident fact, the author means to emphasize quietly Julian's correct treatment of Constantius' satellites.

This last detail aptly illustrates the relationship between the author's veracity and his partiality to Julian. Ammianus is genuinely loath to proceed by way of lies and distortion. The end he is pursuing is the discovery of historical truth and its subsequent exposition 'sine ira et studio': *utcumque potui veritatem scrutari, ... narravimus ordine casuum exposito diversorum ...* (15.1.1); *... opus veritatem professum numquam, ut arbitror, sciens silentio ausus corrumpere vel mendacio* (31.16.9). The second of these statements, which elegantly combines the profession of intellectual integrity with the modest admission of potential mistakes, implicitly poses the problem. If the qualities of such eminent emperors as Titus, Trajan, Antoninus Pius and Marcus Aurelius were really united in the person of Julian (16.1.4), that fundamental fact not only has to be reported, but it will also illuminate the account of his deeds. Ammianus certainly did not compromise the integrity of his work through deliberate lies, but he may be guilty of occasional dissimulation: does 20.4.13 really provide an adequate summary of the conversations at the dinner to which Julian had invited the officers of the eastbound auxiliaries? Does the extremely brief account of the campaign against the Atthuarii in ch. 10 not deny the reader information which might be less than favourable to Julian? Such doubts are counterbalanced by other instances, e.g. when in the first sentence of ch. 4 Constantius' demand for more troops is ascribed to his jealousy of Julian, but the reality of the Persian menace is also explicitly stated.

Apart from *mendacium* and *silentium*, however, there is a third even more complicated factor, of which the author perhaps was not even consciously aware, viz. the suggestive handling of true facts. In the selection and ordering of these, in the emphasis laid on some of them, in the implicit suggestion of causes and consequences the historian's tendentious ordering of the facts brings out his personal convictions. There is nothing deplorable in that, as long as he is essentially honest and tells things which are really important and 'memoria dignum', in accordance with the 'praecepta historiae': *... non humilium minutias indagare causarum ...* (26.1.1).

Legenda

1 Whereas Dr. De Jonge used the edition of C.U. Clark (Berlin 1910-1915) as the basic text for his commentaries, in our case the lemmata are taken from W. Seyfarth's Teubner-edition (Leipzig 1978), with one alteration: consonantial *u* is always printed as *v* (*venit* instead of *uenit*).

2 For references to Greek authors we follow the abbreviations and indications of books and chapters in H.G. Liddell and R. Scott, *A Greek-English Lexicon*. Passages in Latin authors are indicated according to the system of the *Oxford Latin Dictionary*. For later and Christian authors we follow the *Thesaurus Linguae Latinae*.

Some exceptions to these rules:
- In the case of Caesar, Sallust and Tacitus the division of the chapters in sections in the Teubner-editions has also been taken into account.
- Seneca's *Dialogi* are referred to with the title of the individual works.
- For the Panegyrici Latini Mynors' OCT-edition has been used.
- Calcidius is referred to with Chalcid. and quoted from Waszink's edition.

3 As to secundary literature the following rules are observed:
- References to the six volumes of De Jonge's commentaries are usually given with 'see (the note) ad ...' or 'q.v.'.
- Page-numbers etc. of Szidat's two volumes are only mentioned when the reference concerns another section of the text than the one discussed.
- Books or articles are normally referred to with the name of the author(s), the year of publication and the page(s). The full titles can be found in the bibliography; e.g. with Hagendahl, 1921, 64 is meant H. Hagendahl, *Studia Ammianea*, Uppsala 1921, page 64.
- Occasionally reference is made to commentaries on other authors, e.g. Austin's on Virgil and Koestermann's on Tacitus, or to well-known editions like those in the Budé-series. As a rule these works are omitted from the bibliography.
- Of the following books, which are referred to quite frequently, only the name of the author and the page(s) are given:

    Bitter = N. Bitter, *Kampfschilderungen bei Ammianus Marcellinus*, Bonn 1976.

    Blomgren = S. Blomgren, *De sermone Ammiani Marcellini quaestiones variae*, Diss. Uppsala 1937.

    Ehrismann = H. Ehrismann, *De temporum et modorum usu Ammianeo*, Diss. Strasbourg 1886.

    Fesser = H. Fesser, *Sprachliche Beobachtungen zu Ammianus Marcellinus*, Diss. Breslau 1932.

Harmon	=	A.M. Harmon, *The Clausula in Ammianus Marcellinus*, New Haven 1910 (Transactions of the Connecticut Academy of Arts and Science, 16, 117–245).
Hassenstein	=	G. Hassenstein, *De syntaxi Ammiani Marcellini*, Diss. Königsberg 1877.
Hoffmann	=	D. Hoffmann, *Das spätrömische Bewegungsheer und die Notitia Dignitatum*, 2 vols., Düsseldorf 1969.
Jones	=	A.H.M. Jones, *The Later Roman Empire (284–602). A Social Economic and Administrative Survey*, Oxford 1964 (repr. 1986).
Kühner-Stegmann	=	R. Kühner and C. Stegmann, *Ausführliche Grammatik der lateinischen Sprache*, II, Satzlehre, 2 vols., Hannover 1955[4], 1976[5].
Leumann	=	M. Leumann, *Lateinische Laut- und Formenlehre*, Munich 1977.
Sabbah	=	G. Sabbah, *La méthode d'Ammien Marcellin. Recherches sur la construction du discours historique dans les Res Gestae*, Paris 1978.
Szantyr	=	J.B. Hofmann and A. Szantyr, *Lateinische Syntax und Stilistik*, Munich 1965 (repr. 1972).
Wagner	=	J.A. Wagner, *Ammiani Marcellini quae supersunt*, cum notis integris Frid. Lindenbrogii, Henr. et Hadr. Valesiorum et Iac. Gronovii, quibus Thom. Reinesii quasdam et suas adiecit, editionem absolvit Car. Gottl. Aug. Erfurdt, 3 vols., Leipzig 1808 (repr. in 2 vols., Hildesheim 1975).

The following translations are often referred to with the name of the translator only:

Rolfe	=	J.C. Rolfe, *Ammianus Marcellinus*, with an English translation, 3 vols., London-Cambridge Mass. 1935–1939 (repr. 1971–1972).
Selem	=	A. Selem, *Le Storie di Ammiano Marcellino. Testo e Traduzione*, Turin 1965 (repr. 1973).
Seyfarth	=	W. Seyfarth, *Ammianus Marcellinus, Römische Geschichte. Lateinisch und Deutsch und mit einem Kommentar versehen*, II, Berlin 1983[5].

Veh	= O. Veh, *Ammianus Marcellinus. Das römische Weltreich vor dem Untergang*, übersetzt von O. Veh, eingeleitet und erläutert von G. Wirth, Zurich-Munich 1974.

4 In cases where this is relevant for the interpretation the cursus is indicated as follows:

revocávit in státum : cursus planus
sublátius éminens : cursus tardus
fécit et vectigáles : cursus velox

Chapter 1

In the opening chapter of book 20 Amm. returns to Julian, whom he had taken leave of in 18.3.1 with the eulogistic phrase *haec dum in Galliis caelestis corrigit cura*, followed by *in comitatu Augusti turbo novarum exoritur rerum*, introducing the downfall of Barbatio. In a similar sequence Julian is depicted in ch. 1 as the responsible and competent leader, whereas in ch. 2 Constantius compromises the Roman position in the East by dismissing Ursicinus.

Amm. describes the military situation on the borders of Britain and Gaul as unstable and menacing, which justifies both Lupicinus' mission and Julian's decision to stay in Paris himself. It also helps to explain why later on Constantius' order to transfer troops to the East (20.4.2–3) is resented by the soldiers and looked upon with anxiety by Julian (20.4.4–5).

As Szidat has pointed out (I 42 and 97), Lupicinus' mission to Britain might have been told in connection with Julian's pronunciamento in Paris. That, however, would have made the reader suspicious with regard to Julian's real motives in sending Lupicinus away. Szidat's suggestion that Amm. separates the two events precisely to avoid this suspicion is convincing.

1. 1 *Haec ... rerum series fuit* The opening sentence refers to the content of bks. 18 and 19. *Rerum series* is found only here in Amm., who prefers *series gestorum* (25.8.12, 25.8.15, 27.9.3, 28.1.22, 29.1.4., – *rerum gestarum* in 27.11.7). *Rerum series* is found once in Livy: 21.5.3 *rerum serie ... tractus ad id bellum*. For the similar expressions *ordo rerum* and *– gestorum*, used by Amm. to conclude digressions (14.8.15, 22.16.24, 23.4.15) and in recapitulating sentences (17.13.16, 20.11.1), see Samberger, 1969, 378/9. In 29.3.1 Amm. combines the two expressions: *confunditur ordo seriesque gestorum*. Comparable opening sentences are listed by De Jonge ad 18.1.1.

per Illyricum perque orientem In the fourth century, until the final division of the Empire in 395, the region along the eastern side of the Adriatic, from Epirus to Noricum, normally formed part of one *praefectura Illyrici Italiae et Africae*. During some periods, however, Illyricum was an independent prefecture. Cf. ad 19.11.2 and see Palanque, 1969, who, modifying and rectifying his own earlier opinions (cf. Palanque, 1951 and 1955) finally reached the following conclusion: "Je pense donc que la grande préfecture d'Illyricum a existé de 345 à 361 et de 375 à 379 seulement. Elle ne reparaîtra que fugitivement en 387 ..." (Palanque, 1969, 605). See now also Demougeot,

1981. By *Oriens* can be meant either the *dioecesis Orientis* (more precisely: parts of that diocese, cf. the note ad 18.5.2) or, in a wider sense, the East including the dioceses of *Asiana* and *Pontica* (cf. the note ad 18.6.19). In view of the events described in bk. 19 the former is to be preferred here.

consulatu vero Constantii ... incitatis et bella Amm. combines the three essential elements, time (*consulatu Constantii*), place (*in Britanniis*), and central figure (*Caesar*) in one opening sentence (cf. Chausserie-Laprée, 1969, 41/2). Its structure is complicated by the insertion of participle constructions and the accumulation of subordinate clauses. The sentence may be analysed as follows:
consulatu ... Iuliani
in Britanniis cum Scottorum ... excursus ... vastarent
        rupta quiéte condicta
        et implicaret formido províncias
        cladium congérie féssas
Caesar ... verebatur ire subsídio transmarinis
        hiemem agens apud Parisios
        distractusque in sollicitúdines várias
        (ut rettulimus ... fecísse Constántem)
        ne ... relínqueret Gállias
        Alamannis ... incitatis

consulatu ... Constantii deciens terque Iuliani The year 360. For the use of the multiplicativa *deciens* and *ter* with *consulatu* cf. 14.10.1 *Constantius consulatu suo septies et Caesaris iterum*. In the abl. abs. *Augusto novies seque iterum consule* (16.11.1) the multiplicativa are less surprising. A similar expression is found already in Nepos *Han*. 5.3 *M. Claudium Marcellum quinquies consulem*, TLL IV 570.10; Szantyr 214.

Scottorum Pictorumque The *Scotti* (or *Scoti*), a Celtic tribe of Ireland, settled in Scotland in the course of the fourth century. Together with the *Picti*, who lived in the northern part of Britain, they threatened the Roman provinces according to Amm. not only in 359, but also in 365 (26.4.5) and in 367 (27.8.5 *eo tempore Picti in duas gentes divisi, Dicalydonas et Veturiones*). Cf. Szidat and Todd, 1981, 231–2.

gentium ferarum excursus ... vastarent For the phraseology cf. 14.10.1 *quorum crebris excursibus vastabantur confines limitibus terrae*. *Gentes ferae* is used regularly by Amm. to indicate tribes and peoples on the borders of the Empire: 15.10.2 and 25.4.12 (Germans), 19.2.12 and 18.4.1 (the Persians and their allies), 29.5.44 (Africans), 31.12.8 (Huns). The expression *excursus vastarent* (cf. *formido implicaret* below) is treated in Blomgren 83–94 under the heading of personificatio. It should be noted, however, that abstract subjects with *vastare* are common in all periods of Latin.

rupta quiete condicta   Amm. refers to the expedition of Constans in 343, mentioned immediately below and in 27.8.4. For *quies* 'peace, tranquil conditions' cf. Liv. 2.48.6 *bellum quiete, quietem bello in vicem eludentes*. *Quies* is a goddess in 19.11.6, q.v. *Condicere* 'to agree upon' also occurs in 26.6.14. With this meaning it is found for the first time in Plautus (*Cur.* 5). It reappears with some frequency from Apuleius onwards, TLL IV 139.8 sqq.

loca limitibus vicina   The expression can, of course, refer both to the neighbourhood *trans* and to that *cis* Hadrian's wall, but, as Szidat rightly observes, in 359 the Roman sphere of influence north of the wall will have been the main target of the enemy raids. For an analysis of the defense systems in the different periods of the Roman Empire in general and of the function of *limites* in particular see Luttwak, 1976.

implicaret formido   Amm. uses *implicare* in this way again in 20.4.13 *hocque angore impliciti* and 26.6.20 *adventantium periculorum angoribus implicatus*. It is found often, but not exclusively, in poetry: Verg. *A.* 11.108–9 *quaenam vos tanto fortuna ... implicuit bello*, *Culex* 200 *implicuit* (v.l. *implevit*) *dira formidine mentem*, TLL VII 1.643.28.

provincias   *Britannia prima, Britannia secunda, Maxima Caesariensis* and *Flavia Caesariensis*. Cf. the note ad 14.5.7, Frere, 1967, 210–212 and see, for later developments, Hind, 1975. In one of the lost books Amm. had given a description of Britain (cf. 27.8.4).

congerie   *Congeries* is used by Amm. both in its literal meaning (15.10.4 and 17.12.4 *pruinarum –*, 23.2.8 'hay stacks') and metaphorically, cf. 21.16.11 and 31.15.5 *malorum –*. As TLL IV 276.54 sqq. shows, it becomes more frequent in later Latin prose, e.g. Hier. *Ep.* 77.7; August. *Serm.* 261.10; Macr. *Sat.* praef. 1.4 and 1.5.1.

hiemem agens apud Parisios Caesar   There is no specific reference to the last mention of Julian's whereabouts in 18.2. Samberger, 1969, 439 rightly interprets this as a sign that the narrative about Julian is not simply continued but that we enter a new phase in his history.

Apud Parisios 'in Paris'. *Lutetia* (or *Luticia*, cf. the note ad 15.11.3) is used by Amm. only once (15.11.3), as against *Parisii* twelve times. Cf. Szidat and see the chapter "Et Lutèce devint Paris ... (fin IIIe – fin Ve siècles)" in Périn, 1984, 362–372.

distractusque in sollicitudines varias   Cf. 22.10.1 *quibus distrahebatur multiformibus curis*, 31.7.1 *haec ... Valentem principem in sollicitudines varias distraxerunt*, Liv. 22.7.10 *tot in curas distracti animi ... erant*, Hier. *adv. Iovin.* 1.13 *in multas ... sollicitudinum partes miseriarumque distractus*. TLL V 1.1542.17–44.

verebatur ire subsidio transmarinis   *Vereor* with inf. is found only here in Amm. With this meaning ('to be afraid (to do something)') it is found from Plautus onwards, Szantyr 347. In classical prose *transmarinus* is used as an attribute with *gentes* (Liv. 26.24.4), *vectigalia* (Cic. *Agr.* 2.80), *regiones* (Sen. *Ep.* 17.3); this seems to be the first place where it is used substantively.

ut rettulimus ante fecisse Constantem   Constans was the youngest son of Constantine the Great and Fausta, made *Caesar* in 333 and, together with his brothers Constantine II and Constantius II, declared *Augustus* in 337. In 340 a war broke out between Constans and Constantine II, in which the former was victorious. He ruled as sole emperor in the West until his death in 350. Cf. Seeck, 1901; Moreau, 1959 and *PLRE I*, Constans 3. In 27.8.4 Amm. refers to his description, now lost, of the military campaigns of Constans in Britain, which took place in 343.

rectore   *Rector* is a very general word, used by Amm. for all kinds of high officers and officials. "Rapporté à l'empereur, il sert à qualifier et à exprimer un jugement plutôt qu'une définition. Il figure le responsable, du bon au pire; il entre dans la phraséologie du Chef. Chez Ammien, *rector* a un sens concret, plus affectif que cérébral", Béranger, 1976, 56. Cf. the note ad 14.10.8 and A. and A. Cameron, 1964, 326.

Alamannis ad saevitiam etiamtum incitatis et bella   *Etiamtum* refers to the great victories won by Julian. At the same time it foreshadows the war to be fought against the Alamanni by Valentinian in 369. According to Müller-Seidel, 1955, 235, fear of the Alamanni in 360 was not justified by the facts, but only used by Julian as a pretext for staying in Gaul himself while removing Lupicinus. Cf. Szidat and, in general, Barceló, 1981, 34–49. This view has been contested by Blockley, 1980 (1), 480, who argues that it would have been too dangerous for Julian to leave Lupicinus isolated in Britain with a notoriously fractious part of the western army. Drinkwater, 1983, 378–379, on the other hand, accepted the suggestion, but only with a proviso.

According to him Lupicinus' removal had been arranged not by Julian himself, but by a small group of the Caesar's friends (throughout his paper Drinkwater argues against any direct involvement of Julian in the events leading up to the pronunciamento). See for Amm. on the Alamanni Neuscheler, 1938 and on the history of the Alamanni in general Dirlmeier-Gottlieb, 1976-1984, Christlein, 1979[2].

ad saevitiam ... et bella More examples of this type of inconcinnitas, viz. the combination of substantives in the singular and the plural, in Hagendahl, 1921, 113 sqq.

1.2 *ad haec ratione vel vi componenda* *Vel vi* is a certain emendation by Valesius of *vel* VE, based on the identical expression in the preceding chapter (19.13.2). Müller-Seidel, 1955, 233, interprets this repetition as an indication of a change in Julian's policy towards the barbarians. Julian's more diplomatic approach is to be understood, in her opinion, as part of his preparations to seize power. The phrase may be intended as an apology: Julian gave Lupicinus the same instructions as Constantius had given Lauricius in similar circumstances, thereby showing his adherence to the policy of his superior (19.13.2).

ire ... Lupícinum plácuit As the cursus shows, Amm. accentuates this proper name on the antepenultimate despite the fact that the penultimate is long (Szantyr I 224). Cf. 18.2.7 *Floréntio et Lupícino*, 20.4.9 *abséntis Lupícini*, 20.9.5 *successórem Lupícini*. The same applies to the name Ursicinus.

After the death of his predecessor Severus (who seems to have died shortly after the summer of 358, cf. 17.10.1), Fl. Lupicinus was, in 358 or 359, invested with the office of *magister equitum per Gallias*, or rather (Demandt, 1970, 577 rightly warns against the habit of using later attested titles anachronistically), with the office which in due course of time officially (cf. *Not. Dign. Occ.* 1.7) came to be called the *magisterium equitum per Gallias* (compare for this office the note ad 20.2.1). The official title is not found in Amm., who is somewhat loose and inexact in his use of military titles, for the sake of variety (cf. Rolfe, I, 1935, xxxiv n. 3; De Jonge ad 15.5.36), or to avoid technical terms (cf. Szidat I, 101; A. & A. Cameron, 1964, 326), but also perhaps because at this date terminology was still flexible. It should be borne in mind that this post was created only recently (in 355, according to Demandt, 1970, 573-574, contra Ensslin, 1930, 111). Lupicinus did not occupy his post in Gaul for long: in 360 he was succeeded by Gomoarius (see the note ad 20.9.5 for a possible explanation for this change), but continued his military career in the following years. Cf. for details Seeck, 1927 and *PLRE I*, Lupicinus 6. See also Von Haehling, 1978, 254-255.

In 18.2.7 Lupicinus was mentioned simply as *Severi successor*. Now that he is going to play a role in the events leading up to the proclamation of Julian as Augustus, Amm. characterizes him more fully. The fact that this sketch of character is not very flattering is seen by Rosen, 1978, 420 as an indication of Julian's feelings towards Lupicinus: "Das ungünstige Bild, das Ammian bei seinem Amtsantritt von ihm zeichnet (xx 1, 2), ist sicherer Hinweis, dass er ebenfalls von Beginn an mit Julian nicht gut auskam"; Caltabiano, 1979, 426-7. This predominantly negative characterization of Lupicinus, who is seen as a source of danger for Julian in 20.9.9, is balanced by the description in Libanius (*or.* 1.164).

bellicosum sane ... crudelis Lupicinus is portrayed as every inch a soldier. *Bellicosus* is a positive quality, cf. 19.3.3 *bellicosus homo* about Amm.'s favourite, Ursicinus. His qualities as a soldier, however, are given less prominence than his pride, greed and cruelty. Sabbah 421-8 has shown to what extent Amm. makes use of physiognomical data in describing the outward appearance of his personages. *Supercilia* are, of course, a sign of pride (e.g. Plin. *Nat.* 11.138 *supercilia ... indicant fastum*). In this sense they are mentioned more often by Amm.: 16.12.4 *ardua subrigens supercilia ut saepe secundis rebus elatus*, q.v. The opposite idea is expressed in 27.3.15 *supercilia humum spectantia*. Even the hesitation between greed or cruelty as the dominant characteristic can be traced to the physiognomists. Sabbah 425, n. 79 compares Adamantius 1.6 p. 308 Foerster Ὅσοι δὲ καὶ τὰς ὀφρῦς ἐπαίρουσι ... δυσβούλοι, ὠμόφρονες and p. 309 εἰ δὲ καὶ τὸ μέτωπον ἅμα ταῖς ὀφρύσι σπῷη εἰς τὸ μέσον, κερδαλεώτερός ἐστιν ὁ ἀνήρ. For *ut cornua* cf. 21.16.1 *numquam erigens cornua militarium. Cornua* is used metaphorically for *ferocitas* (TLL IV 973.21-39): Lact. *mort. pers.* 32.3 *at ille tollit audacius cornua*, Porph. Hor. *Carm.* 3.21.18 *per cornua ergo violentiam cerebri intellegi vult*.

de tragico, quod aiunt, coturno strepentem Otto, 1890, 95. The parallel in 27.11.2 may serve as a commentary: *ut videretur* (Probus) *cum sibi fideret, de coturno strepere tragico et, ubi paveret, omni humilior socco*. The Roman senators are qualified as *coturnatos et turgidos* in 28.4.27 (cf. 20.9.9 of Lupicinus *homo superbae mentis et turgidae*). See also 28.1.4. This use of *coturnus* (= *tumor*) is confined to late Latin prose (Ennodius, Cassiodorus, Greg. Tur.), TLL IV 1088.43-53.

super quo diu ambigebatur Diu (diutius, semper) ambigere followed by an indirect question frequently occurs in Amm., e.g. 20.4.11 *cum ambigeretur diutius, qua pergerent via* and 14.6.13, 15.5.10, 21.1.1, 29.6.9. With *super* it is found in 15.9.2 and 31.10.21 *ambigenti super corona capiti imponenda Iuliano Caesari*. See the note ad 14.7.12 on *super = de*, and Szantyr 281 ("allgemein im Spätlatein").

avarus esset potius an crudelis Indirect questions with *potius ... an* are less common than one might expect. In Amm. this is the only instance; TLL II 11, 25-30 and X 2.346.74-347.10.

I. 3 *velitari auxilio* *Velitaris* is used twice by Amm., here adjectivally, in 19.3.1 as a noun; compare 16.11.9 (*auxiliares velites*) and see the note ad 19.3.1 *compositis velitaribus*.

Herulis scilicet et Batavis numerisque See Blomgren 28 on this use of the copulae: (A et B) C-que, and in general Pinkster 1969. On Amm.'s use of appositions see Blomgren 100/1.

It is legitimate to assume that from the beginning the field army created by Constantine consisted of vexillations of cavalry and of legions of infantry, and also of infantry formations of a new type, *auxilia* (Jones 97). Some of these *auxilia*, which operated very often in pairs, seem to have had an even older origin (cf. Hoffmann I 170: "Das *Auxilium* war also im besondern das Werk Maximians"). The history of the *Aeruli* = *Heruli* = *Eruli* and *Batavi* as a pair of auxiliaries (mentioned together also in 20.4.2 and 27.8.6), for example, dates, according to Hoffmann I 156-157, from the time of the Tetrarchy. Although direct evidence is lacking, Hoffmann I 4 tentatively estimates the strength of these new units at ca. 800 men. Cf. for *Heruli* and *Batavi* in general the note ad 16.12.45 and see for the *Heruli* Lakatos, 1978, for the *Batavi* Willems, 1986.

numerisque Moesiacorum duobus Even if Hoffmann I 204 is right in identifying these *numeri* with legions (note, however, the caution with which he proposes his suggestion and the uncertainty as regards the question which legions are meant), one should not translate *numeri* as legions (contra Seyfarth II 1983[5], 85). Cf. Jones 610: "This word (viz. *numeri*) became from the fourth century onwards increasingly common as a general term covering units of all kinds". It is anyhow hazardous to try to estimate the strength of Lupicinus' expeditionary force, as Szidat does.

adulta hieme A Sallustianism, as TLL I 803.11 shows. See the note ad 14.2.9.

Bononiam Boulogne-sur-Mer, headquarters of the *classis Britannica*. Cf. 20.9.9 and 27.8.6. Add to the literature cited by Szidat: Will, 1966 and 1969.

observato flatu secundo Cf. 17.2.3 *observata nocte illuni* and 19.6.7 *observata nocte squalida et interlunio*. The same use of *observare* is found in Liv. 3.22.6

signum observari iussit, Plin. *Pan.* 26.1 *observare principis egressum* and Ov. *Ep.* 7.173 *tempus* (sc. to leave the harbour) *ut observem, manda mihi.* TLL IX 2.205.70 sqq.

ad Rutupias   Richborough, in Kent. In 367 Theodosius, the father of the future emperor, also chose *Rutupiae*, the principal landing point from the continent, to start his British expedition (27.8.6).

The importance of Richborough as a Roman town can be surmised from the approximately 56.000 coins found there (cf. Reece, 1981; see also Johnson, 1981 and Philp, 1981).

Lundinium   London, of course, in the fourth century also called *Augusta* (27.8.7 and 28.3.1, with Merrifield, 1965, 65–66; Frere, 1967, 211; Hind, 1975, 108 and Marsden, 1980, 169).

suscepto pro rei qualitate consilio   Cf. 14.10.9 *suscepto pro instantium rerum ratione consilio* and 26.6.2 *pro cognitorum ageret textu. Qualitas* is used sparingly by Amm., only in 23.6.86 (pearls) *minima autem vel magna pro qualitate haustuum figurantur* (Plin. *Nat.* 9.107 *partum concharum esse margaritas pro qualitate roris accepti*) and in 29.2.5 *de qualitate* (i.e. the sex) *partus uxoris consuluisse. Suscipere consilium* is found in Cicero (*Rep.* 1.42, *Off.* 1.112) and Tacitus (*Hist.* 2.76.1, *Ann.* 4.64.1).

festinaret ocius ad procinctum   Cf. 29.5.9 *ad procinctus ire ocius festinabat*, TLL IX 2.415.17 sqq. In conformity with classical usage *ocius* is frequently used in giving or executing orders (17.13.1, 19.12.5, 20.4.3, 26.1.5), normally without real comparative force, the exception being 22.7.10 *solito ocius*. De Jonge ad 16.11.6 distinguishes three meanings of *procinctus*: 'campaign', e.g. 22.4.6 *Spartanum militem coercitum acriter quod procinctus tempore ausus sit videri sub tecto*, 'fight, battle', e.g. 19.2.6 *rapido turmarum processu in procinctum alacritate omni tendentium* and 'army', as in 18.2.17 *Vadomarius ... mirabatur ... apparatum ambitiosi procinctus*. The second meaning is predominant here.

Chapter 2

This chapter reports the final outcome of the intrigues aiming at the downfall, or at least the removal from active service, of Ursicinus. It thus provides a sequel to the information presented in 18.5.4–5. There it is told that the court clique (*Palatina cohors*) 'starting the old song again in order to ruin us' (*palinodiam in exitium concinens nostrum*) found ways to harm a fine soldier, at the instigation of the eunuchs (*auctore et incitatore coetu spadonum*). They succeeded in having Ursicinus relieved of his Eastern command and replaced by the incompetent Sabinianus. Ursicinus was to take over the post of *magister peditum* attached to the emperor's court, a post which was vacant as a result of the execution of his predecessor Barbatio (18.3.1–4). The real motive behind the last-mentioned change was to have him close at hand as a victim of his enemies' slanderous attacks (18.5.5 *quo praesens rerum novarum avidus concitor, ut iactabant, a gravibus inimicis et metuendis incesseretur*). The present chapter describes how they succeeded because of the emperor's propensity to believe the slanderous talk of the court officials. This aspect of Amm.'s portrayal of Constantius shows great similarity to the topos of the *princeps clausus*, present i.a. in some passages of the *Historia Augusta*, e.g.: *imperator, qui domi clausus est, vera non novit. cogitur hoc tantum scire quod illi* (the courtiers) *loquuntur, facit iudices quos fieri non oportet, amovet a re publica quos debeat obtinere* (HA *A*. 43.4). The second part of this quotation exactly fits Amm.'s presentation of Constantius' handling of the Eastern military command. Cf. Stroheker, 1970 and Chastagnol, 1985.

II. 1 *post Amidae oppugnationem* Amida on the Tigris (modern Diyarbakir), an extremely well-fortified town (cf. the notes ad 18.6.17 and 18.9.1–2) was captured and destroyed in September 359 (19.8.4, 19.9.1; cf. Szidat I 43 n. 14). See further ad 20.11.4 (*Amidam petens*).

Ursicinum The general on whose staff Amm. served for some years and to whom he developed a deep loyalty. See for the details of Ursicinus' career the note ad 14.9.1; Lippold, 1961; Demandt, 1970, 569–572; *PLRE I*, Ursicinus 2 (cf. G. Wirth, *HZ* 216(1973)643), and for the degree in which the relationship with Ursicinus affected Amm.'s work as a historian ("Es muss damit gerechnet werden, dass die Darstellung verschiedener Ereignisse und die Charakterisierung einiger Persönlichkeiten von dem freundschaftlichen Verhältnis des Historikers zu U. her geprägt sind", Lippold, 1961, 1058): Thompson, 1947, 42–55 (who, according to Lippold, ibid., "freilich in seiner Kritik mehrfach zu weit ging" and whose view has recently been challenged also by Crump, 1975, 13–17; Frézouls, 1962 and Nutt, 1973). Cf. also Blockley, 1980 (1), 472–477. For the mentioning of Ursicinus in the Talmud of Jerusalem see Delmaire, 1982.

commilitium principis   This denotes the emperor's court, as in 27.6.1 and 8, 28.3.9, 28.4.20. The term *commilitium* is used by Pliny with reference to the emperor (*Ep.* 10.26.2 and 86 B). But, as Sherwin-White notes ad *Ep.* 10.26.2, Pliny is referring to actual service in the field. *Princeps* is not an official title for the emperor, but to call the use of this term "misleading", as De Jonge does ad 16.12.67, is less correct. See for a more sophisticated approach Béranger, 1976, 53 and 56–58. The term *princeps* is also dealt with in the notes ad 20.4.8 and 20.4.12.

peditum magistrum   Constantine brought about an important change in the military organisation of the empire by creating a large-scale field army, a central striking force, which he placed under the command of two new officers, the *magister peditum* and the *magister equitum* (Jones 97). In the course of the fourth century, however, due to various circumstances an increasing number of local groups was separated from the central army, the most important of which were commanded by officers also called *magistri*.

In the *Notitia Dignitatum* we find four of these regional *magistri militum* (as they were generally called, cf. *Not.Dign.Or.* 1.6–8, 7.1, 8.1, 9.1), in addition to the four (two in the East and two in the West) *magistri militum* attached to the emperor's person, who, to distinguish them from the regional commanders, were styled *in praesenti* or *praesentales* (*Not.Dign.Or.* 1.5, 5.1, 6.1, *Occ.* 1.5–6, 5.1, 6.1).

At the time the *Notitia Dignitatum* was composed there were in the West (to restrict ourselves here to that part of the empire) three *magistri militum*: the *magister peditum in praesenti* (*Not.Dign.Occ.* 1.5), the *magister equitum in praesenti* (ibid., 1.6) and the *magister equitum per Gallias* (ibid., 1.7; see for the latter above, the note ad 20.1.2).

Here Ursicinus is called merely *peditum magister*, not *magister peditum in praesenti* or *praesentalis*, although it is clear that he occupied the post with which, in the terminology of the *Not.Dign.*, the latter title corresponded. Is this an instance of Amm.'s habit, noted above (ad 20.1.2) of using military titles rather loosely? In other words, are we justified in calling Ursicinus in 359 already a *magister peditum praesentalis* (as e.g. Von Nischer, 1928, 430; Hoepffner, 1936, 484; Lippold, 1961, 1061 did; cf. also De Jonge ad 14.9.1)? Rather not. Cf. Demandt, 1970, 577, who points to the fact "dass der Titel *mag.mil.praes.* im 4. Jhdt. nicht ein einziges Mal zu belegen ist", and concludes: "Bei der Fülle von Variationen des Titels in der Literatur, in

Inschriften, Gesetzen und Papyri kann das nur daraus erklärt werden, dass es den Titel *mag.mil.praesentalis* im 4. Jhdt. nicht gab".

As to the hierarchical position of the *magister peditum* compared with that of the *magister equitum* and the regional *magistri militum*: Mommsen, 1889 and Ensslin, 1929, 1930 had argued for the superiority in rank and power of, respectively, the *magister peditum* and the *magister equitum*, while Hoepffner, 1936 held that these two *magistri* were equal in these respects, while all scholars agreed that the regional *magistri* should be regarded as inferior to the *magistri 'praesentales'*. Demandt, 1970, 572, however, defended a "prinzipielle Ranggleichheit der Heermeister ..., die nur durch Übertragung besonderer Aufgaben ... zeitweise unterbrochen wurde", though he admitted the possibility of "ein höheres Ansehen" of the *magistri* attached to the emperor's court (ibid., 573).

successisse enim eum Barbationi praediximus   Cf. *successurus Barbationi* in 18.5.5, where it is also stated that Ursicinus was himself succeeded as *magister equitum* in the East by Sabinianus (*Stetitque sententia ut Sabinianus ... praeficiendus eois partibus mitteretur, Ursicinus vero curaturus pedestrem militiam, et successurus Barbationi, ad comitatum reverteretur*). Cf. also 18.6.1 (*Sabinianus ... decessori suo principis litteras dedit, hortantis ut ad comitatum dignitate afficiendus superiore citius properaret*), where by *dignitas superior* is meant *peditum magisterium* (so, rightly, De Jonge ad loc.) and not the consulate (as Demandt, 1970, 573, suggested; if his hero Ursicinus really had obtained the consulate, Amm. would certainly have said so, here or elsewhere, in less oblique words).

Note that almost immediately after his nomination as successor of Barbatio, Ursicinus, being already *magister peditum* (so, rightly, Szidat following Demandt, 1970, 572; for a different interpretation: Crump, 1973, 94-95 and Blockley, 1980(1), 476), was ordered to return to Mesopotamia; there, however, Sabinianus was now in supreme command (18.6.5 *ad alium omni potestate translata*; cf. 19.3.1 *ex alterius pendebat arbitrio*) – a most awkward situation!

See for Barbatio Seeck, 1899; De Jonge ad 14.11.19; Demandt, 1970, 568-569; *PLRE I*, Barbatio; Von Haehling, 1978, 247.

obtrectatores   Such nasty people "who make verbal attacks on others through envy or malice" (OLD) figure more often in Amm.'s story. Thus Julian was the target of Barbatio, *gloriarum Iuliani pervicax obtrectator* (16.11.7, cf. the note ad loc.). In his short polemic introduction in 15.1.1. Amm. expects to become the victim of such people because of the scope of his work.

disseminantes mordaces susurros Amm. sketches such methods as endemic in Constantius' court, with special attention for the eunuchs: *inter ministeria vitae secretioris per arcanos susurros nutrimenta fictis criminibus subserentes* (14.11.3). In the present chapter the different stages of the *susurri* and the *crimina* are explicitly distinguished.

mordaces is very apt: TLL VIII 1484.40–55 provides a list of examples where *mordax* is used "de verbis (sententiis) detrectantibus", e.g.: *non ego mordaci destrinxi carmine quemquam* (Ov. *Tr.* 2.563), *maledictis mordacibus carpunt publicos mores* (Arnob. *nat.* 1.64.3). For *susurros* see the note ad 20.8.11 *susurrantes*.

propalam ficta crimina subnectentes The verb *subnectere* ('to add', cf. Quint. *Inst.* 7.10.7 *deinde proxima subnectens*) is used only here by Amm. Its synonym *subserere* is more frequent. The difference with the course of events sketched in the words quoted from book 14 in the preceding note should not be overlooked. In the present text the courtiers add their overt (*propalam*) accusation to their preliminary malicious whispering campaign, but in 14.11.3 it is implied that the eunuchs surreptitiously add their whisper to their normal duties in the innermost privacy of the court.

II. 2 *quibus imperator assensus* Amm. portrays Constantius as quite prone to believe unwarranted reports and rumours: *si quid dubium deferebatur aut falsum, pro liquido accipiens et comperto* (14.5.1). Cf. also 21.16.8 *si affectatae dominationis amplam quandam falsam repperisset aut levem, hanc sine fine scrutando, fasque eodem loco ducens et nefas, Caligulae et Domitiani et Commodi immanitatem facile superabat,* 21.16.16 and the note ad 20.9.2. See for a discussion of the term *imperator* in Amm. Béranger, 1976, 56–58.

ex opinione pleraque aestimans The term *opinio* here is the opposite of 'truth, reality' (not mentioned here, but implicit in the whole chapter). For a list of texts where both elements are mentioned cf. TLL IX 2.714.61–715.2, e.g. *Sic est vulgus; ex veritate pauca, ex opinione multa aestimat* (Cic. *Q. Rosc.* 29). Szidat quite plausibly takes *opinio* as Constantius' own prejudice.

insidiantibus patens This idiosyncrasy is sketched in very similar terms in 15.2.2: *ad suscipiendas defensiones aequas et probabiles imperatoris aures occlusae patebant susurris insidiantium clandestinis,* and 15.3.3: *recluso pectore patebat insidiantibus multis*. Again Amm. leaves one half of the opposition unmentioned: Constantius is *open* to the words of conspirators, but *closed* to the righteous defence of their victims. The emperor Valens later took this unfortunate leaf from Constantius' book: *imperator enim promptior ad nocendum, criminantibus patens* (26.10.12).

Arbitionem "Der bedeutendste Heermeister dieser Zeit" (Demandt, 1970, 567), a *magister equitum* (see above, the note ad 20.2.1), who started his career as a common soldier (16.6.1: *a gregario ad magnum militiae culmen evectus*). He was *consul* in 355. See for him Seeck, 1896; De Jonge ad 14.11.2; Demandt, 1970, 567 and 578; *PLRE I*, Arbitio 2 (cf. A. Lippold, *Gnomon* 46(1974)271); Szidat I 106-107; Von Haehling, 1978, 245-246 (For a barbarian origin, suggested by Rolfe, I, 1935, 550, there is no evidence, pace Blockley, 1980 (1), 483).

Florentium officiorum magistrum In the early fourth century we meet the first *magister officiorum*, a minister whose title is untranslatable (cf. for the translation of military and civil titles in general Rosen, 1982, 10-11) and whose functions are difficult to reduce to the same denominator. We can get an impression of his multifarious and miscellaneous duties from the following description: "An der Spitze der Hofbeamten stand der *mag.off.* als Vorgesetzter der Kanzleien (*officia*), dem die Ausführung der auswärtigen Politik und der inneren Verwaltung mit den kirchenpolitischen Angelegenheiten anvertraut war. Ebenso hatte er die Aufsicht über die Grenzbefestigungen und die staatlichen Waffenfabriken. Er war für die Sicherheit des Kaisers verantwortlich und befehligte darum die Palasttruppen, die *scholae palatinae*", Clauss, 1980, 1-2; cf. the note ad 15.5.12.

Florentius, a native of Antioch, was *magister officiorum* in 358/359-361. Cf. Seeck, 1909 ('Florentius 3'); De Jonge ad 15.5.12; *PLRE I*, Florentius 3; Szidat 107-108; Clauss, 1980, 155-157.

quaesitores déderat spectatúros Although the original meaning of *quaesitor* is "a member of an extraordinary commission to investigate a particular case" (OLD), it more usually means "an investigator in a criminal matter" (Berger, 1953, 662). Szidat therefore rightly suggests that this term is deliberately chosen by Amm. to create the impression of a criminal trial of Ursicinus. *Dare* with a pred.acc. means 'to appoint as', cf. Cic. *Ver.* 3.54 *dat iste viros optimos recuperatores*. The use of the pluperfect *dederat* instead of a perf. is caused by the cursus velox: cf. Ehrismann 125. For *spectare* in the sense 'to examine, to investigate' (not as a juridical technical term) cf. the note ad 17.4.5. The use of the part.fut. in a final sense is quite usual in late Latin; cf. Schrijnen-Mohrmann, 1936, 39; Szantyr 390. But in these cases it is more often used predicatively in the nom., e.g. *servituri sequebantur* (19.6.2). An example of the predicatively used acc. is Arnob. *nat.* 1.29.6 *solis ignes constituit ad rerum incrementa futuros*. The present case does not belong to that category, but should rather be paralleled by 28.6.7 *Severum et Flaccianum creavere legatos, Victoriarum aurea simulacra Valentiniano ob imperii primitias oblaturos*.

13

óppidum sit excisum   For the meaning of *excidere* 'to devastate, to destroy' cf. the notes ad 19.9.2 and 20.7.1.

The cognate subst. *excidium* is quite often used to denote the destruction of a town, e.g. *post excidium Troiae* (15.9.5) and concerning Amida *post civitatis excidium* (19.6.12).

II. 3   *quibus ... veritisque*   The period is irregular in that the subject of the abl. abs. (*quibus* = Arbitio and Florentius) is also the subject of the main verb. The normal construction would have been: *qui ... refutantes ... veritique ... * Some early examples of this phenomenon are *B. Afr.* 10.2: *omnibus in exercitu insciis et requirentibus imperatoris consilium, magno metu ac tristimonia sollicitabantur*, and Suet. *Tib.* 31.3: *iterum censente ... obtinere non potuit*. It becomes more frequent in the course of time as a result of the increasing independence of the abl. abs., which gradually developed into a true subordinate clause. Cf. Szantyr 140, Norberg, 1944, 68 n. 2, Serbat, 1979, 353 ("l'AA classique est un syntagme en voie de se transformer en proposition").

quibus apertas probabilesque refutantibus causas   Cf. *causam enim probabilem ponebat in medio, multorum testimoniis claram* (15.6.3) and Cic. *Ver.* 5.173 *splendida est illa causa, probabilis mihi et facilis*. In a short section of his chapter on "le vocabulaire de la démonstration" Sabbah discusses Amm.'s use of *probare* and its cognate nouns, drawing attention to the fact that only *probabilis* "connaît une certaine extension". Apart from the cases where it means 'laudable' or 'commendable' (17.9.6, 23.1.4), it qualifies *argumentum* (15.5.21, 23.5.11, 27.7.4), *documentum* (28.6.30), *defensio* (15.2.2), *ratio* (18.6.1, 22.14.1), with the meaning 'credible' or 'reliable'; cf. Sabbah 388/9; *causas* viz. of the fall of Amida.

Eusebius, cubiculi tunc praepositus   The *praepositus sacri cubiculi*, the superintendent of the sacred bedchamber of the emperor and empress, stood at the head of a highly peculiar group of civil servants, the *cubicularii*, the court eunuchs. In the fourth and fifth centuries these eunuchs, and especially the *praepositus*, often wielded a tremendous power at court, whatever may have been the prestige of eunuchs in society at large. See in the first place Hopkins, 1963 and Guyot, 1980; cf. Dunlap, 1924; De Jonge ad 14.11.21 and 15.2.10; Jones 566-570; Szidat I 108-109.

Eusebius, PSC 337-361, was very influential indeed, as, for instance, Amm.'s sarcastic remark in 18.4.3 can testify: *apud quem, si vere dici debeat, multa Constantius potuit*. Cf. Seeck, 1909 ('Eusebius 5'); De Jonge ad 14.10.5; *PLRE I*, Eusebius 11 (with J.R. Martindale, *Historia* 29(1980)483); Szidat I 108-109; Guyot, 1980, 199-201.

documenta Here this term is used in its juridical sense ("quodcumque in iudicio adfertur ad aliquid probandum" is the relevant description in TLL V 1.1808.76 sqq.). With the same meaning Amm. 18.1.4 *documentorum inopia percitus*, and 18.3.4 *documento convicta non levi*.

suscepissent In late Latin *suscipere* is a synonym of *accipere*; cf. the note ad 17.13.23, Wölfflin, 1904, 174.

Sabiniani Sabinianus, in 359 Ursicinus' successor as *magister equitum* in the East (see above, the note ad 20.2.1) was severely, and perhaps correctly, criticized by Amm. for his ineptitude (18.5.5, 18.6.1, 18.6.7, 18.7.7, 19.3.1). "However, one should always take into consideration Amm.'s admiration for Ursicinus" (De Jonge ad 18.5.5; cf. Rosen, 1968, 26). For a less partial judgement of Sabinianus one should also bear in mind that Amm. himself reports that he had been under imperial orders to adopt a prudent and defensive strategy: *litteras imperiales praetendens, intacto ubique milite, quicquid geri potuisset impleri debere aperte iubentes* (19.3.2). See for Sabinianus Seeck, 1920; Demandt, 1970, 572–573; *PLRE I*, Sabinianus 3; Szidat I 109–110; Von Haehling, 1978, 248.

pertinaci ignavia Amm., a military professional himself, has condensed all his irritation in this marvellous oxymoron; *pertinax* is usually said of actions, whether good or bad, or at least of an attitude implying activity, and seems the very opposite of idleness. Cf. this opposition: *dolores omnes ut insultant ignavis, ita persistentibus cedunt* (25.3.16), where *ignavus* contrasts with *persistens*, a participle very similar in meaning to *pertinax*. Sabinianus was steadfastly persisting ... in doing nothing. For the use of *ignavus* as a term of abuse in the military sphere cf. Opelt, 1965, 190–197.

haec accidisse, quae contigerunt This laconic and at the same time euphemistic formula aptly expresses the incontestable reality of the facts: what has been done cannot be undone; *accidere* and *contingere* are fully synonymous here: although TLL IV 717.75/6 notes that intransitive *contingere* is "saepissime" accompanied by a dative, Amm. rather uses it absolutely, as in the expression *quod contingit*: 14.2.7 (*assidue*), 27.9.8, 30.4.15, 31.16.8 (*raro*), 27.9.5 (*saepe*). Cf. also 15.10.5 *et haec, ut diximus, anni verno contingunt* and for a combination similar to the present text Cic. *Phil.* 2.17 *tibi idem quod illis accidit contigisset*.

a veritate detorti In its metaphorical sense *detorquere* is normally used in malam partem, as in Amm. 14.7.21 *ingenium a veri consideratione detortum*. Here it most probably has a passive sense: fear of Eusebius has averted them from the clear truth; cf. the use of *detorquere* in 21.12.6 and 29.5.49.

inania quaedam longeque a negotio distantia scrutabantur *Inanis* here means 'trifling, unimportant' (as, e.g., in Cic. *Att.* 11.17a.3: *quod inane esset etiam si verum esset, non verum esse*), especially in view of the epexegetical addition: the things scrutinized by the committee of inquiry had nothing whatsoever to do with the point in question. Amm.'s information is very unsatisfactory. What were those trifling details? The committee must have done its work thoroughly, as is implied by the use of *scrutari*, with autopsy on the spot, the *tribunus et notarius* Discenes even making calculations of the enemy's losses (Amm. 19.9.9).

II. 4 *percitus* 'Irritated', as in 19.7.8 (about the Persian king) *his turbinum infortuniis percitus*. Ursicinus loses his temper.

qui audiebatur 'He who was interrogated'; *audire* is without doubt here a juridical t.t., as in 18.1.4: *Numerium Narbonensis paulo ante rectorem, accusatum ut furem, inusitato censorio vigore, pro tribunali palam admissis volentibus audiebat*. As Szidat notes, the expression *qui audiebatur* has deliberately been chosen to continue the impression of a criminal trial rather than a military inquiry.

"etsi me", inquit, "despicit imperator" Ursicinus complains about the want of appreciation of his qualities by the *princeps clausus*; cf. the introduction to this chapter.

negotii tamen est magnitudo Clark had accepted the emendation proposed (without any arguments) by Cornelissen, who added *ea* after *tamen*. Haupt had suggested the addition of *tanta*. Löfstedt, 1950, 13, has convincingly proved that such corrections are unnecessary.

non nisi iudicio principis The importance of the matter demands that the emperor himself take charge of the 'legal proceedings'.

nosci Again a juridical t.t., as in Tac. *Ann.* 6.9.4 *ut ipse cum senatu nosceret*, *Hist.* 2.10.1 *ut accusatorum causae noscerentur*.

velut quodam praesagio It is surprising that these words are put into the mouth of the speaker; they would be more appropriate in the report and the comments of the writer, who, knowing what was to happen afterwards, draws the reader's attention to the prognostic character of the words of the speaker. An example may illustrate this, viz. the reaction of the soldiers after the speech in which Constantius announced the appointment of Julian as Caesar: *dicere super his plura conantem, interpellans contio lenius prohibebat, arbitrium summi numinis id esse non mentis humanae velut praescia venturi proclamans* (15.8.9). The soldiers did not pretend to have any foreknowledge themselves, but this is a note of the author, availing himself of a Vergilian quotation (*A.* 3.66, cf. Hagendahl, 1921, 6). In the present section the expression at issue may be taken to indicate that Amm. has put his own aggressive summary of Ursicinus' complaint into the latter's mouth as *oratio recta*. For it really strains the reader's imagination that for all his irritation Ursicinus could literally have used such insulting terms (the emperor characterized as a mere puppet etc.). The suggestion propounded in the above, viz. that the words *velut quodam praesagio* give expression to the writer's foreknowledge of the events, seems to be refuted by the facts: "Die Vorhersage des Ursicinus traf übrigens nicht ein, wie die Auseinandersetzungen mit den Persern in den Jahren 360 u. 361 n. Chr. zeigen" (Szidat). But Szidat overlooks the fact that *proximo vere* the Romans did, indeed, lose Singara (20.6) and Bezabde (20.7), and that Constantius was unable to recapture the latter town (20.11). Although these losses did not bring about the 'dismemberment of Mesopotamia' (*defrustandae Mesopotamiae*), 1. they were serious set-backs, and 2., more importantly, what matters is not the reconstruction of the facts by modern historians, but Amm.'s bias, who is ready to exaggerate Constantius' adversities: *quas ob res omisso vano incepto hiematurus Antiochiae redit in Syriam aerumnosa perpessus vulnera et atrocia diuque deflenda. evenerat enim hoc quasi fatali constellatione ita regente diversos eventus, ut ipsum Constantium dimicantem cum Persis fortuna semper sequeretur afflictior* (20.11.32).

As for the presentation of one's own words as prophetic, an interesting parallel is Cato *fil.* 1, where the author warns his son against Greek doctors, introducing his description of their probable behaviour upon arrival in Rome with these words: *et hoc puta vatem dixisse.*

amendata didicit fide *Amendare* 'to send away' is a strong term, implying a far, often hidden destination: *familiarissimum suum dimittere ab se et amendare in ultimas terras* (Cic. *Sul.* 57). Amm. uses the verb rather often, in its literal meaning (*amendatis procul Graiorum legatis*, 18.6.18), concerning social status (*maculosos tales appellans et sordidos, et infra sortem amendandos*, 30.8.11), in a translated sense (*angorem animi, quamdiu potuit, amendabat*, 14.10.2).

In his commentary on 18.6.18 De Jonge refers to a note of Servius ad *Aen.* 3.50 *amendare est sub specie legationis aliquem relegare.*

Here the speaker wants to say that the reports in question are completely untrustworthy, 'truthfulness having been sent into exile' (Rolfe's understatement "on no good authority" does not suit the aggressiveness of Ursicinus' words).

ad spadonum arbitrium trahitur Amm. uses the same expression to report that Constantius was trying to get his way in the field of the Christian confession: *ritum omnem ad suum trahere conatur arbitrium* (21.16.18). In the present chapter these words express contempt for a person who is being subjected to the will of others, despicable people at that. Constantius can, in fact, be compared to the barbarian king Chonodomarius: *servus alienae voluntatis trahebatur* (16.12.61). Cf. also Tac. *Hist.* 3.49.4 *nec miles in arbitrio ducum, sed duces militari violentia trahebantur*.

defrustandae Mesopotamiae In the only other instance of the verb *defrustare* in Amm. it concerns a garment: *tunica ... defrustata* (31.2.5), 'cut into small bits'. Amm. means the Roman *provincia* of Mesopotamia. See the notes ad 14.3.1 and 17.5.6.

cum exercitus robore omni In view of *omni* the word *robur* here cannot mean the 'core' or 'pick' of the armed forces, as in Livy 30.8.2 *ipse cum robore exercitus ire ad hostes pergit* and 35.29.12 *cum robore exercitus egressus*. So *exercitus* should be interpreted as a defining genitive.

opitulari For a survey of the career of this verb in Latin literature cf. Landgraf's commentary on Cicero's *pro Roscio*, 71/2. In Cicero it occurs 22 times, but afterwards very seldom before Apuleius. There are hardly any instances in historical prose, none in Caes., Tac., Flor., one each in Sal. (*Cat.* 33.2) and Livy (44.27.5). It has a complement in the dative, in the present case *Mesopotamiae*, for *defrustandae Mesopotamiae* is *not* a gerundive construction, as in August. *civ.* 15.7 *ut eorum non opituletur sanandis pravis cupiditatibus, sed explendis*; *defrustandae* is rather an example of the gerundivum as a part. fut. pass.: 'doomed to be cut into pieces', cf. the note ad 15.5.8, Szantyr 394, Odelstierna, 1926, 6–10 and 17–18.

II. 5 *relatis* From the context one has to supply 'Ursicinus' words' (in § 4); the absence of a subst. or pron. in the abl. abs. is common in late Latin, but here the ellipse is rather harsh. In the examples given by Flinck-Linkomies, 1929, 247–250 the subject, usually one or more human beings, is far easier to supply from the context. It is true that in the present case the addition of a second abl.abs. makes it more easy to supply 'these words' or a similar phrase, for after all the *complura* are added to something. Still one wonders whether *his* should be added. Cf. *his auditis* (16.12.19, 20.5.1, 21.12.19) and *his cognitis* (14.7.13, 31.7.9).

It might also be suggested that *relatis* etc. can be interpreted as a dat. or abl. to denote the object or the cause of Constantius' anger: Liv. 8.31.2 *iratus virtuti alienae felicitatique*, Cic. *Ver.* 5.120 *veniunt amissis filiis irati*. This explanation, however, is less attractive, for Amm. almost always uses *irasci* and *iratus* absolutely, without any complement, the only exceptions being 14.7.14 (*iratus ... quod*) and 30.4.22 (*ut ... solis defensantibus irascantur*).

cum interpretatione maligna   The subst. occurs only here in Amm.; for the expression cf. *suspiciones et interpretationes malignas vocis alienae* (Sen., *De ira* 3.34.1). See also Tac. *Dial.* 3.2 and for some further examples of deliberate distortion of the truth *Ann.* 2.82.1, 13.43.1. Again Amm.'s information is vague and unsatisfactory. If, as seems likely, *compluribus* refers to further utterances of Ursicinus', 'malicious interpretation' could hardly have worsened the bad impression caused by his impertinent words cited in section 4.

iratus ultra modum   Similar expressions in Amm. show that this has to be understood as a very severe criticism: Gallus' wife was *germanitate Augusti turgida supra modum* (14.1.2), the urban prefect Orfitus ruled the city *ultra modum delatae dignitatis sese efferens insolenter* (14.6.1), having been informed about Gallus' conduct, *Constantius ultra mortalem modum exarsit* (14.11.13), Damasus and Ursinus quarreled *supra humanum modum ad rapiendam episcopi sedem ardentes* (27.3.12). Julian's pronunciamento in Paris caused a similar outburst of Constantius: having received the letters brought to him by Julian's ambassadors *ultra modum solitae indignationis excanduit imperator* (20.9.2). In the elogium Constantius' *iracundia* is explicitly mentioned (21.16.9). Cf. also Seager, 1986, 3-4.

discusso negotio   The non-classical meaning 'to investigate' or 'to discuss' is quite frequent in late Latin, cf. the note ad 17.12.15.

nec patefieri ... permissis   A personal passive construction with *permittere*, comparable to *iubere*, has become normal in later Latin; e.g. *innoxius abire permissus est* (Amm. 19.12.12), *si propria retinere permitteretur* (17.10.3). Cf. Szantyr 365, Blomgren 162, De Jonge ad 17.10.3.

Some other examples of the abl. abs.: *ad arbitrium suum vivere cultoribus eius permissis* (30.2.4), *nullo paene redire permisso* (30.7.9).

appetitum calumniis   Julian had been a victim of such attacks too: *contumeliosis calumniis appetitus est a Gaudentio tunc notario* (17.9.7), but in that case the context does not necessarily imply that *calumnia* is used in its strict sense as a juridical t.t., as it undoubtedly is in the present section where it adds one more stroke to the sketch of the investigation as a criminal trial, with 'false accusations' at that. Just like *qui audiebatur* the circumlocution *appetitum calumniis* for Ursicinus is meant to stress his victimization.

deposita militia Though *militia* in the fourth century "was being used more generally to designate not simply military service, but a period in the civil service as well" (MacMullen, 1967, 49), in Amm. (where it occurs 28 times, i.a. in 20.5.7 and 20.8.14) its meaning is restricted to that of *militia armata*, with the possible exception of 22.7.5, where we hear of the *militia* of former *agentes in rebus*.

digredi iussit ad otium This expression denoting retirement occurs only in Amm.: 16.7.6, 25.8.9, 28.6.30 are the other instances; its synonym *discedere ad* (or *in*) *otium* is used in 28.6.25 and 31.10.22.

Agilone "... als einziger Alamanne der ganzen spätrömischen Zeit bis zum Heermeister (*magister peditum*) befördert" (Stroheker, 1975, 35). See Seeck, 1894; De Jonge ad 14.10.8; Demandt, 1970, 569; *PLRE I*, Agilo; Waas, 1971[2], 68-69; Szidat I 111; Von Haehling, 1978, 247-248.

immodico saltu promoto Amm.'s dislike of Alamans (cf. Stroheker, 1965, 31: "gegen die Alamannen ist er von einer auffallend heftigen Antipathie erfüllt") and his admiration for Agilo's predecessor Ursicinus (cf. Szidat) may account for this rather sharp comment, for Agilo's promotion does not seem to have been unjustified, nor unprecedented, though it is out of the normal order.

When only a subaltern officer, Agilo already was highly regarded (cf. 14.10.8: *Latinum ... et Agilonem tribunum stabuli atque Scudilonem ... qui tunc ut dextris suis gestantes rem publicam colebantur*). At an unknown date transferred to the post of officer of one of the palace guards (*tribunus Gentilium Scutariorum*), he must have had still more opportunity to show his competence and to attract the attention of an emperor, who, as Amm. himself acknowledges in his final judgement of Constantius' virtues and faults, was very critical in evaluating someone's merits and never appointed an untried man suddenly to a high position (21.16.3: *in conservando milite nimium cautus, examinator meritorum nonnumquam subscruposus ... et sub eo nemo celsum aliquid acturus in regia repentinus adhibitus est vel incognitus*). Hence, it seems likely that Constantius' choice of Agilo as Ursicinus' successor was a deliberate one, justified by Agilo's abilities (which later were acknowledged by Julian, too; cf. 21.12.16).

But even if Agilo's promotion had been due not so much to personal merits as to other factors (cf. ad 20.5.7), the jump from the post of officer of a palace guard to that of *magister militum* was not without parallel. Usually before becoming *magister* a regimental officer had to serve as *comes rei militaris* or *comes domesticorum* first (cf. Jones 382), but this was no iron law. Silvanus (*PLRE I*, Silvanus 2) and Malarichus (*PLRE I*, Malarichus), for example, both of Frankish origin, were offered a generalship without having fulfilled an intermediate post (see the table in Waas, 1971[2], 10 for other examples), and so Agilo's appointment, though exceptional, was not unique.

One fails to understand why *TLL* VII 1.486.43/4 mentions the present text as an instance of *immodicus* in a vague sense: "sine notione reprehensionis fere i.q. permagnus, ingens sim.", for certainly Amm. criticizes this appointment as extravagant.

Promovere in the meaning 'to advance (a person) to higher rank, promote' occurs only in post-classical and late Latin (cf. *OLD* s.v., 4 and the note ad 17.11.5). Amm. uses it twenty times (e.g. in 20.8.14, 20.9.5, see the note ad loc., and 26.6.7, where the nasty Petronius received a sudden promotion from his son-in-law Valens: *promotus repentino saltu patricius*). Amm. employs *provehere* (first attested in this sense in Vell. 2.69.1, according to the *OLD* s.v., 4b) as a synonym twelve times (e.g. in 20.9.5).

Gentilium Scutariorum Shortly after the battle at the Milvian Bridge Constantine disbanded the *cohortes praetoriae*. Post hoc and probably also propter hoc (cf. Hoffmann I 281, but see Frank, 1969, 48) Constantine founded a new imperial bodyguard, the *scholae palatinae*, among them the *scholae* of *scutarii* and *gentiles*. (A Diocletianic prehistory for some of the *scholae*, viz. the *scutarii* and *gentiles*, does not seem impossible, it is true, cf. Jones 54 and 613; Hoffmann I 281–283, "doch hat man mit Recht schon immer in Constantin ihren eigentlichen Schöpfer gesehen", Hoffmann I 281). Amm., for that matter, sometimes uses "alte Terminologie" (Müller, 1905, 579). In 17.13.10 (q.v.) he mentions a *cohors praetoria* in the time of Constantius.

At the time the *Notitia Dignitatum* was recorded there were twelve of these *scholae*, cavalry regiments of, in all probability (cf. Frank, 1969, 52) 500 men each. During the fourth century most of the *scholares* were Germans. See for them Seeck, 1921; De Jonge ad 14.7.9, 14.10.8 and 15.5.6; Jones 613–614; Frank, 1969; Hoffmann I 279–303; Clauss, 1980, 40–45.

Blomgren 8 opposes Gardthausen's addition of *et*, accepted by Clark; in his opinion the transmitted text can be kept as an "asyndeton bimembre".

With this chapter Amm. sadly takes leave of his revered favourite Ursicinus. The sun has eclipsed. But soon it will shine brightly again with the rise of Amm.'s other great hero, Julian. Eclipses are only temporary, as is expounded in the following digression.

Chapter 3

This chapter offers a long and detailed digression on astronomical matters, occasioned by the anular eclipse of Aug. 28th 360. The first part (§ 1-8) deals with solar and lunar eclipses. It is interrupted by a short explanation (§ 6) of the phenomenon known as 'the two suns' (*sol geminus*, παρήλιον).

In the second part (§ 9-11) Amm. discusses the phases of the moon. Section 12 contains a more general remark on faulty observations caused by the position of the observer on earth.

Digressions on geographical and ethnographical subjects were included by historians since Herodotus, often in order to provide the necessary background for descriptions of battles or military campaigns. Herodotus himself goes well beyond indispensable factual information of this kind and incorporates into his work many digressions that are only loosely connected with the narrated events. Hellenistic authors belonging to the so-called Isocratean school of historiography followed his example. In the fragments of Theopompus for instance we find digressions on the founding of cities, the genealogy of royal families etc. A complete book of his *Philippica* was devoted to *mirabilia*. On this subject see Scheller, 1911, 52-3, and Blockley, 1973. Lucianus *Hist. Conscr.* 19 and 57 warns against excesses in this respect; see Avenarius, 1956, 140-149.

Roman historians followed the example of their Greek predecessors with more or less moderation. Mommsen, 1909, 393, has pointed to Sallust as Amm.'s model, who incorporated a number of geographical digressions into his *Iugurtha*, and, more particularly, into his *Historiae*. Amm., however, does not limit himself to geographical and ethnographical excursions only. Schanz-Hosius IV.1.97 distinguish four types of digressions in Amm., dealing with geography, natural science, philosophy/religion and social conditions. Other classifications are mentioned by Cichocka, 1975, 331-2. The digression in 20.3 naturally belongs to the second type, as well as those on earthquakes (17.7.9), the rainbow (20.11.26), meteors (25.2.5) and comets (25.10.2). Amm. does not explicitly state his motives to present these miniature scientific treatises. They must be connected with his intention to offer his readers encyclopedic learning, as indicated in the opening sentence of the very long excursus on Persia (23.6.1): *quod autem erit paulo prolixior textus, ad scientiam proficiet plenam*. This aim is in accordance with the respect Amm. repeatedly shows for great erudition (cf. 14.6.18, 28.4.14, 29.2.18).

The astronomical digression is only loosely connected with the narrative. It is not introduced by any of the usual formulas enumerated by Emmett, 1981, 20-23. The transition from the description of the eclipse of August 360 is given by the words *quod alias non evenit ita perspicue, nisi cum*. The reader gets the impression that the excursus does not serve to explain that particular eclipse, but rather that the eclipse is introduced to provide Amm. with an excuse to insert the digression. In this respect it differs from the shorter passages on the subject in Dio Cassius (60.26) and Curtius Rufus (4.10.5), quoted as parallels by Szidat I 112. There, as in Cic. *Rep.* 1.23-25, to which we shall return below, the scientific explanation of the eclipse is given or deliberately withheld by persons who play a role in the narrative, in order to allay or exploit the fears of ignorant soldiers.

What were Amm.'s reasons to insert this digression here? Szidat I 43-44 seeks the answer to this question in the composition of book 20. According to him, this chapter separates the fall of Ursicinus, described in ch. 2, from Julian's rise to power, which is the subject of the following chapters. Amm., in his opinion, tries to prevent his readers from asking the awkward question why it is that Julian does not restore Ursicinus to his former position as a leading military figure: "A. muss seinen Helden Ursicinus von der Bühne entfernen, bevor sein anderer Held, Iulian, in einer Weise auftritt, die die Frage nach dem Verhältnis beider provoziert hätte". Sabbah 525-528 has pointed to the alternation between markedly persuasive passages (e.g. 14.7 against the Caesar Gallus or 19.8 on the siege of Amida and Amm.'s flight from that city) and scientific treatises (e.g. 14.8 on the Oriental provinces and 19.4 on the plague). He suggests that in this way Amm. tries to reaffirm that he is an objective, scientifically minded author: "Chaque fois que l'historien pourrait être soupçonné de se laisser entraîner par la passion, il doit chercher à récupérer son caractère préféré, celui de l'homme de science, supérieur et détaché" (p. 526). These explanations are both plausible and in no way mutually exclusive. Still, one cannot help wondering whether the choice of this particular subject for a digression may not have a special significance. Eclipses often figure as omens of future reversals of fate, such as major battles or the death of kings. Demandt, 1970, 495 sqq., demonstrates that in many descriptions of eclipses the chronology is violated in order to suggest a connection between these eclipses and such dramatic events. To quote a few examples: Liv. 30.38.8 does this with regard to the battle of Zama. In 44.37.5 the same author says of a lunar eclipse *Macedonas ut triste prodigium ... portendens movit*, with which the parallel versions in Plb. 29.16.6 and Plu. *Aem.* 17 may be compared. Dio Cassius presents a solar eclipse as an omen of the death of Augustus, 56.29.2/3 τέρατα δὲ ἄρα ἐς τοῦτο αὐτῷ φέροντα οὔτε ἐλάχιστα οὔτε δυσσύμβλητα ἐγεγένητο· ὅ τε γὰρ ἥλιος ἅπας ἐξέλιπε etc. and at 79.30.1 of the death of Macrinus καί μοι δοκεῖ ἐναργέστατα καὶ τοῦτο, εἴπερ τι ἄλλο τῶν πώποτε, προδειχθῆναι· ἡλίου ... γὰρ ἔκλειψις ... ἐγένετο. In Ps. Aur. Vict. *epit.* 12.12 the death of Nerva coincides with an eclipse. In other cases the eclipses are interpreted as indications of the shortness of the reign of an emperor as, for instance, in HA *Gd* 23.2 (Gordianus III) and Aur. Vict. *Caes.* 41.7 (Licinianus). In view of this common practice, it seems legitimate to assume that the eclipse recorded here was intended by Amm. either as a symbol of Ursicinus' downfall or as an omen announcing the death of the emperor. The eclipse was also recorded in China and interpreted as an *omen mortis* of the emperor Mu Ti, who died in 362, cf. Ho Peng Yoke, *The astronomical chapters of the Chin Shen*, Paris 1966, 159.

The basic astronomical facts needed to understand Amm.'s exposition on eclipses are the following. A solar eclipse occurs when the moon comes between the sun and the earth. This means that a solar eclipse can take place only at the New Moon. The moon is eclipsed when it moves into the shadow of the earth cast by the sun. A lunar eclipse, therefore, can only occur at the Full Moon (see figs. 1 and 2).

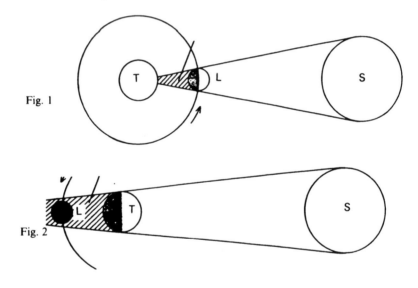

Fig. 1

Fig. 2

The reason why a solar eclipse does not occur at every New Moon is that the moon's orbit plane is slightly inclined to the ecliptic, the plane of the orbit of the sun around the earth (speaking from a geocentric point of view). Thus the moon can pass above or below the sun. For the same reason there is not a lunar eclipse at every Full Moon, as the moon can pass above or below the shadow of the earth. The intersections of the orbit planes of the sun and the moon are called the nodes. The ascending node (ἀναβιβάζων σύνδεσμος) is the point where the moon crosses the ecliptic going from south to north, and the descending node (καταβιβάζων σύνδεσμος) the point where it goes from north to south. Only when the sun is in or near one of the nodes when the moon crosses the ecliptic, sun, moon, and earth are in the same plane, so that they can be on a straight line. If that is the case, an eclipse occurs.

By a coincidence the size and distance of sun and moon are such that, despite the enormous difference in diameter, on earth they appear to have nearly the same angular size. When the center of the moon passes across the center of the sun, the eclipse is called central. As the distance of the sun and the moon to the earth is not constant, their orbits being elliptical, not circular, we must further distinguish between total and anular eclipses. When, at the time of a central eclipse the sun is farthest from the earth and the moon nearest to it, the sun is completely covered by the moon's disk and the solar eclipse is total. When the sun is nearest to the earth and the moon is at its greatest distance, the disk of the moon is smaller than that of the sun. The solar eclipse is then anular. If the center of the moon does not pass across the center of the sun, the solar eclipse is partial.

As the phases of the moon are also treated in this chapter, although they are an altogether different matter, it may be useful to illustrate them in the following diagram:

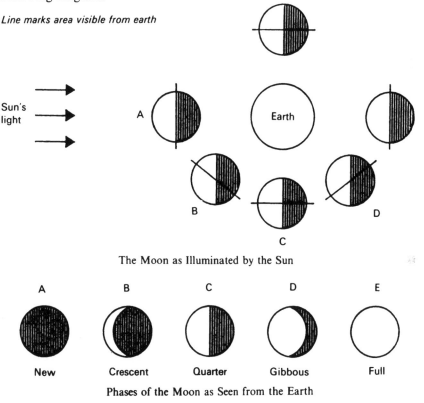

Line marks area visible from earth

The Moon as Illuminated by the Sun

Phases of the Moon as Seen from the Earth

The question of Amm.'s sources is treated by Szidat p. I 113–115. He is certainly right in saying that Amm. follows a number of authors. Very important is his observation that in his choice of technical terms Amm. shows marked similarities with Chalcidius. His conclusion "man wird sich Ammians Quellen daher in dem Ueberlieferungsstrom zu denken haben, der zu Chalcidius führt" must be accepted.

It is a priori probable that Amm. has consulted popular Greek astronomical treatises such as those by Cleomedes, Theon Smyrnaeus and Geminus. Yet there is no evidence of direct imitation of any of these authors. All the astronomical information in this chapter could have been found in the Latin authors who have written on the subject. The one Greek astronomer quoted by name, Ptolemaeus, has in all probability not been consulted directly. Amm.'s rather vague and repetitious account of the phenomena can hardly have been inspired by Ptolemy's highly technical exposition. In this respect, Amm.'s treatment of the subject shows similarities to his digression on earthquakes (17.7.9), where Aristotle, Anaxagoras and Anaximander are quoted *ornatus causa*, as De Jonge remarks in his note ad loc., whereas Amm.'s real sources are Latin authors.

Among the classical authors who have written on the subject of eclipses (Cic. *Rep.* 1.22–23, 6.9–17 (*Somnium*), *Div.* 2.17, *ND* 2.49–56, Plin. *Nat.* 2.41–58, Sen. *Nat.* 1.12 and *Ben.* 5.6.4), Cicero is by far Amm.'s most important source. Indeed, it is only by comparing *Rep.* 1 and the *Somnium* that the correct interpretation of some problematical points in the digression can be reached (see below on § 2 *iter menstruum* and § 8 *circa terrenam mobilitatem*), cf. Den Hengst, 1986. The comparison also helps to understand why Amm. added the enigmatical section 12 to his exposition of eclipses and moon-phases.

To end this introduction we acknowledge again our indebtedness to Szidat, who has been the first to provide a thorough explanation of this difficult chapter. Although we disagree with his findings in some important points, it is only fair to say that his commentary is an indispensable help in interpreting the digression.

III. 1 *Eodem tempore* refers to the year 360, as indicated in 20.1.1 *consulatu Constantii deciens terque Iuliani*. For this reason the solar eclipse of 28-8-360 must be meant. According to Schove 1984, 56–59, the eclipse was anular. From what we must assume was the position of the Roman army on the Eastern border it must have been only a small partial eclipse at sunrise. The inaccuracies in Amm.'s description do not make this doubtful, since, as we shall see, it is not based on personal observation, but rather composed of traditional elements in the description of solar eclipses.

per eoos tractus   The same term is used of the Eastern provinces of the Empire in 28.1.1, 30.2.9, 30.4.8. Cf. 26.6.15 *et in occidentali et in eoo orbe*. Amm. speaks of *eoas partes* in 16.10.1, 18.4.2 and 26.5.2. For the adjective *eous* see the note ad 14.8.4.

caelum subtextum caligine   Cf. 17.4.15 *caelum densitate nimia subtexentis*. The metaphorical use of *subtexere* is certainly poetic, as De Jonge suggests in his note ad loc. He quotes in support Verg. *A*. 3.582 *caelum subtexere fumo*, to which may be added Lucr. 5.466 *subtexunt nubila caelum* and 6.482 *subtexit caerula* (the blue sky) *nimbis*. See also Ov. *Met*. 14.368; Luc. 4.104; Sen. *Phaed*. 956 and V.Fl. 5.413. It is also to be noted that in all these passages, except V.Fl. 5.413, the sky is darkened by clouds or smoke. One might wonder whether Amm. attributes the darkness to two distinct factors, first the clouds, and second, introduced by *accedebat quod*, the eclipse, but the mention of the stars (*intermicabant stellae*) seems to preclude this. If we accept *caelum subtextum caligine* as the effect of the eclipse, we must conclude that Amm. is using this poetic expression in a context where it is not quite appropriate.

a primo aurorae exortu ad usque meridiem   As Szidat, following Ginzel 1899, points out, it is highly improbable that any stars were visible during the eclipse and totally impossible that they were visible for six hours. Demandt, 1970, 476 quotes this passage as a typical example of the tendency to describe partial or anular eclipses as total ("Ausschmückung mit den markanteren Totalitätssymptomen"). The visibility of stars during an eclipse is also reported in Thuc. 2.28 ὁ ἥλιος ἐξέλιπε μετὰ μεσημβρίαν καὶ πάλιν ἀνεπληρώθη γενόμενος μηνοειδὴς καὶ ἀστέρων τινῶν ἐκφανέντων. The phrase *a primo aurorae exortu* also occurs in 27.2.5. Elsewhere Amm. has *a solis exortu*, as e.g. in 17.1.5, q.v. Even in a total eclipse the visibility of the stars lasts no longer than two hours.

intermicabant iugiter stellae   For *intermicare* "to shine or gleam fitfully" (OLD) cf. *intermicante asperginum densitate* 20.11.28, 24.2.5 *splendor ferri intermicans* and Lact. *inst*. 6.20.7 *intermicantibus astrorum luminibus*; TLL VII 1.2222. The verb is listed among Amm.'s poeticisms by Hagendahl, 1921, 19. *Iugiter* 'continually' is found from Seneca onwards (*Nat*. 4.2.20) and is frequent in 4th century prose, TLL VII 2.630-1; see the note ad 17.13.11.

hisque terroribus accedebat quod   Compare the similar opening sentences in the excursus on the rainbow in 20.11.25–6: *et super his iugi fragore tonitrua fulgoraque mentes hominum pavidas perterrebant. 26 accedebant arcus caelestes conspectus assidui,* where *accedebant* introduces a new natural phenomenon, the rainbow. Here, however, *accedebat* does not introduce the eclipse as a new element in the narrative, but rather the misguided reaction of ignorant people to the eclipse. *Terrores* is best taken as 'frightening events', as in 17.7.12, q.v. and 26.10.15, in both cases referring to earthquakes.

penitus lance abrepta Explains the preceding *cum*-clause. *Penitus* proves that Amm. thinks of the eclipse as total (Szidat). *Lanx* for 'the solar disk' is found only here and in § 8.

defecisse diutius solem pavidae mentes hominum aestimabant Again a traditional element. Pliny the Elder, in his hymnical praise of the great astronomers who had discovered the natural causes of eclipses (*Nat.* 2.54 *viri ingentes supraque mortalia ... macte ingenio este, caeli interpretes rerumque naturae capaces, argumenti repertores, quo deos hominesque vicistis*) mentions this fear of the ignorant: *tantorum numinum lege deprehensa et misera hominum mente iam soluta, in defectibus scelera aut mortem aliquam siderum pavente.* Cf. Cic. *Rep.* 1.23, 1.25, and 6.24 *namque ut olim deficere sol hominibus exstinguique visus est, cum Romuli anima haec ipsa in templa penetravit.* Also, Amm. may well have had in mind the famous passage Verg. *G.* 1.466–8.

> *ille (sol) etiam exstincto miseratus Caesare Romam*
> *cum caput obscura nitidum ferrugine texit*
> *impiaque aeternam timuerunt saecula noctem.*

According to Serv. ad loc. the – alleged – eclipse described by Vergil lasted exactly as long as the one under discussion: *solis fuisse defectum ab hora sexta usque ad noctem.* Cf. also Luc. 1.542/3 *gentesque coegit/desperare diem. Diutius* here does not mean *diutius solito* (Wagner), but 'for a long time', or even, as Rolfe says in his note ad loc., "for good and all".

primo attenuatum ... deinde ... auctum ... posteaque ... restitutum A harsh construction; the participles are in apposition to the preceding *solem*. About this use of the participle Blomgren 105 remarks: "iam vero Amm. pro sententia tota saepissime participium apposuisse cognovi". Indeed the participles here are equivalent to a relative clause: (solem) qui (autem) attenuatus ... auctus ... restitutus est. It is to be noted that the past participles describe a development which follows on *aestimabant*. The passage in 31.13.6, quoted by Blomgren, is similar: *conabantur modis omnibus vitam impendere non inultam: adeo magno animorum robore oppositi incumbentibus, ut ...* It is also remarkable that the events denoted by these participles do not explain the preceding sentence *diutius defecisse aestimabant*; on the contrary the reappearance of the sun is described, by which the fears of the common people were allayed. For *attenuare* see the note ad 19.11.3. In addition to the parallels quoted there cf. 21.12.17, 25.1.10, 31.3.8, 31.13.7.

in lunae corniculantis effigiem   The expression is traced by Szidat to Solin. 32.17 *macula quae dextero lateri eius* (sc. the bull Apis) *ingenita corniculantis lunae refert faciem*, imitated by Amm. in 22.14.7 *corniculantis lunae specie latere dextro insignis.* Apul. *Soc.* 1.117 writes *luna corniculata*.

Amm. describes the reappearance of the sun in terms indicating the phases of the moon, for which cf. Thuc. 2.28, quoted above, μηνοειδὴς γενόμενος. *Effigies* is used as a t.t. for the phases of the moon in Plin. *Nat.* 2.80 *easdem effigies paribus edit intervallis* and Mart. Cap. 8.864 *primi luminis effigies*, 8.870 *pleni luminis effigie*.

in speciem auctum semenstrem   *Semenstris* 'half a month old' is not quite accurate, as this would indicate the Full Moon, whereas Amm. means the Half Moon, which he calls *dichomenis* in § 10 and for which the usual terms were *dimidius, dimidiatus* (Le Boeuffle, 1973, 860). As we shall see, Amm. is also confused in his use of the term *intermenstruum*. In Apul. *Met.* 11.4, the only parallel for this use of *semenstris* in the OLD, *semenstris luna* is correct. Apart from the lack of precision in his terminology Amm. is wrong in saying that the sun can have the shape of the Half Moon when reappearing from behind the moon during an eclipse, since it remains crescent-shaped.

posteaque in integrum restitutum   Cf. Obseq. 62 *die toto ante sereno circa horam XI nox se intendit, deinde restitutus fulgor.*

III. 2 *quod alias non evenit ita perspicue, nisi cum*   With this formula Amm. introduces the excursus proper. The words *ita perspicue* are superfluous.

post inaequales cursus   It seems probable that Amm. has in mind Cicero's description of the planetarium (*sphaera*) built by Archimedes (*Rep* 1.22): *in eo admirandum esse inventum Archimedi, quod excogitasset quem ad modum in dissimillimis motibus inaequabiles et varios cursus* (sc. of the sun, the moon and the planets) *servaret una conversio* (sc. of the *sphaera*). *Hanc sphaeram Gallus cum moveret, fiebat ut soli luna totidem conversionibus in aere illo quot diebus in ipso caelo succederet, ex quo et in sphaera solis fieret eadem illa defectio, et incideret luna tum in eam metam quae esset umbra terrae* (cf. *obiectu metae noctis* in § 8), *cum sol e regione* (cf. § 3) ... Lactantius imitates this passage in *inst.* 2.5.18 *in quo ita solem et lunam composuit ut inaequales motus et coelestibus similes conversionibus singulis quasi diebus efficerent.*

Inaequales cursus refers to the courses of the sun and the moon, which are called *inaequales*, because the moon's orbit plane is inclined to that of the sun, the ecliptic. This is the interpretation given by Szidat, and despite the fact that he seems to refer *inaequales cursus* to the moon alone, it should be accepted. The same interpretation is implied by Rolfe p. 10, note 2.

The alternative explanation considered by Szidat is that *inaequalis* refers to the irregularity in the speed at which the moon travels around the earth. In this sense it is found in Germ. *fr.* 2.19–20 *cursus inaequalis cunctis* (sun, moon, planets): *nunc igne citato/festinare putes, nunc pigro sidere sumpto*, see Gain's commentary ad loc., 1976, 124. It should not be rejected offhand, as Szidat does, on the ground that this notion is not found in popular astronomical works and is, therefore, beyond the level of Amm.'s astronomical competence. In Geminos' Εἰσαγωγὴ εἰς τὰ φαινόμενα a long section (18.4–19) is devoted to the ἀνωμαλία τῆς σελήνης. There we find the acceleration of the moon (ἐπίτασις τῆς κινήσεως) and its slowing down (ἄνεσις) (§ 7). If we take *inaequales cursus* to refer to the moon and the sun, the different speeds at which they travel around the earth could be meant. In Amm.'s model, Cic. *Rep.* 1.22, however, this is expressed by the words *in dissimillimis motibus*, as in Cic. *Tusc.* 1.63 (about the same planetarium) *ut tarditate et celeritate dissimillimos motus una regeret conversio*.

iter menstruum lunae Valesius proposed this reading instead of *inter menstruum* VE, *intermenstruum* BAG. He was followed by all later editors. There are, however, strong reasons to retain the ms. reading. *Intermenstruum* means "the period between two lunar months, the time of the New Moon" (OLD), as in Var. *R* 1.37.1 and Cic. *Rep.* 1.25, i.e. the time at which the moon is in conjunction with the sun. *Cum intermenstruum lunae ad idem revocatur initium* would mean: 'When the conjunction of the moon and the sun recurs in the same place again'. The addition of *lunae*, which is, strictly speaking, superfluous, makes it clear that Amm. is thinking not of the time of the *intermenstruum* but of the position of the moon at that moment. *Iter menstruum* produces a statement which is at best ambiguous. In the words of Szidat: "Ohne den Kontext könnte die Wendung ... den synodischen Umlauf des Mondes und die jeweils folgende Konjunktion mit der Sonne bezeichnen". Amm. takes great pains, however, to distinguish between the monthly conjunction and the particular conjunction during which a solar eclipse occurs: *alias non evenit ... nisi cum. Certis temporum intervallis* would be pointless if referring to the monthly conjunction at New Moon, excluded again by *id est cum ... tota repperitur luna sub sole liniamentis obiecta rectissimis*. This is what is expressed without any ambiguity by *intermenstruum lunae ad idem revocatur initium*. A further argument to retain *intermenstruum* is that after his discussion of Archimedes' planetarium, from which Amm. borrowed the phrase *post inaequales cursus*, Cicero describes the conditions under which a solar eclipse occurs as follows (*Rep.* 1.25): *certo illud* (i.e. the solar eclipse) *tempore fieri* (cf. *certis temporum intervallis* below) *et necessario, cum tota se luna sub orbem solis subiecisset; itaque etsi non omni intermenstruo, tamen id fieri non posse nisi intermenstruo tempore*. It should be added that the words *ad idem revocatur initium* are strongly reminiscent of Cic. *Rep.* 6.24 about the Great Year: *ut olim deficere sol hominibus extinguique visus est ... quandoque ab eadem parte sol eodemque tempore iterum defecerit, tum signis omnibus ad idem principium stellisque revocatis* e.q.s. It seems very likely that Cicero's *Rep.* determined Amm.'s phraseology.

One serious difficulty remains. Valesius was moved to his conjecture, however hesitantly ("paene adducor ut credam"), by the fact that in § 11 Amm. says *non nisi tempore intermenstrui deficere visam usquam lunam*. With *intermenstruum* in its proper meaning this is nonsense, as a lunar eclipse only occurs at the Full Moon. For that reason Valesius supposed that Amm. understood *intermenstrui tempus* to mean the period of the Full Moon and he changed the text in § 2 accordingly. It is, however, methodically indefensible to go against a reading which is found in all manuscripts, makes excellent sense in the context of the passage and is in accordance with the model followed by the author, while at the same time attributing a meaning to a word which is unattested elsewhere. We must, therefore, retain the manuscript reading *intermenstruum* and accept the conclusion that in § 11 Amm. makes an embarrassing mistake. As we shall see, it is not the only one in this chapter.

ad idem revocatur initium   Amm. frequently uses *revocare* in a metaphorical sense, e.g. 20.7.11 *nec confixi mortiferis vulneribus plurimi ceteros ab audacia parili revocabant*. See also 15.5.23, 20.8.17, 24.4.17, 24.8.7, 25.3.3. Cf. Cic. *Rep.* 6.24 quoted above.

certis temporum intervallis   Cf. Cic. *Rep.* 1.25 quoted above and, in the same context, Cic. *Rep.* 6.24 *longis intervallis*. Pliny *Nat.* 2.48 writes *stati autem atque menstrui non sunt utrique defectus propter obliquitatem signiferi lunaeque multivagos ... flexus non semper in scripulis partium congruente siderum motu*.

in domicilio eiusdem signi   This refers to the signs of the Zodiac, cf. 26.1.13 *per quae duodecim siderum domicilia sol discurrens* and 31.13.7. Macr. *sat.* 1.12.10 combines *domicilium* and *signum: duodecim zodiaci signis, quorum certa certorum numinum domicilia creduntur*.

tota repperitur luna   In his note ad loc. ("I.e. the Full Moon; cf. § 7") Rolfe confuses lunar and solar eclipses.

liniamentis ... rectissimis   *Liniamentum* here has its geometrical meaning, as in Cic. *de Orat.* 1.187. Elsewhere Amm. uses *liniamenta* of the outlines of the body: 14.6.17, 22.15.13, 24.2.10, 25.4.22, 30.9.6.

in his paulisper consistit minutis   *Consistere* is not found elsewhere in connection with eclipses but is sometimes used for the apparent pause in the movement of the planets (Le Boeuffle, 1973, 916/8). Szidat provides the correct interpretation for *consistere*: "das scheinbare Verweilen des Mondes vor der Sonnenscheibe bei einer Sonnenfinsternis".

quas geometrica ratio partium partes appellat   For the personification of *geometrica ratio*, which in itself is not exceptional, see Blomgren 85–6. The expression is found from Cic. onwards: *Ac.* 2.117 *quodsi (sapiens) geometricis rationibus non est crediturus*, cf. also Chalcid. *comm.* 33 (p. 83.16 Waszink) and Macr. *comm.* 1.20.17; TLL VI 2.1909.84 sqq. *Pars* is the t.t. for one degree of the ecliptic (Le Boeuffle, 1973, 275–6). For *minutum* cf. Firm. *Math.* 2.5.1. *una pars in minuta dividitur sexaginta*. Pliny *Nat.* 2.48 (quoted above) speaks of *scripulae partium*.

III. 3   Having explained in § 2 that solar eclipses do not occur at monthly intervals at the New Moon but only when the moon is on a straight line between the sun and the earth, Amm. goes on to explain that solar eclipses do not occur at yearly intervals either, when both the sun and the moon (*utriusque sideris*) have completed their courses and are in the same sign again (*in unum eundemque finem ... conveniunt*). Although this does not help to understand the phenomenon, it does add a new element, so that it cannot be said that § 3 merely repeats what had been said already in § 2, as Szidat I 117 does.

ac licet ... conveniunt   As was observed by Ehrismann 62–3, Amm. uses the subjunctive after *licet*, when the main verb is in the present or future tense. This is one of the two exceptions to this rule, the other being 28.5.7 *ac licet iustus quidam arbiter rerum factum incusabit perfectum ... pensato tamen negotio non feret indigne*.

conversiones et motus   Borrowed from Cicero *Tusc.* 1.62 *illa non re, sed vocabulo errantia, quorum conversiones omnesque motus qui animo vidit* e.q.s., repeated in 5.69 *totius mundi motus conversionesque*.

scrutatores causarum intellegibilium adverterant   With these words Amm.

refers to the doxographical tradition (Szidat), as in § 8 *opiniones variae collegerunt* and § 11 *doctrina multiplici congruente*. *Scrutari* is one of Amm.'s favourite verbs, used 25 times; *scrutator* is used by him only here. Suet. has it once (*Cl.* 35) as well as [Quint.] *Decl.* p. 364.10 Håkanson. In Statius it is found 4 times, *Theb.* 6.880, 7.720, *Silv.* 3.1.84, 3.3.92. *Intelligibilis* is found for the first time in Apuleius (*Pl.* 1.9) but is frequent only in 4th century writers (Chalcid., Hier., August.). As a rule it is in opposition to *visibilis*, c.q. *sensi(bi)lis* to reproduce the Greek opposition νοητός-αἰσθητός: Hier. *In Is.* 7.10 *νοητά ... quae nos possumus dicere intellegibilia* and Chalcid. *comm.* 302 (p. 304.7 Waszink) *intellegibilia ... sunt, quae intellectu comprehenduntur* (opp. *sensilia*), TLL VII 1.2095–6. Whereas an eclipse can be observed with the senses, the explanation of the phenomenon is a matter for the intellect.

For the use of the pluperfect *adverterant* instead of the perfect see the note ad 14.7.12. To the literature quoted there add Pighi, 1935, 112 sqq. and Szantyr 321. Both Szantyr and Hagendahl, 1921, 121 point to the influence of prose-rhythm on the choice of the tenses. By using the pluperfect Amm. creates a cursus tardus: *intelligibilium advérterant*. For the synizesis in the final syllables of *intelligibilium* see Harmon 223–4.

in unum eundemque finem   Here *finis* indicates the position reached after the completion of a year. In Apul. *Pl.* 1.10 it is used of the completion of the *magnus annus: unde fit ut magnus ille vocitatus annus facile noscatur, cuius tempus implebitur, cum vagantium stellarum comitatus ad eundem pervenerit finem.*

lunari cursu impleto   *Lunaris = lunae* is found in 14.11.25 – *circulo*, 23.6.85 – *aspergine*, 24.5.8 and 31.13.11 – *splendore*, 25.1.16 – *acie*. For *lunaris cursus* and – *globus* (below § 4) see TLL VII 2.1838.18–20 and VI 2.2051.71, 2053.82 respectively.

perenni distinctione   Added to qualify *unum eundemque*. Of course, the sun and the moon stay in their distinct orbits. The same idea is expressed in the next section by the words *parili comitatu obtinentes circulos proprios* and *salvaque ratione altitudinis interiectae*. *Distinctio* and *distinguere* in connection with the stars always mean 'embellish(ment)', see Pease's note ad Cic. *N.D.* 2.15. The meaning 'distance' required here is not found elsewhere in astronomical contexts.

e regione   Used both for the conjunction and for the opposition of the moon and the sun in relation to the earth. Szidat ad loc. quotes as parallels Cic. *Div.* 2.17, *N.D.* 2.103, *Rep.* 1.22.

velut libramento quodam In Seneca *libramentum* is found twice in discussions of eclipses (*Nat.* 1.12.1 and *Ben.* 5.6.4 *si in transcursu strinxit, obducit, modo plus tegit, si maiorem partem sui obiecit, modo excludit totius adspectum, si recto libramento inter solem terrasque media successit*). Other borrowings from Seneca's *Nat.* are pointed out in Gercke's edition, 1907 = 1970, XIX.

igneo orbi et aspectui nostro opponitur media A flowery expression for *inter solem et terram interest*. The sun is called *igneus orbis* in the excursus on the rainbow as well: 20.11.26 *supinantur volubiliter contra ipsum igneum orbem irimque conformant*. For *opponere* in a geographical context see 22.8.13 *arcus utrimque tenues duo ... e regione sibi oppositi*.

III. 4 In this section Amm. introduces the technical vocabulary of astronomy in speaking about the nodes. In this way he summarizes and formalizes the contents of sections 2 and 3.

ad summam 'in short', cf. 15.8.14 and 23.5.22. It is found from Cicero onwards, e.g. *Att.* 7.7.7 *ad summam, "dic, Marce Tulli"*.

astrorum omnium infimus The position of the moon is described in similar terms in Cic. *Rep.* 6.17 *hunc* (sc. solem) *ut comites consequuntur Veneris alter, alter Mercurii cursus, in infimoque orbe Luna radiis solis accensa convertitur* and 18 *gravissimo autem* (sono) *hic lunaris* (cursus) *atque infimus*. Cf. also Chalcid. *comm.* 87 (p. 138.17 Waszink) *lunae globum, qui est infimus proximusque terrae*.

parili comitatu obtinentes circulos proprios The sun, the moon and the planets stay within the belt of the Zodiac: Plin. *Nat.* 2.66 *per hunc* (the Zodiac) *stellae quas diximus* (sun, moon, and planets) *feruntur*. In this respect they may be said to form a *comitatus*, as e.g. in Apul. *Pl.* 1.10 quoted above ad § 3 *in unum eundemque finem*. The sun and the moon are said to travel together along the ecliptic in Macr. *comm.* 1.15.10 *tertia ducta per medium* (zodiacum) *ecliptica vocatur, quia cum cursum suum in eadem linea pariter sol et luna conficiunt, alterius eorum necesse est evenire defectum*. With respect to Venus and Mercury we find the same idea in Chalcid. *comm.* 124 (p. 167.20 Waszink) *parabolas enim quasdam appellat, qui comitatus sunt siderum, ut iuxta solem individui semper Mercurius et Lucifer*, quoted by Szidat. For *circuli proprii* cf. Gem. 12.23 Νυνὶ δὲ ἰδία τίς ἐστιν ἡ περὶ ἕκαστον (planet) σφαιροποιία and 24 οὕτω δὴ καὶ περὶ τὸν ἥλιον καὶ περὶ τὴν σελήνην ἰδία τίς ἐστι ... κίνησις and Chalcid. *comm.* 77 (p. 125.7 Waszink) *propriis circulis per quos feruntur* (the planets) *aequali semper ordinatoque gressu*. From the fact that only in Chalcid. and Amm. *comitatus* and *circulus proprius* are found in astronomical contexts (see, however, Apul. *Pl.* 1.10 quoted above and cf. Cic. *Rep.* 6.17 *ut comites*), Szidat concluded that Amm. "aus dem Ueberlieferungsstrom geschöpft hat, der zu Chalcidius führt" (I 120). This is certainly better than to try to trace the digression to one specific Greek source, e.g. Cleomedes.

iunctim locati The adverb is rarely found in classical prose. The instances quoted in TLL VII 2.648.8 sqq. are mostly from 4th century authors. As is pointed out in the TLL-article, *iunctim locati* prepares *iuncturis* in this section.

ut scienter et decore Ptolemaeus exponit Viz. *Alm.* 6.5. The quotation does not, of course, prove that Amm. had studied Ptolemy. His literal translation of σύνδεσμοι, *coagmenta defectiva*, is found nowhere else. The normal translation *nodus* is used by Lucr. 5.687-8 *ubi anni / nodus nocturnas exaequat lucibus umbras* for the intersection of the ecliptic and the celestial equator. See Le Boeuffle, 1973, 859 sqq. Below Amm. uses *iuncturae* and *articuli* for the nodes.

Decorus is the Latin equivalent of πρέπον, which means that the author writes in a style that suits both his subject matter and his audience. Cicero discusses this stylistic requirement in *Orat.* 70-1: *huius ignoratione non modo in vita sed saepissime et in poematis et in oratione peccatur*. See Lausberg, 1960, 1057, Martin, 1974, 250 and Leeman-Pinkster ad Cic. *de Orat.* 1.144.

ad dimensiones venerint See TLL V 1.1192.68 sqq., where *dimensio* is called a geometrical and astronomical t.t. In the examples quoted there, *dimensio* indicates either the act of measuring, dimensions in the modern sense of the word (e.g. Macr. *comm.* 1.5.9 *omne corpus longitudinis, latitudinis et altitudinis dimensionibus constat*) or a line of intersection, as in Hyg. *Astr.* 1.3 *dimensioque totius ostenditur sphaerae cum ... rectae ut virgulae perducuntur, quae dimensio ... axis est appellata*. *Dimensio* does not indicate the point of intersection, as should be the case here, since it refers to the nodes. Still, the term is found in this context, e.g. in Hyg. *Astr.* 4.14.3 *lunae autem eclipsis sic evenit, cum prope una dimensione sit luna, cum abierit sol sub terram* ("lorsque la lune est sur le même diamètre que le soleil disparu sous terre", Le Boeuffle). Possibly Amm. meant by *dimensiones* the beginning and the end of the line segment connecting the nodes. Cf. Theo Sm. p. 194 ἔσται αὐτῶν (the orbit-planes of the sun and the moon) κοινὴ τομὴ εὐθεῖα, ἐφ' ἧς ἀμφοτέρων (sun and moon) ἐστὶ τὰ κέντρα, ἥτις εὐθεῖα τρόπον τινὰ κοινὴ διάμετρος (*dimensio*) ἔσται ἀμφοῖν· ἧς τὰ ἄκρα, καθ' ἃ τέμνειν δοκοῦσιν ἀλλήλους οἱ κύκλοι, σύνδεσμοι καλοῦνται.

In 26.1.8 Amm. uses *dimensio* in defining the length of the year: *si (sol) a secunda particula elatus Arietis ad eam dimensione redierit terminata*. Here *dimensio* is the equivalent of *cursus*.

ἀναβιβάζοντας - καταβιβάζοντας   Note that the Greek terms are more precise than their modern equivalents "ascending" and "descending" nodes, since the nodes themselves do not ascend or descend, but seem to "send up" and "–down" the moon to the north and the south of the ecliptic.

Graeco dictitamus sermone   Especially when treating scientific subjects Amm. likes to present himself as a Greek by using the first person plural. Cf. 14.11.8 *colligit visa nocturna quas phantasias nos appellamus*, 15.9.2 *Timagenes, et diligentia Graecus et lingua* and 17.7.11. Amm. regularly uses the frequentativum *dictitare* when explaining technical terms or words from other languages: 16.10.8 *catafracti equites, quos clibanarios dictitant*, 21.2.5 *feriarum die, quem celebrantes mense Ianuario Christiani Epiphania dictitant*, 22.4.9 *pabula iumentorum, quae vulgo dictitant capita*. Amm.'s use of *dictitare* does not confirm Fesser's dictum, 1932, 34: "Der unterschiedslose Gebrauch von intensiven und einfachen Formen zeigt wie Amm. ohne inneres Gefühl die Sprache handhabt". In all cases where *dictitare* is found the notion of repetition or usage is explicitly or implicitly present. For frequentativa and intensiva in general see the notes ad 14.2.6 and 14.6.8. About Amm.'s motives to write in Latin see most recently Matthews, 1982, 1122–4 and Calboli, 1983, 33–53.

III. 5 In this section Amm. explains the difference between partial and total eclipses. As Szidat points out, he is the only Latin author apart from Seneca to make this distinction.

si contigua ... praestrinxerint spatia   For *praestringere* cf. Suet. *Aug.* 29 *cum ... lecticam eius fulgur praestrinxisset*. Amm. uses the verb often, see De Jonge ad 14.7.10, who paraphrases it as "transeundo attingere".
   Cf. Sen. *Ben.* 5.6.4 quoted above ad § 3 *velut libramento quodam*. Szidat gives the exact circumstances under which total and partial eclipses occur.

dilutior   'Light' in opposition to *crassatus* below. The effect of the partiality of the eclipse, viz. that it becomes less dark than during a total eclipse, is here transferred to the partial eclipse itself. TLL V 1.1190.63 "in imag. i.q. *manifestus*" is wrong. The word is used with the same meaning in 20.11.28.

qui coactius ascensus vinciunt et descensus   A paraphrase of ἀναβιβάζοντας καὶ καταβιβάζοντας συνδέσμους. *Coactus*, which normally means 'tight', 'stiff' (30.5.14 *coacto gradu*) is chosen here because of the preceding *coagmenta*.

crassato aere   Szidat gives as a parallel 23.5.12 *ex parva nubicula subito aere crassato usus adimitur lucis*. In its normal meaning 'thick', 'dense' *crassatus* occurs in 19.4.6 *affirmant etiam alii terrarum habitu densiore crassatum aera*. The identification of darkness and density is found also in Lucr. 4.349-50 *caliginis aer crassior insequitur* and Sen. *Nat*. 1.2.4 *ob aeris densi obscuritatem*.

ne proxima quidem et apposita cernere queamus   Cf. HA *Gd*. 23.2 *sed indicium non diu imperaturi Gordiani hoc fuit quod eclipsis solis facta est ut nox crederetur neque sine luminibus accensis quidquam agi posset*.

III. 6   The discussion of the solar eclipse is followed by a section on the 'two suns' (*sol geminus*; παρήλιον). Strictly speaking, the subject is out of place as this is a meteorological, rather than an astronomical phenomenon. Szidat concludes from this: "Die Gliederung des Stoffes ist mindestens zu einem Teil Ammians Eigentum" (I 113). But it can be shown that in popular astronomical treatises this subject was regularly treated in connection with the eclipses. In the second book of Pliny's Natural History § 1-101 are devoted to the stars, while § 102-153 deal with meteorology. The discussion on halo-forming and parhelia forms the end of the section on astronomy (§ 99-100). In Seneca *Nat*. 1.11 and 13 the parhelion is discussed, while 1.12 explains the solar eclipse. In 2.6, immediately after the section on eclipses, Cleomedes treats the phenomenon of the sun sometimes remaining visible after it has set, which he explains in terms that are very similar to those used by Amm. in this section: νέφους παχυτέρου πρὸς τῇ δύσει ὄντος καὶ λαμπρυνομένου ὑπὸ τῶν ἡλιακῶν ἀκτίνων καὶ ἡλίου ἡμῖν φαντασίαν ἀποπέμποντος (224.4 sqq. Ziegler). Finally, the description of Archimedes' planetarium in *Rep*. 1.21-25, which helps explain many expressions in Amm.'s excursus, was provoked by Scipio's question concerning the phenomenon of *sol geminus*: 1.19 *Quaesierat ex me Scipio quidnam sentirem de hoc quod duo soles visos esse constaret*. It seems not unlikely that this phenomenon was explained after the section on the planetarium, in which the eclipses played an important role, i.e. in the lacuna following 1.22, as E. Bréguet suggested on internal grounds in a note on p. 260-1 of her Budé-edition of *Rep*. I: "Il faut remarquer que l'explication du double soleil ne pouvait se faire au moyen de la sphère d'Archimède. Etait-elle donnée dans la lacune?" In his commentary on *Rep*., 1984, 102 Büchner also supposes that the *sol geminus* had been discussed in the lacuna. In view of these parallels it is rash to suppose with Boll, art. Finsternisse, RE VI (1909)

2352, that Amm.'s source was Cleomedes on the ground that in his work the parhelion is discussed immediately after the eclipses. This seems to have been common practice. For other discussions of this phenomenon see Pease ad Cic. *N.D.* 2.14 and Le Boeuffle, 1973, 180.

erecta solito celsius nubes For comparative with *solito* see the note ad 14.6.9. Seneca's description runs as follows: *Nat.* 1.11.3 *sunt autem imagines solis in nube spissa et vicina in modum speculi.* The same explanation is offered in 25.10.3 for the appearance of comets: *hanc speciem tunc apparere cum erecta solito celsius nubes aeternorum ignium vicinitate colluceat.* There, as here, *aeternorum ignium propinquitate* refers exclusively to the sun. For Amm.'s use of the plural see Hagendahl, 1921, 73–98.

orbis alterius claritudinem See the note ad 14.6.23 about Amm.'s frequent use of the so-called genitivus inversus; cf. also Szantyr 152.

tamquam e speculo puriore formaverit Seneca *Nat.* 1.5.1 gives two views concerning mirror images: *alii enim in illis simulacra cerni putant, id est corporum nostrorum figuras a nostris corporibus emissas ac separatas; alii non imagines sed ipsa aspici retorta oculorum acie et in se rursus reflexa.* The expression *orbis alterius claritudinem* suggests that Amm. prefers the former explanation. If this is correct, *in speculo* would be more appropriate than *e speculo*.

III. 7 *nunc veniamus* For a collection of transition formulas in Amm.'s digressions, which are usually introduced by *hactenus* or *haec*, see Emmett, 1981, 25.

apertum et evidentem Cf. Hier. *Ep.* 69.9 *tam apertum evidensque praeceptum.* The same combination is found in Claud. Don. *Aen.* 2.550, p. 225, 4 Georgius *quid tam apertum, quid tam evidens.* The phrase may be compared with *ita perspicue* in the opening sentence of the discussion of the solar eclipse (§ 2).

pleno lumine rotundata Rotundatus is found only here in Amm. Vell. 2.59.6 has it in a similar context: *solis orbis super caput eius curvatus aequaliter rotundatusque.*

solique contraria 'In opposition'. For this meaning of *contrarius* cf. Cens. 8.10 *a septimo zodio quod est contrarium* (sc. *primo*).

centum octoginta partibus ... disparatur Amm. uses the same phrase when he speaks about distances on earth, cf. 21.9.6 *venisset Bononiam a Sirmio miliario decimo disparatam et nono*, 22.8.20 *duobus milibus et quingentis stadiis disparatum*, 24.1.3 *ut decimo paene lapide dispararentur a signiferis primis*.

signo septimo As the ecliptic is divided into twelve parts by the signs of the zodiac, *signo septimo* indicates a position opposite the sun, which is *signo primo*.

plenilunium Post-classical for *luna plena*. It is found in Col. 11.2.85 *pridie quam plenilunium sit* and Plin. *Nat.* 2.80 *plenilunio abscondente (stellas)*.

non semper deficit tamen Amm. repeats mutatis mutandis what he has said in § 3 about the frequency of solar eclipses. One would expect him to explain why a lunar eclipse does not occur at every Full Moon. Instead he describes what happens during a lunar eclipse. Szidat observes I 122–3 that in this respect, too, Amm. follows the general practice of Latin authors of not stating under which exact conditions the moon is eclipsed.

III. 8 *circa terrenam mobilitatem locata* This phrase raises a serious difficulty. Szidat rightly rejects all interpretations which would imply that the earth itself is in motion. His tentative solution, viz. that the words could refer to the moon's course around the earth is linguistically impossible and is not supported by the parallel he quotes from Cassiodorus (*in psalm.* 148, 276 sqq. *fabricam quoque caeli quae semper rotabili mobilitate se sustinet*). According to the accepted astronomical theory the celestial sphere revolves around the earth, whereas the earth itself rests at the centre of the universe. The only motion we might think of would be the rotation of the earth around its own axis, a notion which was entertained by Heraclides Ponticus and Aristarchus of Samos, but never found general acceptance. Moreover, the proper term for rotation would be *conversio*, rather than *mobilitas*. A.D. Leeman suggested in a personal communication that the solution is to be found in Cicero's *Somnium*, one of the sources used by Amm. in this digression. In § 17 Cicero describes the universe as consisting of nine concentrical spheres, of which the celestial sphere is the outermost, the terrestrial globe the innermost one. The celestial sphere is called *extumus*, a word found only here in Cicero, who always has *extremus*; it may have inspired Amm.'s phrase (*luna*) *a caelo totius pulchritudinis extima*. About the moon Cicero writes *in infimoque orbe luna radiis solis accensa convertitur* (§ 17) and in § 18 (*cursus*) *hic lunaris atque infimus*. With these passages compare Amm.'s *lunaris globus, astrorum omnium infimus* (§ 4). The words *radiis solis accensa* are echoed in § 8 *quam numquam habere proprium lumen opiniones variae collegerunt*. The description in *Somnium* 17 ends with the sentence *nam ea quae est media et nona, tellus,* *neque movetur et infima est* and in § 18 we read *nam terra nona inmobilis manens*. On the basis of Cicero's description Leeman proposed to read *circa terrenam immobilitatem*, which is paleographically attractive and in accordance with the accepted theory about the earth in the universe.

The adjective *terrenam* is used instead of the genitive *terrae*. *Terrena immobilitas* is equivalent to *terra immota* or – *immobilis* (Chalcid. *comm.* 178 (p. 207.9 Waszink), Apul. *Pl.* 1.11). See Szantyr 152 and Blomgren 83 n. 2, who quotes 26.10.16 as a parallel: *tremefacta concutitur omnis terreni stabilitas ponderis*.

a caelo totius pulchritudinis extima For the gen. qual. see the note ad 16.12.9 *non iacentis animi Caesarem*. *Totus* is equivalent to *summus* here, a meaning for which Löfstedt's comm. on the *Peregr. Aeth.* p. 69 quotes some parallels from late authors. Among his examples, to which may be added CIL 10.4524.3–4 *totius bonitatis femina*, is Claud. Mam. *anim.* 1.13 *habens corpus totius facilitatis maximaeque pulchritudinis*. There is at least one example from the classical period: Cic. *Tim.* 17 *unum opus totum et perfectum ex omnibus totis atque perfectis*. See also the note ad 15.1.2 *tota facilitate*; 26.8.10 *proterviae totius auctore* is another parallel in Amm.

ferienti se subserit lanci In view of the exceptional use of *lanx* 'the solar disk' in § 1 the sun must be meant here. This is awkward, because it could be taken to mean that a lunar eclipse can occur when the moon comes between the sun and the earth. As Amm. has just explained that the moon is eclipsed only when it is full, he would be flatly contradicting himself. "Eine sehr ungeschickte Ausdrucksweise" (Szidat) would be the least one could say about it. After the correct explanation given in § 7 we must suppose that the text should be paraphrased as follows: 'the moon (as seen from the earth) is (fully) exposed to the sun's rays' *(ferienti lanci)*.

Amm. uses *subserere* 11 times. In its literal meaning = *subicere* it is found here and in 15.1.3 and 31.2.3. In 16.7.4 and 29.5.1 *subserere* means 'to insert', 'to add'. In all other instances (14.11.3, 14.11.10, 16.2.4, 25.7.10, 28.4.26, 30.8.12) the notion of surreptitiousness is present, e.g. 14.11.3 *arcanos susurros nutrimenta fictis criminibus subserentes*. See the notes ad 14.11.3 and 15.1.3. Ad 16.2.4 it is mistakenly suggested that *subserere* is a compound of *serere* 'to sow'.

obiectu metae noctis Amm. borrowed the expression from Cic. *Div.* 2.17 *(luna) incurrat in umbram terrae, quae est meta noctis*, as does Boethius *Cons.* 4, carm. 5.8–9 *palleant plenae cornua lunae, infecta metis noctis opacae*. Cf. also Cic. *N.D.* 2.103 *tum ipsa incidens in umbram terrae, cum est e regione solis, interpositu interiectuque terrae repente deficit*. *Terrae obiectu* is found in Plin. *Nat.* 2.47.

in conum desinentis angustum The shape of the shadow cast by the earth is regularly compared to a cone or a spinning-top in Greek and Latin astronomical works: Plin. *Nat.* 2.47 *figuram ... umbrae similem metae ac turbini inverso* and 2.51 *metae exsistere effigiem in cacuminis finem desinentem.* In classical Latin *conus* is rare. It occurs in Cic. *N.D.* 1.24 and Lucr. 4.429 and 5.764 (about the lunar eclipse). Szidat compares again the very similar expressions in Chalcid. *comm.* 90 (p. 143.1 Waszink) *in modum coni desinens in acumen* and Macr. *comm.* 1.15.11.

nigrantibus involvitur globis Cf. Sil. 4.441 *(tempestas) nigrantisque globos ... torquens* and 6.321-2 *nigrantem torquens stridentibus austris/portat turbo globum.* Amm. uses a similar phrase in 17.7.2 *concreti nubium globi nigrantium*, where see De Jonge's note.

ut sphaerae inferioris curvamine circumfusus The lunar eclipse is described as a solar eclipse observed from the moon. The *sphaera inferior* must be the earth, which blocks the sun's rays with its round shape. The same idea is expressed by *mole obsistente terrena. Curvamen* is used again in the digression on the rainbow (20.11.26). There the word has its usual meaning of 'a curved outline'. The meaning required here is 'a curved or circular form'. This meaning is found in Ovid, who uses *curvamen* often: *Met.* 12.95-6 *haesurum clipei curvamine telum/misit in Aeaciden.* Cf. Hagendahl, 1921, 33-4.

Next, in § 9-11 Amm. discusses the phases of the moon. His exposition is in accordance with the traditional distinction of seven phases (see fig. 3 above), which is clearly expressed in Firm. *Math.* 4.1.10: *est itaque luna aut synodica, aut plena aut dichotomos aut menoeides, aut amficyrtos. et per has mutata formas cursum menstrui luminis complet.* Firmicus distinguishes firstly the New Moon and the Full Moon, then the moon in its First and Last Quarter (*dichotomos*). Next he mentions the phases in between, *menoeides*, which comes between Quarter and New Moon, and *amficyrtos*, which comes between Quarter and Full Moon. So there are seven phases in all, as is stated explicitly by Macrobius (*comm.* 1.6.55): *septem ... permutationibus, quas* φάσεις *vocant, toto mense distinguitur (sc. luna): cum nascitur, cum fit* διχότομος, *et cum fit* ἀμφίκυρτος, *cum plena, et rursus* ἀμφίκυρτος, *ac denuo* διχότομος, *et cum ad nos luminis universitate privatur.* Amm. enumerates the phases between New Moon and Full Moon and, for the sake of brevity, says that the moon goes through the same phases again between Full Moon and New Moon. He uses the Greek terms for the moonphases, as do the other late Latin authors who discuss this subject (Firmicus Maternus, Macrobius and Martianus Capella). For the Latin terminology see Le Boeuffle 1973, 856-79 and Soubiran, 1969, 122 in the annotation of his Budé-edition of Vitruvius IX.

Amm.'s terminology is traditional except for the use of *dichomenis* instead of *dichotomos* for Quarter Moon. Szidat I 125 is of the opinion that Amm.'s exposition offers a "bedeutsame und wichtige Erweiterung" (compared with Cleom. 2.5, Firm. *Math.* 4.1.10 and Plin. *Nat.* 2.42), "nämlich die Phase gracilescens". This is certainly overstating the case. Amm. does not speak of a phase *gracilescens* on a par with *menoeides, dichomenis* etc. What is said in § 10 is only that the crescent of the moon, when it reappears after New Moon, is still very slender. The traditional phases stand out by the use of the Greek technical terms (*menoides est appellata, fit Graeco sermone dichomenis, figuram monstrat amphicyrti*). Vitruvius (9.2.3), quoted as a parallel by Szidat, is not to be compared with Amm., as he avoids the traditional terms altogether and speaks in a more technical fashion about the moon in the days after the New Moon as *luna prima, – secunda* and so on. In Macrobius, *comm.* 1.6.55, quoted above, which Szidat mentions as a possible parallel, it is more natural to take the words *cum nascitur* and *cum ... privatur* as a circumlocution of *menoeides* than as the equivalent of a phase *gracilescens*. Macrobius mentions just one phase between New Moon and Quarter. It is utterly unlikely that he should leave out the half-way phase *menoeides* in order to include a phase between *menoeides* and New Moon.

Szidat's qualification of this passage as "sachlich ... fehlerfrei" can only be accepted if the word *intermenstruum* at the end of § 11 is taken to mean 'half-way between two New Moons, i.e. at Full Moon', as Szidat does. As we saw, this is an unattested meaning of *intermenstruum*.

III. 9 *Et cum ad idem signum ... soli concurrerit* *Cum* iterativum with a subjunctive, which we find throughout this section, is discussed by Szantyr 624. For Amm. see the notes ad 14.2.2 and ad 14.2.7. *Concurrere* has its complement in the dative, as in 23.3.5 *mandabatque eis ut ... apud Assyrios adhuc agenti sibi concurrerent*.

aequis partibus The expression is found rather frequently (TLL I 1031.1–8). Here it must be understood in the astronomical sense 'on the same longitudinal degree' (so Szidat), *pars* having the same meaning as in § 7 *centum octoginta partibus ... disparatur. Aequis partibus* is more exact than *idem signum*, one *signum* containing 360 : 12 = 30 *partes*.

obscuratur, ut dictum est As this is the first remark about the phases of the moon, Amm. either inadvertently copied *ut dictum est* from his source or confuses the invisibility of the moon during an eclipse with that during the *intermenstruum*. A possible confusion of this kind was found in § 8 *ferienti se subserit lanci* and will be seen again in § 11 *tempore intermenstrui*. For the first possibility *praediximus* in § 12 will offer a striking parallel.

penitus hebetato candore *Penitus* is used by Amm. mostly with negative verbs like *ignorare, vastare, abolere* (in 22.15.30 it should, therefore, be taken with *oblitteraretur memoria*, not with the words that follow, as all editors do). *Hebetare* is found 18 times in Amm., e.g. 31.1.2 *squalidi solis exortus hebetabant matutinos diei candores*. See De Jonge ad 17.10.2. It is used in Germ. *Arat.* 493 of the sun, in Plin. *Nat.* 2.47 of the moon: *illius* (terrae) *umbra sidus* (= lunam) *hebetari*. For *candor* cf. Apul. *Met.* 11.1 *praemicantis lunae candore nimio*.

et tunc lunae Graece synodos dicitur The text is not above suspicion. As it stands, *tunc ... dicitur* is short for 'then the phenomenon occurs which in Greek is called *synodos*'. Comparable, if less harsh, because of the relative *quae*, is Liv. 40.3.3 *in Emathiam, quae nunc dicitur*. For similar cases see TLL V 1.982.2–15. The phrase may well be a Grecism: X. *HG* 5.1.10 ἔνθα ἡ Τριπυργία καλεῖται. Amm. introduces Greek technical terms in a variety of ways, e.g. 21.1.8 *quae tethimena sermo Graecus appellat*, 17.7.11 *quas Graece syringas appellamus*, 20.3.4 *quos ἀναβιβάζοντας e.q.s. Graeco dictitamus sermone*, 22.15.29 (explaining the word 'pyramid') *ad ignis speciem, tu pyros, ut nos dicimus, extenuatur*, 23.4.10 *quam helepolin Graeci cognominamus*. In view of the last two examples De Jonge's remark at 14.11.8 that 'we' in such cases does not mean 'we Greeks' but "wir Römer mit griechischen Bildung" seems untenable. Compare the note ad § 4 *Graeco dictitamus sermone*, see also A. & A. Cameron, 1964, 324–5.

II. 10 *nasci autem putatur* For the 'biological' terminology (cf. *senescere* in § 11) see Le Boeuffle, 1973, 863–5.

cum ... superiectum egerit solem The reading *gerit* Vm2, kept by Rolfe, is easier to understand than Heraeus' *egerit*. But Amm. uses the perfect subjunctive throughout this section, so *gerit* cannot be correct. The meaning of *agere* must be 'to bring out', 'show' as in [Tib.] 3.7.157 *quippe ubi non umquam Titan super egerit ortus* and Man. 1.827 *quod nisi vicinos agerent* (sc. meteors) *occasibus ortus*. See TLL I 1376.8–36. For *superiectum* cf. 20.11.29 *a nubis similitudine superiectae*.

parva declinatione velut e perpendiculo "with a slight deviation from the plumb-line" (Rolfe, whose text is incorrect in this sentence: the words *et tunc lunae* should follow *candore* in § 9). Amm. uses *ad perpendiculum* in 14.8.11 (q.v.) and 29.2.16, *ex perpendiculo* in 21.16.3 *palatinas dignitates velut ex quodam tribuens perpendiculo*, where it must mean 'scrupulously, with meticulous care'. In an astronomical context it occurs in Vitr. 9.2.1 and Chalcid. *comm.* 88 (p. 140.1 Waszink). Szidat is probably right in taking this as additional proof that Amm. belongs to the same tradition as Chalcidius.

exortus ... videtur   As was said in the introductory remarks, Amm. here describes the first visibility after New Moon. *Adhuc gracilescens* is a predicative participle. Semantically of course, it qualifies *eius (lunae)*. *Videtur* is not a copula here but the passive of *videre*, with *mortalitati* as a dative of the agent. The verb *gracilescere* is used by Amm. four times (also in 17.4.7, 22.8.4, 22.15.29) and is not found in any other author. The abstract substantive *mortalitas* often occurs in elevated passages, mostly in digressions: 14.11.26 on Adrasteia, 14.11.29 on Fortuna, 21.1.8 on Themis, 28.4.12 in the second excursus on Rome. On the use of abstractum pro concreto see ad 14.8.13, 14.11.26, 15.5.16 and 17.7.10. For the dative of the agent with a finite verb see the note ad 18.4.7.

primitus   Cf. 24.2.5 *primo lucis exordio, cum essent hostes iam in contuitu, visi tunc primitus* and 21.9.8 *cum primitus visus adorandae purpurae datam sibi copiam advertisset*. There is a note on *primitus* ad 16.5.14.

porrectius   Amm. uses the comparative again in 21.9.1 *porrectius ire pergebat*, 25.2.6 *porrectius tendere* and 29.5.48 *Firmus equo celsiori insidens sago puniceo porrectius panso*. *Porrectior* is found in Pl. *Cas.* 281 *porrectiore fronte* (opp. *contractior*) and Tac. *Ag.* 35.4 *porrectior acies*.

cornutae (sc. lunae) habitu   The Latin word for the phase *menoeides* is *corniculata* (Apul. *Soc.* 1.117, Mart. Cap. 7.738, cf. *corniculantis* in § 1) or *bicornis* (Chalcid. *comm.* 37, p. 86.14 Waszink). *Cornutus* is also used of the moon in 14.2.2 *luna etiam tum cornuta* and 27.4.5 *formata in cornuti sideris modum*. The only other author to use *cornutus* in this way is Solinus (27.57). The most usual meaning of *habitus* in Amm. is 'clothes'. Here it means 'form', as in § 11 *quem habitum vocamus* ἀπόκρουσιν and 29.5.41 *aciem rotundo habitu figuratam*. See De Jonge's note ad 17.13.9, who distinguishes the meanings 'formation'/'array', 'behaviour'/'attitude' and 'appearance'.

longo ... interstitio   *Interstitium*, 'distance', is not found elsewhere in Amm. TLL VII 1.2280.71 sqq. only mentions parallels from 4th and 5th century authors like Servius, Claudius Donatus, Macrobius and Martianus Capella.

fit Graeco sermóne dichómenis   The usual meaning of διχόμηνις or διχόμηνος is "dividing the month, i.e. at or of the full moon" (LSJ). For that reason Gelenius preferred to read *dichotomos* here. Valesius, however, has pointed out that *dichomenis* is found with the meaning required here in Alex. Aphr. *Pr.* 1.66: ἐν μὲν γὰρ τῷ διχομήνῳ σχήματι ... ἐν δὲ τῷ πανσελήνῳ ... ἐν δὲ τῇ ἀποκρούσει ... ὅτε δὲ ἀφώτιστος ... The other parallel adduced by Valesius, Nonnus *D.* 4.281 ἀμφιφάης, διχόμηνις, ὅλῳ στίλβουσα προσώπῳ evidently refers to the Full Moon. The parallel from Alex. Aphr. is, however, sufficient evidence to keep the reading of V. Note that this use of *dichomenis* for the Quarter Moon has probably suggested the mistaken rendering *semenstris* in § 1 *deinde in speciem auctum semenstrem*. For the accent of *dichomenis* and ἀπόκρουσιν in § 11 see Harmon 212.

II. 11 *procedens ... disiunctissime quintoque signo arrepto* *Disiunctissimus* to indicate a long distance is already found in classical Latin: Cic. *Man.* 9 *in locis disiunctissimis maximeque diversis*. In Amm. it is found 15.8.6 *per disiunctissimas terras* and 29.1.12 *a disiunctissima regione*. Petschenig's *disiunctissima*, not mentioned in Seyfarth's apparatus, is very attractive. *Arripere* 'to reach a position/place' is probably poetic in origin. Cf. Verg. *A.* 3.477 *hanc (Ausoniam) arripe velis*. There are no good parallels in Amm. himself. *Ut ... Corduenam arriperemus* (24.8.5) quoted under the same heading in TLL II 643.24–34 means 'in order to occupy C.'.

figuram monstrat amphicyrti utrimque prominentibus gibbis The Latin word for the gibbous moon is *protumidus*. It is found only in Apul. *Soc.* 1. For *gibbus/gibba* cf. 23.4.4 *ut prominere videantur in gibbas*.

e regione vero cum normaliter steterit contra For *e regione* see the note ad § 3. It is frequent in Amm.: 20.11.28, 21.10.4, 22.8.13, 22.8.20, 22.15.8, 31.15.12, as well as 17.13.20 and 19.7.6 (where *regio* probably does *not* mean 'town-quarter' or 'segment of the wall') q.v. De Jonge. *Normaliter* is not found elsewhere in Amm. Its literal sense is 'at right angles'. In this meaning it is found only in the gromatici. Its meaning here must be 'in a straight line', or rather, as the comparable phrase *e regione velut libramento quodam ... opponitur* (§ 3) suggests, 'exactly', i.e. on a straight line, drawn with the help of a square.

lumine pleno fulgebit The phase of the Full Moon is brought into relief by the change from the present tense to the gnomical future, for which see Szantyr 310 and ad 18.1.3.

domicilium septimi retinens signi Cf. § 2 (*domicilium*) and § 7 (*signo septimo*). *Retinere* is found with the same meaning in 29.1.8 *locoque quem retinebat superior*.

et in eodem tum etiam agens   It would be wrong to interpret *idem* here as equivalent to *modo dictus* (for which meaning see the notes ad 15.5.19–20 and 16.12.21). Amm. stresses that the process called ἀπόκρουσις ('waning') begins when the moon is still in the same sign in which it had become full. *Tum etiam* in Amm. normally refers to past events or situations (16.8.3, 18.9.3, 21.9.7, 21.11.2, 21.15.2, 26.3.4). The only other exception is 21.6.8 *damna Romanis negotiis illaturi, si rebus etiam tum dubiis descivissent ad Persas.* For *agere* with local adjunct, which is very frequent in Amm., see the note ad 16.2.8. Pliny *Nat.* 18.325 also uses it of the moon: *(luna) ... sub terra aget.* TLL I 1403.1–6.

quem habitum vocámus ἀπόκρουσιν   Strictly speaking, ἀπόκρουσις is a process, the waning of the moon, not a phase. The word is used more correctly by Col. 2.10.10 *quinta decima luna, si tamen ea non transcurret eo die solis radios, quod Graeci* ἀπόκρουσιν *vocant.* The process is called *decrescentia* in Vitr. 9.2.2 and, confusingly, *defectus* in Cic. *N.D.* 2.50 *defectibus in initia recurrendo.*

non nisi tempore intermenstrui deficere visam usquam lunam   A real σκάνδαλον for commentators. How is it possible that the author, after explaining correctly the conditions under which lunar eclipses occur only a few sections earlier (§ 7), makes such a gross error as to say that lunar eclipses have been observed only at the New Moon? According to Valesius *intermenstruum* must here mean 'the period between two New Moons, i.e. the Full Moon', and, as we saw, he even changed the text in § 2 accordingly. He was followed by all subsequent editors and translators. Češka, 1972, 16–7 has rightly protested against this interpretation by which *intermenstruum* is given a meaning unattested elsewhere (see TLL VII 1.2222.36–46). Could it be that Amm. understood the phenomena correctly, but was simply mistaken in his terminology (as was the case with *semenstris* in § 1)? Even this is highly unlikely given the order in which Amm. has described the phases of the moon. Having started in § 9 with *lunae synodos* or New Moon, the moon has come full circle at the end of § 11; so it would be perverse to give to *intermenstruum* any meaning other than its normal one: the New Moon. It seems likely that Amm., having insufficiently mastered the subject, carelessly borrowed Cicero's phrase from *Rep.* 1.25 *etsi non omni intermenstruo, tamen id fieri non posse nisi intermenstruo tempore* without realizing that this referred to solar eclipses. Note that only in the context of a solar eclipse the word *usquam* would make sense. Only in the case of solar eclipses does the observer's position on earth play a role. Rolfe and Seyfarth both translate as if Amm. had written *umquam*.

Amm.'s choice of the words *intermenstruum* and *deficere* suggests that with this final remark he intended to integrate the section on the phases of the moon into the main subject of this chapter, the eclipses.

III. 12 The concluding section is not related to the main subject of this chapter and seems to have been added as an afterthought. The opening phrase *quod autem ... praediximus* does not refer to any statement in the digression or, for that matter, in the remaining books of the *Res Gestae*. But for the absence of any trace of damage to our mss. one would be tempted to suppose a lacuna before § 12. As it is, we cannot escape the conclusion that Amm. inadvertently copied the opening words from his source (for a possible context see below). The meaning of the first part of this paragraph, up to *nostris obtutibus*, is clear enough. Amm. explains that it is only from the viewpoint of an observer on earth that the stars are seen to rise and set, whereas in reality they move around the earth without interruption in a uniform, regular motion. The remark on the position of the human observer need not come as a complete surprise, if we realize that Cicero's *Rep.*, and the *Somnium* in particular, is constantly in Amm.'s mind. In § 16 of the *Somnium* Scipio describes the view from the *orbis lacteus*. What strikes him most is firstly that he sees stars which are invisible from the earth (*eae stellae quas esse numquam ex hoc loco vidimus*), secondly the size of the stars (*eae magnitudines omnium quas numquam suspicati sumus*) and thirdly the smallness of the earth (*ipsa terra ita mihi parva visa est, ut e.q.s.*). Macrobius devotes a long chapter (*comm.* 1.16) to these observations; it explains that some stars are invisible from the earth because they are below the horizon. His phraseology is strongly reminiscent of Amm.'s exposition in § 12: *sciendum et hoc, quod umbra terrae, quam sol post occasum in inferiore hemisphaerio currens sursum cogit emitti e.q.s.* (*comm.* 1.20.18). The context Amm. had in mind when he wrote *quod autem ... praediximus* was probably an exposition on lunar eclipses. The relative smallness of the earth is discussed in 16.10: *physici terram ad magnitudinem circi per quem sol volvitur puncti modum obtinere docuerunt.* The fact that two of the problems treated by Macrobius are touched upon in this section makes one wonder if it was not a commentary on the *Somnium* comparable to that of Macrobius that prompted Ammianus to conclude his astronomical digression with these reflections. In the rest of the section, from *nunc caelo infixas* onwards, the text can hardly be sound, as there is no way to construe the infinitives *suspicere* and *arbitrari*. Apart from this textual problem it seems likely that the division *nunc – aliquotiens* corresponds to *nunc – nunc* in the beginning of the paragraph and that again, as so often in this chapter, Amm. repeats the same thought in a different form.

nunc in aethere, nunc in mundo inferiore cursare The distinction between the upper and the lower, the visible and the invisible, halves of the sun's orbit, divided by the horizon, is relevant only for the observer from the earth. *Cursare*, though not found elsewhere in Amm., should not be changed to *versari*, as Bentley proposed, in view of the phrase *solis cursus* in 25.1.18 (cf. also 22.15.31 *sol aestivum cursum extendit*).

sciendum est The expression is repeated in the geographical digression on Persia, 23.6.62: *illud tamen sciendum est* e.q.s. It belongs to scholarly (Macr. *comm.* 1.20.18, quoted above) or would-be scholarly prose. Examples of the latter are to be found in the Historia Augusta, e.g. *OM* 1.4, *Pr* 11.1.

quantum ad universitatem pertinet *Quantum pertinet ad* is found only here in Amm. *Universitas* is used in the excursus on Adrasteia/Nemesis (14.11.25-6 *ut universitatem regere per elementa discurrens omnia non ignoretur*) and in 15.1.4 quoted in the note on *rerumque magnitudini* e.q.s. below. In the meaning 'universe' the word seems to have been introduced by Cicero in his *Timaeus* (§ 6) as a translation of τὸ πᾶν. Macrobius explicitly refers to this rendering in his note on *Somnium* 17 *totius mundi a summo in imum diligens in hunc locum collecta descriptio est et integrum quoddam universitatis corpus effingitur quod quidem* τὸ πᾶν, *id est omne, dixerunt*. It is found also in Plin. *Nat.* 2.11 and Apul. *Mund.* 19.

sed ita videri nostris obtutibus In classical Latin *obtutus* is found only in the singular. Amm. always uses it in the plural, meaning 'the eyes', as in 17.8.5 *sub obtutibus eius*, 21.6.2 - *meis*.

in terra spiritus cuiusdam interni motu suspensa At first sight the addition of *spiritus ... suspensa* to *terra* seems an unnecessary display of erudition, but, here again, a commentary on Cicero's *Somnium* is likely to have played a role, namely on the words *in eam (sc. terram) feruntur omnia nutu suo pondera* (*Rep.* 6.17, see Büchner's commentary ad l.), by which Cicero explains how the earth maintains its position in the center of the universe.

As Valesius saw, Amm.'s terminology is derived from the Stoic theory of the all-pervading πνεῦμα. Szidat also quotes Plin. *Nat.* 2.10 *proximum spiritus quem Graeci nostrique eodem vocabulo aëra appellant, vitalem hunc et per cuncta rerum meabilem totoque consertum; huius vi suspensam cum quarto aquarum elemento librari medio spatii tellurem*. The same idea is found Macr. *Sat.* 1.21.8 *quae natura caeli est cuius ambitu aer continetur qui vehit terram*. As Szidat observes, Amm. speaks of the *spiritus* as a force inside the earth, whereas Pliny, like Macrobius, describes the πνεῦμα as *per cuncta rerum meabilem totoque consertum*. Szidat is probably right in explaining this divergence as the result of careless abridgement by Amm. of the source-text. Amm. may have had in mind the philosophic exposition in Verg. *A.* 6.724 sqq., where in lines 725-26

spiritus intus alit, totamque infusa per artus
  mens agitat molem ...

the ideas of the internal πνεῦμα and its movement are combined. By adding *cuiusdam* Amm. makes it clear that *spiritus* is an approximative rendering of

Greek πνεῦμα. For this use of *quidam* cf. 17.4.7 *est autem obeliscus asperrimus lapis in figuram metae cuiusdam sensim ad proceritatem consurgens excelsam* and 22.15.30 *sunt et syringes subterranei quidam et flexuosi secessus*. In 21.1.8, the excursus on divination, Amm. speaks of the *spiritus* in terms more closely resembling the passage quoted from Pliny: *elementorum omnium spiritus utpote perennium corporum praesentiendi motu semper et ubique vigens*.

rerumque magnitudini instar exigui subditum puncti Amm. has been led to make this observation by Cicero's remark about the smallness of the earth. He borrowed the words either from a commentary on the *Somnium* or directly from Cicero himself, e.g. *Tusc*. 1.40 *persuadent enim mathematici terram in medio mundi sitam ad universi caeli complexum quasi puncti instar obtinere, quod κέντρον illi vocant*. In the *Somnium* Cicero uses *punctum* for the Imperium Romanum: *ut me imperii nostri quo quasi punctum eius (terrae) attingimus paeniteret* (§ 16).

It is one of the basic principles in astronomical treatises. The opening proposition of Euclid's *Phaenomena* runs as follows: ἡ γῆ ἐν μέσῳ τῷ κόσμῳ ἐστὶ καὶ κέντρου τάξιν ἔχει πρὸς τὸν κόσμον. Cf. also Cleomedes 1.11 ὅτι ἡ γῆ σημείου λόγον ἐπέχει πρὸς τὸν οὐρανόν. It is a necessary premiss and it explains why, according to all ancient astronomers, the magnitudes and the configurations of the fixed stars do not differ depending on the observer's position on earth. See R. Goulet (Budé edition), 1980, 204. Amm. extracts a moralizing lesson from it in 15.1.4. Having informed the reader that Constantius referred to himself as *aeternitas mea*, he adds as a comment: *id reputasset legens vel audiens, quod, ut docent mathematici concinentes, ambitus terrae totius, quae nobis videtur immensa, ad magnitudinem universitatis instar brevis obtinet puncti*, where Cic. *Tusc*. 1.40 is even more closely followed than in 20.3.12.

In Gutschmidt's conjecture *subditum*, adopted by Seyfarth in his Teubner-edition, this participle depends on *instar*. Now *instar* is found twelve times in Amm. and there is only one instance of substantival use (15.1.4 quoted above), as against ten cases in which it is used adverbially with a genitive ('in the manner of' 14.1.10, 14.2.2, 16.12.49, 19.12.5, 22.2.5, 23.3.9, 23.4.8, 24.3.12, 26.8.9, 28.6.1). It seems better, therefore, to interpret *instar puncti* as an adverbial phrase and to read *subdita* agreeing with *terra*. See Szantyr 218.

nunc caelo infixas suspicere stellas ... aliquotiens ... discedere suis sedibus arbitrari The combination *nunc – aliquotiens* is found with some frequency in Amm.: 14.2.5, 15.13.4, 20.7.18, 23.6.9, 24.7.7. As we said in the introduction to this section, it repeats *nunc – nunc* in the opening sentence. In the first half of the paragraph, before the parenthesis (*constitutis – puncti*)

Amm. states that while an observer on earth may get the impression that the stars rise and set, in reality they do not move independently but only share in the movement of the celestial sphere around the centre of the universe, i.e. the earth. In the second half the same idea is expressed. At one moment, i.e. during the night, we see the stars in heaven, at other times, i.e. during the day, we are unable to see them and suppose, wrongly, that they have left their places. That this is a misguided opinion is stressed by the words *quarum ordo est sempiternus*, where *ordo* means 'position' as in Man. 1.112 *sideribus vario mutantibus ordine fata*.

This leaves the syntax of the passage unexplained. Erfurdt suggested in his commentary ad loc. that *obtutus*, to be taken from *obtutibus*, should be understood as the subject of *suspicere*. That might be just conceivable. The construction becomes intolerably strained, however, if *obtutus* is to be linked with *arbitrari* as well. Another possibility might be to take *suscipere* and *arbitrari* as dependent on *ita videri*: 'but that it makes this impression on our senses, viz. that at times we see the stars' etc. This is open to the same objection as Erfurdt's suggestion. Moreover, there is no parallel in Amm. for the cataphoric use of *ita*, except in combination with *ut*. An easier solution may be to derive *nos* from *nostris obtutibus* as the subject of *suspicere* and *arbitrari*. If this is what Amm. meant to say, we miss a co-ordinator between *videri* and the following infinitives. As it stands the text admits of no satisfactory grammatical explanation. About its general sense we may with safety assume

a. that the subject of the infinitives must be 'we, human beings';

b. that the infinitives *suspicere* and *arbitrari* develop and specify what had been expressed by the more general *sed ita videri*.

Szidat's explanation of the text is totally different. According to him, it concerns the apparent irregularities in the course of the planets, which is indeed a standard topic in astronomical handbooks since Plato's *Timaeus*. He compares Cic. *N.D.* 2.51, Sen. *Nat.* 7.25.7, Theo Sm. 148.5. Moreover, the phrase *humana visione languente* is in his opinion borrowed from Chalcidius, who uses it in a discussion of this topic: *comm.* 78 *languente visus acie* (p. 125.17 Waszink).

There are two weak points in his interpretation. Firstly, he destroys the internal cohesion of the paragraph by his assumption that in its second half a wholly new subject is brought up. Secondly, he is forced, as he himself admits, to give the term *stellae caelo infixae* a meaning which is diametrically opposed to its normal sense, the 'fixed stars', for which see Le Boeuffle, 1973, 103–4. As a parallel Szidat adduces Chalcid. *comm.* 84 (p. 135.14–19 Waszink): *sed sphaeras esse quasdam quinti illius corporis naturae congruentes easdemque per omne caelum ferri vario diversoque motu ... easdemque omnes perinde ut ceteras stellas minime errantes infixas esse caelo*. Chalcidius discusses here Aristotle's theory that the planets are set in spheres of their own, as the fixed stars are set in the celestial sphere. This is expressed more clearly by Chalcidius' source Theo Sm. 178.17–179.1: σφαίρας δέ τινας εἶναι τοῦ πέμπτου σώματος οἰκεῖον ... ἐν αἷς ἀπλάνων δίκην ἐνεστηριγμένα τὰ πλανητά. In the abridged version of Chalcidius the difference between the celestial sphere and the spheres of the planets is blurred. We are not justified, however, in taking this imprecise rendering of a Greek text as evidence that *stellae caelo infixae* in a different context could refer to the planets. Moreover, the phrase *quarum ordo est sempiternus* does not make sense in a statement about the planets, since they change their respective positions continuously.

humana visione languente   Cf. 16.10.14 *ad cuius* (sc. amphitheatri) *summitatem aegre visio humana conscendit*.

verum ad instituta iam revertamur   Amm. often concludes his digressions with *sed (verum) revertamur ad*: 14.4.7 *ad textum propositum*, 21.1.14 *ad explicanda prospecta*, 23.4.15 and 27.3.15 *ad rerum ordinem (-s)*. See Emmett, 1981, 23–25.

Chapter 4

The first two sections of the chapter deserve careful attention, as they shed some light on Amm.'s conception of his task as a historian. On the one hand he is quite ready to disparage the adversaries of his favourites, Ursicinus and Julian, but on the other the exigencies of historical truth usually prevent him from withholding essential information from the reader. In the present case he was well aware of the dangerous situation on the Eastern border and of Constantius' duty to take adequate measures. At the same time he wanted to stress that ultimately Constantius' jealousy was responsible for the Parisian events. He cleverly combined these two elements by giving the two periods with which the chapter begins (each filling a section in modern editions) a chiastic structure. The first one expounds Constantius' problems, the second explains his measures:
1 the Persian menace – Julian's growing success
2 weakening Julian   – strengthening the Eastern border

Mark especially the agreement of the two exterior terms: *properantem ... prope diem* and *accelerare ... primo vere*. This clearly contradicts Szidat's statement ad 4.1: "Dieser sehr abgeschwächte Gebrauch von properare findet sich häufig bei Ammian. Es kann bis zur Bedeutung von agere verblassen" (I 134). It is true that Amm. uses *properare* (as well as *festinare*) rather often, but the least one can say is that it lends a note of urgency to the action. Szidat seems to confuse his own precise analysis of the situation with Amm.'s way of reporting.

IV. 1 *Properantem ... Persicis* The opening sentence recapitulates 19.11.17 (*Constantinopolim petit, ut orienti iam proximus cladibus apud Amidam mederetur acceptis et ... impetus regis Persarum pari virium robore cohiberet, quem constabat ... per extenta spatia signa moturum*) and indicates once more that a major Persian invasion of Rome's eastern possessions was to be expected soon. Since the Sassanid offensive of 359 it must indeed have been very clear that after a relatively calm period the eastern part of the Roman empire was in real danger again (Szidat I 63–65 gives a good survey of the relations between Rome and the Persians in the first half of the fourth century, Barceló, 1981, 73–104 does the same with fuller details. See for the general background of the struggle between Rome and her eastern neighbours Wirth, 1980/1981; cf. also Pugliese Carratelli, 1976 and Widengren, 1976.

The Persian policy of Constantius II, characterized by a desire to avoid battle, has often been criticized by modern historians following Amm. (19.11.7 and 21.16.15) as the result of timidity (cf. e.g. Seeck, 1923[4], 292). Recently, however, more than one scholar has argued for a different view, crediting Constantius with a prudent, rational and even successful policy in the East (cf. Stallknecht, 1967, 44-48; Warmington, 1977; Leedom, 1978, 141-145; Wirth, 1980/1981, 342; Barceló, 1981, 85 and 97, and in general Lightfoot, 1981).

ferre suppetias An archaic expression, which occurs a few times in Plautus and then again in Apuleius. It is not used by Sal., Livy, Tac., Flor., but Amm. employs it ten times, i.a. 16.4.3, where De Jonge has a short note. Cf. *Gron. Comm. on Apul.* 6.27 (149, 14-20).

turbando Turbare and its cognate subst. *turbator* are frequently used to denote the unsettlement of a quiet and peaceful situation: *Silvanus ... composita forte turbabit* (15.5.7), *ne super turbando Armeniae vel Mesopotamiae statu quicquam moveretur* (17.14.1), *ipsum otii turbatorem petebat* (29.5.45), *per has provincias molientem otium turbare commune* (30.7.10). Here *turbando* functions as part. fut. pass.: 'doomed to be unsettled'.

perfugae concinentes exploratoribus Concinere as a synonym of *congruere* or *consentire* is found quite often in late Latin. The origin of this metaphoric use can be illustrated by Cic., *Rep.* 2.69: *ut enim in fidibus aut tibiis atque ut in cantu ipso ac vocibus concentus est quidam tenendus ex distinctis sonis ... sic ex summis et infimis et mediis interiectis ordinibus, ut sonis, moderata ratione civitas consensu dissimillimorum concinit.* The unanimity of deserters is stressed as important in 18.6.8 *constanti asseveratione perfugis concinentibus*, where, as De Jonge notes, one has to understand *concinentibus inter se*.

The word *explorator* is regularly used by Amm. to designate military scouts, sometimes of the enemy (16.11.9, 25.7.1), more often of the Romans themselves. In the latter case, however, it is not always clear whether (semi-)barbarians, temporarily employed by the Romans, are meant (so, it seems, in 18.7.9, 29.5.40 and 31.16.2) or, as here, patrolling and scouting forces of the regular Roman army (so, it seems, also in 18.6.17, 19.3.3, 21.7.7, 21.13.1, 31.9.2 and 31.12.11). Cf. for the latter Fiebiger, 1909 and Neumann, 1967 (note that their reference to Zosimus 3.14.3 ἅμα τοῖς ὑπ' αὐτὸν κατασκόποις χιλίοις, needs qualification; in the corresponding passage in Amm., 24.1.2, one reads *excursatores*, not *exploratores*) and see Szidat I 134-135.

Rosen, 1968, 46 has rightly observed that one should not without due consideration accept Amm.'s representation of the facts whenever he ascribes certain information to the reports of *exploratores* ("Vorsicht ist daher überall dort geboten, wo er '*exploratores*' oder '*speculatores*' als Zeugen anführt"), but there is no need to question Amm.'s words here.

urebant Valesius refers to Hor. *Ep.* 2.1.13-14:
urit enim fulgore suo qui praegravat artis
infra se positas

In his comments on this somewhat vexed phrase Brink approvingly quotes Lambinus: "id est, qui virtute, aut arte aliqua ceteris omnibus, qui eandem artem, ac virtutem colunt, antecellit, illis acerbum dolorem commovet, sibi odium et invidiam conflat". The OLD s.v. *uro* 7 mentions this meaning: "to cause to burn or smart with resentment, jealousy, grief, anxiety etc.". A good example of a case of jealousy is Livy 40.15.1 *ad id, quod doles, quod invidiā urit, reverteris*. In the survey of the Emperor Valentinian's vices Amm. remarks: *invidia praeter haec ante dictus medullitus urebatur* (30.8.10). Jealousy is implied in the present text too, the more so because Amm. often stresses Constantius' envy of Julian's Gallic exploits. In 17.11.1 he relates how the court circles fall in with these feelings by disparaging Julian, which inspires him to add some instructive paragraphs on the evil aspects of jealousy.

Iuliani virtutes These fell victim to the slanderous talk just referred to: *virtutes eius obruere verbis impudentibus conabantur ut segnem incessentes et timidum et umbratilem* (17.11.1). In view of this and the present context one has to understand that *virtutes* expresses Julian's military qualities.

per ora gentium diversarum The oldest example of this image is Ennius' famous *volito vivos per ora virum* (*var.* 18), and it returns throughout Latin literature, the first time in Catullus' *an ut pervenias in ora vulgi?* (40.5). But Julian is even on the lips of men all over the world (*diversarum*)! As Sabbah 267 remarks, the contents of the phrase are reminiscent of Lib. *Or.* 18.90 ... πάσης φωνῆς ταὐτὸν ᾀδούσης, ὡς οὐχ ὅπλων ταυτὶ μᾶλλον ἢ τῆς ἐκείνου διανοίας

fama celebrior Cf. *fama vero ... per Illyricos omnes celebrior fundebatur* (21.9.3), *quod latior fama vulgarat* (16.8.8), *ut crebrior fama vulgarat* (26.3.4), *ut locuta est pertinacior fama* (28.1.30).

per ora ... fama ... effundebat The phrase as such is Ammian's; he has combined three existing expressions, all referring to human speech. For *effundere* in this respect cf. *eos per ipsos dies effudi, si ita vis, honores in mortuos* (Cic. *ad Brut.* 1.15.8).

adoreas celsas *Adorea* appears only once in classical Latin:
ille dies Latio tenebris
qui primus alma risit adorea
(Hor. *Carm.* 4.4.40-1)

Its meaning and etymology caused some uncertainty already in antiquity, witness these curious statements: *Gloriam denique ipsam a farris honore adoriam appellabant* (Plin. *Nat.* 18.14) and TURNUS ADORO *id est iuxta veteres, qui adorare adloqui dicebant: nam ideo et adorea laus bellica, quod omnes eum cum gratulatione adloquebantur, qui in bello fortiter fecit* (Serv. auct. ad *Aen.* 10.677). Its general meaning seems to be 'military glory'. Amm. may well have borrowed this word from Solinus: the only other occurrence *ultimus Catilina claras gloriarum adoreas sempiternis maculis obumbravit* (25.3.13) is a clear reminiscence of *nisi heres in posteritatis eius successione Catilina tantas adoreas odio damnati nominis obumbrasset* (Solinus 1.105). The list of occurrences in TLL I.813.56-814.35 shows that the plural is quite usual.

Celsus is often used by Amm. in a literal sense, about mountains, hills etc., but in a number of cases it means 'sublime, lofty, proud', the opposite of 'humble, lowly': *dux meriti celsioris* (25.8.11), *videreque licebat celsum ferocia barbarum* (31.13.4) and about Jovian, referring to the derivation of his name (*Iuppiter, Iovis*), *militem celsi nominis* (23.5.13).

post Alamanniae quaedam regna prostrata Amm. is very fond of this construction; cf. De Jonge ad 14.1.1; Szantyr 243; Helttula, 1985.

Julian's victories over the Alamanni (see for the history of this people above, ad 20.1.1) are recorded in 16.2, 16.11-12, 17.1, 17.10 and 18.2. The word *Alamannia* is used by Amm. twice, here and in 30.3.1.

receptaque oppida Gallicana Of the approximately forty-five (so Julian, *Ep. ad Ath.* 279 a and Lib. *Or.* 12.48; Zos. 3.1.1 speaks of forty) towns in Gaul which had been sacked by the Germans, almost forty were recovered by the end of 359 according to Julian ibid. (280d: τότε δὲ ἀνειλήφειν ἐλάττους ὀλίγῳ τῶν τεσσαράκοντα). See Amm. 16.2.12 (*primam omnium Brotomagum occupavit*; cf. Lib. *Or.* 18.46), 16.3.1 and 18.2.4 for the names of some of these towns and cf. Hoffmann I 343-344.

a barbaris For Amm. on barbarians recently: Dauge, 1981, 330-352, Bonanni, 1981, Jacob, 1982, Frézouls, 1983 and Wiedemann, 1986.

post ... excisa In the speech thanking Julian for his consulship Claudius Mamertinus relates that, in order to raise Constantius' jealousy, Julian's adversaries saw to it that Julian's praises were sounded everywhere, *in omnibus conventiculis quasi per benivolentiam illa iactantes: Iulianus Alamanniam domuit, Iulianus urbes Galliae ex favillis et cineribus excitavit* (*Pan.* 3.4.5).

quos tributarios ipse fécit et vectigáles   The perf. instead of the pluperfect is caused by the cursus velox. The technical distinction which can be made between *tributarius* and *vectigalis*, 'subject to direct and indirect taxes' respectively, or 'subject to taxation' ("pflichtig zu Staatssteuer") as against 'subject to rates' ("pflichtig zu städtischen Abgaben", cf. Mommsen, 1910 (= 1899), 259, n. 2), seems to be only secondary. Here the words denote complete subjection, like the Livian *vectigalis stipendiariusque* (see for *stipendium/stipendiarius* as synonym of *tributum/tributarius*: Grelle, 1963; *stipendiarius* does not occur in Amm., *tributarius* is used by him six times). Cf. Weissenborn-Müller ad Liv. 21.41.7: "Hier soll beides die gänzliche Abhängigkeit bezeichnen". For some examples of the way Julian treated defeated barbarians see 17.1.13, 17.10.4 and 17.10.9, where it is stated that he forced Germans to deliver food and building supplies.

IV. 2 *haec et similia*   This vague expression is very frequent in Amm. Livy uses it only once: *haec et his similia* (*pr.* 8).

ne augerentur in maius   In view of 16.10.17 *de fama querebatur ut invalida vel maligna, quod augens omnia semper in maius erga haec explicanda, quae Romae sunt, obsolescit* one might be tempted to interpret these words as referring to *fama*, but in what follows it is implied that Constantius is taking measures against the further growth of Julian's successes as such. The translations of Rolfe ("fearing that their fame would grow greater") and Seyfarth ("befürchtete, Julians Ruhm könne noch weiter anwachsen") do not seem to be correct.

stimulante ... Florentio   Not *adhortante, monente* or *auctore*: Amm. wants to stress that emotional motives rather than rational calculation were responsible for the events. Livy uses the verb more than 40 times, often with *ira* as agens. Its emotional connotation is obvious in the other four instances in Amm., the agentes being *conscientia* (15.8.2 and 21.15.4), *fiducia* (16.12.3) and *invidia* (22.13.2). The present text, in which a human person is the stimulator, can be compared with *domi uxore Tullia inquietum animum stimulante* (Liv. 1.46.2) and *stimulabat aegrum amore uxor socerque* (Liv. 30.11.3).

In 20.4.7 Amm. more explicitly makes Florentius, *praefectus praetorio* of the Gauls since 357, responsible for the withdrawal of troops from the defence of Gaul, although he there too puts in a proviso by using *putabatur* (*Perpendebat enim ad relationem suam, quam olim putabatur misisse, abstrahendos e Galliarum defensione pugnaces numeros barbarisque iam formidatos*). From 20.8.20 we learn that Florentius, according to Amm., had often treated Julian rudely and consequently was afraid of him (*quem saepe tractatum asperius formidabat*).

Julian himself, in retrospect, traced his enmity with Florentius to an incident which occurred in 358/359 (καὶ μικρὸν ὕστερον καὶ Φλωρέντιος ἦν ἐχθρὸς ἐμοὶ διὰ τὰς πλεονεξίας, αἷς ἠναντιούμην, *Ep. ad Ath.* 282c, cf. Lib. *Or.* 18.84–85), but at that time relations between the Caesar and the prefect were strained already (cf. Amm. 17.3.2–6; Jul. *Ep. ad Ath.* 280a). The reason for this may be sought in temperamental incompatibility (after all, Julian was not easy to get on with; in the words of Bowersock, 1978, 19: "It is not surprising that a man of such a complex nervous temperament, superstitious and calculating, easily wounded in his pride, should have had few friends"), in Florentius' loyalty to Constantius (Athanassiadi-Fowden, 1981, 69 dubbed him "the spokesman of Constantius' policy in Gaul"), in Florentius' narrow-mindedness (cf. Bidez, 1930, 166) or the like (the explanation of De Vos, 1910, however, is too far-fetched), but part of the tension between the two men must undoubtedly have been structural, the result of the appointment of a Caesar with limited competence (cf. Valensi, 1957, 83–84; Blockley, 1972, 447 ff.) in an area where the *praefectus praetorio* played the role of a vice-emperor, cf. 17.3.4 *cui Augustus summam commiserit rerum*; note, however, that according to De Jonge ad loc. *summa rerum* there does not have a general, but rather a technical meaning).

A territorial praetorian prefecture of the Gauls had grown up in the reign of Constantine. Not only did this emperor from 312 onwards transform the *praefectura praetorio*, among other things depriving the prefects of their military functions, he also broke with the tradition that a praetorian prefect was always attached to an emperor's person, and appointed some prefects to govern fixed areas. The first person definitely attested as *praefectus praetorio per Gallias* is C. Annius Tiberianus (Hier. *Chron.* s.a. 336, cf. *PLRE I*, Tiberianus 4), but it is possible that the Gauls had been in the charge of a separate prefect ever since Crispus had been appointed Caesar in 317 (Jones 100–103, 126; for further details: Ensslin, 1954; cf. also De Jonge ad 14.7.9).

See for Florentius (he was *PPO Illyrici* a. 360–361 and *consul* in 361): *PLRE I*, Florentius 10 and cf. Seeck, 1909 ('Florentius 2'), De Jonge ad 16.12.14, 17.3.2, 18.2.4, Szidat I 136–137 and Von Haehling, 1978, 100–101. For the term *praefectus* (*praetorii/-io*) see Van Leijenhorst, 1986.

Decentium tribunum et notarium Decentius is mentioned also in 20.4.11 and 20.8.4 (but not in 20.4.5; see the commentary ad loc.). In 364–365 he was *magister officiorum* (though his title is given nowhere). Cf. Seeck, 1901; *PLRE I*, Decentius 1 and Clauss, 1980, 151–152.

Tribuni et notarii were, as their name implies, originally shorthand writers. Presumably during the reign of Licinius and Constantine the imperial stenographers, until then indiscriminately called *exceptores* or *notarii*, came to be called (*tribuni et*) *notarii* as members of a newly formed *schola notariorum*. This was the start of a series of considerable changes which occurred in the course of the fourth century: imperial shorthand writers saw their tasks extended, their status raised, their numbers grown etc. At the end of the century knowledge of shorthand was probably not even required any more from most *tribuni et notarii*. See for them Teitler, 1985.

auxiliares ... trecentenos According to Julian in *Ep. ad Ath*. 282d Constantius' demand meant the withdrawal from Gaul of all his most efficient troops, while Libanius (*Or*. 18.90, cf. *Or*. 12.58) amplifies Julian's statement by arguing that only inferior troops were allowed to stay with the Caesar in Gaul. Amm.'s words on this issue, on the other hand (here and in 20.4.7: *abstrahendos e Galliarum defensione pugnaces numeros barbarisque iam formidatos*), are less outspoken.

It is important to know, though difficult to assess, whether or not Julian (and, in his wake, Libanius) is exaggerating the number and strength of the troops ordered by Constantius to march off (τὸ στρατιωτικὸν ἄπαν ἀδιακρίτως τὸ μαχιμώτατον). If he is not, one should, however, not automatically conclude (as, for example, Geffcken, 1914, 49–50 and Seeck, 1920–1923$^{2-4}$, IV, 281–282 did) that Constantius was not justified in strengthening the Persian frontier by weakening the defense in the West. Even if Julian was right in stating that he was going to be deprived of all his most experienced soldiers, Constantius' policy can be defended by pointing to the fact that "the military crisis on the eastern frontier was a perfectly reasonable explanation for the shift of troops from a front now calm to one that was not" (Bowersock, 1978, 47; see in general the literature cited ad 20.4.1).

It is not to be denied that Constantius' demand that reinforcements be sent would, if granted, weaken the strength of Julian's army. It is difficult, however, to indicate precisely what the implications were for the army which remained in Gaul.

Among other things this depends on the exact meaning of *lectos ex numeris aliis trecentenos*: assuming that by *auxiliares milites* the four subsequently mentioned *auxilia* are meant, the *Heruli* and the *Batavi*, the *Celtae* and the *Petulantes*, and that *numerus* is a general term covering units of all kinds (see above, ad 20.1.3), *lectos ... trecentenos* might mean: 300 men from each of all other regiments, i.e. including other auxilia (stated differently: *lectos ... trecentenos* stands in opposition to *Herulos ... Celtas*, not to *auxiliares milites*). In that case Julian's army, loosing four complete *auxilia* and detachments from all other units, would, indeed, have been weakened considerably.

However, as Szidat points out, another interpretation of *lectos ... trecentenos* is possible in view of 20.4.3 (*Et super auxiliariis quidem et trecentenis*). In 20.4.3, Szidat argues, the *auxiliarii* and the *trecenteni* stand in opposition to each other, which suggests that this must also be the case in 20.4.2. In other words: the *trecenteni* of 20.4.3 and, accordingly, of 20.4.2 do not belong to the *auxilia*. According to Szidat, therefore, *lectos ... trecentenos* in 20.4.2 should be rendered as: 300 men from each of the other regiments, i.e. the non-auxiliary regiments. In that case Julian would have had less reason to complain about loosing the *Heruli, Batavi, Petulantes* and *Celtae* because he presumably (cf. for *auxilia* under Julian's command Hoffmann I 203-204) still had at his disposal some other *auxilia* maintained at full strength.

Szidat's argument is attractive, but not cogent. The *auxiliarii* and *trecenteni* in 20.4.3 stand not so much in opposition to each other as, taken together, to the *Scutarii* and *Gentiles*, which category of troops Amm., surprisingly enough, had not mentioned in the preceding section. *Super auxiliariis quidem et trecentenis* simply takes up again *auxiliares ... trecentenos* of 20.4.2, leaving Amm.'s precise meaning obscure. One cannot but conclude that in giving information about the transfer of Julian's troops Amm. is not as clear as one might wish.

In this respect one further point should be stressed. While Amm. is silent about any previous transfer of troops to the East, thus creating the impression that Constantius' request in 360 was unusual and excessive, it is known from Jul. *Ep. ad Ath.* 280d (ἔπεμψα τῷ Κωνσταντίῳ τέτταρας ἀριθμοὺς τῶν κρατίστων πεζῶν, τρεῖς ἄλλους τῶν ἐλαττόνων, ἱππέων τάγματα δύο τὰ ἐντιμότατα; cf. Lib. *Or.* 12.58 (not 18.90-94, pace Paschoud, 1979, 84)) that also on an earlier occasion soldiers of the army in Gaul had been ordered to head east. Cf. for this also Zos. 3.8.3-4, with Paschoud's excellent note ad loc.

abstracturum For this use of the part. fut. in a final sense see above ad 20.2.2.

cumque Petulantibus Celtas For the sake of variation Amm. uses the preposition *cum*. There is no difference in meaning with the preceding *et*, for, like the *Heruli* and *Batavi*, these *auxilia* (cf. *Not.Dign. Or.* 9.26, *Occ.* 5.160, 161, 205) normally operated as a couple (see 20.5.9; 21.3.2; 22.12.6 and 31.10.4). In fact, as an auxiliary unit the *Celtae* never occur alone in Amm., while we meet the *Petulantes* only twice without their companions, in 20.4.18 (*Maurus nomine quidam ... Petulantium tunc hastatus*) and in 20.4.10 (*apud Petulantium signa*). With regard to the latter case, however, it should be noted that in the parallel passage in *Ep. ad Ath.* 283b Julian mentions the *auxilia* together: πρὸς τοὺς Πετουλάντας τουτουσὶ καὶ Κελτούς. Cf. also 20.4.20 *signa Petulantium ingressus atque Celtarum*.

The meaning of the names of these units and their provenance is disputed. Was *Petulantes* merely a fancy name (Jones 98), having nothing to do with the Latin words *petulans* and *petulantia*? (Contrast e.g. Jullian, 1926, 85 n. 6: "Quant aux *Petulantes*, le nom ne me paraît avoir rien de commun avec le mot latin *petulans*: c'est un arrangement de quelque vocable géographique ou ethnique des basses terres" with Seyfarth, 1983[5], 195 n. 28: "Die ersteren (= *Petulantes*) hatten ihren Namen wahrscheinlich nach ihrem widerspenstigen und leichtfertigen Benehmen, ihrer *petulantia*"). As for the *Celtae*, must we conclude that, in spite of their name, they were not Gauls? (So Jullian, 1926, 44 n. 7 and, on different grounds, Hoffmann I 136-137, 150-151).

The question is discussed at length by Hoffmann, loc.cit., who argues for a German origin of both the *Petulantes* and the *Celtae*. Part of his argument is certainly correct: it does not do to infer (as, e.g., Müller, 1905, 582 and Neumann, 1965, 531 did) from Amm. 20.4.13 that the *Petulantes* and *Celtae* must have been Gauls. But the rest of his argument is largely an elaboration of a theory concerning other auxiliary units, the *Cornuti* and *Bracchiati*; this theory, put forward in 1935 and again in 1959 by Alföldi, is based upon his interpretation of shield emblems in the *Notitia Dignitatum*. Its weakness has been shown by Grigg, 1983, and, consequently, Hoffmann's arguments for a German origin of *Petulantes* and *Celtae* can not be deemed decisive.

hac specie ... ut Other expressions denoting 'pretext' are *specie tenus* (14.1.5 and 14.7.5), *per speciem* (16.11.7, 21.11.2, 29.5.19). Amm. uses them relatively rarely in comparison with Livy and especially Tacitus.

primo vere Rolfe ad loc.: "This would hardly have been possible; cf. *adulta hieme*, in 20.1.3". As a matter of fact it is clear from 20.8.1 *adulto vere* that Constantius did not start his campaign early in spring. See for chronological matters Szidat I 43 ff.

in Parthos As is remarked in the note ad 15.1.2 (cf. also Seyfarth, II, 1983[5], 198 n. 62), Amm. calls the Persians indiscriminately now *Persae* then *Parthi*. Julian in his *Second Oration* (63a-b) goes further, denying the most dangerous enemies Rome had in the East the right to call themselves Persians: διασώζουσι γὰρ καὶ ἀπομιμοῦνται τὰ Περσικὰ οὐκ ἀξιοῦντες, ἐμοὶ δοκεῖν, Παρθυαῖοι νομίζεσθαι, Πέρσαι δὲ εἶναι προσποιούμενοι etc.

IV. 3 *super ... cogendis* As was noted ad 20.1.2, in late Latin *super* is common as synonym of *de*; with a gerundive construction cf. 19.12.9 *quod super adipiscendo interrogasse dicebatur imperio*, where De Jonge notes that the first specimen of this construction is Hor. *Saec*. 18-19 *decreta super iugandis/feminis*. The use of *cogere* stresses the compulsory character of the measure in question.

In addition to Szidat I 138 ("Ammianus gebraucht nur selten den Fachterminus *auxilium* ... sondern umschreibt mit *auxiliaris* als Adjektiv ... oder als Substantiv") it should be noted that besides *auxiliaris* Amm. uses also *auxiliarius*, as a noun here, adjectivally in 18.2.6.

conventus est   This is the only instance in Amm. of transitive *convenire* as a synonym of *adire, admonere, rogare*, in which meaning the verb occurs since Apuleius.

transisse ... compertus   The earliest example of *comperire* in a nom.c.inf. with personal subject is Sal. *Hist.* 2.92 *eo postquam Pompeius ... adventare compertus est*.

perducere ... iubetur   It is an affront to Julian that a member of his *comitatus* is given orders by the central government; *perducere* is an adequate term: 'to conduct to a destination'.

Sintula   Mentioned by this name again in 20.5.1 (*ducente Sintula*), but called Gintonius in Jul. *Ep. ad Ath.* 282 d (ἐπιτάξας τοῦτο τὸ ἔργον Λουππικίνῳ τε καὶ Γιντωνίῳ). Seeck, 1920-1924$^{2-4}$, IV, 282 and 1927, 259 gets round the difficulty by calling him Gintonius Sintula. Cf. *PLRE*, I, Sintula; Waas, 1971, 107-108 ("vielleicht Germane").

stabuli tunc tribunus   By using the word *tunc* Amm. seems to imply that Sintula, like for instance Agilo (14.10.8 and above, ad 20.2.5), later occupied another post than that of chief stable master, but evidence for this is lacking.

The *tribunus* (later *comes*)*stabuli* commanded a corps of grooms and equerries (*stratores*) and was responsible for the levy of horses not only for the court but for the cavalry as a whole (Jones 372-373, 625). Presumably (cf. Clauss, 1980, 21, who is less positive than De Jonge ad 14.10.8) he was subordinated to the *magister officiorum*.

IV. 4 *conticuit*   The choice of this verb, which usually means 'to stop speaking', seems prompted by the alliteration with *concedens* at the end of the sentence. Julian 'did not utter a word of protest'.

acquiéverat Iuliánus   The pluperfect is probably due to the cursus velox, cf. Hagendahl, 1921, 122, but it might also be interpreted as having its full sense: Julian had acquiesced in Constantius' decision and therefore he did not say anything.

potioris arbitrio According to Amm. Julian and those around him behaved correctly in this respect. Even the soldiers who attended his installation as Caesar scrupulously respected the hierarchy: *eumque ut potiori reverentia servaretur, nec supra modum laudabant nec infra quam decebat* (15.8.16). With *potiori* Constantius is meant, cf. De Jonge ad loc. (Rolfe's rendering of this sentence goes completely astray).

nec dissimulare ... nec silere Mark the chiastic position with respect to *conticuit hisque adquieverat*.

ut ... nullas In classical Latin the rule would have prescribed *ne ... ullas*. But in later Latin *ne* tends to be ousted by *ut non* in such clauses. Cf. Szantyr 535 and 643/4. An example in Amm. is 22.5.4 *quod agebat ideo obstinate, ut ... non timeret ... plebem*.

laribus Amm. is rather fond of the metonymical use of this word, which in earlier Latin literature is mainly restricted to poetry.

sub hoc ... pacto Hoffmann I 142 takes this at face value: "... unter der ausdrücklichen Bedingung, dass sie einzig in Gallien und nicht jenseits der Alpen, geschweige in entfernteren Räumen eingesetzt würden". This is undoubtedly the purport of Amm.'s words. But even if he exaggerates the official character of the condition, the Germans' wishes must have been quite clear.

verendum esse ... ne As the Empire was in constant need of military manpower, this danger was considerable. The German tribes supplied many soldiers: *saepe adsueti transire ad nostra*.

The fear Julian expressed here did not, for that matter, prevent him from persuading his barbarian soldiers to cross the Alps when he himself needed their assistance in the East! Cf. 21.5.1 ff. and 25.4.13 (*exhortatum eum supplici contione militem Gallicanum pruinis assuetum et Rheno peragratis spatiis regionum extentis per tepentem Assyriam ad usque confinia traxisse Medorum*).

militares In later Latin this word is sometimes used as a substantive. There are a few instances in Amm., e.g. 14.7.5 *militares avidi semper turbarum*, 21.16.3 *militarium aliquis*.

ad nostra The use of *noster* as a synonym for *Romanus* is quite usual since early Latin, as indeed is the substantivized plur. masc. *nostri* ('our compatriots'). The use of the plur. neutr. in this way is a quite frequent idiosyncrasy of Amm. This extension of Latin idiom, in which *sua* was already normal, may have been inspired by Greek τὰ ἡμέτερα, cf. Kühner-Gerth, Satzlehre I 266, Schwyzer-Debrunner, Syntax 202.

Instances of *ad nostra* ('to Roman territory') can be found in 18.6.16 and 20, 20.8.13, 24.1.10, 30.7.6. Its counterpart *ad sua* ('home, to his (or 'their') territory'), in combination with the verb *redire* (or a synonym), can be found in 17.2.4, 17.5.1, 17.8.5, 18.6.6, 19.9.1, 20.7.8, 21.4.5, 23.5.3, 26.3.5, 28.5.12, 29.3.4, 29.5.18, 30.7.9.

IV. 5 *loquebatur* Amm. may very well want to stress the durative or iterative aspect: Julian 'kept saying' or 'said repeatedly'. But it is a well-known fact that he has a tendency to avoid the forms of the perf. pass. (Ehrismann 14–16); there are only three instances of *locutus (-a) est*: 21.1.13, 26.1.1 and 28.1.30. In the present case rhythmic considerations should not be left out of account: *loquebátur in cássum* is a specimen of the cursus planus.

in cassum This expression occurs very seldom in classical Latin, e.g. only twice in Livy (2.49.8, 10.29.2). Cf. the notes ad 14.2.9 and 20.7.8.

tribunus In view of 20.5.1 (*etiam illi quos antegressos rettulimus, ducente Sintula*) there can be hardly any doubt about the identity of this tribune: Sintula must be meant, the *tribunus stabuli* just (20.4.3) mentioned and not Decentius, the *tribunus et notarius* mentioned in 20.4.2 (contra, e.g., Müller-Seidel, 1955, 227; Jones 127 and 573; *PLRE I*, Decentius 1).

parvi querelas Caesaris ducens Augusti iussis obtemperabat The tribune's conduct perfectly demonstrates the subordinate position of Julian as a Caesar of Constantius, rightly stressed by Blockley, 1972. Cf. also De Jonge ad 15.8.11 and Valensi, 1959, 79–84. The article written by Lesuisse in 1961 ("Le titre de *Caesar* et son évolution au cours de l'histoire de l'Empire") is not very helpful for the Later Empire, but see for Caesar in Late Antiquity in general Straub, 1970 and in Amm. in particular Béranger, 1976, 55–56; cf. for Augustus De Jonge ad 17.3.4 and Béranger, 1976, 53–55.

iussis In these sections Amm. emphasizes Constantius' responsibility for the way things went. He did not consult, but he ordered, cf. *iussos* (2), *cogendis* (3), *iubetur* (3), *praeceptis* (6).

lecta According to his instructions (*excerpere quemque promptissimum*) the tribune does indeed choose the pick of the bodyguard.

vigore corporumque levitate This type of the *figura* ἀπὸ κοινοῦ "wo der zwei

Substantiven gemeinsame Genitiv dem zweiten Gliede durch -*que* angehängt wird" is discussed by Hagendahl, 1922, 85, who also quotes *vigore corporum ac levitate confisi* (14.2.9). This parallel does, indeed, prove the ἀπὸ κοινοῦ character of the present expression. Consult also Szantyr 835.

cum isdem   For the purely anaphoric use of *idem*, which grew steadily in later Latin, consult TLL VII 1, 204-206, Szantyr 188, De Jonge ad 15.5.19, 20.

spe potiorum erectus   This is a variation of the more usual construction of this verb in cases of hope or desire. Cf. Cic. *Phil.* 3. 32 *populumque Romanum ad spem reciperandae libertatis erectum*, Livy 33.3.12 *erigi ad aliquam spem poterant*; Amm. has some examples too: *ad meliorem expectationem erectus* (14.11.12), *ad cupidinem altioris fortunae erectos* (29.2.9). In the present text, however, it does not mean 'roused to the hope', but 'cheered by the hope'. Cf. the note ad 16.8.5 *spe potiorum*.

erectus   Clark accepts Bentley's emendation *erectis*. Szidat declares his adhesion with a reference to Amm. 17.13.34. Pighi, 1935, 123/4, however, defends V's reading, explaining it as expressing Sintula's hope of promotion. Seyfarth, accepting this, returns to V in his Teubner edition. In order to make a reasoned choice one must take some other passages into account. Amm. has *spe potiorum* in three other cases: 16.8.5, 17.13.34 and 27.12.7. The official Rufinus, having contrived the downfall of many by his intrigues, *spe potiorum ad imperatoris pervolat castra* (16.8.5), the soldiers cheered Constantius after his speech *aucta spe potiorum et lucri* (17.13.34), the Armenians Cylaces and Arrabannes, failing to persuade the queen and people of the besieged city Artogerassa to surrender, changed their course, *spe potiorum erecti* (27.12.7). In the latter two instances *potiora* may very well mean 'profits', 'rewards' or something in that vein. Presumably Szidat's defence of *erectis* is founded on this. In the first case, however, it is far more likely that Rufinus is trying to advance his career; he is hoping 'to be promoted', cf. Wagner's comment: "ut altius ascenderet". Such a sense tallies with two other passages in Amm.: in 20.5.7 Julian, dealing with the system of promotion, says that he will see to it that only because of merits a person *ad potiorem veniat gradum*, and *ad potiora festinans* (29.3.6) means 'striving after promotion'. Such a meaning fits the present passage too: Sintula hopes for a promotion and therefore most obediently acts upon Constantius' orders. There is nothing wrong with V's *erectus*.

IV. 6 *Et quia*   The conjunction *quia* occurs more than 70 times in Amm. In 30 of these cases it is preceded by *et*, at the beginning of a period. In fact, in that position it rarely occurs without *et*, e.g. 17.3.1, 26.5.15. This phenomenon illustrates how *et* and *-que* lost their semantic value: cf. Löfstedt, 1933, II 342, Szantyr 483. A telling parallel of *et quia* in this respect is the frequency of *cumque* in Amm.; cf. Bitter 172.

residuis Amm.'s use of this word is remarkably frequent. It does not occur in Caes., Curt., HA and only a few times in Livy. Normally it qualifies things, abstract or concrete, hardly ever persons, but Amm. often uses it in the latter way, either as an adjective or substantivized. The only example in Tacitus provides a parallel: *quem ultra honorem residuis nobilium* (*Ann.* 11.23.3). There it possibly has its original meaning ('the remainder of the nobility'), but it may very well be employed as a synonym of *reliquus*, which is often the case in Amm., as De Jonge points out ad 16.12.35.

mitti praeceptis One of the growing class of verbs used in a personal passive construction in later Latin is *praecipere*, cf. Szantyr 365. Some examples with an inf. pass. in Amm. are *antistes a Constantio ad comitatum mitti praeceptus est* (15.7.6), *perque elogium principis torqueri praeceptus* (19.12.9).

perque varias curas animum versans Amm.'s rather sparing use of *versare* (in the general sense 'to turn over in the mind') shows a large grammatical variety: *multa mente versans et varia* (17.8.2), *et tandem multa versantibus nobis sedit consilium* (19.7.6), *in varia sese consilia diducens et versans* (20.11.24), *multa cum animo versans* (29.5.7). Such instances are Virgilian reminiscences, cf. especially

  atque animum nunc huc celerem nunc dividit illuc
    in partisque rapit varias perque omnia versat
        (*A.* 4.285/6 = 8.20/1)

In his notes ad loc. Pease lists many parallels, among which the present expression in Amm.

barbara feritas For this stereotype see above ad 20.1.1 *gentium ferarum*.

iussorum ... auctoritas TLL II 1231–1233 has a long list of occurrences where *auctoritas* is ascribed to things, esp. words and institutions. Some examples in Amm.: *prohibente auctoritate sacrorum* (14.10.9), *quod medicinae quoque admittit auctoritas* (16.8.2).

urgueret Blomgren's tentative proposal (63 note 1) to keep V's *urguet* deserves attention, if not approval. After all, *cum* with the indic. praes., when the verb in the main clause is a past tense, already occurs in classical Latin: *sed, cum redeo, Hortensius venerat* (Cic. *Att.* 10.16.5), *cum occiditur Sex.*

Roscius, ibidem fuerunt (Cic. *S. Rosc.* 120). Landgraf ad loc. refers to a similar case of *ubi* in Caes. *Gal.* 2.9.2; cf. Szantyr 621.

absentia magistri equitum Szidat suggests that Julian was keen on the presence of Lupicinus and Florentius because he wanted to show his readiness to cooperate with Constantius and his faithful servants. But in that case one does not really understand why their absence contributed so much (*maxime*) to his uncertainty and hesitation. It seems more likely that Julian, not wanting the burden of unpopular measures to rest only on his own shoulders, intended the presence of these high authorities to show that they fully shared the responsibility.

dubietatem The first occurrence of this late Latin word is in Eutropius. Amm. uses it three times: 22.14.4, 25.10.12, and in this section, where it means 'hesitation'.

Viennam Early in the fourth century Vienne was the capital not only of the *provincia Viennensis* but, presumably (cf. Nesselhauf, 1938, 84), of the *dioecesis Viennensis* as well. In the course of the century, however, the organization of the diocese changed and its administrative centre moved westward (so Chastagnol, 1970, 287-290, deviating from the opinion of earlier scholars, e.g. Nesselhauf, 1938, 84 n. 5). Accordingly, the diocese was renamed *Aquitania* or *Quinque* (later *Septem*) *Provinciae*, while the *vicarius* of the diocese transferred his residence from Vienne to, probably (Chastagnol, 1970, 287-290), Bordeaux. Soon Vienne even lost her prominent position in the *provincia Viennensis*, too, and was overshadowed by Arles. All this meant a gradual diminishing of Vienne's importance: "Le transfert du vicaire à Bordeaux nous explique aussi le rôle plus modeste qui devient celui de Vienne en Gaule dans la seconde moitié du IVe siècle. La grande période de Vienne est le début du siècle", Chastagnol, 1970, 289.

Nevertheless, in Julian's time Vienne was one of the most important cities of the *provincia Viennensis*, mentioned by Amm. before Arles in 15.11.14: *Viennensis civitatum exultat decore multarum, e quibus potiores sunt Vienna ipsa et Arelate et Valentia.* Cf. the note ad 15.8.21 and see for the earlier history of Vienne Pelletier, 1982; Vienne in the later empire is dealt with by Pelletier, 1974.

specie annonae parandae Whatever the truth of Amm.'s assertion that the grain supply was only a pretext Florentius used in order to escape possible troubles among the soldiers in the vicinity of Julian, the grain supply of the army was, of course, very important and belonged to Florentius' tasks (cf. Jones 371). Failure to fulfil this task could seriously endanger the position of a prefect, as is demonstrated by an incident which took place in 354 and was surely known to Florentius: when the usual supplies had not been brought to the soldiers assembled in Chalon, the praetorian prefect, Rufinus, was exposed to extreme danger and forced to explain personally to the troops why the supply of provisions had been interrupted (14.10.4: *Unde Rufinus ea tempestate praefectus praetorio ad discrimen trusus est ultimum. Ire enim ipse compellebatur ad militem ... ut satisfaceret atque monstraret, quam ob causam annonae convectio sit impedita*).

It may perhaps seem strange that Florentius went to Vienne *alimentariae rei gratia* (20.8.20; a variation of the expression *specie annonae parandae* used here) in view of 18.2.3, where it is explicitly said that the grain for the Rhine army was regularly brought over from Britain: *annona a Britanniis sueta transferri*. The deviation from what is called the normal practice (*sueta*) in 18.2.3 might even be regarded as a corroboration of Amm.'s suspicion about Florentius' intentions.

The grain for the army, however, did not only come from Britain, as is testified by Amm. himself in 17.8.1: *antequam ex Aquitania ... veheretur annona*. Cf. 17.9.2 and 17.10.9.

See for other meanings of the word *annona* the note ad 14.7.11.

ut se militari eximeret turba The translations of Rolfe ("to escape troubles in the camp") and Seyfarth ("um sich den unruhigen militärischen Treiben zu entziehen") may be right: *turba* and *militaris* can mean 'riot' and 'caused by the soldiers', respectively; cf. also Tac. *Hist.* 4.46.1 *inter quae militaris seditio prope exarsit*. But with this meaning *turba* is usually in the plural: *militares avidi saepe turbarum* (Amm. 14.7.15), *turbarum acerrima concitatrix* (21.13.12), *nullas ciere potuit turbas* (20.9.9). With one exception (25.3.23) the singular in Amm. always denotes a 'mass' or a 'throng', cf. especially 21.10.1: a *militaris et omnis generis turba* escorted Julian to his palace.

Therefore it is perhaps better to render the phrase under discussion by: 'in order to withdraw from the (restless) mass of soldiers'; cf. also *illud non veniet in dubium quin se exemerit turbae et altius steterit quisquis despexit lacessentis* (Sen. *De ira* 3.25.3). Of course, Florentius went away because he foresaw the rioting: *motusque militares timentis praefecti* (20.4.9).

IV.7 *perpendebat* In Roman narrative style (historiography and epic) the predicate often takes the first place, cf. Szantyr 403. Amm. even has a predilection for this arrangement, as Bitter 174 notes. In the present case both this first position and the durative imperfect add weight to the semantic value of the verb *perpendere* ('to assess carefully'), stressing the calculated motive of Florentius' absence.

ad relationem suam   This adjunct has to be linked with *abstrahendos*, not with *perpendebat*, as in Seyfarth's translation. TLL I 553.32/3 mentions the expression in a list of instances of *ad* used to denote *causa* (*"usus cognatus cum notione* secundum *atque vi temporali"*). Rightly so: Florentius fully realized that it was his own report which had prompted the forthcoming removal of troops, cf. also Blomgren 167/8; "*relatio* is official intelligence from a lower to a higher instance, especially to the emperor" (De Jonge ad 15.5.13).

putabatur   Amm. repeats his restriction *ut ferebatur* (20.4.2).

abstrahendos   The inf. fut. pass. does not occur in Amm. A regular substitute, used more often in late Latin, is the gerundivum with *esse*. Cf. Szantyr 312/3, Ehrismann 73, De Jonge ad 14.11.19.

Galliarum   See 15.11.1–18, with De Jonge's commentary for a description of the Gallic dioceses.

pugnaces numeros   The *auxiliares milites* and *lecti ex numeris aliis trecenteni* of 20.4.2. See for *numerus* above, the note ad 20.1.3.
   Obviously *pugnaces* is meant to be a positive quality, like *bellicosus* in 20.1.2, of which it is a synonym; cf. *Vetranionis mors viri pugnacis* (25.1.19), about one of Julian's officers.

barbarisque iam formidatos   The ideal of all Roman power through the ages, cf.
   et formidatam Parthis te principe Romam
         (Hor. *Ep.* 2.1.256).
This verb, which does not occur in Caes. or Livy and only once in Tac., is quite frequent in Amm. De Jonge has a note ad 17.12.9.

IV. 8 *suscepisset*   For *suscipere* as a synonym of *accipere* see above ad 20.2.3.

monentis petentisque   Synonymous verba monendi are often coupled in this way. Hagendahl, 1924, 184/5 provides some examples, among which a remarkable parallel to the present text: *imperatoris scripta suscipiebat assidua, monentis orantisque ut ad se veniret* (14.11.9).

venire acceleráret   The choice of this verb, which is rarely used by Amm. (only 20.4.2, 26.7.14 and here), is prompted by the cursus velox, which would have been impossible with *festinare* or *properare*.

rem publicam consiliis iuvaturus   A thoroughly Roman phrase! It was an immemorial tradition for those invested with authority to seek the advice of others before taking a decision. The rule was followed by *patres familias*, magistrates, kings, emperors, etc. Tarquinius proved to be a real tyrant by trying criminal cases *sine consiliis per se solus* (Liv. 1.49.4); cf. Liebenam, 1901, 915–922; Crook, 1955. As a counterpart of this rule of conduct friends had the duty not only to provide material assistance, but also to help with their advice: the expression *consilio* (or *consiliis*) *iuvare* is in fact quite frequent. Some examples: *nunc ego te quaeso ut me opera et consilio iuves* (Pl. *Trin.* 189), *aut consolando aut consilio aut re iuvero* (Ter., *Hau.* 86), quoted at the end of a letter (*Fam.* 7.10.4) by Cicero, who has elsewhere recorded this thought: *consilio iuvare cives et auxilio aequa in laude ponendum est* (*Top.* 71). The abl. plur. also occurs: *studioque altisque iuvabat / consiliis* (Stat., *Silv.* 2.6.51/2), and about the pseudo-Agrippa Postumus: *quamquam multi ... sustentasse opibus, iuvisse consiliis dicerentur* (Tac. *Ann.* 2.40.3). So Florentius is urged to fulfil a time-honoured Roman duty, and to make the appeal more urgent, he is not asked to assist a person, but the commonwealth itself. Shrinking from this is pure desertion.

obstinatissime It should be noted that in Latin *obstinatus* is by no means only used in a deprecatory sense. At least originally, it could denote praiseworthy determination and stubbornness: *sed obstinata mente perfer, obdura* (Catul. 8.11), *quo terrore cum vicisset obstinatam pudicitiam* (Liv. 1.58.5). Gradually, however, it tended to be used more negatively, rather like English 'obstinate', especially in Christian authors.

pavore mente confusa The causal force lent to this expression by Rolfe ("for his mind was disturbed by fear") is quite possible: Florentius obstinately refuses to comply with Julian's pertinent request, because he experiences the latter's emphasis on his obligations as menacing and frightening. A concessive sense, however, is not out of the question: Florentius is disobedient, although the clear reference to a duty inherent in his function makes him feel ill at ease. This meaning of *confundere* ('to confound, to disconcert') is quite normal, also in Amm., e.g. *confundente metu consilia* (17.12.19), but here it may very well be a Virgilian reminiscence:
   hic mihi nescio quod trepido male numen amicum
      confusam eripuit mentem   (*A.* 2.735/6)

scripta Both the context and other occurrences imply that Julian's letters are meant here. Cf. the sentence just quoted from 14.11.9 at the beginning of this section in the note ad *monentis petentisque* and *imperatoris scripta perferentes et munera* (17.5.15), *ibique principis scripta suscepimus* (18.6.5), *militiaeque rectoribus insinuare novi principis scripta* (25.8.12). De Jonge ad

16.9.4 calls this meaning "exceptional"; it is indeed unusual, but it does occur a few times in Ovid: *a! quotiens dubius scriptis exarsit amator* (*Ars* 3.481), *Antoni scripta leguntur* (*Pont.* 1.1.23), *Am.* 2.18.28 and 30, *Rem.* 717/8.

ab imperatore nusquam diiungi debere praefectum A somewhat peculiar statement, for, as Jones 101 remarks, "it does appear that Constantine did break with the tradition that a praetorian prefect was always attached to an emperor's person" (cf. the note ad 20.4.2). But Amm.'s mention of a *praefectus praetorio praesens* (14.1.10 and 23.5.6) seems to imply that the praetorian prefect was sometimes a regular member of the *comitatus*.

in ardore terribilium rerum A bold extension of the figurative use of *ardor* in cases like *in medio ardore belli* (Liv. 24.45.4), *in ardore pugnae* (Curt. 8.2.38), *in medio ardore pugnandi* (Veg. *mil.* 4.46) and *ardor proelii* (Amm. 16.12.24). Gel. 19.1.7 has *ardor ille periculi* and Amm. 16.12.28 *ardor negotii* (concerning a difficult stage of the battle of Strasbourg). In the examples quoted *ardor* relates to a critical and perilous situation, which is the case here too, for *terribiles res* refers to the menace of mutiny (a comparable use of *aestus* can be found in 22.2.2 *post exemptos periculorum aestus*).

procurare This is a vexed textual question. The verb occurs throughout Latin literature with the meaning 'to look after, to attend to', but never absolutely (Pl. *Truc.* 878 *nunc puero utere et procura, quando pro cura aes habes* is an easily understandable ellipse.). The context calls for a verb or an expression conveying Florentius' duty and most probably beginning with *pro-* in view of the presumable word-play with *proiceret* and the strong alliteration in the last part of this section (of the 36 words 10 begin with *p*, 7 of these with *pr*). Löfstedt's defence of *procurare* as a military term did not convince Clark, who was evidently not sufficiently impressed by the various emendations either (such as *procurrere*, praised by Valesius: "quam equidem coniecturam valde probo" and therefore printed † *procurare*. Pighi, 1935, 72 defended *procurare* with a reference to Veg. *mil.* 3.3 *sed fidelis horreorum custodia et erogatio moderata consuevit sufficere pro copia, maxime si ab initio procuretur*. But also in this instance *procurare* is not really used absolutely. Therefore Seyfarth's leaving out Clark's crux is too optimistic, nor is any of the emendations really convincing, although a variation of one of Clark's own suggestions has some attractiveness: ⟨*provincias*⟩ *procurare* would tally with the alliteration, anticipate *provinciarum interitum* and precisely because of the many words beginning with *pr(o)-* could fall victim to a scribe's negligence.

All things considered, however, Clark's crux still seems hardly open to question.

dissimulasset Wagner's explanation "negligeret" is not incorrect, but his reference to 21.3.2 *quod ne dissimulatum redivivas bellorum materias excitaret* is not very helpful, since there is no question of an inf. as complement. In fact in late Latin *dissimulare* with inf. means 'not to take the trouble to', almost even 'to refuse': *taceas licet et salutationi respondere dissimules* (Symm. *Ep.* 9.36), *creator quidem deus infideles homines et ad se dissimulantes venire dicitur excaecare* (Rufin., *Adamant.* 2.21), *ad eum venire dissimulans* (Sulp. Sev., *dial.* 1.14.4).

proiceret insignia principatus In his *Ep. ad Ath.* 283a Julian himself also mentions his intention to resign his office (διενοούμην - μάρτυρες δὲ αὐτοί - πᾶσαν ἀπορρίψας τὴν βασιλικὴν πολυτέλειαν καὶ παρασκευὴν ἡσυχάζειν, πράττειν δὲ οὐδὲν ὅλως). Referring to Amm. 24.3.7 and 25.4.12, Szidat notes that Julian was quite prone to such a "Rücktrittsdrohung". Here the wording is quite dramatic, and recalls the action of soldiers when fleeing or refusing duty: *proicere arma*. Cf. *de his agitur etiam qui arma proiciunt in pace; placuit abstineri eos a communione* (*Conc. Arel.* can. 3).

Amm. uses the expression *insignia principatus* also in 14.11.3 (... *ad magistri equitum liberos principatus insignia transferantur*) and in 27.6.4 (*Gratianum filium suum, adulto iam proximum, insignibus principatus ornare meditabatur*). Cf. 15.6.3, 31.12.10 and 31.15.2 and see for the literal meaning of these *insignia* Alföldi, 1980³.

As Béranger, 1976, 53 has pointed out, *principatus* can be used by Amm. not only to denote the supreme power of an *Augustus*, but of an *Augustus* in spe as well: "Chez Ammien, le terme s'applique à un pouvoir de fait, indépendamment de la théorie et de l'opinion, légal ou illégal, légitime ou légitimé, pouvoir inconditionnel, de droit divin, empire au sens d'autorité souveraine, règne. Le mot n'éveille aucun souvenir de passion partisane. Nul ne représente un principat idéal comparativement avec un autre. *Principatus* ne recouvre même pas le pouvoir conféré, mais il correspond aux étapes qui le précèdent et l'annoncent, aux degrés de l'ascension vers le trône, pronunciamentos, promotions hiérarchiques, dignités, influence personnelle dominante, voire menaçante". Cf. 20.4.12 where *princeps* refers to Julian, then still a Caesar.

gloriosum esse Julian's threat of desertion is surprising for a man who *oppetere dimicando gloriose magis optabat* (Amm. 17.1.14). But Amm. points out that in this case precisely the continued discharge of his imperial obligations could result in ignominy, the Gallic provinces being doomed to destruction. Therefore, desertion and, as its consequence, death would paradoxically enhance his reputation more than fulfilling a catastrophic duty, which after all would also result in his death, ordered by Constantius (*iussa*).

iussa morte oppetere As De Jonge notes ad 17.1.14, in classical Latin *oppetere* without *mortem* in the meaning 'to die' is restricted to poetry. In later Latin it is quite normal and a modal or causal ablative may even be added to express the manner of death: *hoc genere oppetit mortis* (Amm. 15.5.32), *publica morte oppetiverunt* (28.1.16), *quo gloriosa morte fortes oppetant* (Prud. *perist.* 10.65). Cf. also Hagendahl, 1921, 64. Julian means to say that his disobedience inevitably implies that his death will not be natural or self-chosen, but 'ordered' (by Constantius).

quam "Deest *magis* vel *potius* more Graeco" (Wagner). But this occurs already in archaic Latin, and is quite frequent in late Latin. Cf. Szantyr 593 and the note ad 20.7.18.

ei provinciarum interitum Clark and Seyfarth have heeded Valesius' categoric statement: "Ego vero non dubito quin legendum sit, *quam ei provinciarum interitum assignari*". All the same V's *et provinciarum* is not unfitting the context: Julian thinks it better for his reputation to die after desertion, which will be punished by execution (*iussa morte*), than to die while sticking to his post, and then have the responsibility for the Gallic catastrophe a l s o (*et*) ascribed to him. The use of *assignari* without a dative seems a little awkward, however, and Gelenius' *sibi* is too neat to be true, so that *ei* is indeed quite likely. The use of the oblique cases of *is* instead of *se* and *sibi* occurs already in classical Latin and its frequency grows in late Latin. Cf. Szantyr 175. Besides, in this case the use of *ei* might betray that the reflection is Amm.'s own rather than Julian's. With this text the passage means that Julian prefers disobedience with the certainty of execution to accepting Constantius' demands, which will cause the ruin of the provinces to be attributed to himself.

vicit Usually in such a context this concerns a deliberation: *haec sententia, quae tutissima videbatur, vicit* (Liv. 21.6.8), *vicit pars quae sortiri legatos malebat* (Tac. *Hist.* 4.8.5), *vicit tamen ad ultimum coetu seniorum urgente, dedendi sese consilium* (Amm. 17.13.21), *vicit sententia melior* (24.7.2). The prevalence of Florentius' obstinacy is parallelled by Valens: *vicit tamen funesta principis destinatio* (31.12.7).

rationabiliter A very purposeful term! Whereas jealousy, fear, egoistic calculation etc. abound in the circles of the emperor and his henchmen, Julian is portrayed as acting in accordance with reason and common sense.

parere ... reluctantis De Jonge ad 19.2.15 and 19.8.5 characterizes the comparatively infrequent verb *reluctari* as poetical and post-classical. Amm.

uses it in contexts implying strong or stubborn resistance: *destinatius* (25.5.3), *pertinaciter* (25.8.17, 25.10.11) and *incredibili pertinacia* (17.2.2) are some parallels of *contentione maxima* in the present text. The construction with an inf. as a complement is not parallelled, for in Claud. *In Ruf.* 2.353/4

equites illinc poscentia cursum
ora reluctantur pressis sedare lupatis,

reluctari evidently has a different meaning. In Amm.'s case the construction is probably inspired by the analogy of *recusare*, which verb is combined with an (acc.c.)inf., as *reluctari* in the present text, or with a noun-clause, as is the case with *reluctari* in *pertinaciter reluctantis ne in curuli sella veheretur* (25.10.11).

IV. 9 *inter has tamen moras absentis Lupicini motusque militares timentis praefecti* At first sight *moras* seems to refer to the loitering of the two high officials. But this could only concern Florentius, for Lupicinus had been sent to Britain by Julian himself (see above 20.1.2) and Amm. has not mentioned any recall, which would warrant criticism of Lupicinus in case of delay. Possibly Amm.'s wording is somewhat careless, but there might be a better explanation. The expression *inter moras* occurs three more times: 17.10.3, 28.6.13, 29.1.4, the second of which is quite interesting: *inter tales tamen consulendi moras exspectandique responsa*; this evidently does not mean that the consultations were delayed, but rather that the delay was caused by, or perhaps even consisted in, the consultations and the waiting for replies. Such a sense fits the present context quite well too, especially when *absentis* and *timentis* are considered to carry the weight of the phrase: 'during these delays which were caused by Lupicinus' absence and the prefect's fear for riots among the soldiers'. Seyfarth's rendering tallies with this. Amm. has a predilection for the (poetic) plural of *mora*, using it twice as often as the singular.

consiliorum Gardthausen's *consili⟨at⟩orum* is quite wrong. Amm. uses *consiliator* nowhere else, *consiliarius* seven times, all in the singular. Besides, the emendation is not necessary at all. Wagner's explanation "consiliantium" is fully satisfactory. He could have referred to other passages where *consilium* is used in a 'res pro persona' manner, such as *consilium patriae legumque oriundus rogator* (Lucil. 853 M), *esse illi matrem et aviam, propiora consilia* (Tac. *Ann.* 4.40.2).

adminiculo For this figurative use cf. *si ingenium eius nullis alienarum artium adminiculis inniti videretur* (Tac. *Dial.* 2.6, with Gudeman's instructive note ad loc.), *nullisque artium bonarum adminiculis fulta* (Gel. 7.2.8).

ancipitique sententia fluctuans Amm.'s continued emphasizing of Julian's hesitation aims at persuading the reader that the pronunciamento was by no means a preconceived plan of Julian's. Comparable expressions of uncertainty are *in hoc aestu mentis ancipiti* (15.5.30), *haec operientibus illis et ancipiti cogitatione districtis* (18.4.7), *sed fluctuantes ambiguitate mentium in diversa rapiebantur* (17.13.7). There are quite a few examples of the use of *fluctuare* or *fluctuari* concerning the human mind in all stages of the Latin language, both in prose and in poetry. It denotes agitation (*magnis curarum fluctuat undis*, Catul. 64.62, imitated by Verg. *A.* 8.19) or irresolution (*fluctuansque animo*, Liv. 1.27.6).

et sollemniter Both Clark and Seyfarth print this emendation of *vita sollemni* (V). As De Jonge notes ad 16.12.36 *dato igitur aeneatorum accentu sollemniter signo*, the adverb *sollemniter* can be the equivalent of *ex more*. In Rolfe's opinion this adverbial adjunct ("in the usual manner") is to be linked with *egressos*, but Seyfarth's "er ordnete in der üblichen Form an" is more likely to be right. As regards Heraeus' *et*: this can excellently be defended by a reference to 14.11.4 *id ut optimum factu elegit: et Ursicinum primum ad se venire summo cum honore mandavit*. Blomgren 38 lists this among a series of examples of *et* explicativum. So grammatically and stylistically *et sollemniter* is quite sound and it satisfactorily fits the context, too. Nevertheless, its rather large deviation from V's *vita sollemni* is a little perturbing. Gelenius has *via sollemni*, regarded as a reasonable conjecture by Valesius "equidem non damno", although, with an eye to 14.2.15, he had earlier ventured *tessera data sollemni* himself. Blomgren 38 note 2 agrees with Gelenius, pointing to 26.6.18, where V has *vitam* for the evidently correct *viam*. The meaning 'course of action' or 'method' is, of course, quite normal; Amm. has some examples too: *nullam ad tuendam salutem viam superesse* (27.10.9), *provinciam omni fallaciarum via prodere* (28.6.3), and in combination with *consilii: viam consilii mei salutarem* (21.5.6), *novam consilii viam* (22.12.8), *consiliique eius viam* (26.2.8). Therefore, *via sollemni* could very well be a variation of *sollemni more* (30.10.5).

e stationibus ... in quibus hiemabant Cf. *milite locato per stationes hibernas* (14.1.1), *milite disperso per stationes hibernas* (16.11.15). For the meaning, '(winter)quarters' consult the note ad 17.10.10: "*statio* has here a general meaning = ± garrison, etc.".

disposuit In the meaning 'to ordain, decide' this verb occurs quite frequently, witness the list in TLL V 1425.56 sqq. under the general heading latiore sensu "recedente notione dividendi, praevalente voluntatis: i.q. ordinare quomodocumque". De Jonge has devoted three substantial notes to Amm.'s use of *disponere*: ad 16.10.16, 16.11.4 and 16.12.23. The second of these is especially useful for the present case.

IV. 10 This is a highly interesting section in that it shows something of Amm.'s use of his material. Julian himself reports this incident in quite frugal terms: καὶ γράφει τις ἀνώνυμον ⟨γραμμάτιον⟩ εἰς τὴν ἀστυγείτονά μοι πόλιν πρὸς τοὺς Πετουλάντας τουτουσὶ καὶ Κελτούς (Jul. *Ep. ad Ath.* 283 b). In Zosimus' version both the writer and the pamphlet have been pluralized: some officers are said to have spread them among the soldiers who were bound to leave for the East (τῶν δὲ ταξιάρχων τινές ... ἀνώνυμα γραμμάτια τῶν στρατιωτῶν ἐν μέσῳ κατὰ τὸ λεληθὸς διαρρίψαντες ... 3.9.1).

Julian's letter to the Athenians covers three subjects: abuse of Constantius, laments about the betrayal of the Gallic provinces (πολλοὶ δὲ ὑπὲρ τῆς Γαλλιῶν προδοσίας ὀδυρμοί) and complaints about the dishonour suffered by Julian himself. Zosimus reports only the last point, but in a more elaborate and even pathetic way; the pamphlets are said to refer to the danger to which Julian, that great champion, would soon be exposed (εἰς ἔσχατον ἥξει κινδύνου). For Amm.'s presentation of the events at Paris this element was unusable, because it could justify the suspicion that revolutionary tendencies were at work in Julian's own surroundings, whereas Amm. is constantly endeavouring to lay all responsibility on Constantius' shoulders. So in contrast to Zosimus he selected the second point of the list of contents, cleverly dramatizing it by the use of oratio recta and keeping the writer completely anonymous. In this way he gives a voice to the oppressed themselves, which must convince the reader of the spontaneity of the events. Ascribing the outburst to the officers, as Zosimus does, would not have suited his purpose at all.

famosum ... libellum The only occurrence in Amm. "The expression *famosi libelli* is not frequently attested, but appears to be a semi-technical term for the jurists" (F.D.R. Goodyear ad Tac. *Ann.* 1.72.3). Here Amm.'s use of the term is remarkable in that it provides a glimpse of an element deliberately suppressed, viz. the abuse of Constantius.

inter alia multa Judging from Julian's words (πολλὰ μὲν ... πολλοὶ δὲ ...) one may perhaps conclude that the size of the pamphlet was quite substantial. With the expression as such Amm. explicitly informs the reader that he has made a choice among the contents.

ut noxii pellimur et damnati Amm. makes the anonymous writer follow the pattern of the complaints raised in ch. 2, where Amm.'s choice of words aims to present the investigation of the fall of Amida as a trial of Ursicinus. Here, too, the measures in question are presented as taken by a criminal court, which in this case has sentenced the accused to deportation.

caritates TLL III 462.43-60 prints a list of instances in which *caritas* denotes a person. This occurs most frequently as a title of address, mainly in Christian texts (*suggestum caritati tuae*, Hier. *ep.* 101.2); cf. O'Brien, 1930, 51-53; Svennung, 1958, 80; Zilliacus, 1964, 176.

Used in another way, as in the present text, it is quite characteristic of Amm., who has 13 instances, among which 18.5.2 *cum coniuge, liberis et omni vinculo caritatum*, where De Jonge has an instructive note.

internecivas ... pugnas Amm. uses this strong adjective ('fought to death, murderous'), which is relatively rare in other authors, quite often, to define *bellum* (18.7.7, 26.10.9), *certamen* (19.1.9, 22.16.15, 23.1.2, 31.7.15), *hostis* (25.9.10, 29.5.23), *rebellatrix* (14.8.2), *populatio* (28.6.10), or substantivized: *interneciva minantibus barbaris* (26.5.12). The adverb *internecive* occurs twice (27.9.6, 30.3.7), both times concerning devastation.

IV. 11 *quo textu ad comitatum perlato lectoque* Amm. uses *textus* in two different meanings:
1 as a synonym of *series* to denote a train of events: *tali textu recte factorum* (17.13.25), *hoc comperto textu gestorum* (27.12.11), *mandaratque ... pro cognitorum ageret textu* (26.6.2).
2 'written text', often indicating a passage in his own history: *post gesta quae superior continet textus* (19.13.1), *residua quae secuturus aperiet textus* (15.1.1). This can be compared to a phrase at the beginning of the Vita Max., where the author announces that he will not economize on the space devoted to great emperors, *quorum res gestae plures atque clariores longiorem desiderant textum* (HA, *Max.* 3.1). Other written texts are denoted by *notarum textus obelisco incisus* (17.4.17) and *textu lecto iussorum* (21.4.5).

Neither of these meanings is classical and Amm. seems to be the first author to use them on a large scale. The lemma in Krebs-Schmalz II 660 is quite instructive about the semantic development.

ad comitatum Derived from *comes*, a travelling companion, *comitatus* is sometimes used by Amm. quite literally, as a collective term for persons accompanying or escorting someone (15.8.18 *comitatu parvo suscepto*, 19.1.3 *multiplici vertice dignitatum et gentium diversarum comitatu sublimis*, 31.10.14 *arma imperatorii comitatus*). Usually, however, the word has a more impersonal sense: 'the emperor's (here, of course, 'the Caesar's) headquarters', 'the court'. In this sense Amm. uses the term without further qualification (as here and in 15.7.6, 16.8.7, 18.5.5, 18.6.1, 21.12.2, 25.10.9, 26.5.7, 28.2.9, 28.3.9, 28.5.12, 28.6.9, 28.6.16, 28.6.20, 28.6.27, 28.6.29, 30.1.3) or with the addition of *imperatoris* (14.5.8, 16.11.15, 16.12.66), *principis* (15.3.9, 22.11.7, 28.1.41), *Augusti* (15.8.18, 16.6.1, 17.2.3, 18.3.1) and the like (*Constantii* in 17.11.1, *eius* in 28.1.26).

More so than *palatium*, which is often used without any difference in meaning (cf. the notes ad 14.5.8 and 17.11.1), the word reflects the travels of the imperial court. Cf. Jones 366: "Down to the death of Theodosius the Great, while the emperor still normally took the field in major wars, and sometimes made tours of inspection in the frontier areas, the *comitatus*, the group of ministries which were attached to the emperor's person and formed the central government, was in fact a migratory body". See also Millar, 1977, 42–43.

contemplans rationabiles querelas It is tempting to assume a construction with a predicative accusative: "although he found the complaints reasonable" (Rolfe), but there are no other instances where *contemplari* is constructed in this manner, so that Seyfarth's translation has to be accepted as more correct: "Julian überdachte ... die berechtigten Klagen der Soldaten". The implication that *contemplans* is an example of the late Latin use of the part. praes. with preterite force (Szantyr 387) is, however, unnecessary: Julian had the complaints in mind, when he gave his orders to depart with their families.

It is remarkable that Amm. usually uses *querelae* to refer – implicitly or explicitly – to justifiable complaints, as in the present case and in 17.9.6 and 29.6.1 *et erat ratio iusta querelarum* or 29.2.20 *perpetuum numen ratione querelarum iustissima commoventes*.

cum familiis A constitution promulgated in 349, *Cod. Theod.* 7.1.3, concerning soldiers who had received imperial permission for their families to come to them (*quicumque militum ex nostra auctoritate familias suas ad se venire meruerint, non amplius quam coniugia, liberos, servos etiam de peculio castrensi emptos neque adscriptos censibus ad eosdem excellentia tua dirigi faciat*), is taken by Szidat to prove that Julian did nothing unusual ("nichts Aussergewöhnliches") in allowing the soldiers to take their families with them.

Szidat's assumption is rather unlikely. The very issuing of *Cod. Theod.* 7.1.3 points to special circumstances (cf. Jones 630), while the circumstances in 349 certainly differed from those in 360 in at least one respect: the soldiers meant in *Cod. Theod.* 7.1.3 must at first have departed *without* their families. It seems better to regard the very mentioning of *cum familiis* as a hint that Julian, far from doing something quite normal, was granting a special privilege.

clavularis cursus In the later Roman Empire the postal service consisted of two divisions, the express post or *cursus velox*, and the slow wagon post, the *cursus clavularis* or *clavularius*. Cf. e.g. *Cod. Theod.* 8.5.62, a. 401: *usurpa-*

tionem cursus publici penitus iussimus amputari, scilicet ut excepta magnitudine tua praesumendi velocis et clavularii cursus nullus habeat potestatem. "The wagon post was mainly used for carrying the foodstuffs levied for the *annona*, but also for the uniforms and arms destined for the troops, and for timber and building stone for public works" (Jones 831).

The organisation of the system with its network of posting stations (*mutationes* and *mansiones*) was very expensive to maintain. The costs, moreover, tended to rise because of the extravagant use made of the service by officials and its illegal usurpation by private persons, notwithstanding frequent attempts of successive emperors to counteract abuse: the title '*de cursu publico*' is one of the longest in the Theodosian Code (cf. Jones 830–834 and Clauss, 1980, 45–51) – incidentally, the term *cursus publicus*, which is regularly used by modern writers to describe the postal service in the Early Empire too (see, in general Seeck, 1901; Holmberg, 1933; Pflaum, 1940; Kornemann, 1954 and Van Ooteghem, 1959), is not attested before the fourth century (see for this Mitchell, 1976, 112).

Through minute legislation Julian himself, too, tried to ease the pressure on the postal services and relieve the cities, which bore the main costs, of a considerable burden (cf. Seston, 1943; Bowersock, 1978, 75; Athanassiadi-Fowden, 1981, 105 and in the first place Pack, 1986, 169 ff., who combats the view that Julian's measures differed much from those of his predecessors.

cum ambigeretur diutius, qua pergerent via   The discussion took place in the *consistorium*, as is clear from *ad comitatum*. Mark that Amm. mentions these consultations only now, tacitly suggesting that the previous decisions had all been taken by Julian personally. The reason for this is clear: these decisions all testified to his prudence and submission to the emperor, but now a most disputable and even ominous measure has to be reported and Amm., true to his purpose, ascribes it to others.

per Parisios   Why *per Parisios*? What had Decentius in mind when he proposed that the troops should be led by way of Paris? Did he not see or did he not want to see, some scholars wondered, that to lead the soldiers to Julian's headquarters would further the chances of a usurpation? Did the man who was supposed to be one of Constantius' agents "with the unerring misjudgement of the chairborne administrator" (Browning, 1976, 101, cf. Norman, 1969, 341) make a very momentous mistake? Or was Decentius not that stupid? Was he perhaps not stupid at all? The latter view is defended by Blockley, 1972, 451, who puts forward a theory to the effect that Decentius, far from being stupid, acted very shrewdly, the *notarius* secretly being in league with Julian.

Direct evidence to prove or disprove Blockley's theory is lacking – which is to be expected, if Decentius really was a clever double agent – and the circumstantial evidence Blockley adduced is not very impressive (cf. Szidat I 148), but at any rate one thing seems clear: though he never says so, Amm. apparently wants his readers to think that to lead the troops by way of Paris was asking for trouble and that, consequently, Decentius, not Julian, was to be held responsible for the subsequent course of events.

Amm.'s wording, it should be stressed, implies more than it actually says. Amm. is only suggesting that Decentius' advice was the decisive step which finally led to the pronunciamento. Libanius, *Or.* 18.96, on the other hand, is more explicit.

In Libanius' version (in which, incidentally, Decentius' name is missing; there is, however, no reason to reject Amm.'s more precise information in this respect) the possibility of a usurpation forced upon Julian by the soldiers is explicitly mentioned: the troops were concentrated in Paris, though Julian himself, Libanius asserts (οἶμαι), had wanted them to march off by another route lest the soldiers should react in the way they did: παρῄνει τοῖς ἐξ Ἰταλίας ἥκουσιν ἑτέραν ἄγειν τοὺς στρατιώτας πολὺ τῆς πόλεως, ἐν ᾗ καθῆστο καὶ διέτριβεν, ἀπέχοντας. ἐδεδίει γάρ, οἶμαι, μὴ δράσειαν, ὃ καλῶς ποιοῦντες ἔδρασαν). Mark that, like Amm., Libanius does not mention the considerations of those who opted for Paris.

Curiously enough, in our third testimony on this matter things are stated rather differently. Julian in his *Ep. ad Ath.* 284a does, indeed, mention the discussion concerning the route which the soldiers were to take: ἐσκοποῦμεν ἐνταῦθα, ποίαν ὁδὸν αὐτοὺς χρὴ βαδίζειν, διττῆς οὔσης, and draws attention to the fact that he was of a different opinion than the others (note the plural; Decentius' name again is missing): ἐγὼ μὲν ἠξίουν ἑτέραν τραπῆναι, οἱ δὲ αὖθις ἀναγκάζουσιν ἐκείνην ἰέναι. So far his representation of the facts tallies with that of Libanius. Keeping silent about his own point of view, he rather surprisingly hints at the reason why the others insisted (ἀναγκάζουσιν) on a rendez-vous at Paris, viz. fear that choosing *the other route* should bring about mutiny among the troops and consequent disturbance: μὴ τοῦτο αὐτὸ γενόμενον ὥσπερ ἀφορμήν τινα στάσεως τοῖς στρατιώταις παράσχῃ καὶ ταραχῆς τινὸς αἴτιον γένηται, εἶτα στασιάζειν ἅπαξ ἀρξάμενοι πάντα ἀθρόως ταράξωσιν.

All this is rather puzzling. Julian, unlike Amm. and Libanius, at least pays some attention to the arguments adduced by Decentius cum suis (if indeed these arguments are correctly reproduced, which is of course by no means certain), but his version, too, leaves many questions unanswered; for instance, he does not explain (though he admits the possibility: ἐδόκει τὸ δέος οὐ παντάπασιν ἄλογον εἶναι τῶν ἀνθρώπων) why there should be a mutiny if Paris were avoided (see for some suggestions Seeck, 1920–1923[2-4], IV, 285; Drinkwater, 1983, 382).

The historical truth behind Amm.'s statement concerning Decentius' proposal is difficult to assess. Amm.'s own words are rather lapidary and those of Julian and Libanius are not very helpful, both of whom were, of course, not impartial (cf. for the propaganda in Julian's *Ep. ad Ath.* Caltabiano, 1974; see also Tumanischvili Bandelli, 1980) and give conflicting views at that. As to Amm.'s intentions, his words do not offer any problem: Amm. wants to emphasize that Julian had nothing to do with the usurpation and subtly forces this opinion upon his readers.

ubi morabatur adhuc Caesar nusquam motus This is by no means an otiose piece of information. Amm. stresses the fact that Julian had not yet taken action to meet and influence the soldiers in question. For *moveri* 'to move into some direction, to depart' cf. 16.3.2 (about Julian) *non ante motus est exinde*, 30.5.1 *Valentinianus a Treveris motus*. Although *nusquam* could be interpreted as a colloquial variant of *non* (cf. Szantyr 337), here its most probable meaning is 'to no place, in no direction', as in 29.6.18 *undarum magnitudine nusquam progredi permittente* and 31.12.17 *nusquam ire permissi*.

IV. 12 *et ita est factum* Although Amm.'s style is quite varied, such lapidary phrases are rare. The present one is repeated in 28.6.17, where it also winds up the preliminaries of a fatal action. A nice parallel is provided by the laconic phrase at the end of the description of the way of life of the aristocrats at Rome: *haec nobilium sunt instituta* (14.6.24).

in suburbanis In classical Latin *suburbanum* means 'a country estate near a city (usually Rome)', but in late Latin its meaning has changed to 'suburb'. Ad 16.10.14 De Jonge mentions a number of instances. The local detail is important: it underlines the information provided at the end of the preceding section (*ubi morabatur* etc.). Julian met the soldiers on Parisian territory.

princeps occurrit ex more laudans The division of these words into commata deserves close attention. Both Clark and Seyfarth combine *ex more* with *laudans*, the former accentuating this by accepting Heraeus' suggestion to add *et* after *occurrit*. Valesius, however, pointed to Julian's own words ὑπήντησα κατὰ τὸ νενομισμένον αὐτοῖς (*Ep. ad Ath.* 284b), which in his opinion necessitated a punctuation *princeps occurrit ex more*, the more so because other texts too make mention of such a custom. Valesius' view becomes even more convincing when one takes two further facts into account:
1 rhythmically this punctuation presents no problems: *occúrrit ex móre* and *láudans quos agnoscébat* providing a cursus planus and velox, respectively;
2 it suits Amm.'s purpose much better: not the fact that he praised individual soldiers needs a justification, one could hardly expect a Roman

general to act otherwise, but his going to meet the troops might raise the suspicion of a deliberate revolutionary purpose: therefore Amm. states that this was (Julian's) normal custom. Cf. also Sabbah 308 note 48.

princeps is used here by Amm. to denote Julian, still a Caesar (so called in the preceding section), while earlier in this book, 20.2.1, it referred to Constantius, here called *Augustus*. See for the way Amm. employs imperial titles Béranger, 1976, and for *princeps* above, ad 20.2.1 and 20.4.8.

singulos This is a topos in the description of generals; some examples: Sal. *Cat.* 59.5 (about Catiline) *ipse equo circumiens unumquemque nominans appellat*, Tac. *Ann.* 1.71.3 (about Germanicus) *facta singulorum extollere*, Plin. *Pan.* 15.5 *Inde est quod prope omnes nomine appellas, quod singulorum fortia facta commemoras*; HA *AS* 21.7 *denique cum inter militares ageretur, multorum dicebat et nomina*; it also occurs in epic texts: Verg. *A.* 11.731 *nomine quemque vocans*, and outside the military sphere: *die senatus numquam patres nisi in curia salutavit et quidem sedentis ac nominatim singulos nullo submonente* (Suet. *Aug.* 53.3). In Petronius' *Cena* Ganymedes praises the politician Safinius for this reason: *et quam benignus resalutare, nomina omnium reddere, tamquam unus de nobis* (44.10). For further examples cf. Vretska ad Sal. *Cat.* 59.5.

factorumque fortium singulos monens For this genitive with *monere* cf. Goodyear ad Tac. *Ann.* 1.67.1 (*temporis ac necessitatis monet*): "*moneo* thus with a genitive, on the analogy of *admoneo, commoneo, commonefacio* (Kühner-Stegmann II 1.472–3), is confined to T., here and 2.43.4, apart from his imitator Ammian (20.4.12)". The last part of this quotation implies an unprovable suggestion.

animabat lenibus verbis This meaning of *animare* (= *animum confirmare*) is not classical; cf. also 19.11.2 *similium spe fidenter in effectus animabitur prosperos* and 15.8.6 *hac animati fiducia*. Quintilian would have approved of the *lenia verba*, for (*ut*) ... *in conciliando lenitas, in movendo vis exigi videatur* (12.10.59). Cf. Liv. 25.24.15 *ut adloquio leni pellicerent hostis ad dedendam urbem*. In a similar situation Julian mixed this method with stronger language: *sermone cum leni tum aspero et minaci hortabatur ad deditionem defensores* (24.1.8).

alacri gradu A variation of *celeri gradu* (20.11.19, 25.10.12, 27.8.2, 30.5.1), *agili gradu* (23.5.1), *concito gradu* (29.5.11). It denotes eagerness implying quickness, cf. the formula in TLL I 1473.39–40: "fere i.q. mobilis, acer, promptus, saepe gaudio commotus, incitatus". Other instances in Amm. are 17.10.2 and 22.2.2.

pergerent Heraeus' addition *ire* presumably aims at restoring a normal cursus: *pergerent ire*, because *gradu pergerent* results in a rhythm which occurs very rarely: Harmon 168 mentions only six cases in a total of 3272 cadences in book 21.

Amm. does, indeed, sometimes add *ire* (21.9.1, 26.6.16, 29.5.9), but he also uses *pergere* alone.

ubi potestas est ample patens et larga If (pace Clark, who adds a crux) this rather striking phrase is correct; it should be linked progressively, *ubi* being used with antecedent enclosed: the soldiers were to receive their rewards 'there, where' a generous authority awaited them. Concerning *est* it should be noted that throughout Latin literature, but especially in archaic and late Latin, specimens of the indicative in subordinate clauses of oratio obliqua can be found; cf. Szantyr 548 and De Jonge ad 16.10.17. Hassenstein 37/8 treats a number of cases in Amm., e.g. the following sentence, the structure of which bears some similarity to the present text: *proficisci pellexit ... saepius replicando quod ... eum videre frater cuperet patruelis, si quid per imprudentiam gestum est, remissurus.* (14.11.11).

In the present text the effect of the ind. praes. may be to present this remarkable phrase as a direct quotation; possibly with a tinge of irony, it refers to Constantius' generosity (*larga*), adding his accessibility and readiness to put it into practice (*ample patens*). There are no parallels for the latter expression.

IV. 13 Another very interesting section, the contents of which are not parallelled by anything in Julian's own report to the Athenians. Entertaining the officers of the eastward bound troops seems a rather suspect action, but Amm. explains that the invitation to dinner was prompted by Julian's *comitas* (*ut honoratius tractaret*) and *liberalitas* and not by any attempt to bribe them into mutiny against the Augustus.

utque honoratius procul abituros tractaret Amm. means to say that the departure of the troops in question was certain and that on its eve Julian wanted to treat the officers to a dinner in order to honour them appropriately; *honoratius* seems to have the full force of the comparative: it was an additional honour in continuation of the courteousness with which Julian had treated them.

ad convivium proceribus corrogatis The verb is almost a t.t.: the same expression occurs in 18.2.13, 29.6.5, 31.5.5 and only in 30.6.4 is *corrogare* used in a different context.

The term *proceres*, as Szidat observes, is normally used by Amm. for leading men of barbarian origin, *Sarmates* (17.12.16), *Galli* (25.5.2), *Armeni* (30.1.9) and *Quadi* (30.6.2). On account of this and considering the context Szidat concluded that by *proceres* here "keine Truppenführer der Legionen gemeint sind, sondern lediglich Führer der Auxilien, wahrscheinlich sogar nur die der Celten und Petulanten". This may be true, but not necessarily so. In the first place, the use of the word *proceres* is not restricted to barbarians. In 19.9.6 it definitely denotes Romans (this is admitted by Szidat) as it does in other sources (some examples are quoted in the note ad 17.12.16). More importantly, however, there is no reason to assume that Julian would seek to mollify only the officers of the *auxilia* and leave those of the other units (cf. 20.4.2) out of account.

petere iure ... edixit The use of *edicere* implies the official character of Julian's generosity. There are only a few parallels for the construction *c. inf.*, i.a. Liv. 27.24.3 *ipsos extemplo dare ... edixit*. That emendations have been suggested for *iure* is understandable in that it is indeed rather difficult to explain. If it is accepted in the text, it could either be regarded as a synonym of *cum ratione* (cf. TLL VII 2.698.69 sqq.), as in Cic. *Fin.* 5.33 *iure igitur gravissimi philosophi initium summi boni a natura petierunt* or taken in its literal sense. In the latter case Amm. could have intended it to emphasize the legality of the question Julian put to the officers: they were invited to ask only what he could possibly grant within his competence.

si quid in promptu esset The translations of Rolfe ("any request that was in their minds") and Seyfarth ("wenn sie solche (= Bitten) auf dem Herzen hätten") are only superficially attractive. The expression *in promptu* never has such a meaning and besides Julian's words would be very rash indeed. The phrase rather limits the possible wishes to Julian's competence: he gives the officials leave to ask anything which is lawfully (*iure*) within his powers (*in promptu*). Such a meaning would perfectly suit Amm.'s obvious purposes in this chapter. The only other passage where Amm. uses the expression is 14.2.18 *congesta undique saxa telaque habentes in promptu*: the warriors had the projectiles mentioned 'at their disposal'.

liberaliter Julian's *liberalitas* is praised in the in memoriam portrait: *liberalitatis eius testimonia plurima sunt et verissima* (25.5.15). Mamertinus also took care to mention it: *imperatoris nostri posterior liberalitas vincit priorem* (*Pan.* 3.22.3). The origin and structure of *liberalitas* as a virtue of emperors is discussed by Kloft, 1970.

fortuna quaedam inclemens It is tempting to interpret this phrase as 'a particularly unkind fortune' after the manner of *incredibili quodam studio*

(Cic. *de Orat.* 1.14; cf. Leeman-Pinkster ad loc.) and similar instances. This use of *quidam* is treated by Kühner-Stegmann II 1.643 and Szantyr 196 (cf. also OLD s.v. *quidam* 2). The word order, however, seems to oppose this explanation, for in such cases the substantive occupies the final position. Another paraphrase, which also suits the context, is the following: 'some stroke of bad luck which treats us harshly'. There is an interesting parallel in *Cod.Theod.* 13.9.5, where shipowners who cannot meet their obligations because of shipwreck are excused, *quia excludere casus et inclementem non possumus cohibere fortunam.*

Amm. uses *fortuna/Fortuna* (there are more than a hundred occurrences) in a variety of senses. "By far the most common occurrences are of *fortuna* personified as the hostile and unpredictable power in the history of states and the lives of men" (Naudé, 1964, 83), but in other cases the word is only vaguely personal or it is used as a metaphor for a condition of life or a state of affairs (ibid., 79). See for *fortuna* as *inclemens* 31.8.8 *de te, Fortuna, ut inclementi querebatur et caeca,* for the concept of fortune in Amm., apart from Naudé, Camus, 1967, 176–184 and in general Cupaiuolo, 1984.

moderato rectore   Amm. has Julian himself mention this quality in his final speech: *civilia moderatius regens* (25.3.17).

terris genitalibus   As Hoffmann 151 and Szidat rightly observe, not only Gaul is meant (so, e.g. Müller, 1905, 582; Alföldi, 1959, 175 n. 33 and Neumann, 1965, 531), but also the regions beyond the Rhine (cf. 20.4.4 *laribus transrhenanis*). See however Sabbah, 1983, who, discussing the attachment of Julian's soldiers to "la patrie Gauloise", stresses again the Gaulish character of the army ("En dépit de la présence en son sein d'un fort élément germanique, cette armée reste, même ethniquement, une armée à prédominance gauloise", p. 163).

dispararet   This verb is often used by Amm. to denote geographical distances: *oppidum quod centesimo lapide disparatur* (18.7.9), *promuntorium duobus milibus et quingentis stadiis disparatum* (22.8.20), see above ad 20.3.7. Here it is used, however, to express the separation of men from one another. There are only few examples of this, scattered through Latin literature, the oldest being Pl. *Rud.* prol. 10 *is nos per gentis aliud alia disparat.*

hocque angore impliciti   In his list of *perturbationes* Cicero defines *angor* as *aegritudo premens* (*Tusc.* 4.18), a definition which suits the present context quite well: the *proceres* left Julian 'on tenterhooks' (*suspensi*) because of their distress; having come home they feel deeply depressed. For *impliciti* see above ad 1.1 *implicaret formido.*

in stativa solita cessarunt Thus Seyfarth's version of this locus conclamatus, both in his bilingual edition and in the Teubneriana. If one wonders how this is to be understood, his translation presents the following solution: "gingen sie in ihre gewöhnlichen Quartiere". This, however, does not render *cessarunt*, but Gelenius' *recesserunt*, which is a rather smooth solution of the textual problem. Besides, one does not really understand why the *stativa* need to be called 'usual'. Presumably Amm. wants to stress that nothing unusual *happened*, not that the encampment was normal. If *cessarunt* is to be kept it can only mean 'they took no action, they were idle (or resting)' and this, together with Mommsen's *ut in stativis solet*, results in a text which may be possible: 'They were inactive, as is normally the case in an encampment'. There remains, however, the grave difficulty that this would suit the common soldiers much better than their officers, so that a sudden change of subject would have to be assumed. The same problem mars Češka's ingenious conjecture *vita in stativis solita cessarunt* (1972, 18). Moreover *vita* denotes a 'manner of life' (18.7.7 *more vitae remissioris*, 19.9.9 *vita parcior*) rather than specific activities, as implied by this suggestion. A few times the verb *cessare* has a single abl. as a complement, e.g. Plin. *Nat.* 2.224 *nam nec aquarum natura miraculis cessat*. In Amm. the present text would be the only instance. Clark's crux († *ut in stativi solita cessarunt*) still seems inevitable.

IV. 14 In this section Amm. firmly emphasizes the loud noise, using stronger expressions than Julian himself in the letter to the Athenians: *fremitu ingenti, horrendis clamoribus concrepabant, iterata magnitudine sonus*. Neither Libanius nor Zosimus pays special attention to the shouting as such.

nocte vero coeptante This agrees with Julian's own chronological indication ὀψίας δὲ ἤδη περὶ ἡλίου δυσμάς (*Ep. ad Ath.* 284 b), but not quite with Libanius' ἑσπέρας ἤδη, μᾶλλον δὲ περὶ μέσας νύκτας (*Or.* 18.97) or Zosimus' report that the events took place after the soldiers had been banqueting νυκτὸς ἄχρι βαθείας (3.9.1).

in apertum erupere discidium Blockley, 1973, 64 very tentatively suggests "a certain parallelism" with Tac. *Ann.* 1.28.1 *noctem minacem et in scelus erupturam*. Pace Szidat's adhesion this reminiscence is very doubtful. Even Livy 2.45.10 seems a closer parallel: *rem ad ultimum seditionis erupturam*, but one should rather look for passages where *erumpere* is used of "persons breaking out in a specified form of conduct" (OLD), as *in omne genus crudelitatis erupit* (Suet. *Tib.* 61.1). In this connection another Tacitean phrase deserves to be introduced for comparison with the present expression: *erupere legionarii in perniciem auxiliorum* (*Hist.* 2.68.2).

insperata res Throughout Latin literature *insperatus* is used of "neutral or undesirable events" (OLD), as in *insperato et necopinato malo* (Cic. *Tusc.* 3.28). Another instance in Amm. is 17.12.4 *vitantes exitium insperatum.*

ad tela convertuntur et manus A similar expression is used in Tac. *Ag.* 25.3 *ad manus et arma conversi*; cf. also *ad vim, ad manus, ad arma confugere* (Cic. *Ver.* 2.1.82) and *manus et arma* (Tac. *Ag.* 33.5).

palatium Situated on 'l'île de la Cité'. See for this Szidat, contra Seyfarth, 1983⁵, 196 n. 37.

spatiis eius ambitis This is more emphatic than Julian's sober τὰ βασίλεια περιείληπτο (*Ep. ad Ath.* 284 b).

ne ad evadendi copiam quisquam perveniret The same "affected turn of phrase" (De Jonge) is used in 17.2.3 *ut ... nullus ad erumpendi copiam facile perveniret.*

Augustum Iulianum horrendis clamoribus concrepabant The verb *concrepare* is normally used to denote the sound of wind instruments: *bucinae* (21.12.5, 25.8.2), *litui* (14.7.21, 28.1.4), *tubae* (16.12.27, 29.5.39) or of arms: *arma* (19.2.6), *hastae* (25.3.10). Only a few times the human voice is concerned: 14.6.25 (about men who are quarreling), 26.10.3 (cheering). Both Rolfe ("they hailed Julian as Augustus") and Seyfarth ("riefen Julian zum Augustus aus") consider *Augustum Iulianum* to be a construction with a double acc., which is, indeed, possible with verbs of shouting: *solos felicis viventis clamat in urbe* (Hor. *S.* 1.1.12), but rather unlikely in the present case, because *concrepare* seems unapt for such a construction. It is preferable to take into account that, when the words which are shouted are not quoted literally, the contents of the cry are given in the acc., cf. *infantem ... 'Io triumphe' clamasse* (Liv. 24.10.10) and *infantem ... triumphum clamasse* (Liv. 21.62.2), *victoriam conclamant* (Caes. *Gal.* 5.37.3) and also *audito Baccho* (Verg. *A.* 4.302) "when she hears the cry *Euoe Bacche*" (Austin ad loc.). In the present case the soldiers shouted '*Iulianus Augustus*'. The correctness of this explanation can be proved by a reference to 25.5.6 *antesignani clamare quosdam Iovianum audientes Augustum, eadem multo maius sonabant*, where *eadem* obviously refers to the contents of the shouting, viz. '*Iovianus Augustus*'. Curiously enough, both Rolfe and Seyfarth base their translation of this passage on this explanation. Finally, it should not be overlooked that the soldiers have not yet *seen* Julian. That only happens the next morning.

destinatius As De Jonge notes ad 17.2.2, *destinate* and its comparative figure only in Amm. as synonyms of *pertinaciter (-ius)*.

dum lux promicaret Amm.'s expressions for 'daybreak' are large in number. Hagendahl, 1921, 102/3 provides a list. The verb occurs only here.

adigentes expectareque coacti ... progredi compulerunt Amm. wants to emphasize the strong pressure put upon Julian, which he could relieve only temporarily by forcing the soldiers to wait. Julian himself is much more vague about the precise order of events. The tumultuous scene starts ὀψίας δὲ ἤδη περὶ ἡλίου δυσμάς (*Ep. ad Ath.* 284 b) and the next more or less precise indication of time is that a soldier gave him his neck-chain ὥρᾳ που τρίτῃ σχεδόν (284 d). The difference between Julian's somewhat confused report and Amm.'s much more clear-cut account is caused by a difference of purpose. For Julian the all-important stimulus to yield to the soldiers was Zeus' τέρας which he had prayed for. Zeus' exhortation is enough to turn the balance: ἠνώγει πεισθῆναι καὶ μὴ προσεναντιοῦσθαι τοῦ στρατοπέδου τῇ προθυμίᾳ (284 c). This divine incentive not to oppose the will of the army warrants the correctness of Julian's conduct and decision. For Amm., however, it is first and foremost the course of events which shows that Julian is blameless.

It is interesting to make a comparison with Libanius' handling of this matter, or rather with the accounts given by Libanius on three different occasions. In *Or.* 13 and *Or.* 12, panegyrics addressed to Julian himself in July 362 and on the first of January 363, respectively, Libanius conforms himself to what seems to have been the official doctrine, giving the gods their due (ταυτὶ δὲ ... ὑπὸ τῶν θεῶν ἐκυροῦτο, *Or.* 13.34; θεοῦ δὲ τοῦτο, *Or.* 12.59), while in *Or.* 18.96–99, composed some years after Julian's death, he does not make any mention of divine interference and comes closer to Amm.'s rendering (cf. for further details Petit, 1956, 479–481).

quo viso In classical Latin this would have been *quem visum, quem* being the direct obj. of *appellavere*. Cf. the note ad 20.2.3 *quibus ... refutantibus*.

iterata magnitudine sonus Seyfarth's rendering "wiederholten sie ihre lauten Rufe" implies that *sonus* is a specimen of the genitivus inversus, *magnitudine sonus* being the equivalent of *magno sonu*. This solution is, indeed, necessary when *iterare* is taken in its literal sense, as in the only other occurrence in Amm.: *quibus saepe eadem iterantibus*. But the present expression rather seems to be the climax in the trio *fremitu ingenti – horrendis clamoribus – iterata magnitudine sonus*: the sound has now reached its loudest proportions. Rolfe renders "they redoubled their shouts", which tallies with TLL VII 2.549 75–80, where the present expression is mentioned among a few instances where *iterare* practically means 'to redouble, to increase', e.g. *iterabo metum* (Sen. *Tro.* 626), *iterare culpam gaudebant* (Tac. *Hist.* 3.11.2). Amm. always uses *sonus* as a noun of the u-declension. Cf. Neue-Wagener I, 1902, 786.

Augustum appellavere It is not until now that Julian is actually hailed as Augustus. Mark Amm.'s insistence on the soldiers' orderly behaviour. The sound is enormous, but no longer riotous and unruly, as it was during the night. Now they acclaim a man whom they see (*quo viso*) and their cheering is unanimous (*consensione firmissima*).

consensione firmissima A reference to Eutr. 10.15.1, *consensu militum Iulianus factus Augustus est*, might be added to the parallels cited by Szidat in his note. Szidat rightly stresses the importance of the military with respect to fourth century appointments to the imperial dignity. *Consensio* or *consensus militum* and *consensus universorum* (cf. for this Instinsky, 1940) had become practically the same.

IV. 15 *mente fundata* The same expression to denote steadfast resolution is used in 29.5.46 *quem Theodosius fundata mente intuens torvum*. Cf. also *fundato pectore mansit immobilis* (14.9.6) and *mentibusque fundatis et compositis* (21.12.7). TLL VI 1562.69 sqq. provides a few other examples, especially in Seneca, i.a. *bene fundatae mentes* (*de ira* 2.21.7).

universis resistebat et singulis This resistance is also reported by Julian himself: ἀντέσχον εἰς ὅσον ἠδυνάμην (*Ep. ad Ath.* 284d) and by Libanius: τοῦ μὲν οἷς ἡγεῖτο κωλύσειν διεξιόντος (*Or.* 18.98). The combination of *universi* and *singuli* is used more often in situations of heightened common interest: *adnitendum singulis universisque* (Liv. 27.13.12), *haec singuli, haec universi, ut quemque dolor impulerat, vociferantes* (Tac. *Hist.* 3.14.1), *congruit sedulo singulos atque universos pro dignitate publica providere* (Apul. *Met.* 3.3.3)

From the Early Principate onwards a candidate who was offered the imperial throne was supposed to refuse this honour at first, even if he was eager to accept, as is demonstrated at length by Béranger, 1948 and 1953, 137-169 (cf. Wickert, 1954, 2258-2264 and 1974, 70-71). The ceremonial *recusatio*, Béranger argues, was considered to be proof of legitimacy and to dispel any suspicion of usurpation of the throne, and was, therefore, of the utmost necessity for anyone who aspired to become emperor. This is not to say, however, that an emperor designate could not have motives other than political: "Iulian folgte mit der *recusatio* ... nicht nur einer politischen Tradition, sondern offensichtlich fühlte er sich auch von seiner Bildung und philosophischen Haltung her dazu gedrängt" (Szidat I 151).

nunc manus tendens oransque et obsecrans   Only Amm. has this pathetic detail. The outstretched hands especially have a dramatic effect, cf. *manusque tendentes flentesque orabant* (25.9.2), *manus tendentes orantesque* (31.15.9) and Liv. 3.50.5 *supinas deinde tendens manus, 'commilitones' appellans orabat*. Cf. Sittl, 1890, 50/1.

aliquid indecorum   In classical Latin, too, *aliquid* in a subordinate clause beginning with *ne* can be found in cases of "Fernstellung" (Szantyr 194). As to *indecorum* instead of the partitive genitive, the classical rule does, indeed, prescribe *aliquid utile*, but *aliquid boni* (Szantyr 58). This is, however, no iron rule, as Löfstedt, 1942, I 136 sqq. has demonstrated. Among other things, Löfstedt draws attention to the remarkable fact that, in spite of his general predilection for the use of the genitive, Tacitus often chooses the "appositive Gliederung" (Szantyr l.c.) in such cases.

It should be stressed that *indecorum* is by no means a weak term or a euphemism. Its force may perhaps best be demonstrated by a reference to a list of synonyms in Cic. *Fin.* 3.14 *si nihil malum, nisi quod turpe, inhonestum, indecorum, pravum, flagitiosum, foedum*.

temeritas et prolapsio   The latter occurs only here in Amm. In the only instance in classical Latin, Cic. *Cael.* 41, it is used in a somewhat palliating sense: 'stumble', but in the present text this is less likely in view of the combination with *temeritas*, which has the character of a hendiadyoin. Besides, Amm.'s use of the verb *prolabi* also points to a stronger meaning: *numquam ad deteriora prolapsam* (17.5.14) and *ad haec ... scelesta prolapso* (18.8.6). To choose unglorious conduct (*indecorum*) would be a sign of 'reckless degeneration'.

discordiarum materias excitaret   Amm.'s use of *materia* (once *materies*: 19.4.2) is not divergent from classical usage. It occurs in a literal sense, e.g. *facibus et omni materia, qua alitur ignis, petitae* (24.6.5), and quite often metaphorically ('source', 'ground', 'cause'): *sedata iurgiorum materia* (16.12.16), *huius concilii convocandi materia* (21.13.10). Amm. has a certain liking for the plural, cf. especially 20.9.9 *suspicio quod ... novarum rerum materias excitaret*, 21.3.2 *ne ... redivivas bellorum materias excitaret*.

haecque adiciebat   The difference between sections 15 and 16 should be noted. In section 15 Julian focuses on their sense of honour, and only when this has proved successful (*tandem sedatos*) he addresses them with his mild concessions (*leniter allocutus*). The way Julian is said here to have approached the soldiers forms a nice contrast to Amm.'s rather curt description in 16.12.64, when, after the battle at Strasbourg, Julian was for the first time offered the title of *Augustus: ut agentes petulantius milites increpabat id se nec sperare nec adipisci velle iurando confirmans*. Since 357 the situation had changed indeed!

IV. 16 *Cesset ira* The termination of the soldiers' enraged and revolutionary conduct is the condition for the fulfilment of their wishes, not the other way round.

quaeso The parenthetical use of *quaeso*, "added for urgency or from politeness" (OLD), is found throughout Latin literature. Its correctness is emphasized by Cic. *Att.* 12.6a.2 '*quaeso' illud tuum, quod erat et* εὐπινὲς *et urbanum*. Amm. has it a number of times in speeches of emperors and twice (17.5.14 and 20.8.11) in a letter.

dulcedo vos patriae retinet For, as Cicero wrote to Marcellus, *nec locus tibi ullus dulcior esse debet patria* (Cic. *Fam.* 4.9.3).

redite iam nunc ad sedes Blockley's (1980(2)) rendering "winter quarters" may be correct, cf. *ad sedes revertens hibernas* (17.2.1), but it seems far more likely that the dwelling-places of the mutineers are meant. This is the normal meaning, which can also be found in Amm.: *omne iuventutis robur relictum in sedibus* ('at home') *acciverunt* (14.2.12) and *rex quidem Parthus, hiemem Ctesiphonte acturus, redit ad sedes* (29.1.4). In the present text *sedes* refers to (*dulcedo*) *patriae*, while (*nihil* ...) *transalpinum* repeats *insueta peregrinaque* ... *loca*. Besides, Julian's promise can be considered to honour the pledge reported in section 4 of this chapter: *relictis laribus transrhenanis, sub hoc venerant pacto ne ducerentur ad partes umquam transalpinas*.

nihil ... transalpinum Cf. the note ad *aliquid indecorum* (20.4.15).

hocque ... competenti satisfactione purgabo The verb *purgare* with a blameworthy action as direct object and an abl. instr. can be used in two ways: 1. 'to wipe out by another deed', as in *virtute dedecus purgatura ardens copia nostrorum erupit* (19.11.14), 2. 'to excuse by an apology or defence': *ut factum firma defensione purgarent* (27.5.1). The present text is an instance of the latter use. Julian's words imply a confidence in Constantius' inclination to pardon which contrasts rather sharply with Gallus' expectations in this regard: *nec satisfactionem suscipiet aliquam nec erratis ignoscet* (14.11.7). But the difference is, of course, due to Amm.'s purpose in this chapter. He is continually out to emphasize Julian's loyalty to Constantius, whom he commends to the soldiers as generous (12) and now as most reasonable. The emperor's acceptance of the apology is guaranteed by Julian personally (*ego*).

IV. 17 In Amm.'s account the facts reported in sections 17 and 18 are presented as the inevitable result and culmination of the course of events. This account is most akin to Zosimus' cool and succinct registration: καὶ ἐπί τινος ἀσπίδος μετέωρον ἄραντες ἀνεῖπόν τε σεβαστὸν αὐτοκράτορα, καὶ ἐπέθεσαν σὺν βίᾳ τὸ διάδημα τῇ κεφαλῇ (3.9.2), which, however, lacks Amm.'s narrative strategy. The episode of the shield, which is absent in Julian's own story, is further referred to in Libanius' pathetic utterance: ὢ μακαριάς ἀσπίδος, ἣ τὸν τῆς ἀναρρήσεως ἐδέξατο νόμον πρεπωδεστέρα σοι παντὸς εἰωθότος βήματος (*Or.* 13.34). See the note ad *impositusque scuto pedestri* below.

conclamabatur After *resistebat* and *adiciebat* (§ 15) this is the third instance of the ind. imp. used to sketch a situation, which is finally wound up by the result *coactus est*. The absolute use of *conclamare* is treated in TLL IV 70.68 sqq. ("absolute positum continet notionem vel approbationis gaudiique vel lamentationis vel furoris sim."). Some examples: *conclamat omnis multitudo* (Caes. *Gal.* 7.21.1), *conclamant Haedui* (ib. 7.38.6), *conclamant vir paterque* (Liv. 1.58.12). These examples further illustrate the tendency of this verb to take the first place in a sentence; other instances are Liv. 30.21.10, 34.61.8, 37.49.5, Tac. *Hist.* 2.68.3, *Ann.* 1.8.5.

uno parique ardore The same expression can be found in 20.11.21, 21.12.9, 24.1.1. Amm. wants to emphasize the continued unanimity, which he had first mentioned at the end of section 14 (*consensione firmissima*).

nitentibus universis ... assentire coactus est Once more (cf. ad 20.4.15) the idea of *recusatio* is implied. Cf. Jul. *Ep. ad Ath.* 284d: ἐπεὶ δὲ οὔτε εἷς τῶν πολλῶν ἠδυνάμην κρατεῖν etc. and Lib. *Or.* 13.34: ὡς καλὸν μὲν σοῦ τὸ διωθεῖσθαι τὴν δόσιν. As to *nitentibus* Amm.'s only further absolute use of this verb is in the expression *facere nitique poterant* (19.8.1, 24.4.15, 26.1.6).

maximoque contentionis fragore It is difficult to ascertain the precise meaning of *contentio*, a word which Amm. does not use frequently. It can denote physical exertion, as in *acri contentione pugnabat* (24.2.13), or fighting, as in *eoque producta contentione* (19.8.2, cf. the note ad loc.). In the present case the expression is completely paralleled by *magno contentionis fragore* (25.6.13), where the situation is quite similar too: soldiers strongly refuse to comply with the demands of the emperor, and even threaten to use violence. Therefore it seems best to regard these two instances of *contentio* as belonging to the list in TLL IV 674.52 sqq. ("i.q. studium certationis, cupiditas certandi, contumacia"). Since *fragor*, which is more often used of arms, shields, thunder etc., can denote the sound of the human voice and of shouting (*ululantium undique Persarum intonante fragore*, 20.7.14), the present expression can be rendered by 'with the loud noise of their protest'. It is, however, more plausible to regard *contentionis* as a gen. inversus: 'with their loud and noisy protest'.

probrosis conviciis mixto Such treatment fell to Danielus and Barzimeres after their failure to capture the Armenian king: *probrosis lacerati conviciis* (30.1.16). The same can be expressed by a hendiadyoin: having asked for an interview with their countryman in Roman service Ormizdas, the men of Pirisabora *propinquantem probris atque conviciis ut male fidem incessebant et desertorem* (24.2.11). These cases show that the soldiers are indeed fiercely harassing Julian. Besides, it should not be forgotten that with *conviciis* the noisy atmosphere is further emphasized, for TLL IV 873.18 rightly defines this word as "exprobratio cum clamore facta". Cf. Zonaras, *Epit.* 13.10.12 ἠπείλουν διαχειρίσασθαι αὐτόν, εἰ μὴ πείθοιτο.

impositusque scuto pedestri The phrase is, of course, reminiscent of the Tacitean *impositusque scuto more gentis*, said of the Canninefate Brinno (Tac. *Hist.* 4.15.2), but, apart from the resemblance, the difference between Amm. and Tac. should be noted. Unlike the Canninefates (*more gentis*) and other German peoples (cf. Treitinger, 1956[2], 22; Straub, 1939, 231), the Romans were not accustomed to elevate their emperors to the shield, in spite of Alföldi's arguments for the contrary (Alföldi, 1980[3], 172; his view has been convincingly refuted by Ensslin, 1942, 293 ff. but is accepted by, among others, Selem, 1971, 89-91).

It is no doubt true that some sort of elevation formed part of the Roman coronation ceremony. When Julian was appointed Caesar in 355, he was presented to the troops while standing on a platform (*tribunali ad altiorem suggestum erecto*, 15.8.4) and Valentinian in 364 also mounted a tribunal to accept the imperial dignity before the assembled soldiers (*permissusque tribunal ascendere celsis structum*, 26.2.2). This part of the proceedings at a coronation ceremony may be seen as "die zeremonielle Erhöhung des neugewählten Herrschers" (Rosen 1978, 410 with n. 15; Szidat), though perhaps the reason for it should not be sought too far. It is quite natural that when spectators are invited to attend a spectacle they are given an opportunity to see it in the best possible way. In any case, the mounting of a platform is quite different from the elevation to the shield. In 360 Julian's soldiers, barbarians for the most part, put their own mark upon the coronation. They thus introduced a new element into the ceremony, which was to survive until late in Byzantine times (though, according to Ostrogorsky, 1955, not uninterrupted; see, however, Teitler, 1987; cf. also Brightman, 1901; Boak, 1919 and Walter, 1975). See further the introductory note to ch. 5.

Julian's elevation to the shield is also attested in Libanius (*Or.* 13.34 ὦ μακαρίας ἀσπίδος) and Zosimus (3.9.2 καὶ ἐπί τινος ἀσπίδος μετέωρον ἄραντες). Julian himself is silent about it, or at any rate not explicit. The question is if the words ἐπὶ τῶν ὤμων ἔφερον in *Ep. ad Ath.* 285c are meant literally (for an example of an emperor, though admittedly still a child (sc. Gordian III), carried on the shoulders of an enthusiastic throng see Herodian 7.10.8: ἀράμενοι ἐπὶ τῶν ὤμων διὰ μέσου τοῦ πλήθους ... ἀνάγουσιν ἐς τὸ Καπετώλιον) or as an allusion to the elevation to the shield. If the latter interpretation is chosen, one should assume (as Rosen, 1978, 411 n. 16 does) that the chronological order of Julian's account is inexact.

The omission of this element in Julian's presentation of the facts is quite understandable. Julian probably felt too embarrassed at having been subjected to a manifestly barbarian ritual to mention it in his letter to the Athenians (cf. Paschoud in his note ad Zos. 3.9.2).

On the other hand, it seems questionable if one should follow Rosen and regard Amm.'s wording, more specifically the Roman t.t. *scuto pedestri*, as significant in this respect as Julian's silence. Rosen, 1978, 410 believes that by using the very words *scuto pedestri* Amm. tried "den Gedanken an eine fremde Sitte und an die Beteiligung der Germanen ... fernzuhalten". It seems too far-fetched, however, to believe that "der vollständige Terminus technicus für den Langschild des römischen Legionärs einen Gegensatz (implizierte) zu Nichtrömern und ihrer Bewaffnung", and was, therefore, deliberately chosen by Amm. in order to influence his readers.

sublátius éminens The comparative is needed for the cursus tardus. The general use of the comparativus pro positivo is treated by Hassenstein 30, Hagendahl, 1921, 135 sqq., De Jonge ad 14.6.12, 14.10.9, 16.7.8, Szantyr 168/9.

nullo silente After *uno parique ardore* this again stresses the unanimous character of the proclamation. Sabbah 185 note 41 refers to 15.8.15, where Constantius' announcement of the appointment of Julian as Caesar is greeted with enormous joy (*immane quo quantoque gaudio Augusti probavere iudicium*), but also with some opposition, which precludes complete unanimity (*praeter paucos*). Commenting upon this scene, Sabbah notes "Ammien peut avoir ... voulu ménager une gradation entre cette scène et celle de la proclamation de Julien à Lutèce, cette fois par le consentement *unanime* des troupes".

Augustus renuntiatus The only instance of this verb in Amm. During the Republic it is used for the official announcement of the outcome of an election: *L. Murenam consulem renuntiavi* (Cic. *Mur.* 1). In later Latin it hardly occurs with this or a similar meaning. The nearest parallel is HA *DI* 5.3: *impetravit ut hostis Severus renuntiaretur.*

iubebatur As in the case of *poscebatur* at the end of this section, the imperf. may have been chosen to express the repetition of these requests, but, as De Jonge notes ad 14.2.14, 17.7.4, 17.10.6 and 19.10.1, Amm. tends to avoid the composite forms of the perf. pass. Together with the other passive forms in this section of which Julian is the grammatical subject (*coactus est, impositus, renuntiatus, poscebatur*), *iubebatur* shows that Julian was simply in no position to prevent the inevitable development of things and that he did not play an *active* role.

iubebatur diadema proferre If Ps. Aur. Vict. *epit.* 35.5 (*iste primus apud Romanos diadema capiti innexuit*) is to be believed, Aurelian was the first emperor who wore the *diadema* (or *corona*; cf. e.g. 26.2.3 *principali habitu circumdatus et corona*, 31.10.21 *ambigenti super corona capiti imponenda*, Socr. *HE* 3.1.35 στέφανος βασιλικός), which formed, at any rate since Constantine, a normal part of the imperial *insignia* (cf. in general Mau, 1905; Dellbrueck, 1933 and Alföldi, 1980³, 263 ff.). Originally any band wound about the head, the diadem in Hellenistic times (cf. Ritter, 1965) was white with decorated edges, while in the later Roman Empire it was made of purple and sometimes set with jewels and pearls. For example, at the quinquennial games celebrated at Vienne Julian is said to have worn a magnificent diadem set with gleaming gems: *ambitioso diademate utebatur lapidum fulgore distincto* (21.1.4).

At these quinquennial games late in 360 Julian acted as an Augustus. As a Caesar he apparently did not wear the diadem (though earlier Caesares possibly did, cf. Mau, 1905, 304): *negansque umquam habuisse*, cf. Socrates, *HE* 3.1.35'Ὡς δὲ στέφανος βασιλικὸς οὐ παρῆν; Zonaras, *Epit.* 13.10.14 ἐκεῖνος μὲν μὴ ἔχειν ἐξώμνυτο. At any rate he was not able to bring out (*proferre*) one – to do so would, of course, have been highly suspicious.

The soldiers were not able to offer a real diadem either. It would be wrong, as Szidat rightly observes, to follow Selem, 1971, 90 in interpreting the words used by Julian in his *Ep. ad Ath.* 284d, οὔτε τὴν πρόσρησιν οὔτε τὸν στέφανον προσιέμην, as implying that a diadem was available, and thus to construct a contradistinction between Julian's and Amm.'s version.

Cf. for "La couronne de Julien César" also Piganiol, 1938 (Piganiol's main point in that article, though not of any importance here, is based on a misunderstanding of Amm. 21.1.4).

uxoris colli ... vel capitis It is very difficult to understand why both Clark and Seyfarth have refused to accept the obvious insertion of *decus*, suggested by Heraeus and Petschenig in view of Verg. *A.* 10.135 *aut collo decus aut capiti.* Amm.'s text contains many Virgilian reminiscences, cf. Hagendahl, 1921, 1–15 ("De Ammiano Vergilii imitatore"). Julian's wife Helena (*PLRE* I, Helena 2), a sister of Constantius, was with Julian in Paris (cf. Julian, *Ep. ad Ath.* 284c: ἔτι τῆς γαμετῆς ζώσης μοι), but died afterwards. See for her Aujoulat, 1983.

IV. 18 *primis auspiciis* In the three other cases where Amm. uses this expression, it concerns towns or fortifications: Rome (14.6.3), Laodicia, Apamia and Seleucia (14.8.8), a *munimentum* near the Neckar (28.2.2). Here Julian wants to assert that his reign as an emperor will get off to a bad start, if it is accompanied by the wrong ornaments.

aptari muliebri mundo Presumably this is an oxymoron. The verb is rarely constructed with the abl. and in these cases it concerns persons or things being equipped with arms or other equipment: Liv. 9.31.9 *ut quisque liberaverat se onere aptaveratque armis,* Verg. *A.* 8.80 (about ships) *remigioque aptat.* In Amm. there are two other instances: 23.4.11 (about a *testudo) ferreisque clavis aptata,* 24.4.16 *aptatae ligneis sagittis ballistae.* In the present case the 'equipment' consists of a woman's adornment; *mundus* in itself usually denotes womanlike attire, but the adjective *muliebris* is regularly added, here with a strong depreciatory connotation, as is shown in Julian's subsequent refusal of the *equi phalera: id quoque turpe esse.* This use of *muliebris* is quite frequent, cf. TLL VIII 1568.47 sqq. ("saepe cum nota vitii vel debilitatis"). Julian's protest tallies with his disparaging remark about the usurper Silvanus, who filled his own soldiers with disgust: θῆλυν δὲ οὐχ ὑπομένοντες ὁρᾶν ἐνδεδυκότα στολὴν τὸν δείλαιον, ἐπιθέμενοι σπαράττουσιν (Jul. *Or.* 2.98d). This reference is aptly provided by Blockley, 1980(2), 16, in a note ad Amm. 15.5.16. The only other author who mentions Julian's refusal of a woman's ornament as a makeshift diadem is Zonaras *Epit.* 13.10.14 τινῶν δὲ κόσμον αἰτούντων γυναικεῖόν τινα, ἵν' ἐκ τούτου σχεδιασθείη διάδημα, παρῃτήσατο τοῦτο ὁ Ἰουλιανὸς ὡς ἀπαίσιον οἰωνόν.

equi phalera quaerebatur The singular is surprising, since *phalerae* normally occurs only in the plural, as indeed was V's reading before the correction by the second hand. It seems more correct to retain *phalerae* and to adapt the verbal form to this: *quaerebantur.* A different emendation is proposed by Szidat, who, noticing that V has *aequi,* wants to read *aeque,* which would be the only occurrence of this word in Amm., unless Gelenius' *abundant aeque* (23.6.31) is right. Szidat's main motive is the difficulty to imagine how a horse's ornamental disc (*phalera* sing.!) could function as a substitute for the *diadema.* Without *equi* the word *phalera* would refer to a soldier's military decoration, worn on a neck-chain. But, as Szidat admits himself, it is hard to understand why Julian would label the use of such a decoration as *turpe*. In the circumstances this would be highly tactless. Besides, one can very well imagine that a horse's ornament had to be fetched, but it is difficult to believe that a soldier's decoration was not immediately available on the spot or spontaneously offered as the *torques* was. Horses' *phalerae* were made of precious metals: the silver captured by the Carthaginians after the battle at Cannae *plurimum in phaleris equorum erat* (Liv. 22.52.5), and Julian's mount Babylonius even had *auro lapillisque ornamenta distincta* (23.3.6). See for a survey of *phalerae* found in the Rhine Brouwer, 1982. All problems are solved if in the present text the plural *phalerae* is read and understood as a belt with some gold or silver discs, which is quite imaginable as an emergency substitute for the *diadema*.

uti coronatus speciem saltem obscuram superioris praetenderet potestatis The first six words are a marginal addition in V by a second hand. There is no decisive reason for suspicion, although two details are rather remarkable: 1. *coronatus* is the first example of the meaning "insigne regium imponere" (TLL IV 991.31 sqq.), the only other instance in Amm. being *ita, inquit, imperator, a civitatibus residuis coroneris* (25.9.4), 2. although at first sight *obscuram* seems easily understandable, with the approximative meaning 'vague dim, unclear' (cf. Seyfarth: "einen, wenn auch unvolkommenen Anblick"), it is very difficult to find an exact parallel. TLL IX 169.58 – 170.7 lists a number of cases where "color, aspectus fuscatus" is concerned, e.g. *cum caput obscura nitidum ferrugine texit* (Verg. *G.* 1.467), *obscurisque genis* (Juv. 6.131), but in all these instances actual darkness is meant. The other possibility would be to regard *obscuram* as the equivalent of *humilem* or *ignobilem*. This is a very normal meaning of *obscurus*, concerning men's reputation, their extraction and indeed their person. With this meaning the chiastic word order, with juxtaposition of *obscuram* and *superioris*, is more effective: 'an albeit lowly outward appearance of his higher power'. Although this solution may appear attractive, it should be noted that Amm. uses *obscurus* with this meaning only about men's extraction: *ausus eripere virginis non obscurae pudorem* (15.7.5), *iuxta nobiles et obscuri* (19.12.7), or the importance of townships: *oppida non obscura* (22.8.16).

Petulantium tunc hastatus ... draconarius The exact meaning of the terms Amm. uses to qualify Maurus is disputed. Does *hastatus* hint at Maurus' rank at the time of the pronunciamento? At first sight this seems to be the case, *Petulantium tunc hastatus* standing in opposition to *postea comes* and *hastatus* being the name of one of the ranks into which the centurionate was subdivided (cf. Von Domaszewski-Dobson, 1967², 90); Zonaras' τις τῶν ταξιάρχων seems to point in the same direction. Seyfarth followed this line of thought, as appears from his translation "damaliger Unterführer der Petulanten". TLL VI 2556.36.40 expresses doubts.

An objection can, however, be raised against this meaning of *hastatus*. In the military units which went back to the Principate (legions, cohorts, *alae*) the old rank of centurion was preserved, it is true, but in the types of formation dating from the third and fourth centuries (vexillations, *scholae* and the units to which the *Petulantes* belonged, the *auxilia*) the grades were quite different (Jones 634). No centurions, let alone *hastati*, are attested in these units in the later Roman army.

Müller, 1905, 611 already saw this and proposed a different interpretation (not quite adequately reported by Szidat I 155), stressing the connection between the words *hastatus* and *draconarius*. Referring inter alia to Amm. 16.12.39 where the dragon held by the *draconarius* is said to be fitted to the top of a very long *hasta* (*purpureum signum draconis summitati hastae longioris aptatum*) and to Vegetius, *mil.* 1.20, where the *hasta* of the *draconarius* is also mentioned (*quid ipsi draconarii et signiferi, qui sinistra manu hastas gubernant, in proelio facient?*), Müller believes that "der *draconarius* habe von der *hasta longior* in der Soldatensprache den Namen *hastatus* geführt". In other words, *hastatus* and *draconarius* here are nearly synonyms, used together in one sentence for the sake of variety. Müller is followed by e.g. Rolfe, who renders *hastatus* by "standardbearer".

Whatever the meaning of *hastatus* (needless to say that Müller's view, too, is far from definitely proved), the meaning of *draconarius*, 'carrier of the dragon', is fortunately less problematical. The *draco* as a standard, probably Dacian in origin, was generally introduced in the fourth century. Cf. the note ad 15.5.16.

Another problem concerning the function of Maurus in the army still needs some comment. In 31.10.21 Amm. speaks of him in his capacity of *comes* (sc. *rei militaris*; see the next note) and refers back to the events of 360 and Maurus' role in them: *dum inter eius (i.e. Iuliani) armigeros militaret*. These words are clearly in contradiction with Amm.'s earlier statement, though they correspond with the words of Socrates *HE* 3.1.35 (εἷς τῶν δορυφόρων), in that they describe Maurus as one of the imperial bodyguards, rather than a standard-bearer of the *Petulantes*. Szidat's proposal to solve this problem is excellent: Maurus was probably promoted to serve as one of Julian's bodyguards shortly after the pronunciamento as a reward for his help in making Julian emperor. Amm. 31.10.21 and Socrates *HE* 3.1.35 reflect this later situation.

postea comes Cf. for Amm.'s habit of mentioning an officer's or official's later career e.g. 17.6.3 (*postea consul*); 21.4.2, 21.10.6, 25.10.9, 28.2.5. As to *comes*: here the post of *comes rei militaris* ("ein Titel der selten in dieser Vollständigkeit gebraucht wird", Seeck, 1901, 662) must be meant, first attested under Constans. "The title seems to have been given to officers commanding groups of *comitatenses*, ranging from substantial army corps to a couple of regiments, allocated to a special task or assigned to a particular area" (Jones 124). De Jonge has several notes on various other sorts of *comites*, cf. ad 14.5.1, 14.7.9, 14.11.19, 15.5.4, 17.10.5, 18.3.5, 19.1.9.

Whether the post of *comes rei militaris* was the culmination of Maurus' career (so e.g. *PLRE I*, Maurus 2 and Szidat) or only the stepping-stone to the *magisterium militum* (so e.g. Ensslin, 1930, 2396) is disputed. For the latter view, however, there is no direct evidence.

qui rem male gessit apud Succorum angustias This anticipation of an event which took place in 378 is quite remarkable. Obviously Amm. wants to avoid creating a favourable impression of Maurus on the reader's part. His dislike of this man becomes fully clear in 31.10.21, where he is pictured as *venalis ferociae specie et ad cuncta mobilis et incertus*, which is immediately followed by a reference to the present section. Unfortunately there are considerable textual problems; Seyfarth's version runs as follows: *is est, quem praeteritorum textu rettulimus ambigenti super corona capiti imponenda Iuliano Caesari, dum inter eius armigeros militaret, arroganti astu fidenter torquem obtulisse collo abstractam* (Clark puts a crux after *Caesari, arroganti astu fidenter* is Heraeus' correction of V's *adrogantia custodiret*). This passage is important for the precise understanding of Amm.'s appraisal of the present incident, and especially to ascertaining the meaning of *confidenter*.

Only Amm. mentions the name of the soldier in question. In other accounts he is anonymous: οὐκ οἶδα οὕτινός μοι στρατιώτου δόντος (Jul. *Ep. ad Ath.* 284d), ἀνήρ τις μέγας καὶ τἄλλα βέλτιστος ὄπισθεν αὐτῷ παραστὰς οἷον εἶχε στρεπτὸν περὶ τῇ 'κείνου τίθησι κεφαλῇ (Lib. *Or.* 18.99), τις τῶν ταξιάρχων (Zon. 13.10.15); Zosimus even ascribes the action to the soldiers in general: καὶ ἐπέθεσαν σὺν βίᾳ τὸ διάδημα τῇ κεφαλῇ (3.9.2). The last two accounts agree with Amm.'s version in that it is emphasized that Julian was simply forced to accept this culmination of the pronunciamento.

apud Succorum angustias One of the narrow passes leading from Thrace to the northern provinces, half-way between Serdica and Philippopolis. In a brief digression (21.10.3–4) Amm. describes the topography. Cf. Oberhummer, 1931.

torquem, quo ut draconarius utebatur A *torques*, a twisted neck-chain (see the literature cited by Szidat for a description of the *torques* of late antiquity, to which may be added Roes, 1947), could be awarded to a Roman soldier as a decoration for valour (cf. Maxfield, 1981, 86-89). In the case of Maurus, however, Amm.'s wording (*quo ut draconarius utebatur*) seems to imply that the *torques* could also be a distinctive mark connected with a certain function. Speidel, 1985, 286, drawing attention to an interesting parallel in Prudentius' *Perist.* 1.65: *aureos auferte torques, sauciorum praemia*, said by two Christian martyrs who must have been *draconarii* (cf. 1.34-36: *Caesaris vexilla linquunt, eligunt signum crucis / proque ventosis draconum, quos gerebant, palliis / praeferunt insigne lignum, quod draconem subdidit*), combines the two possibilities: "Perhaps standard bearers were selected only from those who had been awarded torcs".

Though in some of the sources the coronation with the *torques* is not mentioned (cf. Zos. 3.9.2 ἐπέθεσαν σὺν βίᾳ τὸ διάδημα τῇ κεφαλῇ; *Art. Passio* 19 τό τε διάδημα περιτίθεται; Theophanes *Chron.* p. 46.33 De Boor διάδημα περιθέμενος) or even deliberately suppressed (cf. Libanius *Or.* 12.59 λιθοκόλλητον ταινίαν φέρουσάν τι καὶ αὐτὴν καρποῦ θαλαττίου, *Or.* 13.33 τὸν ἐκ λίθων στέφανον – *nót* the *torques*, pace Rosen, 1978, 412 – and for the idea of deliberate concealment *Or.* 18.99, quoted below, and Petit, 1956, 479-481), the fact is beyond any doubt whatsoever. Apart from Amm. (here and in 31.10.21) it is attested by Julian himself (*Ep. ad Ath.* 284d οὐκ οἶδα οὔτινός μοι στρατιώτου δόντος μανιάκην περιεθέμην), Libanius (*Or.* 18.99 φεύγοντος δὲ τὴν ταινίαν τὴν χρυσῆν ... ἀνήρ τις μέγας καὶ τἆλλα βέλτιστος ὄπισθεν αὐτῷ παραστὰς οἷον εἶχε στρεπτὸν περὶ τῇ 'κείνου τίθησι κεφαλῇ), Socrates (*HE* 3.1.35 Ὡς δὲ στέφανος βασιλικὸς οὐ παρῆν, εἷς τῶν δορυφόρων, ὃν εἶχε περιτραχήλιον ἑαυτοῦ στρεπτὸν λαβών, τῇ κεφαλῇ Ἰουλιανοῦ περιτέθεικε) and Zonaras (*Epit.* 13.10.14 ἐπεὶ δέ τις τῶν ταξιάρχων χρύσεον ἐφόρει στρεπτόν, λίθους ἔχοντα χρυσοδέτους, τοῦτον λαβόντες τῇ ἐκείνου προσήρμοσαν κεφαλῇ – Ensslin, 1942, 269 n. 1 is probably right in assuming that Zonaras' description is partly the result of his imagination: "Der Eidelsteinschmuck ist Zutat des Byzantiners"; but see Rosen, 1978, 412).

Mentioned for the first time in connection with Julian's usurpation in 360, a coronation with the *torques* is reported more often in later cases (in Amm., with regard to Firmus, in 29.5.20: ... *cum tribunis, e quibus unus torquem pro diademate capiti imposuit Firmi*; note, however, the scepsis of Kotula, 1970, 141 ff. See for other Late-Roman and Byzantine sources Ensslin, 1942), which induced Alföldi 1980[3], 172 to conclude: "Dass die Oströmer diese Sitte von dem Apostaten gelernt und übernommen hätten, wird wohl niemand annehmen wollen, und so bleibt nichts anderes übrig, als die Torqueskrönung in eine noch ältere Zeit zurückzuführen". This view, accepted by e.g. Treitinger, 1956[2], 22 has been convincingly (pace Selem, 1971, 90 and 108-110) refuted by Ensslin, 1942, 268-282. Like the elevation to the shield the coronation with the *torques* had no precedent in the history of the Roman emperors. It was surely the result of a coincidence, a makeshift contrivance for lack of a diadem (cf. also Rosen, 1978, 411-412).

capiti Iuliani imposuit confidenter The final position of adverbs is sometimes caused by rhythmical reasons, but often a more classical position would not preclude a regular cursus. Therefore Blomgren 110 rightly concludes "Ammianum non rhythmi potissimum causa, sed praecipuo quodam insolentioris verborum ordinis studio tam saepe adverbia loco ultimo collocasse". This unusual word order may also be due to the wish to lay particular stress on the adverb. The present instance is an excellent example: wanting to put Maurus' action in an unfavourable light, Amm. emphasizes *confidenter* by its position. The adjective *confidens* tends to be used in malam partem, as was already noted by Cic. *Tusc.* 3.14 *confidens mala consuetudine loquendi in vitio ponitur, ductum verbum a confidendo, quod laudis est*. This fact is borne out by the list of cases in TLL IV 209.79 – 210.29 and the use of the adverb *confidenter* is in keeping with this. Some clear examples in Amm. are 14.1.9 (about Gallus roaming about the inns in Antioch) *haec confidenter agebat in urbe ubi pernoctantium luminum claritudo dierum solet imitari fulgorem*, 16.11.12 *confidenter nefanda multa temptabat*, 31.10.5 (about the Germans) *sublati in superbiam nostra confidentius irruperunt*. In the present text, therefore, *confidenter* should not be rendered by "boldly" (Rolfe) and most certainly not by "entschlossen" (Seyfarth): 'Maurus had the daring arrogance to put his own neck-chain on Julian's head'. There is reason to doubt Heraeus' emendation *fidenter* in 31.10.21.

In Amm.'s version it is undoubtedly Maurus who placed the *torques* on Julian's head. In some of the other sources (see the preceding note) and notably Julian's *Ep. ad Ath.* 284d Julian crowns himself, a version which is preferred by Rosen, 1978, 415, contrary to the communis opinio. In a balanced note Szidat opts for the traditional view.

trusus ad necessitatem extremam Elsewhere Amm. uses similar expressions to indicate that someone is in dire straits, e.g. *ad discrimen trusus est ultimum* (14.10.4), *trudente ipsa necessitate* (16.12.6), *ultima trudente necessitate* (29.1.3). Julian says that he refrains from mentioning any candidate for his succession *ne ... ad discrimen ultimum trudam* (25.3.20). Here Amm. wants to express that for Julian there was no safe solution but to accept his proclamation and to promise the usual *donativum*.

For the use of the expression *necessitas extrema* by Sallust and Tacitus cf. Fesser 11.

si reniti perseverasset The only example of this verb in classical Latin is Liv. 5.49.2 *cum illi renitentes pactos dicerent sese*. After that it is used by several post-classical authors, although not with great frequency. Amm. has more than 15 instances, usually absolute, but a few times with a dat., as 19.3.2 *quibus Sabinianus renitebatur ut noxiis* (cf. the note ad loc.).

quinos omnibus aureos argentique singula pondo Since Constantine introduced a new gold coin, its full name, *aureus solidus* or *solidus aureus*, was usually abbreviated to *solidus* (cf. Regling, 1927, 920). Amm., however, still prefers the old name *aureus* (16.5.14, 25.8.15) or *aureus nummus* (24.4.26, 26.7.11), though not always (pace Regling; cf. 28.1.18 *denis modiis singulis solidis indigentibus venundatis*). This gold coin, struck at 72 to the pound and weighing 4,55 grams, kept its weight throughout the fourth century.

As to the pound of silver, there is some doubt whether the gold and silver coins in the fourth century maintained any stable relationship. This might explain the fact that part of the donative was paid in bullion and not in coins. It would seem that the gold and silver ratio fluctuated so severely that the government found some difficulty in adjusting the coinage to the changes, and therefore sometimes paid silver in bullion. Eventually the silver currency was even abandoned altogether (Jones 439-440).

An accession donative was expected of a new emperor ever since the Early Principate (cf. Fiebiger, 1905) and could sometimes, in anticipation, play an important role in the events leading up to a usurpation (cf. Elbern, 1984, 62-63). The sum distributed in 360, 5 *solidi* and 1 lb. of silver, continued at that figure until 578, except that Tiberius Constantine paid the whole sum in gold – nine *solidi* (Jones 624 and 670). It was called *augustiaticum* (cf. Hendy, 1985, 481). According to Hendy, l.c., it is "highly likely that the precise amount of the *augustiaticum* should be taken back at least as far as the tetrarchy, and quite possibly even further".

IV. 19 *cura constrictus* A strong expression implying that a person is in the shackles of a certain thought or feeling. Cf. *dum rei publicae non solum cura sed quaedam ... procuratio multis officiis implicatum et constrictum habebat* (Cic. *Ac.* I 11), *superstitione constricti* (Quint. *Inst.* 12.2.26), *licet maiore venturi pavore constringerentur* (Amm. 25.8.14), *maioreque venturi pavore constrictus* (31.3.7).

futuraque celeri providens corde Cf. Amm. 16.12.55 *celeri corde futura praevidens Caesar*. The nimbleness of the human mind in general is sometimes hinted at in philosophic texts: *nulla est celeritas quae possit cum animi celeritate contendere* (Cic. *Tusc.* 1.43), *celeri et volucri cogitatione divina perlustrat* (Sen. *Helv.* 11.6).

nec diadema gestavit After Julian's categoric statement *negansque umquam habuisse* (above, section 17) this is either superfluous or elliptic. In the latter case the text would imply that he had in the meantime procured a *diadema*.

nec procedere ausus est usquam   Possibly this is the only instance in Amm. where, because of the motion implied in *procedere, usquam* means 'to any place'. But *procedere* can also be regarded as elliptic for *procedere in publicum* ('to appear in public'), cf. *nec processit in publicum* (14.7.10, cf. also 26.6.16), in which case *usquam* has its normal meaning.

nec agere seria   With *seria* Julian's public and military duties are meant, as becomes clear from the following two quotations from his portraits by Amm.: ... *explorate rei publicae munera cuncta curabat. Post quae ut ardua et seria terminata, ad procudendum ingenium vertebatur* (16.5.6), *explorabat per semet ipsum vigiliarum vices et stationum, post haec seria ad artes confugiens doctrinarum* (25.4.5).

In his zeal to prove Julian's innocence Amm. now even reports an alarming neglect of necessary duties.

IV. 20   The incident which is reported in the last three sections of this chapter can also be found in the accounts of Julian (*Ep. ad Ath.* 285a sqq.) and Libanius (*Or.* 18.102), albeit with considerable differences in the details. But apart from these the most remarkable element is the fact that both Julian and Libanius definitely refer to some conspiracy to murder the newly acclaimed Augustus, whereas Amm. refers only vaguely (*clam interemptum*) to such a possibility. This implies the suggestion that the *decurio* who was responsible for the emotional reaction of the soldiers had merely lost his nerve. Evidently Amm. wants to prevent his readers from suspecting that the soldiers were not as unanimous in their support for Julian's elevation as he has emphatically described them in the preceding text.

accidentium varietate perterritus Iulianus   In Szidat's view *accidentium varietate* refers to "einen Umschwung in der Stimmung eines Teiles der Truppen" contrived by Constantius' supporters. While it is doubtful that the words in question could really have such a meaning, it is unlikely that Amm. would (cryptically) mention any dissension among the troops and at the same time be silent about the conspiracy causing it. This would not at all tally with Amm.'s aim to convince the reader that the soldiers' unconditional consensus was the decisive and indeed the only cause of the pronunciamento.

In fact, the expression in question must be interpreted in a wholly different way. The sentence *sed cum ... Iulianus* chiastically recapitulates the preceding section, as becomes clear from the deliberate addition of the subject *Iulianus*, which from a purely grammatical viewpoint is superfluous, as there has not been any change in subject since *qui trusus* in section 18. Now *cum ad latebras secessisset occultas* summarizes the second half of section 19 (*nec diadema gestavit* etc.), and *accidentium varietate perterritus* is a short formula for the contents of the first half. The expression *accidentium varietas* denotes the whole situation with its various aspects and its consequences for the future, as becomes clear from the parallel in 23.1.2 *accidentium varietatem sollicita mente praecipiens*, one of the phrases by which the wide range of Julian's worries and intentions is expressed in that section. Concerning *perterritus* it should be noted that the verb is sometimes used clausulae causa, as in 19.2.14 *sanguine et pallente exspirantium facie perterrente* (cf. the note ad loc.) or for reasons of alliteration, as in 18.8.9 *quidam cuneorum densitate perterriti petebant proximos Tauri montis excessus*. Neither is the case here, and as the simplex is by no means ousted by the compositum in Amm., *perterritus* should be given its full force: according to Amm. Julian was 'intensely frightened'.

aliqui palatii decurio The three *palatii decuriones* (cf. for the term *Cod. Theod.* 6.23.1, *Avell.* 19.1), also called *consistorii decuriones* (cf. *Cod. Theod.* 6.2.26) or simply *decuriones* (cf. *Cod. Theod.* 6.23.1-4; not to be confused with the *decuriones* who were members of municipal councils), each headed a *decuria* of *silentiarii*, who, among other things, served as ushers in the palace. From a comparison of Amm. and Julian, *Ep. ad Ath.* 285b, τις τῶν ἐπιτεταγμένων τῇ προόδῳ τῆς ἐμῆς γαμετῆς, it would appear that in 360 the wife of a Caesar had a personal *decurio*. An empress in the fifth century apparently had one. Const.Porph. *Cer.* 1.86 mentions four *silentiarii* of the empress Ariadne (cf. Jones 571-572; Seeck, 1901 and Seeck, 1927).

qui ordo est dignitatis As De Jonge notes ad 19.1.3 *dignitas* in late and legal Latin is a general term to indicate official rank, dignity or office, as well as the persons possessing such a rank. The gen. *dignitatis* should be explained as a gen.qual. "ohne Attribut" (Szantyr 70). An interesting list of such genitives can be found in Löfstedt, 1942, I 281/3. For *ordo* with the meaning 'class' see the note ad 20.5.7.

As a rule the offices indicated by the term *dignitas* formed the higher military and administrative posts. Jones 377-378 discusses the difference between *dignitates, honores* or *administrationes* on the one hand and service in the lower echelons of the army or civil service, *militia* in its technical sense, on the other. In Amm. the functions of a *praefectus urbi* (14.6.1), a *corrector* (15.5.14), a *magister sc. militum* (18.5.5, 26.5.11), a *comes* (19.13.2, 25.10.9), a *tribunus* (26.4.2, 29.3.7) and a *protector atque tribunus* (30.7.3) are termed a *dignitas*.

These *dignitates* could be classified on account of different criteria. For example, in 21.16.3 Amm. mentions *palatinae dignitates*; in 14.10.4 he makes a distinction between military and civil *dignitates*; in 18.6.1, 21.16.1 and 28.4.23 we find *superiores, celsiores* and *mediocres dignitates*, respectively.

Ultimately a fixed rank and merit for each separate office was precribed, as is evidenced, for example, by *Cod.Theod.* 6.5.1-2, headed by the title: *ut dignitatum ordo servetur* (see for this Löhken, 1982).

As to the rank of *silentiarii* and their *decuriones*, by the time Amm. wrote his history they had presumably already achieved rather high official standing. By the early fifth century, at any rate, they ranked high, as is clear from some laws pertaining to them in the Theodosian Code (6.23.1-4). In 360, however, their rise to prominence can only have just begun. In *Cod.Theod.* 8.7.5, 326-354, they are still classed with *ministeriales* and *paedagogiani*, who, together with other *castrensiani*, carried out the menial services of the palace. Hence it must have been in the second half of the fourth century that the holders of the office of *silentiarius* and their *decuriones* saw their *militia* upgraded and become a *dignitas*.

Therefore, Amm.'s addition *qui ordo est dignitatis* lends a specific tinge to his account in that he emphatically ascribes the incident to a high-placed official. Possibly he wants to show that Julian's rise to the title Augustus was favourably received in high court circles, too.

pleniore gradu It is difficult to decide whether the comparative has its full force or is the equivalent of the gradus positivus. The expression *pleno gradu* can be found a few times in Livy (4.32.10, 9.45.14, 34.15.3, 34.16.2) and in Sal. *Iug.* 98.4. For the military sphere the pace of this 'Geschwindschritt' has been determined quite exactly by Vegetius: *pleno autem gradu, qui citatior est, totidem horis* (i.e. 5 hours) *XXIIII milia peragenda sunt; quidquid addideris, iam cursus est* (*mil.* 1.9). Since for such a dignified person as a *palatii decurio* running is out of the question, *pleniore gradu* is the fastest pace he can allow himself.

signa Petulantium ingressus According to Julian the man shouted his alarming message κατὰ τὴν ἀγοράν (*Ep. ad Ath.* 285b). With *signa* Amm. means either the centre of the camp, where the standards were kept in an *aedicula* (cf. Stat. *Theb.* 10.176/7 *ventum ad consilii penetrale domumque verendam / signorum*), or perhaps the camp in general, as in 21.4.5 *Vadomarium ... rectori militum arte custodiendum apud signa commisit*.

facinus indignum turbulente exclamat It is quite usual that *exclamare* is accompanied by the literal text of the shouts: 15.5.34 *ut ... populus incertum relatione quadam percitus an praesagio 'Silvanus devictus est' magnis vocibus exclamaret*, 20.9.6 *exclamabatur undique vocum terribilium sonu 'Auguste Iuliane'*. A literal quotation seems quite feasible in the present case too, but obviously editors are of a different opinion: they presumably regard *facinus indignum* as an accusative denoting the contents of the cry (cf. the note ad

20.4.14 *Augustum Iulianum ... concrepabant*). It is worth remarking that the adj. *turbulentus* and the adv. *turbulente(r)*, which are used quite often by Cicero, are rare in historical prose: there are no instances in Sal., Flor. and HA; Caes. and Tac. provide one example each, Livy three. Amm., however, has 14 occurrences. Its meaning in the present section is debatable. One can choose a passive sense: 'agitated, disturbed by passion' or an active one: 'unruly, riotous'. An example of the first interpretation is 17.4.4 where Amm. says about the Persian king Cambyses: *qui dum inter praedatores turbulente concursat, laxitate praepeditus indumentorum, concidit pronus*, but when the Iuthungi *obliti pacis et foederum quae adepti sunt obsecrando Raetias turbulente vastabant* (17.6.1), they were obviously behaving 'riotously'; as De Jonge notes ad loc., they were "violating the quiet peace". In the present text the first meaning is most likely: Julian's complete retirement from the scene – mark that he is not merely said to stay in the palace, but to have withdrawn into *latebras occultas*, a detail wholly absent in his own version – has caused the *palatii decurio* to fear the worst and to voice this fear in a state of great agitation.

pridie Augustum eorum arbitrio declaratum clam interemptum Again this differs from the versions of Julian and Libanius, who both portray the shouting man urging the soldiers to support the Augustus against the conspiracy: μὴ προδῶτε τὸν αὐτοκράτορα (Jul. *Ep. ad Ath.* 285b), (the soldier) συνεκάλει τὸν ὄχλον εἰς ἐπικουρίαν (Lib. *Or.* 18.102). Amm.'s suppression of the conspiracy compels him to report a different phrase, and a dramatic one at that. Like *renuntiare* (see above ad 20.4.17) *declarare* was an official term to announce the election of a magistrate: *igitur comitiis habitis consules declarantur M. Tullius et C. Antonius* (Sal. *Cat.* 24.1). Unlike its synonym *renuntiare* it is used more often by Amm.: having hailed Valentinian as Augustus, the soldiers urged *confestim imperatorem alterum declarari* (26.2.3), and at Valentinian's request the soldiers *Gratianum declararunt Augustum* (27.6.10). It is also used in a 'republican' sense: *Varronianus ... cum Ioviano patre declaratus est ... consul* (25.10.17).

The verb *interimere* is one of a long list of *verba interficiendi*, made up by Hagendahl, 1921, 101/2.

IV. 21 *quos ignota pari sollicitudine movebant et nota* The combination or juxtaposition of *notus* and *ignotus* is not uncommon: *date viam mihi, noti ignoti* (Pl. *Cur.* 280), *si me non omnes noti ignotique monuissent* (Cic. *Ver.* 2.1.31), in Amm.: *notos pariter et ignotos ad faciendum fortiter accendebat* (16.12.29). An example of the neutr. plur. is Sen. *Helv.* 6.6 *(mens) cogitationes suas in omnia nota atque ignota dimittit*. Amm.'s remark is akin to Tacitean reports on mob behaviour, such as *vulgus, ut mos est, cuiuscumque motus novi cupidum* (*Hist.* 1.80.2).

pars crispantes missilia, alii minitantes nudatis gladiis   For *pars ... alii* cf. TLL I 1642.56–81 and De Jonge ad 19.5.6. Presumably the use of *crispare*, which also occurs in 14.2.7 and 27.10.12, is a reminiscence of Verg. *A*. 1.313 (= 12.165) *bina manu lato crispans hastilia ferro*.

Minari and *minitari* with a single abl., the menaced person not being mentioned, is rare: *qui ferro minitere* (Enn.*Ann*. 131 Sk.), *minari interdum ferro* (Sal. *Cat*. 23.3), *minabatur ferro potius quam utebatur* (Amm. 25.4.8).

As noted by Müller, 1905, 606, Amm. does not supply detailed information on arms and armour. For the various types of swords used in the imperial Roman army see Hazell, 1981.

diverso vagoque ... excursu   Amm. uses *vagus* in other places to indicate disorderly behaviour: 15.12.4: the Gauls tend to drunkenness and then *raptantur discursibus vagis* ("rush about in aimless revels" Rolfe), 23.6.80: the Persians have supple and flexible bodies, *vagoque incessu se iactitantes, ut effeminatos existimes*. But *vagus* is also an apt term in the military sphere: *deriguntur acies, pari utrimque spe, nec ut olim apud Germanos, vagis incursibus aut disiectas per catervas* (Tac. *Ann*. 2.45.2), *globus autem dicitur qui a sua acie separatus vago superventu incursat inimicos* (Veg. *mil*. 3.19). So in the present text *vago* emphasizes the chaotic and undisciplinary character of the action.

ut in repentino solet   Blomgren 118 note 2 explains that Amm. uses *subitus* and *repentinus* "nulla differentia". The words *in repentino* are rather difficult to interpret exactly. The translations of Rolfe ("in a sudden commotion") and Seyfarth ("bei plötzlichen Vorfällen") assume a substantivation: *repentino* is obviously regarded as an abl. sing. neutr. Although this may not be impossible, one would have expected the abl. plur. or a phrase comparable to the other places where Amm. uses the expression *ut solet*, e.g. *ut solet in dubiis rebus* (15.5.31), *ut in arduis necessitatibus solet* (26.9.9). Cf. also 18.8.8, 25.1.1, 30.1.5, the note ad 15.5.31 and Fesser 4, who assumes Sallustian influence. Another explanation would be to take *in repentino* to be an adverbial expression meaning 'suddenly'. OLD s.v. *repentinus* 1 c mentions two instances of *de repentino*, both in Apuleius: *Fl*. 16 (24.1 Helm), *Soc*. prol. 3. There does not seem to be another example of *in repentino*. The number of adverbial expressions with *in* increases greatly in Late Latin. The nearest parallel is perhaps *in continenti* ('immediately') e.g. in Tert. *Apol*. 23.11 *etiam illud in continenti cognoscetis*, Cypr. *Ep*. 80.1.2 *rescripsisse Valerianum ad senatum ut episcopi et presbyteri et diacones in continenti animadvertantur*. Cf. Schrijnen-Mohrmann, 1936, I 144 and Heumann-Seckel, 1907, s.v. *continens* 2.

Perhaps the most likely solution is to assume that *excursu* is to be linked with *diverso vagoque* and *repentino*: 'with a chaotic sally in different directions, as is usually the case when such a sally is made all of a sudden'.

occupavere volucriter regiam   Amm. uses the mainly poetic adj. *volucris* in such expressions as *velocitate volucri* (14.11.26, 19.4.7) or *celeritate volucri* (17.13.6). The adverb occurs in 14.6.20 (where, however, it is an emendation by Gronovius), 17.1.12 (where De Jonge notes: "only in Amm.?"), 21.9.6, 28.6.21, 29.1.18. The speed expressed by *volucriter* concurs with Julian's account: καὶ πάντες εἰς τὰ βασίλεια μετὰ τῶν ὅπλων ἔθεον (*Ep. ad Ath.* 285b, cf. also Lib. *Or.* 18.102), but the occupation of the palace is only reported by Amm. As to *regiam*, it is remarked ad 16.8.11 that the word is synonymous to *comitatus* (see above, 20.4.11) and *palatium* (cf. the note ad 20.4.14).

excubitores perculsi   The correctness of Szidat's remark "Mit den excubitores sind ... die einzelnen auf Wache stehenden Soldaten gemeint. Es ist eine blosse Funktionsbezeichnung ..." is perhaps best illustrated by the situation during the night in which Maximianus made his unsuccessful attempt on Constantine's life *rari excubitores erant et ii quidem longius* (Lact. *mort.* 30.4). Another interesting parallel is Suet.*Cl.* 42.1 *excubitori tribuno*, to be compared with Suet.*Ner.* 9: *excubanti tribuno*.

tribuni et domesticorum comes   In the Suetonian passages just quoted a *tribunus* of the praetorian guard is meant. It is likely (cf. Szidat) that the *tribuni* in the present text were officers of the fourth- and fifth-century counterpart of the praetorian guard, the *scholae palatinae* (see for these above, ad 20.2.5). Hence both the *excubitores* and the *tribuni* mentioned here were probably *scholares*.

Whether or not the *domesticorum comes* had any connection with the *scholae palatinae*, is disputed. Jones 372 did not see any: "Of the functions of the *comes domesticorum* nothing is known save that he commanded the corps of officer cadets, the *domestici et protectores*". Frank, 1969, 88-89, however, followed by Szidat, suggests that the *comes domesticorum* exercised a de facto command over all the palace troops, his own *schola domesticorum* as well as the *scholae palatinae* which were nominally headed by the *magister officiorum*. This view has been contested by Clauss, 1981, 41, who argues, not very convincingly, that the *magister officiorum* held the supreme command over the *scholares*, de iure ánd de facto.

Excubitor nomine   Although there is no indication of any difficulty in the mss, this gives considerable cause for suspicion: the name *Excubitor* is not known from other sources and the mentioning of *excubitores* in the immediately preceding text increases the doubts. Szidat has tried to solve the problem in an ingenious way; he proposes to read *excubitor nomine* and to ascribe the meaning "dem Scheine nach, dem Namen nach" to *nomine*; the whole expression would be a sarcastic qualification of the highly placed *comes*, regarding him as "nur dem Scheine nach Wächter". Undoubtedly *nomine* may have such a meaning, but only in a context in which the contrasting reality is explicitly expressed: *terrestre praesidium non re, sed nomine* (Cic. *Ver.* 2.5.87). There are no examples of this in Amm.; Szidat's only parallel is 31.7.4, where it is stated about the then *domesticorum comes* Richomeres: *ductans cohortes aliquas nomine tenus*. But in this case it is, of course, *tenus* which clearly defines the meaning of the expression. A variation of Szidat's solution would be to keep *Excubitor* as a proper name and to assume an implicit paronomasia. In the ars rhetorica paronomasia making use of proper names is considered to be a legitimate technique: Arist. *Rhet.* B 23, 1400 b 17 sqq., Cic. *Inv.* 2.9.28 *ut si dicamus idcirco aliquem Caldum vocari quod temerario et repentino consilio sit*, Quint. *Inst.* 6.3.55 (referring to Cic. *Ver.* 2.1.121) *malum sacerdotem qui tam nequam verrem reliquisset, quia Sacerdoti Verres successerat*. But in the present text the pun would be very cryptic because of its elliptic character. The most likely explanation is that at some point in the tradition of the text the name of the *comes* was misread and adapted to the preceding word *excubitores*. The original name may have had a similar beginning, e.g. *Exsuper(ant)ius* (cf. PLRE I 321/2, II 447/8) or ending (*Victor nomine*, Amm. 31.12.6, 31.13.9).

veritique versabilis perfidiam militis The rare adjective *versabilis* is used by Amm. in a literal sense: *evadendi spe repagulis versabilibus illiduntur* (19.6.4, about wild beasts in their cages, cf. the note ad loc. for the technical problem involved), but also figuratively: *fortuna versabilis* (23.5.19). This is reminiscent of Sen. *Tranq.* 11.10: *scito ergo omnem condicionem versabilem esse*. Amm., however, has also extended its use to persons: 14.11.2 about Constantius' courtiers, 16.8.4 about a slave-woman, 15.5.15 even of the emperor: *sciens animum tenerum versabilis principis*. Cf. also the note ad 14.3.1 and 19.11.1. For *perfidiam* cf. Tac. *Hist.* 2.27.2: *ad postremum Valens e petulantia* (of the soldiers) *etiam perfidiam suspectabat*.

evanuere ... dispalati For *evanuere* cf. De Jonge ad 19.9.6; *dispalari* ('to stray off in several directions') is a rare verb. Amm. has a few instances, to indicate disorderly flight (15.4.8, 24.7.2) or nomadic life (31.2.10), and figuratively in *quo dispalato foedo terrore* (16.12.1, cf. the note ad loc.).

IV. 22 In this last section the divergence from Julian's own description of the incident reaches a culmination. Julian sketches a scene of great gaiety: when the soldiers found him alive and well, they embraced him and carried him on their shoulders, καὶ ἦν πως τὸ πρᾶγμα θέας ἄξιον, ἐνθουσιασμῷ γὰρ ἐῴκει (*Ep. ad Ath.* 285c). Next he relates his great pains to prevent the conspirators (τοὺς Κωνσταντίου φίλους) from being lynched. Because Amm. has suppressed any indication of a conspiracy he has no reason to mention this detail.

Instead of the joyous scene in Julian's letter to the Athenians Amm. reports that all the sound and fury changes into peaceful silence, culminating in the remarkable vignette of the new Augustus in all his hieratic glory, with which the whole chapter is wound up in an astonishing way. For this finale not only differs considerably from Julian's report, it is also very difficult to reconcile with the picture of a much bothered and even frightened (*perterritus*, section 20) man sketched hitherto. But perhaps Amm. wanted to show that Julian's complete acceptance of his new status with the inherent paraphernalia was the inevitable outcome of the soldiers' continued pressure.

quieti stetere paulisper armati The use of *stare* with a predicative adj. occurs quite often in Livy, e.g.: *principio pugnae quieti steterant* (2.30.14), *aliquamdiu intenti utrimque steterunt* (9.32.5), *cum in concursu quieti stetissent in cornibus* (25.41.6), *itaque steterunt scutis innixi* (28.15.5), *pauci stabant impavidi equi* (37.20.12). Amm. has a few examples too: *stabat immobilis* (15.2.3, where the expression is figuratively used, 24.6.6, 25.1.13), *immobiles stabant* (19.2.5). In most cases it concerns a situation on the battlefield.

armati This word occurs quite frequently as a synonym of *milites*: *gravidus armatis equus* (Enn. *trag.* 72 Jocelyn, the oldest instance), *quotannis singula milia armatorum bellandi causa ex finibus educunt* (Caes. *Gal.* 4.1.4), *armatis in litora expositis* (Liv. 37.28.8). Amm. also has many instances, e.g. *ipse cum armatis die noctuque inter propugnacula visebatur et pinnas* (16.4.2), *convocatis armatis simul atque plebeiis* (29.5.56). For some examples in Vegetius cf. the note ad 17.9.3.

interrogati The agens is not mentioned. This is not surprising, for the attention of the author is fully centered on the soldiers and their reactions.

diu tacendo haesitantes The use of the abl. gerundii as the equivalent of the part. praes., which can be found already in classical Latin, increases considerably in the course of time. Cf. Koestermann ad Sal. *Iug.* 1.2, Austin ad Verg. *A.* 2.6, Fedeli ad Prop. 1.1.9, De Jonge ad Amm. 19.1.10 and Szantyr 379-380. The verb *haesitare* is used rather sparingly by Amm.; it can denote indecision, as in 17.13.21: *diu haesitabant ambiguis mentibus, utrum oppete-*

rent an rogarent or uncertainty, as in 18.7.2: *confirmavimus animos haesitantium* (cf. De Jonge's explanation of this passage). In view of *super salute* the last-mentioned meaning is the most suitable here. It is not necessary to regard *haesitantes* as an instance of "praeteritaler Gebrauch des Part. Praes." (Szantyr 386), as in Tac. *Ann.* 11.35.2: *apud quos praemonente Narcisso pauca verba fecit*, a phenomenon which greatly increased in later Latin, for in the present text *non antea discesserunt quam* is the equivalent of *remanserunt donec*.

super salute principis Clark proposed to add *novi* clausulae causa. This addition, which results in a cursus planus: *príncipis nóvi*, can be defended on palaeographical grounds, *non* causing the omission of *novi*, and tallies with Amm.'s usage: *novi principis scripta* (25.8.12), *aureos scilicet nummos, effigiatos in vultum novi principis* (26.7.11). Baehrens, 1925, 49 rejected Clark's addition, "weil zur Bezeichnung des Kaisers, um dessen Schicksal die Soldaten sich aufrichtig kümmern, das Prädikat *novi* zu kalt wirkt. Besser wäre schon *principis* ⟨*sui*⟩". The latter suggestion is palaeographically much less plausible, whilst the 'sentimental' argument is very unconvincing. Baehrens also doubts the necessity of an addition c.c.: "Aber es scheint erst nach *discesserunt*, nicht auch vor *non* eine Klausel vorzuliegen". This is more relevant and it should further be noted that the addition of *novi* is by no means necessary for the contents of the phrase.

asciti in consistorium The use of *asciscere* is somewhat remarkable. Normally the verb denotes promotion to a certain rank: *in societatem imperii asciscere cogitabat* (15.8.1) and with a different construction: *ascivit sibi pari potestate collegam* (27.6.16), or the admittance to someone's fellowship or counsel: *ascitus in amicitiam* (14.6.13), *ascito Lupicino in consilium* (18.2.11), *periti iuris altrinsecus asciscuntur* (28.4.26, about people engaged in divorce proceedings). In the present text such things are out of the question, the soldiers are only admitted in order to behold their favourite with their own eyes; *ascitus postea in palatium* (16.7.6) is no parallel: the retired chamberlain Eutherius is obviously summoned to the palace for counsel. It is necessary to assume a more general meaning for *asciscere* here ('to introduce, to receive'). The feasibility of this can be proved by these passages: *susceptus ad consessum vehiculi* (15.8.17), *nec in consessum vehiculi quemquam suscepit* (16.10.12), *ascitumque in consessum vehiculi* (22.9.13). In these phrases *asciscere* is obviously a synonym of *suscipere*.

From the beginning of the Principate the emperor had always consulted his *consilium*, an informal body of friends and advisers (cf. Crook, 1955 and Millar, 1977, 110–122). The name given to it from the time of Diocletian onwards was *consistorium*, since the members no longer sat down but stood in the emperor's presence. Its membership was dependent on the emperor's choice but normally included the principal civil and military officers of the *comitatus* (cf. the note ad 20.4.11), former holders of these offices, and also *comites consistoriani*, who held no office. It functioned both as a council of state and as a high court of justice (Jones 333–341; cf. De Jonge ad 14.7.11; Kunkel, 1968/69; Graves, 1973; Weiss, 1975 and De Bonfils, 1982.

In most other cases where Amm. speaks about the admittance of persons to the *consistorium*, an actual meeting of the emperor and his counsellors is meant, but here *consistorium* clearly denotes the room where such meetings are held, as in 25.10.2: *cum horrendo stridore sonuerunt in consistorio trabes*. Cf. *at ille sedebat super solium in consistorio palatii* (*Vulg. Esth.* 5.1).

quam ... fulgentem eum augusto habitu conspexissent This final picture comes completely ἐξ ἀπροσδοκήτου, to the soldiers, but also to the reader who has grown accustomed to Amm.'s report of Julian's cautious and even timid course. The verb *fulgere* can express the bright glow of garments: *Hispani linteis praetextis purpura tunicis, candore miro fulgentibus, constiterant* (Liv. 22.46.6), *indumentis plerique eorum ita operiuntur lumine colorum fulgentibus vario* (Amm. 23.6.84), but it can also be applied to the persons wearing them: *qui fulgent purpura* (Cic. *Cat.* 2.5), *ut auro et purpura fulgamus* (Liv. 34.3.9), *nonnullos fulgentes sericis indumentis* (Amm. 28.4.8).

In classical Latin the substantive *habitus* sometimes occurs as a synonym of *vestitus*: *anulo equestri Romanoque habitu* (Hor. *S.* 2.7.53/4), but in late Latin this becomes frequent. Amm. provides a few examples too: *per quietem deducentia se habitus tragici* ("in tragic garb", Rolfe), *figmenta viderat multa* (19.12.10, cf. the note ad loc.) and about the imperial robe: *hunc loci principalis circumferens habitum* (27.6.6). The latter is also denoted by means of the adj. *augustus*: *en, inquit, habes, mi Gratiane, amictus, ut speravimus omnes, augustos* (27.6.12). Cf. also 26.7.13 and, about the *signa*, 30.5.13.

Though in 26.2.3 (*principali habitu circumdatus et corona*) and 27.6.11 (*corona indumentisque supremae fortunae ornatum*) Amm. explicitly mentions the diadem apart from the rest of the imperial garb, Szidat is right in assuming that by *augusto habitu* here both the purple *paludamentum* (see below, ad 20.5.4) and the diadem (above, ad 20.4.17) must be meant (compare the words from 27.6.11 just quoted with *amictus ... augustos* in 27.6.12). As a Caesar Julian was already entitled to wear the *avita purpura* (15.8.11). He now apparently for the first time put on the crown which shortly before he still refused to wear: *nec diadema gestavit* (20.4.19).

Concerning *conspexissent* it should be remarked that the coni. is fully normal after *ante* (...) *quam* in late Latin and also in Amm., cf. De Jonge ad 19.9.5, Szantyr 600. But in Amm. the usual preterite tense is imperf., as can be demonstrated by some close parallels of the present text: *nec discedere quisquam ... permissus est, antequam ... remearent nostri captivi* (17.12.20), *non ante discessit quam ... armatos ibi locaret* (20.7.16). In fact *conspexissent* is the only case of the coni. of the pluperfect, which comes in for some censure by Ehrismann 52 ("male plusquamperfectum pro imperfecto collocatum est"), who overlooks both similar instances in Livy (*Achaei non antea ausi capessere bellum quam ab Roma revertissent legati*, 35.25.3) and the exigencies of the clausula: *habitu conspicerent* would have been an unsatisfactory conclusion of the chapter from that point of view.

Chapter 5

After finally presenting himself to his troops as Augustus, Julian confirms his position by pronouncing a formal *adlocutio*. That this form of address is to be interpreted as an unmistakable sign of his acceptance of the imperial dignity, is shown by a comparison with the introduction to the address given by Julian to the army on the eve of the battle of Strasbourg. There Amm. explains why Julian declines to give a formal speech to the troops (16.12.29): *et alioqui vitabat gravioris invidiae pondus, ne videretur id affectasse, quod soli sibi deberi Augustus existimabat.*

Both the *adlocutio* itself and the ceremony that goes with it, contain a number of standard elements as is evident from a comparison with the other *adlocutiones* in the *Res Gestae*: 14.10.11–15 (Constantius), 15.8.5–8 (Constantius), 17.13.26–33 (Constantius), 21.5.2–8 (Julian), 21.13.10–15 (Constantius), 23.5.16–23 (Julian), 26.2.6–10 (Valentinian), 27.6.6–9 (Valentinian). The emperor addresses his troops, standing on a *tribunal* or, if the speech is given in the field, on any elevated place. He is surrounded by the standards and banners and by the officers. With respect to this last detail, it is significant, as Szidat points out (I 171), that in the present case Julian is surrounded for his safety by armed soldiers instead of high-ranking officers, which shows that his position is not yet consolidated completely. *Adlocutiones* are depicted on coins and on the arch of Galerius in Saloniki (Szidat I 169–170 with references, to which may be added Gabelmann, 1984, 117 and 203).

The *adlocutio* contains the following elements:
§3 Introduction
§4–5 Past exploits of the army under Julian's command
§6 Call for armed support, should Constantius resist the nomination of Julian as Augustus
§7 Promise to suppress corruption and to judge claims to promotion only on the basis of personal merit.

The following standard topics may be observed:
1 The *captatio benevolentiae*: §3 *propugnatores mei reique publicae fortes et fidi*, with which cf. *commilitones mei fidissimi* (14.10.13), *optimi rei publicae defensores* (15.8.5), *Romanae rei fidissimi defensores* (17.13.26), *fortissimi milites* (23.5.16), *provinciarum fortissimi defensores* (26.2.6).
2 The description of their past exploits in §4–5, which is in fact a *captatio* in another form, may be compared to 14.10.14: *arduos vestrae gloriae gradus, quos fama per plagarum quoque accolas extimarum diffundit,* 17.13.26 *recordatio rerum gloriose gestarum omni iucunditate viris fortibus*

113

gratior ... posteritatis memoriae iusta ratione mandandum, 23.5.18 *quae de nobis magnifice loquatur posteritas*. See also Demandt, 1965, 40.

3 The promise of *brevitas*: §3 *perstringere pauca summatim*, with which cf. 14.10.13 *accipite aequis auribus quae succinctius explicabo*, 15.8.5 *tamquam apud aequos iudices succinctius edocebo*.

4 Value attached to the judgement of the troops: §7 *sub reverenda consilii vestri facie*, cf. 27.6.8 *vestraeque maiestatis voluntas*.

The actual proposals or demands put forward by the emperor tend to be somewhat obscured by the acts and graces with which he approaches his audience. As in this *adlocutio* by Julian, in 14.10.12 Constantius makes a transition from the introduction to the actual proposal by speaking about the measures which the situation requires: *remedia cuncta quae status negotiorum admittit*.

The reason for the inordinate length of the passage in which Julian dwells on his past military successes in Gaul is obvious. His primary concern in this speech is to secure the loyalty of the troops; he is quite successful, as sections 8–9 show. The last section (§10) provides, as one might say, the divine sanction of the pronunciamento. It is a highly interesting version of an event told by Julian in his *Ep. ad Ath.* 284C. In assigning this sanction to the *Genius populi Romani*, a deity of a distinctly Roman and political nature, Amm. dissociates himself from Julian's more mystical religiosity. It may be added that the Christian poet Prudentius thought the conception of the *Genius populi Romani* dangerous enough to devote a long passage of his *Contra Symmachum* (II 370–453) to its refutation.

V. 1 *his tamen auditis* Amm. often resumes the narrative with *tamen* (Gr. δ' οὖν). Cf. e.g. 16.5.16, 17.10.3, 19.12.1, 20.4.9. Also in a continuous narrative *tamen* has at times only connective force, as in 16.9.2, 16.11.4, 17.7.1, 19.9.2. The loss of the adversative force of *tamen* is a common feature of late Latin texts. Löfstedt, 1911, 28–29 compares the *Historia Augusta* with Amm. in this respect.

quos ... rettulimus In 20.4.5. The troops under the command of Sintula are said to be relieved (*iam securi*) when they return to Paris, which may be seen as an additional argument to retain the ms. reading *erectus* in 20.4.5. If they had left for the East hoping for rewards, their reaction would have been less positive (Pighi, 1935, 123).

edictoque, ut ... convenirent in campo For the abl. abs. without a nominal ablative see Fesser 6, De Jonge ad 19.11.13 and Szantyr 141.

Futura luce is not found elsewhere in Amm. He has *lux secuta* (23.3.8, 25.5.1, 29.5.47, 31.11.4), – *sequens* 19.6.13, – *postera* 19.6.1 and 21.13.8. TLL VII 2.1911.51 sqq. Cf. Hagendahl, 1921, 102/3 for similar expressions.

in campo This is a military term for an open space used for parades, exercises and assemblies, cf. 20.9.6, 21.2.1, 21.13.9, and 27.6.5; TLL III 214.83–215.3. The importance of the *campus* in the process of urbanisation in Italy and the western provinces and its role in the social and cultural life of the towns there is discussed by Devijver-Van Wonterghem, 1984 and 1985.

ambitiosius solito For *solito* with comparatives see Fesser 23. It seems best to take *ambitiosius* as an adverb, as Szidat does, not as an adjective defining *tribunal* (so De Jonge ad 14.7.6 and TLL I 1855.23). This is the first formal speech delivered by Julian as an Augustus. It is appropriate that his outward appearance is explicitly mentioned. The word order, as Szidat rightly observes, is also in favour of this interpretation, *ambitiosius solito* forming a cursus tardus which concludes the phrase beginning with *progressus princeps*. *Ambitiosius* may refer both to Julian's suite, as in 26.2.11 after a speech by Valentinian: *circumsaeptum aquilis et vexillis agminibusque diversorum ordinum ambitiose stipatum*, and to his dress, for which compare 21.1.4 *quinquennalia Augustus iam edidit et ambitioso diademate utebatur lapidum fulgore distincto* and 18.8.5, where *ambitiose praegrediens agmen* is explained in what follows by *sublata tiara, quam capiti summo ferebat honoris insigne*.

signis aquilisque circúmdatus et vexíllis A description of the emperor's retinue is a topos in the introduction to a speech. See Pighi, 1935, 121–123. For the banners and standards see the note ad 15.5.16 *draconum* and Seston, 1969.

saeptusque tutius Amm. has *tuto* only twice (19.9.5 and 20.11.8), *tutius* 13 times. It is without real comparative force here, as in 26.9.2 *quo* (oppido) *praesidiis tutius communito* and 30.3.5 *saeptus ... multitudine castrensium ordinum tutius prope ripas accessit*. For this use of the comparative see Hagendahl, 1921, 135 sqq., De Jonge ad 15.2.3 and Szantyr 168/9.

armatarum cohortium globis Cf. for *cohors* and *globus* the notes ad 14.2.12 and 16.12.49, respectively. Note that *globus*, "a tightly packed crowd of infantrymen" (De Jonge) is used also of cavalry: *equestres turmae divisae per globos*, 24.4.9. As noted above, Amm. is not very precise in his military terminology.

V. 2 *cumque interquievisset paululum* For *cumque* see the note ad 16.12.37, Pighi, 1935, 76–81 and Szantyr 475. The verb *interquiescere* is very rare, see TLL VII 1.2263.40. Note that Seyfarth's text results in a sentence-ending ‿ ‿ ‿ ‿ ‿, which is extremely rare. It occurs only six times in the 3272 cases examined by Harmon 168. Therefore Damsté's *paulisper* is tempting, but it may be that Amm. is following Gellius: 2.2.9 *patrum iura interquiescere paululum et conivere*, or Cicero: *Brut.* 91 *cum haec dixissem et paulum interquievissem*.

dum alte contemplatur praesentium vultus The phrase could be subordinate to *visos*. It seems more natural, however, to connect it with the preceding *interquievisset* and to connect *visos* with *omnes* taken substantivally as the object of *incendebat*. *Alte* is interpreted as equivalent to *ex alto* by Agozzino, 1972, 68 in his commentary ad loc. (cf. 19.11.10 *imperatore ex alto suggestu iam sermonem parante* and 11 *ex alto despiciens*) and translated in this sense by Rolfe, Seyfarth and Veh. This is probably correct, although it must be noted that Amm. never uses *alte* in this meaning. As an alternative we may consider the meaning 'deeply'. Cf. 26.1.11 *hocque alte considerato*, 30.4.12 *altius ... iura callere*, 21.14.5 *alteque monstrare*. Julian studies the expression on the faces of the soldiers intently and sees that they are in high spirits (*alacres et laetos*). For this meaning of *alte* cf. Gel. 2.12.3 *qui penitus atque alte usum ac sententiam legis introspexerunt* and Tac. *Ann.* 1.32.3 *militares animos altius coniectantibus*, TLL I 1785.69. As *alte* with this meaning seems to occur exclusively in connection with conceptual verbs, it is safer to accept Agozzino's view that it is the equivalent of *ex alto*. For parallels see TLL I 1784.30 sqq. For *contemplari* cf. 15.5.12 *contemplans diligentius scripta* and 24.2.12 *quae defensores intentius contemplati*.

alacres omnes visos et laetos For the word order see Hagendahl, 1924, 187/8.

quasi lituis verbis ... incendebat The word *lituus* is often used metaphorically by Amm., as in 19.12.1 *inflabant litui quaedam colorata laesae crimina maiestatis* and 29.1.14 *internarum cladum litui iam sonabant*. Cf. also 14.7.21, 23.5.15 with Fontaine's note (nr. 117) and 28.1.14. It probably refers not so much to the loudness of Julian's voice as to the inspiring contents of the speech. Cf. Sen. *de ira* 3.9.2 *quis autem ignorat lituos et tubas concitamenta esse?*

ut intellegi possit is best taken with *simplicibus*. The direct, frank address is suited to the audience. Cf. 25.4.13 *exhortatum eum simplici* (Val., *supplici V*) *contione militem Gallicanum* and Fontaine's note ad loc. (nr. 580). Cf.

Valentinian's speech (26.2.7): *pacatis auribus accipite, quaeso, simplicioribus verbis, quod conducere arbitror in commune.* For the idea of *simplicitas* see Hiltbrunner, 1958, 15–106.

V. 3 *res ardua poscit et flagitat*   Amm. frequently uses *arduus* for the difficult tasks of the emperor, especially in military matters: 15.8.6 (speech of Constantius) *quod nos per disiunctissimas terras arduae necessitates astringunt*, 22.10.1 *iudicialibus causis intentus non minus quam arduis bellicisque*, 24.1.1 *difficultates arduae belli. Res ardua* is found from Cicero onwards: *Off.* 1.66 *res ... vehementer arduas plenasque laborum.* For *poscit et flagitat* cf. the climax in Cic. *Ver.* 5.71 *nemo erat quin ... reliquos non desideraret solum, sed etiam posceret et flagitaret* and *Planc.* 48 *posco atque adeo flagito* (Hagendahl, 1924, 183).

propugnatores mei reique publicae fortes et fidi   For the literal meaning of *propugnator* see the note ad 20.6.2. For its metaphorical use see 19.12.17 *principis, propugnatoris bonorum et defensoris* with the note. Szidat quotes i.a. Cic. *Dom.* 129, *Sest.* 137, Tac. *Ann.* 12.42.3 and CIL 6.5127.62 = *Inscr.* Dessau 8393. For *mei reique publicae*, implying that the well-being of the state is linked with that of the emperor, see Agozzino ad 15.8.14 and Szidat. For *res publica* in Amm. see Béranger, 1976, 49–51. The combination *fortes et fidi* is traced by Pighi, 1936 (1), 14 nt 6 to Sal. *Cat.* 20.3. It is also found in 15.6.3 (Silvanus) *militem allocutus est, fortis esset et fidus.*

qui mecum pro statu provinciarum vitam ... obiecistis   This leads up to the description of their campaigns in Gaul. The same emphasis on the provinces is found in Valentinian's speech 26.2.6 *provinciarum fortissimi defensores.* For *obicere* in this sense cf. 20.8.6 *iamque inde uti me creatum Caesarum pugnarum horrendis fragoribus obiecisti* in Julian's letter to Constantius, and again in a speech by Julian 25.3.18 *me velut imperiosa parens consideratis periculis obiecit res publica.* It may be a reminiscence of Verg. *A.* 8.144/5 *me, me ipse meumque / obieci caput.* In a similar context Amm. writes *prodigere vitam* (16.12.50, q.v.).

quoniam Caesarem vestrum firmo iudicio ad potestatum omnium columen sustulistis   The phrase *firmo iudicio* stresses the *consensus militum*, Rosen, 1978, 420 and n. 57. Amm. often uses *columen/culmen* for the imperial dignity: *imperiale* – 15.5.16, 21.16.11, 30.4.2, *principale* – 14.1.1., *augustum* 15.5.17, 20.8.21, 25.8.8. See the notes ad 14.1.1 and 15.5.17. It is a poetical metaphor according to Agozzino, who quotes Cic. *poet.* 11.21 and Catul. 63.71. TLL III 1736.40 sqq.

perstringere pauca summatim This is repeated with a slight variation from 14.6.2 *summatim causas perstringam* 'to touch upon', for which meaning cf. e.g. Cic. *Ver.* 4.105 *breviter perstringere*. Amm. uses *perstringere* of rivers and seas 'to flow past' (16.12.54, 22.8.3, 22.8.26); in 20.7.9 and 29.1.32 it means 'to touch lightly'. A curious use of the word is found in 16.9.2 and 21.3.5, where it is coordinated with *fallere: fallendi perstringendique gnaros* and *ad perstringendum fallendumque*, for which expression see Hagendahl, 1924, 184. Amm.'s predilection for adverbs ending in -*im* is discussed by De Jonge ad 15.5.24, 16.2.6, 17.4.7. For other historians see Vretska ad Sal. *Cat.* 4.2.

ut remedia permutatae rei iusta colligantur et cauta As is to be expected in historiography, Amm. uses *remedium* nearly always in a metaphorical sense (16.5.8, 16.7.10, 16.12.12, 21.1.13, 27.6.4 and 29.2.28 are the only exceptions; in 19.12.14 it refers to an amulet). As a rule it refers to measures to remedy a difficult situation, as e.g. in a speech by Julian 16.12.12 *statum nutantium rerum ... aliquotiens divina remedia repararunt* (where see the note) or 28.6.6 *remedia quaerere damnorum*. Here, of course, as in 14.10.12 quoted in the introduction to this chapter, the word does not imply that the circumstances are unfavourable. *Permutatae rei* refers to Julian's nomination as Augustus. It may be compared with 15.3.7 *optatam permutationem temporum*, 21.14.1 – *temporum*, 26.6.9 – *status praesentis* and 29.2.17 *imperii*.

The separation of two coordinated adjectives, nouns or verbs by a noun or a verb is a prominent feature of Amm.'s style. Pighi, 1935, 119–120 gives a list of examples taken from book 20, showing clearly that very often the cursus dictates the word order.

Colligere in its intellectual meaning "ratiocinatione percipere" (TLL III 1617.10 sqq.) is found from Ovid onwards. Amm. uses it in 15.8.16 *cuius oculos ... vultumque ... contuentes, qui futurus sit colligebant*, 17.1.12 *id nimirum sollerti colligens mente* and 26.1.13 *spatiis duodecim mensuum et sex horarum magna deliberatione collectis*. A good parallel is *HA OM* 1.5 *ex parte, ut ex ea cetera colligantur*.

V. 4 *vixdum adolescens* Julian was born in 331 or 332. In 1977 Bowersock criticized Browning, 1976, 32 and the authors of the *PLRE* for reviving without new evidence the traditional birth date of 332. He was apparently unaware that the discussion had been re-opened in 1971 by Gilliard, who adduced powerful arguments for rejecting 331. The ancient evidence is succinctly set forth by Paschoud ad Zos. 3.5.3.

specie tenus purpuratus, ut nostis, vestrae tutelae nutu caelesti commissus Julian speaks in the same vein in 21.5.3 *arbitrio dei caelestis vobis inter ipsa iuventae rudimenta permixtus*. In his final account of Julian's merits Amm.

returns to the issue of his limited power as a Caesar: 25.4.25 *iuvenis iste ad occiduam plagam specie Caesaris missus.* For comparable passages see Szidat. The expression *specie tenus* is used by Amm. in 14.1.5, 14.7.5, 19.9.9, 22.3.9 and 26.5.1 *alter* (Valens) *honori specie tenus adiunctus.* See the note ad 17.7.5 *collo tenus.*

purpuratus In 356, when he was appointed Caesar, Julian was clothed by Constantius in the *amictus principalis* (15.8.10), that is to say, the *avita purpura* (15.8.11). Cf. Julian, *Ep. ad Ath.* 277a: τὸ χλανίδιον περιεβλήθη τοῦ καίσαρος. The imperial cloak, *paludamentum* (21.5.12, 26.6.15), *paludamentum purpureum* (23.3.2) or *purpura* (15.5.18, 15.8.11, 21.9.8), was the most conspicuous sign of monarchical authority from the Early Principate onwards (cf. Mommsen, 1887³, 432–433, Alföldi, 1980³, 167–169). Its colour (cf. Gipper, 1964 and, though less relevant for the present case, Edgeworth, 1979), throughout antiquity used as a status symbol (cf. Reinhold, 1970), enjoyed its greatest vogue in the Roman world and became of special importance since Diocletian introduced the ceremony of the adoration of the purple (15.5.18), cf. Avery, 1940, Reinhold, 1970, 60 ff. In the fourth century purple became increasingly limited to the emperor and his relatives and the use of purple by anyone else could give rise to the suspicion of high treason (cf. Brok, 1982) or usurpation (cf. Elbern, 1984, 76–78).

The word *purpuratus* occurs six times in Amm., i.a. in 17.11.1, where it is said that Julian was called by the soldiers not only a *loquax talpa* and a *litterio Graecus,* but also a *purpurata simia,* which is a Greek expression: πίθηκος ἐν πορφύρᾳ, quoted by Erasmus in his *Adagia* 1.7.10. See Leutsch-Schneidewin, 1839, I 303 (Diogenianus 7.94) and II 614 (Apostolius 14.32). There, as in 21.1.4 (*xystarchae similis purpurato*), *purpuratus* is used attributively. As a secondary predicate we find it in 14.11.10 *antegressus est Galerius purpuratus* and in 25.9.13 *multo postea apud Constantinopolim visus est subito purpuratus.* In all these cases *purpuratus* has its literal sense, 'clad in purple'. This notion is still prominent in 15.5.27 too, (*adorare sollemniter anhelantem celsius purpuratum*), as is evident from 15.5.16: *cultu purpureo a draconum et vexillorum insignibus ad tempus abstracto,* and in the present text. In Late Antiquity the substantive *purpuratus* came to be synonymous with *princeps* and *imperator,* as is shown by Rösger, 1980 and Del Chicca, 1982.

Ut nostis accentuates the experiences and knowledge shared by the speaker and his audience, as in 15.8.8, 17.13.28 (with the note), 25.3.18 (speeches) and 18.8.6 *ut nosti* (conversation).

Although *tutela* more often indicates protection offered by the commander than protection received by him (e.g. 14.10.12 *nihil non ad sui spectare tutelam,* 18.6.2 *relictus ad sui tutelam,* and the note ad 17.13.24, where Veg. *mil* 3.10 is quoted: *dux ergo ... cuius fidei atque virtuti ... tutela urbium, salus militum ... creditur*), here the roles seem to be reversed and Julian deferentially describes himself as being committed in his youth to the army as a ward. The words *nutu caelesti* seem to be an echo of Constantius' words (15.8.10) when he presented Julian as his Caesar to the army: *ergo eum praesente nutu dei caelestis amictu principali velabo*. The divine guidance in Julian's elevation to the throne is a recurrent theme, both in his own writings (for which see Szidat) and in the *Res Gestae*, e.g. 22.2.5 *principatum ... deferente nutu caelesti*.

numquam a proposito recte vivendi deiectus sum A comparison with the opening sentence of Julian's letter to Constantius (20.8.5) suggests that this somewhat self-righteous phrase refers to his loyalty towards the Augustus. In the death bed scene (25.3.17) his impeccable behaviour both as a private citizen and as emperor is emphasized: *vel cum in umbram et angustias amendarer, vel post principatum susceptum animum immaculatum ... conservavi*. Valentinian recommends his son Gratian in similar terms: 26.2.7 *quem ab ineunte adolescentia ... splendide integreque vixisse experiundo cognostis*. The Caesar Gallus is an example e contrario: 21.13.11 *qui cum a iustitia per multa visu relatuque nefaria defecisset* ... Amm. uses *propositum* frequently, mostly in the sense of 'purpose', 'objective', as in 22.14.2 *nusquam a proposito declinabat*, often with a genitivus explicativus, as here and e.g. 21.12.6 *proposito pugnandi detortos*. With reference to his own work we find e.g. 23.6.74 *ne ... a proposito longius aberremus* and in the extended sense of 'scope' in 22.15.32 *opusculi nostri propositum excedentia*. Its post-Aug. meaning "chosen mode of conduct" (OLD s.v. 2) (cf. Vell. 2.2.2 *vir ... proposito sanctissimus*), which is also found in Amm., as in 23.6.2 *in melius mutato proposito*, develops into 'inclination' (15.2.4 *inexplebili quodam laedendi proposito*) or even 'character' (18.3.6 *Barbatio subagrestis arrogantisque propositi*, 29.4.1 *morum eius et propositi cruenti*). In some of these shades of meaning it is the parallel of Greek προαίρεσις. In fact, that is the word used by Julian himself in describing his attitude toward Constantius, *Ep. ad Ath.* 280 D μάρτυρας καλῶ τὸν Δία καὶ πάντας θεοὺς ... ὑπὲρ τῆς ἐμῆς προαιρέσεως εἰς αὐτὸν καὶ πίστεως, quoted by Agozzino. In the meaning 'chosen mode of conduct' it can be regarded as the synonym of ἦθος, cf. Chalcidius' rendering of ἔμενεν ἐν τῷ ἑαυτοῦ κατὰ τρόπον ἤθει (Pl. *Tim.* 42 e 5–6) by *cum in proposito rerum creator maneret* (Chalcid. 38.10–11 Waszink).

For *deiectus sum* cf. 28.4.1 *numquam ab humanitatis statu deiectus* and Aquila rhet. 24 p. 30 Halm *a proposito deiectus*, TLL V 1.400.28 sqq.

vobiscum in omni labore perspicuus A typical virtue of the good army commander, cf. e.g. Sal. *Jug.* 7 (Jugurtha) and Liv. 21.4 (Hannibal), often mentioned by Amm. in connection with Julian. For a list of passages, also from other contemporary authors, see Szidat.

cum dispersa gentium confidentia ... persultaret Amm. uses *dispergi* 'to spread about' again in 29.6.9 *malorum similium dispersa formidine*. For this meaning see TLL V 1.1407.42 sqq. As it is often used of rivers and seas, it leads up to the comparison of the barbarians with a flooding river in the next section.

For *gentes* see the note ad 20.1.1 and for *confidentia* the note ad 20.4.18 *confidenter*. Like the adverb, the noun and the adjective are used in a negative sense, as in 16.12.2 about the Alamanni: *erexit autem confidentiam caput altius attollentium* and 31.10.5 (Germani) *sublati in superbiam nostra confidentius irruperunt*, 21.10.1 about Julian *ut erat in rebus trepidis audax et confidentior* seems to be the only exception to this rule.

post civitatum excidia peremptaque innumera ... milia For the coordination of a participle and an abstract verbal substantive see Laughton, 1964, 89-92. Other examples are *nec multa cruoris effusio nec confixi ... vulneribus plurimi ceteros at audacia parili revocabant* (20.7.11) and *post reseratas angustias abitumque militis tempestivum* (31.8.6). Amm. uses *excidium* always of cities or camps, once (31.10.3) of the empire as a whole. For *innumerus* see Hagendahl, 1921, 50 and the note ad 14.11.29.

quae semiintegra sunt relicta *Semiinteger* seems to be a neologism coined by Amm. For similar word formations see Camus, 1967, 32 sq. The perfect tense, where we would expect the pluperfect, is probably chosen for metrical reasons.

cladis immensitas persultaret A remarkable example of Amm.'s use of personification. *Immensitas* is used only twice in Cicero and once in Apuleius. In later Latin it occurs with some frequency, see TLL VII 1.449.20 sqq. *Persultare* seems almost a terminus technicus for the overrunning of provinces by barbarians. Compare Liv. 34.20.6 (Lacetani) *memores quam saepe in agro eorum impune persultassent* and Tac. *Ann*. 11.9.1 *Hibero exercitu campos persultante*. Here, it is another reminiscence of Constantius' speech when he presented Julian to the army: 15.8.6 *persultant barbari Gallias*. Cf. also 14.2.5, 16.12.5 with the note, 17.13.27, 25.6.8, 26.5.11.

et retexere superfluum puto Amm. uses this type of praeteritio several times, e.g. 23.6.62 *quas nunc recensere alio properans superfluum puto*. For *retexere* cf. 28.6.18 *suas civiumque et finitimorum retexentes aerumnas*. Agozzino quotes parallels from Statius (*Theb*. 3.338) and Apuleius (*Met* 9.17, *Apol*. 61).

hieme cruda rigentique caelo Cf. 27.12.6 *rigente tunc caelo. Hieme cruda* is found also in Min. Fel. 34.12 and Paneg. 4.36.5

opere Martio A poetical expression, for which compare Verg. *A*. 5.284 *operum haud ignara Minervae*. Amm. repeats it in 31.7.2 *opere ... Martio saepe recte compertas*.

indomitos antea When Constantius addresses his troops to inform them of Julian's usurpation, he gives a different account: 21.13.13 *levium confidentia proeliorum quae cum Germanis gessit semermibus*, in which Sabbah 369 suspects the influence of Greg. Naz.

cum iactura virium suarum reppulimus Alamannos The use of *suus* instead of *eius/eorum*, which is found already in classical prose, becomes more frequent in Late Latin, see Szantyr 175. A very similar case is 31.10.4 *quos ... cum Petulantibus Celtae non sine sui iactura afflictos graviter*. For the use of the indicative in indirect questions see the note ad 14.6.2.

V. 5 *nec praetermitti est nec taceri* The insertion of *est* was suggested by Pighi, 1935, 95/6, who quotes parallels from Tertullian and Valerius Maximus for *est* + inf. pass. It should be noted, however, that there is no parallel for *est* + infinitive in Amm., except 30.4.8 *at nunc videre est*, which is a very common expression (Szantyr 349). In view of 25.9.7 *nec vituperari est aequum nec laudari* and the very similar phrase *illud tamen nec praeteriri est aequum nec sileri* (29.3.9), it seems decidedly better to accept the reading of G *nec praetermitti est aequum nec taceri*. Cic. *Catil*. 1.14 *quod ego praetermitto et facile patior sileri* may have served as a model.

cum ... illuxisset ille beatissimus dies A poetical turn of phrase repeated with unmistakable irony in 28.4.31 *exoptato die equestrium ludorum ... illucescente*. Julian was, deservedly, proud of his achievement in the battle at Strasbourg (August 357). Ἐμαχεσάμην οὐκ ἀκλεῶς, he wrote to the Athenians (279b). Bitter 56–101 and Blockley, 1977 have analysed Amm.'s description of the battle in book 16, while Hatt-Thévenin-Vogt, 1980 has written a history of Strasbourg, from the origens to the invasion of the Huns. Cf. also De Jonge ad 15.11.8.

vehens quodam modo ... libertatem Amm. uses *quodam modo* with metaphorical expressions, e.g. in 14.6.17 *tacita quodam modo lege*, 25.4.14 *ipsis quodam modo cervicibus Fortunae* or proverbial phrases: 16.12.47 *pares enim quodam modo coiere cum paribus*. Parallels for this use of *quodam modo* can be adduced from Livy, e.g. 32.20.2 *obtorpuerant quodam modo animi* and Tacitus, e.g. *Ag*. 32.2 *paucos numero ... clausos quodam modo ac vinctos di vobis tradiderunt*. Here *quodam modo* does not qualify *vehens perpetuam libertatem*, but is added because it is a metaphor, be it a time-honoured one.

me discurrente Repeated in 23.5.25 (numeri Gallicani) *memores aliquotiens eo ductante perque ordines discurrente cadentes vidisse gentes aliquas, alias supplicantes.* For *discurrere* see the note ad 20.6.2.

ususque diuturnitate fundati We find the same phrase, without gen. inversus, in 16.12.43 *usu proeliorum diuturno firmati*. The expression in the present text is traced by Fletcher, 1937 (2), 382, to Sal. *Hist.* fr. 3.87 M, where the inhabitants of a besieged town resort to cannibalism: *parte consumpta reliqua cadaverum ad diuturnitatem usu sallerent* ('made salty'). Amm. uses the phrase in a similar sense in 17.8.2 *ad usus diuturnitatem excoctum, buccellatum* ('soldier's biscuit'). In the present text, however, it means 'experience', as in 25.4.10 *fortitudinem certaminum crebritas ususque bellorum ostendit*. TLL VI 1562.29 wrongly comments "de corpore hominis".

velut incitatos torrentes hostes abruptius inundantes The comparison of an invading army to a torrent is traditional, see Bitter 136, n. 414, and compare 31.10.21 *tamquam exaestuare sueti torrentes ... vagarentur* and 31.5.12 *inundarunt Italia ... Teutones ... cum Cimbris*, which may have been inspired by Pomp. Trog. Iust. 38.4.15 *Cimbros ... more procellae inundasse Italiam*. See also 16.3.3, 19.5.5, 31.15.10 and TLL VII 2.248.56-64. The adverb *abruptius* combines the notions of suddenness and danger. See the note ad 17.7.8.

fluminis profundo submersos The combination of a neuter adjective or participle with a noun in the genitive is frequent in Amm. With a plural substantive the adjective is always in the plural. If the substantive is singular the adjective is either in the singular or in the plural: 14.2.6 *hoste ... rupium abscisa volvente*, 14.6.4 *ad tranquilliora vitae discessit*, 18.8.7 *editiora collis*, 25.2.3 *obscuro noctis*, 31.9.2 *per montium celsa silvarumque densitates*. With *fluminis profundo* in particular cf. 14.11.29 *ad Cocyti profunda mergentes* and 27.12.11 *per silvarum profunda*. It is a poeticism found frequently in historians, Szantyr 152, De Jonge ad 14.2.6.

paucis relictis nostrorum According to Amm. in 16.12.63 the Romans lost less than 250 men. Cf. also 17.1.14, where the war against the Alamanni is compared to the Punic wars and the battles against the Teutones, with the difference that it was won *dispendiis rei Romanae ... levissimis*.

celebri ... laude Well paraphrased by Wagner: "memoriam eorum laudibus celebrando".

V. 6 After the elaborate commemoration of their past exploits, Julian returns to the measures announced in section 3 in connection with his accesion to the throne. The speech to the troops in 21.5.2-8 shows exactly the same pattern. There, after the introduction in section 2, Julian describes in section 4 their exploits in Gaul, for which he promises them eternal fame: *haec laborum ... Galliae ... posteritati per aetatum examina commendabunt*, and in section 5 he speaks of his higher ambitions now that he is emperor: *altius affecto maiora* ("I am aiming higher at greater deeds", Rolfe), qualified by *si fortuna coeptis affuerit*. In the present text Julian speaks with less confidence. He asks the soldiers for their help, now that they have made him an Augustus, *si quid adversum ingruerit*. The text is corrupt after the words *in rem publicam meritis*. V reads *que gentibus cunctis plene quem* (*quam* BA), on the basis of which Heraeus conjectured *quae gentibus cunctis plene ⟨iam cognita sunt, si eum⟩ quem*, which gives good sense. *Nec* before *posteritatem* remains isolated, but that is not exceptional (*nec = ne quidem* is "fast allgemein im Spätlatein", Szantyr 450, see also the note ad 14.10.3). Madvig balanced *nec* by inserting *nec dubito quin*. Bentley took Gelenius' G which reads *in gentibus cunctis si plene quem*, as his starting-point, and wrote *ingentibus cuncti si plene quem*, which is a correction rather than a conjecture. As this reading is closest to the text of the mss., it deserves serious consideration. The only objection against it is that *plene ... virtute gravitateque defendatis* seems less natural than e.g. *plene cognita sunt*.

quem altiore fastigio maiestatis ornastis Amm. uses *fastigium* a few times in its literal meaning 'top', 'summit'. The only parallel for the present use is 14.11.29 *in amplissimum fortunae fastigium*. *Fastigium* 'high position' is found from Livy onwards, e.g. 35.12.10 *ex altiore fastigio rex quam tyrannus detractus*, TLL VI 322.32 sqq. *Ornare* is here combined with the abstract *fastigio*, while in similar contexts it usually refers to the imperial insignia: 26.4.3 *decoreque imperatorii cultus ornatum*, 27.6.11 *corona indumentisque supremae fortunae ornatum*, 30.7.4 *indutibus imperatoriae maiestatis ... ornatus*.

si quid adversum ingruerit *Adversus* is frequently found in euphemisms: 16.12.34 *si quid contigisset adversum*, 24.8.7 *ne quid adversum accideret*. Julian obliquely refers here to possible counter measures by Constantius. *Ingruere* is used in connection with possible dangers since Livy: 7.25.9 *si qua externa vis ingruat*. Agozzino correctly calls it a poeticism, cf. e.g. Verg. *A* 2.301 and 8.535. In Amm. cf. 18.6.6 *si fortuna sequior ingruisset* and 30.8.14 *si fors ingruisset inferior*. See the notes ad 16.2.7 and 18.6.6. For *quid adversum/adversi* see the note ad 20.4.15 *aliquid indecorum*.

V. 7 *ut autem rerum ... ordo servetur* The last section of the speech contains both a warning and a promise. No sudden promotions are to be expected after the nomination of the new emperor either in the army or in the civil service. The general policy is formulated in *rerum integer ordo servetur*, specified by *praemia virorum fortium* for the military, *honores* for the civil servants, chiastically repeated by the words *civilis iudex – militiae rector*. The promise to promote persons only because of their personal merits is, of course, traditional, as Szidat illustrates with a number of parallels from the Cod. Theod. The record of an emperor in this respect is important for Amm.'s final judgment about him, cf. 21.16.1, 25.10.15, 30.9.3 and 31.14.2 (Demandt, 1965, 49). When presenting Gratian as Augustus to the troops Valentinian promises: *librabit suffragiis puris merita recte secusve factorum* (27.6.9).

Amm. uses *ordo* in four main meanings. Most often it is found in a military context: 'rank', 'order', a more specific use being *'primi ordines'* for the lower-ranking officers, for which see the note ad 16.12.20. Next in frequency comes *ordo* as a term indicating the different classes in society, more specifically the higher classes (senators and curiales, see the note ad 18.6.2). The third meaning is 'order, series of events', for which compare 17.13.16 with the note. Closely similar is the expression *fatorum* -, c.q. *fatalis ordo* (15.3.3, 19.11.15, 23.5.5, see the note ad 16.1.1). Finally, in *rerum integer ordo* the idea of 'regularity', 'normal procedure' seems predominant. With this shade of meaning *ordo* is found in 22.12.7 *sine fine vel praestitutis ordinibus* and 31.15.15 *nullo ordine iam sed per procursus pugnabatur*.

honores ambitio praeripiat clandestina   As some officials tried to do under the reign of Valens: 30.4.2 (iudices advocatique) *qui tenuiorum negotia militaris rei rectoribus vel intra palatium validis venditantes aut opes aut honores quaesivere praeclaros*. Valens is nevertheless called *ultor acer ambitionum* in 31.14.2.

sub reverenda consilii vestri facie   Julian addresses his audience in terms usually reserved for the senate: 14.6.6 *patrum reverenda cum auctoritate canities*, 16.10.5 *senatus officia reverendasque patriciae stirpis effigies*. The phrase *sub ... facie* is strange. In the numerous expressions with *facies*, mostly in biblical texts, meaning 'in the presence of –', the preposition *sub* is never used according to TLL VI 53.40 sqq. As a possible model TLL s.v. 51.58 quotes Tac. *Hist* 2.54.2 *publici consilii facie*, adding "i.e. simulatione". If Amm. imitates Tacitus here, as seems probable, he modifies the meaning of the phrase, as he did in § 5 *usus diuturnitas*.

civilis ... iudex ... militiae rector   *Iudex* is used by Amm. most frequently in its usual sense of 'judge'. Sometimes (17.12.21, 27.5.6, 27.5.9, 31.2.25, 31.3.4) we find it in the sense of 'chief' or 'ruler' of barbarian peoples. Quite often (in this book, apart from the present text, in 20.8.14 and 20.9.1) it means 'official', 'functionary', that is to say, 'civil official'. Only once (29.4.5) a military officer is meant. Normally the word in itself suffices to denote a civil functionary, but sometimes this notion is made explicitly clear by the addition of the word *civilis*, as in the present case, or *ordinarius*, as in 16.8.13 and 20.8.14. For *civilis* compare for example 26.1.3: *potestatum civilium militiaeque rectores*. The phrase *militiae rector* is a favourite of Amm., as is evidenced by 15.5.2, 18.3.1, 25.8.12, 26.4.1 and 26.5.2. De Jonge has notes on *iudex* ad 15.5.18, 16.5.13, 16.8.13, 17.12.21 and 18.6.12. See for *rector* and *militiae* the notes ad 20.1.1 and 20.2.5, respectively.

alio quodam ... suffragante   Both Veh and Seyfarth seem to take *alio quodam* as a neuter. This may not be impossible (cf. 30.5.12 *alio quoque in eum perniciose composito*), but in view of *quodam* and the penalty announced for those who would act as *suffragatores* it is decidedly better to translate with Rolfe "through anyone supporting him beyond his merits". In other instances of *suffragante/-ibus*, except in 30.7.4 *contextu suarum quoque suffragante virtutum*, there is always a human agent: 15.2.8 *Eusebia* -, 16.6.3 *cubiculariis* - (with note), 26.7.6 *Agilone genero* -, 28.1.27 *Victorino*. Cf. 29.3.6 (*suffragatori magistro equitum Theodosio*) and 22.6.5 (*lex est promulgata, qua cavetur nullum interpellari suffragatorem super his, quae eum recte constiterit accepisse*). The latter passage refers to a law of Julian, *Cod. Theod.* 2.29.1, which, differently assessed by modern scholars, seems to be crucial for the proper understanding of Julian's attitude towards the practice of *suffragium*. For details see Goffart, 1970, Barnes, 1974, Andreotti, 1975 and Liebs, 1978. Cf. in general De Ste. Croix, 1954, Collot, 1965, Schuller, 1980 and Veyne, 1981.

ad potiorem veniat gradum   For *potior* cf. 20.4.4 *Iulianus potioris arbitrio cuncta concedens*, 26.6.13 *potiorem locum obtinebant* and for *gradus* 21.16.14 *potestas in gradu*, 28.1.42 *ad gradus potestatum excelsos* and 29.1.8 *secundum inter notarios adeptus iam gradum*.

non sine detrimento pudoris   For this 'loss of face' cf. 17.5.12 *nihil pudori nostro praeruptura vel maiestati*.

eo qui ... petere temptaverit, discessuro   Szantyr 139 discusses this use of the future participle in abl. abs. *Petere* is a terminus technicus 'ask for favours', as is shown by the heading of Julian's law in the *Cod. Theod.* quoted above: *si certum petatur de suffragiis*.

V. 8   The reaction of the troops is one of the standard elements in Amm.'s description of speeches by emperors. The soldiers demonstrate their approval in two ways, by shouting and making a terrible noise with their shields. With this section we may compare the response to Constantius' address in which he proclaimed Julian as Caesar in 15.8.15 *militares omnes horrendo fragore scuta genibus illidentes ... inmane quo quantoque gaudio praeter paucos Augusti probavere iudicium.* Julian's *adhortatio* in 16.12.9–12 elicits this response: *ardoremque pugnandi hastis illidendo scuta monstrantes in hostem se duci ... exorabant.* His speech in 21.5.2–8 meets with the following reaction: *hoc sermone imperatoris vice alicuius oraculi comprobato mota est incitatius contio et ... unanimanti consensu voces horrendas immani scutorum fragore miscebat.*

The unanimity or near unanimity of the soldiers, expressed in this section by *uno prope modum ore*, is also a recurring element, as is shown by *militares omnes* and *unanimanti consensu* in the passages just quoted, with which may be compared 17.13.34 *contio omnis*, 26.2.11 *flexit imperator in suam sententiam universos* and 21.13.16 *omnes post haec dicta in sententiam traxerat (?) suam.*

hac fiducia spei maioris animatus For *animatus* see the note ad 20.4.12 The demonstrative *hac* refers to Julian's speech: 'the confidence caused by this speech'.

Spes maior, 'better prospects' is found only here in Amm. Its negative counterpart is *spes inferior*, as in 20.11.11 *cum spes nostrorum inferior cuncta maerore compleret*. With the phrase as a whole cf. 15.8.6 *persultabant barbari Gallias ... hac animati fiducia quod* e.q.s. *Spei maioris* is best taken as a gen. obiectivus dependent on *fiducia*.

dignitatum iam diu expers et praemiorum *Dignitas* is often accompanied by a defining genitive (15.5.14 *correctoris*, 26.4.2 *tribunatus*, 30.7.3 *protectoris*) or an adjective (18.6.1 *dignitate afficiendus superiore*, 28.4.23 *cum dignitate licet mediocri cervice tumida gradiens*). Here *dignitas* has the general meaning of 'high position'. See also ad 20.4.20. The expectation of promotions and rewards had not been prompted explicitly by Julian, but the soldiers were of course well aware of the regular practice in situations like this. The usurper Procopius proceeds with less dignity in 26.6.16 *opesque pollicitus amplas et dignitates ob principatus primitias processit in publicum.*

hastis feriendo clipeos sonitu assurgens ingenti In 15.8.15 Amm. makes a distinction between *genibus illidere scuta* as *prosperitatis indicium plenum* and *hastis ferire clipeos* as *documentum irae et doloris*. The first action is interpreted by Amm. as an omen of success (not as a sign of complete approval as all translators have it, following Heyne's Prolusio de Ammiano Marcellino, p. CXXXVIII in the Introduction to Wagner-Erfurdt's commentary; this meaning of *prosperitas* is unattested). The second action is taken to be a sign of anger and resentment. At first sight *ira et dolor* seem out of place in the present text.

De Jonge in his note ad 15.8.15 follows Pighi, 1936 (1) 62 nt. 3, who was of the opinion that the distinction made there by Amm. does not apply to all cases in which he mentions this practice: "Il fatto è che la distinzione d'Ammiano...riguarda l'uso ordinario, senza escludere altri casi". The fact, however, that Amm. mentions *ira et dolor* twice in a similar context does not speak in favour of this solution: 14.2.17 *hastisque feriens scuta, qui habitus iram pugnantium concitat et dolorem* and 25.3.10 *miles ad vindictam ira et dolore ferventior involabat hastis ad scuta concrepans*. It seems best therefore to accept, with Szidat, Seyfarth's interpretation, 1983[5], 197 n. 49, that the soldiers gave vent to their resentment about the situation during the reign of Constantius, who had offered them no prospect of promotions or rewards. In this way they showed their readiness for battle in Julian's service, as they had done after his adhortatio before the battle of Strasbourg: 16.12.13 *ardoremque pugnandi hastis illidendo scuta monstrantes*. In this respect again the proclamation of Procopius described in 26.6.16 reads like a parody: *circumclausus horrendo fragore scutorum lugubre concrepantium*, as the soldiers in this case held their shields above their heads to protect themselves against stones thrown at them from roof-tops.

The usual expression for striking spears against shields is *concrepare armis* (TLL IV 94.30 sqq.), which is found from Sisenna onwards (*hist*. 64 *conglobati et collecti concrepant armis*). The action is not specifically Roman. Caesar mentions it as a sign of assent among the Celts: *Gal*. 7.21.1 *conclamat omnis multitudo et suo more armis concrepat, quod facere in eo consuerunt, cuius orationem approbant*. Tacitus relates the same about the Germans: *Ger*. 11 *sin placuit* (sc. oratio) *frameas concutiunt: honoratissimum assensus genus est armis laudare*. Cp. also Liv. 28.29.10, Verg. *A*. 8.3 and 12.332.

For *sonitu assurgens ingenti* cf. the very similar passage following Constantius' speech to his troops in 17.13.34: *contio omnis alacrior solito aucta spe potiorum et lucri vocibus festis in laudes imperatoris assurgens*. In all probability *assurgere* is used metaphorically by Amm. (29.6.11 *ad arripienda quae urgebant acri nisu assurgens*) and other authors, e.g. Verg. *A*. 10.94/5 *nunc sera querelis/haud iustis adsurgis et inrita iurgia iactas*, Florus *Epit*. 1.36.10 *in ultionem ... adsurgit*, August. *gen. ad litt*. 4.28 *a cognitione creaturae in laudem creatoris adsurgitur*, TLL II 938.74 sqq.

dictis favebat et coeptis *Coeptum*, used substantivally, is found frequently in Amm., but also in classical authors, especially Ovid, Livy and Tacitus, TLL III 1430.3 sqq.

V. 9 *ne turbandae dispositioni consultae tempus saltem breve concederetur* Seyfarth translates: "In der Absicht, auch keinen Augenblick Zeit zu verlieren, um eine so reiflich überlegte Anordnung zu stören". Indeed, a somewhat sarcastic comment seems appropriate, since the request of the Petulantes and the Celtae violates the policy declared by Julian in section 7 above. This, however, attributes a meaning to *concedere*, viz. 'to leave unused', 'to lose', for which no certain parallel can be found. Therefore Rolfe's translation "lest even an instant should be allowed to interfere with so resolved a purpose" seems preferable. For this meaning of *concedere* cf. Cic. *Arch.* 13 *quantum ... ad ipsam requiem animi et corporis conceditur temporum* and Sal. *Jug.* 61.3 *neque id tempus ... quieti aut luxuriae concedit*. This would mean that the soldiers interpret Julian's *disposito* as some kind of promise and that they do not realize that his warnings against unjustified intercession apply to themselves also. Thus the Petulantes and the Celtae, who had played a decisive role in Julian's pronunciamento, decide to make hay while the sun shines.

Elsewhere Amm. uses the gerund with *ad* after *concedere* (27.12.8 *biduumque ad deliberandum ... sibi concedi*) or a predicative gerund as in 20.8.14 *militiae moderatores promovendos arbitrio meo concedi est consentaneum*. There is no parallel for the gerundive construction in the dative used here.

For *turbare* see the note ad 20.4.1 and for *dispositio* the note ad 16.12.12. The meaning required here is 'arrangement', 'ordinance', referring to the declaration of policy in section 7. *Consultus*, 'well-considered', is found in contemporary texts, e.g. *Cod. Theod.* 8.5.20 (a. 364) *consultissimam legem* and Symm. *or.* 7.5 *causas consultissimae placiditatis tuae*, TLL IV 585.33 sqq. Amm. has the expression *opera consulta*, 'after due deliberation' in 14.10.5 and 29.1.3. Cf. also 23.2.2 *cum primam consultae rationes copiam praebuissent* and see the note ad 16.12.10, where *Cod. Iust.* 9.44.1 is quoted: *quarta bonorum omnium parte multatus aculeos consultissimae legis incurrat*.

pro actuariis obsecravere Petulantes et Celtae The *actuarii* were the regimental quartermasters (cf. Kubitschek-Seeck, 1894, De Jonge ad 15.5.3, Jones 626-628, 672-674), who enjoyed a dubious reputation (cf. e.g. Aur. Vict. *Caes.* 33.13 *genus hominum praesertim hac tempestate nequam, venale, callidum, seditiosum, habendi cupidum atque ad patrandas fraudes velandasque quasi ab natura factum* and Amm. 25.10.7 *ex actuario ... fraudum conscius et noxarum*), but perhaps not so much with the soldiers as with the state and the provincials whom they cheated in the interest of their units (Jones 628). This may account for the demands made on their behalf by the Celtae and the Petulantes (cf. for other possibilities Szidat). In 355 *Dynamius quidam actuarius sarcinalium principis iumentorum* (15.5.3) recieved a governorship as a reward for treachery (15.5.14).

recturi, quas placuisset, provincias mitterentur As a rule, *obsecrare* in Amm. is followed by *ut* (14.7.5, 15.5.10, 30.1.6, 31.4.12), see the notes ad 14.5.7 and 19.11.6 and Szantyr 529–530 on the omission of *ut* after verba orandi. Most often, when the dative with *placet* is not expressed, a decision of the emperor is meant, e.g. in 14.11.1 *acciri ... eundem placuerat* (sc. Constantio) *Gallum,* 19.11.6 *paratique intra spatia orbis Romani, si id placuerit* (sc. Constantio), *terras suscipere longe discretas.* This is also the case in 15.8.3, 16.3.1, 17.12.16, 20.1.2 and 20.4.11. It seems natural, therefore, to translate 'to whichever provinces he (Julian) might choose' rather than "they might choose", as Rolfe does.

quo non impetrato abiere nec offensi nec tristes Julian's rejection of the demands of the Petulantes and the Celtae forms a very effective ending to Amm.'s description of the events surrounding his accession to the throne. On the one hand it shows that Julian is in no way a puppet of the troops that had made him emperor and, on the other, that the soldiers are so devoted to him that they accept this rebuff without resentment or loss of enthusiasm.

Quo/hoc (non) impetrato is used by Amm. in 15.5.3, 15.7.10, 27.7.8, 31.5.7, 31.12.8; with *parum* in 30.2.6. The phrase occurs already in classical authors, see TLL VII 1.599.77 sqq. *Abiere nec offensi nec tristes* recalls the phrase *dolore duplici suspensi discesserunt et maesti* in 20.4.13, after their kind reception by Julian. Now even his refusal of favours is accepted without protest.

V. 10 After the description of the events on a purely human level Amm. ends with the divine justification of Julian's accession to the throne. Here again his reluctance is underlined. The fact that the appearance of the *genius publicus* is told at the end of the account of Julian's elevation does not necessarily mean that Amm. attached little importance to the role played by the gods, as Szidat, following Straub, 1939, 60, thinks. On the contrary, the insistence of the *genius publicus*, which is brought into relief by the use of direct speech, seems calculated to take away the last doubt as to the justification of Julian's action.

As far as literary texts are concerned, the term *genius publicus* is found, apart from Prud. *c. Symm* 2.429/30 *fluctibus his olim fatum geniusve animusve/publicus erravit,* only in Amm. In inscriptions and on coins we find *genius populi Romani.* Szidat I 179 gives literature about the *genius,* to which may be added Camus, 1967, 163, Schilling's article on *Genius* in the *RAC* 10, 52–83, Fontaine's note nr 512 ad 25.2.3, MacCormack, 1975, and the chapter "Le genius populi Romani" in Béranger, 1975, 411–427 and Neri, 1984, 29–34 and 1985, 40–43.

Amm. again introduces a *genius,* in all probability the *Genius Augusti,* on two other momentous occasions, in 21.14.2, where its disappearance is interpreted by Constantius as an *omen mortis*, and in the events leading up to the death of Julian himself (25.2.3). In 23.1.6 Amm. tells us about an offering made by Julian on the first of January in the *Genii templum* at Antioch, an *interpretatio Romana*, as Fontaine calls it in his note ad loc. (nr. 26) of the Τυχεῖον. Although the Genius is already mentioned by Livy, who informs us that sacrifices to him were ordered at the beginning of the Second Punic War (21.62.9), it is only in the literature of the late fourth century that we find more numerous references to this divine power. Servius speaks about the *genius urbis Romae* in his note ad *Aen.* 2.351.

Symmachus in his *rel.* 3.8 says: *ut animae nascentibus ita populis fatales genii dividuntur*. Prudentius combats this view in a long passage of his *contra Symmachum* (2.370–453) culminating in the words *qui nusquam est nec fuit umquam* (2.386). The cult of the *genius* of the family is expressly forbidden in *Cod. Theod.* 16.10.12: *Nullus omnino ... in nulla urbe sensu carentibus simulacris vel insontem victimam caedat vel secretiore piaculo larem igne, mero genium, penates odore veneratus accendat lumina, imponat tura, serta suspendat*.

Julian himself in his *Ep. ad Ath.* 284C mentions divine intervention during the events leading up to his declaration: προσεκύνησα τὸν Δία. γενομένης δὲ ἔτι μείζονος τῆς βοῆς (sc. of the soldiers outside the palace) ... ᾐτεόμην τὸν θεὸν δοῦναι τέρας. αὐτὰρ ὅ γ' ἡμῖν δεῖξε καὶ ἠνώγει πεισθῆναι. Both the moment at which the divine will manifests itself and the form the manifestation takes differ in the two versions. Julian only mentions the τέρας at the time when the soldiers proclaimed him Augustus, in Amm. it is a dream Julian had during the night before. Despite these differences it seems best, pace Neri, 1985, 41, to suppose that Amm. refers to the same revelation as the one Julian hints at in his letter. It is important for an understanding of Amm.'s portrayal of Julian that he presents the event in a thoroughly romanized form, stressing its political rather than its religious importance, in conformity with his general practice in writing about Julian, for which cf. Selem, 1964. Amm.'s version is modelled on Suet. *Gal.* 4.3 *somniavit Fortunam dicentem, stare se ante fores defessam et, nisi ocius reciperetur cuicumque obvio praedae futuram*, followed by Cassius Dio 64.1.2.

Nocte tamen ... iunctioribus proximis rettulerat imperator With *tamen* the narrative is resumed. The abl. temporis *nocte* must be linked with *visum*, not with *rettulerat*, as this would imply that during the night preceding the proclamation Julian had given an unequivocal indication of what was going to happen. This would be totally incompatible with the purport of ch. 4. The occasion on which Julian told his intimate friends about his dream is left unspecified, and the pluperfect *rettulerat* is used instead of the perfect, for which see the notes ad 20.3.3 and 20.4.4. The expression *declaratio Augusta* is found only here. For *declarare* in this sense cf. 21.6.4, 26.2.3. *Iunctioribus proximis* occurs also in the account of the manifestation of the *Genius Augusti* in 21.14.2: *post haec confessus est iunctioribus proximis.*

per quietem aliquem visum The words *per quietem* show that the vision occurred in a dream. Cf. 15.3.5 *si per quietem quisquam, ubi fusius natura vagatur, vidisse aliquid amico narrasset,* 30.5.18 *nocteque quam lux ereptura eum vita secuta est, ut per quietem solet, videbat coniugem suam absentem sedere passis capillis amictu squalenti contectam* and 15.6.2, 19.12.10, 25.10.17, 31.1.3. De Jonge has a note on *quiescere* and *quies* ad 18.2.11. Amm. attaches great importance to *divinatio*, as these passages show. He offers general speculations on the subject of *divinatio* in 21.1.7–14, a digression of which the last three sections are devoted to dreams. See the chapter on *divinatio* in Camus, 1967, 200–222.

ut formari Genius publicus solet I.e. as a young man, holding a *cornucopia* in his left hand and a *patera* in his right. Aurelian had erected a golden statue of the *genius* on the *Rostra* (Platner-Ashby, 1929,247). Representations on coins may be seen in Callu, 1960, who discusses the role of the *genius* on the basis of numismatical and literary fourth-century evidence on pp. 105–112.

haec obiurgando dixisse *Obiurgando* serves as a manner adjunct subordinated to *dixisse*. For this use of the gerund see Vester, 1983, 190 sqq. with lit. Amm. uses *obiurgatorio sonu* in 14.7.12, 15.7.4, 18.8.5 and 30.6.3.

olim, Iuliane, vestibulum aedium tuarum observo latenter For *olim* = *iamdudum* cf. 14.6.6 *et olim licet otiosae sint tribus pacataeque centuriae.* Amm. elaborates on Suetonius' words (*Gal.* 4.3) *stare se ante fores defessam.* For *observare* in this meaning cf. Pl. *As.* 273 *vae illi qui tam indiligenter observavit ianuam.*

augere tuam gestiens dignitatem A very strong expression, for which compare 18.6.20 *remeare ad nostra ardenti desiderio gestiebat.* De Jonge has notes on *gestire* ad 16.10.1 and 17.11.1, TLL VI 1961.46 sqq.

aliquotiens tamquam repudiatus abscessi *Repudiare* with a personal object is found only here in Amm. Elsewhere (27.12.16, 29.5.11, 31.4.13) the objects are requests or orders. See the note ad 17.13.5. A parallel to the present passage is Pac. *trag.* 342 (p. 120 Ribbeck) *te repudio nec recipio: naturam abdico: i, facesse!*

si ne nunc quidem recipior sententia concordante multorum Again based on Suet. *Gal.* 4.3: *nisi ocius reciperetur.* The abl. abs. explains *ne nunc quidem* and is said in anticipation of 4.14 *Augustum Iulianum horrendis clamoribus concrepabant.* For *concordare* cf. 31.4.7 *concordante omni posteritate,* Iust. 5.3.3 *concordante civitate* and Sidon. *epist.* 3.3.1 *concordantibus civium votis.* There is no evidence in the TLL for Agozzino's characterization of the expression as a "tecnicismo giuridico".

ibo demissus et maestus The collocation is found again in 30.1.2 *inter quos erat Terentius dux demisse ambulans semperque submaestus* and in the scene of Julian's death 25.3.15 *circumstantes allocutus est demissos et tristes.* Hagendahl, 1924, 176 points to the influence of Cicero in this and similar instances, cf. Cic. *Sul.* 74 *maerentem demissum adflictumque,* TLL V 493.57 sqq. Agozzino is probably right in explaining these words as a veiled threat that Julian's life, and consequently the well-being of Rome, is in danger, if he refuses to take the purple. When the *genius* finally takes leave of Julian this is described in the following words: *vidit squalidius* ('dimly'), *ut confessus est proximis, speciem illam Genii publici, quam cum ad Augustum surgeret culmen conspexit in Galliis, velata cum capite cornucopia per aulaea tristius discedentem* (25.2.3).

id tamen retineto imo corde, quod tecum non diutius habitabo Agozzino rightly calls attention to the simple, unadorned style of this sermocinatio. For *quod* + verbum sentiendi Agozzino quotes Löfstedt, 1911, 116. See also Szantyr 576. De Jonge has notes on the subject ad 14.7.14 and 14.11.11. For the use of the future imperative see Vairel, 1975, 283–292. *Imo corde* is rather rare. Amm. has it again in 29.5.15 *fessus aerumnis gemini proelii Firmus imoque aestuans corde.* Cf. Verg. *A.* 10.464/5 *sub imo corde*; TLL IV 941.65 sqq.

Chapter 6

The description of the Persian king's successful sieges of Singara and Bezabde occupies the centre of the whole book. As was stated in the Introduction, it forms the hinge of the diptych consisting of chapters 4–5 and 8–9, respectively. Sapor's successes ought to have persuaded Constantius to come to terms with Julian, but, as becomes clear in ch. 8–9, he failed to do so, with all harmful consequences.

In his report of the two sieges Amm. uses many traditional and even stereotyped phrases, but he handles this almost formulaic language with skilful variation.

VI. 1 *Haec dum per Gallias agerentur intente* In many other places Amm. has the classical indic. praes. after *dum* meaning 'while', e.g. *dum haec in oriente aguntur* (14.5.1), *dumque haec aguntur in Galliis* (15.5.17). The use of the coni. imperf. occurs already in Livy: *dum praedae magis quam pugnae memores tererent tempus, triarii Romani ... ad praetorium redeunt* (2.47.5). Its frequency increases in the course of time (cf. Szantyr 613/4) and Amm. too has quite a few instances of the coni. imperf., e.g. *haec dum oriens diu perferret, ... Constantius ... Valentiam petit* (14.10.1, cf. the note ad loc.). But in 'formulaic' phrases, as the present text, the indic. praes. is usual, the only parallel of the coni. imperf. being 24.4.21 *dumque haec luce agerentur ac palam*. The positivus *intente* occurs only here; the comparative is used to express watchfulness in 24.2.12, 24.2.19 and 28.4.34, whereas in 24.8.2 *resistebat intentius princeps* it has the same meaning as in the present case: 'with great energy'. For the final position of *intente* cf. Blomgren 108.

truculentus rex ille Persarum The adj. *truculentus* denotes the outward show of aggressiveness which is horrifying to the senses: *quam taeter incedebat, quam truculentus, quam terribilis aspectu* (Cic. *Sest.* 19), *quo truculentior visu foret* (Tac. *Hist.* 4.22.2), *vocibus truculentis strepere* (Tac. *Ann.* 1.25.2). Such instances can also be found in Amm.: 17.13.8 and 29.1.23 about the human voice, 25.1.14 about an elephant's mouth. But it is also used to characterize rulers: *rursus Armeniam Radamistus invasit, truculentior quam antea* (Tac. *Ann.* 12.50.2); together with *crudelis, dirus, immanis, nefandus* etc. it belongs to the stereotyped picture of a tyrannic emperor (cf. Opelt, 1965, 166/8). In this way it is used by Amm. about Maximinus (14.1.8), Gallus (14.11.8) and Valentinian (28.1.20).

It is not surprising that Sapor, too, is given a negative epithet for in the digression devoted to the Persian empire its rulers are called *reges eiusdem gentis praetumidi* (23.6.5). Sapor II, son of Hormisdas II, became king at a very early age in 309/310. He died in 379. He waged war with Rome from 336 down to 378, with occasional interruptions. See Amm. 17.5.4-6 for the Persian aims as stated by Sapor in a letter to Constantius. Cf. Seeck, 1920; De Jonge ad 14.3.1; *PLRE I*, Sapor II, Lightfoot, 1981, 130-134.

incentivo Antonini adventu Craugasii duplicato   The subst. *incentivum* occurs regularly in later Latin as a synonym of *incitamentum* or *stimulatio* (TLL VII 1.872.79 sqq.). It is an idiosyncrasy of Amm. to portray persons themselves as an *incentivum: cuius acerbitati uxor grave accesserat incentivum* (14.1.2, cf. the note ad loc.), *cuius diritati adiectum erat incentivum exitiale socer Petronius* (26.6.7), cf. also 22.11.5 and 29.3.1; in the other cases it refers to men's actions or words (27.8.10, 31.7.7), as presumably in the present text, although it might be feasible to regard *Antonini* as a gen.explic.: the incentive consisting of (the defection of) Antoninus was doubled by (that of) Craugasius.

As a result of severe financial difficulties, extensively expounded by De Jonge ad 18.5.1, Antoninus (*PLRE I*, Antoninus 4), a former merchant, then a *rationarius apparitor Mesopotamiae ducis* and finally a *protector*, went over to the Persians in 359. He became one of the leading advisers of the Persian king. Craugasius (not in *PLRE I*; cf. Baldwin, 1976, 119), a distinguished citizen of Nisibis, deserted to the Persians at the prompting of his wife who was the captive of Sapor (Amm. 18.10.1-3, with the note, and 19.9.3-8). As an adviser of Sapor he held the second place after Antoninus, *ut ait poeta praeclarus, longo proximus intervallo* (19.9.7).

ardore obtinendae Mesopotamiae flagrans   This use of *ardor* ('eager desire') with a gerundi(v)um-construction is poetical: *quaerendique mihi nominis ardor erat* (Ov. *Tr.* 1.1.54). It is, however, by no means absent in prose: *crescit ardor pugnandi* (Liv. 2.45.9). Amm. also has a few instances: *succrescente paulatim ardore bellandi* (20.11.19), cf. 19.2.9 and 29.5.29. In general, as De Jonge notes ad 17.4.9, 18.2.3 and 18.4.1, Amm. uses the gerundivum-construction sparingly. Unfortunately his work is not part of the corpus on which Aalto's survey of the use of gerundium and gerundivum is based, so that exact statistical data are not available (Aalto, 1949).

For Amm.'s use of *ardor* cf. also Bitter 151 note 472 and see above the note ad 20.4.8.

dum ageret cum exercitu procul Constantius   In this case the subj. is in conformity with classical usage, the temporal clause being part of Sapor's reflections and thus virtual oratio obliqua. Amm. has not put the adverb in final position, for the emphasis is rather on Constantius. The fact that the Roman emperor is at a considerable distance, stimulates the Persian king to action.

When Sapor pushed into Mesopotamia, Constantius was still in Constantinople (not "on the Danube", as Crump, 1975, 50 has it; cf. Szidat I 45). As Crump, 1975, 50 observes, Rome's enemies occasionally timed their attacks to coincide with a temporary weakening of the imperial forces in certain regions.

armis multiplicatis et viribus   For the juxtaposition of *arma* and *vires* cf. Tac. *Dial*. 37.3 *ex his intellegi potest Cn. Pompeium et M. Crassum non viribus modo et armis, sed ingenio quoque et oratione valuisse* with Gudeman's note ad loc. Amm. is rather fond of the combination: *pondere armorum oppressus et virium* (14.10.14), *arma viresque parabat* (18.4.1), further 17.13.27, 18.2.17, 18.9.4.

transmisso sollemniter Tigride   Referring to 18.7.1, Wagner explains *sollemniter* as: "sacris in ponte factis". This explanation is very much open to doubt. The passage referred to (*in medio pontis Anzabae hostiis caesis extisque prosperantibus transiere laetissimi*) evidently concerns a special occasion rather than the usual practice in crossing a river. As De Jonge notes ad 16.12.36, *sollemniter* is a synonym of *ex more*. Therefore it can be used in all contexts where the normal course of events is reported, in the military sphere (16.12.36, 25.1.17, 26.6.12), concerning justice (14.7.21), oaths (21.5.10), proskynesis (15.5.27), and indeed also in religious matters: 21.2.5 *sollemniter numine orato discessit*, 23.6.35 (about the Magi), but in both the lastmentioned cases the religious ceremony is explicitly referred to. In the present text such a meaning is quite improbable; it is far more likely that the 'usual manner' concerns the technique of crossing rivers: *Euphrate navali ponte transmisso* (23.2.7), cf. also 17.1.2 with De Jonge's note and 27.5.6.

oppugnandam adoritur Singaram   The construction of *adoriri* with an inf. is quite normal and occurs very often in Livy, e.g. *castra Servili consulis adorti sunt oppugnare* (2.51.6), but the gerundivum is attested only in Amm.: *alii ferratas portarum obices effringendas adorti* (21.12.13), *oppidum ... quod eruendum adorti* (25.8.5) and the present text.

For Amm.'s treatment of sieges consult Crump, 1975, 97–113, whose conclusion is worth quoting: "Considered as a whole, the historian's treatment of sieges reflects the same interests and emphases found in his narrative of other operations. His desire to entertain as well as to enlighten prompts him to describe siege warfare at some length and also to make those descriptions as dramatic as possible. His reports are frequently a curious blend of colorful generalizations and precise fact. In their most extreme form the florid passages suggest the multiplicity of confused events in a struggle without clarifying the direction which those events are taking. Machines roar, missiles fly, soldiers struggle and fall; but the result of this conflict is not immediately clear. Such sections betoken the literary man's goal of impressing his audience at once with the polished eloquence of his own style and with the heroic grandeur of beleaguering operations. On cursory reading, the effect seems more appropriate to the work of a rhetorician than to that of a historian. But further study of the narratives reveals historical insight as well" (p. 111). See below the relevant notes ad 20.7.15.

Singara, modern Beled-Singar, presented the first major obstacle to the Persians when they sought to invade Roman territory from the Tigris valley to the south-east. Its geographical position is sketched by Amm. in section 9. Add to the passages cited by Szidat ("Ammian erwähnt die Stadt noch 18,5,7 u. 19,2,8"): 18.9.3, 19.9.9, 20.6.9, 20.7.4, 25.7.9 and 25.7.11, and consult, apart from the modern literature given in Szidat, De Jonge ad 18.5.7, Fontaine, 1977, 258 n. 647 and 648 and Lightfoot, 1981, 83–84.

usuique congruis omnibus ... munitam Amm. has a predilection for *congruus*, which occurs once in Plautus (*Mil.* 1116) and after that in Apuleius and later authors. Together with *victu(i)* it occurs in 16.4.4, 16.12.12 (cf. De Jonge's note), 24.5.12, 29.5.15, 31.5.1, with *usui* in 23.2.5 (Bentley's emendation) and 30.3.3; cf. also *omnibus ad usum congruis* (25.1.4). In these cases the meaning of *congruus* has virtually developed from 'fit for, suitable for' to 'necessary for'.

qui regionibus praeerant In the first place the *dux Mesopotamiae* must be meant (cf. *Not. Dign. Or.* 1.47; 36.1). The highest civil official in the province of Mesopotamia was the *praeses* (cf. *Not. Dign. Or.* 1.93).

VI. 2 *propugnatores* This is one of the normal terms to denote the defenders of a besieged town, occurring already in classical Latin prose: *nec prius ille est a propugnatoribus vacuus relictus locus* (Caes. *Gal.* 7.25.4), *deiectisque propugnatoribus occupantur muri* (Liv. 28.19.18). Cf. the note ad 19.2.9.

per turres discurrebant et minas The verb *discurrere* is used quite often by Amm. It can indicate the unruly behaviour of a riotous mob: *plena omnia discurrentis turbae* (19.11.11), but it also occurs as a military t.t. (cf. 16.12.28 and the note ad 16.12.21), either to denote the commander's active omnipresence on the battlefield: *inter confertissima tela me discurrente* (20.5.5, cf. the note ad loc.) or, as here, the energetic action of defenders on the walls of their town: *defensores ultro citroque discurrunt* (24.4.22). In this way it is also used in Caes. *Civ.* 3.105.4: when at Antioch the sounds of an approaching army were heard, this had the following effect: *ut in muris armata civitas discurreret*.

The word *minae* is used only twice by Amm. with its usual meaning 'threats, menaces': *frendendo minas tumidas intentantes* (15.4.9) and 27.2.3. In the other four cases it indicates "something projecting, like *pinnae*, 'battlements'" (Austin ad Verg. *A.* 4.88/9): *celsarum turrium minas* (24.2.19 and 29.6.11), *in qua excellebant minae murorum* (24.2.12). One cannot but agree with Hagendahl's suggestion that, together with the present text, these are reminiscences of Verg. *A.* 4.88/9 *minaeque murorum ingentes* (Hagendahl, 1921, 10, cf. also 25).

tormentaque bellica As De Jonge ad 17.1.12 (cf. his note ad 18.7.6) points out, *tormenta* included several different sorts of machines. A description of some of these *machinae* (this word is sometimes used as a synonym of *tormenta*, cf. e.g. 19.5.2, with the note, and 19.2.8 *tormentorumque machinis*) is given by Amm. in 23.4.1–13. See on this, apart from the literature cited by Szidat, Tomei, 1982.

cunctisque praestructis The verb *praestruere* is more than once used by Amm. with the meaning 'to take precautions, to make preparations', e.g. 21.5.13 *his ... ut poscebat negotii magnitudo, praestructis*, 24.1.1 *praestructis omnibus quae difficultates arduae belli poscebant*. De Jonge has substantial notes on the use of this verb by Amm. and other authors ad 16.6.1 and 16.11.3

parati propellere It is difficult to establish Amm.'s criteria in choosing between *pellere* and its compounds. The simplex occurs more than once in a military sphere: *utque facile defensuri moenia pellerentur* (20.11.20), *primoque conflictu barbarorum pluribus pulsis et interfectis* (29.5.51), 16.12.42, 18.8.9, 23.6.3, 25.1.18, in other cases it concerns expulsion or exile: *ut noxii pellimur et damnati* (20.4.10), 14.6.19, 18.3.1, 19.11.1, 25.9.5, 27.12.4, 28.4.32, 31.4.2, 31.5.17; *propellere* seems to be more appropriate for warfare: *hostem propellere laborabant* (16.12.37), 15.5.4, 16.12.32, 19.5.1, but in 17.7.13 it concerns the effect of earthquakes and in 22.15.11 the course of the Nile. In the present text Amm.'s choice of *propellere* is stimulated by the cursus: *paráti propéllere*.

si moenia subire temptasset The subj. is caused by virtual oratio obliqua, *temptasset* representing the indic. fut. ex. of the oratio recta, according to the rule set forth by Kühner-Stegmann II 2.181/2. The present text is one of those cases where "das Verb des Hauptsatzes zwar kein eigentliches Futur, aber futurischen Sinn enthält", e.g. *utrique mortem est minitatus, nisi sibi hortorum possessione cessissent* (Cic. *Mil.* 75), explained by Poynton ad loc. with the help of a simplified reconstruction of the oratio recta: "moriemini nisi cesseritis". Another example in Amm. is 16.1.1 *colligere provinciae fragmenta iam parans, si affuisset fortuna flatu tandem secundo*, although in that case *tandem* points to the added element of impatience. In the present text there is no such complication; the defenders of Singara thought: 'multitudinem propellemus, si moenia subire temptaverit'.

VI. 3 *per optimates suos propius admissos*   The use of the term *optimates* for the aristocracy of non-Roman peoples occurs already in classical Latin authors such as Cicero (e.g. *Tusc.* 1.108: *in Hyrcania plebs publicos alit canes, optimates domesticos*), Nepos and Livy (e.g. 24.23.10: *crimina serebant in senatum optimatesque* of Syracuse). De Jonge has notes on a similar use in later authors ad 16.12.26 and 17.12.11. The Persian aristocrats were allowed to approach by the defenders of Singara, perhaps even granted an audience; *admittere* occurs in Amm. in two senses: 'to become guilty of': *admissi flagitii metu exagitati* (14.3.4), and 'to grant access': *admissus in consistorium* (16.7.2). Cf. also De Jonge on 19.11.7 (Constantius) *cunctos admisit*: "thus *admittere* is to admit to an audience, *adire* to be given an audience".

pacatiore colloquio flectere defensores   Such attempts by the besieging party are reported more than once by Amm.: Crump, 1975, 101 note 18 and Bitter 19 note 47 list a number of cases. The Persian King has evidently become more prudent than at the start of the siege of Amida, when he rode up to the gates thinking *quod visu statim obsessi omnes metu exanimati supplices venirent in preces* (19.1.4). There are few examples where *pacatus* meaning 'peaceful' is used of words. Livy has a few instances, e.g. *ubi nihil pacati respondebatur* (28.3.5), where in a similar situation it concerns the words of the besieged, *pacatum responsum* (2.26.5). Cf. also Cic. *Brut.* 121.

matutinae lucis exordio   This is one of Amm.'s many expressions for dawn, listed in Hagendahl, 1921, 102/3.

signo per flammeum erecto vexillum   The adi. *flammeus* is used in two ways by Amm.: 1. literally, concerning fire or heat: *casus flammeos* ('the risks of ignition') *pertimescens* (20.7.13), *ut flammeos detrectet et missiles casus* (23.4.11), *miles solis cursu flammeo diu lassatus* (25.1.18), 2. to indicate a colour; about a horseman: *cuius vertici flammeus torulus* ('headband') *aptabatur* (16.12.24), about one of the parts of the rainbow: *ostendit aspectum flammeo propiorem* (20.11.28). The normal colour of the flag which served as a signal for battle, was red, cf. the 'flag' in 19.5.5: *mane sago punici coloris elato, quod erat subeundae indicium pugnae*. Strictly speaking, *flammeus* does not mean 'red' but rather denotes a reddish shade of orange: "*flammeus* est un orange vif, très proche du rouge, étincelant" André, 1949, 115). But, as André also notes, a "glissement de sens" towards 'red' can be ascertained, cf. *externo iam flammea murice cerno / tegmina* (V. Fl. 5.360/1). For *vexillum* in the meaning 'flag' cf. 24.6.5 *sublato vexillo, ut iussum est, evolant e conspectu quinque subito naves*, 27.10.9 *stetit regibilis miles, vexillum opperiens extollendum, quod erat opportune subeundae indicium pugnae* and in general Dennis, 1982.

circumvaditur civitas This is the only instance of this rare verb in Amm. The other cases, four of which can be found in Livy, never concern the encircling of a town, the nearest parallel being *immobiles naves et loca ignota plus quam hostem timentes circumvadunt* (10.2.12).

vehentibus scalis cf. 20.7.6 (with note) and 20.11.21. Attempts to scale the walls had only a remote chance of success. Cf. Crump, 1975, 109-110.

obiectu vinearum pluteorumque tectis For *vineae* and *plutei* cf. De Jonge's substantial note on 19.5.1; *obiectus*, "the act of placing something in the way of something else" (OLD) is normal already in classical Latin. Szidat refers to Caes. *Civ.* 2.15.3 *plutei obiectu* (where *obiectu* is an emendation of *obiecto*).

ad fundamenta parietum ... subvertenda The normal meaning of *paries* is 'wall of a house or building', which is especially proved by the proverbial expressions gathered by Otto, 1890, 265/6, among which a phrase in Amm.: *ideoque etiam parietes arcanorum soli conscii timebantur* (14.1.7). Other passages in Amm. where *paries* has this sense are 22.8.34 (of a temple), 22.15.30 (of caverns), 27.9.10, 28.4.12 (of private houses), 29.5.54 (not specified). But in other cases, 20.11.10, 21.12.6, 23.4.13, 31.6.4, there cannot be any doubt that the walls of a town are meant. In one case this is made explicit, when a multitude of soldiers (*numerus magnus*) is said to be *affixus parietibus moenium aedibusque continuis* (31.15.4): *moenium* must clearly be a gen. expl. But perhaps the last-mentioned text explains this equalization of *parietes* and *moenia* as caused by the presence of buildings bordering directly upon the town-walls.

Efforts to undermine a city's fortifications usually failed because artillery fire drove the sappers away despite their attempts to protect themselves behind *vineae* and *plutei* (cf. 20.11.8, 21.12.6). In 24.4.21, on the other hand, Amm. provides some information concerning the successful effort to undermine the foundations of Maiozamalcha. Cf. Crump, 1975, 109.

VI. 4 *superstantes propugnaculis celsis* The verb *superstare*, which implies a relatively high position, preponderantly occurs in military situations, by far the most usual form being the part. praes. Livy uses the word 10 times, in 6 cases in combination with *armatus*. The position can be on top of a wall during a siege: *neque illos muri neque superstantes armati arcere queunt* (Livy 26.44.9), even on the ruins of a wall: *armati ruinis superstantes instar munimenti erant* (Livy 38.7.5), or, in a city guerilla, any high object: *superstantes maceriis hortorum Vitelliani ... subeuntes arcebant* (Tac. *Hist.* 3.82.3). Often a *turris* is concerned: Livy 32.17.17, 37.40.4 (on the back of elephants), Tac. *Hist.* 4.30.1, Amm. 20.7.13, 21.12.10; Amm.'s only other instance concerns a *tribunal* (20.9.6).

For *propugnaculum*, 'rampart, bulwark', see De Jonge ad 16.4.2 and Rebuffat, 1984.

lapidibus eminus telorumque genere omni Szidat may well be right in assuming that Amm. means artillery here. But this is not proved, as he supposes, by the occurrence of *eminus*. It is true that *eminus* is used in such cases: *eminus confixi tormentis* (21.12.10), but in other situations it is used about arrows and other missiles: *visos eminus barbaros Romani sagittis aliisque levibus iaculis incessebant* (27.1.3), *missilibus obvios eminus lacessens* (14.2.5).

ad interiora ferocius se proripientes arcebant The first five words are interpreted by Wagner as meaning "muris audacius appropinquantes hostes". Amm. uses *interiora* to indicate the remote parts of a country (24.2.1, 24.7.6, cf. Liv. 42.39.1 *Perseus in interiora regni recepit se*), the centre of enemy's ranks (24.6.11) and the interior of a city (27.12.6). None of these instances is exactly paralleled by the present text, but on the basis of the general meaning which can be gathered from the various cases, viz. 'the inner part of a certain territory', here the sense could be that the Persians surged forward to the immediate neighbourhood of the walls. So Wagner's paraphrase seems quite correct. At the same time Valesius' emendation of a phrase in 14.2.18 is corroborated: the defenders of Seleucia took up their positions on the walls with stones and missiles at hand, *ut si qui se proripuisset interius* (*terius* V, *citerius* Gronovius), *multitudine missilium sterneretur et lapidum*.

The use of the tenses of the main verbs in the sections 3 and 4 is completely in accordance with classical rules: the perf. hist. *dedit* and the praes. hist. *circumvaditur* (the use of the praes. is furthered by Amm.'s dislike of the perf. pass., which in this case is unlikely, if not impossible) indicate two successive events, the imp. *arcebant* sketches the ensuing situation.

VI. 5 *diebus aliquot* The abl. of duration occurs already with some frequency in classical Latin, cf. the examples provided by Kühner-Stegmann II 1.360/1.

"Der erste Schriftsteller, der den durativen Abl. in grösserem Umfang verwendet, ist Caesar (B.Civ.), dann Prop., Ov. und die Prosaiker seit der Zeit des Tiberius" (Löfstedt, 1933, II 448, who should also have mentioned Livy). Amm. has the abl. a few times, e.g. *orabant haruspices saltem aliquot horis profectionem differri* (25.2.8), but the acc. with or without *per* is more frequent, e.g. *ibi moratus aliquot dies* (23.3.2), *per quinque dies et noctes* (17.7.8).

hinc inde This asyndeton does not occur before Seneca and Tacitus. Amm. has a great liking for it, as TLL VI 2805.38/9 notes very briefly "14.9.3 et saepe", using it more than 15 times. The usual meaning is 'on (from) either (every) side'.

fervente certaminum mole Exactly the same expression is used in 25.1.18. Amm. uses *moles* in various ways: literally, to indicate size or quantity of concreta: *moles saxeae* (19.2.7, 'enormous stones'), *moles excitabantur altissimae* (19.6.6, about earthworks), figuratively for the weight of problems and dangers: 14.11.9 *inter has curarum moles immensas*, cf. Tac. *Ann.* 12.66.1 *in tanta mole curarum;* 19.6.9 *cum unum in locum totam periculi molem conversam ... advertissent*, cf. Livy 27.40.6 *et unum in locum totam periculi molem, omne onus incubuisse.* Such a meaning does not fit the present text, where *moles* rather denotes difficulty and exertion. It is paralleled by 27.10.14 *haud parva mole certatum est*, which is a Tacitean reminiscence: *haud parva mole certatum* (*Hist.* 3.77.4). This meaning tallies with *fervente*, the verb *fervere* being used "de rebus quae studiose aguntur" (TLL VI 592.63 sqq.), as in Amm. 18.6.8 *speculatores apparatus omnes apud hostes fervere ... affirmabant,* 31.15.5 *fervente itaque tot malorum congerie;* cf. also 24.4.20.

In all probability *mole certaminum* has to be explained as a case of gen. inversus, so that the phrase commented upon can be rendered by 'when laborious fights were in full progress'.

propinquante iam vespera An abl. abs. with *vespera* as subj. to denote the time of day is used in seven other cases by Amm.: *incedente* (24.1.6, 31.11.4), *ingruente* (19.7.5), *propinquante* (26.2.1, 27.2.6) and *tenebrante* (19.8.5, 25.8.18). In the present text the indication of time is by no means otiose: it is remarkable that after some days of intense fighting the battering-ram is introduced only at dusk.

admotus aries robustissimus Remarkably enough, this is the first time Amm. mentions the use of a battering-ram (cf. Crump, 1975, 105/6). Concerning the overall construction of the sentence, it should be noted that the bringing in of the ram, which might have been regarded as a decisive event, is subordinated to *feriebat* by way of the participial construction. In fact, one would rather have expected *aries admotus est, qui feriebat*. But Amm. obviously prefers a series of main verbs in the imp. (*pugnabatur ... feriebat ... dimicabatur ... convolabant*) sketching the background for the final event *vicit* (6).

The *aries* is one of the machines discussed by Amm. in his excursus in 23.4.1-13 (cf. the note ad *tormentaque bellica* in 20.6.2). The others are the *ballista*, the *scorpio* or *onager* and the *helepolis*.

orbiculatam turrim feriebat   The adi. is a rarity. Half of the instances listed in TLL IX 2. 905.48-74 concern a type of apple which was regarded as a luxury: *malis orbiculatis esse pasti videntur* (Cic. *Fam.* 8.15.1). The two other cases in Amm. denote the form of a row of shields (24.8.7) and of a circle of carts (31.2.18). The last-mentioned phrase proves that *orbiculatus* is purely a synonym of *rotundus* and *teres*, which adjectives are used in a similar expression in 31.7.5 and 31.15.5, respectively. The round form of a *turris*, occurring only here in Amm., is known from a number of places. Lander, 1984 distinguishes three sub-divisions and reckons the Singara-type among "those referred to as 'U-shaped', in which two parallel walls project from the outer face of the curtain and are joined at the other end by a complete half-circle" (p. 217; see for Singara p. 226 and fig. 238 on p. 227). Once a specific position is mentioned: *angularem turrim* (24.2.12) and in four cases the height is stressed: 19.5.4, 24.2.19, 24.4.19, 29.6.11.

unde reseratam urbem obsidio superiore docuimus   The verb *reserare* indicates the opening of the gates or entrances of a city: *reseratisque portis egressi* (20.7.3), *reserata latenter postica* (20.11.22), *civitatis aditu reserato* (27.12.8), but it can also be used of the conquest of a besieged city: *indicabat autem Coloniam Agrippinam ... pertinaci barbarorum obsidione reseratam magnis viribus et deletam* (15.8.19), *hoc Marte Cyzico reserata* (26.8.11), cf. also 26.10.4. There are no earlier examples for this, for in Verg. *A.* 12.584 *urbem alii reserare iubent* it is an action of the inhabitants themselves. The closest parallel is Tac. *Hist.* 3.2.4 *iam reseratam ... Italiam, impulsas Vitellii res audietis* (Heubner ad loc. refers to Cic. *Phil.* 7.2, which, however, should rather be compared with Verg. *A.* 12.584 just quoted).

Michael, 1880, 6 note 1 mentions this sentence as one of Amm.'s references to lost books not figuring in the relevant list in Gardthausen's edition (vol. 1, Leipzig 1874, 1-4). Szidat ("Es ist nicht auszumachen, auf welche Eroberung Singaras Ammians Bemerkung Bezug nimmt") is, rightly, more circumspect than Rolfe ("it happened in 348") as to the date of the event in question.

VI. 6 *ad quam conversa plebe dimicabatur artissime*   Amm. uses *plebs* to denote various large groups: 1. the common people of Rome: *nunc ad otiosam plebem* *veniamus et desidem* (28.4.28), cf. 14.6.26, 19.10.2, 27.3.8, also in a historical sense: *cum proscriptorum locupletes domus diripiendas Romanae plebei Marius dedisset et Cinna* (30.8.9), 2. a foreign nation: *Vadomarii plebs* (16.12.17, cf. De Jonge's note), 3. the flock of a bishop: *dissidentes Christianorum antistites cum plebe discissa* (22.5.3); this tallies with Christian usage, cf. Cypr. *ep.* 50.2 *successorem plebi cui antea praefuerat Zetum in locum eius* (a schismatic bishop) *episcopum esse constitutum*, 4. the mass of common soldiers, especially of non-Roman peoples: *ex arce innumeram cernimus plebem* (19.6.1), *ululante barbara plebe ferum et triste* (31.12.11), 16.2.9 with De Jonge's note, 25.6.3, 31.5.5, but once of Roman soldiers: *concrepantibus centuriis et manipulis cohortiumque omnium plebe* (26.2.3). This use of *pleb(e)s* is hardly paralleled: *plebes omissis armis per agros palatur* (Tac. *Hist.* 4.70.4), *castrorum in plebe merebat* (Luc. 6.144, interpreted by Housman ad loc. as "ante gregarius"). Presumably in the present text Amm. means both masses of soldiers, attackers and defenders, for the fighting went on *artissime*: 'in a very narrow space'. Bitter 151 note 471 refers to Sal. *Iug.* 68.4 *quam artissume ire*.

facesque cum taedis ardentibus et malleolis   As this is the only occurrence of *taeda* in Amm., it is not possible to define the difference with *fax*, unless it concerns the material, for a *taeda* strictly speaking consists of pinewood; *faces* are mentioned together with *malleoli* in 20.7.10, 24.4.16 and 27.3.8. The *malleolus*, which in this specific sense is called a "telum incendiarium" in TLL and a "fire-dart" in OLD, is mentioned a few times in classical Latin, e.g. Cic. *Cat.* 1.32 *desinant ... malleolos et faces ad inflammandam urbem comparare*. A vague description is provided in Veg. *mil.* 4.18, and a much more detailed one in Amm. 23.4.14, which is thoroughly discussed by Brok, 1975, 1976 and 1978.

ad exurendum imminens malum undique convolabant   Seyfarth correctly renders *imminens malum* by "das drohende Ungeheuer"; *malum* is used as a synonym of *monstrum* to denote dangerous beasts more than once by Pliny in the *Naturalis Historia* and by Seneca in his tragedies: *saeva Lernae monstra, numerosum malum* (*Herc. F.* 241), *totiens uno latrante malo* (*Med.* 354, about Scylla), cf. Amm. 22.15.15 about the crocodile: *exitiale quadrupes malum*, a phrase which seems ultimately to derive from Plin. *Nat.* 8.89 *crocodilum habet Nilus, quadrupes malum*, presumably via Solinus 32.22 *crocodilus malum quadrupes*. *Imminens* could be interpreted as 'overhanging', but with this sense *imminere* is rather used about hills, mountains or large buildings; it is better to explain it as referring to the threatening nearness of the *aries*, which is pressing closely, cf. *mater dum imminentium hostium terrore percita fugeret* (18.6.10) and especially Liv. 21.7.7 *turris ingens imminebat*. It is an idiosyncrasy of Amm. to use *convolare* "de rebus" (TLL IV 888.28.32), which in five cases are missiles and once (23.5.14) flames. Only once (17.13.22) it concerns people.

nec sagittarum crebritate nec glandis hinc inde cessante This has the character of a topos; perhaps its strongest expression is 19.2.8 *sagittarum creberrima nube auras spissa multitudine obumbrante* (cf. the note ad loc.); in other cases Amm. likes to use *crebritas*: 16.12.43 *iaculorum*, 20.11.12 *lapidum atque fundarum*, 20.11.21 *missilium*, 19.6.9 and 25.3.11 *sagittarum*, 19.7.8 *telorum*. Concerning *glandis* it should be noted that normally the collectively used singular denotes the acorn, whilst in the case of the missiles the plural is usual. TLL VI 2031.16-35, however, lists a number of deviations from this rule, e.g. Liv. 38.21.7 *sagittis glande iaculis incauti ab omni parte configebantur*. Other cases in Amm. are 24.2.15, 31.7.14. Hagendahl, 1921, 114 suggests that the inconcinnitas of plural and singular, a phenomenon which occurs quite often in Amm. (cf. the list on pages 113/4), is here due to the rarity of the gen. plur. *glandium*. *Glandes*, normally made of lead, were often labeled with an appropriate inscription. Cf. Kromayer-Veith, 1928, 410 and fig. 125. For *hinc inde* see above ad 20.6.5.

omne prohibendi commentum Amm. has the word *commentum* ('device', 'design', 'strategy' etc.) more than 15 times, in one other place with the gen. of the gerundium: against burning naphtha *nullum inveniet humana mens praeter pulverem exstinguendi commentum* (23.6.16).

coagmenta fodiens lapidum recens structorum madoreque etiamtum infirmium So the opinion of the local authorities about Singara's means of defence (*ut existimavere*, above in section 1) was too optimistic.

The expression *coagmenta fodiens lapidum* is repeated in 20.7.13; the *coagmenta* are the joints between the stones, which are the potential weak spots in walls. Usually the direct object of *struere* in its literal sense is a structure which is the result of the action: a town (18.9.1), walls (23.6.23), roads (15.10.7), a bridge (18.2.14, 27.3.9), a tribunal (26.2.2) etc. The present text is the only instance in Amm. where the building materials are meant and *struere* means 'to arrange', 'to pile up', cf. Caes. *Civ.* 2.10.4 *lateres qui super musculo struantur*.

The words *madore etiamtum infirmium* prompted Valesius to refer to 30.1.10 *infirmati periculoso madore*, which, however, concerns a completely different situation, viz. the crossing of a river. Much more to the point is his reference to Sal. *Hist.* 4.16 *quasi par in oppido festinatio et ingens terror erat, ne ex latere nova munimenta madore infirmarentur*. In the present text the congruence of the adj. *infirmium* with *lapidum* poses a problem: *lapis* does not mean 'brick', for which the normal Latin word is *later(culus)*, cf. Amm. 24.2.12 *minae murorum bitumine et coctilibus laterculis fabricatae*, cf. also *latericios aggeres* (23.4.5). As it is not possible to imagine stones being weak through moisture the expression calls for a different explanation. It is either a case of enallage, so that *infirmium* in reality qualifies the *coagmenta* rather than the stones, or *lapides structi* should be explained as 'the stone constructions (of the walls)'. Also in the latter case, of course, the weakness lies in the open spaces between the stones, which had been filled with mud and other materials which still were wet.

VI. 7 *ferro certatur et ignibus* The combination of *ferrum* and *ignis* or – less frequently – *flamma* or *incendium* occurs often in descriptions of warfare. Livy provides many instances, e.g. *ferro ignique vastantem agros legati ... adeunt* (8.1.7), *omnia ferro flammaque miscet* (1.29.2). Usually the predicate is a verb denoting devastation and ravage, as in Amm. 24.4.30 *ita omnibus ferro incendioque consumptis*. The inconcinnitas of singular and plural (cf. Hagendahl, 1921, 113) is paralleled by *ferro violarent et flammis* (17.1.4), cf. also Tac. *Ann.* 1.51.1 *quinquaginta milium spatium ferro flammisque pervastat*.

cum patuisset iter in urbem For this expression cf. Liv. 21.28.4 (Galli) *qua patere visum maxime iter, perrumpunt*, Tac. *Hist.* 3.68.3 *interclusum aliud iter, idque solum quo in sacram viam pergeret patebat*. The verb *pate(sce)re* is also used in an objective, purely geographic sense: *iter longissimum patet, mercatoribus pervium* (23.6.60), *Succorum patescunt angustiae* (27.4.5).

periculi ... magnitudo An instance of genitivus inversus, like *undarum magnitudo* (14.2.15, 22.8.30), *moenium Augustoduni magnitudo vetusta* (15.11.11), *magnitudo furentium incubuit procellarum* (17.7.3, pace De Jonge, who regards *magnitudo* as a synonym of *multitudo*), *quos ... dolorum absumpserat magnitudo* (27.2.8), *magnitudine iacturarum Pamphyliam afflictabant et Cilicas* (27.9.6), *praesidiorum magnitudine communitus* (29.5.34), *caedibus incendiorumque magnitudine cuncta flagrabant* (31.6.7).

ululabili clamore sublato The same expression occurs in 24.1.7. The verb *ululare* and its cognate nouns are regularly used to denote the war-cries of non-Roman nations: *tum vero suo more victoriam conclamant atque ululatum tollunt* (Caes. *Gal.* 5.37.3), *Galli occursant in ripa cum variis ululatibus cantuque moris sui* (Liv. 21.28.1), *atque, ut mos est, ululante barbara plebe ferum et triste* (Amm. 31.12.11). Other instances in Amm. are 14.2.5, 16.11.8, 19.5.5 (see De Jonge's note), 19.11.10, 20.7.14, 28.5.6. Cf. also Bitter 139–140.

cuncta oppidi membra complebant Commenting on Prop. 3.2.6 (*saxa*) *sponte sua in muri membra coisse ferunt* W.A. Camps notes about *membra*: "used of various kinds of component parts, e.g. the rooms of a house or timbers of a ship". This laconic statement seems to do less than justice to Propertius' remarkable phrase, which can be regarded as an example of the further development of the figurative use of *membrum*. Cicero and Lucretius use this word to denote the parts of the kosmos: Lucr. 5.244 and 381, Cic. *N.D.* 1.100 and 2.86 (cf. Pease's notes). Amm. seems to be the first author to use the term about the state: *rei publicae membra totius* (15.3.3 and 18.5.1), the walls of a town (not in the same way as Propertius, however): *docuerat quae moenium appeteret membra* (20.7.9) and, several times, to denote the parts of a town: *urbis* (15.7.5, 16.10.14), *civitatis* (25.9.5, 27.3.7, 29.6.18). In these cases *membrum* is obviously no more than a synonym of *pars*. Cf. the note ad 15.7.5.

Although the imperf. *complebant* may very well have been chosen to sketch the background for the events reported in what follows, viz. the slaughtering and capturing of the inhabitants, it should be noted that *mémbra complevérunt* does not produce a regular cursus.

caesisque promisce paucissimis Commenting on what happened after the fall of Amida (19.8.4 *pecorum ritu armati et imbelles sine sexus discrimine truncabantur*), Bitter 53 note 159 lists a number of verbs (*sternere, truncare* etc.) and expressions (*ut pecora, sine aetatis ullo discrimine* etc.) used by Amm. in similar situations. In the present text the indiscriminate slaughter is limited: the victims are 'very few'. Amm.'s other instances of this superlat. prove that it should be taken literally: in 17.5.15, 30.5.16, 31.11.1 it is used about days, 21.14.3 notes that only a very small number of men have actually seen a *genius*, in 23.6.1 it is said that *paucissimi* have provided a reliable geographic description of Persia and finally, 24.3.1 reports the losses sustained during an enemy attack.

residui omnes For Amm.'s use of *residuus* cf. the note ad 20.4.6.

ad regiones Persidis ultimas sunt asportati For *Persis* cf. the notes ad 14.8.5 and 16.10.16. In the long geographical digression about the provinces of Persia (23.6) Amm. uses both genitives: *Persidis* (1, 22, 23) and *Persidos* (27, 36, 73). The verb *asportare* with the meaning 'to deport' occurs a few times in Livy, e.g. *omnia passim mulierum puerorumque qui rapiuntur atque asportantur ploratibus sonant* (29.17.16). Cf. also Amm. 17.2.4 *cum captos comperisset et asportatos*. The subsequent fate of the defenders of Singara is not known. Szidat, who follows Christensen, may be right in assuming that the Sassanid kings had always been prone to take advantage of the technical superiority of captured Romans and that for this reason the garrison of Singara was led away. Another theory has been put forward by Müller, 1905, 577 and, in his wake, by Hoffmann I 236. They suggest that the captives were ransomed after the peace treaty of 363 and were afterwards used to reinforce the legions to which they formerly belonged (these legions still existed in the time the *Not.Dign.* was written; cf. the note on *prima Flavia primaque Parthica* in the next section).

VI. 8 *Tuebantur autem hanc civitatem* At first sight one would have expected a pluperfect, as the story of the siege and capture of Singara was wound up in section 7 and this phrase refers to a situation before these events. Sections 8 and 9, however, should not be regarded as a continuation but as a retrospect, at the beginning of which some information about the defence forces is supplied in the usual tense, viz. the imperf. This status of sections 8 and 9 is also illustrated by the use of parenthetical *autem* (cf. Szantyr 473).

prima Flavia primaque Parthica These legions had been created by Constantine and Septimius Severus, respectively (cf. Hoffmann I 236 and 413-414). The First Flavian, according to Hoffmann, 236-237 to be identified with the *I Flavia Gemina* of *Not. Dign. Or.* 8.40 and not with the *I Flavia Constantia* of *Not. Dign. Or.* 7.44 (as Müller, 1905, 577 would have it), apparently was sent to Singara some time before the Persian attack to assist the First Parthian which was normally alone responsible for the defense of the town (so Hoffmann, 237 and 414 contra Ensslin, 1942, 60; Lightfoot, 1981, 74 however regards the First Flavian as the permanent garrison of Singara). The First Parthian should be identified with the *I Parthica Nisibena* of *Not.Dign. Or.* 36.29.

indigenae plures For *indigenae* cf. De Jonge ad 17.12.18 and especially 18.9.3. The meaning 'very many', which *plures* has here, is paralleled in earlier literature, e.g. Plin. *Ep.* 5.3.11 (about friends) *quos plures habere multis gloriosum* and the expression *pluribus verbis*, 'at great length' (Cic. *Clu.* 53, *Ver.* 1.135, *Rab. Perd.* 7). Cf also Krebs-Schmalz II 311 s.v. *plures*.

cum auxilio equitum For *auxilium* cf. ad 17.1.13 and 19.3.1.

illic ob repentinum malum clausorum The last two words are Clark's emendation of V's *ad inclusorum* (the early editions have *malum inclusorum*). There have also been some attempts to extend *ad* into a substantive (*aditum, adsultum, adventum hostium*), but Clark's proposal is more plausible, in view of *malo repentino* in 15.4.7 and 30.7.10 and Amm.'s regular use of *claudere* in the meaning 'to blockade, to besiege', e.g. *(aries) clausorum hebetaverat mentes* (20.11.11). Baehrens, 1925, 47 also agrees on account of the resulting cursus. As it stands, the phrase is somewhat elliptic: Amm. presumably wants to say that these horsemen took refuge in Singara 'because of the sudden disaster' (viz. the attack by Sapor) and then were 'blockaded'.

vinctis manibus ducebantur In the sphere of arrest and captivity the verb *ducere* can be used absolutely without the mention of the particular goal: *Mens Bona ducetur manibus post terga retortis* (Ov. *Am.* 1.2.31, in a *triumphus*), *vinctae pone tergum manus; laniata veste, foedum spectaculum, ducebatur* (Tac. *Hist.* 3.84.5, Vitellius to his execution), *et ducebatur intrepidus* (Amm. 14.9.6, the Edessan orator Eusebius to his execution), *post terga vinctis manibus ducebantur* (19.9.2, Roman officers after the fall of Amida). In the present case the deportation to the outlying districts of Persia is meant.

As the imperf. *ducebantur* refers to *sunt asportati* in the narrative proper, *ducti sunt*, which would have resulted in a normal cursus in this colon, would have been more likely. As has been noted before (e.g. De Jonge ad 19.10.1, above ad 20.4.4), Amm. uses the perf. pass. very sparingly, in the case of *ducere* only four times: *ductus est* (14.7.20, 19.12.9, 30.6.3), *ducti sunt* (31.4.11).

VI. 9 *Nisibin* For Nisibis in Mesopotamia (a town of the same name in the Persian province of Aria is mentioned in 23.6.69) see the notes ad 14.9.1 and 18.6.8. See also Szidat and Fontaine's notes 675 and 680–688 ad ch. 8 and 9 of book 25.

sub pellibus agens These soldiers were staying 'in tents'; the expression occurs in earlier authors: *sub pellibus hiemare constituit* (Caes. *Civ.* 3.13.5), *sub pellibus haberi coepti sunt* (Liv. 23.18.15), *retentusque omnis exercitus sub pellibus, quamvis hieme saeva* (Tac. *Ann.* 13.35.3). The first and third of these quotations show that during the winter season the expression contrasts rather sharply with a normal sojourn *in hibernis.* Cf. Amm. 19.11.4 with the note, 23.3.8 and 25.2.3.

intervallo perquam longo The adverb ('exceedingly'), which is used rather sparingly by earlier authors (e.g. twice by Livy, three times by Tacitus) has gained a greater frequency in Amm., who uses it more than 20 times. Cf. the notes ad 15.2.4 and 18.2.2. As Seyfarth, 1983[5], 197 n. 56 points out, it was not so much the distance between Nisibis and Singara, amounting to about 120 kilometres, which made it difficult to aid Singara in time of trouble, but rather the configuration of the geography mentioned in the next sentence.

alioqui As in the other four cases in Amm. (14.10.4, 15.3.10, 16.12.29 with De Jonge's note, 21.13.2) the adverb here means 'moreover', 'besides'. In the present case it turns the retrospect into a short digression about Singara's difficult geographical position in general.

temporibus priscis Amm. uses this indication in other digressions to denote days long past: 15.11.1, 22.16.1, 23.6.23, 25.9.11; cf. also 28.5.11.

licet Amm. is very fond of this word. He uses it more than 25 times with the classical subj., a little less frequently with the indic., which is a normal phenomenon in late Latin, and on a vast scale to give a concessive force to an adj., subst. or partic. Cf. Ehrismann 62-64, Szantyr 605 and the notes ad 14.1.5, 14.6.6, 14.11.6 and 16.10.11.

locavit antiquitas Cf. *docente antiquitate* (21.13.13), *ut antiquitas docet* (27.4.4), (provincias) *quas Venetas appellabat antiquitas* (31.16.7). This personification is not mentioned by Blomgren in the relevant chapter of his study (p. 83 sqq.). It occurs already in classical Latin: *errabat enim multis in rebus antiquitas* (Cic. *Div.* 2.70). Cf. also Cic. *Leg.* 2.27, *Tusc.* 1.26 and the note ad 17.2.1.

dispendio tamen fuit rei Romanae The word *dispendium*, which originally meant 'expenses' in the purely financial sense, later had a more general meaning: 'losses, injury, harm etc. to life and goods'. It does not occur in classical prose, but is used quite frequently by Symm. and Amm. The latter's instances concern losses sustained during military operations, e.g. 17.13.28 *absque nostrorum dispendio*, ib. *post aerumnosa dispendia*, harm done by dishonesty, e.g. 30.1.2 *dispendiis saepe communibus pasti*, damage incurred due to raids, e.g. 27.12.2 *nationem ... dispendiis levibus afflictabat*. Losses to the Roman state are meant in 26.5.6 *omnisque hic annus dispendiis gravibus rem Romanam afflixit*, and also in 17.1.14 and 29.4.6. The present text also belongs to that category. Cf. also the note ad 16.12.41.

aliquotiens interceptum The adverb, which does not occur in Caes. or Tac., once in Sal. and 17 times in Livy, is a great favourite of Amm., who uses it nearly 90 times, usually "fere eadem vi qua *saepe*" (TLL I 1617.45/6). The verb *intercipere*, which originally implied that a person (or a thing) was prevented from reaching his destination (*per insidias intercepti duo quaestores Romani* (Liv. 21.59.10), *intercepti centum equites* (Tac. *Hist.* 2.17.2), *interceptas litteras* (Liv. 24.31.6), *interceptis Antei litteris* (Tac. *Ann.* 16.14.2)), acquired various other meanings already in classical Latin, e.g. 'to occupy': *Sardiniam ... fraude Romanorum ... interceptam* (Liv. 21.1.5). It should be noted that in such cases (e.g. Liv. 26.51.12, 36.31.10) a fraudulent action brings about the occupation. In Amm. this corollary is no longer present: *interceptis castellis aliis vilioribus* (20.7.17), *locisque recuperatis, quae olim barbari intercepta retinebant ut propria* (20.10.3).

"How many times Singara fell to the Persians is uncertain" (Lightfoot, 1981, 83, discussing the available evidence, i.e., apart from Amm., Ruf.Fest. 27).

Chapter 7

VII. 1 *Exciso itaque oppido* For the destruction of cities Amm. uses forms belonging to *ex(s)cindere* and to *excidere*. The TLL distinguishes as follows (V 2.1240.34) "formas stirpis perf., ubicumque vi 'delendi' in prosa orat. leguntur, quominus ab -scindere derives, per se vix impediaris ..., quamvis hic illic dubites, de utro verbo agatur ..., praesertim in Amm. qui 25ies -sus, numquam -ssus praebeat, sed in praes. nonnisi -scindere uti videatur". It seems probable that Amm. considered these forms to belong to the same verb. For *excidium*, which is a derivative of *ex(s)cindere*, see the note ad 19.9.2.

Nisibin prudenti consilio vitans Concerning Nisibis see the note ad 20.6.9 and Fontaine's notes 647, 675 and 680-688 in his commentary on books 23-25.
In 19.9.9 Amm. had already mentioned the heavy losses incurred by Sapor at Nisibis. During the campaign of 359 Sapor and his vassal kings had also by-passed it: 18.7.8 *reges Nisibi pro statione vili transmissa*. Amm. has many ablatives of manner with *consilio*, e.g. 25.8.11 and 27.12.17 (*prudenti*), 14.11.4 (*concordi*), 21.8.3 (*sollerti*), 31.8.5 (*non absurdo*). *Consilium prudens* is found already in Cicero (*Att.* 10.8.2), quoted in the note ad 17.9.2.

memor ... quae saepius ibi pertulerat Sapor made three attempts to capture Nisibis, in 337, 346 and 350, all without success. Cf. Ruf. Fest. 27: *ter autem a Persis est obsessa Nisibis*, with Eadie, 1967, 149-151; see also Lightfoot, 1981, 92-103. Cf. the note ad 14.9.1.

dextrum latus itineribus petit obliquis Instead of taking the route to the central parts of Mesopotamia, Sapor went to the North, as can be seen on the map in Dillemann, 1962, 149. A very similar description of the king's line of march is given in 18.10.1 *a Bebase loco itinere flexo dextrorsus ... ut transiturus Amidam*. *Obliquus* "at an angle to the general direction" (OLD 3) is well illustrated by 25.8.2 *undarum occursantium fluctus obliquis meatibus penetrabant*. Cf. also 16.2.10 *tramite -o* and 29.5.50 *per tramites ... -os*. Expressions like these are found already in Caesar, e.g. *Civ.* 1.70.5 *-o itinere*, and Livy, e.g. 5.16.5 *-is tramitibus*; 41.2.2 *-is itineribus*.

Bezabden, quam Phaenicham quoque ... appellarunt ... retenturus As Dillemann, 1962, 84 explains, Amm. is mistaken in identifying Bezabde and Phaenicha (the latter town is called Pinaka by Strabo in 16.1.24 and described as κράτιστον ἔρυμα, which Amm. has followed in the present text: *munimentum impendio validum*), but, though most scholars assume that Bezabde stood on the same site as Jazirat Ibn-Omar, mod. Cizre, "the exact location ... has not been satisfactorily identified" (Lightfoot, 1983, 190). Lightfoot himself, however, who visited the area in 1980 believes to have found the site on the west bank of the Tigris, opposite Jazirat.

In 20.11 Amm. relates how Constantius tried in vain to recapture Bezabde. After Julian's death, the region of Zabdicene, of which Bezabde was the capital (beth = house, cf. Sozom. 2.13 Ζαβδαῖον χωρίον and see Fraenkel, 1899), was ceded to the Persians by Jovian (25.7.9). For that reason Amm. adds *tunc nobis obtemperantium* at the end of this section.

As Crump, 1975, 72 observes, Amm.'s description of the Persian (20.7) and Roman (20.11) attacks on Bezabde is largely limited to the beleaguering operations themselves. The same holds good for the siege of Singara described in 20.6. In contrast, relating the events leading to the fall of Amida in bks. 18 and 19, Amm. not only devotes eight chapters to the siege proper, but also five chapters to the maneuvering preliminary to the investment of the city. The reason for this difference is obvious. The loss of Bezabde and Singara did not have a smaller impact on the conflict between Rome and Persia than the fall of Amida, but in the incidents at Amida Amm. was personally involved.

institutores The first author to use this substantive is Tert., according to TLL VII 1.1998.38. It is found almost exclusively in Christian authors. In Amm. it never means 'teacher', but always 'founder', as in 14.8.6 (nomina) *quae eis Assyria lingua institutores veteres indiderunt*, and 17.4.2, where see the note.

vi ... retenturus At first sight *retenturus* is surprising, as *retinere* is always used by Amm. in its classical meaning 'to retain (what is already in one's possesion)', as in Liv. 26.5.1 *Hannibalem diversum Tarentinae arcis potiundae Capuaeque retinendae trahebant curae*. This is how Amm. used the verb in 20.10.3 *quae olim barbari intercepta retinebant ut propria*. This makes Müller's *reseraturus*, or rather Novák's *recepturus*, very tempting. Still, it seems just possible to interpret the text as it stands: 'to retain it after having won the defenders by promises'. In that case *illectis* is to be taken zeugmatically with *vi*.

For the gen. inversus *promissorum dulcedine* cf. 18.6.20 *dulcedine liberalium studiorum illectus* and the note ad 20.6.7 *periculi ... magnitudo*.

munimentum impendio validum As De Jonge ad 16.12.58 explains, *munimentum* 'fortress', is a general word, not a specific technical term. Note that Bezabde is not only called *munimentum* (here and in §16), but also *municipium* in 7.1, *castra* (see the note ad 7.2) and *oppidum* in 7.11, apparently for the sake of variety. For comparable cases see 18.10.1, 25.7.9 and 27.12.6. *Impendio* is found in comedy, Cic. *Ep.* and becomes more frequent from Gellius onwards, mostly with adverbs in the comparative, as in Ter. *Eu.* 587 *impendio magis animu'gaudebat mihi*. With the exception of Iul. Val. 3.28 all combinations with adjectives quoted in TLL VII 1.544.32 sqq. are from Amm.

in colle mediocriter edito A description of the geographical position of Bezabde is given by Szidat. *Mediocriter* is found in a comparable context in Col. 2.16.4 (campus) *mediocriter proclivis*. Amm. uses the word again in his description of the physical appearance of the emperor Valens: *incurvis cruribus exstanteque mediocriter ventre* (31.14.7).

vergensque in margines Tigridis Strabo 16.1.24 πρὸς δὲ τῷ Τίγρει. For the expression cf. 23.6.72 *dextrum vergens in latus Indis obiecta*. Livy has *vergere* very often in geographical descriptions, e.g. 38.4.2 *urbs qua murus vergit in campos et flumen*.

loca suspecta Cf. 16.3.3, 26.5.14 and 31.8.5 *suspecta loca acutius observantes*; Liv. 32.16.15 *noctu ab ea parte quae minime suspecta erat impetu facto ... urbem cepit*.

duplici muro vallatum As in the case of Pirisabora (24.2.12 *duplicibus muris*) and Maiozamalcha (24.4.10 *munitum muris duplicibus oppidum*) the easier approach to Bezabde was protected by a double wall. This detail does not, however, play an important role in the description of the siege of these towns, but seems to be mentioned primarily to stress the strength of the cities under attack. As Crump, 1975, 97–98 notes, Amm. wishes to show the difficulty which a beleaguering army would encounter in trying to capture one of the towns, but he makes this point only to heighten interest, not to explain specific events or stratagems.

ad cuius tutelam tres legiones sunt deputatae The garrison is mentioned before the actual siege begins; in the chapter about Singara it came at the end. *Deputare* is found only here in Amm., but seems to be quite normal in military contexts: Veg. *mil.* 3.4 *ad agendum aliquid ... aut ad castella urbesque deputet muniendas atque servandas*.

secunda Flavia secundaque Armeniaca et Parthica itidem secunda Of these units the Second Parthian (see, however, Lightfoot 1981, 74, who argues for the Second Flavian) in all probability formed the permanent garrison of Bezabde, responsible for the defence of the town and its surroundings. Likewise, it had been the task of the First Parthian to defend Singara (20.6.8).

Presumably soldiers of the Second Flavian and Second Armenian legions were only quite recently sent to Bezabde in order to assist their colleagues of the Second Parthian there. One should compare for this the situation at Amida in 359, which Amm. sketches in fuller detail: the regular garrison at Amida was formed by the Fifth Parthian (18.9.3 *cuius oppido praesidio erat semper Quinta Parthica legio destinata*), while six additional legions were sent to the threatened town from elsewhere (*sed tunc ingruentem Persarum multitudinem sex legiones raptim percursis itineribus antegressae muris astitere firmissimis*).

Whether the additional forces were complete legions, as Amm.'s wording both here, in 18.9.3 and in 20.6.8 seems to imply, is not fully clear. Hoffmann I 236 ff. and 420 ff., who has raised this question, adduces powerful arguments in support of the view that *secunda Flavia* does indeed refer to a legion of the field army, but that, on the contrary, of the Second Armenian, which was stationed on the Upper Euphrates, only a detachment was sent to Bezabde.

The Second Parthian was founded by Septimius Severus and stationed not in Mesopotamia, but in Alba, near Rome. It is a matter of debate whether it was transferred from Italy to the Eastern front in the course of the third century (so e.g. Jones 57; cf. Seyfarth, II, 1983[5], 198 n. 60) or was at some time disbanded and afterwards newly founded by Diocletian (so e.g. Hoffmann I 414, q.v. for other suggestions). What happened to this legion after the fall of Bezabde is not clear either. Its fate is nowhere explicitly stated. A *legio secunda Parthica*, however, is mentioned in the *Not. Dign., Or.* 36.30. Perhaps the suggestion regarding the resurrection of the First Parthian after the fall of Singara (above, ad 20.6.8) also applies to the Second Parthian, as well as to the Second Flavian and Second Armenian.

The Second Flavian should be identified with the *secunda Flavia gemina* of *Not. Dign., Or.* 8.41 (so Hoffmann I 236 ff.) rather than with the *secunda Flavia Constantia Thebaeorum* of *Not. Dign., Or.* 7.45 (Müller, 1905, 577). As its name implies, the latter legion was probably a creation of Constantine.

In the *Not. Dign.* (*Or.* 7.50) the Second Armenian is reckoned to belong to the *pseudocomitatenses*, that is, to those units which were transferred from the frontier to the field armies without having their status upgraded to that of the *comitatenses*. The title *pseudocomitatenses* is first attested for the year 365 and was applied, it would seem, to the units evacuated from the regions ceded by Jovian to the Persians (Jones 609 and Hoffmann I 405 ff.)

cum sagittariis pluribus Zabdicenis The presence of indigenous troops in these outposts is mentioned also in the case of Singara (20.6.8 *indigenae plures*) and Amida (18.9.3 *cuius oppidi praesidio erat semper V Parthica legio destinata cum indigenarum turma non contemnenda*). Among the *indigenae* at Amida there had also been archers, as in Bezabde: *Aderat comitum quoque sagittariorum pars maior, equestris videlicet turmae ita cognominatae, ubi merent omnes ingenui barbari, armorum viriumque firmitudine inter alios eminentes* (ibid.), but whether the *sagittarii Zabdiceni* were mounted like their colleagues at Amida is not stated. Amm. explicitly mentions mounted archers elsewhere (16.12.7 *equites ... turmae, inter quas catafractarii erant et sagittarii*, cf. the note ad loc., and 29.5.20 *equites quartae sagittariorum cohortis*), but also knows of an infantry troop of bowmen (31.12.2 *peditibus sagittariis*).

For *Zabdiceni* see the note above concerning Bezabde. Szidat is probably right in assuming that "*Zabdiceni* ist eine reine Herkunftsbezeichnung für die Soldaten und kein Truppennahme".

municipium Originally denoting an Italian community which had received *civitas sine suffragio*, *municipium* had long ceased to be a specific term. "The universal grant of Roman citizenship by Caracalla in A.D. 212 should presumably in theory have raised all cities of the East which were not colonies to the rank of *municipia*. In fact no change of status is perceptible ... the constitutional origin of the various classes of cities was forgotten" (Jones, 1979 = 1940, 134).

VII. 2 *primo ... impetu cum agmine catafractorum* Probably this was not a real attack, but rather a reconnaissance with the added intention to intimidate the Zabdiceni. The *catafracti*, mail-clad horsemen, were eminently suited to that purpose, as the classical description in 16.10.8 shows: *catafracti equites, quos clibanarios dictitant, personati thoracum muniti tegminibus et limbis ferreis cincti, ut Praxitelis manu polita crederes simulacra, non viros* e.q.s. A graffito found in Doura-Europos and reproduced in Ghirsmann, 1962, 51, perfectly matches this description. The *catafractarii* are probably to be identified with the *cohors regalis* in 19.1.4–5, where Sapor's behaviour is described in very similar terms. The *catafractarii* seem to have played a role already during the battle of Gaugamela, according to Walbank in his note ad Plb. 16.18.6. In Latin literature they are mentioned for the first time in Sal. *Hist.* 4.64 *et sequebantur equites catafracti*, TLL III 592.38 sqq. Livy gives the Latin term: *equites loricatos, quos catafractarios vocant* (35.48.3). Though this form of armour had been invented in the East (Iul. Val. 1.35 *cataphractis ... quod armaturae genus Orientis inventio est*) mail-clad horsemen were by no means only found in the armies of Eastern peoples (for those cf. Rubin, 1955). Apparently *catafractarii* formed part of the Roman army since the time of Hadrian (cf. Eadie, 1967, 167).

In Amm. *catafractus* or *catafractarius* is used of Persians (18.8.7, 19.7.4, 24.6.8, 25.3.4, 25.6.2, 29.1.1; cf. 19.1.2 *ferreus equitatus*) and to denote cavalry in the Roman army (16.10.8, 16.12.5, 16.12.7, 16.12.38, 16.12.63, 22.15.16, 28.5.6). Of particular interest is 16.10.8, quoted above, with its equation of *catafractarii* and *clibanarii*. Cf. Eadie, 1967, 172 with n. 63 and Hoffmann's comment (267): "Damit darf es als sicher gelten, dass die Bezeichnung *equites clibanarii* in fachgerechter Anwendung nicht einfach ein Synonym von *equites catafractarii* ist, wie man früher mitunter gemeint hat (so e.g. De Jonge ad 16.2.5 and 16.10.8), sondern dass sie insonderheit für die nunmehr zusätzlich im Heere eingeführten Panzerreiter rein orientalischer Prägung gilt, die von den tatsächlich nur halbgepanzerten römischen catafractarii geschieden werden müssten".

See on this and related matters Speidel, 1984, who discusses a recently published gravestone from Claudiopolis in Bithynia with a reference to *vexillatio equitum catafractariorum clibanariorum*, the only known Latin inscription mentioning *clibanarii*.

castrorum ambitum Bezabde is called *castra* again in 20.7.8, 20.7.16 (*-ambitum*) and 20.11.18. In all probability we must add 23.5.18, see the note on *amissionem castrorum* below (§16). In the same way Davana is called *castra praesidiaria* in 23.3.7. In many cases *castra* has become part of the name of a permanent settlement. For *castra* thus used cf. 15.11.3 (*castra Constantia*), 18.2.4 (*castra Herculis*), 18.6.9 and 25.7.9 (*castra Maurorum*), 31.11.6 (*Martis castra*). See TLL III 561.3–42. For *castra* in other senses see the notes ad 16.8.1 and 16.12.66.

prope labra ipsa fossarum venit *Labrum* is found with this meaning since Sisenna *hist*. 103 *in labro summo fluminis*, TLL VII 2.811.77 sqq.

audentius The distance between Sapor, who came within the reach of missiles from *ballistae* and of arrows, and the defenders of Bezabde can only be conjectured. As McLeod, 1965 has demonstrated, ancient bowmen were quite accurate up to 50–60 metres, while their effective range extended from 160 to 350–450 metres.

ballistarum iactibus crebris et sagittarum This is Eyssenhardt's suggestion for V's *actibus cretis*. Both words are uncertain. *Ictibus* is a possible alternative for *iactibus* in view of e.g. 20.11.22 *ictus varii ballistarum* and 31.13.1 *rotatis ictibus iaculorum et sagittarum*. Also, *certis* instead of *crebris* should not be rejected on the ground of the king's not being wounded, since this is because of the protection offered by the shields rather than because of inaccuracy on the part of the defenders. Tac. *Ann*. 14.37.1 *postquam in propius suggressos hostis certo iactu tela exhauserat* may have been Amm.'s model.

With the *ballista* as described in 23.4.1-4, wooden arrows tipped with a large iron point (*sagittam ligneam spiculo maiore conglutinatam*; cf. 24.4.16 *aptatae ligneis sagittis ballistae*) were fired. For literature on the subject see Szidat II 16 and cf. the note ad 20.6.1 (*tormentaque bellica*). Drawings of the ballista secundum Ammianum are to be found a.o. in Rolfe, II, between 328 and 329 and in Fontaine, 1977, fig. 1.

The *sagittae* mentioned in the present text, however, shot no doubt by bowmen using ordinary bows rather than machines, will have been different from those fired by *ballistae*. They, too, contained iron parts, cf. 24.2.13 (*harundines ferratas*), 31.7.14 (*harundinibus armatis ferro*) and 31.15.11 (*nervis ferrum lignumque conectentibus*).

densitate opertus armorum in modum testudinis contextorum For *opertus* 'protected' cf. 19.7.3 *machinarum operti tegminibus* (siege of Amida) and 24.4.15 *qua velut testudine ... operiebantur aptissime*; TLL IX 2.686.34. Julian found himself in a similar predicament during the reconnaissance of a stronghold near Ctesiphon: 24.5.6 *oppetisset ... ni ... scutorum densitate contectus evitato magno discrimine discessisset*. Here, as in the passage just quoted, the *testudo* was made of shields (cf. Kromayer-Veith, 1928, Pl. 51, fig. 144), but, as Bitter 129-130 n. 392 observes: "Die *testudo* war offensichtlich für Ammian kein fest fixierter Terminus..., sondern mehr eine Art Metapher für jedes dichte Gefüge der Linien, das mit Hilfe der Schutzwaffen abgesichert wurde. Die *testudo* erscheint bei ihm sowohl bei der Zernierung als auch in der Feldschlacht (16.12.44, 24.4.15, 31.7.12). Die Feststellung stützen ausserdem die von ihm verwendeten Umschreibungen: *in testudinis formam* (29.5.48,cf. 31.7.12) oder *in modum testudinis* (16.12.44, 20.7.2)." Apart from the passages cited so far the word occurs in 20.11.8, 23.4.11, 24.2.17 and 26.8.9, which are not treated in the note ad 16.12.44, nor by Bitter.

abscessit innoxius As in the present text, *innoxius* is most often used in a passive sense by Amm. It has an active meaning in 20.11.13 *ut ignis in eas laberetur innoxius*, 27.2.2, 27.9.5. See the note ad 14.7.8. *Innocuus* is far less common. It is passive in 16.2.6, q.v., 17.8.5, 25.6.13 and 29.1.36, active in 18.7.5 and below in section 6.

VII. 3 *ira tamen tum sequestrata* Sapor sees an attack on his person as a sacrilegious act: *quasi in sacrilegos violati saeviens templi* (19.1.6). For *sequestrare* see the note ad 17.13.29. In its metaphorical sense 'to put aside' it is found mostly in later Latin, e.g. Macr. 7.11.2 *sequestrata verecundia*. Amm. has it in 18.1.1 *sequestratis ... sollicitudinibus* and 29.1.36 *quibus post haec cognita sequestratis*.

caduceatoribus missis ex more Cf. 31.12.14. Servius *Aen.* 4.242 writes: *secundum Livium legati pacis caduceatores dicuntur* and indeed the word is very common in that author, cf. TLL III 32.69 sqq. The practice referred to (*ex more*) was sometimes successful, as Bitter 19 n. 47 observes. See 18.10.2 (Reman et Busan), 21.12.19 (Aquileia) and 24.2.21 (Pirisabora).

ut vitae speique consulturi obsidium deditione solverent *Vitae speique* should not be taken as a hendiadys. If the town is captured, many will lose their lives; those who are spared will have no future (*spes*). For *consulturi* we may compare Constantius' veiled threat in 20.9.4 *si saluti suae proximorumque consulit tumenti flatu deposito* e.q.s. In classical prose a ptc. praes. would have been used in a case like this. Amm., however, often prefers assimilation : 14.6.2 *summatim causas perstringam numquam a veritate sponte propria digressurus*, 24.3.7 *moriar stando, contempturus animam quam mihi febricula eripiet una.*

supplices victori gentium semet offerrent The titles of the Sassanid king are mentioned in 19.2.11: *Persis Saporem saansaan appellantibus et pirosen quod rex regibus imperans et bellorum victor interpretatur*; see the note ad 17.5.3. *Se offerre* is used in the same sense in Caes. *Gal.* 7.89.2 *se illis offerre seu morte sua Romanis satisfacere, seu vivum tradere velint.* In 22.7.10 we are told how all the peoples of the world pledge obedience to Julian: *ab australi plaga ad famulandum rei Romanae semet offerentibus Mauris.*

VII. 4 *quod cohaerenter sibi iunctos duxerant ... ingenuos* The word *cohaerenter* is used of men standing closely together, as in 29.5.48. Amm. uses it three times in descriptions of the coat of mail of the *catafracti* (16.10.8, 24.2.10, 24.6.8), once of a race horse rounding the turning-post closely (28.4.30) and finally of the athlete Milo, holding apples tightly in his fist (30.7.2). Florus has *cohaerenter* in a temporal sense: *non continuo, nec cohaerenter, sed prout causae lacessierant, Epit.* 1.33.5.

Ingenuus may mean no more than 'free-born'. Amm. calls himself an *ingenuus* in 19.8.6 and possibly alludes to himself as such in 14.6.21. See Rosen, 1982, 15–17, for interpretations of this biographical fact, and the notes ad 18.9.4 and 19.8.6.

telum nemo contorsit nec super pace respondit In view of 19.1.7 *contorta ballista* and 31.15.12 *lapidem contorsit ingentem* we must interpret *contorquere* as 'to shoot' (with a *ballista*) rather than 'to throw'. *Nec respondit* may be paraphrased as 'but, on the other hand, nobody answered either'. A similar adversative force seems to be implied in § 6 *nec nostris innocui* and 23.5.17 *nec erravere diu manes eius inulti.* See further Bitter 21 n. 52 on *respondere super.*

VII. 5 *datis indutiis die totius et noctis*   Such cessations of hostilities are a fixed element in siege-descriptions; cf. 20.6.3, 20.11.9 and the note ad 20.8.9.

For the genitive *die* see Gel. 9.14, 3–9 and Neue-Wagener, 1902, I 569–572. It is also found in 24.2.11, 30.1.5 and, possibly, 25.10.4.

Persarum populus omnis   Amm. uses *populus* regularly in the sense of 'militaris multitudo', sometimes in opposition to the leaders, as in 14.10.14 *Alamannorum reges et populi*, 18.2.14 *perculsi reges eorumque populi* with the note and 31.6.1 *Sueridus et Colias, Gothorum optimates, cum populis suis*.

adortus avide vallum   For *avide* "de ira et impetu pugnantium", see TLL II 1430.65 sqq. quoting i.a. Liv. 34.15.4 *si quis extra ordinem avidius procurrit*. Amm. has it several times: 16.12.33 (*avidius*), 21.15.1, 31.12.16 (*avidius*). In 24.5.6 he relates how Julian found himself in a dangerous position during the siege of a fortress: *pauloque avidius intra telorum ictum repertus*.

acriter minans ac fremens   See Bitter, 141 for a collection of the remarks about intimidating noises uttered during attacks both by barbarians and by the Romans.

VII. 6 *eaque re sauciabantur plerique Parthorum, quod*   Gardthausen's *atque ea re* is closer to V's *et quae re*. Moreover, *eaque re* would suggest a reference to the preceding words *vi magna resistentibus oppidanis*, whereas in fact *ea re* is to be connected with the following *quod*-clause, as in 17.10.9, 18.1.2, 18.3.6, 21.13.16, 29.3.4, 31.10.13. *Sauciare* is much less frequent in Amm. than *vulnerare* (4 : 25). In two of the four instances it is used metaphorically: 14.11.17 *sauciabantur eius sensus* and 24.1.4 *sauciabatur salus hostium*. It has its literal meaning in 31.15.7.

pars scalas vehentes, alii opponentes vimineas crates   Scaling ladders and hurdles of osier figure in every siege-description. Cf. e.g. 20.6.3 *quibusdam vehentibus scalas ... plerisque obiectu vinearum pluteorumque tectis iter ... quaerentibus*, 20.11.21 *scalas vehentibus multis* and the following passage about the siege of Aquileia (21.12.13) *quidam elatis super capita scutis ... alii vehentes ... scalas ... pectora multiformium telorum ictibus exponebant*. For *cratis* in military contexts see TLL IV 1111.67 sqq. and the note ad 19.7.3.

velut caeci pergebant introrsus   The adverb *introrsus* must mean here 'into enemy territory' and, therefore, within range of the artillery of the defenders, as in 20.6.4 *ad interiora ferocius se proripientes*. A similar interpretation imposes itself in 19.9.1 *Persae qui tendere iam introrsus ... prohibebantur*. This seems better than to translate 'further inland' or words to that effect (Sabbah, Seyfarth). Tac. *Ann.* 2.25.2 *Caesar pergit introrsus* may have provided the model; TLL VII 2.83.17.

nec nostris innocui   After mentioning the losses on the Persian side and their cause (*ea re quod*), Amm. proceeds to tell about the defenders. *Nec* has the meaning *neque autem, - tamen*, as in § 4. The reason for their heavy losses is given in the next sentence, for which see the note ad 20.6.6 *sagittarum crebritate*.

stantes confertius perforabant   Amm. has only the comparative *confertius* (19.6.9, 24.1.2, 24.7.7, 27.1.3), never *confertim*. For *perforare* cf. 16.12.49 and 31.5.9 *obvios hastis perforabant et gladiis*.

partibusque ... digressis   As a rule, Amm. uses *partes* in the plural for the opposing sides in a siege-description, as in 19.2.14 and 19.3.1. When he uses the singular, as in § 8 *post communes partis utriusque luctus* and in 31.10.14, he does so in order to emphasize that the losses are heavy on both sides. Livy prefers the singular in descriptions of battles and sieges. Cf. the note ad 19.2.14.

appetente postridie luce   This expression for daybreak is found only here in Amm.; in 14.2.2 he writes *cum appeterent noctes*. The phrase occurs in Caes. *Gal.* 7.82.2 *cum lux appeteret* and with some frequency in Livy, never in Cicero.

hinc inde concinentibus tubis   Of the musical instruments used for military purposes Amm. mentions the *tuba*, the *lituus* and the *bucina*. He further speaks of *cornicines, liticines, aeneatores* and of *classicum* and *bucinum*. "Ob wir aber Amm. in jedem Falle die richtige Angabe der Instrumente zutrauen dürfen, steht dahin; er scheint es vielmehr mit seinen Bezeichnungen nicht genau genommen zu haben" (Müller, 1905, 597). Cf. the notes ad 14.1.1, 16.12.27, 19.6.9, and see in general Behn, 1912.

For *concinere* cf. 21.13.9, Liv. 9.32.6 *concinuntque tubae et signa inferuntur*, Tac. *Ann.* 1.68.3 *datur cohortibus signum cornuaque ac tubae concinuere*. Amm. more often uses *concinere* metaphorically, e.g. 20.4.1, q.v.; for *hinc inde* see the note ad 20.6.5.

nec minores strages utrubique visae sunt   Another topos in descriptions of sieges, cf. 20.6.5 and in this section *aequa iactura*. A similar dramatic picture is found in 19.2.10 *ita strages stragibus implicatas ... ne vespertinae quidem hebetaverunt tenebrae, ea re quod obstinatione utrimque magna decernebatur*.

The word *strages* illustrates "die pietätslose Sprache der antiken Historiographie" (Bitter 156 n. 490), which counts the victims on a battlefield not by numbers, but by heaps of corpses, *aggeres* (16.12.54, 17.13.12), *acervi* (19.1.9, 31.13.6) or *strages*. The otherwise comparatively rare adverb *utrubique* is used bij Amm. no less than ten times. It occurs in a military context e.g. in *B. Afr.* 93.1: *dum haec utrubique geruntur* and Liv. 10.39.4 *praeda opulenta utrubique est parta*.

ambobus obstinatissime colluctatis *Ambo* seldom refers to two groups of people. Among the rare examples is 21.12.11 *datoque signo in receptum ex more ambo digressi.* Cf. Verg. *A.* 7.470 *ambobus Teucrisque ... Latinisque*, 12.136, 12.190, Liv. 2.7.1 *ambo exercitus Veiens Tarquiniensisque* and Stat. *Theb.* 11.369/70 *en utraque gentis/turba rogant ambaeque acies.* For *obstinatissime* cf. Bitter 153–154 n. 482. *Colluctari* is found from Sen. Mai. onwards. It becomes more frequent in later Latin (TLL III 1656.70 sqq.). Amm. writes *colluctari cum* in 21.15.3, 30.4.19, 31.6.4, 31.7.16. The verb is used absolutely, as in the present text, in 30.6.6 *animam diu colluctatam efflavit*.

VII. 7 The story about the Christian bishop, whose name, Heliodorus, is known from Persian martyr acts (Braun, 1915, 110 sqq.), has been discussed by a number of scholars with very different conclusions, most recently by Hunt, 1985, 196 and Neri, 1985, 60–61. The question is not so much whether or not the bishop betrayed his city to Sapor, as it is extremely unlikely that the leader of a Christian community should have chosen the side of the Persians, Sapor being a notorious persecutor of the Christians in his empire. The story about their treatment during the deportation as told in the martyr acts bears ample testimony to this. The problem is rather why Amm. gives such a detailed version of a rumour which he qualifies as unfounded himself. Sabbah, in his chapter on 'les techniques de l'argumentation', 1978, 405–453 follows Angliviel de la Beaumelle, 1974, 19, who was of the opinion that both the attention given by Amm. to the rumours and his terminology (*asseveratione vulgata multorum; hocque exinde veri simile visum est quod*) suggests that Amm. did not wish his readers to reject the rumours without further thought. It may be added that when an author presents his readers with different interpretations of an action, the one mentioned last is usually intended to stick with them, as Ryberg, 1942 has shown in her article on Tacitus' Art of Innuendo. Some comparable passages in Amm., though not the present one, are discussed by Roselle in her dissertation, 1985 (formerly (1976) on microfilm), 230 sq. She concludes that "innuendo is important to Tacitus; to Amm. it is relatively unimportant". Readers of the chapter just quoted from Sabbah's great study will be inclined to disagree. In the present story one gets the impression that Amm. deliberately withholds his personal opinion. That in itself, it should be added, is in this particular case a sign of anti-Christian bias in Amm. Blockley, 1975, 132–133 takes Amm.'s words *suspicio vana quaedam, ut opinor* at face value. According to him, the bishop's attempt to end the hostilities serves to bring into relief Sapor's mad aggressiveness. He is certainly right in pointing out the contrast between *placido sermone* and *efferata vesania*. Still, the relatively little attention given to this contrast makes it a secondary theme at best.

secuto die otio ... atributo   Again a standard element, for which see the note ad § 5 *datis indutiis*.

post aerumnas multiplices   Amm. is very fond of *aerumna(e)*, which he uses no less than 44 times. De Jonge has notes on it ad 15.4.10, 16.12.51 and 17.3.1. Quintilian considered it an archaism (*Inst.* 8.3.26), but from the second century onwards it became increasingly common in prose; TLL I 1066.51.

cum magnus terror circumsisteret múros   *Terror* means 'terrifying situation, danger', as in 17.13.28 *terrore nullo relicto post terga*, 26.10.15 *horrendi terrores per omnem orbis ambitum grassati sunt subito*. The phrase may have been inspired by Verg. *A.* 4.561 *nec quae te circumstent deinde pericula cernis*. Amm. has *circumstare* in 19.2.13 and, possibly, in 30.2.8 *rem Romanam alius circumsteterat metus*. His choice of *circumsistere* is probably dictated by the cursus; TLL III 1166.43 sqq.

Christianae legis antistes   De Jonge has a long note about this phrase ad 15.7.6, in which he gives parallels from the *Cod. Theod.* for *lex* in the meaning *religio*. *Antistes* is used for bishop in 21.16.18, 22.5.3, 27.3.15 and 29.5.15. In 23.6.24 and 22.14.8 it refers to pagan priests.

exire se velle gestibus ostendebat et nutu   For the alternation of plural and singular see Hagendahl, 1921, 113–4. The nearest parallel to the present text is Min. Fel. 37.12, where *gestibus et nutibus* is used of actors. In Amm. we find *ut gestibus indicabant et vultibus* (17.13.3). *Nutus* is elsewhere used in connection with the deity (31.10.18) and powerful persons (27.9.4).

acceptaque fide, quod redire permitteretur   Cf. 19.9.5 *accepta fide quod, si ... licuerit, sequetur coniugem libens*, where mood and tense of the or. recta are retained. De Jonge has a note on *quod* ad 14.10.14. He quotes Kallenberg, 1868, 12: "ubicumque apud Amm. quod cum conj. conjunctum exstat, tempus praeteritum antecedit". The rule is not convertible, as 19.9.5 quoted above shows. Livy has the abl. abs. *accepta fide* no less than eight times, e.g. 38.9.4 *Amynander ... fide accepta venerat in castra Romana*.

usque ad tentoria   Vm' reads *adusquead*, which the corrector Vm² changed into *usque ad*, but, according to Hagendahl, 1921, 69-70 Amm. prefers the poetic *adusque*. In fact, he writes *adusque* 112 times, against 3 instances of *usque ad*. It is safer, therefore, to read *adusque* with Novak.

VII. 8 *suadebat placido sermone discedere Persas ad sua*   The construction of *suadere* with an object in the accusative and an infinitive is found in classical prose from Pliny's letters onwards; it becomes more frequent in Late Latin (Szantyr 356, Hassenstein 49). Amm. writes *suadere aliquem* followed by an inf. without a direct object or *suadere alicui* followed by an inf. with a direct object: 29.1.21 *cuius metu vel in mare nos ire praecipites suadet Theognis*, 27.12.6 *Cylaces ... suadebat ... defensoribus et reginae motum Saporis ... lenire*. A remarkable switch in the construction can be seen in 31.6.4: *tunc Fritigernus ... abire negotio imperfecto suasit ... suadensque ut ... adorerentur*.

post communes partis utriúsque lúctus   *Luctus* here has the sense of *iactura, clades*. The present text is listed among the "exempla audaciora" in TLL VII 2. 1740.24 sqq., where it is suggested that Verg. *A.* 10.755/6 *aequabat luctus et mutua Mavors / funera* provided the model.

formidari etiam maiores affirmans forsitan adventuros   The addition of the last two words, which are strictly superfluous, is a good example of 'Satznachtrag' in Amm., for which see Bitter's precise observations on p.185-189. The use of the ptc. fut. in this way can be seen also in 14.6.2 *et quoniam mirari posse quosdam peregrinos existimo haec lecturos forsitan (si contigerit)*.

sed perstabat incassum ... disserendo   *Perstare* occurs only here in Amm., who probably imitates Verg. *A.* 2.650 *talia perstabat memorans*. For the archaism *incassum* see Wölfflin, 1885, 14, Krebs I 264 and the notes ad 14.2.9 and 20.4.5.

efferata vesania regis obstante   A very strong expression indeed. Amm. uses *efferatus* of Gallus (14.1.10, 14.7.2), again of Sapor (27.12.11) and of Valentinian (28.1.11). *Vesania* is also applied to barbarians in 14.2.15 (Isaurians) and 31.5.13 (unspecified).

non ante castrorum excidium digredi ... adiurantis   The omission of the subject-accusative when it is identical with the subject of the main verb is a common feature in Amm. De Jonge in his note ad 15.7.4 quotes as parallels 15.2.8, 15.5.14, 19.12.12, 20.4.17 and 28.6.21. Szantyr 364 explains it as a Grecism which found its way first into the language of poetry, later also into prose.

VII. 9 *perstrinxit tamen suspicio vana quaedam episcopum, ut opinor, licet asseveratione vulgata multorum* The various meanings of *perstringere* in Amm. are given in the note ad 20.5.3. Rolfe translates "incurred the shadow of a suspicion". *Tamen* is added, because although the bishop's mission had no effect for the city, it did prove harmful for his reputation. Parentheses of the type *ut opinor* are very rare in Amm. He introduces them in letters and speeches (20.8.17, 21.6.2, 23.5.19, 26.2.9, 27.6.9). Speaking in *propria persona* Amm. has them in 16.10.15 on the beauty of the Forum Traianum, 22.15.4 on the sources of the Nile, 22.8.1 and 28.6.1 on the appropriateness of a digression and, finally, in the sphragis 31.16.9.

Blockley, 1975, 133, has drawn attention to Amm.'s treatment of a comparable controversy in 22.13.1–5. The Christians are held responsible for the conflagration of the sanctuary of Apollo Daphnaeus. Amm. mentions another version according to which the philosopher Asclepiades was to blame. The alternative version is introduced with the words *ferebatur autem licet rumore levissimo*. The parallel is striking, as is the difference between *rumor levissimus* and *asseveratio multorum*; Seyfarth's translation "wenn auch viele Gerüchte ihn als wahr verbreiteten" is inadequate. Better is Rolfe's "though circulated confidently by many". Cf. Plin. *Nat.* 29.61 *quaedam pudenda dictu tanta auctorum adseveratione commendantur, ut praeterire fas non sit*.

The word *episcopus* is one of the many instances in which Amm. uses Christian terminology without qualifications. Indeed, there is no reason to doubt that Amm. was "perfectly familiar with the Christian way of life, Christian teaching and Christian vocabulary" (A. and A. Cameron, 1964, 323), although now and then he refers to things Christian seemingly as an outsider, as in 14.9.7 *inductus est (ut appellant Christiani) diaconus* or 31.12.8 *Christiani ritus presbyter (ut ipsi appellant)*. See for a discussion of Amm. as a representative of a school of writers of large-scale contemporary histories "driven to devise a modus vivendi, albeit somewhat quaint and artificial, between the Christian world in which they lived and the classical world of which Tradition obliged them to write" the article by A. and A. Cameron quoted above.

quod clandestino colloquio Saporem docuerat At first sight *clandestinus* is surprising, as the bishop had shown his desire to negotiate with Sapor in full view of the Zabdiceni and the Persians. The word must be understood, however, as part of the allegations against the bishop. His enemies must have suggested that the bishop officially acted as a mediator, but secretly revealed the weak spots in the defences of Bezabde. In classical Latin the use of the AcI with *asseveratio* would have made unambiguously clear that this is not a statement by the author himself. Amm. uses both the subjunctive and the indicative in sentences introduced by *quod* after verba declarandi. See Hassenstein 37 and De Jonge ad 17.5.8.

quae moenium appeteret membra   See the notes ad 15.7.5 *urbis membra* and 20.6.7 *cuncta oppidi membra.*

ut fragilia intrinsecus et invalida   A good example of Amm.'s abundantia sermonis, Cf. 18.2.15 *saepimenta fragilium penatium.* For *intrinsecus* see the note ad 17.7.6.

hocque exinde verisimile visum est, quod   *Exinde* normally has a temporal meaning. Here it is causal, to be connected with *quod,* as *postea* shows. See the note ad 16.12.38. *Verisimile,* either written as one word or as two words, is found, apart from the present text, only in 17.1.12.

intuta loca carieque nutantia   Cf. 16.4.2 *clausa ergo urbe murorumque intuta parte firmata* and 31.15.6. De Jonge has a note on *caries* ad 16.2.1 *muros ... carie vetustatis invalidos. Caries* is used metaphorically in Amm.'s vehement attack on the emperor Valens in 29.2.14 *rectoris imperii caries tota stoliditatis apertius est profanata.*

cum exsultatione magna velut regentibus penetralium callidis   It is remarkable that in the sequel of the chapter no mention is made either of these weak spots or of the exultation of the enemies. Blomgren 93 rightly rejects Clark's *maligna,* conjectured for metrical reasons, adducing a substantial number of similar colon-endings. *Penetralium callidis* sounds highly poetical. It may be an echo of Verg. *A.* 2.508 *medium in penetralibus hostem.* For *callidus* + gen. cf. 15.10.5 *locorum callidi,* 27.10.7 *ductantibus itinerum callidis,* Tac. *Hist.* 2.32.1 *nemo illa tempestate rei militaris callidior habebatur.*

contemplabiliter   'accurately', as in 20.11.15 *neve ferire muros assultibus densis contemplabiliter posset.* The adjective is found in 30.5.16 and 23.4.2 *quarum prope unam assistit artifex contemplabilis* "the gunner who aims the shot", as Rolfe correctly translates. It seems best to interpret *contemplator* (19.1.7, q.v.) in the same way; TLL IV 646/7.

machinae feriebant hostiles   According to Szidat *machinae* here should be taken to mean 'rams' and not 'hurling machines' (contra Seyfarth 1983[5], II, 103). The text of Amm. does not warrant this interpretation. On the contrary, the use of the plural *machinae* militates against it, for in § 13 we are told that only one ram made its way to the wall.

VII. 10 *quamquam angustae calles difficiliorem aditum dabant* Quamquam, balanced by *tamen* in the main clause, suggests that the *ballistae* and *scorpiones* mentioned here are those of the attacking Persians, or possibly those of both the attackers and the defenders. A comparison with 20.11.12, where a similar situation during the second siege of Bezabde is described, makes the second alternative more attractive: *dum instrueretur aries ... tormenta nihilo minus et lapidum crebritas atque fundarum ex utraque parte plurimos consumebant.*

Servius *Aen.*4.405 *calle angusto* gives the following etymology of *callis*: *semita tenuior callo pecorum praedurata.* Liv. 22.14.8 confirms the association with small cattle: *nos ... pecorum modo per ... devias ... calles exercitum ducimus.* In Amm. the word *callis* is found three more times (18.8.11, 30.1.15, 31.10.9), of which the first describes a very similar situation: *in arduo sitam* (Amidam) *unoque ascensu perangusto meabilem, quem ... molinae ad calles artandas* (*V*; *aptandas* Clark) *aedificatae densius constringebant.*

aptatique arietes aegre promovebantur Aptare means either 'to bring into position for use' or 'to make ready'. For the first meaning cf. e.g. 19.7.2 (towers) *quorum in verticibus celsis aptatae ballistae*, compared by De Jonge ad loc. with 19.5.1 (towers) *quarum fastigiis ballistae locatae sunt singulae*, from which he concludes that *aptare* has the reduced meaning 'to place in a suitable manner'. As *promovebantur* shows, the rams are not yet in the desired position, so the second meaning must be preferred, for which 20.11.11 is an excellent parallel: *molem arietis magnam ... quae subito visa aptataque faberrime* e.q.s. (where *faberrime* does not refer to its "geschickte Anwendung" (Seyfarth), but to "the skilful manner in which it was put together" (Rolfe). For *aptare* see also the notes ad 18.7.6 and 20.4.18 and TLL II 326.58–66, for *promovere* as a military t.t. the note ad 20.11.15.

manualium saxorum ... metu arcente In Sis. *hist.* 23 *manualis lapides dispertit* the adjective is found for the first time. Tacitus has it in *Ann.* 4.52.1 *manualia saxa iacere*, Amm. uses it again in 24.2.14. *Manualia saxa* contrasts with *saxa molaria* in § 12.

nec ballistae tamen cessavere nec scorpiones We find *cessare* in similar contexts, e.g. 20.6.6 and 20.11.12. Amm. is probably inspired by Verg. *A.* 2.467/8 *nec saxa nec ullum/telorum interea cessat genus.* Cf. also Liv. 30.14.16 *nec pila ab antesignanis cessabant.* For the *ballista*, see ad 20.7.2. The *scorpio, quem onagrum sermo vulgaris appellat* (31.15.12), was a one-armed stone-throwing machine. A description is given by Amm. in 23.4.4–7, but, as De Jonge notes ad 19.2.7, without a reconstruction of any kind, in a drawing or "in natura", Amm. is difficult to understand. Cf. the illustrations in Rolfe, II, between p. 328 and 329, and Fontaine, IV.2, fig. II, but consult in the first place Marsden, 1971, 249–265.

Crump's observation (1975, 103) that Amm. never specifically mentions the *scorpio* as a battering weapon used to break down towers and walls of a beleaguered city, but that he does describe occasions on which defenders of a city fired scorpions to wreck the engines and counterworks of their approaching enemies, is correct. Crump is wrong, however, in stating that Amm.'s principal reason to mention the *scorpio* in the present text was the fact that its utilization at Bezabde was unusual. According to Crump, the *scorpio* was used at Bezabde in a remarkable way in that it checked the approach of the enemy's rams by bombarding them not only with stones but with flaming wicker baskets coated with tar and asphalt as well. He apparently (like Rolfe and Kiechle, 1977, 255) takes *quali ... ardentes* as a direct object of *torquentes*, on a par with *lapides crebros*, but Szidat is, of course, right in pointing to the fact that *quali ... ardentes* is another subject of *cessavere* and that, accordingly, the baskets were thrown by hand, not fired by the scorpions.

qualique simul ardentes A verb like *iacti sunt* must be supplied from *nec cessavere*. The word *qualus* is found nowhere else in Amm. Vegetius mentions *quali* amongst the necessary implements for defending fortifications, along with mattocks and drag-hoes, which suggests that these baskets were normally used for trenching (*mil.* 1.24). A similar use of such baskets is described by Caesar *Civ.* 2.11.2: *cupas taeda ac pice refertas incendunt easque de muro in musculum devolvunt.*

pice et bitumine illiti Pitch was used also for fire-darts: 21.12.10 *contortis malleolis madentibus pice. Bitumen* is mentioned as a building material in 23.6.23 (Babylon) and 24.2.12 (Pirisabora). As Amm. tells us, it was found in large quantities in Assyria near Lake Sosingites (23.6.15). For its use during a siege see Veg. *mil* 4.8 *bitumen sulphur picem liquidam oleum ... ad exurendas hostium machinas convenit praeparari.* For the use of bituminous materials for military purposes see Forbes, 1964, I 105-111.

quorum assiduitate per proclive labentium We have already been told that Bezabde was situated on top of a hill (20.7.1). *Quorum assiduitate labentium* is an extreme specimen of a gen. inversus instead of *quibus assidue labentibus.* Amm.'s desire to present this technical information in an elevated style also shows itself in the comparison *velut altis radicibus fixae.* The comparison would indeed be more appropriate as an illustration of inflexibility under pressure (as in its model Verg. *A.* 4.445/49) rather than of incapacity to advance, the emphasis being on the effectivity of the burning wicker baskets in bringing the battering ram to a halt, at least temporarily. For similar comparisons see 19.2.5 and 25.1.13.

malleoli et faces iactae destinatius For *malleoli* see the note ad 20.6.6; for *destinatius* ad 20.4.14. This use of *destinate, destinatius* is found exclusively in Amm. (TLL V 1.761.59-63).

VII. 11 *caderentque altrinsecus multi* In Amm. *altrinsecus* always means 'on both sides', which is the normal meaning in later Latin (TLL I 1771.66 sqq.).

ardebant magis oppugnatores ... exscindere The precise meaning of *magis* is difficult to establish. It may be the equivalent of *tamen* or *nihilo minus*, thus balancing the preceding concessive clause, or it may contrast the attackers with the defenders: 'the attackers in particular'. For the adversative interpretation of *magis* no certain parallel can be adduced. For the second meaning 25.1.14 is a possible parallel: *elephantorum ... formidandam speciem ... vix mentes pavidae perferebant, ad quorum stridorem odoremque et insuetum aspectum magis equi terrebantur* (the horses in particular, in contrast with *mentes pavidae*). *Ardere* is followed by an infinitive also in 15.5.29, q.v., 22.12.2 and 31.8.4, Szantyr 347, Hassenstein 49.

ante brumale sidus Strictly speaking, *brumale sidus* is Capricornus, as is explicitly stated in Germ. fr. 4.38. Amm. uses this poeticism loosely for 'winter', as in 16.12.15 (with note), 22.13.4 and 27.12.12. The expectation that it would take all the rest of the year to capture Bezabde turned out to be too pessimistic. On the chronology of Sapor's campaign see Dillemann, 1961, 113 (contra Seeck, 1906) and Szidat I 44-45 and 60.

rabiem regis *Rabies* is found for the first time with the meaning 'frenzy of battle' in Sal. *Hist.* 1.55.19 *ea desperatio Tuscis rabiem magis quam audaciam accendit*. In Amm. it is found in the same contexts as *vesania*, which we found in connexion with Sapor in § 8. It is applied to barbarians: 14.2.14 *concepta rabie saeviore quam desperatio incendebat et fames* (Isaurians), 16.5.16, 27.9.1, to wild animals: 24.5.2 *ursos, ut sunt Persici, ultra omnem rabiem saevientes*, to Gallus 14.1.10 *ad rabiem potius evibrabat* and to Valens in 29.1.27. Sapor must have been extremely irritable during sieges; cf. 19.8.1 (Amida) *ira et dolore exundans nec fas ullum prae oculis habiturus*.

nec multa cruoris effusio nec confixi ... plurimi A coordination of a nomen actionis and an Ab urbe condita-construction, as in 20.5.4. For *cruor* see the note ad 20.11.7. In classical authors *effusio* (et sim.) *sanguinis* is more common, e.g. Cic. *Mil.* 101, Verg. *A.* 7.788, Tac. *Hist.* 4.32.2.

ab audacia parili revocabant *Parilis* is rare in Amm.: 20.3.4 *parili comitatu*, 21.6.2 *parile obsequium*, 23.3.5 *ad parilem potestatem*. In these cases it offers a

169

metrically convenient alternative for *par*, which Amm. uses 61 times. See Hagendahl 1921, 44. For *revocare* see the note ad 20.3.2.

VII. 12 *diu cum exitio decernentes postremo periculis obiectavere semet abruptis* The action expressed by *decernentes* precedes *obiectavere semet*, as is underlined by *postremo*. We find an exact parallel for this use of the present participle in § 15 of this same chapter: *ancipiti diu exitio renitentes, postremo ... disiecti sunt.* Even more notable is *diuque flagrans* in § 16, which follows *gaudio elatus* to which it is prior. De Jonge has a note on the present participle "replacing the missing part. perf. act." ad 16.2.6. See also Szantyr 386/7. *Cum exitio* is a modal ablative, as in 18.8.14 *aliis cum exitio sauciis* q.v.. The perfect tense of *obiectavere* seems to anticipate the decisive event in the siege, the attack of the battering-ram (as in 20.6.5 *admotus aries*). The numerous examples of *pericula abrupta* listed in TLL I 142.72 are nearly all from Amm. De Jonge has a note on *obiectare* ad 19.7.5.

denso saxorum molarium pondere 'A dense hail of heavy stones', gen. inversus with hypallage of *densus*, comparable in both respects with 25.10.4 *curarumque ponderibus diversis afflictum. Saxa molaria* are opposed to *minuta* in Sen. *Ep.* 82.24. The battle between Hercules and Cacus in Verg. *A.* 8.250 is fought *ramis vastisque molaribus*.

fomentisque ignium variis ire protinus vetabantur In 21.12.10 we find *fomes* with the same meaning: *vario fomite flammarum incessebantur*. Vegetius mentions *sarmenta ... aliaque fomenta flammarum* in *mil.* 4.24 and *-ignium* in 4.44; TLL VI 1019.63 sq. *Vetare* + infin. with impersonal agent is already classical: Hor. *Sat.* 1.1.24/5 *ridentem dicere verum / quid vetat?*, Sen. *Ben.* 5.6.5 *quibus* (diebus) *sol intercursu lunae vetetur omnes radios effundere*.

VII. 13 *umectis taurinis copertus exuviis* *(H)umectus* is a rare word, found e.g. in Cato *Agr.* 6.3, Var. *L* 5.24 and Apul. *Soc.* 10. In 20.11.13 we find an exact parallel: *quod umectis coriis et centonibus erant opertae materiae*.

minus casus flammeos pertimescens aut tela As *casus* never seems to mean simply 'fall' in Amm., Wagner is probably right in interpreting *casus flammeos* as "pericula ex ignibus coniectis". The same idea is expressed in 23.4.11 (the *helepolis* is covered with ox-hides and young branches) *ut flammeos detrectet et missiles casus*.

antegressus omnes repsit nisibus magnis Even more clearly than in 20.6.6 Amm. describes the battering-ram as a live animal, no doubt prompted by its name (cf. *onager, scorpio*). (*Repere* generally means 'to move with difficulty'.

Lucan, in a passage that shows great similarity to the siege-description in Amm., uses *repere* of movable siege-towers (3.458 sqq.). It also occurs in Amm.'s description of how he climbed the hill of Amida (18.8.11). For *nisibus magnis* cf. 19.1.6 with the note and 29.5.28.

coagmenta lapidum fodiens turrim laxatam evertit   Repeated verbatim from 20.6.6. The effect of the battering-ram is described as follows in 23.4.8: *concidunt structurae laxatae murorum. Laxare* is used in the same context by Curt. 4.4.12 *crebris arietibus saxorum compage laxata*; TLL VII 2.1071.70.

superstantes ... mortibus interiere diversis et insperatis   For *superstare* see the note ad 20.6.4. *Diffracti*, according to De Jonge ad 19.2.7 an archaism, must mean 'smashed' by falling stones and beams, cf. 28.6.14 *in puteum aquis vacuum sese coniecit, unde costa diffracta levatus*. On the numerous adjectives and participles with *in-* De Jonge has a note ad 14.6.15, on *in- speratus* in particular ad 16.2.7.

inventoque tutiore ascensu   Amm. avoids *tuto* both as an adjective and as an adverb (see note ad 20.5.1 *tutius*). *Invento tuto* would have been less elegant. *Ascensus* is used more often by Amm. for entering a beleaguered city: 20.11.9 *ascensus undique temptabatur* and 31.15.13 *ascensumque in muros ex latere omni parantes*.

II. 14 *Trepidis ... superatorum auribus*   Cf. Stat. *Theb.* 9.35 *trepidas...Polynicis ad aures*. A whole list of transferred epithets of this type is given in TLL II 1514.5 sqq., e.g. Verg. *A*. 4.428 *cur mea dicta negat duras demittere in aures?* and in Amm. 14.11.4 *cum haec ... sollicitas eius aures everberarent*. *Superatorum* implies that the defenders are doomed, despite their valiant efforts.

ululantium undique Persarum intonante fragore   This, too, is topical, cf. 20.6.7 *Persarum agmina ... ululabili clamore sublato* with the note ad loc. In 16.10.9 *intonante fragore* refers to the thunderous welcome given to Constantius as he entered Rome; see De Jonge's note ad loc. and the notes ad 20.4.17 and 20.8.6.

artius proelium intra muros exarsit   *Artius* does not mean "vehementius" (pace Wagner), but refers to close combat, as is evident from 25.1.18 *quibus saepe languidis in conflictu artius pes pede conlatus graviter obsistebat pugnare fortiter eminus consuetis*. For possible literary models see Bitter 151.

hostium nostrorumque catervis   As De Jonge remarks ad 16.2.6, *caterva* is

171

normally used of barbarian or mercenary troops, as in 17.12.16 – *confluentium nationum et regum*, 19.6.8 – *Persarum*, 31.5.15 *in Scythicarum gentium* –. See also TLL III 609.65 sqq. In the present passage it refers also to the Romans, probably on account of the disorderly character of the fighting.

confertis inter se corporibus 'in serried ranks'. The phrase is best illustrated by 16.2.6 *barbaros in se catervatim ruentes ... confertis lateribus observabat* and 16.12.38 *ni conferti illi sibique vicissim innexi stetissent immobiles*. For a discussion of these and similar expressions see Bitter 147. The allitteration *catervis certantibus comminus cum confertis inter se corporibus* lends vividness to the description of the fighting.

hinc indeque stricto mucrone As Szidat notes, the description of the final stage in the siege of Bezabde resembles that of the fall of Amida: 19.8.4 *stricto comminus ferro cum sanguis utrubique immensis caedibus funderetur* e.q.s. The expression *stricto mucrone* may have been inspired by Verg. *A.* 2.449 *strictis mucronibus*.

VII. 15 *magna ... mole ancipiti diu exitio renitentes* Here, as in 20.6.5, *moles* refers to the exertions of the defenders. *Ancipiti exitio* is best taken as a dative dependent on *renitentes* (for which verb see the note ad 20.4.18), not as an abl. abs. In that case the meaning would be 'with uncertain outcome' ("mit zweifelhaftem Erfolg", Seyfarth). The distinction, however, between *exitium* 'death' and *exitus* 'outcome', which in later Latin tends to get blurred (TLL V 2.1530), is maintained throughout in Amm. The expression seems to combine the idea of a fight against death, as in 25.3.8 *magno spiritu contra exitium certans*, with the notion that the fight remained undecided for a long time, as in 20.6.5 *pugnabatur eventu ancipiti diebus aliquot*. The sentence in 16.2.13 *cum ... exitioque hostes urgerentur ancipiti* is no real parallel, because there *anceps* means 'from both sides', as the preceding *in bicornem figuram acie divisa* shows.

plebis immensae ponderibus effuse disiecti sunt *Plebs* can refer to the common soldiers, normally to barbarians, as in 16.2.9 *Alamannicam ... plebem* (q.v.), 16.12.34 and 27.2.1, but sometimes also to the Roman army, as in 25.2.1 *imae quoque militum plebi* and 26.2.3 *cohortiumque omnium plebe*. The combination with *pondus* also occurs in 18.8.8 *trudente pondere plebis immensae* and 29.5.41 *Isaflenses pondere catervarum ingentium inclinati sunt*. This use of *pondus* is found already in Liv. 30.34.2 *pugna Romana stabilis et suo et armorum pondere incumbentium in hostem*. In 22.8.18 the expression *acrique concertatione effuse disiectae* is used again, more appropriately this time, as it refers to a battle in the open field.

et post haec ... concidebant   The Persians treat the Zabdiceni more harshly than the inhabitants of Singara (20.6.7 *caesisque promiscue paucissimis*). Indiscriminate slaughter is another standard element in siege-descriptions. Compare e.g. 19.8.4 *pecorum ritu armati et inbelles sine sexus discrimine truncabantur* (with the note) and 24.4.25 *sine sexus discrimine vel aetatis, quidquid impetus repperit, potestas iratorum absumpsit*. A general discussion of the relation between these topical elements and historical reality may be found in Sabbah 584–594.

abreptique sinibus matrum ... trucidabantur   The 'distributio' of the victims – normally infants, women and elder people are mentioned – goes back ultimately to *Il.* 22.62–65 and, in all probability, to the lost description of the fall of Troy in the Ilioupersis. In his illuminating essay on this subject Paul, 1982, 148 quotes Ogilvie's pertinent remark that "almost all Livy's accounts of captured cities are variations on the Ilioupersis theme". A list of parallel passages in Amm. is given by Bitter 53 n. 159. The reading *ipsae quoque matres* of VE BAG (VE write *ipse*) results in a sentence that is less than perfect, but cannot be rejected out of hand because of the virtual consensus of the mss. The most elaborate version of this topos is 31.6.7 *abstractisque ab ipso uberum suctu parvulis et necatis raptae sunt matres* e.q.s.

inter quae tam funesta gens rapiendi cupidior   The same combination of thoughts is found in 19.9.2 *inter haec tamen funera direptionesque*. *Gens* refers to the Persians, as e.g. in 25.1.13 *cuius artis* (archery) (*fiducia ... gens praevaluit maxima*. Amm. possibly chooses to refer to them in this way, because wealth and greed are distinctive features of the Persians as a nation; see Fontaine's note 351 ad 24.3.4. As Rolfe points out, *cupidior* is real comparative here: the Persians preferred plunder to bloodshed.

II. 16   *gaudio insolenti elatus*   There is a remarkable similarity between Sapor and his opposite number Constantius. After the liquidation of Silvanus (15.5.35) the emperor is described as *inaestimabili gaudio re cognita princeps insolentia coalitus et tumore*. In 17.11.3 Amm. calls the Persians *gentem insolentia semper elatam*. Cf. also Liv. 42.60.2 *insolens laetitia* and Curt. 4.6.26 *insolenti gaudio ... elatus*.

diuque desiderio capiendae Phaenichae flagrans   On Amm.'s mistaken identification of Bezabde with Phaenicha see the note ad 20.7.1, and for the preterite force of *flagrans* ad 20.7.12 *decernentes*. The present participle is particularly confusing as it is coordinated simply by -*que* with *elatus*, which it both precedes and explains.

munimenti perquam tempestivi This repeats what had been said about Bezabde in §§ 1 and 11 of this chapter. *Tempestivus* is found with its usual meaning 'at the proper time', 'timely', in 15.5.33, 19.8.6 and 31.8.6. Four times we find it in personal remarks by the author: 15.9.1 *Galliarum tractus et situm ostendere puto nunc tempestivum* 17.4.1, 28.1.43, 28.1.57 (adv.) and twice in speeches: 25.3.15 *advenit ... abeundi tempus e vita, impendio tempestivum,* and 27.6.6. The meaning required here is 'convenient', i.e. 'of strategic importance', which is unattested in Amm. as well as in Sal., Liv., Verg. and Tac. Probably, *tempestivus* must be taken as a synonym of *opportunus*, as in 25.7.9 *Castra Maurorum, munimentum perquam opportunum* and 30.5.2 *Carnuntum ... perquam opportunum.*

For *perquam*, an archaism used 22 times by Amm., see the note ad 15.2.4.

non ante discessit, quam ... locaret Sapor's enthusiasm and pride do not diminish his effectivity as a military leader. Amm. insists on his measures as an implicit criticism of the state in which the Romans had left Singara, which had necessitated hasty repairs (Szidat ad 20.6.6) and had ultimately led to its fall. On the other hand, the account of Sapor's activities prepares the reader for the unsuccessful siege of Bezabde by Constantius, which will be told in ch. 11. There the criticism is made explicit: 20.11.6 *loca quae antehac incuria corruperat vetustatis.* In 21.13.1 mention is made of plans for yet another siege: *obsidione gemina Bezabden aggressurus.*

alimentisque affatim conditis Amm. has *affatim* 5 times, in four of which (14.10.11, 20.7.16, 24.5.12, 24.7.6) it refers to food stocks, as in Sal. *Jug.* 54.6 *obsides frumentum et alia affatim praebita.* It is probably an archaism, TLL I 1173.63. On adverbs ending in *-im* see the notes ad 15.5.24 (*cursim*), 16.2.6 (*catervatim*), 16.7.4 (*carptim*), 17.4.7 (*sensim*) and 19.5.4 (*furtim*).

insignes origine bellique artibus claros The bravery of these elite troops is indicated in 20.11.16–18 and 21.13.2. *Ars belli* or *-bellica* is common in Livy, e.g. 25.40.5 *omnis belli artes edoctus* and 27.16.1 *non arte belli par Romano Tarentinus erat*; TLL II 663.60–78.

amissionem castrorum ingentium Amm. calls Niniveh *ingens civitas* in 18.7.1 and speaks of the *ingens circumitus* of Amida in 19.3.1. *Amissio* is found since *Rhet. Her.* 1.14.24 *exercitus amissione*; cf. also Cic. *Pis.* 40 *oppidorum turpis amissio.* It becomes more common in later Latin; TLL I 1917.37 sqq. When in a speech to his soldiers (23.5.18) Julian mentions *inultae caesorum exercituum umbrae et damnorum magnitudines castrorumque amissiones,* he is probably thinking of Amida, Singara and Bezabde, as Fontaine says in his note ad loc.

(nr 122). It is the only other instance of *amissio* in Amm., which is a further argument in favour of Bentley's *castrorum*.

ad eadem obsidenda viribus magnis accingerentur De Jonge has a note on *accingere* ad 17.5.8. *Accingi ad* is found in 30.2.7 and 31.8.10, with abl. instr. in 17.5.8, 18.4.1, absolutely in 27.2.1 and 27.6.12. Cf. Liv. 28.41.8 *quin igitur ad hoc accingeris?*, Tac. *Hist.* 4.79.1 *antequam hostes ... ad spem vel ad ultionem accingerentur*; TLL I 303.46. On *magnis viribus* see Bitter 76, n. 220.

VII. 17 *Latius se ... iactans* TLL VII 2.1020.61 mentions a few cases of *latus*, "accedente colore gloriandi", among which Sen. *Ep.* 76.31 *cum praesente populo lati incesserunt*. Of Sapor Amm. says *latius semet extentans* (17.5.2 with De Jonge's note). Examples of *iactare* 'to boast' and its derivatives are to be found in 15.3.2, 16.8.4 and 31.2.22 *nec quicquam est quod elatius iactant*; cf. Cic. *Catil.* 1.1 *quem ad finem sese effrenata iactabit audacia?*, TLL VII 1.58.81 sqq.

quidquid aggredi posset The subjunctive may be explained as part of the virtual or. obliqua. Moreover, as Szantyr 562 remarks, it becomes more and more frequent after *quisquis* since Livy. De Jonge has a note on it ad 17.3.2. *Aggredi posset* seems equivalent to *aggrederetur*; it belongs to the category of which TLL X 2.140.69 sqq. says "exempla inter vim possibilitatis et temporis futuri ambigua", where we find i.a. 14.6.2 *mirari posse quosdam peregrinos existimo*, 20.8.7 *miles ... cum nullas sibi vices a Caesare ... rependi posse contemplaretur* and among the "exempla certiora" 20.11.3 *adiurans animam prius posse amittere quam sententiam*. Note that even in the present text and in the example quoted last the notion of 'possibility', 'contingency' is still present. That notion becomes very dim in the examples quoted in TLL X 2.141.59 sqq. of *poterit* + infin., e.g.14.7.5 *invito rectore nullus egere poterit victu*. Cf. also 24.3.6 and 30.2.8. Szantyr 313/4 considers these examples of *possum* + infin. a periphrasis of the future tense. The development of the Romance future tenses is treated in detail by Pinkster, 1985.

interceptis castellis aliis vilioribus For *intercipere* see the note ad 20.6.9. *Vilis* (for which see the note ad 19.9.5) is used of a *statio* in 18.7.8 *Nisibi pro statione vili transmissa*, cf. 23.6.72 *hic quoque civitates sunt inter alias viles*.

Virtam The geographical position of Virta (= Syriac Birtha 'fortress') is disputed. Dillemann, 1962, 298/9 followed by Szidat and Seyfarth II, 1983[5], 198 n. 69, identifies the place with Biredjek on the eastern bank of the Euphrates, opposite to Zeugma.

This identification would imply that Sapor, after having captured Singara and Bezabde, both situated in the eastern part of Mesopotamia, marched through the whole of the Roman province in order to reach the Euphrates and attack Virta. Some objections may be raised against this supposition.

In the first place, a march from Bezabde on the Tigris towards the Euphrates would have meant that Sapor deliberately left his rear unguarded, notably leaving Nisibis (cf. § 1) undisturbed. This, it is true, does not seem inconceivable, certainly not in view of the fact that Sapor's self-confidence was increased after his successes at Singara and Bezabde. There is, however, a more serious reason to doubt the correctness of Dillemann's assumption. Amm. remarks that Virta was situated on the outer frontier of Mesopotamia: *in extremo quidem Mesopotamiae situm*. Dillemann, 1962, 299 takes this to mean: in the *western* part of the Roman province, that is, he wants to see *in extremo* viewed from the Persian stand point ("située sur l'Euphrate, *in extremo quidem Mesopotamiae situm* par rapport à Bezabdé d'où venait Sapor"), which is rather odd. Moreover, he does not take into account the subordinate clause introduced by *sed* which qualifies *in extremo*. Its adversative force is most simply inderstood if Virta was situated near the Tigris: Virta's position near the frontier with Persia was dangerous, but nevertheless defendable, thanks to the inaccessibility of the terrain and its strong walls. For such a Virta on the Tigris see Ptol. *Geogr.* 5.18 and Georg. Cypr. 937 Gelzer, cited by Fraenkel, 1899. Cf. also Procop. *Aed.* 2.4.20, who mentions a town called Βιρθὸν in the neighbourhood of Amida near the Tigris.

velut sinuosis circumdatum et cornutis "with salient and re-entrant angles" (Rolfe), cf. Veg. *mil.* 4.2 *Ambitum muri directum veteres ducere noluerunt, ne ad ictus arietum esset expositus, sed sinuosis anfractibus* e.q.s. *Velut* serves to apologize for the uncommon adjectives *sinuosus* and *cornutus*, as in 16.12.57 *velut luctante amnis violentia* or 17.7.14 *tunc enim necesse est velut taurinis reboare mugitibus*. In Amm. we find *cornutus* twice of the moon, 20.3.10 and 27.4.5. It is used nowhere else of fortification.

instructioneque varia Instructio is late and altogether rare; TLL VII 1.2007.76 sqq.quotes among the few examples August. *Epist.* 243.1 *ad bellandum ... instructione decem milium idoneum esse*.

inaccessum A neologism in Vergil (*A.* 7.11 *inaccessos ... lucos*), which became rather popular in later Latin. Amm. has it eleven times; Hagendahl, 1921, 47.

VII. 18 *quod cum omni arte temptaret*   *Quod* refers to *oppidum*, cf. e.g. 26.7.12 *aditus ... per quos provinciae temptantur arctoae*. With a personal subject we find *temptare* in 20.11.2 *audiebat enim saepius eum temptatum a rege Persarum*. This use of *temptare* (OLD s.v. 9 "to make an attempt on") is also found in classical authors: Caes. *Civ.* 3.40.1 *simul ... scalis et classe moenia oppidi temptans*, Liv. 27.39.14 *quam ipse frustra eandem illam coloniam ... temptasset*, Verg. *A.* 8.231/2 *ter saxea temptat/limina nequiquam*.

poenas cruciabiles minitans   *Cruciabilis* is not found before Gellius and Apuleius. Amm. uses it several times, e.g. 28.1.3 *minantesque defensoribus cruciabiles neces* and 29.1.24 *post cruciabiles poenas*.

nunc ... nunc ... aliquotiens   This *variatio* is typical of Amm.; see the note ad 20.3.12 and TLL I 1617.55–58.

multis acceptis vulneribus quam illatis   For *quam = magis quam* see the note ad 17.12.19 and Szantyr 593/4. It is characteristic of Tacitus in particular: *Ann.* 5.6.3 *ne memoriam nostri per maerorem quam laeti retineatis* and 14.61.4 *si id rebus conducat, libens quam coactus acciret dominam*.

Chapter 8

Before turning to the detailed comments on this chapter it is worth while to take the structure of the book and the sequence of events in Amm.'s narrative into account.

The first two short chapters each report a particular event in the Western and Eastern half of the empire, respectively, viz. Lupicinus' mission to Britain and Ursicinus' troubles at the imperial court. After the digression about the eclipses in ch. 3 the next two chapters provide a precise account of the usurpation at Paris. Next, chapters 6 and 7 describe events in Mesopotamia, viz. the siege and fall of Singara and Bezabde. Having sketched these serious misfortunes in the East, Amm. now starts his description of the negotiations between Julian and Constantius, to which chapters 8 and 9 are devoted.

Referring to the structure just sketched, and especially to the place occupied by ch. 6 and 7, Sabbah 479/480 suggests that Amm. aimed to obscure the simultaneity of the negotiations and Sapor's all too successful actions in Mesopotamia, "en donnant ainsi l'impression qu'elles furent toutes antérieures aux tractations diplomatiques entre Julien et Constance, rapportées seulement et en bloc en 20.8 et 9". There may be some truth in this, but, as Sabbah points out himself, collecting the events in East and West into larger units is a quite natural method for a historian, one which had also been employed by Tacitus and which, for that matter, is defended by Amm. himself in 26.5.15 and 29.5.1. In addition, it should be noted that Amm. certainly does not conceal the simultaneity of events, cf. 20.6.1 *haec dum per Gallias agerentur.*

In the first sections of the present chapter it becomes quite clear that Amm. is not out to cheat the reader in chronological matters. The situation and the state of mind of the two protagonists, Constantius and Julian, are briefly sketched in sections 1 and 2, respectively, and in both cases explicit temporal expressions make clear, at least to the attentive reader, that the author returns to a time before the events in the spring and summer of that year (*eo anno*): *hiemem apud Constantinopolim agens* (§ 1) and *apud Parisios hibernis locatis* (§ 2). Mark that in both sections the tenses of the main predicates characterize this passage as a short sketch of the background of the events, the report of which starts only in section 3 with the perfects *statuit* and *dedit*.

VIII. 1 *intra Tigrim ... et Euphraten*   Seyfarth's text is wrong here: *intra* should be changed into *inter*. *Euphraten* is the only acc. form of that river, but besides *Tigrim* (also in 23.3.6) two other forms are used: *Tigrin* (19.5.4.) and, most frequently and parallel with the gen. *Tigridis* and the abl. *Tigride, Tigridem*. According to Dillemann, 1961, 299 the expression is to be taken quite literally: between Bezabde on the Tigris and Virta on the Euphrates. See, however, the note ad 20.7.17 for the geographical position of Virta.

metuens expeditiones Parthicas Obviously *metuens* has to be regarded as placed in causal subordination to *hiemem agens*. Originally *expeditio*, as TLL V 2.1626.26 notes, meant "militum expeditorum in hostem iter", its 'light order' being nicely illustrated by Liv. 3.12.5 *egregia facinora nunc in expeditionibus nunc in acie*, but it gradually came to denote a full-scale campaign, cf. Amm. 22.12.1 about Julian: *expeditionem parans in Persas*.
For *Parthicas* cf. the note ad 20.4.2 *Parthos*.

apud Constantinopolim The eastern capital was *vetus Byzantium, Atticorum colonia*, according to Amm. in 22.8.8. The latter statement does not seem to be correct. Of the various founders named in the sources Megara has the best claim (cf. Legon, 1981, 78 ff.). For the history of Constantinople in the fourth and fifth centuries Dagron, 1974 is fundamental. De Jonge ad 14.7.19 and 19.11.17 cites some older works.

impensiore cura The same expression occurs in 17.10.7, 19.6.6 and 26.1.1. Cf. Tac. *Hist*. 1.31.3 and Ov. *Met*. 2.405/6 *Arcadiae tamen est impensior illi / cura suae* (according to Bömer ad loc. the first example of the comparat. of *impensus*). De Jonge ad 17.10.7 lists some variations, such as *pleniore cura* (20.10.3).

limitem instruebat eoum omni apparatu bellorum As stated at the end of the introduction to this chapter, the imperfects *instruebat* and *poscebat* express the fact that in this section Constantius' circumstances are sketched. The expression *apparatus bellorum* is also found in 18.5.8, where, however, *apparatus* has its original verbal sense 'preparation'. Here it denotes 'equipment', as in Caes. *Civ*. 3.44.1 *omnem apparatum belli, tela arma tormenta, ibi collocaverat*. The gen. sing. *belli* is usual in Livy (some 10 instances) and occurs twice in HA (*A*. 26.4, *Max*. 11.9). Amm.'s use of the gen. plur. in the present case is paralleled by such instances as *magna perdidit instrumenta bellorum* (26.7.12) and *disiectis bellorum officinis* (31.16.7). See for the eastern frontier during Constantius' reign in general Frézouls, 1981 and Lightfoot, 1981 and for Constantius' eastern policy the note ad 20.4.1 *properantem ... Persicis*.

tirocinia cogens The same abstractum pro concreto occurs in 19.11.7, 21.6.6, 30.6.1, 31.4.4, 31.10.17. The only earlier example is possibly Liv.

40.35.12, where, however, as De Jonge notes ad 19.11.7, *contemptum tirocinium* may denote the enemy's contempt for the recruits' inexperience.

Though we know of some individuals who volunteered for the army, most of the civilian recruits were conscripts of one type or another (cf. 21.6.6: *indictis per provincias tirociniis*), the main source being the regular conscription which was apparently instituted by Diocletian (For this and what follows: Jones 607 ff., cf. De Jonge ad 17.13.3). It was annual (cf. 31.4.4 *pro militari supplemento, quod provinciatim annuum pendebatur*), but recruits were not levied every year from every province, a tax, the recruit money (*aurum tironicum*) being exacted in some instead. The rate at which recruits were assessed on the provinces, is unknown and it is impossible to tell exactly how severe the levy was. Conscription of citizen recruits, however, does not seem to have been very popular (cf. 19.11.7 *aurum quippe gratanter provinciales corporibus dabunt*, with De Jonge's note) and certainly was not the only source of recruitment. Apart from citizens the Roman government enlisted barbarians. Some of them were volunteers, others prisoners of war or *dediticii* or *laeti* (see for the latter categories below, the note ad 20.8.13), drafted into Roman formations. Still others belonged to contingents furnished under treaty by tribes in alliance with the empire and serving under their own chiefs.

The latter practice, apparently hinted at in this section with the words *auxilia..Scytharum*, underwent a considerable change after the battle at Adrianople in 378, when Theodosius the Great had to sign a treaty with the Goths. This was the beginning of an ever-increasing use of federates in a new sense, barbarian hordes which were either homeless or were assigned land within the empire. See for recruitment in general Gigli, 1947.

statariae pugnae per orientales saepius eminuere procinctus Livy twice uses the adi. *statarius* about soldiers in a battle: *statarius uterque miles, ordines servans* (9.19.8) and 22.18.3. In Amm. the only other occurrence also concerns the fight itself: *impares nostris ... congressione stataria* (14.2.8). For this Livy rather uses the adi. *stabilis*: *pugna Romana stabilis* (30.34.2), 28.2.7, 31.35.6, cf. also Tac. *Ann.* 2.21.1 (*multitudo*) *coacta stabile ad proelium*. Interpreting the present expression Forcellini's lexicon notes in the lemma *statarius*: "qua pede collato pugnatur et immobili, σταδία μάχη". Cf. *Il.* 13.314 ἐν σταδίη ὑσμίνῃ and the note ad 14.2.8.

Kiessling rightly emended V's *enimuere* (m 1) or *emicuere* (m 2) into *eminuere*. The reading of V's second hand would have been the only occurrence in Amm. of *emicare*. Another instance where *eminere* is used about events is 14.1.3 *eminuit autem inter humilia ... nefanda Clematii cuiusdam Alexandrini nobilis mors repentina*. Both Clark and Seyfarth wrongly ascribe a conjecture *eminuerunt* to Wagner: this is merely a comment on *emicuere*, which was printed in the text.

For the different meanings of *procinctus* (here 'campaign') cf. the note ad 20.1.3.

auxilia ... Scytharum In the sources for the history of the later Roman Empire *Scythae* is a general designation of the nomadic tribes of the north of Europe and Asia, beyond the Black Sea. Procopius, for instance, speaking in *Goth.* 8.5.6 of the Goths called Tetraxitae (οἱ Τετραξῖται καλούμενοι Γότθοι) says: οἳ δὴ καὶ Σκύθαι ἐν τοῖς ἄνω χρόνοις ἐπεκαλοῦντο, ἐπεὶ πάντα τὰ ἔθνη ἅπερ τὰ ἐκείνη χωρία εἶχον, Σκυθικὰ μὲν ἐπὶ κοινῆς ὀνομάζεται. Amm.'s wording in 22.8.42 (*gentesque Scytharum innumerae, quae porriguntur ad usque terras sine cognito fine distentas*) is also rather vague, while Synesius in a speech delivered before the Emperor Arcadius in 399 still less exactly uses Σκύθαι for barbarians in general (*De Regno*, 19 and passim).

In view, however, of the growing importance of the Goths in the history of the fourth century, it seems to be a not altogether wild guess to suppose that when *Scythae* are mentioned in the sources, Goths are often meant (cf. Wolfram, 1979, 21 ff.). The following line of argument can perhaps corroborate this idea, at least as far as the present text is concerned.

Like Constantius and later Valens (*Scytharum auxilia festina celeritate mercante*, 30.2.6), Julian employed 'Scythian' auxiliaries in his army (23.2.7): *cum exercitu et Scytharum auxiliis*), pace Libanius (οὐ γὰρ ᾤετο δεῖν ὁ βασιλεὺς Σκύθας καλεῖν εἰς ἐπικουρίαν, *Or.* 18.169). Now, because it is likely that the *Scytharum auxilia* in Julian's army in 363 were identical with those enlisted by Constantius in 360, and because the *Scythae* of Julian seem to have been Goths (if indeed, as Paschoud, 1979, 178 n. 71, believes, οἱ Γότθοι mentioned by Zosimus in 3.25.6 are to be identified with the *Scythae* of Amm. 23.2.7), the *Scytharum auxilia* of the present text may have been Goths too.

It is to be noted, on the other hand, that this is by no means certain. Amm. is not always as vague as he is here and he sometimes does specify the origins of barbarian auxiliaries. In 27.4.1, for instance, he states that *Gothi* had furnished the usurper Procopius with soldiers: *Valens ... arma concussit in Gothos ... quod auxilia misere Procopio civilia bella coeptanti* (needless to say that the *auxilia* of the text just quoted and of the section under discussion differ from those mentioned in 20.1.3; see the commentary ad loc.).

mercede vel gratia The expression is reminiscent of 16.12.26, where this is said about the troops of the Alamannic kings: *armatorumque milia triginta et quinque, ex variis nationibus partim mercede, partim pacto vicissitudinis reddendae quaesita*. The term *merces* is regularly used to denote the payment of mercenaries: *factum esse uti ab Arvernis Sequanisque Germani mercede arcesserentur* (Caes. *Gal.* 1.31.4), *Gallica auxilia mercede sollicitabantur* (Liv. 10.18.2), *mittit qui auxilia mercede facerent* (Tac. *Ann.* 6.33.2), *relicta plebe quam coegerat magna mercede* (Amm. 29.5.34). Cf. also 30.2.6: *Scytharum auxilia ... mercante*. As to *gratia*, one is reminded of the fact that the Roman government was sometimes (not only in the Later Empire, as Luttwak, 1976, 33 points out) forced to subsidize barbarian tribes in order to keep them quiet. Cf. e.g. 25.6.10, 24.3.4 (*auro quietem a barbaris redemptare*) and Julian's reproach that Constantius was too much in the habit of trying to conciliate the barbarians (λίαν εἰωθότι θεραπεύειν τοὺς βαρβάρους, *Ep. ad Ath.* 280b).

loca suspecta The same expression to denote points of danger is used in 16.3.3, 20.7.1 (cf. the note), 26.5.14, 31.8.5.

adulto vere Cf. *primo vere* in 20.4.2.

e Thraciis In 27.4.11–12 Amm. distinguishes between Thrace in the wider sense, that is to say the diocese, and Thrace in the narrower sense, viz. one of the provinces which formed the diocese: *Thraciae omnes ... sex provinciae ... inter quas prima ... Thracia speciali nomine appellatur*. When referring to the diocese, Amm. as a rule uses the plural (on this see Zawadzki, 1976, who argues that the singular as a designation of the diocese gradually disappeared in the fourth century; in Amm. the proportion of plural to singular is 34:7, rather than 23:6, as Zawadzki, followed by Szidat and Marié, 1984, 241 n. 185, holds).

Thrace was one of the twelve dioceses into which Diocletian had grouped the provinces of the empire. Its organisation underwent very little change in the period up to its abolishment by Anastasius (cf. Jones 373–374 and Velkov, 1981). Amm. gives a description of Thrace in two digressions, 22.8 and 27.4.

VIII. 2 This section is remarkable for Amm.'s very strong insistence on Julian's lack of confidence and determination caused by fears, with which he returns to the purport of the narrative in sections 19–21 of ch. 4, cf. especially *accidentium varietate perterritus Iulianus* (20.4.20).

Inter quae This is the relative counterpart of *inter haec*, which occurs twice as frequently. Amm. uses these pronominal expressions more often than *interea* (only 5 times) or *interim*. The latter adverb is a great favourite with Livy, who also has a fair amount of instances of *inter haec*. Cf. ad 14.6.1.

summa coeptorum quorsum evaderet, pertimescens Cf. 21.12.10 *summa coepti prudentis aliorsum evasit* and 21.13.9 *summa itaque coeptorum quorsum evaderet ambigens*, where *summa* has the same meaning as here: 'sum total', 'result'. For *quorsum* cf. 17.2.2 (with the note), 27.3.1, 31.16.1. This is the only instance in Amm. of an indirect question as a complement of *pertimescere*, which is usually accompanied by a direct object and twice (17.2.3, 31.5.2) by a clause introduced by *ne*. The present case is an extension of the classical use of *pertimescere*, which is hardly surprising in view of the fact that *timere* and *metuere* are regularly combined with indirect questions: *haec quo sint eruptura timeo* (Cic. *Att.* 2.20.5).

erat anxius In itself this phrase is not impossible: cf. *sollicitus erat et anxius* (28.4.1) and Sal. *Cat.* 46.2 *anxius erat dubitans ... quid facto opus esset*. All the same, as the main predicate of the period it is rather a flat expression, especially in comparison with the words preceding it. This unsatisfactory state of affairs is mended perfectly by the emendation c.c. suggested by Heraeus and accepted by Clark: *haeserat anxius*. There are two parallels in Amm.: *anxia cogitatione quid moliretur haerebat* (14.11.6) and *haerebat anxius qua vi ... terras eorum invaderet repentinus* (18.2.1). It is true that in both these instances *anxius* is followed by an indirect question, but in the present case such a clause, dependent on *pertimescens*, has already preceded. The tense of *haeserat* is quite suitable too, for it refers to Julian's thoughts before the events reported in the following sections.

numquam assensurum Constantium factis multa volvendo considerans The use of an acc.c.inf. with *considerare*, which also occurs in 14.1.10, 21.4.1, 24.1.8, 26.4.3, is not frequent, although it can be found already in classical Latin, e.g. *considerare debes nihil tibi esse committendum* (Cic. *Fam.* 6.12.5). The equivalence of the abl. gerundii and the part. pres. can be illustrated by comparing *multa volvendo* with 26.4.3 *multa secum ipse diu volvens* (also in coordination with *considerans*!). Here the phrase emphasizes Julian's hesitation.

apud quem sordebat ut infimus et contemptus As the whole of the preceding part of the period reports Julian's fears and feelings, it is tempting also to regard this relative clause as being part of his thoughts. But this seems to be precluded by the absence of the subj., which is required in virtual oratio obliqua. The adiectival use of the part. perf. *contemptus*, which according to TLL IV 645.7 is equivalent to *contemnendus*, is found more often in Amm.; the contempt may be based on moral considerations: *feritate contemptior* (16.7.8), *ut cunctator contemptus* (28.1.44) or a person's relative lack of power: *contemptus ut comitantibus paucis* (21.8.2). In the present case, however, *sordebat* and *infimus* prove that Julian fears being despised for social reasons; for *sordere* cf. 14.7.6 *vulgi sordidioris*, Livy 4.25.11 *adeo se suis etiam sordere nec a plebe minus quam a patribus contemni* and Gudeman ad Tac. *Dial.* 32.4; *infimus* as a term denoting social position can be illustrated by Pl. *Capt.* 305 *me qui liber fueram servom fecit, e summo infumum* and Livy 1.47.11 *fautorem infimi generis hominum ex quo ipse sit*.

Whether the contents of the relative clause are to be regarded as Julian's thoughts or as a statement by the author, in either case it must be doubted whether what is said in the clause is true. For it is unlikely and even incredible that Constantius should think about Julian as a person belonging to the lowest classes of society. Feelings of fear or jealousy can readily be believed, but the utter contempt suggested by Amm. strains the imagination.

VIII. 3 *circumspectis itaque trepidis rerum novarum exordiis* Some other examples of *circumspicere* denoting the thorough examination of a dangerous situation: *timidis et omnia pericula circumspicientibus* (Cic. *Mil.* 95), *circumspectis difficultatibus* (Liv. 28.6.12), *circumspecta infrequentia militis* (Tac. *Ann.* 14.33.1), *anxia sollicitudine stringebatur, reputans multa et circumspiciens quibus commentis Alamannorum et Macriani regis frangeret fastus* (Amm. 28.5.8). The use of *res novae* implies that Julian was perfectly aware of the revolutionary character of his rise to imperial power: the expression is used about Barbatio (18.3.1), Valentinus (28.3.4) and, especially, Procopius (17.14.3, 25.7.10, 26.5.8). When actions are concerned, Amm. usually has the plural *exordia*: *Gallicani procinctus exordia* (17.8.1), *inter exordia ipsa coeptorum* (21.7.1), whilst in other cases the singular is found: *primo lucis exordio* (24.2.5).

legatos In section 19 they are mentioned by name, viz. Pentadius, *officiorum magister*, and Eutherius, *cubiculi tunc praepositus*.

gesta docturos For this use of the part. fut. cf. the note ad 20.2.2 *spectaturos*.

eisque concinentes litteras dedit For *concinere* see above the note ad 20.4.1 *perfugae concinentes exploratoribus*. Referring to the way in which Constantius was informed about the behaviour of Gallus (14.9.1 and 14.10.2) Sabbah 171 notes: "Selon l'habitude du temps, Herculanus a transmis le rapport de son supérieur en le complétant et en le confirmant verbalement. Ainsi font également Euthérius et Pentadius, chargés par Julien de confirmer la lettre adressée par le César à Constance". In the present section, however, the facts are set forth the other way round: the letter is meant to elucidate the situation and its consequences more clearly than the oral report. In section 19, however, the order sketched by Sabbah is followed. See below the note ad loc.

The comparative *apertius* should be taken literally, as in the two other instances in Amm.: *rebus ipsis id apertius monstrare concedens* (31.14.4) and 29.2.14; the positivus *aperte* occurs more than 30 times.

quidve fieri oporteat deinceps   As is noted in TLL V 404.37 sqq., since Sal. *deinceps* gradually became a synonym of *postea*. Cf. also the notes ad 17.5.11, 19.4.6, 19.6.3.

monens apertius et demonstrans   Mark the chiastic placing with regard to the preceding cola: *monens* refers to *quidve fieri oporteat deinceps* and *demonstrans* to *quid actum sit*.

VIII. 4 *quamquam eum haec dudum comperisse opinabatur*   It is difficult to understand why both Clark and Seyfarth print a full stop after *demonstrans* in section 3; thus, the present sentence has to be regarded as a main clause, which *quamquam* characterizes as the correction of a preceding statement: *quamquam quid loquor?* (Cic. *Cat.* 1.22), *Romanus ... Volscum primo impetu perculit; quamquam cessere magis quam pulsi hostes sunt* (Liv. 2.65.1–2). It would, however, be the only instance of *quamquam correctivum* in Amm. and, besides, there is no reason why the sentence should not be attributed a normal sense as a concessive clause: Julian sent a message to Constantius, although he expected the latter already to have been informed of the facts. Another possibility could be to athetize *et quamquam* in the locus conclamatus in the last part of this section, and to take *tamen ... scripsit* as the apodosis of the present sentence. In that case, too, it would be a normal concessive clause.

As to *quamquam* the facts are as follows: it occurs 27 times, 18 times preceded by *et* (see above the note on *et quia* in 20.4.6). In 8 cases it is followed by a subj., elsewhere by an indic. Ehrismann 60–62 has attempted to detect a system in the use of the modi, but he has to admit exceptions to the rule he proposes, which seems rather ominous in the case of such a small corpus.

Amm. uses *dudum* quite frequently, but only in four instances combined with *iam*. But, as in classical Latin, also without *iam* it can mean 'long ago', 'for a long time': *militesque intenti dudum ac parati ... clamore sublato decurrunt* (Liv. 24.39.4).

relatu Decentii olim reversi   In the three other cases *relatu* is supinum: *visu relatuque horrendum natum est monstrum* (19.12.19), 16.10.15, 21.13.11. It is a comparatively rare word, dealt with by De Jonge in his note on 16.10.15. His rendering of *relatus* in the present case ("message") is not correct, it should rather be 'account', 'report' (provided by Decentius personally). It should not be confused with *relatio*, which denotes an official dispatch: cf. the notes ad 16.11.7 and 20.4.7.

Decentius' return to the East has not yet been mentioned. By adding *olim*, which here is a synonym of *dudum*, Amm. suggests that he had left Gaul soon after the usurpation.

et cubiculariorum recens de Galliis praegressorum   Strictly speaking, *cubicularii* were servants of the bedchamber (*sacrum cubiculum*) of the emperor and empress, but the term is also used in a wider sense to denote the court eunuchs in general. See the literature cited ad 20.2.3 *Eusebius, cubiculi tunc praepositus*. They could be entrusted with "more delicate missions, which required an agent of greater authority" than the normal functionaries (Jones 401).

At first sight Gelenius' *regressorum* seems to suit the context better, but in fact it is not necessary to get rid of *praegressorum*: travelling from Gaul, these eunuchs had only recently 'preceded' Julian's envoys.

qui ad Caesarem aliqua portavére sollémnia   Wagner notes: "h.e. tributorum in Galliis exactorum debitam partem Iuliano attulerant, (quae eadem *sollemnium* significatio est XXII, 7)". He refers to *annua complentes sollemnia* (22.7.10) and might also have mentioned 17.3.5, where *sollemnia* means 'the regular payment of taxes'; cf. the note ad loc. The expression *aliqua sollemnia* is rather vague, however, and Szidat may be right in interpreting it as a reference to the annual contributions by Constantius to meet the expenses of Julian's household, although his argument that *cubicularii* have nothing to do "mit der Finanzverwaltung" is not at all conclusive. As was stated in the preceding note, the services of such functionaries could be used for different kinds of tasks.

The perf. *portavere* is one of the many instances of the use of the perfect in a relative clause, where a pluperfect would have been used in classical Latin. In the present case the cursus seems to be the main reason. Cf. Ehrismann 31/2.

et quamquam non repugnanter nec arrogantibus verbis quidquam tamen scripsit, ne videretur subito redundasse   It is perhaps useful to provide the text of the locus conclamatus as it is found in V: *et quamquam non repugnant certant* (*repugnanter tamen* m 2) *nec arrogantibus verbis quicquam scripsit ne videretur subito redundasset* (*repuggnasse* m 2). The general purport seems to be clear: in his letter Julian keeps a low profile. The problems, however, are as considerable as the proposals for emendation are numerous. These either consist in additions or in changes. Szidat adheres to the first method, adding (with Novák) *nova referret* after *quamquam* ('although he reported a revolution') and (with Selem) *reus* before *redundasse*[*t*]. If such corrections are regarded as too drastic, two problems in the first part of the sentence have to be addressed: 1. there are no other instances in Amm. of *quamquam* with an adverb, 2. *repugnanter* and *arrogantibus verbis* must be in contrast with one another, as Wagner rightly remarks, drawing the following tentative conclusion: "fortasse aliud verbum pro *repugnanter* Ammianus posuerat, cui significatio inesset ea, ut Iulianus non *demisse* quidem, immo aperte scripserit". Petschenig's *repigranter* ('putting on the brakes') and Heraeus' *obsecundanter* intend to meet this demand. Seyfarth has not accepted these suggestions, but merely follows Pighi's transposition of *tamen*, which is put after *quidquam*, but without the comma (before *tamen*) which is essential for the latter's interpretation. Cf. Pighi, 1935, 98-101. The translation illustrates Wagner's problem: "Sein Schreiben war zwar nicht in widersetzlichem Ton gehalten, aber auch nicht in anmassenden Worten". This is, of course, most unsatisfactory. The only possible explanation of *repugnanter* is to accept a close link with the immediately preceding sentence: Julian wrote 'without opposing' the reports of Decentius and the eunuchs and thus openly admitting the usurpation, but 'not in arrogant terms'. The transposition of *tamen* is unnecessary, provided a comma is printed after *repugnanter*.

What impression was Julian trying to avoid (*ne videretur*)? The choice of *repugnasse* would imply the suddenness of the rebellion, but this relates to the contents of the letter, not, as is clearly the purport of the preceding sentence, of its style. Valesius' choice of *reclinasse* (the v.l. in S) suffers from the same defect (he interprets this verb as the equivalent of ἀφηνιάζειν and ἀναχαιτίζειν, about a horse throwing off its rider). On the other hand, *redundasse* would be the only instance of the verb in Amm., with an unprecedented sense, too: 'superbia efferri'. In view of *subito* it is less likely to be a rhetorical t.t. here, as in Cic. *de Orat*. 1.20 *efflorescat et redundet oportet oratio*.

All in all, Clark's crux before *repugnanter* may be a shade too pessimistic, if the interpretation suggested above ('opposing Decentius' account') is acceptable, but the crux before *repugnasse* seems hardly contestable.

nec arrogantibus verbis In his *Ep. ad Ath*. Julian himself more than once emphasizes his deferential attitude vis-à-vis Constantius: σκοπεῖτε δὲ ὅπως καὶ γενόμενος αὐτοκράτωρ ἔτι θεραπευτικῶς αὐτῷ προσηνέχθην ἐξ ὧν ἐπέστειλα (281c) and οὔπω καὶ τήμερον ἐν ταῖς πρὸς αὐτὸν ἐπιστολαῖς τῇ δοθείσῃ μοι παρὰ τῶν θεῶν ἐπωνυμίᾳ κέχρημαι (285d).

erat autem litterarum sensus huiusmodi Cf. *sensuque intellecto scriptorum* (18.6.17) and especially 17.5.2 (about Sapor's letter to Constantius) *litteras ... quarum hunc fuisse accepimus sensum*. To denote the tenor of a speech or a written document other writers make use of *sententia*: *imperator Romanus in hanc fere sententiam respondit* (Liv. 30.31.1), *misere ad Cerialem epistulas, quarum haec sententia fuit* (Tac. *Hist*. 4.75.1), *litteras ad senatum composuit quarum sententia in hunc modum fuit* (Tac. *Ann.* 3.52.3), *litteras ... quarum sententia haec fuit* (HA *Max.* 12.5). The expression shows that Amm., following the normal practice of historians, has composed the text himself on the basis of whatever information may have reached him. As Bowersock, 1978, 52 remarks, "there is no reason to regard" the letter "as an authentic fragment of Julian's own writings". In fact, the only other source mentioning this particular letter, pace Seyfarth, II, 1983⁵, 198 n. 72, is Zonaras *Epit.* 13.10.16–18, a passage which contains a few remarkable parallels with Amm.

VIII. 5 Although, as Pighi, 1936 (2), 32–34 notes, in the whole of the *Res Gestae* some 50 letters are mentioned, in only three cases does Amm. provide the text or, rather, a paraphrase. Two of these can be found in ch. 5 of book 17, where the contents of the reciprocal letters of Sapor and Constantius are reported. Obviously this means that the present letter is deemed very important by Amm.: it belongs to the class of *negotiorum celsitudines* (26.1.1). Bidez incorporates the text as no. 17b in his edition of Julian's letters, not regarding it as a literal transcript, however, but as "la version visiblement très libre d'Ammien". This expression deftly masks the problems, viz. whether Julian did indeed send a letter and, if so, what its precise contents were.

As was stated just now in the last note on the preceding section, there is no explicit mention of a letter in the works of Julian, Libanius or Zosimus. But, apart from the fact that it is, generally speaking, likely that a written document was handed to the emperor, the letter is clearly reported by Zonaras, whose short summary of the contents shows some striking similarities with Amm.'s text. It seems reasonable to regard these details as reliable elements in Amm.'s version, but at the same time it should be emphasized that they are incorporated in a well-thought-out composition which, both in its wording and purport, tallies completely with the author's narrative. The description of the events at Paris in sections 7–10 fully squares with the one provided in 20.4.10 sqq. On the whole the letter is an important part of Amm.'s presentation of Julian, whom he continually portrays not as a rash revolutionary striving after the fall, or at least the disparagement, of his rival, but as a responsible ruler, who for the sake of the empire asks for nothing else than cooperation.

There is also a striking 'negative' similarity between the narrative in ch. 4 and the letter. In both cases all references to a divine sign or the will of the gods (cf. οἵ τε τοῦτο βουλόμενοι γενέσθαι θεοί, *Ep. ad Ath.* 284d) are conspicuously absent. Julian's vision of the *genius publicus* was only reported *iunctioribus proximis* (20.5.10, cf. the note ad loc.) and has no 'public' function in Amm.'s version of the events. It is difficult to decide whether the absence or in any case the inconspicuous nature of the part played by the divine world is to be ascribed to Julian's official stance in the original letter or to Amm.'s narrative conception.

The structure of the letter is carefully devised, as a brief analysis may show:
- 5-6 Julian's loyal services to the empire and to Constantius during the campaigns in Gaul,
- 7-10 account of the events at Paris: causes and final results.
- 11-12 plea to accept the situation and assurance of a continued respect for Constantius' authority,
- 13-16 proposals and promises for the future,
- 17 insistence on the need for unity and cooperation.

The beginning, middle and end of the letter are devoted to the good relationship between Julian and Constantius: these sections encompass the two passages which contain the tangible realities of the situation. At the same time there is a clear line from the past via the present to the future.

Ego quidem This strong emphasis laid on his personal loyalty helps prepare the introduction of those truly responsible in section 7 (*miles*). The occurrences of *ego* are comparatively rare: 10 times, of which 4 concern the author himself.

propositi mei fidem Cf. above the note ad 20.5.4 *numquam a proposito recte vivendi deiectus sum*.

non minus moribus quam foederum pacto Julian's mode of conduct is firmly consistent because of his loyalty to the arrangements made with Constantius and to an even greater extent thanks to his normal behaviour. The gen. *foederum* can be interpreted as a gen. explicativus, perhaps even as a gen. inhaerentiae (Hagendahl, 1924, 192-202, Szantyr 63). The expression presumably refers to the directives which Constantius gave in the speech held after he had clothed Julian in the imperial purple (15.8.12-14) or to the manual which he had sent Julian and which the latter regularly consulted: *cum legeret libellum assidue, quem Constantius, ut privignum ad studia mittens, manu sua conscripserat* (16.5.3).

quoad fuit The laconic brevity with which the dissolution of the existing agreement is mentioned is quite remarkable, but in itself consistent with the euphemistic *si quid novatum est nunc* in section 7. Julian can allow himself these expressions, because in sections 7 and 8 he explains that the terms of the agreement were no longer tenable.

unum semper atque idem sentiens Constantius uses the same expression in a speech to his soldiers: *vos unum idemque sentientes* (17.13.33). De Jonge ad loc. refers to Cic. *Cat.* 4.14 and 4.19, where the expression is also used. To these can be added Cic. *Phil.* 3.32 and 14.16. These parallels suggest that the phrase which at first sight might be considered to stress Julian's consistency, should perhaps rather be taken as a reference to his harmonious relationship with Constantius.

ut effectu multiplici claruit evidenter The term *effectus* either refers to the implementation of some plan: *effectu res difficillima* (24.4.10), *utque celeritas effectum negotii faceret tutum* (28.2.5), or to the result or effect: *negotii plenus effectus* (15.12.5), *hoc prospero rerum effectu* (27.2.4). Cf. also the note ad 17.4.14. In view of the context the second meaning should be chosen here. For *clare(sce)re* meaning 'to be (come) obvious or evident' cf. 16.5.14, 17.2.1, 17.9.7, 24.3.13 and De Jonge ad 17.1.14. The phrase *claruit evidenter* is illustrated by *nuntiis crebris* and *documentis assiduis* in the next section.

VIII. 6 *iamque inde uti* This combination of the classical *iam inde (ab)*, 'continuously (from)', and the temporal conjunction *ut* occurs only in Amm. Apart from the present text the other instances are 15.11.6, 17.9.6, 22.16.6. Wagner's explanation ("i.e. ex quo") is not incorrect, but should be supplemented: Julian stresses the loyalty of his line of conduct 'from the very moment he was appointed Caesar': November 6, 355 A.D.. Cf. Amm. 15.8.17: *Haec diem octavum iduum Novembrium gesta sunt, cum Arbitionem consulem annus haberet et Lollianum.*

pugnarum horrendis fragoribus This is a very stereotypical phrase; *fragor* is often used to denote the uproar of the battlefield, e.g. 16.1.1 *pugnarum fragores*, 27.10.12 *bellum fragore terribili concitantes*, 31.5.13 *post bellorum fragores immensos*, 31.10.8 *horrifico ... fragore terrente*. There is a tendency to add strong adjectives, *horrendus* being one of them: 26.6.16, 31.12.12 and, in other contexts, 15.8.15, 22.8.14. Cf. also Liv. 21.58.5 *inter horrendos fragores*, 29.14.3 *cum horrendo fragore*.

potestate delata contentus For the position of Julian as a Caesar of Constantius, see the literature cited ad 20.4.5 (*parvi ... obtemperabat*).

currentium ex voto prosperitatum nuntiis crebris Cf. *cunctis igitur ex voto currentibus* (17.9.1), *hoc rerum prospero currente successu* (17.13.24). De Jonge ad 17.9.1 quotes Tac. *Hist.* 3.48.3 *cunctis super vota fluentibus*. To this can be added Tac. *Dial.* 5.6 *rebus prospere fluentibus* (cf. Gudeman's note), *Ann.* 15.5.3 *nec praesentia propere fluebant*. Cf. also Cic. *Off.* 1.26.90 and Seyffert-Müller ad Cic. *Lael.* 12.43 (p. 306), where some examples of *ire* with this meaning ('to proceed', 'to develop') are given. For *currere* as a synonym of *evenire* or *procedere* TLL IV 1518.68 sqq. provides only post-classical instances.

The plural of *prosperitas* is rare. Amm. has three instances: *prosperitatibus summarum rerum elati* (17.4.6), *prosperitates similes adventare* (24.6.16). An early example is Cic. *N.D.* 3.88 *improborum ... prosperitates*. It should be noted that in Amm. the singular does not always mean 'prosperity', but can also denote a particular instance of good luck: *inopina prosperitate elatus* (25.5.9), *erectus prosperitate nimia* (31.9.2).

For *nuntiis crebris* cf. 17.11.1 *erat enim necesse, tamquam apparitorem, Caesarem super omnibus gestis ad Augusti referre scientiam.*

ut apparitor fidus Cf. the text just quoted and 16.7.3, where Eutherius is said to be convinced that Julian *apparitoremque fidum auctori suo* (i.e. Constantius) *quoad vixerit fore*. The idea has the character of a topos emphasizing the subordinate position of the Caesares: *Diocletiano et eius collegae ut apparitores Caesares ... obtemperabant* (14.11.10); cf. also the note ad 20.4.5. Even Valens, who had been proclaimed Augustus, was very compliant towards his brother Valentinian, *in modum apparitoris* (26.4.3).

For the literal meaning of *apparitor* ('clerk', 'servant') cf. the note ad 15.7.3.

periculis meis assignans For the meaning of the verb here, "imputare alicui auctori" (TLL II 893.74), cf. 28.5.14 *ut solent Aegyptii casus eius modi suis assignare rectoribus*, and for a non-human 'auctor' 15.5.35 *hoc quoque felicitatis suae prosperis cursibus assignabat.*

cum documentis assiduis constet Dealing with "le vocabulaire de l'évidence", Sabbah 398 ascribes to *documentum* a "caractère d'évidence, c'est-à-dire de clarté qui s'impose à l'esprit"; about *constare* he says: "il est surtout fréquent dans les applications historiques, pour rappeler une vérité admise". There is nothing new or exclusive in this: *constat*, 'it is an established fact', is normal already in classical prose, especially in Livy, and TLL V 1. 1807.13 sqq. provides a long list of mainly post-classical instances where *documentum* can be regarded as "fere i.q. exemplum quod probat aliquid, probatio, interdum fere i.q. experimentum".

diffusis permixtisque passim Germanis The former of the two participles is not difficult to understand: the Germans 'had swarmed' through Gaul, cf. the same phrase in Julian's obituary: *diffusis per nostra Germanis* (25.4.25); *permixtis*, however, is more difficult to explain exactly: the verb *permiscere* can denote the forming of a combination or alliance, as in *Gothi Hunis*

Halanisque permixti (31.16.3), or the intermingling of two or more groups, e.g. *cum ... permixtum senatui esset populi concilium* (Liv. 21.14.1). In such cases, however, the people or group with which the combination is made is explicitly stated. Rolfe and Selem assume that Amm. refers to the unity and alliances among the Germans themselves, witness their respective translations "interallied" and "uniti fra loro", but perhaps it is more likely that the Germans had 'infiltrated' in Gaul and that the two participles together emphasize that the German danger loomed everywhere.

in laboribus me semper visum omnium primum, in laborum refectione postremum   This seems a reminiscence of the famous phrase in Livy's portrait of Hannibal: *princeps in proelium ibat, ultimus conserto proelio excedebat* (Liv. 21.4.8). Hannibal is mentioned by Amm. in four passages: 15.10.10 and 11, 18.5.6, 22.9.3, 25.1.15. Livy seems to have been Amm.'s source, which is especially clear in the second passage mentioned: *Maharbal lentitudinis increpans Hannibalem, posse eum vincere, sed victoria uti nescire, assidue praedicabat* (18.5.6), which evidently derives from Liv. 22.51.4 *vincere scis, Hannibal, victoria uti nescis*. In Florus' report of the same incident (1.22.19) the sentence has a different structure.

VIII. 7   *sed bona tua venia dixerim*   Cf. *bona hoc tua venia dixerim* (Cic. *Div.* 1.25), *bona venia tua dixerim* (Liv. 28.43.7). Pease ad Cic. *N.D.* 1.59 *bona venia me audies* provides a list of occurrences of this polite phrase, to which can be added Cic. *de Orat.* 1.242, Livy 6.40.10, 29.17.6, Pliny *Ep.* 5.6.46.

si quid novatum est nunc, ut existimas   Amm. uses *novare* only once in a 'neutral' sense, stating about Constantius in the latter's obituary: *nihil circa administrationum augmenta praeter pauca novari perpessus* (21.16.1). In all other cases it expresses revolutionary actions or the violation of loyalty, e.g. 29.6.5, where it is told that Marcellianus ruthlessly executed *Gabinium regem nequid novaretur modeste poscentem*. Julian's addition *ut existimas* curiously anticipates Constantius' judgement, which in the next chapter is expressed in precisely such terms: *nihil novatorum se asserens suscepisse* (20.9.4).

aetatem sine fructu conterens miles   The first example of *aetatem conterere* is Pl. *Bac.* 781 (ut) *in pistrino aetatem conteras*; cf. also Cic. *de Orat.* 1.219 and Amm. 14.6.13.

olim deliberatum implevit   The addition of *olim* ('since long ago') intensifies the meaning of *deliberare*, which implies careful thought. For *implere*, 'to carry out' cf. *quidquid pro re publica mandaverit, impleturi* (16.10.21), *quidquid geri potuisset, impleri debere aperte iubentes* (19.3.2) and the note ad 14.1.5.

fremens secundique impatiens loci rectorem In the section of the lemma *fremere* devoted to the human voice TLL VI 1283.3 sqq. lists all five such occurrences in Amm. as "praevalente sensu furendi, furenter irascendi". For 16.8.7 (Constantius' rage on learning about a plot), 16.12.37, 20.7.5, 31.7.8 (war-cries) this is correct, but the present instance rather belongs to the cases "praevalente sensu indignandi" (ib. 1282.54 sqq.). *Impatiens* usually has a complement in the gen.: *differendi* (31.10.7), *dolorum* (23.3.6), *laborum* (31.14.5), *morarum* (14.10.3, 19.6.7, 21.10.2, 28.1.9), *otii* (22.12.2), *proeliorum ... et laborum* (27.10.10), *quietis* (28.3.4). The present text provides the only example of the acc. Löfstedt, 1942, I 255 agrees with Blomgren 135, who remarks that in the present case the gen. has been avoided because of the gen. *secundi loci* ("duplicem genetivum propter ambiguitatem displicuisse"). In itself this observation is correct, but it may be added that in the cases mentioned there is a preference for the gen. plur., where this is possible, presumably because of the generalizing character, and that in none of the instances a person is concerned.

As for *rector*, see the note ad 20.1.1.

Julian throws the full responsibility of the events upon the soldiers, in complete agreement with Amm.'s account in ch. 4 and also with the following passage in Zonaras' version of the letter: ἀπολογούμενος ὡς οὐχ ἑκὼν προήχθη πρὸς τὴν τῆς βασιλείας ἀνάρρησιν, βιασθεὶς δ' ὑπὸ τῶν στρατιωτῶν μὴ βουλομένων στρατεύεσθαι ὑπὸ Καίσαρι, ἀλλ' ὑπὸ βασιλεῖ (*Epit.* 13.10.16).

cum nullas sibi vices a Caesare diuturni sudoris et victoriarum frequentium rependi posse contemplaretur The immediate sequel of the text just quoted from Zonaras provides a striking parallel: καὶ ἵν' ἔχοιεν ἐξ αὐτοῦ ἀξίας τῶν πόνων τὰς ἀμοιβὰς ἀπαιτεῖν. Mark the close similarity: ἀμοιβάς – *vices*, 'requital', which is the more remarkable as it is the only instance of *vicis* with this meaning in Amm.

For *sudoris* ('labour', 'exertion') cf. Liv. 7.38.6 *victor exercitus ... qui suo sudore ac sanguine inde Samnites depulisset*, 2.48.2 and Tac. *Ger.* 14.3. Other instances in Amm. are 17.13.31 *quae sudore quaesivit et dexteris*, 17.2.1 (with De Jonge's note), 17.9.6, 28.4.21. A curious case is Caes. *Gal.* 7.8.2 *ita viis patefactis summo militum sudore*, where most editors prefer the v.l. *labore*, O. Seel (Teubner 1961) even reporting about *sudore*: "quod defendere nemo ausus est".

The verb *rependere* occurs only here, in contrast with *contemplari*, which is quite frequent, especially with an acc.c.inf. as complement; cf. the note ad 17.13.6.

III. 8 *cuius iracundiae nec dignitatum augmenta nec annuum merentis stipendium id quoque inopinum accessit* The often latent difference between *ira* ('rage') and *iracundia*, which can denote a more permanent state of anger or resentment, is quite clear here: the soldiers' persistent discontent develops into a furious rage because of a new occasion for indignation.

In 21.2.3 *dignitatis augmentum* denotes Julian's 'increase in status', in 17.12.20 the addition (consisting in the crowning of a king) to the freedom restored to the Sarmatians. Cf. also *incrementa dignitatum* (23.6.5). Here the soldiers complain about the absence of any 'promotion'. Amm. refers to 20.5.8 *dignitatum iam diu expers et praemiorum*.

The words *nec annuum merentis stipendium* clearly repeat 17.9.6 *sudoribus Gallicanis miles exhaustus nec donativum meruit nec stipendium*, where just as in the present text *merere* denotes the actual drawing of the soldiers' pay. In the middle of the fourth century the soldiers were chiefly (not exclusively, as Seeck, 1920–1923$^{2-4}$, II, 257 thought) paid in kind (cf. 22.4.9 *vicenas diurnas ... annonas totidemque pabula iumentorum, quae vulgo dictitant capita*), but they received some money wage too, in theory paid annually (ibid.: *annuum stipendium grave*). This pay was supplemented by donatives, also paid in cash, on the birthdays and accession days (see above, ad 20.4.18) of the emperors, and on their consulates, and by occasional presents, such as rings, bracelets, fibulae, silver plates and the like. See on this De Jonge's note ad 17.9.6, Jones 623–624 and Delmaire, 1977, 312–315.

Amm. rather likes *inopinus*, using it more than 20 times. It is a mainly poetic word, which first occurs in Verg. *A*. 5.857 *vix primos inopina quies laxaverat artus*.

ad partes orbis eoi postremas   This repeats the complaint raised in the *famosus libellus* in ch. 4.10: *nos quidem ad orbis terrarum extrema ut noxii pellimur et damnati*. For *orbis eoi* cf. 14.8.4, 25.8.14, 26.5.15, 27.1.1.

assueti glacialibus terris   The adj. was originally mainly poetic: *glacialis hiems* (Verg. *A*. 3.285), *extremis Scythiae glacialis in oris* (Ov. *Met.* 8.788).

separandique liberis et coniugibus   For the gerundivum as part. fut. pass. cf. above the note ad *opitulari* (20.2.4).

egentes trahebantur et nudi   The combination of *egens* and *nudus* is used in a few other texts to add to the pathetic picture of somebody's plight: *nudus atque egens ad extremum fugit e regno* (Cic. *Rab. Post*. 39), Apul. *Apol*. 75.8, 92.2.

solito saevius efferati   Amm. is rather fond of the abl. comp. *solito*. Cf. De Jonge ad 14.6.9, Szantyr 108 and see above 20.3.6 and 20.5.1; Livy has some ten instances. The whole phrase sketches the soldiers' rage in strong terms: 'they behaved with abnormal aggressiveness as furious wild beasts'.

palatium obsidere   In all but two cases in Amm. the verb concerns the siege or a blockade of towns and other strongholds. This proves that Julian is using a forceful expression, akin to the phrase which sketches the true position of Procopius at the time of his usurpation: *cum honore quidem, sed in modum tenebatur obsessi* (26.6.14). Some early editions unnecessarily change *obsidere* into *obsedere*. Some composita of *sedere* (*sidere*) sometimes have a perf. with the vowel *i*, although the *e* is more usual (Neue-Wagener, 1902, III 414/6). The phrase refers to 20.4.14 *petiverunt palatium*.

Augustum Iulianum vocibus magnis appellantes et crebris   This repeats 20.4.14 *Augustum Iulianum horrendis clamoribus concrepabant*; see above the note ad loc.

III. 9   *cohorrui, fateor, et secessi*   Occurrences of *cohorrescere* are scarce throughout Latin literature. The only other instance in Amm. is 16.10.9. Parenthetical *fateor* is used very frequently, often in a rather weakened sense, as the lists in TLL VI 1. 336.70 sqq. show. In his scathing comments on F. Skutsch's attempt to explain a disputed verse in Statius' *Silvae* (2.1.67 *muta domus, fateor, desolatique penates*, cf. H.-J. Van Dam ad loc.) A.E. Housman (*CQ* 1906, 40 = *Classical Papers* II 643) distinguishes two meanings: "it means to confess or concede something which one might be thought willing to deny ... and it means to declare something which one has the power to conceal". The former of these meanings is quite suitable in the present text.

amendatusque, dum potui, salutem dilatione quaeritabam   Amm. uses *amendare* in contexts concerning complete hiding: (ut) *in secretis se secessibus amendaret* (16.12.58, Valesius' emendation), *silvarum se latebris amendarunt* (27.10.15), *semet abstrusius amendarunt* (28.1.49), 25.10.7, 29.5.53, 30.7.7.

After *potui* V has *salutemus latione*, which has caused several conjectures. Gelenius' *salutem mussatione* is very attractive from a paleographic point of view. The verb *mussare* ('to whisper'), which occurs already in Ennius (*Ann.* 344), is by no means rare, and in Verg. *A*. 11.345 *dicere mussant* it is obviously a synonym of *dubitare*. 'Hesitation' would also fit the present text; unfortunately, however, it would be the first (and possibly the only) instance of *mussatio* in Latin literature. Therefore, Wagner's suggestion (of which he is quite proud: "cuius emendationis non est quod me poeniteat") is preferable: *salutem simul dilatione quaeritabam*, although Seyfarth may well be right in accepting Kiessling's removal of *simul*. Amm. uses *dilatio* in five other places.

For *quaeritabam* cf. the short notes on this verb ad 14.7.7 and 17.7.4.

cumque nullae darentur indutiae As is only natural in a history which deals with a great deal of fighting and warfare, *indutiae* occurs regularly in Amm., denoting a discontinuation of hostilities, either formally agreed or brought about spontaneously. It is used metaphorically only once, when Amm. relates how during his frenetic journey westward the restless Gallus at times found some rest *per indutias naturae* (14.11.17). In the present text *indutiae* has its normal meaning, as Julian describes the soldiers' actions also in full military terms: *palatium obsidere*.

libero pectoris muro, ut ita dixerim, saeptus The use of *pectus* to denote someone's mind or personality is quite normal. Some examples in Amm.: *ut erat angusti pectoris* (19.12.5), *veloci vigore pectoris excitus* (24.6.5), *recto pectore (quod dicitur)* (17.5.9). The last quotation refers to proverbial usage, for which Otto, 1890, 269–270 can be consulted. The present expression is not proverbial, as the addition of *ut ita dixerim* clearly shows; *libero* is remininiscent of *ore et pectore libero docuit gesta* (16.8.7), but that phrase does not present any difficulty, whereas *libero pectoris muro* is hard to explain. Hitherto Julian had sought safety in hiding behind the material walls of his palace, now he decides to seek the shelter provided by his frank and open mind. If this explanation is plausible, *libero* is a case of enallage (for other examples cf. Blomgren 146–7). The metaphorical use of *murus* is paralleled by Cic. *Cat.* 4.23, where Cicero says that as long as the memory of his consulate is kept alive, *tutissimo me muro saeptum esse arbitrabor.* Julian is well aware of the audacity of the expression: *ut ita dixerim* belongs to the "locutiones excusantis se vel corrigentis" (TLL V 1. 975.81 sqq.). A similar case in Amm. is 22.11.3 *iram in Georgium verterunt episcopum, vipereis (ut ita dixerim) morsibus ab eo saepius appetiti.*

molliri posse tumultum Cf. 27.12.17 (ut) *turbas consilio prudenti molliret,* 31.12.9 *se popularium saevitiam mollire non posse.* See also the note ad 17.10.1 *lenito ... tumultu.*

sermonibus blandis This refers to 20.4.16. Cf. also Valens' method: *militem stipendio fovebat et alimentis, et blanda crebritate sermonum* (31.11.1).

VIII. 10 *mirum in modum* This is one of the originally colloquial "Ausdrücke des Staunens und Verwunderns in intensiver Verwendung" (Hofmann, 1951, 78). Like the other expressions, it is found a few times in Cicero's correspondence (e.g. *Att.* 1.14.6, 7.3.1), but also in other authors, e.g. Caes. *Gal.* 1.41.1, Plin. *Nat.* 6.85, Plin. *Ep.* 4.12.6. This is the only occurrence in Amm., who has *miro modo* in 31.2.24.

eo usque provecti, ut Amm. uses the expression *eo usque ... ut* also in 23.6.6, 26.7.13, 27.2.6 and 28.6.21. It can be found in classical prose, Livy has a few instances, but Tacitus uses it more often, cf. especially *Ann.* 2.55.5 *eo usque corruptionis provectus est ut.*

precibus vincere This is a stereotypical phrase, cf. Ov. *Met.* 1.377/8 *'si precibus' dixerunt 'numina iustis / victa remollescunt'*, Liv. 23.8.4 *victusque patris precibus lacrimisque*, 30.12.22, 42.22.7, Suet. *Tib.* 37.4 *nec ut revocaret umquam ullis populi precibus potuit evinci.*

contiguis assultibus The subst., which is very rare in earlier authors (cf. R.D. Williams ad Verg. *A.* 5.442), occurs 11 times in Amm. It refers to animals in 15.2.4, 24.8.5, 29.3.3, the Symplegades in 22.8.14, flames in 23.1.3. The other instances are in military contexts, e.g. a siege. Such a meaning is implied in the present text: Julian says he was assaulted by the soldiers. For the use of *contiguus*, "aus nächster Nähe" (Seyfarth), cf. *ut contigui magis directioresque ictus fiant* (Gel. 9.1.2).

The phrase repeats in more explicit form what is expressed in 20.4.17 by *probrosis conviciis mixto* and in 20.4.18 by *trusus ad necessitatem extremam iamque periculum praesens vitare non posse.* The same idea is to be found in Zonaras, *Epit.* 13.10.12 (quoted above, ad 20.4.17).

mecumque ipse contemplans Both Clark and Seyfarth accept Cornelissen's correction of V's *contestans*. This is indeed plausible: *contemplari* is quite frequent in Amm., especially the partic. praes., which occurs 15 times; there are two examples of a *quod*-clause as a complement (both, however, preceded by an antecedent): 23.5.11 and 29.4.1. Nevertheless Pighi's defense of *contestans*, which would be a hapax in Amm., is interesting. He points out the variety of verbs used by Amm. to denote reflection (*commentari, disputare, pensare, volvere* etc.) and concludes that there is no reason not to add *contestari* to this list. Its meaning would be "affirmare" or "aperte ostendere" and the whole phrase would be equivalent to "sibi ipse affirmans" (Pighi, 1935, 104-106).

quod ... libens declarabitur princeps Like many predicatively used nouns, *libens* is the essential element of the phrase. It contrasts with Julian's own position: he gives in to the soldiers only *victus*, cf. *Caesar assentire coactus est* (20.4.17).

Amm. frequently has a *quod*-clause where classical Latin would have used an acc.c.inf. Ehrismann 66 provides the curious information that in 80% of the cases *quod* depends on a partic. or inf. He also notes that in 75% of the occurrences the indicative is used in the *quod*-clause (ib. 67). Some examples of the indic. fut.: *moxque accepta fide quod si tuto licuerit, sequetur coniugem libens, evasit* (19.9.5), *quod ... proletarios lucrabitur plures* (19.11.7), *addentesque quod ... tristes sollicitudines, si huic irrisioni superfuerit, excitabit* (30.1.17).

For Amm.'s use of *princeps* see above ad 20.2.1, 20.4.8 (*principatus*) and 20.4.12.

vim lenire speratus armatam Rejecting Gelenius' *sperans*, Löfstedt, 1907, 76–78 proposes to correct V's *superatus* into *speratus*, to be understood in an active sense. He draws attention to the deponential conjugation of many verbs in late Latin, especially in the case of "Verba des Glaubens, der Gefühlsstimmung und ähnlicher Bedeutung", with Amm. 29.4.5 *idque, quod acciderat, suspecti* as his crown witness. It must be admitted that the acceptance of *suspecti* (V *suspencti*) can imply the emendation *speratus*: in both cases the part. perf. of these verbs, which Amm. uses in a passive sense in other places, would for once be deponential. Paleographically *speratus* is far more attractive than Heraeus' *posse ratus*, which is accepted by Clark. From that point of view, however, Petschenig's *sic paratus* also deserves consideration, although Löfstedt finds it "der Bedeutung nach etwas gekünstelt". It would testify to more strength of purpose in Julian than *speratus*, which is quite possible in the context.

VIII. 11 *Gestorum hic textus est* For *textus* see above the note ad *quo textu* (20.4.11).

quaeso See above ad 20.4.16.

accipito ... existimes ... admittas ... adverte ... suscipito Although Szantyr 341 remarks that the process of confusing the imperat. praes. and fut. which started in post-classical Latin "führt recht bald zu ihrem völlig unterschiedslosen Gebrauch", it should be noted that in the present case *accipito* and *suscipito*, at the beginning and the end of the series, refer to the events at Paris (sections 7–10) and the future line of conduct proposed by Julian (sections 13–17), respectively. As was shown in the short analysis of the letter (see above the first note on section 5), these are the parts which are concerned with the facts and their consequences, and thus form the essence of the letter.

nec actum quidquam secus existimes Amm.'s use of *secus*, 'otherwise', 'differently', tallies with normal Latin practice. The other half of the antithesis can be mentioned or implied in the context: *secus quam* (22.14.1, 28.5.5), *secus atque* (20.11.24), *si secus accidisset* (15.5.19), *neque secus evenit* (26.9.4), *iure vel secus* (22.6.2), *recte vel secus* (23.5.22), *recte secusve* (27.6.9,

29.2.24). The last examples show that it can be employed euphemistically with the connotation 'badly', 'wrongly'. That is precisely what *secus* means when used absolutely ('contrary to what is right or desirable'): *coepta secus cadebant* (Tac. *Ann.* 2.80.1, cf. also Koestermann ad *Ann.* 2.50.2), *siquid factum sit secus aut dictum* (Amm. 22.10.4); in the other instances in Amm. it qualifies *gesta* (15.5.38, 17.11.1, 21.4.3, 27.7.9). From this it may be concluded that here, too, *secus* has such a sense: Julian wants to state that he has not acted wrongly.

susurrantes perniciosa   Amm. is the first historian who takes great interest in whispering. Both the noun (*susurrus*) and the verb occur in different contexts, but almost always with a negative connotation, the whispers contrasting with honest sincerity, especially at Constantius' court: *imperatoris aures occlusae patebant susurris insidiantium clandestinis* (15.2.2). This obviously was the suspicion harboured in the circle of Ursicinus (see above the note ad 20.2.1) and Julian.

secessiones principum   The normal sense of *secessio* is 'withdrawal', 'abstinence of participation', as in the only other instance in Amm.: *quorum perfidia vel secessione Pannoniarum nudatum est latus* (30.5.3), where it is the equivalent of 'desertion'. The only other example of the meaning 'dissension' or 'rift' seems to be Liv. 28.20.10 *aperta discordia secessionem inter Carthaginienses atque Hispanos fecit*.

adulatione vitiorum altrice depulsa   The verb *adulari* and its cognate nouns (*adulabilis, adulatio, adulator*) abound in post-classical prose. Amm. also has many instances, ascribing this practice especially to Constantius' surroundings: *sufflantes adulatores ex more Constantium id sine modo strepebant* (17.4.12). After a reasonable start Valens, too, became a victim: *adulationum perniciosis illecebris captus* (27.5.8). For the expression cf. 15.5.38 *quae res perniciosa vitiorum est altrix* with De Jonge's note. In the same section Amm. elucidates which behaviour should be preferred to *adulatio*: *ea demum enim laus grata esse potestati debet excelsae, cum interdum et vituperationi secus gestorum pateat locus*. But alas! Constantius was *magniloquentia elatus adulatorum* (16.12.69).

excellentissimam virtutum omnium adverte iustitiam   Cf. Cic. *Off*. 3.28 *haec* (sc. *iustitia*) *enim una virtus omnium est domina et regina virtutum*, Chalcid. *comm.* 267 *iustitia, virtutum omnium principalis* (272.22 Waszink), and above all Cic. *N.D.* 1.4 *una excellentissima virtus iustitia* with Pease's list of parallels, which makes clear that the formula goes back to Arist. *Eth. Nic.* 5.1.15 (1129b 27-28) καὶ διὰ τοῦτο πολλάκις κρατίστη τῶν ἀρετῶν εἶναι δοκεῖ ἡ δικαιοσύνη. There is no such pronouncement in Plato, pace Szidat, whose references are wrong. The verb *advertere* occurs already in classical authors with the meaning 'to pay attention to': *diligentius signa morbi advertunt* (Var. *L.* 10.46), *pericula nostra advertit* (Tac. *Ann.* 14.43.3).

condicionum aequitatem Cf. *fortuna condicionumque aequitate spem successus secundi fundante* (17.5.8), although in the present text *condicionum* is a gen. inversus, as in 17.8.3 *oppositaque condicionum perplexitate* and 18.2.19 *pacem condicionum similitudine* ('on the same terms') *meruerunt*.

bona fide The paraphrase in TLL VI 1.680.20 sqq. "ita ut ei actioni (quam enuntiati verbum exprimit) bene confidi possit" is quite suitable here. Cf. Ov. *Rem.* 649 *sed meliore fide paulatim extinguitur ignis*, Stat. *Silv.* 5 praef. *bona fide deos colit*.

statui Romano prodesse In classical Latin *status*, often with a depending genit. (*civitatis, rei publicae, rerum* etc.), is very frequently used to denote the political situation or the constitution. Examples of such a use can be found in Amm. too: 14.5.4 (*orbis terrarum*, 20.5.3 and 21.4.6 (*provinciarum*), 27.6.12 (where *statum* is Heraeus' emendation, *Romani imperii*), 31.7.1 (*Armeniae*). The present expression, however, differs from these cases. The earliest parallel is Tert. *Resur.* 24.18, where Tertullian, discussing 2 Thess. 2.1–7, says that the enigmatic *qui nunc tenet* (ὁ κατέχων ἄρτι) is none other than *Romanus status*, which cannot have any other meaning than 'the Roman state'. After that the expression can be found in Aur. Vict. *Caes.* 24.9 and 39.48. For a full discussion of *status* in a political sense cf. Köstermann, 1937, who draws attention to the fact that the words in the present text occur in a letter, "also in einem Abschnitte des Werkes, der sich durch eine gepflegtere Diktion auszeichnet" (p. 239). This is not very convincing, as the letter does not show any appreciable differences with Amm.'s usual style. Neither Köstermann nor Suerbaum, 1977[3], 163, mentions the parallel in Zonaras: καὶ ἀξιῶν δέξασθαι τὴν τῆς ἀρχῆς κοινωνίαν, εἰς ὠφέλειαν ἐσομένην τῇ πολιτείᾳ (13.10.17), which is the final proof that Amm. does, indeed, mean the 'Roman state'.

caritate sanguinis As regards the family connections of Julian and Constantius (τὼ γὰρ ἡμετέρω πατέρε γεγόνατον ἀδελφὼ πατρόθεν, Jul. *Ep. ad Ath.* 270c), see the stemmata 2 and 3 in *PLRE I*, 1129–1130 with the relevant lemmata and cf. De Jonge in his comm. on bk. 14, p. 43 and 46.

The contrast between Julian's appeal to *caritas sanguinis* here and his open enmity towards his nephew in the *Letter to the Athenians* is illuminating. In *Ep. ad Ath.* 281b Julian openly accuses Constantius of the murder of his relatives in 337: τὸν φονέα πατρός, ἀδελφῶν, ἀνεψιῶν. Cf. for this Lucien-Brun, 1973 and Klein, 1979.

It is worth noting that Julian apparently abstained from any attempt to legitimate his usurpation by pointing to the fact that he belonged to the Constantinian dynasty. On this see Rosen, 1978, 425-427.

fortunae superioris culmine See above the note ad 20.5.3 (*quoniam ... ad potestatum omnium columen sustulistis*).

III. 12 *ignosce enim* Zosimus 3.9.3 also makes mention of Julian's asking for pardon, but the similarity is superficial, as in that passage the granting of this request is presented as a preliminary to Julian's renouncement of the title Augustus: οἷς εἰ παράσχοι συγγώμην, ἕτοιμος ἔφασκεν εἶναι τὴν τοῦ Καίσαρος ἔχειν ἀξίαν, ἀποθέμενος τὸ διάδημα. In Amm.'s version, however, there is no question of any willingness on Julian's part to return to the preceding situation. Julian rather urges Constantius to accept things as they stand, promising his future compliance with the orders of the senior Augustus.

The lacuna after *enim* has occasioned several conjectures, although surprisingly *mihi* has not been suggested, cf. 18.8.6 *ignosce mihi*. There is, of course, no certainty that the lacuna is not much larger. One might imagine Julian first asking pardon for the course he had taken and then continuing with the reasonableness of the soldiers' demands.

quae cum ratione poscuntur Cf. *quae rationabiliter poscebantur* (20.4.8). The expression *cum ratione* is a rarity, it occurs only here in Amm. and further in Sen. *De ira* 1.6.1, *Brev.* 18.6.4, *Ben.* 2.34.4.

avide tua pracepta deinde quoque suscepturus Here Julian is exaggerating his politeness, as can be illustrated by Liv. 27.12.6 *imperata non impigre solum, sed etiam avide exsecuti*.

One is reminded of the booklet with instructions for the newly appointed Caesar which Constantius, as if sending a stepson to the university, had written with his own hand (*libellum..quem Constantius, ut privignum ad studia mittens, manu sua conscripserat*, 16.5.3).

III. 13 *equos praebebo currules Hispanos* Again the similarity with Zonaras is remarkable: ἐπαγγελλόμενος δὲ καὶ τοὺς ἀμιλλητηρίους ἵππους ἐξ Ἰσπανίας, ὡς ἔθος, καὶ τοὺς ἐπιλέκτους ἄνδρας ἐκ τῶν Γαλλιῶν ἐτησίως στέλλειν αὐτῷ (13.10.18). Spain was famous for its horses: *cum sit dives equini pecoris Hispania* (Symm. *Ep.* 4.58) and above all its racehorses. In view of the continuous task of the emperor and other authorities to provide amusement Julian's generous offer is quite invaluable, although the emperor had studs at his disposal in the eastern part of the empire, e.g. the famous one of Palmatius in Cappadocia (cf. *Cod. Theod.* 15.10.1, Jones 706).

In the two other passages where the adiect. is used with reference to chariot racing, it is spelt *curulis* (14.6.26, 21.10.2). The spelling *currulis* is called a "jüngere Bildung" by Walde-Hofmann I 317 s.v. *curulis*, whilst Ernout-Meillet I 286 s.v. *curro* note: "adj. de l'époque impériale, qui s'est substitué sans doute à *curulis*, specialisé dans un sens particulier, et dont le rapport avec *currus* n'était plus senti". That Constantius was fond of horse-races is implied in Jul. *Misop.* 340a–b, where it is said that he used to spend whole days in the hippodrome while Julian, who hated the races (μισῶ τὰς ἱπποδρομίας), was glad to get away soon. See on chariot racing, apart from the literature cited by Szidat, Humphrey, 1986 (primarily archeological).

miscendos Gentilibus atque Scutariis adolescentes Laetos quosdam, cis Rhenum editam barbarorum progeniem, vel certe ex dediticiis, qui ad nostra desciscunt The interpretation of this phrase causes a number of difficulties. First, does Amm. draw a distinction between *laeti* (this orthography is preferable to that with capital L) and *dediticii*, in other words, does the apposition which explains *laetos quosdam* end with *progeniem* or include the words *vel certe ex dediticiis ... desciscunt*? Günther, 1975 (1), 344 and 1975 (2), 225, followed by Szidat, opts for the latter and subsumes the *dediticii* under the *laeti*: "Ammianus Marcellinus charakterisiert sie (i.e. the *laeti*) als Leute, die entweder in Gallien von germanischen Eltern geboren sind oder aus den Reihen der im Kriege unterworfenen Germanen (*dediticii*) stammen, die in Römische Dienste traten". This does not seem to be correct. If Amm. had wanted to say this, he probably would have added another *vel* before *cis Rhenum* and he certainly would have omitted *certe* (not rendered in Günther's translation). It is, especially in view of *certe*, much more likely to see in the *laeti* and *dediticii* two distinct groups. For service in the regiments of *Gentiles* and *Scutarii* (see for them the note ad 20.2.5), Julian promised to supply Constantius with *laeti* or at any rate (viz. if it was not possible to supply *laeti*; see for this below) with *dediticii*. Who, then, were the *laeti* and the *dediticii*?

As for *dediticii*, the word (cf. TLL V 1.264.10 sqq.) is defined by Gaius (1.14) as follows: *vocantur autem peregrini dediticii hi qui quondam adversus populum Romanum armis susceptis pugnaverunt, deinde victi se dediderunt*. In Amm. the word can still have this meaning. It is used to denote barbarians from without the empire (but see 21.10.1 and 31.6.5, where this is not the case) who had surrendered themselves to the Romans (cf. *Corp. Gloss. Lat.* 4.51; 5.188: *dediticius si barbarus tradat se Romanis*), in 21.4.8 Alamans (*quosdam occidit, orantes alios praedamque offerentes, dediticios cepit*), in 24.2.22 the inhabitants of Pirisabora.

These *dediticii* surrendered unconditionally, which left them without rights at the mercy of the Romans (see in general Schulten, 1901, Jones, 1960 and Wolff, 1976, 210-218). One of the possible obligations of barbarians after a *deditio* was to provide soldiers for the Roman army, as is demonstrated by 31.10.17, where the Lentienses are ordered to give their strong young men to be mingled with Roman recruits: *post deditionem, quam impetravere supplici prece, oblata, ut praeceptum est, iuventute valida nostris tirociniis permiscenda ad genitales terras innoxii ire permissi sunt*. Julian's proposal to supply Constantius with *dediticii* does, therefore, seem to have been in accordance with normal practice.

In the three examples cited from Amm. thus far, the *dediticii* were obtained by the Romans after an actual campaign. The addition in the present text of *qui ad nostra desciscunt*, however, may be seen as an indication that the *dediticii* Julian intended to send to Constantius were "the victims of intertribal wars or domestic feuds" (Jones 620) among the barbarians themselves, rather than the result of Roman campaigns. Whatever their origin, Amm.'s wording (*laetos ... vel certe ex dediticiis*) suggests that they were merely second-choice and that *laeti* were to be preferred.

But who were the *laeti*, mentioned by Amm., apart from the present text, in 16.11.4 (*Laeti barbari ad tempestiva furta sollertes ... invasere Lugdunum incautam*) and in 21.13.16 (*Arbitionem ... iter suum praeire ... praecepit, et cum Laetis itidem Gomoarium*), and attested for the first time in *Pan.Lat.* 8.21 (*tuo, Maximiane Auguste, nutu Arviorum et Trevirorum arva iacientia Laetus postliminio restitutus et receptus in leges Francus excoluit*)? An Alamannic tribe? So Chiabò, 1983, 425, not distinguishing between 16.11.4, 20.8.13 and 21.13.16 (cf. Simpson, 1977, 519: "a tribal unit independent of Roman authority" and Rolfe's "a savage tribe" in 16.11.4 and "a tribe of barbarians" in the present case). Seyfarth, I, 1983[5], 298 n. 143, on the other hand, draws a distinction: "An der vorliegenden Stelle (i.e. 16.11.4) handelt es sich um einen alamannischen Stamm, nicht um Angehörige der römischen Armee, die in Gallien angesiedelt waren wie 20.8.13 und 21.13.16", while De Jonge in his note ad 16.11.4 only refers to the last mentioned interpretation and does not consider at all the possibility that the *laeti* were a tribe (see for the many suggestions concerning the controversial problem of the *laeti*, apart from the literature cited by Szidat, Lassandro, 1979, Milani, 1979 and Bulla, 1983).

Support for the view that *laeti* was the name of some tribe would seem to be provided by Zosimus, who says about the usurper Magnentius: γένος μὲν ἕλκων ἀπὸ βαρβάρων, μετοικήσας δὲ εἰς Λητούς, ἔθνος Γαλατικόν, παιδείας τε τῆς Λατίνων μετασχών (2.54.1). Zosimus' wording suggests that he considered the *laeti* to be a tribal group (ἔθνος), but it certainly does not imply that in his eyes the *laeti* were an Alamannic or at any rate a German tribe. The sixth-century historian not only distinguishes (μὲν ... δὲ) between the *laeti* and the barbarians from whom Magnentius was descended (i.e. Germans from across the Rhine), but he explicitly speaks of an ἔθνος Γαλατικόν. The natural inference is that he regarded the *laeti* not as barbarians (to take ἔθνος Γαλατικόν as an elliptic expression for 'a barbarian tribe, settled on Gallic soil' clearly strains the evidence), but as Gauls, members of the Gallo-Roman population, among whom Magnentius could receive a Roman education (παιδείας τε τῆς Λατίνων μετασχών). Since, however, in the fourth century Amm. called the *laeti* 'barbarians' (16.11.4) and 'the offspring of barbarians' (20.8.13), Zosimus' remark about the ethnic origin of fourth century *laeti* must be wrong. This raises the question if his calling the *laeti* an ἔθνος is perhaps wrong too. If so, what is the alternative?

Cod. Theod. 13.11.10, in combination wit *Not. Dign. Occ.* 42. 33–44, helps to answer the last question. In the constitution of Honorius, written in 399 A.D., mention is made of *terrae laeticae*, lands set aside for the settlement of barbarians who sought refuge in the empire (*ex multis gentibus sequentes Romanam felicitatem se ad nostrum imperium contulerunt, quibus terrae laeticae administrandae sunt*) and from the *Notitia Dignitatum* it can be inferred that the territories of various cities in Gaul comprised such lands. Moreover, the *Notitia* makes it clear that the settlers who were planted on these lands had to supply the Roman army with contingents of troops under prefects (Cf. e.g. 42.36: *praefectus laetorum Francorum, Redonas Lugdunensis tertiae*, 37: *praefectus laetorum Lingonensium per diversa dispersorum Belgicae primae*, 38: *praefectus laetorum Actorum, Epuso, Belgicae primae*). This justifies the conclusion that the term *laeti* denoted the status of barbarian immigrants under particular conditions of settlement, viz. the supply of soldiers to the Roman army, a meaning which perfectly suits the present context and is also applicable in the other passages were *laeti* are mentioned, with the exception of Zos. 2.54.1. As Schönfeld, 1925, 446 already said, *laeti* "ist ein Standes-, kein Volksname".

qui ad nostra desciscunt Livy has many instances of *desciscere ad*, e.g. 25.1.2 *anno priore ad Poenos desciverant*. In Amm. it occurs also in 14.3.4, 15.2.3, 19.5.5, 21.6.8, 26.7.17, 31.15.4. For *nostra* 'our (= Roman) territory' see above the note ad 20.4.4 *ad nostra*.

spondeo non modo grato, verum cupio quoque The verb *spondere*, which is regularly used by Cicero and Livy, but does not occur in Tacitus, is found 15 times im Amm.

Seyfarth prints V's text, fully disagreeing with Clark, who follows Gelenius in adding *animo* after *grato* and reading *cupido* instead of *cupio*. The most obvious problem is *grato*, but accounting for his constitution of the text in the present passage, Seyfarth cheerfully points to *Corp. Gloss.* 2.35.51 Goetz *grato* ιδεως (presumably = ἡδέως) and concludes that it is a variant of the normal adverb *grate*. "Die Steigerung verläuft von *spondeo* zu *cupio*, nicht aber von *grato animo* zu *cupido animo*" (Seyfarth, 1967, 219). Setting aside the rather weak basis for *grato*, it is somewhat difficult to understand that a wish or desire (*cupio*) could be stronger than a pledge (*spondeo*), a problem which does not arise in Gelenius' text, in which the pledge is given not only gratefully, but even eagerly.

III. 14 *praefectos praetorio* Julian kept his word, accepted only Constantius' nominee for the post of *praefectus praetorio*, Nebridius (*PLRE I*, Nebridius 1, cf. the note ad 14.2.20), who was appointed later in the year (*in locum Florentii praefectum praetorio Nebridium tum quaestorem eiusdem Caesaris promoverat*, sc. Constantius, 20.9.5), and refused the others (*nulloque arbitrio eius promotorum suscepto praeter Nebridium*, 21.1.4). After Nebridius' refusal to support Julian's march against Constantius, he was dismissed (21.5.11–12).

tua nobis dabit clementia Like *aeternitas, benignitas, excellentia, felicitas, prudentia*, etc., this is one of the usual titles of address of the emperor in the later Roman empire: *si divinae clementiae tuae merita cogitentur* (Symm. *Rel.* 13.1), *vestrae tantum clementiae liberum est inique elicita rescripta rescindere* (ib. 44.1). Cf. Svennung, 1958, 75 and 87, Zilliacus, 1964.

residuos ordinarios iudices militiaeque moderatores For *residuus* as a synonym of *reliquus* see above ad 20.4.6.

Apart from *ordinario iure* (22.2.3) *ordinarius* is only used by Amm. to denote 'civil' authorities in contrast to military officers: *in ordinarias dignitates asperum* (14.10.4), *inter ordinarios iudices Rufinus primus praefectus praetorio, et inter militares equitum magister Arbitio* (16.8.13), *cunctae castrenses et ordinariae potestates* (21.16.2).

For *iudex* as a general term to denote high officials see above the relevant note ad 20.5.7. The term *moderator* is also used for different kinds of 'rulers': in a general sense 17.4.11 *moderatori cum iucunditate aculeos quoque innasci debere*, to denote a provincial governor 30.1.6 *provinciae moderator*, an emperor 26.1.3 *moderatorem quaeritabant diu exploratum et gravem*. It is also used in the military sphere: 18.7.7 *lectissimus moderator belli internecivi* (sarcastically about Sabinianus). All this tallies with the varied usage in earlier authors: *contionum moderatores* (Cic. *Sest.* 125), *moderatoresque publici consilii* (Liv. 2.23.11), *ingentis exercitus septem per annos moderator* (Tac. *Ann.* 4.18.1). In the military sphere Amm. normally uses *militiae rector* (see above the note ad 20.5.7).

promovendos arbitrio meo concedi est consentaneum   For the gerundivum as a complement of *concedere* cf. Cic. *Ver.* 2.1.38 *bona quaedam proscriptorum in agro Beneventano diripienda concessit*, Quint. *Inst.* 1.10.29 *nam poetas certe legendos oratori futuro concesserint*, Amm. 31.12.8 *petentis propalam ut sibi suisque ... habitanda Thracia sola ... concederetur.*

The expression *consentaneum est*, 'it is fitting (or proper)', with an (acc.c.) inf. as a complement occurs already in classical Latin, especially in Cicero.

itidemque stipatores   As De Jonge notes ad 16.10.2 and 17.13.6, *stipator* is not a t.t.; *stipatores* are all those who are 'in close attendance', e.g. Constantius' retinue on his arrival in Rome (16.10.2), but quite often during military actions. Although Szidat's suggestion regarding the present text ("... dass Ammian mit den stipatores ebenfalls Beamte auf hoher Ebene meint") is attractive, its correctness is open to doubt in view of 27.10.10 (about Valentinian) *nullo potentium in conscientiam arcani adhibito, remota multitudine stipatorum*, where obviously *potentes* and *stipatores* are different groups.

stultum est enim   A remarkably strong expression in a generally polite letter. Amm. uses this word and its cognates very rarely: in 16.4.2 *stulte* concerns a rash military action, in 16.12.40 flight is said *irriti conatus stultitiam indicare*. In 22.8.33 *stultus* occurs in a short lexicographical digression. Julian's use of this forceful term lends urgency to the request in question: it is absurd to attach fully unknown men to the emperor's person.

eos latus imperatoris ascisci   Obviously agreeing with Pighi, Seyfarth prints V's text. Clark prefers *eos ad latus*.

In his substantial argument Pighi, 1935, 117 finally points to some indications of a more or less prepositional use of *latus*, foreshadowing Italian 'allato', Rumanian 'alaturi' etc. Szantyr 236 is sceptical, and it should be noted that precisely 'allato' presupposes the addition of *ad*.

Seyfarth is consistent in that he also accepts V's *ascito honorum verticem eo* in 26.2.7, again rejecting the addition of *ad* or *in*. This conservative view of the text, however, is contradicted by Amm.'s further use of *asciscere*: 14.6.13 *ascitus in amicitiam*, 16.1.1 *in collegium fastorum a consule octiens Augusto ascitus*, 16.7.6 *ascitusque postea in palatium*.

VIII. 15   The contents of sections 15 (*tirones*) and 16 (*auxilia*) take up and underline what has been said earlier: Constantius' sending for *auxiliares milites ... et lectos ex numeris aliis trecentenos* (20.4.2); Julian's promise never to send troops beyond the Alps (20.4.16); the tribute Julian paid his soldiers for their courage and the way they had endured hardships in defending Gaul (20.5.3, 20.8.7). Moreover, Amm. skilfully brings in a new element in order to put Constantius' request for soldiers in a still more unfavourable light, by ending section 16 with the statement that the provinces of Gaul, rather than being able to send part of their defending troops away, themselves needed more aid from without.

Hoc sane sine ulla dubitatione firmaverim This is an almost literal quotation of Cic. *Brut.* 25 *hoc vero sine ulla dubitatione confirmaverim.* Amm. has a certain predilection for *firmare* as a synonym of *affirmare* ('to assert') instead of the more usual *confirmare*; e.g. *ut ipse firmavit* (15.6.2), *fortiter fecisse firmatur* (17.6.3), *pondus paulo minus ... quam ille firmarat* (29.3.4). As in these instances, the use of *firmare* in the present text is caused by the cursus: *dubitatióne confirmáverim* would be irregular.

tirones ad peregrina et longinqua Galli mittere Whereas this is the only instance of the substantivized neutr. plur. *peregrina* in Amm., *longinqua*, which occurs already in classical Latin (e.g. Cic. *Man.* 32: *sed quid ego longinqua commemoro?*), is found several times, cf. the note ad 17.13.2.

Clark's suspicion of *Gálli míttere* has resulted in a crux after *mittere* in his text. In his critical apparatus he suggests to create a normal cursus by the emendation *transmittere*. Pighi, 1935, 103 has another remedy: *longínqüa Galli mittere*, leaving *Galli* without accent, which seems rather strange.

Although the phrase as such at first sight offers no grounds for suspicion, it must be admitted that Harmon 168 lists only 6 instances of this irregular cadence in a total of over 3200. An emendation seems feasible. A palaeographically plausible solution could be *longinqua a Gállia míttere*.

ne ... desperatione pereant impendentium The difference between sections 15 and 16 should be noted. Whereas section 16 deals with the inopportuneness to send Gallic reinforcements from a purely military point of view, the present section dwells on the psychological impact of such a measure. The continuous disasters of the past (*diuturna perturbatione casibusque vexati gravissimis*) have corroded the resilience of the Gauls (*affliguntur praeterita recordantes*). Further losses would entail their utter demoralization.

The expression *desperatione impendentium* is somewhat remarkable. Usually the gen. obiect. with *desperatio* concerns a thing or a person whose safety is despaired of or a goal the realization of which is regarded as unlikely: *desperatio rei publicae* (Cic. *Mur.* 50), *desperatio ... apiscendi honoris* (Liv. 4.6.10), *salutis rata desperatione* (Amm. 19.2.4). Neither of these categories fits *impendentium*, since *impendere* in this sense always has the connotation of some threatening evil, either explicitly, as in *formido malorum impendentium*

(14.1.6) or implicitly, as in *pro captu rerum ... impendentium* (31.7.1). To solve the problem the following passages can be adduced: *ex praeterito casu impendentia formidantes* (17.12.9), *ubi et praeteritorum recordatio erat acerba, et expectatio tristior impendentium* (25.4.25), *haec lacrimosa ... impendentiumque spes atrocior provincialium* (26.6.9). All these cases are similar to the present passage in that awkward experiences of the past are coupled with a gloomy outlook concerning the future. From this it can be concluded that in the present text *desperatio* is used as a synonym of *formido, expectatio tristior* and *spes atrocior*. Whereas the 'neutral' substantives *expectatio* and *spes* must be qualified by a negative epithet, *desperatio* in itself is a negative concept which needs no further qualification. Its meaning here is 'fearful anticipation' or 'gloomy prospect'.

It is worth noting that Julian does not ascribe revolutionary intentions to the Gauls but, rather, despondent and pessimistic feelings. The danger consists of demoralization, not rebellion.

VIII. 16 *nec Parthicis gentibus* The fact that this is another argument against sending the reinforcements asked for is expressed by *nec*, 'neither'.

The chiastic structure of this section (*Parthicis gentibus ... hinc × hae provinciae ... externis*) aptly suits Julian's reasoning, the gist of which is that the measures called for should be taken the other way round: the Gauls ought to receive, not to send reinforcements.

cum adhuc nec barbarici sunt impetus interclusi Presumably Gelenius interpreted *cum* as causal, witness his choice of the coni. *sint* (and, for that matter, *indigeant*), but *cum* should rather be regarded as temporal ('at a time when'). Besides, even causal *cum* can be combined with the indic., cf. Ehrismann 58, De Jonge ad 14.2.13, Szantyr 624/5.

si dici, quod verum est, pateris In itself this has to be regarded as a polite formula, like *de primo primum, si placet, disputemus* (Cic. *Part.* 70), *ego illam, si pateris, adiungam* (Sen. *Ep.* 117.5), *si dici liceat verum* (Amm. 21.13.10); cf. also such phrases as *pace tua dixerim* (Cic. *Tusc.* 5.12) and above in section 7 *bona tua venia dixerim*. In view, however, of Constantius' alleged tendency to believe false reports (see above the relevant note ad 20.2.2) the formula may well have a sarcastic ring.

hae provinciae Seyfarth fails to report that V has *haec*, which is not a unique case, witness *haec regiones* (14.8.4, 23.6.10, 23.6.14). In 15.11.12 many mss. have *haec provinciae*. This form of the nom. plur. fem. is by no means impossible, cf. the instances listed in Neue-Wagener, 1902, II 417/8 and the explanation in Leumann 468/9. In the present case Seyfarth's correction is founded on the ms H and the editions B and G.

externis indigent adiumentis et fortibus As a complement of *indigere* Amm. uses the gen. sing. (14.8.14, 21.9.2) and abl. plur. (23.6.82, 31.2.3, 31.2.19), the only exception being *magnitudine indigens impensarum* (30.8.8).

The placing of the two adjectives follows the type *fidus defensor et cautus* (15.2.5), cf. also Hagendahl, 1924, 187 sqq. Pighi, 1935, 120/1 finds fault with this because of their different character, *externis* being a determinative adj., *fortibus* a qualifying one: "utrumque ad *adiumentis* referri absurda res est, ut si ⟨⟨Gallicana oppida et excisa⟩⟩ dixisset". For a 'correct' combination he refers to Cic. *Fin.* 5.59 (ut) *adiumentis externis et adventiciis uteretur*, regarded by him as Amm.'s model, which is quite possible in spite of the wholly different context (cf. also 23.2.1).

In order to solve this problem Pighi suggests to take *fortibus* as the abl. of the substantivated *fortia*, not, however, in its classical sense 'deeds of valour' (e.g. Verg. *A.* 8.509 *seraeque ad fortia vires*), but as a late Latin synonym of *vires*, for which he adduces a few instances in Commodian and Prudentius. He could have added that Romance 'forza', 'fuerza', 'force' etc. are generally regarded to derive from *fortia* (cf. Leumann 269).

Pighi concludes: "igitur *adiumentis et fortibus* idem est quod ⟨⟨armis et uiribus⟩⟩". Pace Szantyr 154, who is inclined to accept this ingenious construction, it cannot claim a high degree of credibility. In the reliable examples of *fortia* with this meaning it only concerns the nom./acc. neutr. plur., which of course is the origin of its Romance derivations, and the abl. seems rather unlikely. Besides, there are no occurrences of the nom./acc. in Amm. Finally, the addition of the qualifying adj. *fortis* is quite opportune in the context; at the end of the sentence it once more stresses the Gauls' plight: the help they are in need of should be 'strong'.

III. 17 In this concluding section Julian winds up his argument with a fully Roman reference to past experiences, which provide excellent examples for the future. The style becomes more florid, with an emphatic geminatio (*scio enim scio*) and no less than four cases of "Synonymenhäufung": *poscens et rogans, conclamatas et perditas, fortunate beateque, ultimo tempori posteritatique.*

Haec hortando, ut aestimo, salutariter scripsi poscens et rogans A parenthetical formula with verba sentiendi is a frequent phenomenon since the oldest phases of Latin literature. Here *ut aestimo* lends a touch of modesty to the summarizing first phrase of the section, contrasting with the emphatic character of the final appeal (*scio enim scio*).

Hagendahl, 1924, 184/5 notes that the coupling of synonyms is especially frequent with the "verba monendi sive orandi". The difference between *haec hortando* and *poscens et rogans* should be noted. The first expression refers to the contents of the letter ('in insisting on these measures'), *poscens et rogans* to its tone: Julian is not presenting decisions or uttering menaces, but 'making requests'. The adverb *salutariter* occurs only here in Amm.

scio enim scio Hagendahl, 1924, 190 notes only two other examples of geminatio in Amm.: 23.5.23 (at the end of a speech) and 28.4.9 (in an urgent cry). As to *enim*, this particle can, of course, be regarded as having a confirmatory or causal meaning: Julian is proposing these measures, 'since' he knows the lessons of the past. These lessons, however, do not really concern the different proposals and appeals in sections 13-16, summarized in *haec hortando*. The phrase *scio enim scio* should rather be regarded as introducing the last expression of Julian's general insistence on a good relationship between the rulers, which is put into words in the beginning, the middle and the end of the letter (see above the introductory note ad 20.8.5). Therefore, it is better to assume that *enim* is used asseveratively here, as Verg. *A.* 8.84 *tibi enim, tibi, maxima Iuno*.

ne quid sublatius dicam The *ne dicam*-formula (cf. TLL V 1.976.58-70, Kühner-Stegmann 2.1.825) is used to reject a stronger expression than the one chosen. As Brink notes ad Hor. *Ars* 272 it "often emphasizes what it apparently apologizes for". Usually it concerns one particular term, e.g. *quod positum est in alterius voluntate, ne dicam libidine* (Cic. *Fam.* 9.16.3), *his forsitan artibus divinabat, ne dicam somniabat* (Tert. *An.* 28.5), but the rejection can also be expressed by means of a comparative: *nos hoc ⟨non⟩ defendente, ne dicam gravius, adflixerat* (Cic. *Att.* 9.5.2, 'to use no harsher phrase'). Although *sublatus* can be employed about a state of mind, either positively (16.4.5 *sublato animo*, 'with spirits raised') or negatively (15.12.1 *sublatius insolentes*, 'arrogantly insolent'), here it is, rather, a stylistic term, as in *nihil enim umquam de me dixi sublatius* (Cic. *Dom.* 96), cf. also Cic. *Brut.* 201. As *ne dicam* always refers to the preceding text, Julian's words imply that he refrains from using a 'loftier' expression than *scio enim scio*.

cum imperio congruens In his Teubner edition Seyfarth returns to this (corrected) reading in V, which Clark had changed into *quam imperio congruit*. Although it must be admitted that there is no other example in Amm. of *congruere cum*, Clark's emendation is difficult to understand: which terms would be loftier (or, with a different explanation of *sublatius*, more arrogant) than is fitting for imperial power? Wagner's explanation of V's text, in which *congruens* presumably is taken as an acc. sing. neutr. defining *quid*, is not satisfactory either: "ne Augusta dignitate superbius uti velle tibi videar". It seems more likely to take *congruens* as a nom. sing. masc.: the verb *congruere* can concern the harmony of a person and a concrete or abstract entity: *si aliquem nacti sumus, cuius cum moribus et natura congruamus* (Cic.

Lael. 27), *si rebus gestis congruere voluerunt* (August. *Civ.* 3.25). If this is right, Julian is saying that his conviction that agreement between the rulers is necessary is 'harmonious with his imperial dignity', either as a Caesar or as a junior Augustus, the word *imperium* being suitable for both and the expression having been chosen for its ambiguity.

quas rerum acerbitates iam conclamatas et perditas As Blomgren 83 note 2 remarks (not using the term, however), *rerum* is a case of gen. inversus. The synonymity of *conclamatas* and *perditas* is nicely illustrated by Serv. *A.* 2.233: *et bene de peritura civitate 'conclamant' dixit, quia semper res perditae 'conclamatae' dicuntur.* There is one other instance in Amm. of *conclamatus* with this meaning: *salutarem quendam genium affulsisse conclamatis negotiis* (15.8.21); cf. also 18.6.18.

concordia vicissim sibi cedentium principum In his letter to the Athenians Julian ascribes his insistence on harmonious cooperation between Constantius and himself to the unanimous feelings of his soldiers (ἅπαντα τὰ παρ' ἐμοὶ τάγματα), who sent letters to Constantius with this purport: ἱκετεύοντα περὶ τῆς πρὸς ἀλλήλους ἡμῖν ὁμονοίας (*Ep. ad Ath.* 286a). Valentinian later saw the need for such harmony very clearly too, choosing Valens as his colleague, *ut germanitate, ita concordia sibi iunctissimum* (30.7.4). The words *sibi cedentium* may punningly refer to *secessiones* in section 11: *principes* should not be *secedentes*, but rather *sibi cedentes.*

revocávit in státum For the indic. in indirect questions cf. the note ad 14.6.2 In the present case the cursus planus has influenced the choice of the mood.

cum appareat maiorum exemplo nostrorum The causal clause contains the ground for Julian's strongly expressed conviction: his knowledge of the past (cf. 23.5.21 *haec ut antiquitatum peritus exposui*) has provided him with a clear understanding of history. Szidat is probably right in seeing in this phrase a reference to the *concordia* which existed under the Tetrarchy, but the concept is, of course, older. Cf. the obvious Sallustianism in 26.2.8 (*concordiae ... per quam res quoque minimae convalescunt*) and see Straub, 1939, 36–42 and Béranger, 1969. To Szidat's references HA *Car.* 18 should be added.

It is interesting to note that Amm. here makes Julian still express his hope for a restoration of the harmony between himself and Constantius, that in 21.1.1 he represents Julian as being in doubt whether to try every means for inducing Constantius to come to an understanding (*ambigens, utrum Constantium modis omnibus alliceret in concordiam*) and that finally in 21.10.7 he relates that Julian had lost all hope that Constantius could ever be brought into harmony with him (*numquam credens ad concordiam provocari posse Constantium*).

moderatores haec et similia cogitantes   For *moderatores* see above the note ad 20.8.14, for *haec et similia* ad 20.4.2.

fortunate beateque vivendi repperire quodam modo viam   Cf. Cic. *Brut.* 9 (with the same coupling of synonyms) *ei mihi videntur fortunate beateque vixisse*. For *quodam modo* see above the note ad 20.5.5.

ultimo tempori posteritatique   Amm. uses *ultimus* quite often, in a geographical sense (15.13.4 *in ultimis terrarum suarum terminis*) or to denote a degree (14.2.6 *ex necessitate ultima*), but rarely about time (19.2.5 *a sole itaque orto usque diei ultimum*). Hagendahl, 1924, 173 lists the present expression with those in which there is no difference in meaning between the two parts of the "Synonymenhäufung", but it does not seem to be such a clear-cut instance as e.g. *ad tristitiam versus est et maerorem* (21.3.1). Perhaps it rather has the character of a hendiadyoin: harmonious rulers will live on in people's memory until 'the very last phase of the time to come'.

VIII. 18   Ammianus Marcellinus is a proud historian, who has set himself high standards. For the facts he presents this is his rule: *non falsitas arguta concinnat, sed fides integra rerum absolvit* (16.1.3). In cases of uncertainty he does not fail to mention this, by a vague nom. c. inf. (with *dicitur, fertur, firmatur*) or by a more definite phrase: *ut iactavere rumores incerti* (15.5.4), *ut prodidere rumores assidui* (15.7.7), *ut loquebatur pertinax rumor* (16.6.3, 26.4.4). The present section contains the most explicit statement in this vein, and at the same time provides ample reasons for suspicion. As Valesius already noted, in Zonaras' version Julian's nasty letter to Constantius was handed to Leonas when the latter returned from his unsuccessful mission to Paris: ὑπέστρεψε μετὰ γραμμάτων τοῦ τυραννήσαντος, ἀναιδῶς ὀνειδιζόντων τὸν αὐτοκράτορα καὶ ἐπιπληττόντων ὡς πλεῖστα ἐξαμαρτόντα κατὰ τοῦ γένους αὐτοῦ καὶ ἀπειλούντων αὐτὸν γενήσεσθαι τιμωρὸν τῶν ἀδίκως παθόντων (13.10.28). Now it is true that one of Amm.'s methods was interviewing eyewitnesses (15.1.1 *perplexe interrogando versatos in medio*) and that he was well acquainted with one of the envoys, Eutherius, who also had an excellent memory (16.7.5 *immensum quantum memoria vigens*), but his chronological placing of the letter is rather unlikely. Its insulting purport would have precluded any possibility of success for the plea in the official letter, with the consequence that that letter could only be regarded as a propagandistic effort. According to Zonaras, however, the offending letter was sent after it had become fully clear that Constantius rejected Julian's proposals, which seems a far more natural chronology.

offerendas clanculo misit obiurgatorias et mordaces The adverb *clanculo* is found since Apuleius, while the older form *clanculum* occurs quite often in Plautus. Amm. has two other instances of *clanculo*: 21.12.13, 26.6.5. In the translations it is assumed that *clanculo* qualifies *offerendas*, but it seems more likely to regard it as determining the affair as a whole: unlike the official letter, the contents of which, presumably for propagandistic reasons too, were disclosed, this nasty message was kept secret.

Amm.'s other instances of *obiurgatorius* all concern sound: 14.7.12, 15.7.4, 18.8.5, 27.1.5, 30.6.3 *sonus*, 16.12.55 *clamor*. In Cic. *Att.* 13.6.3 it also qualified a letter. For *mordax* cf. the note ad 20.2.1. The combination of the two adjectives emphasizes the aggressiveness of the letter. Zonaras' brief indication of the contents is fully credible: Julian's letter to the Athenians contains similar complaints (270c sqq.).

quarum seriem nec scrutari licebat There are no other examples in Amm. of the *series* of a letter. With the meaning 'text' or 'contents' it occurs a few times in the *Coll. Avell.*, e.g. 83.298 *sicut series eiusdem testatur epistulae*, 144.5 *quid igitur facere debeant et litteris nostris et libelli, quem direximus, serie continetur*. Cf. also *Cod. Theod.* 9.34.10 *famosam seriem scribtionis* and Joh. Cass. *Coll.* 19.12.3 *sacrae series lectionis*. In one other pasage Amm. avails himself of *scrutari* to denote his historical research: 15.1.1 *utcumque potui veritatem scrutari*.

Clark has corrected V's *scruta licunt*. His choice of the imperf. *licebat* is presumably caused by rhythmic considerations and the parallelism with *decebat*. On the other hand, *licuit* would be nearer the ms reading and fully in line with Amm.'s usage, cf. 15.1.1 *ea quae videre licuit per aetatem*. The indic. perf. records a fact in the past, whereas the imperf. *decebat* describes the background of such a fact: Amm. was refused permission to study the letter in a situation in which, in any case, decency precluded its publication. A further argument for perf. *licuit* could be that it tallies better with the following *si licuisset*.

nec, si licuisset, proferre decebat in publicum In itself the preceding phrase *nec scrutari licebat* would have been sufficient. No reader could reasonably criticize the author for not having access to the secret imperial archives. The addition of the present sentence is intriguing. It certainly is not the equivalent of statements in which Amm., like other historians, sets forth his rule not to go into unimportant details which are *narratu minus digna* (27.2.11); cf. also 14.9.9, 26.1.1 (one of his most explicit pronouncements), 28.1.15 and Den Hengst, 1981, 44-46. Here, however, Amm. is not saying that the information withheld is insignificant, but that it is indecent, which is remarkable, since the exact purport of the letter would doubtless further the understanding of the course of events in general and Constantius' policy in particular. Amm. is obviously heeding the rule *sunt aliqua quae fieri non oportet, etiam si licet* (30.8.8), presumably in order to reduce the damage to Julian's reputation, although on a later occasion he does not hesitate to criticize another letter of Julian's rather sharply: in abusing Constantine's memory he was acting *insulse nimirum et leviter* (21.10.8).

VIII. 19 The improbability of the contents of section 18 now becomes even more clear. It is very difficult to imagine that Julian would have sent such an important delegation (*viri graves*) with ample powers to negotiate (*fidenter acturi*), while at the same time completely undermining the earnestness of this diplomacy by an inopportune letter.

Ad id munus implendum This does not only refer to the preceding section, but also to *legatos ad eum mittere statuit gesta docturos eisque concinentes litteras dedit* in section 3.

Pentadius officiorum magister At first sight the choice of the former *notarius* (cf. Teitler, 1985, 159–160) Pentadius (*PLRE I*, Pentadius 2) may seem surprising. He was one of Julian's enemies (*Ep. ad Ath.* 282b: γίνεταί μοι δυσμενής) who had urged Julian to accept Constantius' demands for troops (ibid., 283c–d), and was, therefore, not likely to defend Julian's case before his cousin. By sending this partisan of Constantius as his envoy, Julian may have wanted to demonstrate that he had a clear conscience, but, on the other hand, he may simply have wanted to get rid of him (so Szidat). See for his office the note ad 20.2.2, and for the man, apart from the literature cited by Szidat, Clauss, 1980, 180 and Kuhoff, 1983, 200 and 416 n. 15.

Eutherius cubiculi tunc praepositus This highly respected eunuch (*PLRE I*, Eutherius 1; cf. the note ad 16.7.2) forms the exception to the established prejudice that all eunuchs were to be despised as stained with some vice or other. To put it in Amm.'s words: *inter vepres rosae nascuntur et inter feras nonnullae mitescunt* (16.7.4). Add to the literature cited by Szidat: Guyot, 1980, 201–202 and see the note ad 20.2.3 (*Eusebius, cubiculi tunc praepositus*).

post oblatas litteras relaturi nullo suppresso, quae viderunt This is a more natural order than the one implied in the phrase just quoted from section 3: the messengers' oral report is a supplement to the official letter, not the other way round. Cf. Suet. *Aug.* 49.3 *Commodius id* (viz. the furnishing of carriages in which messengers were to travel) *visum est, ut qui a loco idem perferunt litteras, interrogari quoque, si quid res exigant, possint*.

Nullo as an abl. of *nihil* occurs already a few times in earlier post-classical Latin, e.g. *nullo magis exterritus est quam quod* etc. (Tac. *Ann.* 3.15.2, cf. Nipperdey's note ad loc.); cf. also the note ad 14.1.4, Neue-Wagener, 1902, II 527.

In classical Latin the coni. pluperfect (*vidissent*) would have been used here. Concerning the tense (perf. instead of pluperfect) cf. Ehrismann 31/2, De Jonge ad 14.3.4. The use of the indic. is dealt with in Hassenstein 37/8 and Szantyr 548.

et super ordine futurorum fidenter acturi Amm. uses *ordo* with a gen. plur. more than once to denote a sequence of events. In this sense it is a synonym of *series*, cf. *ordo seriesque gestorum* (29.3.1). These are the instances: *casuum* (15.1.1), *fatorum* (15.3.3, 16.1.1; cf. also 19.11.15, 23.5.5 *ordo fatalis*), *gestorum* (14.8.15, 20.11.1), *rerum* (17.13.16). Possibly Verg. *A.* 7.44 *maior rerum mihi nascitur ordo*, quoted in 15.9.1, was the example for this usage.

As was pointed out in the note ad 20.4.18, *confidenter* generally has an unfavourable meaning, implying arrogance or the neglect of proportions. The simplex *fidenter*, however, usually does not imply any disapproval, 15.1.3 (about the self-exaltation of Constantius) being an exception. Normally it denotes a justified degree of confidence or courage (sometimes in the face of high authorities, e.g. when Valentinian consulted his *primores* about the choice of a partner, *Dagalaifus tunc equestris militiae rector respondit fidentius*, 26.4.1), or confidence derived from an official mandate: *quo fidenter ad haec patranda digresso* (18.2.3).

The difference between *confidenter* and *fidenter* is well illustrated by a passage in 29.1.6. A certain Palladius had been arrested on a charge of attempted poisoning; during the investigation *exclamabat Palladius confidenter levia esse haec*, and that he could give more important information. He then was invited to speak out: *iussusque docere fidenter quae norat*. The addition of *fidenter* indicates that his exposition was now backed by those who were in charge of the proceedings.

In the present text *fidenter* means that the envoys, being fully authorized by Julian, were to conduct the negotiatons with Constantius without any undue fears and with justified self-confidence.

III. 20 *Auxerat inter haec coeptorum invidiam Florenti fuga praefecti* This section returns to the information provided in 20.4.2 and 6-8. Florentius' absence from Paris, in spite of Julian's urgent appeals, is now flatly styled a 'flight'. The loss of his *praefectus praetorio* was a serious set-back for Julian's schemes (*coeptorum*), greatly adding to the odium of the whole affair. For this meaning of *invidia* ('odium', 'unpopularity') cf. *res in invidia erat* (Sal. *Iug.*

25.5), *magna cum invidia novi principatus* (Tac. *Hist.* 2.64.1), *invidiam cientes Iuliani memoriae principis* (Amm. 26.4.4). Usually Amm. employs *invidia* in an active sense ('envy', 'jealousy', 'hatred'). It should be noted that the present section is Amm.'s first explicit reference to the fact that the events at Paris did not meet with such general enthusiasm as he had suggested until now. Mark especially the pluperfect *auxerat*.

velut praesagiens concitandos motus In some other cases too an expression indicating someone's foreboding is mitigated by *velut*: 15.8.9, 20.2.4 and 30.4.11. The gerundivum *concitandos* has the sense of a part. fut. pass. or even an inf. fut. pass., cf. above the note ad *turbando* (20.4.1) and also ad *abstrahendos* (20.4.7).

ob militem, ut sermone tenus iactabatur, accitum This is somewhat difficult to understand, possibly at least partly due to the fact that the text commented on in this and the preceding lemma is not wholly certain, V providing *concitando motus ut militem ut* (G has *ob* instead of the first *ut*). It could mean that Florentius' fear of disturbances was based on mere rumours about the summoning of troops and that he fled to Vienna before this actually took place. But this is not satisfactory, since in his report of the events Amm. leaves no doubt about Constantius' demand, which he presents as an absolutely certain fact. One is further reminded of some phrases in chapter 4, which express Amm.'s reserves when he mentions the belief that Constantius acted on Florentius' advice: *stimulante, ut ferebatur, praefecto Florentio* (20.4.2) and *relationem suam quam olim putabatur misisse* (20.4.7). The parallelism with the report in sections 6 and 7 of chapter 4 about the motive of Florentius' flight allows a similar interpretation in the present case, albeit of a somewhat elliptic character: Florentius feared that he might fall victim of the soldiers' anger at his alleged advice to Constantius to withdraw troops from Gaul.

Amm. is rather fond of expressions with *tenus*, especially in a metaphorical sense. In this he differs from other historians: in Sal., Curt. and HA *tenus* does not occur. Livy and Tacitus have only a few instances in which it is used metaphorically: Liv. 34.5.4, Tac. *Ann.* 15.6.4, 15.45.2. In Amm., on the other hand, there are only three cases in which it has a literal meaning, all concerning parts of the body: 14.4.3 *pube*, 17.7.5 *collo*, 28.2.4 *mento*. In all other cases *tenus* restricts the reality of the relevant statement: *rumore* (14.5.3, 16.11.13, 26.1.4), *specie* (cf. above the note ad 20.5.4), *suspicione* (21.16.6, 22.3.3, 25.4.3), *verbo* (26.1.8, 26.4.4, 30.4.17). The present case is paralleled by 16.11.13 *illud tamen rumore tenus ubique iactabatur*.

alimentariae rei gratia divelli causatus a Caesare For the importance of the grain supply and Florentius' responsibility see above the note ad 20.4.6 *specie annonae parandae*.

Apart from *divulsa compage* (14.7.16), which, of course, is a wholly different case, this is Amm.'s only instance of *divellere*. Its use by other authors in reporting the separation of persons shows that it is rather a strong term ('to force away from'), especially suiting emotional situations: *eo maiore a te dolore divellor* (Cic. *Mil.* 99), *divelli liberos a parentum complexu* (Sal. *Cat.* 51.9), *si ab uxore carissima et tot communium liberorum parente divelleretur* (Tac. *Ann.* 3.34.6).

The pathetic excuse, however, cannot conceal that it is a mere pretext. TLL III 704.67 thus defines the meaning of *causari*: "causam afferre vel veram vel fictam". In Amm.'s usage the emphasis is firmly on the second half of the alternative. In the present text the sham character of the excuse is clearly shown by the addition of the real reason of Florentius' absence: his fear of Julian.

quem saepe tractatum asperius formidabat   For the relations between Julian and Florentius see above the note ad 20.4.2 *stimulante (ut ferebatur) praefecto Florentio*.

III. 21 *eum ad Augustum culmen evectum*   This is a very stereotypical phrase, cf. *ad magnum militiae culmen evectus* (16.6.1), *ad praefecturae culmen evectus* (28.4.3). Cf. also *culmen celsum* (22.1.2), *imperiale* (15.5.16, 21.16.11), *principale* (14.1.1). Concerning the present expression, it is difficult to understand why Clark and Seyfarth print *augustum* in 15.5.17 and 25.8.8, but *Augustum* in 21.5.5 and 25.2.3. In all four cases Amm. means the imperial dignity, which only in 15.5.17 is illegally pursued. Cf. also the note ad *quoniam ... potestatum omnium columen sustulistis* (20.5.3) above.

versus in metum   For this use of *vertere* consult OLD s.v. *vertere* 21 b ("to cause a person to pass into a new frame of mind"). Amm. does not mean 'fear of Julian', which had already been expressed in the preceding section (*formidabat*), but 'fear of death'.

ut longe disiunctus   Selem's translation brings out the meaning excellently: "approfitando della notevole lontananza": like ὡς c. part., *ut* expresses the personal considerations of the subject, as in 14.7.12 *ut iniusta perferens et indigna*; elsewhere, too, the verb *disiungere* is used to denote a geographical distance: *cum ab Italia freto disiunctus esses* (Cic. *Ver.* 1.154), *a vespera Issiaco disiungitur mari* (Amm. 22.15.2), *Canopus inde duodecimo disiungitur lapide* (22.16.14). See also above the note ad 20.3.10 on *disiunctissime*.

necessitudine omni relicta   With the concrete (post-classical) meaning 'relatives', 'close connections', *necessitudo* normally occurs in the plur., e.g.

17.1.6 *ad opitulandum suis necessitudinibus avolarunt*. The present 'collective' case is paralleled by *necessitudine omni recuperata* (19.9.7, cf. the note ad loc.).

venit ad Constantium itineribus lentis   Such expressions occur mainly in the military sphere: *itineribus lentis* can be found in 31.5.4, 31.16.1, its counterparts are *i. celeratis* (31.11.3), *i. festinatis* (14.7.10, 26.7.1) and the classical i. *magnis* (cf. Sal. *Cat.* 57.1) (25.8.5, 26.7.3, 28.1.54, 28.6.16, 29.5.17). The slowness of Florentius' progress may be due to his wish to play a waiting game and to watch carefully how many partisans Julian could muster outside Gaul, but Szidat's suggestion that Florentius was continuously rousing the feelings of imperial functionaries against Julian is perhaps to be preferred in view of what follows.

Remarkably enough, at the beginning of the next chapter (20.9.1) Julian's envoys are also said to have travelled *itineribus lentis*.

Iulianum ut perduellem multis criminibus appetebat   This can refer to the time after his arrival, the sense being that he was accusing Julian in the presence of Constantius. In that case, however, the preceding final clause (*utque se nulli obnoxium culpae monstraret*) loses much of its significance. For Constantius, Florentius' dissociating himself from Julian's plans and his return to the legal emperor would be a sufficient indication of his loyalty. This would be much less clear to the local authorities whom he met while travelling to the Orient. So presumably Amm. means that Florentius was attacking Julian during this eastward journey in order to convince his various hosts of his rejection of Julian's usurpation. The imp. *appetebat* can be interpreted in an iterative sense: at each stage of his journey he heaped abuse on Julian.

Amm. has a great liking for the archaic word *perduellis*, which does not occur in Sal., Curt. and HA, five times in Livy, only once in Tac. (*Ann.* 14.29.2). Varro's definition *perduelles dicuntur hostes* (*L.* 7.49) needs further precision in Amm.'s case, for usually he denotes usurpers with this term: Silvanus (15.5.19), Procopius c.s. (26.5.11, 26.7.13, 26.8.1), Firmus (29.5.36, 52, 55), and once more Julian: one of Constantius' flatterers kept asking him *ut Iuliani ad eos mitteret caput, perduellis ingrati* (22.14.4).

For *appetere*, 'to assail' in a non-physical sense cf. 17.9.7 *contumeliosis calumniis appetitus est a Gaudentio tunc notario*.

VIII. 22 *bene Iulianus cogitans et prudenter*   Amm. praises Julian's *prudentia* in his necrology: *prudentiae eius indicia fuere vel plurima* (25.4.7). His intellect was well-trained: *per omnia philosophiae membra prudenter disputando currebat* (16.5.6), which enabled him to react sagaciously: *prudenter motus ex tempore ... ait* (18.1.4). The present passage, too, refers to his clever reasoning rather than to his wisdom: Julian was reflecting 'intelligently' on the situation. For further passages illustrating this quality of Julian cf. Pauw, 1972, 119-120.

scirique volens The passive inf. deserves attention. Julian's intention was not so much to show Florentius his lack of ill-feeling towards him (which would have been expressed by *eum scire volens*), but rather to make a favourable impression on the public opinion.

quod praesenti quoque pepercisset The coni. plusquamp. expresses past unreality, the protasis *si praesens fuisset* having been replaced by *praesenti*.

caritates eius cum re familiari intacta For *caritates* see above the relevant note ad 20.4.10. Political opponents could fare far worse: 14.5.9 *proscripti sunt plures, actique in exsilium alii* (Magnentius' supporters), 26.10.14 *proscriptiones et exsilia et quae leviora quibusdam videntur, quamquam sint aspera, viri pertulere summates* (Procopius' party). Apart from the fact that Julian was as yet not in a position to enforce such measures, he possibly also wanted to demonstrate his putting into practice the rule of conduct which he set before the eyes of his greedy soldiers: *nec pudebit imperatorem, cuncta bona in animi cultu ponentem, profiteri paupertatem honestam* (24.3.5).

In *Ep. ad Ath.* 281b Julian prides himself on leaving alone the property of his opponents: ἀφελόμενος δ' οὐδὲν τῶν ὑπαρχόντων ἐκείνοις. His general mildness towards enemies is praised in a section of the necrology (25.4.9). His clemency was reminiscent of that of Antoninus Pius: *clemens ut Antoninus* (16.1.4). Cf. further Pauw, 1972, 122; Blockley, 1975, 75.

publico cursu usu permisso For the state-controlled *cursus* see above the note ad 20.4.11. The succession of ablatives is slightly awkward and has prompted some attempts to smoothe the text. There is, however, no real problem: *publico cursu* is an abl. instr. with *vehi, usu permisso* an abl. abs.

ad orientem vehi tutius imperavit Both Clark and Seyfarth print Novák's emendation *vehi* for V's *redi*, preferring it to G's *redire*. Presumably the reason is their doubt whether the journey could properly be called a 'return'. Florentius, however, was a *comes* of Constantius and probably belonged to the Eastern half of the Empire.

For *tutius* see above the note ad 20.5.1.

Chapter 9 Introduction

In this chapter we hear first (§ 1–2) about the experiences of Julian's envoys, Pentadius and Eutherius, during their voyage and at the court of Constantius. Theirs is an unenviable task. The hostility of the provincial governors towards them prepares the reader for the intimidating audience given them by Constantius, who is depicted in very negative terms. As might be expected, Constantius shows himself wholly unwilling to compromise (§ 3–4). In a show of force, presented by Amm. with a touch of irony (*velut magnis viribus fretus*, § 5), he even appoints a number of officials in the West, as if no change in the distribution of power had occurred. In the second part of the chapter (§ 6–8) the reception of Constantius' envoy, Leonas, is reported. The contrast could not have been greater. Leonas is received with due respect (§ 6) and sent back unharmed (§ 8). Moreover Julian is not portrayed as having the unpleasant task of rejecting Constantius' proposals, but in a unanimous show of their devotion to Julian (§ 7) the army and the *provinciales* make it quite clear that there is no way back. The last two sections (§ 9–10) mention some of Julian's measures. He acts in complete accordance with what he had written to Constantius. The awesome Lupicinus, who had been conveniently absent at the time of the pronunciamento, is discreetly taken care of when he returns from Britain, to nip any revolutionary plans in the bud.

IX. 1 *nec minore studio secuti legati* The ablative of manner probably refers to the speed at which the envoys travelled, or, rather, would have travelled if the provincial magistrates had not caused delays. For similar expressions with *studio* cf. 14.2.20 *studio properabat ingenti*, 21.12.9 *veloci studio*, 30.1.6 *festinato studio*, 30.5.13 *celeri studio*. The *legati* are Pentadius and Eutherius, as is said in 20.8.19.

haec secum ferentes, quae praediximus I.e. both the official letter reproduced in 20.8.5–17 and the secret letter mentioned in 20.8.18

intentique ad viandum Amm. uses *intentus* in the absolute sense 'unremitting' in 22.16.13 *septingenta voluminum milia Ptolemaeis regibus vigiliis intentis composita*. Cf. also *studio intento* (18.2.14, 25.4.1). It is followed by *in* + abl. once: *omnium oculis in eo contuitu pertinaci intentis* (16.10.4), if V's reading *in eo* is correct; see De Jonge's note. We find *in* + acc. in 22.2.4. It occurs with the adverb *aliorsum* twice: 14.10.7, 19.11.8, with *ad* three times: 24.5.7 *prohibitoribus acriter ad resistendum intentis*, 28.1.55, 31.5.9. The most frequent construction is with the dative, sometimes of the gerund: 15.4.8 (=

16.12.49) *vulneribus declinandis intenti (-us)*, which was introduced bij Livy, e.g. 1.56.1 *intentus perficiendo templo*; Szantyr 377. For *viare* see the note ad 19.8.10.

cum venirent ad iudices celsiores, oblíque tenebántur For *cum* iterativum with coni. see the note ad 20.3.9. *Oblique* here means 'by chicaneries'. Usually *obliquus* refers to ambiguous language, as in 23.5.9 *oblique destinaverat mare* (subj. the Delphic oracle) and 29.1.35 *per ambages obliquas*. This metaphorical use is found from Seneca onwards, e.g. in Tac. *Ann.* 2.55.1 *oblique Germanicum perstringens*, Suet. *Dom.* 2.3 *obliquis orationibus et edictis*. See the note ad 15.5.4 *verbis obliquis* and TLL IX 2.103.50 sqq. On *obliquus* in its literal sense see the note ad 20.7.1.

ad iudices celsiores As is noted ad 20.5.7, *iudex* is repeatedly used by Amm. in the sense of 'official', more specifically 'civil official'. Combined with *celsus* the word is found once, in 28.4.33, where high officials are distinguished from those of lower rank: *iudicibus celsis itidemque minoribus*. For *celsus* thus used (see the note ad 20.4.1 for a different sense) one should compare *celsae potestates* in 14.1.10, 14.10.10, 16.12.14, 23.5.15, where the phrase is to be taken as an abstractum pro concreto, and 30.9.3: *scrupulosus in deferendis potestatibus celsis*. See also 21.16.1: *erga tribuendas celsiores dignitates impendio parcus*.

Neither in the example last quoted nor in the present text does the comparative seem to have its full force (cf. for the comparativus pro positivo the note ad 20.4.17). It is better to take *iudices celsiores* as equivalent to *iudices celsi* than to suppose that Amm. wanted to say that only officials of a rank superior to that of Pentadius and Eutherius, who were *magister officiorum* and *praepositus sacri cubiculi*, respectively, tried to detain the envoys. As for the reaction of the provincial magistrates, it was to be expected that the envoys, bringing the news of Julian's usurpation, would not be welcomed with open arms by officials who had to take into consideration the legitimate emperor's feelings and to fear reprisals if they chose the wrong side. Compare the reaction of the senators in Rome some time later to a letter of Julian which was full of complaints about his relative: *Exclamatum est enim in unum cunctorum sententia congruente "auctori tuo reverentiam rogamus"* (21.10.7).

morasque ... perpessi diuturnas et graves The same coupling of adjectives is found in 21.5.4 *iacturas ... diuturnas et graves*. The latter probably refers to the haughty and threatening attitude of the provincial governors. Cf. the description of the Persians as *magnidici et graves ac taetri* in 23.6.80.

transfretati per Bosporum Amm. uses *transfretare* transitively, as in the present text, of crossing rivers, (18.5.3 with note, Tigris, 19.8.9. Euphrates, 31.4.5 Danube) and straits (22.6.4 Bosporus). For *per* to indicate the place of the crossing cf. 21.7.7 *per Capersanam Euphrate navali ponte transcurso.* Gellius, speaking about a peculiarity in the style of Asinius Pollio (10.26.1), writes *eosque qui fretum transmiserant, quos transfretasse dici solitum sit, transgressos dixit.* In 22.8.13 Amm. distinguishes two Bospori, the Thracian and the Cimmerian, and displays some mythological lore: *hac causa Bospori vocitati, quod per eos quondam Inachi filia, mutata (ut poetae loquuntur) in bovem, ad mare Ionium permeavit.*

itineribusque lentis progressi The phrase is surprisingly repeated from 20.8.21 q.v. In normal terrain, a private voyager who had no access to the government post covered approximately fifteen to twenty miles a day on foot, about twenty-five to thirty in a carriage. Government officials, having the facilities of the *cursus publicus* at their disposal, could do better. At an average of five miles an hour they covered some fifty miles in a normal day's travelling. Cf. Ramsay, 1925, Eliot, 1955 and Casson, 1979, 188-189.

apud Caesaream Cappadociae Mazaca or Eusebia-under-the-Argaeus (cf. Strabo, 12.2.7: τὰ Μάζακα, ἡ μητρόπολις τοῦ ἔθνους· καλεῖται δ' Εὐσέβεια καὶ αὕτη, ἐπίκλησιν ἡ πρὸς τῷ Ἀργαίῳ· κεῖται γὰρ ὑπὸ τῷ Ἀργαίῳ ὄρει, mod. Erçiyeç Daği) was created by the Cappadocian kings to be their capital, though its site had many disadvantages, which Strabo details at great length. The city saw its name changed to Caesarea by Archelaus in 12-9 BC and was made the capital of the province of Cappadocia in AD 17. Cf. Jones, 1971[2], 177-179, Veh, 1980, 167 and the literature cited by Szidat.

opportunam urbem et celebrem For *opportunus* 'well situated' see the note ad 20.7.16 *munimenti perquam tempestivi.* After Strabo's criticism of the site of Caesarea the adjective comes as a surprise. It is either added thoughtlessly as a stock epithet, or Amm. was of the opinion that history had proved the founders right. The large number of inhabitants and visitors is also mentioned in 21.10.2 *ad exemplum urbium matris populosae et celebris* (Sirmium), which gives support to Bentley's conjecture *celebritate (celeritate* V) in 16.10.6 about Rome: *cum se vertisset ad plebem stupebat qua celebritate omne ... genus confluxerit Romam.*

IX. 2 *intromissi* Like *admittere, intromittere* is often used with reference to the admission of people to the *consistorium* cf. 14.1.6, 22.5.3, 28.1.25 *qui cum intromissi in consistorium haec referrent,* 30.6.2 *in consistorium Equitio suadente sunt intromissi.*

hisque recitatis ... excanduit imperator Constantius' reaction is in accordance with Amm.'s description of his temper, cf. 20.2.5 *iratus ultra modum* with the note. For an earlier example of Constantius' rage see 14.11.13: *Constantius ultra mortalium modum exarsit*. The present text is echoed in Zonaras, *Epit.* 13.10.20: ἐκεῖνος οὐδὲν ὑπ' ὀργῆς ἀπεκρίνατο, pace Szidat ("Constantius' heftige Reaktion wird durch Zonaras ... nicht bestätigt"). Constantius' reaction resembles that of Valentinian as described in 29.1.10 *gestorumque volumine imperatori recitato de more, prodigiosa feritas in modum ardentissimae facis fusius vagabatur*. *Excandescere* is used of daylight in 21.10.2 and 26.6.14, of anger in 30.5.10 *in immensum excanduit urente irarum nutrimenta ... Leone*. The verb is used absolutely in this sense from Cicero onwards: *Fam*. 8.12.2 *id postquam resciit, excanduit*; TLL V 2.1200.80 sqq.

limibusque oculis eos ad usque metum contuens mortis See TLL VII 2.1427.22 sqq. for the rare adjective *limus* (the alternative form *limis* seems to be based on a misinterpretation of the expression *limis* (sc. *oculis*). Its meaning is defined by Don. Ter. *Eu*. 601 as follows: *cum igitur dissimulant se homines videre quod vident et non recta facie sed transversa intuentur limes dicuntur aspicere*. As Gow explains ad Theoc. 20.13, the Greek equivalent λοξός is used of angry glances (Solon fr. 34.16 νῦν δέ μοι χολούμενοι / λοξὸν ὀφθαλμοῖς ὁρῶσι πάντες ὥστε δήιοι) and of a shy or suspicious look. The first possibility is found in the comparable phrase in 31.7.11 *torvitate mutua bellatores luminibus se contuebantur obliquis*. In the present text the second notion may also be intended, as a sign of Constantius' suspicious and insincere character. The elder Pliny (*Nat*. 8.52) tells about the lion: *cetero dolis carent et suspicione, nec limis intuentur oculis, aspicique simili modo nolunt*. With *ad usque metum* we may compare 30.8.3 *nonnullis ad usque discrimina vitae vexatis*.

IX. 3 *perculsus tamen ardenter cunctatione stringebatur ambigua* Amm. conveys the impression that Constantius was lacking in resolve and that the decision to turn his attention to the war against the Persians was due to his advisers. In fact, Constantius' problems must have been only too real, as Julian's pronunciamento had probably weakened the Roman position vis-à-vis the Persians. Sabbah 479-80 points out that by separating the narrative of the war in Mesopotamia (chs. 6-7) from the negotiations between Constantius and Julian (chs. 8-9) Amm. glosses over the simultaneity of these events and prevents the reader from asking unwelcome questions about Julian's co-responsibility for the setbacks on the Eastern front. Although Amm. cannot be proved guilty of distorting or deliberately withholding chronological data, Sabbah's estimate of the effect of his composition on the reader seems plausible. For a different interpretation of Amm.'s motives to present the facts in this order see the general introduction.

Ardenter suggests anger rather than consternation. *Perculsus* is indeed used four times of angry persons (16.7.1, 16.12.3, 30.6.3, 31.12.3 *imperator procaci quodam calore perculsus*). As *ardere* and its derivatives frequently denote eagerness and haste in Amm., there is also a contrast with the following words. *Cunctatione ambigua* is not, strictly speaking, a specimen of Amm.'s abundantia sermonis like 28.5.8 *anxia sollicitudine stringebatur*, because the adjective provides the extra information that Constantius was hesitating between two options, as in 21.12.21 *curis altioribus stringebatur multa utrimque pertimescens*. On *stringere* see the note ad 20.11.2.

acies Technically, *acies* should refer to an army in battle array, Veg. *mil.* 3.14 *acies dicitur exercitus instructus*. Amm. uses *acies* in this way in 14.2.6, 14.6.17, and 16.2.12. In 31.4.7 *memoriae veteres Medicas acies ductantes ad Graeciam* we have a parallel for the more general meaning 'armies', which, according to TLL I 404.39–55 is poetical. Cf. e.g. Verg. *A.* 7.642–3 *quae quemque secutae / complerint campos acies*.

haesitansque diu perpensis consiliis For *haesitare* see the note ad 20.4.22. Here the verb denotes indecision. *Perpendere* suggests a careful weighing of the alternatives, cf. e.g. 22.9.9 *causarum momenta aequo iure perpendens suum cuique tribuebat* and 24.4.26 *divisa itaque perpensis meritis et laboribus praeda*.

flexus est quorundam sententiis utilium suasorum *Flectere* is mostly used of negative influences: *venalis et flecti a veritate pecunia facilis* (16.9.2). This is not the case here, as *utilium* shows. The interest of the state prevails over the emperor's personal animosity. We find an exact parallel for this honourable behaviour in Valentinian's decision not to turn against Procopius before he had dealt with the Alamanni: 26.5.13 *utilitate rei perpensius cogitata in multorum sententias flexus*. The phrase *utilium suasorum* is somewhat ambiguous. In view of 14.1.8 *utilia suadendo* it seems possible to interpret *utilium* as a gen. obi. Cf. also 30.9.4 *boni pravique suasor ... admodum prudens*.It seems more natural, however, to take *utilium* as an adjective. It may well be used of persons, as in 16.12.24 *utilis praeter ceteros ductor*. *Suasor* is not uncommon in classical authors, e.g. Cic. *Phil.* 2.29 *quid enim interest inter suasorem facti et probatorem*? and Tac. *Hist.* 3.2.4 *idem suasor auctorque consilii ero*. Constantius is normally represented by Amm. as susceptible to bad and flattering advice. Cf. e.g. 14.5.4 *Accedebant ... proximorum cruentae blanditiae exaggerantium incidentia* and the note ad loc. See also 14.5.5 and 21.16.16.

iter orientem versus edixit   Cf. 31.10.3 *Gratianum orientem versus mox signa moturum*. This use of *versus* with adpositional force occurs also in Sal. *Cat.* 56.4 *Catilina ... modo ad urbem, modo Galliam versus castra movere*. *Edixit* means that Constantius issued marching orders (called *tessera expeditionalis* in 23.2.2), cf. 21.5.13 *per tesseram edicto itinere in Pannonias* and 31.11.2 *itinere edicto per tesseram*.

IX. 4 *legatos absolvit*   *Absolvere* in the sense of "debitis vel propositis factis a se dimittere" (TLL I 172.76) is found only in Comedy, e.g. Pl. *Am.* 1097 *quaeso apsolvito hinc me extemplo* and in Amm., who uses it of envoys in 17.1.1. as well, q.v.

Leonam quaestorem suum   Leonas was already an important person at court in 355 (cf. *PLRE* I, Leonas; Seyfarth, II, 1983[5], 199 n. 86: "Leonas wird sonst nicht genannt", is wrong). As *quaestor sacri palatii* (the full title is not found in Amm.) he must have been Constantius' chief legal adviser, his main task being the drafting of imperial constitutions. In this capacity the QSP, whose office, according to Zos. 5.32, had been created by Constantine, gradually became more important than the *magistri* of the *scrinia* (below, ad 20.9.8). See Jones 104 and 368; Guilland, 1971; De Bonfils, 1981 (on Leonas, p. 190–195) and cf. the note ad 14.7.12.

cum litteris datis ad Iulianum pergere celeri statuit gradu   Amm.'s terminology *dare litteras (alci) ad*, as in 17.5.2, is in conformity with classical usage, cf. Cic. *Att.* 4.1.1 *fuitque cui recte ad te litteras darem*. For manner expressions with *gradu* see the note ad 20.4.20 *pleniore gradu*. Amm. has a predilection for AcI (pass) after *statuere*, as in 14.7.5 *disponi quidquam statuit*, 22.12.8 *corpora statuit exinde transferri*. A parallel for an AcI (act.) is to be found in 25.8.3 *navigia ultro citroque discurrere statuit*.

nihil novatorum se asserens suscepisse   Constantius echoes Julian's words *siquid novatum est nunc* in 20.8.7 q.v. A negative connotation is intended here, as in 21.10.8 where Julian criticizes the policy of Constantine *ut novatoris turbatorisque priscarum legum*. For *asserere* see the relevant note ad 17.11.4. *Suscipere* 'to acknowledge' = *accipere* for which see the note ad 15.5.5 and Wölfflin, 1904, 174.

si saluti ... consulit   For the use of the indicative in subordinate clauses of or. obliqua see the note ad 20.4.12.

tumenti flatu deposito   A fine specimen of Amm.'s abundantia sermonis not registered by Hagendahl. *Flatus* is found for the first time in this sense in

Verg. *A.* 11.346 *flatusque remittat* (Turnus). It is late and poetical, as the examples quoted in TLL VI 883.56-79 show.

intra Caesaris se potestatem continere praecipiens This tallies with Julian's statement in his *Ep. ad Ath.* 286C, that in his letters Constantius still addressed him as *Caesar* (ἔτι νῦν μοι ὡς Καίσαρι γράφει) and with the versions of Libanius (*Or.* 18.106: πάντως δεῖν ἀφίστασθαι τῆς τιμῆς καὶ διὰ πάντων εἶναι τὸν πρότερον) and Zonaras (*Epit.* 13.10.21: καὶ συμβουλεύων ἀποσχέσθαι τοῦ μὴ προσηκόντως γενομένου καὶ εἰς τὸ πρότερον ἐπανελθεῖν σχῆμα, ὃ παρ' αὐτοῦ εἴληφε). Zosimus, on the other hand, represents Constantius as far more severe against his relative: ὡς προσήκει Ἰουλιανὸν τοῦ ζῆν ἀντεχόμενον ἀποθέσθαι πρὸς τῇ βασιλείᾳ καὶ τὸ τοῦ Καίσαρος σχῆμα, καταστάντα δὲ ἰδιώτην ἑαυτὸν τῇ προαιρέσει τοῦ βασιλέως ἐκδοῦναι 3.9.4).

IX. 5 *utque id facile formido intentatorum efficeret* It is difficult to decide whether *intentatorum* is to be taken as a gen. obi. or subi. As *formido* usually has the subjective meaning 'fear' in Amm., the former seems more attractive, but 17.5.14 *formidines quae nobis intentantur* leaves room for doubt. For *intentare* see the notes ad 15.4.9 and 18.6.16.

velut magnis viribus fretus Szidat rightly remarks that Amm. stresses Constantius' arrogance rather than his legitimate right to give orders to Julian. At the same time *velut* indicates that there is an element of bluff in Constantius' handling of the situation.

in locum Florentii Florentius' flight (20.8.20, cf. 20.4.2) had cleared the way for the appointment of a new praetorian prefect, as Julian himself realized (20.8.14).

praefectum praetorio Nebridium ... promoverat Amm. writes either *promovere alqm ad* followed by the name of the new assignment or *promovere* with double acc., as in the present text. Cf. e.g. 16.11.2 *Barbatio post Silvani interitum promotus ad peditum magisterium* with 17.6.2 *B. in locum Silvani peditum promotus magister*. The alternation of pluperfect and perfect in *promoverat – provexit*, the exact opposite to what classical usage would have prescribed, is a good example of Amm.'s indiscriminate use of these tenses. It cannot be accounted for on metrical grounds. Harmon 236 proposed *promovebat* for that reason. Since, however, it seems hazardous to change the text on metrical grounds only and because the resulting alternation of imperf. and perf. would produce another anomaly, it is better to leave the text as it stands.

Although Nebridius was not one of Julian's supporters (cf. *Ep. ad Ath.*

283C: καὶ γὰρ οὐδὲ ἄλλος τις παρῆν τῶν δοκούντων εὔνως ἔχειν ἐμοί, Νεβρίδιος δέ etc.), his nomination was accepted in conformity with Julian's promise to acquiesce in Contantius' choice of praetorian prefects (20.8.14 and 20.9.8). See for Nebridius' career (he was a former *comes Orientis* and became later *PPO Orientis*), apart from the literature cited by Szidat, the note ad 14.2.20 and De Bonfils, 1981, 195-203, for the office of *quaestor* the note ad section 4 (*Leonam quaestorem suum*). See also Von Haehling, 1978, 66.

Felicem notarium officiorum magistrum The appointment of Felix (*PLRE I*, Felix 3), one of the *notarii* who were promoted to the post of *magister officiorum* (cf. Clauss, 1980, 22 and for the *notarii* in general the note ad 20.4.2), was not accepted by Julian. The newly proclaimed emperor wanted to nominate his own officials and officers (20.8.14) and had already chosen Anatolius (20.9.8 *magistrum enim officiorum iam pridem ipse Anatolium ordinavit*). However, in 362 Julian made Felix *comes sacrarum largitionum*. Cf. Seeck, 1909, 2167; Clauss, 1980, 154 and Kuhoff, 1983, 200-201 and 416-417 n. 16.

Gomoarium ... magistrum provexit armorum Gomoarius, a former tribune of the *schola Scutariorum* (21.8.1 *cum Scutarios ageret*) had been sent to replace Lupicinus as *magister equitum per Gallias* (cf. for this title and the equivalent used here the note ad 20.1.2) before (so, rightly, Szidat, but see *PLRE I*, Lupicinus 6) any news of Julian's usurpation had reached Constantius: *antequam sciretur huiusmodi quidquam*. Why Lupicinus had to be replaced is not clear. Demandt, 1970, 573 tentatively suggests that he may have been chosen by Constantius to succeed Sabinianus as *magister equitum* in the East, but direct evidence for this is lacking. Another explanation might be that Constantius appointed Gomoarius *magister armorum* when he ordered Lupicinus to bring the detachments from Gaul to the East (20.4.3).

The nomination of Gomoarius was not rejected (this corroborates the view that Gomoarius had been sent to Gaul prior to the Parisian proclamation, for otherwise he would have met with the same fate as the *notarius* Felix), but Julian later dismissed the man, suspecting him of having secretly betrayed Vetranio in former years (21.8.1); Gomoarius thus became his bitter enemy (21.13.16 *ut contemptus in Galliis erat Iuliano infestus*).

Gomoarius probably was a German (see Lippold in *Gnomon* 46 (1974) 270, following Waas, 1971[2], 84-85, criticizing *PLRE I*, Gomoarius).

antequam sciretur huiusmodi quidquam Amm. has *antequam* 35 times (always followed by coni. except in 22.15.26), *priusquam* only once (19.2.12). *Prius* and *quam* are separated in 17.3.2, 20.11.3, 29.1.18. See the note ad 14.6.23 and Szantyr 600.

IX. 6 *postridie principi progresso in campum*   The alliteration, repeated at the end of the clause by *pariter et plebeia*, may well be the reason for the separation of the indirect object *principi* from *offerre*. For *campus* see the note ad 20.5.1 *convenirent in campo*.

cum multitudine armata pariter et plebeia   The role played by the civilians in this carefully staged mass meeting is stressed again in § 7. Szidat quotes 15.5.25 and 26.6.17 as parallel instances for the support of the civilian population.

tribunali, ut emineret altius, superstanti   Julian repeats the ceremony described in 20.5.1, with this difference that there is no longer any need for military protection. Moreover, his position makes his superiority to Leonas visible. For *superstare* see the note ad 20.6.4.

Leonas ... scripta iubetur offerre   Zonaras' account of Leonas' mission differs from that of Amm. In it (*Epit.* 13.10.21–28) Julian and Leonas meet in private after the latter's arrival in Paris (ἀπελθὼν οὖν ὁ κοιαίστωρ πρὸς τὸν Ἰουλιανὸν τοὺς λόγους αὐτῷ τοῦ Κωνσταντίου ἀπήγγειλεν), while during their conversation Leonas shows himself reluctant to discuss Constantius' demands openly in front of Julian's soldiers (ὁ δέ γε κοιαίστωρ φοβηθείς, ὡς, εἰ τοῖς στρατιώταις τοῦτο ἐκφήνειεν ὁ Ἰουλιανός, παρὼν αὐτὸς διασπασθήσεται παρ' αὐτῶν). He asks Julian to refrain from this (ἐδεῖτο μή τι τούτων τῷ στρατιωτικῷ κοινώσασθαι ὄχλῳ). Julian's response to Leonas' request is not mentioned, nor is his actual conduct. Zonaras confines himself to saying that Leonas gave up hope that he would be able to accomplish any of the things he was ordered to do and returned to Constantius with a letter from Julian (ἀπογνοὺς μέντοι δυνήσεσθαί τι τῶν αὐτῷ προστεταγμένων ἀνύσαι, ὑπέστρεψε μετὰ γραμμάτων τοῦ τυραννήσαντος).

Zonaras' words differ from those of Amm., but are not incompatible with them (as Rosen, 1978, 439–440 thinks: "Ob Leonas tatsächlich vor der Versammlung Julian den Brief überreicht hat, wie Amm. XX 9.6 behauptet, ist nach Zonaras' Worten unwahrscheinlich"). "Both authors highlighted different aspects of the same series of events" (Dimaio, 1980, 164). It seems best to assume that Julian first saw Leonas in private and afterwards had the proposals of Constantius recited before the assembled townsmen and soldiers, in the presence of Leonas.

replicatoque volumine   *Replicare* here has its original sense 'to unroll', as in Cic. *Corn* 1 fr. 44 *replicate, ipsa sunt; legite*, which leads to the meaning 'to read, study': *antiquitates replicando complures* (16.7.8), *annalibus replicatis* (25.9.9) and 'to disclose' *haec quae tradidit recens memoria replicabo*

(23.5.17). The most common meaning in Amm. is 'to repeat', e.g. 14.11.11 *saepius replicando quod ... cuperet*. See the notes ad 14.7.5 and 16.12.3.

edicti The use of this word suggests that Constantius' message was not a private letter but was meant to be posted in public. Edicts, issued by virtue of the emperor's *ius edicendi*, contained general legal norms laid down both for officials and for private citizens. They occasionally, as here, referred to certain immediate circumstances. See Kipp, 1905, 1947; Berger, 1953, 447-448 and Millar, 1977, 252-259.

cum ventum fuisset The impersonal passive indicates that Julian is not reading the passage out himself, as Rolfe's translation suggests. This is confirmed by the preceding words *legi ... coepto*. For the correct procedure compare *Conc. Carth.* a. 411, 1.4.72 sqq. *Marcellinus, vir clarissimus, tribunus et notarius, dixit: "... Unde nunc edictorum meorum per ordinem forma recitetur". Martialis exceptor recitavit* e.q.s.

IX. 7 *exclamabatur undique vocum terribilium sonu "Auguste Iuliane"* The acclamation of Julian as Augustus, described in similar terms in 20.4.14 *Augustum Iulianum horrendis clamoribus concrepabant* and again at the end of that section with the words *iterata magnitudine sonus Augustum appellavere consensione firmissima*, is repeated here for the benefit of Leonas and indirectly, of course, of Constantius. The intimidation (*vocum terribilium sonu*), expressed by *horrendis clamoribus* in 20.4.14 and directed against Julian, is in the present text intended for Leonas.

The imperfect *exclamabatur* implies that the cries were repeated several times. For *sonu* cf. the note ad 14.6.18.

ut provincialis et miles et rei publicae decrevit auctoritas In older editions these words are printed as part of the acclamation. Clark and Seyfarth limit the acclamation to the vocative *"Auguste Iuliane"*. This would be in accordance with the form of the acclamation in 20.4.14 quoted above. Still it seems more natural to interpret the *ut*-clause as a whole, with Rosen, 1978, 416-7, as Amm.'s free rendering of the *acclamationes* than as Amm.'s personal comment, as Szidat does. In the first place, the 'decision' of the provincials and the authority of the state have not been mentioned before. In 20.4.14 only the unanimity of the troops has been stated explicitly. Secondly, Rosen rightly observes that *quibus auditis* and *haec eadem indicantibus* in the following section seem to refer to more than just the vocative *"Auguste Iuliane"*. Szidat's objection that the *ut*-clause "formal deutlich davon abgezetzt ist" is in itself correct, but does not take into account that Amm. usually presents acclamations indirectly. Cf. e.g. 22.9.14, on Julian's arrival in Antioch, *votis excipitur publicis miratus voces multitudinis magnae salutare sidus illuxisse eois partibus acclamantis* and 23.2.4, on his departure from this city *itum felicem reditumque gloriosum exoptans oransque ut deinde placabilis esset et lenior*; cf. also 26.7.17. Moreover, as a rule acclamations consist of several cola, as these examples show. This impression is confirmed by acclamations on inscriptions (Roueché, 1984), in the *Cod. Theod.* and above all in the *Historia Augusta*. The acclamations in these biographies, though not authentic in content, as is generally agreed, give an adequate idea of their formal structure. Most of them pretend to be part of the proceedings of the senate, but there are a few acclamations by soldiers: *Dd.* 1.6 *Macrine imperator, di te servent, ... Antoninum diu vivum omnes rogamus* e.q.s., and by civilians: *Q* 9.2 *Saturnine Auguste, di te servent*. Acclamations by veterans are recorded in *Cod. Theod.* 7.20.2: *Auguste Constantine, di te nobis servent: vestra salus nostra salus: vere dicimus, iurati dicimus*. In view of these examples it seems plausible that the *ut*-clause is the indirect form of acclamations like *provincialis decrevit, miles decrevit, rei publicae decrevit auctoritas*, as Rosen has suggested. For the subject as a whole see Alföldi, 1980³, 3-118, in particular 79-88 and 92; Klauser in RAC I 216-233 with literature, to which add Burian, 1980 and Baldwin, 1981.

Ulpian (*dig.* 50.16.190, quoted in the note ad 17.3.5) defines *provincialis* as follows: *provinciales eos accipere debemus qui in provincia domicilium habent, non eos qui ex provincia oriundi sunt*. As Szidat remarks, the term probably refers to all the inhabitants of the *praefectura Galliarum*, who must have shown their loyalty to Julian by sending embassies from their various cities. In comparison with the acclamation in 20.4.14 the demonstration described in the present text stresses the total support both from the civilian population and the army. *Auctoritas rei publicae* expresses this consensus, summarizing and transcending *provincialis* and *miles*. Amm. has borrowed the phrase in all probability from Plin. *Pan.* 1.2 *imperio senatus, auctoritate rei publicae ad agendas ... gratias excitamur*. Further parallels are given in TLL II.1228.37 sqq.

recreatae quidem, sed adhuc metuentis ... excursus This looks like an addition from Amm. himself, repeating both Julian's restoration of order in Gaul (cf. 17.4.1 *inter haec recreandarum exordia Galliarum*) and the persistent fear of the Alamanni (20.4.10 *caritates vero nostrae Alamannis denuo servient*). For *redivivus* cf. 21.3.2 *quod ne dissimulatum redivivas bellorum materias excitaret* and 28.1.1 *in eois tractibus bella rediviva consurgunt*. *Excursus* is Amm.'s normal term for barbarian invasions into Roman territory, cf. the note ad 17.4.3.

IX. 8 *revertit incolumis* It is in small touches like the addition of *incolumis* that

Amm. betrays his bias in favour of Julian. Contrast the honourable welcome given to Leonas and his safe return home with the treatment of Pentadius and Eutherius, who at one moment feared for their lives.

solusque admissus est ... Nebridius For *admittere* 'to appoint' compare 26.7.6 *aliique plures ad aulae varios actus et administrandas provincias sunt admissi.*

aperte praedixit In 20.8.14.

Anatolium ordinavit *Ordinare* has the same meaning in 22.11.4 *is ... episcopus Alexandriae est ordinatus.* For *ordinare* 'to give orders' see the notes ad 14.3.1 and 16.11.6; for the meaning 'to manage' see ad 17.12.17. The verb has its original sense 'to draw up (in formation)' in 20.11.18 *inter armatos, qui portabant ignes, amplioribus ordinatis.* It is also used for drawing up a will (21.15.5 *Constantium voluntatem ordinasse postremam,* cf. 28.4.22).

libellis antea respondentem A *magister libellorum* (*Not. Dign. Or.* 19.10) or *magister libellorum et cognitionum sacrarum* (*CIL* 6.510 = Inscr. Dessau 4152) – for those are the technical terms which Amm. as usual avoids – controlled the *scrinium libellorum,* one of the *scrinia* which together served as a general secretariat of the *comitatus.* There were four of them according to *Not. Dign. Or.* 19 (cf. the note ad 15.5.4), but the number sometimes varied. As appears from *Not. Dign. Or.* 19.11 the *magister libellorum* was responsible for preparing trials and dealt with petitions (*cognitiones et preces tractat*). It is not easy, however, to define exactly the competence of the various *scrinia.* Their tasks often overlapped.

During the Principate the *magistri scriniorum* were very important (cf. Millar, 1977, 213 ff.), but since Constantine had created the office of *quaestor sacri palatii* (see the note ad 20.9.4), their importance gradually declind. Cf. for the Later Empire Bury, 1910; Jones 505-507, 575-578 and Clauss, 1980, 16-18.

Anatolius, a close friend of Julian (cf. *PLRE I*, Anatolius 5) was apparently appointed as soon as Pentadius had gone (cf. 20.8.19). He was not replaced by Constantius' nominee Felix (cf. 20.9.5) but remained *magister officiorum* until the day he died. He was killed in the same battle as Julian. See for the man, apart from Szidat, Clauss, 1980, 145 and Kuhoff, 1983, 425 n. 53.

et quosdam alios Neither Libanius (*Or.* 18.104: ἄρχοντάς τε ἐπὶ τὰς πόλεις ἐξέπεμπεν ἀντὶ πονηρῶν μὲν ἀγαθούς, ἀντὶ δὲ σκαιῶν πεπαιδευμένους) nor Sozomen (*HE* 5.1: ἄρχοντας μὲν τοὺς ὑπ' αὐτοῦ χειροτονηθέντας ἤμειβεν) nor Zonaras (*Epit.* 13.11.1: πολλοὺς εἰδὼς ἐν τοῖς αὐτῷ συνοῦσι τὰ Κωνσταντίου φρονοῦντας πάντας ἐκεῖθεν ἐξήλασεν) is more specific.

ut ... utile videbatur et tutum   The third of the traditional deliberative τέλη is mentioned in 15.4.1 *digestis diu consiliis id visum est honestum et utile*.

IX. 9 *timebatur Lupicinus*   Lupicinus, the *magister equitum per Gallias* (cf. for this title the note ad 20.1.2), had been sent to Britain in order to fight against the Scots and the Picts while Julian was passing the winter in Paris (20.1.1–2). Whether this assignment was a deliberate move of Julian and/or of Julian's friends to get rid of an enemy, is disputed (above, ad 20.1.2), but it is at any rate clear from the present section that Lupicinus was no friend of Julian and was thought to be capable of harming Julian's interests.

Whatever he may have been planning, nothing came of it according to Amm. (*nullas ciere potuit turbas*). In *Ep. ad Ath.* 281A Julian states that Lupicinus actually plotted against him and was therefore arrested (Λουππι-κῖνον, φησί, καὶ τρεῖς ἄλλους ἀνθρώπους κατέσχες· οὓς εἰ καὶ κτείνας ἤμην ἐπιβουλεύσαντας ἔμοιγε φανερῶς etc.), but this apparently happened after Lupicinus' return from Britain. It meant, incidentally, in no way the end of Lupicinus' career. He was *magister equitum* in the East under Jovian and Valens and *consul prior* in 367 (for literature see the note ad 20.1.1).

Of Lupicinus' achievements in Britain nothing is recorded and one can only speculate about his exploits there (Todd, 1981, 231: "as he was soon back in Gaul some success was clearly gained") and about the motives which made Constantius replace him by Gomoarius (20.9.5, with the note ad loc.). It is even more speculative to suppose that Lupicinus was the owner of the so-called Mildenhall treasure, a fourth-century hoard consisting of thirty-four silver objects found near Mildenhall in Suffolk in 1942, which, according to Painter, 1973, 173 may have been hidden by Lupicinus' family or entourage in 360.

Lupicinus is characterized as *homo superbae mentis et turgidae*, which varies *supercilia erigentem ut cornua* in 20.1.2, q.v. for a more favourable judgment of Lupicinus by Libanius.

eratque suspicio, quod   We find the same construction in 20.7.9. In classical prose *suspicio* is followed by an infinitive: Cic. *Fam.* 12.15.5 *ipsi magistratus veniebant in suspicionem ... demorati esse*, or by AcI: Liv. 37.7.12 *ea ... remissio animi suspicionem dempsit novare eum quicquam velle*, or by *quasi*: Suet. *Tit.* 5.3 *unde nata suspicio est quasi desciscere a patre ... temptasset*.

novarum rerum materias excitaret   For *materia* see the note ad 20.4.15 *discordiarum materias excitaret*.

notarius Bononiam mittitur   We have no information about the date of this measure. If indeed the most important motive to send Lupicinus to Britain was to remove him from the stage before Julian took the purple, it seems likely that the measure was taken immediately after the pronunciamento in February, not after Leonas' visit to Paris.

The growth of numbers, success and prestige of imperial *notarii* during the fourth century was temporarily interrupted by Julian, who disliked the way they were employed for all sorts of activities which had nothing to do with their original task as stenographers. This is not to say, however, that Julian did not occasionally use *notarii* for special missions too. See Teitler, 1985, 68-69; for *Bononia*, above, ad 20.1.3.

observaturus sollicite, ne   Instead of the classical construction with *ut* or *qui* in final clauses Amm. regularly uses a future participle after *mittitur*, e.g. *Eutherius ... mittitur statim post eum, si quid finxerit, convicturus* 16.7.2; cf. 24.1.6, 25.9.12, 27.12.13, 30.1.14; Szantyr 390. *Observare ne* is the equivalent of *curare ne*, as in 18.1.1 *diligenter observans ne quem tributorum sarcina praegravaret*, for which see TLL IX 2.214.13 sqq. Julian used similar tactics against the troublesome Egyptians after ordering them to cross to Calchedon: *quibus transgressis mandatum est navigiorum magistris ... ne qui transfretare auderet Aegyptium* (22.6.4).

fretum oceani transire permitteretur   The term *fretum oceani* for the Channel is possibly borrowed from Tacitus *Ag.* 40.2 *in ipso freto Oceani*. In Amm. *Oceanus* without an adjective refers to the Atlantic Ocean: 15.4.4 (Rhenus) *Oceani gurgitibus intimatur* If he wants to indicate the Eastern or Northern part of the *Oceanus*, he employs adjectives: 22.8.11 *qua sol oceano exsurgit eoo*, 31.2.1 *ultra paludes Maeoticas glacialem oceanum accolens*. For the personal passive construction of *permittere* see the note ad 20.2.5; Szantyr 365.

antequam horum quidquam sciret   A slightly varied repetition of 20.9.5 *antequam sciretur huiusmodi quidquam*. There Constantius must be supplied as the Agent.

nullas ciere potuit turbas   A somewhat cynical euphemism for 'was arrested'. Julian himself does not make a secret of this precautionary measure in *Ep ad Ath.* 281A, quoted above.

Chapter 10

Szidat's suggestion that it is Amm.'s implicit intention in this chapter to show that Julian was in no way preparing himself for an armed conflict with Constantius, whereas the latter was occupied by the nagging question *utrum in Persas an contra Iulianum moveri iuberet acies quibus fidebat* (20.9.3), may very well be correct. This should, however, not eclipse the author's explicitly stated purpose, viz. to illustrate the respective military accomplishments of the two protagonists after the events at Paris. Julian's rise immediately proves to be salutary for the empire: his increased confidence (cf. *Laetior* in section 1) is an asset during the successful campaign across the Rhine. Amm.'s account especially stresses the swiftness of the actions. From this report few readers will gather the real duration of the operations, which took three months: ἐκείνης μοι γενομένης τριμήνου τῆς στρατιᾶς Jul. *Ep.* (26.414b). Libanius also suggests that things went quickly: ... ἐλθὼν δ' ἐπὶ τὸν ʽΡῆνον καὶ δείξας τοῖς βαρβάροις τὴν κεφαλήν ... (*Or.* 18.105).

Julian's swift success contrasts sharply with Constantius' protracted and finally fruitless siege of Bezabde, reported in ch. 11. Right at the beginning of that chapter Amm. explicitly and emphatically draws attention to this contrast, stating about Julian's actions: *quae dum ita prospere succedunt*. The contrast is further illustrated at the end of the report of the respective campaigns. Both retire to winter quarters (*hiematurus*): Julian goes to Vienne, having vanquished the Atthuarii, strengthened the *limes*, recovered and fortified places which had been taken by the *barbari*. Constantius repairs to Antioch *aerumnosa perpessus et gravia* (11.32).

X. 1 *celsiore fortuna militisque fiducia laetior* The use of *fortuna* accompanied by an adj. meaning 'high' to denote the imperial dignity is first attested in Tacitus, e.g. *Ann.* 2.72.2 *summae fortunae* (cf. also *Ann.* 15.1.4). To Szidat's references should be added *fortuna superioris* (15.6.3) and *supremae fortunae* (27.6.15). Concerning *fortuna principalis* his reference should be corrected to 31.12.10; this too is a formula used by Tacitus, cf. *Hist.* 2.59.3, with Heubner's note.

The gen. *militis* can either be subi., as in *erecta barbarorum fiducia* (21.3.3), or obi., as in *sui rectorisque fiducia* (23.5.15). The former suits the context much better and besides tallies with *angebat fiduciam militis* (25.4.10, about Julian).

The comp. *laetior* occurs more often in Amm., but curiously enough only in 23.3.6 and 25.3.8 it concerns a person.

ne intepesceret neve ut remissus argueretur et deses In three other cases a precaution is expressed by *ne intepesceret*: 14.7.18, 21.7.2 and 31.15.3. The second of these has a person as subject, interestingly enough Constantius, whose considerations in that context are comparable: *ne intepesceret aut omississe belli videretur aliud latus*. Rulers should be active in the military sphere and besides demonstrate this activity clearly, in order to prevent any misunderstanding, such as befell the Latini who despised Ancus Martius, thinking *desidem Romanum regem inter sacella et aras acturum esse regnum* (Liv. 1.32.3). In his necrology Amm. takes care to show that Julian's military ardour left nothing to be desired (25.4.10 sqq.). The final clause just quoted from 21.7.2 clearly shows that Müller-Seidel's interpretation of the present text is partly incorrect: "Julian wollte nämlich – so heisst es dort – den Eifer der Soldaten nicht erkalten lassen. Er wollte sie bestätigen, um sie weiter und enger an sich zu binden" (1955, 235). The immediate sequel is correct: "und um selbst nicht nachlässig und träge zu erscheinen".

The negative sense of *remissus* is parallelled by *more vitae remissioris fluxius Sabinianus agens* (18.7.7), which pictures the guilty negligence of Ursicinus' bête noire (see above the note ad 20.2.3). *Amm.* uses *deses* more often than other authors. It tends to be coupled with another negative adj. (cf. Liv. 21.16.3, Tac. *Hist.* 2.21.4): *ignavus* (24.3.2), *iners* (30.1.16), *malignus* (22.12.3), *otiosus* (28.4.28), *pervicax* (29.6.3), and is quite apt to express scorn: *Romanumque ut desidem increpans* (28.6.19), cf. also 15.8.13 and Tac. *Hist.* 2.21.4, quoted above.

legatis ad Constantium missis In regarding this phrase as a reference to 20.9.8 *Leonas cum Iuliani litteris...revertit*, Szidat I 47 overlooks Amm.'s use of the plural. Besides, Leonas was not a *legatus* of Julian but of Constantius. The *legati* of the present text are Pentadius and Eutherius (20.8.19), who are also referred to as such in 20.9.1 and 4. This does, indeed, imply a problem, as is pointed out by Szidat. At face value Amm. seems to report that Julian marched out to the German border (*egressus est*) immediately after the departure of Pentadius and Eutherius, presumably in February. In that case it would have to be assumed that he returned to Paris after the expedition in order to receive Leonas there in June (cf. Piganiol-Chastagnol, 1972[2], 138 with note 5); this involves an altogether unlikely sequence of events and does not tally with section 3 of this chapter, where it is told that after the campaign Julian *Viennam hiematurus abscessit*. The problem, however, is not unsoluable: it has less to do with chronological order than with Amm.'s composition.

At the end of ch. 8 we had left Julian in Paris, to follow Pentadius and Eutherius on their eastward journey. The outcome of their mission and the way Constantius reacted to it are sketched in the opening sections of ch. 9.

After having told this, Amm. continues his account of the exchange of messages between Julian and Constantius with a description of the next step taken by Constantius, viz. the sending of Leonas, and of Leonas' meeting with Julian (20.9.4-8), only to return in ch. 10 to other events which had taken place after Pentadius and Eutherius had been sent to the East.

In fact, meanwhile Julian had been planning an expedition across the Rhine, a campaign which probably began in July (cf. 17.8.1 *opperiensque Iulium mensem, unde sumunt Gallicani procinctus exordia*). Because the emphasis in the present short chapter is entirely on the speed of Julian's operations, Amm. does not waste many words on any preparatory measures, fully in accordance with his habit of taking "a great deal for granted, e.g. in the prior organization of campaigns" (Austin, 1979, 164). Obviously it must have taken some time to prepare the attack on the Franks and to furnish the army with all the equipment that the business in hand demanded (*omnique apparatu, quem flagitavit instans negotium*), enough time, it seems, to allow Julian to meet Leonas in Paris before his departure to Germany.

in limitem Germaniae secundae In his enumeration of the provinces of Gaul in 15.11.7 et seq., Amm. begins with *secunda Germania*, fortified by the wealthy and populous cities of Cologne and Tongres. The province was called *Germania inferior* (cf. 15.11.6) before Diocletian reorganised the provinces of the Empire (see for its history during the Principate Rüger, 1968 and also Bechert, 1982). It belonged to the diocese of the Gauls, which, together with Spain, *Viennensis* (later: *Aquitania* or *Quinque Provinciae*, still later *Septem Provinciae*, cf. the note ad 20.4.6) and Britain fell under the jurisdiction of the *praefectus praetorio per Gallias* (see for him the note ad 20.4.2, for the provincial organisation ad 15.11.1-18 and in general Nesselhauf, 1938).

The stability of the lower Rhine frontier (cf. for *limes* the notes ad 17.13.1 and 18.2.17), repeatedly disturbed in previous years and even after Julian's recapture of Cologne in 356 (16.3.1-2) still threatened (cf. 17.2.1), had been restored to a great extent by Julian's recent successes (cf. 17.8 and 17.9), notably his recovery, repair and fortification of a number of cities along the Rhine, among others *Tricensima* (18.2.3-4). But even now the area near the frontier was not sacred from barbarian intrusion (*inquietorum hominum licentius etiam tum percursantium extima Galliarum*, 20.10.2).

There is no reason to underestimate the seriousness of the barbarian inroads into Roman territory nor to see in Julian's attempts to stop them primarily a move in the struggle for power against Constantius. Libanius, *Or.* 18.105 (ἐλθὼν δ' ἐπὶ τὸν ῾Ρῆνον καὶ δείξας τοῖς βαρβάροις τὴν κεφαλὴν καὶ δευτέροις ὅρκοις τὰς ὁμολογίας ἐνδήσας ἔτρεχεν ἐπὶ τὸν ἀκούσιον ἀγῶνα) does not warrant Szidat's statement that the campaign against the Franks "deutlich (verknüpft war) mit den Vorbereitungen für den Marsch gegen Constantius".

See for the defense of this part of the Roman Empire in general Luttwak, 1976, in particular Schönberger, 1969, Von Petrikovits, 1971 and Johnson, 1983.

quem flagitavit instans negotium   Amm. regularly uses *flagitare* with a non-personal subject (viz. the relevant situation in the context): 20.11.9 *quotiens flagitabat necessitas*, 22.15.1 *quoniam tempus videtur hoc flagitare*, 16.12.28, 17.13.1, 20.5.3, 21.12.3, 25.1.16, 27.8.2, 31.4.1. There are some examples of this in earlier authors, e.g. *magnam exercitationem res flagitat* (Cic. *Orat.* 229).

For *instans negotium* cf. *rigore itaque instantium negotiorum anceps* (21.7.1).

Tricensimae oppido propinquabat   About the verb *propinquare* Heubner ad Tac. *Hist.* 2.18.1 remarks: "Tac. macht von dem Simplex weitaus häufigeren Gebrauch als die Prosaiker vor ihm"; Livy has only two instances: 21.46.4, 28.37.7; Amm., on the other hand, does not use *appropinquare*. It is worth noting that this is the only case of a main verb in the imperf. in this chapter; all the other main predicates are indic. perf.: *egressus est* (§ 1), *pervasit* (§ 2), *superavit* (§ 2), *dedit* (§ 2), *venit* (§ 3), *abscessit* (§ 3). This adds to the purpose of the narrative sequence: Julian 'was nearing' Tricensima, when he suddenly crossed the Rhine and attacked the Atthuarii; *propinquabat ... subito pervasit* is very much akin to a 'cum inversum'-construction. This suggestion is slightly weakened, however, by the fact that 5 of the 6 instances of finite *propinquare* in Amm. are imperf., while there is only one example of the perf.: *propinquasse* (17.13.5). The verb occurs more than 30 times, the part. praes. especially being in frequent use.

In 359 seven *civitates* along the Rhine which had been destroyed and abandoned a long time before (*multo ante*, 18.2.3; presumably 352 or 355, cf. Hoffman II 68 n. 584) were recovered by Julian, who ordered the repair of their walls (*receptarum urbium moenia reparari*, 18.2.5). One of these cities was *Tricensima*, or *Tricensimae*, as some (e.g. Rüger, 1979, 499 n. 2) prefer to read with Vm2 in 18.2.4.

The name *Tricensima* is clearly derived from the *legio XXX Ulpia Victrix*, stationed from about 120 A.D. until 352 or 355 (so Hoffmann, loc. cit.) in the neighbourhood of modern Birten, ancient *Vetera* (*Vetera II*, that is, the fortress built to replace *Vetera I*, destroyed by Julius Civilis in A.D. 70). Near *Vetera* was situated *Colonia Ulpia Traiana*, not far from the present-day Xanten, founded by Trajan between 98 and 106 (cf. Hinz, 1975 and 1976).

The site of *Tricensima* is disputed. It has been identified as Birten/*Vetera* (e.g. by Zöllner, 1970, 20: "Mit *Tricensima* ist kaum die alte *Colonia Traiana* umweit Xanten gemeint, sondern eher das benachbarte Lager der dreissigsten Legion bei Birten") and as Xanten/*Colonia Ulpia Traiana* (e.g. by Johnson, 1983, 146: "At Xanten, the site of the late Roman fort of *Tricensima* has been located within the area of the *Colonia Ulpia Traiana*"). Rüger, 1979, however, rejects the view that an older settlement was rebuilt. He plausibly argues that the course of the Rhine had changed to such a degree that Julian had to look for a new place to erect his fortress. "Der Platz dieser ammianischen '*civitas*' ist archäologisch noch nicht nachgewiesen. Er lag entlang dem Xantener Rheinufer ..., jedenfalls nicht in der CUT" (p. 524). See for *Tricensima* also the note ad 18.2.4.

X. 2 *regionem subito pervasit Francorum, quos Atthuarios vocant* The use of *pervadere* c.acc. with this meaning is by no means widespread. In a figurative sense it is better known: *cum ex eo pavor ac trepidatio totam urbem pervasisset* (Liv. 21.14.2), *horror pervaserat universos* (Amm. 29.1.27). The meaning it has here, viz. 'to force one's way aggressively into something', seems typical for Amm. Its objects are towns and houses (14.1.6, 24.2.13, 28.2.11), provinces, regions etc. (21.13.6, 26.6.11, 31.3.1) and more generally *aliena* (23.1.7) and *cuncta* (18.4.1). Cf. for *subito* 17.8.4: *subito cunctos* (i.e. some Salian Franks) *aggressus tamquam fulminis turbo perculsit*, and see Szidat.

"Der fränkische Stammesbund – von einem solchen ist unbedingt zu sprechen, nicht von einem politisch oder ethnisch von Anfang an einheitlich organisierten Stammesverband – bildete sich aus dem Zusammenwirken von Kleinstämen der Istwäonengruppe" (Zöllner, 1970, 2). In 17.8.3 another of those tribes is mentioned: *Francos, eos videlicet quos consuetudo Salios appellavit* (see the note ad loc.; cf. also the note ad 15.5.11).

The name of the *Atthuarii* appears for the first time in Velleius Paterculus (2.105.1). Strabo (7.292) calls them *Chattuarii* (Χαττουάριοι). An identification with the *Chasuarii* of Tac. *Germ.* 34 or with the *Marsi* (the latter is defended by Gutenbrunner, 1972, 75) is disputed (cf. Schmidt, 1940[2], 425).

inquietorum hominum licentius etiamtum percursantium extima Galliarum Julian's action was not a rash deed of a military adventurer, but a necessary protection of Roman interests, as the circumstantial description of the enemy implies. The adi. *inquietorum* expresses their rejection of the *pax Romana*, cf. Liv. 22.21.2 *ipsorum Hispanorum inquieta avidaque in novas res sunt ingenia*, Tac. *Ann.* 1.68.1 *haud minus inquies Germanus*.

Amm.'s frequent use of the adv. *licenter* (and its compar. *licentius*) is remarkable. It occurs only three times in Sallust and Livy, a little more often in Tacitus, but more than 30 times in Amm., of which the following concern barbarian raids in the borderland of the Empire: 15.5.2, 16.12.5, 19.11.1 (q.v.), 21.4.6, 23.6.7, 27.1.1, 28.6.3, 30.2.8, 31.5.17, 31.7.4, 31.9.3. It is a small testimony to the growing problems to restrain restless neighbours of the Empire: these nations acted 'freely, according to their own wishes'.

This is the only instance of *percursare* in Amm. It is a rare verb, which also occurs only once in Livy (23.42.10) and Tac. (*Ann.* 15.8.2).

Concerning *extimus* TLL V2.1994.25-42 provides an interesting table in which its frequency is compared with *extremus* and it is shown that its occurrences form a small percentage of the total. Several authors in different periods do not use it, e.g. *Rhet. Her.*, Caes., Verg.; Cicero has one instance (referred to in Amm. 20.3.8) against 325 of *extremus*. In Amm. the proportions are a little different: 16 instances of *extimus*, 56 of *extremus*. The first occurrence of the substantivized n.pl. is Plin. *Nat.* 6.217 *Apuliae extuma*. Another example in Amm. is *super Thraciarum extimis* (22.8.1); *extima limitum* (17.13.27) is somewhat different. Cf. De Jonge ad loc.

quos adortus subito nihil metuentes hostile   By repeating *subito* Amm. adds to the impression of great speed in Julian's operations. The combination *nihil hostile*, which also occurs in Sal. *Iug.* 91.4, Liv. 5.39.2, 6.26.5, 30.6.3, 37.53.28, 42.14.3, Tac. *Hist.* 3.86.3, 4.20.4, is further used by Amm. in 15.5.25, 27.9.7, 29.5.19 and 29.6.6..

scruposa viarum difficultate arcente   This is one of the combinations of gen. inversus and enallage treated by Blomgren 146-7, who provides this formula: "adiectivum, quod re vera ad genetivum pertinet, ad nomen principale accommodatur". Another case of enallage in book 20 is *libero pectoris muro* (20.8.9), cf. the note ad loc. The adi. *scruposus* occurs once more to denote a rugged landscape: *per asperitates scruposas* (31.8.4).

nullum ad suos pagos introisse meminerant principem   One of the many opportunities for 'auxesis' is offered according tot Arist. *Rhet.* A 9.1368a 10-11, εἰ μόνος ἢ πρῶτος ἢ μετ' ὀλίγων ἢ καὶ μάλιστα πεποίηκεν. Cf. also Cic. *de Orat.* 2. 347 *sumendae autem res erunt aut magnitudine praestabiles aut novitate primae*, Quint. *Inst.* 3.7.16 *dum sciamus gratiora esse audientibus quae solus quis aut primus aut certe cum paucis fecisse dicetur*. Of the instances aptly quoted by Szidat *Pan.* 7.8.4 is especially interesting: *Romana trans Rhenum signa primus barbaris gentibus intulit*. By making the fact in question the object of the Atthuarii's thought, Amm. elegantly incorporates this rhetorical technique into his report.

Seyfarth rightly agrees with Blomgren 170 and Frassinetti, 1966, 300-1, both of whom reject Clark's emendation *adhuc*, quoting among other texts Sal. *Cat.* 28.1 *salutatum introire ad Ciceronem*. Cf. also Amm. 14.6.12, where, however, *introieris* is an emendation.

Although *pagus* is used about a geographical entity anywhere in the world (e.g. in 23.6. 15, 17, 27, 44, in the description of the Persian empire), it most often concerns Germany.

The inf. praes. in an a.c.i. as complement of *memini*, quite normal in pre-classical Latin (e.g. Enn. *Ann.* 11 Sk. *memini me fiere pavom*) and not unusual in classical Latin, does not occur in Amm.

superavit negotio levi The phrase *levi negotio* (or, as here, *n.l.*) occurs only in Amm. 16.12.22 (q.v.), 25.1.5, 26.6.10, 27.10.10, 31.8.5, cf. also *levi labore* (18.1.2) and *opera levi* (17.13.28).

pacem ex arbitrio dedit The expression *ex arbitrio* does not occur frequently, only once more in Amm.: *ex arbitrio suo* (21.8.1). Much more usual is *ad arbitrium*, used by Amm. in 14.8.6, 15.5.5, 16.10.14, 18.4.2, 19.12.5, 20.2.4, 25.4.19, 26.1.12, 30.2.4. The addition of *ex arbitrio* is quite important: Amm. wants to stress that peace is made on Julian's terms. At the same time it contrasts nicely with *licentius*: the situation has been normalized in a very satisfactory manner.

hoc prodesse possessoribus finitimis arbitratus This addition of Julian's consideration deserves attention. Amm. wants to prevent the reader from drawing the conclusion that the expedition's successes were not fully exploited, perhaps as a result of Julian's lack of vigour and perseverance. On the contrary, the final settlement was dictated by him and besides served the interests of the landowners in the borderland between Gaul and Germany. The phrase betrays Amm.'s prejudices. "He considers the protection of the propertied classes to be one of the first duties of government" (Momigliano, 1974, 1401).

The first occurrence of *possessor* used absolutely as a t.t. with the meaning 'owner of a farm' is Fron. *Aq.* 9.5 (TLL X2.104.47 sqq). The other instances in Amm. are 17.3.1 (cf. the note ad loc.), 18.5.3, 22.15.13, 29.5.11. The second of these concerns the former *protector* Antoninus, who, in order to prepare his desertion to the Persians, settled as a *possessor* on the bank of the Tigris. This was an excellent pretext, for nobody dared to ask him *causam veniendi ad extremas Romani limitis partes*: the interests of a landowner were obviously deemed to run parallel to those of the Roman empire.

It could be asked what kind of advantage for the *possessores* Amm. precisely had in mind, when he wrote the present phrase. Peace alone will not do, for, though the constant pillaging expeditions of the Germans must have driven many landowners in the frontier provinces to abandon their estates in despair ("Abandoned lands, *agri deserti*, are a constant theme of imperial legislation from before Diocletian's time to that of Justinian", Jones 812), it is obvious that not only *possessores* would have benefited by peaceful conditions. There must have been a more specific advantage.

Perhaps the intereststs of landowners, who "seem to have been perennially short of tenants" (Jones 817), were best served by an increase of their labour force and it is likely that Amm. alludes here to the allocation of barbarian prisoners to their estates. Cf. Jones 794: "... often the government, when it made a large haul of barbarian prisoners, preferred not to sell them as slaves, but tot distribute them to landlords as *coloni*, thus making them and their descendants eligible for conscription into the army". Jones refers inter alia to Amm. 31.9.4, where it is said that the Roman general Frigeridus spared the lives of Gothic prisoners, but banished them to Italy, where they were to work in the fields (*rura culturos*). Cf. also 28.5.15.

As to the meaning of *possessor*, it is to be noted that in Late Antiquity the word could be used with a still more technical meaning than simply 'owner of land' to denote an *emphyteuticarius* or a *perpetuarius*, i.e. a person to whom an estate was leased for life or in perpetuity, respectively. On this see Jones 788 ff., who remarks on p. 791: "The holders on emphyteutic and perpetual leases were no doubt usually rich men; lands so leased were often in bad condition and needed considerable capital outlay, which ruled out the poor man. Moreover, they were a form of investment only slightly less attractive than freehold land. For though they were burdened with a perpetual rent, they were free, if state or church lands, as they usually were, from superindictions, extraordinary levies and *munera sordida*. It is probable that many *emphyteuticarii* and *perpetuarii* were at the same time private landlords on a large scale".

The *possessores finitimi* of the present text too may have been not only owners of private estates but holders of emphyteutic or perpetual leases as well. In both capacities they would have welcomed an increase of their agricultural manpower.

X. 3 The succinct narrative now becomes even more concise and lapidary. Precise details are lacking, so that many questions are left unanswered, e.g. how a journey by boat along the Rhine as far as Rauraci was combined with a thorough inspection, repairs included, of the *limes*, which, the farther southward they traveled, was many miles away.

per flumen The various translations are correct ("by way of the river", "zu Schiff auf dem Fluss", "attraverso il fiume"), as the parallels in 14.2.19, 18.2.12 and 24.1.4 prove. A march along the river's banks would have been expressed differently: *Severo duce misso per ripam* (17.8.4), *per contrarias ripas leniter incedentes* (18.2.10).

In *Ep. ad Ath.* 280a Julian boasts of having collected a fleet of six hundred

241

ships during his second and third years as Caesar in Gaul: ἑξακοσίων νηῶν ἀνήγαγον στόλον. Four hundred of them he had had built in less than ten months (ὧν τὰς τετρακοσίας ἐν οὐδὲ ὅλοις μησὶ δέκα ναυπηγησάμενος) and he brought them all into the Rhine (πάσας εἰσήγαγον εἰς τὸν Ῥῆνον), where he used them repeatedly. Indeed, "auch der letzte Herrscher der Constantinischen Dynastie hatte zur Flotte ein enges Verhältnis" (Kienast, 1965, 147).

In the Later Empire the Rhine fleet (*classis Germanica*), which had been created in the reign of Augustus (see for its early history, apart from Kienast, Starr, 1960[2], 141 et seq.) seems to have consisted mainly of small, swift boats (cf. 17.1.4: *navigiis modicis et velocibus octingentos imposuit milites*), called *lusoriae naves* (17.2.3; 18.2.12). During excavations at Mainz in the winter of 1981–82 some fourth-century examples of these ships have been found (cf. Höckman, 1982).

explorans diligenter et corrigens This use of *corrigere* is remarkable. Amm. has a number of instances where the verb means "aliquid in pristinum vel aequum statum reducere" (TLL IV 1037.77), but these always concern circumstances and to "remedy an undesirable situation" (OLD s.v. 4) aptly fits the various contexts, in almost all cases the quenching of rebellion and similar troubles or the solving of military problems (15.5.2, 16.1.2, 17.13.26, 18.3.1, 19.13.2, 21.3.2, 21.12.2, 25.4.25, 26.1.13, 27.2.1, 27.3.12), a few times dishonest practices (18.1.2, 27.7.1), once the breach of the terms of a treaty (27.12.18). A concrete object, as in the present text, is not attested anywhere else in Amm., nor in any other author. Could this be a grecism? Cf. Hdt. 7.208.2 ἔσω ... τοῦ τείχεος, τὸ ἀνορθώσαντες εἶχον ἐν φυλακῇ.

ad usque Rauracos In the territory of the *Rauraci* (cf. Caes. *Gal*. 1.5.4 e.a.), near modern Basle, a colony was founded by L. Munatius Plancus in 44 B.C. It was strengthened by Augustus and henceforth called *Augusta Rauraca*, modern Augst (see Martin-Kilcher and Zaugg, 1982, and cf. the notes ad 14.10.6 and 15.11.11). After 260, in the wake of the Alamannic incursions, the city was largely abandoned. Under Diocletian it was succeeded by a new settlement, *Castrum Rauracense*, nearer the Rhine (*ad supercilia fluminis Rheni*, 14.10.6; De Jonge ad loc. prefers to see in the *Rauracum* of 14.10.6 the *colonia*, not the *castrum*), modern Kaiseraugst (for recent archaeological reports concerning Augst and Kaiseraugst: T. Tomasevic-Buck, 1982 and 1982/1983). Together with Besançon it was the chief city of the province *Maxima Sequanorum* (15.11.11: *Apud Sequanos Bisontios videmus et Rauracos, aliis potiores oppidis multis*).

barbari intercepta retinebant ut propria This information is extremely vague. The absence of any geographic and quantitative details is striking. For *intercepta* see above the note ad *aliquotiens interceptum* (20.6.9).

pleniore cura There are only two other instances of the compar. of *plenus* in Amm.: *pleniore gradu* (20.4.20), *plenius designabo* (26.1.7).

per Besantionem Besantio, modern Besançon, was the provincial capital of *Maxima Sequanorum* (cf. 15.11.11 with the note). Its name occurs for the first time in Caesar (*Gal.* 1.38.1: *Vesontionem, quod est oppidum maximum Sequanorum*), whose description of the city on the river *Dubis*, modern Doubs, probably served as a model for Julian in his letter to Maximus, *Ep.* 26.414c.

Viennam Cf. the note ad 20.4.6.

Chapter 11

The succinct tenth chapter having dealt with Julian's swift successes in Germany, due in no small degree to his freshly gained confidence, the present long chapter sketches Constantius' lengthy but unsuccessful attempt to regain Bezabde. Amm. provides an extensive, though not in all respects clear report of the military operations, in which especially the chronological details leave something to be desired. In this report the different phases of the siege are sketched in traditional and even almost formulaic language. It should be added, however, that the author quite skilfully varies this traditional terminology.

It is definitely suggested that Constantius' final failure was not merely caused by the course of the military actions, but that Constantius' personality also had something to do with it. At the beginning of the chapter much attention is paid to the pains taken by Constantius over manipulating the Armenian king Arsaces, which certainly does not testify to the emperor's resolution. The same lack of confidence comes to the fore in the last part of the chapter, where Constantius' uncertainty and finally his utter confusion are portrayed.

At the end of the chapter, however, the psychological contrast between the two protagonists is overarched by the prominent manifestation of heavenly signs: dark clouds, continual rain, thunder and lightning are experienced as terrifying by the Roman soldiers. To crown it all, the frequent sight of rainbows makes it clear that a change of (political) climate has taken place. Amm. briefly elucidates the nature of this phenomenon in a digression which aptly winds up the whole book, in which Julian's rise to the status of Augustus is the central event.

XI. 1 *ordo gestorum* Cf. the note ad 20.1.1 *rerum series*.

quae dum ita prospere succedunt et caute For the combination of *prospere* and *succedere* cf. Liv. 44.31.6 *quia prima successerant prospere* and Amm. 21.16.15 *ita prospere succedentibus pugnis civilibus tumidus*. The adv. *caute*, which rarely occurs in other historians (twice in Livy, Tac. and HA, three times in Curt.) is quite frequent in Amm. Combined with another adv. it takes a similar position in the colon in 21.12.6 *sensim incedentes et caute* and 26.6.3 *iniuncta civiliter agens et caute*. In the present text it is by no means otiose: Julian's successes in Gaul were not the result of rash and inconsiderate actions.

ascitum Arsacen Without any explanation Seyfarth here differs from Clark, who prints V's *adcitum*. Perhaps he thought that *accire* was only suitable to express the summoning of a subordinate person, but cf. 14.11.1: when Constantius considered how to deal with Gallus, *acciri mollioribus scriptis ... eundem placuerat Gallum*. The verb *asciscere* can indeed mean 'to invite', 'to summon', but then it is usually accompanied by an adjunct: *ascitusque postea in palatium* (16.7.6), although this is no iron rule: *ancilla ascita notarum perita* (18.3.2).

According to *PLRE I* the king of Armenia mentioned here is Arsaces III, son of Tigranes VII. His chronology is uncertain. *PLRE* gives as Arsaces' regnal years c. 350–364, but refers to alternative dates proposed by Baynes, 1910: 339–369.

The chronology of Arsaces (he is mentioned again by Amm. in 21.6.8, 23.2.2, 23.3.5, 24.7.8, 24.8.6, 25.7.12, 27.12.3, 5, 9 and 12, but not in 23.6.5, pace Chiabò, 1983, 74) and of the other kings of Armenia in this period is a vexed problem indeed (cf. Hewsen, 1978/79, 100: "Further studies must be undertaken ... before the chronology and genealogy of the fourth-century Arsacids may be considered to be as firmly settled as those of the third"), but it is not the only problem.

For instance, was the Arsaces of the present text the third king of that name, as *PLRE* has it, or the second (so, among others, Asdourian, 1911, 147; Grousset, 1947, 134 and Garsoïan, 1971, 346)? And was his father's name really Tigranes VII or rather Tiran II (Baumgartner, 1895; Ensslin, 1937) or perhaps Tiridates IV (Hewsen, 1978/79, 124)?

The status quaestionis concerning these and related matters has recently been set forth by Hewsen, 1978/79 in an article which sheds new light on what seems to be the main crux, viz. the discrepancies between Amm. and the Armenian sources (cf. Garsoïan, 1967, 297: "Les sources classiques et arméniennes, surtout Ammien Marcellin d'un côté et P'awstos Buzand de l'autre, se contredisent systématiquement"). Hewsen argues (p. 101 et seq.) that thus far scholars have wrongly approached the problem from the standpoint that the regnal dates found in Movsēs Xorenac'i are unreliable but that his genealogical data and those of P'awstos Buzand are correct. According to him it is the other way round: the chronological indications of Xorenac'i are for the most part valid, but it is the genealogical data of both Xorenac'i and P'awstos Buzand which are erroneous.

Suggesting that most of the trouble has been caused by the insertion of two third century kings into the fourth-century regnal list, Hewsen gives a new chronology for the fourth century and arrives at the following conclusions as regards Arsaces. He was born c. 310 as son of *tiran* (not a personal name, but a kind of title) Tiridates IV the Great; acceded to the throne as Arsaces II in 337, but was driven out of his kingdom in the same year; was restored some time in 338 (or possibly as late as 339) by intervention of Constantius II; reigned until his death in 367.

Hewsen's revised genealogy and chronology will no doubt be the starting point for any further research (see for some slight criticism Lightfoot, 1981, 327-328).

Armeniae From the context it is, of course, clear that here by *Armenia* the Arsacid kingdom of Armenia is meant. Note, however, that Garsoïan, 1971, 344 (cf. Lightfoot, 1981, 186 ff.) warns against the tendency "to treat fourth century Armenia as a single religious and political unit, as a toponym with an invariable, unified content identified with the northern Arsacid kingdom". Fourth-century Armenia, she argues (p. 343), consisted of a number of separate units. Apart from the kingdom in the north it comprised the autonomous satrapies of the south, which had passed into the Roman orbit as a result of the peace of A.D. 298, and the cis-Euphratine province of Armenia Minor (for the latter, see below, section 4).

summaque liberalitate susceptum See above the note ad *liberaliter* (20.4.13) and cf. also the similar phrases in 23.2.1 and 30.2.6.

praemonebat et hortabatur For the coupling of two verba monendi cf. Hagendahl, 1924, 185. There are two other instances of *praemonere* in Amm.: 19.12.19 (where, however, it has a different meaning, as De Jonge notes ad loc.) and 29.2.8. Here it means 'to forewarn'.

ut nobis amicus esse perseveraret et fidus The loyalty of the Armenian king to the Romans is emphasized with the same words in 25.7.12 (*amico nobis semper et fido*), where Amm. expresses his indignation about the way Arsaces was left in the lurch by Emperor Jovian, which eventually (cf. 27.12.3) caused his death. Amm.'s description of Arsaces' attitude towards the Romans contrasts sharply with that found in the Armenian sources, notably P'awstos Buzand (for references see Asdourian, 1911, 147-154; Grousset, 1947, 138-143).

Garsoïan, 1967 attempts to explain the Armenian historians' hostility toward Arsaces by pointing to religious motives. In her view the religious policy of Arsaces and his son must have been Arianizing, in accordance with the Arianism of Constantius II and Valens, and thus gave offence to P'awstos Buzand and other orthodox Armenian historians: "La présence d'une politique parallèle à la cour d'Arménie justifierait en même temps les louanges d'Ammien, officier païen qui apprécie la fidélité des souverains sans s'intéresser à la question doctrinale, et la condamnation des sources ecclésiastiques arméniennes qui le contredisent" (p. 300).

For the place of Armenia between Rome and the Sassanid kingdom, see in general Lightfoot, 1981, 186-210 and Garsoïan, 1985.

XI. 2 *fallaciis et minis et dolis* As Blomgren 24 notes, in combinations of three or more terms Amm. has a predilection for polysyndeton with *et*.

Romanorum societate posthabita In earlier authors *posthabere* usually means 'to treat as less important', 'to regard as inferior', as in the famous instance at the beginning of the Aeneid, *posthabita ... Samo* (Verg. A. 1.16) or Tac. *Hist.* 4.7.1 *ne aliis electis posthabitus crederetur*. In Amm., however, the meaning of *posthabere* has developed into 'to pay no attention to', 'to renounce': *ancillari adulatione posthabita* (16.2.2), *omni causatione posthabita* (18.6.5., 'without any excuse'), *aviditate rapiendi posthabita* (23.5.21). In the present passage the Persian king tries to persuade Arsaces to break with the Romans altogether, not merely to attach less importance to his alliance with them.

suis rationibus stringeretur Presumably *rationes* here means 'interest', as in Sal. *Cat.* 44.5 *consideres quid tuae rationes postulent*, or, in a somewhat weakened sense, Amm. 31.14.6 *in his privatis cotidianisque rationibus* ('affairs'), cf. also 26.2.9. The verb *stringere* is used by Amm. in several contexts, but always with the meaning 'to bind', 'to hamper'. It denotes captivity in 16.6.3 *vinculis sunt exutae personae quae stringebantur ut consciae*, 31.8.7 *quarum stringebat fera captivitas manus*, a strong physical hold in 21.2.1 *quam retinens valida manu stringebat*, preoccupation by worries etc., as in 17.3.1 *magnis curarum molibus stringebatur*, 21.12.21 *curis altioribus stringebatur*, 25.3.17 *gravis flagitii recordatio stringit*, the monopolization of a person's attention in 16.12.1 *cum ille ... perficiendi munimenti studio stringeretur*, the binding by an oath: 21.5.11 *iuris iurandi nexu ... se stringi posse*. All these examples illustrate that the expression under discussion strongly emphasizes the binding character of the obligations: the Persian king aims to make Arsaces the prisoner of his own interests. This wording of the phrase of course expresses the Roman point of view.

XI. 3 *qui crebro adiurans* Although it might just be possible to regard the action of the present participle as simultaneous with *muneratus* ('when Arsaces received his rewards, he kept repeating his oath'), it is far more likely that *adiurans* is an example of the use of a part. praes. as a substitute for the missing part. perf. act., a regular phenomenon in late Latin, cf. the note ad 16.2.6 and Szantyr 387. In that case the action of *adiurans* is prior to that of *redit*.

animam prius posse amittere quam sententiam In classical Latin the expression *vitam amittere* is more usual, with a few exceptions in Sallust: *cavete inulti animam amittatis* (*Cat.* 58.21), *aerumnas cum anima simul amisisti* (*Iug.* 14.23), but Szidat's assertion about the present text ("... geht offensichtlich auf Sall. Cat. 58.21 zurück") is overconfident. Amm. has a similar phrase in 17.3.2 *animam prius amittere quam hoc sinere fieri memorabat* and in 17.13.23. For *posse* see the note ad 20.7.17 *quidquid aggredi posset.*

muneratus cum comitibus, quos duxerat The verb *munerare* does not frequently occur in earlier Latin, and, when it does, at times as a deponens; Cf. the note ad 14.7.4. It is accompanied by the same complements as *donare*. The addition *quos duxerat* is quite important: Arsaces was trusted so much that he was not compelled to leave behind any hostages.

nihil ausus temerare postea promissorum The mainly poetic verb *temerare* is aptly used here, in that its object is "protected by religious sanctions" (OLD s.v.). Amm. uses it on two other occasions: 19.1.6 (cf. the note ad loc.) and 30.3.2. Cf. also 29.5.43 *temeratorem quietis* ('the violator of peace', about the rebellious Firmus).

obligatus gratiarum multiplici nexu Constantio Cf. *obligatum gratia* (15.5.33) and *beneficiis obligatus erat crebris et multis* (21.5.11). The binding character of the obligation is stressed by the addition of *nexu*; thus, the phrase balances *rationibus stringeretur* in the preceding section. Other examples of *nexus* in a transferred sense with an added gen. explic. are 15.3.4 (*calumniarum*), 21.5.11. (*iuris iurandi*) and 29.2.22 (*germanitatis*).

At first sight Amm. seems to report the diplomatic manipulation of the Armenian king in a factual and neutral, perhaps even favourable way: in view of the forthcoming operations it is a wise policy to bind the king of such a strategic country. In 23.2.1, however, Julian assumes a much more confident and proud attitude. When embassies from many nations arrive to offer help he answers *nequaquam decere adventiciis adiumentis rem vindicari Romanam.* He does, indeed, want to employ the assistance of Arsaces, but the latter is almost treated as a subordinate who is told to wait for orders: *Arsacem monuerat ... ut ... iubenda operiretur*. In view of this, it is quite possibly with some disgust that Amm. mentions Constantius' 'binding' of the king with all kinds of favours. It testifies to Constantius' anxiety and lack of confidence, which contrasts rather sharply with Julian's self-assurance.

Arsaces was granted immunity from taxation, as is shown by *Cod. Theod.* 11.1.1 (a. 360, Jan. 18): *Praeter privatas res nostras et ecclesias catholicas et domum clarissimae memoriae Eusebii ex consule et ex magistro equitum et peditum et Arsacis regis Armenorum nemo ex nostra iussione praecipuis emolumentis familiaris iuvetur substantiae.*

Olympiada ... Constantis The chronology of Olympias (*PLRE I*, Olympias 1), daughter of the former praetorian prefect Ablabius (*PLRE I*, Ablabius 4, cf. A. Lippold in *Gnomon* 46 (1974) 271 and Martindale, 1980, 474) is, like that of her husband, much disputed. Various dates have been suggested (cf. Lightfoot, 1981, 202 et seq.) for the political union between her and the Armenian king Arsaces. The terminus post quem is 350, the year when Constans died, the terminus ante quem is furnished by a passage in Athanasius' *Hist.Ar. ad Mon.* 69, written in 358 and mentioning the marriage in for Arsaces rather unflattering terms: τὴν δὲ μνηστὴν αὐτοῦ (sc. Constans) τὴν Ὀλυμπιάδα βαρβάροις ἐκδέδωκεν (sc. Constantius).

An interesting piece of evidence, suggesting 356-358 as the date for the marriage, might be seen in the issue of a series of contorniates (see Alföldi, 1943, pl. III.1-2; IV.1.2) with the effigy of Olympias, the mother of Alexander the Great. Perhaps these contorniates were issued in order to commemorate the union of Arsaces and Olympias. See on this Piganiol-Chastagnol, 1972², 111 n. 3 and Garsoïan, 1967, 305 n. 33: "Même si nous acceptons la thèse d'Alföldi, *Die Kontorniaten* (Leipzig, 1943) et voyons dans le cycle d'Alexandre un thème favori, il est intéressant qu' Olympias, avec la devise OLYMPIAS REGINA, n'accompagne son fils que sur les toutes premières émissions (c. 356-358). Ensuite, les Alexandres restent toujours nombreux, mais Olympias disparaît et la devise n'est jamais répetée".

As Amm.'s wording (cf. also the quotation from Athanasius above) makes perfectly clear, the marriage of Olympias, a Roman noblewoman and the former fiancée of a Roman emperor, was considered to be a great honour for Arsaces. The Armenian king, however, must have been married more than once. In 27.12.5 Amm. mentions an *uxor* of Arsaces. She is called *regina* in 27.12.6 and mother of the future king of Armenia, Papa, in 27.12.9. Apparently this woman was not the same person as Olympias (pace Rolfe in his note ad 27.12.5). Amm. does not give her name, but the Armenian sources do. She was called Pharandzem (*PLRE I*, Pharandzem) and is said to have poisoned Olympias (P'awstos Buzand, 4.15, Movsēs Xorenac'i, 3.24).

The date of Olympias' death is, again, disputed, but in view of the present text she cannot have died before 360 (pace Baynes, 1955, 194, who dates her death between 354 and 356).

praefecti quondam praetorio The semi-adiectival use of *quondam* is also found in 18.6.18 *Hadriani quondam Romani principis*, 22.8.41 *ducis quondam Thessali*, 26.5.14 *sub patre Cretione quondam comite*, 31.13.18 *Ursicini patris, magistri quondam armorum.*

ei copulaverat coniugem In two other cases the verb also concerns matrimony: 15.8.18, 21.15.6. This use is post-classical. The other instances are 23.4.5, where it has a literal meaning, and 31.9.5, where it concerns homosexual relations.

quo dimisso a Cappadocia The verb *dimittere* is unexpectedly rare in Amm., the only other instances being 19.9.4 and 29.3.9. On rhythmical grounds it seems more likely to take the quoted text as a colon, than to regard *a Cappadocia* as an adjunct to *venit*. Besides, in the latter case one would rather have expected the name of the town Constantius departed from (viz. Caesarea, cf. 20.9.1), matching the names of the other towns of the journey, whilst it is quite natural to say that Arsaces returns from Cappadocia to Armenia.

XI. 4 *ipse per Melitenen ... Edessam venit* A description of the ancient route between Caesarea (cf. 20.9.1) in Cappadocia and Melitene is given by Hild, 1977, 84-103 (maps on p. 86 and 87), who distinguishes a northern and a southern variant. French, 1983, 71-101 (map on p. 99) deals with the roads between Melitene and Samosata. See in general for this part of the empire Veh, 1980.

Melitene, *minoris Armeniae oppidum* (cf. 19.8.12), modern Eskimalatya, was since the days of Vespasian the base of the *Legio XII Fulminata* and so it remained at least until the end of the fourth century. Around the original legionary camp a substantial settlement developed which is said to have been granted municipal rights by Trajan (Mitford, 1980, 1186). While in earlier days it belonged to the province of Cappadocia, Melitene became part of *Armenia Minor* when in the Diocletianic reorganization of the empire Cappadocia was split in two and its eastern half was attached to *Armenia Minor*. The latter province was in its turn divided into *Armenia I* and *Armenia II* before the end of the century (probably in 386, cf. De Jonge in a "Nachtrag" on p. 147 of his comm. on book XIV). Melitene was situated in *Armenia Secunda*.

While *Lacotena* was a wayside station rather than a fort (cf. Mitford, 1980, 1191), *Samosata*, modern Samsat, was more important. It had been the capital of the kingdom of Commagene (*Commageni quondam regni clarissimam sedem*, 18.4.7), which was finally annexed in A.D. 72 by Vespasian. In 14.8.7 (cf. the note ad loc.) Amm. gives the name it took as a Roman province: *Commagena, nunc Euphratensis*.

Edessa, modern Urfa, an ancient Macedonian colony (in the second century B.C. officially known as Antioch) and later the capital of the Arab tribe of the Osrhoeni, "has been in many ages the principal city of northern Mesopotamia. At the end of the third century, after Galerius' victory over the

Persians, it became the capital of the new province of Osrhoene. As such it had an equal importance as an administrative centre and military headquarters. It played a complementary role to that of Nisibis, the major fortress of the province of Mesopotamia proper. While the latter stood as a bulwark of the Roman limes, Edessa acted as a base where fresh supplies of men and material could be gathered" (Lightfoot, 1981, 77). It is mentioned by Amm. in 18.5.7 (see the note ad loc.), 19.6.12, 21.7.7 (*uberem commeatibus et munitam*) and 21.13.1. Add to the literature cited by Szidat: Drijvers, 1977.

rei cibariae abundantes copias The expression *res cibaria*, which is very rare in earlier Latin (only Pl. *Capt.* 901 and Gel. 6.1.8) occurs five times in Amm., the other cases being 21.6.6, 23.3.6, 27.10.6 and 29.5.13. The last instance most resembles the present text: *ubi abunde rei cibariae copiam condi effecit*.

post aequinoctium egreditur autumnale Having left Constantinople in the late spring of 360 (*adulto vere*, 20.8.1), Constantius marched to Caesarea in Cappadocia (20.9.1), where he hesitated long (20.9.3) before taking the decision to wage war against the Persians instead of against Julian. It took him some time to depart from Cappadocia and reach Edessa, where again he lingered away his time (*diu moratus*), so that it was only after the 21st of September that he set out on his way to Amida. See for chronological matters Szidat I 43 ff. Cf. also the note ad 17.1.10.

Amidam Once a very small city (*civitatem olim perquam brevem*, 18.9.1), Amida had developed into a major military post since Constantius, when he was still a Caesar, had surrounded it with strong walls and towers. Its capture and destruction in 359 (cf. the note ad 20.2.1) must have been a heavy blow for the emperor, who had wished it to be named after himself (*suoque nomine voluit appellari*, 18.9.1). Amida seems to have been rebuilt during the reigns of Valentinian, Valens and Gratian. Cf. Lightfoot, 1981, 80 sqq.

XI. 5 *moenia favillis oppleta collustrans* As in 17.1.10 *superfusae nives opplevere montes*, the verb *opplere* here means 'to cover completely'. For *collustrans* cf. Verg. *A.* 3.651 *omnia collustrans*, Tac. *Ann.* 2.45.3 *equo conlustrans omnia*. These examples show that the verb is used when a person surveys a wide space or a large quantity of things, as is also the case in the other instances in Amm.: 16.10.14, 24.5.3 and 27.10.10.

flebat cum gemitu This is the only example in Amm. of an emperor shedding tears. It is open to question, however, whether Amm. reports the incident with sympathy and does not rather regard Constantius' sorrow as crocodile tears in view of Ursicinus' strong feelings about the responsibility for the fall of Amida. See above the notes on ch.2. The famous story about Scipio Aemilianus' tears for the destruction of Carthage (ὁ Σκιπίων ἀπροσποιήτως ἐδάκρυεν, Diod. 32.24) and his quotation from Homer is wholly different from the present text. Cf. Astin, 1967, 251-2 (relevant texts) and 282-7 (discussion).

quales miseranda civitas pertulerat clades For the hyperbaton cf. Blomgren, passim, but especially p. 25 n. 2; for the indic. in an indirect question cf. Hassenstein 38, Szantyr 538 and the note ad 14.6.2.

Ursulus ... qui aerarium tuebatur Ursulus (*PLRE I*, Vrsulus 1), "eine von Ammianus Marcellinus hochgeschätzte Persönlichkeit" (Lippold, 1965, 1148), a man of praiseworthy severity (*severitatis ... non improbandae*, 16.8.5), fearless and bold (*intrepidus ... ore et pectore libero*, 16.8.7), was *comes sacrarum largitionum* from 355-361.

The *comes sacrarum largitionum*, formerly called *rationalis rei summae* or *summarum* (the earliest recorded *comes sacrarum largitionum* is Nemesianus in 345, provided that *Cod.Theod.* 11.7.5 is addressed to a central, not to a diocesan *comes;* see for this below) headed one of the three independent financial departments (the other two being those of the praetorian prefects and the *res privata*), each responsible directly to the emperor and each with its own revenues, treasury and administrative staff (see in general Jones 411 sqq.). He was responsible for a number of taxes, for the mints and the mines and for the payment of cash *stipendia* and donatives to the army and civil service (cf. the note ad 14.7.9 and Delmaire, 1977).

Amm. never uses the full official title, availing himself of a paraphrase as in the present case, in 21.8.1 (*et Mamertino largitiones curandas*) and in 21.16.3 (*qui ... largitiones ... esset recturus*) or leaving out the adjective *sacer*, as in 14.7.9 (*Domitiano ex comite largitionum praefecto provecto*), 16.8.5, 22.3.7 (both about Ursulus) and 23.1.5 (*Felice ... largitionum comite*). Such avoidance of precise technical terms is Tacitean, cf. Syme, 1958, 343-344 and Blockley, 1973,72, and see also the note ad 20.1.2 (*ire ... Lupicinum placuit*).

The leaving out of *sacer* sometimes causes confusion, since diocesan *comites largitionum* were under the disposition of the central *comes sacrarum largitionum* and it is not always immediately clear whether the *CSL* or one of his subordinates is meant. Presumably a diocesan functionary is meant in 18.5.2 (*largitionum comite ad alterius gratiam infestius perurgente*, cf. *PLRE I*, Anonymus 144) and in 22.9.11 (*Iulianus ... ad largitionum comitem ... inquit*, cf. *PLRE I*, Anonymus 143), and certainly 27.7.5, where Amm. explicitly mentions the diocese of the former *comes largitionum* Diocles (*Dioclis ex comite largitionum Illyrici*).

dolore percitus Amm. has a predilection for *percitus*, often combining it with an abl. causae, e.g. *formidine* (27.5.3), *indignitate* (14.2.1), *ira* (16.10.7, 17.10.6, 25.7.4, 27.7.7), *terrore* (18.6.10); cf. also 14.11.23 *irrevocabili ira princeps percitus et dolore*, 28.6.19 *ira percitus et dolore*.

en quibus animis In the other seven instances of *en* the oratio recta is indicated by *inquit*. Cf. the note ad 16.12.31, to which it should be added that Livy uses *en* on twelve occasions. One of these can be compared to the present text, in that *en* accompanies an indignant phrase: *en inquam fando audistis* etc. (10.8.10). A similar use can be found in Suet. *Aug.* 40.5.

stipendium Cf. the note ad 20.8.8.

imperii opes iam fatiscunt In classical Latin the verb was dep., e.g. *simulacraque fessa fatisci* (Lucr. 5.308), the first instances of active forms occurring in Verg., e.g. *(tellus) ... manibus iactata fatiscit* (*G.* 2.249); cf. Flobert, 1975, 201–2. Amm.'s instances are treated by De Jonge in his notes ad 18.6.13 and 19.9.9.

quod dictum ita amarum Ursulus' caustic remark is clearly meant to insult the soldiers; cf. Quintilian's definition: *est et amarum quiddam, quod fere in contumelia est positum* (*Inst.* 8.3.89). For *ita* qualifying an adi. or adv. with reference to a preceding statement cf. Cic. *Ver.* 2.61 *an ita parva est pecunia?*, *Sest.* 114 *ita vehementer*, Amm. 15.4.8. *in quo casu ita tristi et inopino*, 19.11.1 *inter haec ita ambigua*.

militaris multitudo Amm. often uses the adi. with a subst. denoting a group or a crowd. Similar cases are the combinations with *cuneus* (23.5.8) and *numeri* (14.7.19, 17.13.34, 23.2.2, 26.1.6). Cf. De Jonge ad 17.12.6 and see above the note ad 20.4.6 (*ut se militari eximeret turba*). TLL VIII 952. 20–41 shows that this is normal Latin usage.

postea apud Calchedona recordata Ursulus in 361 fell victim to the passion of the judges (*causas vehementius aequo bonoque spectaverunt*, 22.3.2) at a trial of adherents of Constantius after the latter's death. Amm. criticizes Julian sharply for this injustice and also reports the objections of many others. Julian defended himself by saying that *eum militaris ira delevit, memor quae dixerat (ut ante rettulimus), cum Amidam vidisset excisam* (22.3.8).

ad eius exitium consurrexit Cf. *consurrectum est in perniciem eorum qui deseruerant proelia* (17.13.13 with the note).

XI. 6 *contis consertis* Thus Seyfarth's rather improbable emendation of V's *concis consertis*. Indeed, *contus* 'pike' occurs a few times in Amm.: 25.1.13, 25.3.4 (and 31.7.6, where, however, it is an emendation), and the verb *conserere* denotes the formation of a close order in 16.12.37 *frontem artissimis conserens parmis*, but, as Szidat remarks, neither of these words is ever used to describe a marching order. Therefore *cuneis* (Gelenius) *confertis* (Lindenbrog), accepted by Clark, should be preferred. Normally *cuneus* denotes (part of) an attacking formation, and Veg. always uses it in such a context. As Szidat remarks, however, a few times it occurs in the description of a marching order, though not in 19.13.1 *confertique in cuneos densos per furta et latrocinia finitimos afflictabant*. Such a meaning is feasible for 17.12.9 *iunctis densius cuneis* and 31.9.3 *congregatusque in cuneos*. For this last passage cf. Kromayer-Veith, 1928, 596: "Eine ähnliche dichtgeschlossene Marschform sind auch die *cunei*, von denen Ammian (XXXI 9) beim Rückzug des Frigeridus ... spricht".

Bezabden Cf. 20.7.1.

fixis tentoriis vallo fossarumque altitudine circumsaeptis The expression *tentoria figere* also occurs in Veg. *mil.* 2.7 and Amm. 18.2.10 and 24.4.2. Other examples of *altitudo* c. gen. plur. are *aggerum* (20.11.13, 21.10.4, 27.4.3), *arborum* (16.1.5), *montium* (24.7.5, 29.5.44, cf. Liv. 21.30.6), *silvarum et montium* (31.4.13). With *fossarum* it occurs also in 24.4.12 (*altitudines*) and 24.5.12. Not in all these cases the gen. can be explained as gen. inversus, but for *fossarum* no other explanation is possible, *fossarum altitudine* being the equivalent of *fossis altis*.

The word *circumsaeptus* occurs in different situations, about the victims of an attack: *a Saracena multitudine circumsaepti* (25.6.9), denoting an honourable entourage: *circumsaeptum aquilis et vexillis* (26.2.11), or protection: *Persarum regem armatorum centum milibus circumsaeptum* (19.6.11). In all cases the complete enclosing of a person or object is expressed.

obequitans castrorum ambitum longius The verb *obequitare* occurs 15 times in Livy, usually combined with a dat., as in Amm. 19.1.5 and 24.1.1. The acc. is used in 24.2.9, in a phrase which closely resembles the present passage, referring to Julian at the start of the siege of Pirisabora: *cuius obequitans moenia imperator et situm obsidium omni cautela coeptabat*. For *castrorum ambitum* see above the note ad 20.7.2. With *longius* Amm. indicates that Constantius kept far from the walls, riding 'at a considerable distance'. Such a meaning is also present in 16.12.38 (Julian seeing that his cavalry was getting ready for a flight), 22.16.16 (a dog barking around a lion), 24.7.7 *insultantesque nobis longius Persae* ('at a long range').

docebatur relatione multorum   At first sight it seems surprising that *docebatur* is the only main verb in this period, but on reflection it does indeed contain the main statement: Constantius finds out that the careful measures taken by the Persians sharply contrast with permanent negligence on the Roman side. In view of *multorum* the imperf. has to be regarded as intentional: Constantius repeatedly received the same information. For the use of *relatio* to denote a communication to a higher authority cf. the notes ad 16.11.7 and 20.8.4 (*relatu*).

instaurata esse firmius loca   After having captured Bezabde the Persians had firmly repaired the shattered parts of the walls: *labefactata murorum parte reparata firmissime* (20.7.9). The use of *instaurare* to denote the restoration of cities or buildings is not classical. The first instances of this meaning can be found in the Panegyrici, whilst in HA it occurs a number of times. Amm.'s instances concern forts (17.9.1, cf. the note), a temple (23.1.2), buildings (27.3.10, 29.6.19, 31.14.4) and cities (28.3.7).

quae antehac incuria corruperat vetustatis   Suddenly Amm. makes use of official terminology. Cf. the following phrases in inscriptions about *milliaria* (*columnae*): *aetate et incuria corruptam adque dilapsam restituerunt* (CIL 8.22016), *longa incuria corruptam adque dilapsam restituerunt* (ib. 22073), and also the formula *vias et pontes vetustate corruptas restituerunt* (CIL 3.3726 and 10629). In other passages Amm. uses *corrumpere*, *incuria* or *vetustas* without such technical connotations. For *incuria* cf. Wölfflin, 1887, 408–9, who inter alia quotes *Cod.Theod.* 15.1.20: *vel incuria vel vetustate*. Presumably, however, in the present text *vetustas* has a somewhat different meaning: functioning as a personification, it is equivalent to *veteres*, 'former generations'. In 20.7.9 Amm. avails himself of non-official language: *intuta loca carieque nutantia*.

XI. 7   The attempt to persuade the defenders of a besieged town to surrender is a stereotyped element in the reports of sieges. In this book it can also be found in 6.3 (see the note ad loc.) and 7.3.

ante fervorem certaminum   This expression is typical for Amm., who uses *fervor* with a literal meaning only in 25.4.10 and 31.12.13. In the other instances it is accompanied by a gen. of a subst. denoting fighting: *proelii* (16.2.13), *proeliorum* (18.2.3., 19.2.12), *pugnarum* (17.13.26), *certaminum* (16.12.43, 17.13.13); cf. Bitter 150.

erat necessario praestruendum For Amm.'s use of *praestruere* see above the note ad 20.6.2.

condicione posita dupla This is the only instance of *duplus* in Amm., listed in TLL V 1.2282.49-50 as one of the cases where the adi. denotes "duo diversi generis".

cogebat moenium defensores The use of *cogere* is remarkable. Indeed, TLL III 1525.76 sqq. notes that at times this verb is equivalent to "compellere, invitare, orare sim." and in col. 1530.66-69 mentions the present text with the addition "i. invitabat", but an inspection of the instances which are quoted reveals that the connotation of force or constraint is never lacking; cf. e.g. Cic. *Fam.* 1.9.18 *cumque eum nec persuadendo nec cogendo regi vidisset*. The same holds true for Amm., cf. 14.9.1 about Ursicinus: *dispicere litis exitialis crimina cogebatur*. Obviously in the present text *cogebat* is used de conatu (for other cases cf. Ehrismann 27), but the meaning of the verb itself should not be detracted from: the Roman emperor is accustomed to have things his own way, his proposals are compelling (so he thinks).

alienis sine cruore concessis TLL IV 1242.1-26 provides useful statistical information about the relative frequency of *sanguis* and *cruor* throughout Latin literature. Instances of the former form a clear majority (e.g. Verg. 108:23, Liv. 99:16, Tac. 96:11), from which rule Amm. does not essentially differ (35:21). The expression *sine cruore* also occurs in 21.16.12 and 26.7.5. For *cruor* cf. also the note ad 17.10.9.

dignitatibus augendos et praemiis Some similar passages in which *augere* c.abl. means 'to provide with', implying a case of promotion, are Cic. *N.D.* 3.87 *aut honoribus aucti aut re familiari* (cf. Pease's note), *Planc.* 22 *se augeri dignitate arbitrabatur*, Tac. *Ann.* 6.8.2 *illius propinqui et adfines honoribus augebantur*, Amm. 25.10.9 *auctus comitis dignitate*, 26.5.11 *eodem Aequitio aucto magisterii dignitate*.

The parallel adduced by Szidat, 24.1.9, is not quite apt in all respects. The commander of captured Anatha, a fortress on the Euphrates, was given the rank of tribune, it is true, but the *castellum* was set on fire and its inhabitants were sent to a city in Syria.

atque cum illi destinatione nativa reniterentur This meaning of *destinatio* (viz. 'determination') does not occur before Silver Latinity, e.g. Tac. *Hist.* 2.47.3 *praecipuum destinationis meae documentum*, *Ann.* 12.32.1 *ducem destinationis certum*. Amm. uses it in a neutral sense: 19.3.1 *hac partium destinatione pugnatur*, or with a positive or negative qualification: 26.8.12 *verecundia et destinatio gloriosa*, 31.12.7 *funesta principis destinatio*. The adi. *destinatus* and the adverb *-e* (or *-ius*) can have a similar sense: 17.2.2 *destinatis barbarorum animis*, 18.2.7 *Florentio et Lupicino ... destinate certantibus*. Cf. the note ad 17.2.2. The adi. *nativus* occurs rarely in historical prose, not in Sall., Liv., HA, once in Caes.: *silvam ... pro nativo muro obiectam* (*Gal.* 6.10.5) and Tac.: *nativo in specu* (*Ann.* 4.59.1). Its meaning in these instances is the most usual, viz. 'natural', 'provided by nature'. Amm., however, only uses the word with the sense 'inborn' about human behaviour: 15.8.3 *prudentia*, 16.12.14 *calor* ('hotness of temper'), 16.12.61 *mos*, 17.13.23 *feritas*, 24.1.13 *affabilitas*. For *reniti* see above the note ad 20.4.18.

ut clare nati periculisque et laboribus indurati There are some textual problems in this phrase. In the first place *clare nati*, which evidently refers to *insignis origine* (20.7.16), has been deemed suspect by some editors, presumably because they found the qualification 'illustrious by birth' fitting for a group of envoys from Rome (23.1.4), but not for all the defenders of a rampart. The emendations, however, are not attractive: Gardthausen's *clarentes* ('famous'?) is unlikely, because *clarere* is not used of living people before August., and *damnati* (in two early editions) strikes the wrong note: the men of Bezabde are not presented as desperadoes, but as stubborn fighters. The reference to 20.7.16, where the defenders are sketched as a corps d'élite, seals the matter. Further, *et* is an editorial addition, but even Blomgren 17, who tends to defend most cases of 'asyndeton bimembre', regards it as plausible here. Finally, *indurati* is Valesius' emendation for *in*, which is quite plausible in view of 14.2.14 *legiones bellicis sudoribus induratae* and 21.16.3 *pulvere bellico indurati*. In spite of some uncertainty it may be concluded that Amm. may well have written the present phrase.

There are examples of the combination of *labor* and *periculum* in several authors (e.g. Cic., Sen., Tac.), but it occurs with especially great frequency in Livy.

cuncta obsidioni congrua For *congruus* see above the note ad 20.6.1.

XI. 8 In the following description of Constantius' siege of Bezabde many elements are reminiscent of the reports of Sapor's conquest of Singara and Bezabde in chapters 6 and 7, and of Amm.'s other descriptions of warfare; cf. Bitter's summaries of these "Topoi in den Kampfberichten" (119 sqq.). These stereotyped elements lend a somewhat uniform character to these descriptions, although it should be noted that Amm. shows himself capable of stylistic variety: the present chapter, too, contains phrases which do not occur elsewhere.

densis itaque ordinibus Not without reason the description is started with this phrase. Whereas in chapters 6 and 7 the lively variety of methods used by the Persians is stressed, here attention is drawn to the massive and uniform character of the Roman attack. The phrase as such is not found elsewhere in Amm., but it can be parallelled by e.g. *densior et ordinibus frequens miles* (16.12.49), *conferti acieque densiore contracta* (17.13.8), *confertis ordinibus* (31.13.3). A traditional element lacking here is an expression denoting daybreak, as *matutinae lucis exordio* (20.6.3), *ante alterius lucis initium* (20.7.5).

cum tubarum incitamentis The rousing of the soldiers by the blast of trumpets is mentioned more than once, e.g. *tubarum perciti clangore castrensium* (19.6.9), *tubarum minacium accendente clangore* (27.10.12), *incitamento tubarum* (21.12.12); cf. the note ad 19.6.9. The subst. *incitamentum* occurs quite often in Tac., but not in a similar expression. Cf. also the note ad 20.7.6 *(hinc inde concinentibus tubis)*.

latera oppidi cuncta adortus alacrius miles Instances of *latus* to denote a side of a town are by no means frequent. It can be found in *B. Afr.* 78.2 *ab oppidi lateribus*, Liv. 44.31.3 *a latere urbis*, Amm. 14.6.16 *per latera civitatis cuncta* (where, however, it has a somewhat different meaning, viz. 'quarter'), 18.9.2 (about Amida) *a latere quidem australi*.

The phrase as a whole can be compared with 20.7.5 *Persarum populus omnis adortus avide vallum*. As Bitter 137/8 remarks, Amm. has a great liking for *alacer* and its cognates to denote the fighting spirit of the soldiers. A few examples: *Alamanni bella alacriter ineuntes* (16.12.46), *ad celsiora ducebatur alacrior miles* (17.1.5), *rapido turmarum processu in procinctum alacritate omni tendentium* (19.2.6).

legionibus in testudines varias conglobatis The general purport of this phrase is clear: the attacking soldiers are divided into several protecting shield-formations. Cf. also Tac. *Ann.* 13.39.3 *hos in testudinem conglobatos subruendo vallo ducit*. The precise meaning, however, is more difficult to ascertain. There are not many occurrences of *legio(nes)* without an accompanying adi. or numeral, e.g. *cum legiones iam pugnaturae congrederentur* (26.7.15), where it means 'troops', 'forces', more specifically 'infantry', as in *Tertiacorum equestris numerus a legionibus incusatus est* (25.1.7). This meaning can be paralleled with some examples in Livy, where there is also a contrast with cavalry: *legiones ipse dictator, magister equitum suos equites ducit* (3.27.6), *mihi legiones peditumque pugna curae erunt* (8.38.16). The adi. *varias* too deserves attention. It normally expresses variety and can usually be rendered by 'different', 'multifarious', 'changeable' etc. There is no reason to regard it as a kind of loosely used synonym of *plures* or *plerique*, witness also the well-known combination with *multus*, e.g. Sal. *Cat.* 51.35 *in magna civitate multa et varia ingenia sunt*, a combination which is also favoured by Amm.: 18.2.2, 20.11.30, 28.4.15, 29.1.17, 29.2.24, 31.3.1. In the present text, therefore, *testudines varias* should not be translated by "numerose testuggini" (Selem) or "(zu) mehreren Schildkröten" (Seyfarth), but by 'tortoise formations of different size and shape'. For Amm.'s non-technical use of the term *testudo* cf. the note ad 20.7.2.

paulatim tuto progrediens Bitter 120/1 mentions many instances of the slow or fast pace of an advancing force. In a few cases the wariness of the proceedings is noted: *mandabat ... ut ... tutius graderentur* (21.8.4). The present text is parallelled by *sensim incedentes et caute* (21.12.6, in a similar situation). Cf. also Bitter 134 n. 404.

subruere moenia For another effort to undermine the fortification of a city see 20.6.3 (with note).

telorum omne genus in subeuntes effundebatur As in 20.6.4, this is a clear Virgilian reminiscence: *telorum effundere contra/omne genus Teucri* (*A.* 9.509/510).

nexu clipeorum soluto The *testudines* just mentioned were of course formed by the shields of the soldiers, cf. Liv. 32.17.13 *in constructam densitate clipeorum testudinem*. Strictly speaking, *clipeus* denotes the small round shield used in old times. Here, as in other passages in Amm., it simply means 'shield' in general, like its much more frequently used synonym *scutum*, which is an anachronism itself; cf. De Jonge ad 14.10.8 *Scutariorum*.

in receptum canentibus signis Amm. uses the classical dat. of *receptus* only once: *cumque receptui caneretur* (24.4.11). Other instances of his idiosyncratic *in receptum* are 19.11.15 (cf. the note), 21.12.11, 25.1.18. The verb *canere* is used absolutely with *signa* as subject in a number of cases in Livy, e.g. 7.40.10 *istinc signa canent*, 24.15.1 *signa coeperunt canere*, and also a few times in Sal., e.g. *Cat* 59.1 *signa canere iubet* (cf. Vretska's note ad loc.).

XI. 9 *laxatis deinde ad diem unum indutiis* Cf. 16.12.19 *cum nullae laxarentur indutiae* (consult the note ad loc.), 31.7.8 *nihil post haec inter partes praeter indutias laxatum est breves*. TLL VII 2.1074.42 sqq. lists these cases as examples of *laxare* as the equivalent of *concedere*, like e.g. Cypr. *Ep.* 55.19.1 *faciles ad communicationem temere laxandam*. For *indutiae* see also the notes ad 20.7.5 and 20.8.9 above.

259

tertia luce For other instances of *lux* as a synonym of *dies* see above the note ad 20.5.1 *futura luce*. It should be noted that in all these cases, as in the present one, the early morning is meant. Mark the contrast with *decimo die* in section 11, which implies another time of day than daybreak.

milite curiosius tecto Forms of the adi. *curiosus* or the adv. *curiose* are not very frequent in Latin historiographic literature; there are no instances in Caes., Sal., Liv., Tac.; HA has some examples and in Amm. there are three further occurences: 22.12.8, 23.6.1, 26.3.5.

elatis passim clamoribus This traditional element is dealt with by Bitter 139 and note 424.

licet ... latebant For *licet* see above the note ad 20.6.9.

sub obtentis ciliciis, ne conspicerentur ab hostibus Cilicia are (Cilician) rugs or blankets made of goat's hair. Their purpose during sieges is described by Veg. *mil.* 4.6 *Deinde per propugnacula duplicia saga ciliciaque tenduntur impetumque excipiunt sagittarum* and by Amm. himself in 24.2.10 *per propugnacula ciliciis undique laxius pansis, quae telorum impetus cohiberent.* Apparently the screening of the defenders was only a secondary advantage.

lacertos fortiter exsertantes Like *exserere* the verb *exsertare* often has a part of the body as object: *linguam* (Quad. *hist.* 10b, 208.9 Peter), *ora* (Verg. *A.* 3.425, Amm. 14.9.3). The other examples in Amm. are *bracchium* (26.2.3) and *lacertos* (14.2.7).

subiectos incessebant This use of *subiectus* to denote the attacking enemy at the foot of the walls is remarkable. It may either be an extension of the geographic sense, as in *rivus ... subiectus castris Scipionis* (Caes. *Civ.* 3.37.3), *in subiectis septentrioni spatiis* (Amm. 22.15.5), or perhaps be regarded as a kind of graecism. In Greek ὑπεῖναι means 'to be underneath', but also 'to be subjected to', as in Apoll. Dysc. *Synt.* 3.32 (292.26) κτῆμα βασιλέων οἱ ὑπόντες. For a similar use of *subiectus* by Veg. see below the note on *cadebant* in section 10.

XI. 10 *et vimineae crates cum procederent confidenter* For *vimineae crates* see above the note ad 20.7.6. Whereas in section 8 the soldiers were said to advance (*progrediens*) protected by their *testudines*, here the covering *crates* themselves are advancing. It is a different case from 14.6.17 *omne textrinum incedit,* where *textrinum* equals *textores* (see the note ad loc.); here *crates* does not mean the soldiers covered by these wickerwork constructions: they are so completely hidden underneath them, that the onlooker in fact seems to witness the advance of the mantlets themselves.

As was pointed out in the note ad 20.4.18, *confidenter* usually has the connotation of (somewhat) rash boldness. This is perfectly possible here too: the attackers are approaching the wall with excessive daring and this almost costs them dearly.

essentque parietibus contiguae For *paries* as the wall of a town see above the note ad 20.6.3. The crux printed by Clark behind *contiguae* is presumably caused by dissatisfaction with the cursus: *pariétibus contíguae*. The problem could be solved by regarding *contiguae* as trisyllabic: *cóntiguae*. It should be admitted, however, that in comparable cases as 14.2.3, 14.8.13, 28.2.7, 29.5.11 and 31.14.1 *contiguus* is treated as a quadrisyllable. In general, as Harmon 224 points out, synizesis in Amm. is much less common than dialysis.

dolia desuper cadebant, molae et columnarum fragmenta For *cadere* expressing the landing of projectiles which are shot or thrown with a definite aim cf. Veg. *mil.* 4.29 *sed ex alto destinata missilia ... in subiectos vehementius cadunt* and Amm. 19.2.13 *nulla* (tela) *frustra mittebantur inter hominum cadentia densitatem*. Blomgren 23 provides parallels and thus convincingly rejects Heraeus' proposal to add *et* before *molae*. As to the size of the projectiles cf. 20.7.12, where the defenders of Bezabde try to prevent the advance of the enemies *denso saxorum molarium pondere* and 31.15.13 *contrusis per pronum saxis et columnarum fragmentis et cylindris*.

hiatuque violento disiectis operimentis This use of *hiatus* is by no means trite. It normally denotes
1 the splitting of the earth, as in Cic. *N.D.* 2.14 *repentinis terrarum hiatibus*, cf. Amm. 17.7.13, 23.6.17.
2 a wide-opened jaw, as in Lucr. 5.24/5 *magnus hiatus/ille leonis*, cf. Amm. 16.10.7, 25.1.14.
3 greediness, cf. Amm. 29.1.19. The present text has only one parallel in Amm., viz. about a gaping wound: *dilatato vulneris hiatu* (29.5.42), but here the action of splitting up the *crates* is meant.

The adi. *violentus* suits such a meaning very well, as in similar cases like 23.4.5 (*concussio*), 24.2.12 (*ictus*).

For *operimentum* cf. Varro's simple definition (in a passage dealing with the requisites of the bed) *quibus operibantur, operimenta dixerunt* (*L.* 5.167). In Amm. the word denotes a table-cloth (16.8.8), the lobe of a liver (22.1.2.), the canopy of a wagon (31.2.18), the covers of horses (24.6.8), the cuirass of soldiers (24.2.10). Here it refers to the *crates*.

evadebant This is the final instance of a series of seven cases of the ind. imp., beginning with *temptabatur* in section 9. In view of *decimo die* in the next section these imperfecta should be interpreted as iterative: Amm. has been describing the daily routine during seven days.

XI. 11 *Decimo itaque, postquam pugnari coeptum est, die* The chronological aspect of Amm's description leaves much to be desired. In fact this is the second and also the last precise information in this respect. The other indications are both scarce and vague. The watchfulness of both parties is said to have taken *dies et noctes* in § 13; in section 16 *in audaciam ruere praecipitem* presumably opens a new phase, which seems to be interrupted by *nocturnae tenebrae* in § 20; sections 21-23 describe a day's fighting between *prope ipsum crepusculum* (§ 21) and *vespera* (§ 24); after that *serum tempus* (§ 24) precludes all-out attacks, and finally the emperor abandons the siege *ingravescente hiemis magnitudine* (§ 31).

A further problem is posed by the tenses of the verbs in sections 11 and 12. In sections 9 and 10 the iterative imperfectum was used (see the preceding note), in sections 11 and 12 one finds instances of the pluperfect, after which Amm. returns to a series of imperfecta. Ehrismann 12 regards *placuerat, hebetaverat* and *cessaverat* as instances of pluperfect pro perf., which is a somewhat unsatisfactory solution as only in the last case the cursus could be regarded as the reason of the choice. The other explanation would be to consider sections 9-15 as one continuous report about the first phase of the siege, between the Roman attempt to climb the walls (§ 9) and the sally of the defenders (§ 16). In order to make clear the dominating part played by the *aries* in the second half of this report, Amm. returns to a moment before its presence on the battlefield, when it *had* been decided to fetch it, which *had* not put an end to the *temeritas* and *consilium* of the fighting parties.

In classical Latin, in cases where a definite interval of time is expressed, *postquam* is usually, but not always, accompanied by the pluperfect: *undecimo die postquam a te discesseram* (Cic. *Att.* 12.1.1). The present text is parallelled by 16.10.20 *tricensimo postquam ingressus est die*.

cum spes nostrorum inferior cuncta maerore compleret Valesius was in no doubt that *interiora*, which can be found in some later manuscripts, provides the correct text. Agreeing with this Wagner put forward the following explanation: "cum spes tantum nobis cresceret, quantum oppidanis minueretur". It is indeed possible to use *interiora* for the town inside the walls: *cum socio ad interiora susceptus* (27.12.6), but the implication is wrong. Despondency was prevailing among the Romans, as is proved by *itaque*, which refers to the bad results mentioned in section 10.

There are no parallels for *inferior spes* denoting 'gloomy prospects'. In

25.8.11 *homo inferioris spei ad sublimiora provectus* it expresses the low social status of the person in question. In the present case *inferior* is obviously equivalent to *mala* or *peior*, as in 30.8.14 *si fors ingruisset inferior*. Cf. also the note ad *hac fiducia spei maioris animatus* (20.5.8).

molem arietis magnam For the gen. cf. Verg. *A*. 2.32 *et molem mirantur equi* (and also *ib*. 2.150).

quam Persae quondam Antiochia pulsibus eius excisa relatam reliquerant apud Carrhas The ram was very old indeed, for Antioch had been taken by the Persians a hundred years earlier, in A.D. 256 or A.D. 260 (Cf. Downey, 1961, 256: "our literary sources... appear to confuse the two captures of the city"). Amm. alludes to these events in 23.5.3, while Libanius states (*Or*. 15.16) that in his time the effects of the burning of the city by Sapor I were still apparent. Consult for Antioch in the fourth century, apart from Downey, in the first place Liebeschuetz, 1972 and cf. the notes ad 14.1.6 and 19.8.12. De Jonge ad 18.7.3 has a note on Carrhae, ancient Harran, known for the defeat of Crassus in 53 B.C.

aptataque faberrime In itself this phrase does not pose any problems. The verb *aptare* means 'to prepare', 'to fix', cf. Verg. *A*. 4.289 *classem aptent taciti*, Liv. 21.27.8 *paratas aptatasque habebat pedes lintres* and above 20.7.10 *aptatique arietes* (q.v.). The fem. gen. here is due to *moles*. The adv. *fabre* does not occur in classical Latin; there are some instances in Apul., e.g. *gemmis faberrime sculpendis* (*Fl*. 15), the other cases in Amm. are 19.5.4 (consult De Jonge's note), 23.5.1, 29.3.4, 31.13.14. Finally, *-que* adds an emphatic parenthesis (cf. OLD s.v. *-que* 11b): the defenders suddenly saw the big ram, which was most skilfully assembled 'at that'. The difficulty, however, consists in the fact that the putting together of the ram, which had been taken to pieces (*dissolutus*) to facilitate transport, is only told in the following section: *dum instrueretur...omni arte*.

clausorum hebetaverat mentes For *clausi* to denote the besieged, cf. 20.6.8 (see the note ad loc.) and 20.7.3. With the meaning 'to amaze', 'to stun' the verb *hebetare* has either the persons themselves as obj. (27.2.6, 28.6.4) or their *mens* (25.7.3, 28.1.54) or *sensus* (28.2.13); cf. also the note ad 19.7.4.

In his list of cases where the ind.plusquamperfecti is used in the apodosis of an anreal conditional clause (note ad 14.3.2) De Jonge rightly has not incorporated *hebetaverat...ni...praeparassent*. The protasis should rather be linked with *prolapsas*: they were (truly) stunned and they would have considered surrender, if etc.

ad usque deditionis remedia paene prolapsas For the frequent metaphorical use of *remedium* see above the note ad 20.5.3. The accompanying gen. is usually a gen.obi.: *communiumque remedium aerumnarum* (15.8.21), but the present phrase can be parallelled by *celeritatis remediis* (21.13.14): in both cases the gen. can be explained as subi. or explic.

As was suggested in the preceding note, *prolapsas* can be taken as the equivalent of 'quae prolapsae essent'. The verb implies the falling into something objectionable: *ad deteriora* (17.5.14), *in vitia* (28.3.8), *ad unum...errorem* (29.5.23). Cf. also the note ad 20.4.15 (*temeritas et prolapsio*).

opponenda minaci machinae According to TLL IX 2.772.30 this is the only place where the neutr.pl. of *opponendus* is used "pro subst.". For *machina* to denote the ram see 20.6.3 *machinas*.

XI.12 *dum instrueretur aries vetustus et dissolutus* Amm. quite often uses a coni.imp. after *dum*; cf. Ehrismann 47 sqq., who wrongly mentions this sentence as a case where *dum* means "während": he should have listed it with the instances of the sense "so lange als". Amm. clearly means that all the usual actions of the siege continued all the time while the Romans were mounting the ram. The sequence *instrueretur...defensabatur* seems caused by the mere wish for variation. For *instruere* as a synonym of *aptare* see the note on *aptataque faberrime* in the preceding section. It is difficult to determine whether the choice of *vetustus* instead of *vetus* is important. Amm. does not use *vetustus* very often and in some of these cases it refers to a very distant past: the huge walls of Autun (15.11.11), the kings of old (17.5.5), a fortress (20.7.17), temples (22.9.5), Egypt (22.15.2), Roman buildings (27.3.10). So perhaps the tentative conclusion could be that Amm. wants to emphasize the archaic appearance of the ram. For *dissolvere* in a technical sense cf. Suet.*Cal.* 57.1 *simulacrum Iovis quod dissolvi transferrique Romam placuerat*.

vineae firmitudine summa defensabatur Cf. *nulla murorum firmitudine communitas* (23.6.35), and also *murorum firmitate cautissimas* (14.8.13), *propugnaculorum firmitate muniebatur* (24.4.10). These examples show that *firmitas* and *firmitudo* are used by Amm. to denote the strength of a protecting cover, so that from that point of view Heraeus' emendation of *veniet* into *vineae* is feasible. At first sight Gelenius' *vi et* looks more attractive (cf. Hagendahl, 1921, 125), but there are no other combinations of *vi* and a synonym in Amm. and there is only one instance of *vi* with the gen. of persons: *vi barbarorum excisas* (17.10.9).

lapidum crebritas For this topos see above the note ad 20.6.6 *nec sagittarum*.

plurimos consumebant The meaning 'to kill' for *consumere* is quite normal. Usually the agens is a more or less lasting process, cf. Cic.*Prov.*5 *incuria, fame, morbo, vastitate consumpti*. Examples of this can be found in Amm. too: *consumebatur angore* (26.10.14), (ut) *diuturna consumeret fames* (31.7.3). Amm., however, uses *consumere* also in cases of violent death: 26.3.3 *abscisa cervice consumptus est*, 31.11.5. For this there are only few parallels in classical Latin, e.g. B. *Afr.*94.1 *Iubam Petreius facile ferro consumpsit*.

aggerum moles These *aggeres*, "battering-walls, which are built in such a way, that their upper ends are at least on the same level with the town walls" (De Jonge ad 19.5.1; cf. Crump, 1975, 106-107) are mentioned again in § 13 (*aggerum multitudine*), § 16 (*aggeribus cumulatius excitatis*), § 16 (*aggeribus quos erexerunt Romani*), § 20 (*in ipsis aggerum summitatibus*), while the synonym *aggestus* is used in § 20 (*per sublimes aggestus*) and § 23 (*unius aggesti*). Against such *aggeres* the besieged could build similar ramparts as a counter-measure. Cf. e.g. 19.6.6: *duo tamen aggeres celsi Persarum peditum manu erecti...contra quos nostrorum quoque impensiore cura moles excitabantur altissimae fastigio adversae celsitudinis aequatae* and 19.8.1: *cumque...pugna per aggeres celsos muris proximos temptaretur, ex aggestis erectis intrinsecus...nostri...resistebant* (The *aggestus* of 20.11.20 were built by the attackers, pace De Jonge loc.cit.).

In the present case the *aggeres* were composed of flammable bundles of branches and reeds supported by beams (cf. § 23); the mounds at Amida seem to have consisted, at least in part, of earth (cf. 19.6.6, 19.8.1-4). Cf. Crump, 1975, 108.

adolescebat obsidio Bitter 151 note 470 regards this metaphoric use of *adolescere* as Tacitean. De Jonge ad 14.2.9 *adulta nocte* makes a simular suggestion. It is indeed a fact that Tac. has many such instances, e.g. *Amm.*2.50.1 *adolescebat interea lex maiestatis*.

decernentes sub imperatoris conspectu Other passages in Amm. where *decernere* is a pure synonym of *pugnare* (cf. TLL V 1.139.63 sqq.) are 16.12.49 *inter quos decernebant et reges*, 18.8.9 *fortiter decernentes*, 19.2.10 *obstinatione utrimque magna decernebatur* (see the note ad loc.), 20.7.12 *diu cum exitio decernentes*.

For the topos of the general's knowing of the individual soldiers cf. above the note ad 20.4.12 *singulos*.

spe praemiorum Rewards in the form of military decorations (*armillae, hastae purae* etc., cf. Maxfield, 1981) are hardly mentioned by Amm. Apart from the *torques* (but see the note ad 20.4.18 for an alternative interpretation), we hear of them only twice. After the capture of Maiozamalcha *obsidionales coronae* were given to those who had fought valiantly (24.4.24), while some time later after a successful battle against the Persians Julian presented many of his soldiers with other crowns: *navalibus donavit coronis et civicis et castrensibus* (24.6.1, cf. for this Heus, 1982). Of monetary rewards we hear more often. Cf. 24.3.3 (*argenteos nummos centenos viritim pollicitus*), 25.1.6 (*remuneratus est, ut decebat*), 25.10.10 (*munerati redire iubentur ad signa*). Cf. Müller, 1905, 620-621.

nudantes galeis capita   Robinson, 1975, 13-144 is devoted to the classification of the different types of helmets used by Roman soldiers. For *galeae* in Amm. see Müller, 1905, 603-604 and the notes ad 16.12.54 and 19.8.8. Cf. § 21: *conisque galearum minacius nutans*.

sagittariorum hostilium peritia fundebantur   Cf. 19.5.5 *tela summa peritia dispergebant* with De Jonge's note. *Fundere* as a synonym of *prosternere* is mainly poetic: Verg.*A.* 9.592 *fortemque manu fudisse Numanum*, Ov.*Met.* 13.85/6 *hunc ego.../ingenti resupinum pondere fudi*. Other examples in Amm. are 24.2.14, 24.4.5, 29.5.14.

XI. 13 *proin dies et noctes intentae vigiliis cautiores stantes utrubique faciebant*   This is a somewhat puzzling sentence and difficult to interpret exactly. Presumably Amm. wants to say that as a result of the many losses suffered (*proin*) both parties kept watch for days and nights on end, which brought a higher degree of prudence (*cautiores*) with it.

Whereas *proinde* is used more than thirty times by Amm., this is the only instance of *proin*. These proportions do not essentially differ from those of *exin* (9 times) and *exinde* (more than sixty occurrences). If *dies et noctes intentae* should indeed be interpreted as a so-called ab urbe condita-construction, it is one of few examples in the nom. in Amm.; cf. Blomgren 88 note 2.

Heraeus' emendation *pauciores*, which is accepted by Clark, is not probable. The only other instance of *paucior* occurs in section 18 of this chapter, whereas *cautior* can be found in 15.10.5, 16.12.9, 17.5.1, 29.6.2. It seems likely that Amm. wanted to report the increase of watchfulness rather than the diminishing of the numbers: possibly section 12 has illustrated the *temeritas* mentioned at the beginning of that section, and now in section 13 it is the turn of the *consilium* as its counterpart. Further, the phrase *cautiorem facere* can be parallelled by Liv. 36.12.7 *fraus cautiores, non timidiores Thyrreenses fecit* and August. *C.D.* 12.20 *sive nos faciat cautiores diligentior ipsa tractatio*.

aggerum altitudine iam in sublime porrecta For *altitudo* + gen. see above the note ad 20.11.6. The expression *in sublime porrectus* also occurs in 22.14.4 and 29.5.37.

malleolos atque incendiaria tela torquentes For *malleolos* see above the note ad 20.6.6. This is the only instance of *incendiarius* in Amm.; in earlier authors it is used as a subst. meaning 'fire-raiser'.

laborabant in cassum For *in cassum* see above the relevant note ad 20.4.5.

quod umectis scortis et centonibus erant opertae materiae plures V's *cortis* is corrected by Petschenig into *coriis*, an emendation which is rightly printed by Clark: the term is used in comparable situations in 23.4.11 and 24.6.8. Cf. also Veg.*mil.* 4.14 *testudo ... quae, ne exuratur incendio, coriis vel ciliciis centonibusque vestitur.* For *centonibus* see also De Jonge's note ad 19.8.8, the only other passage where *cento* occurs, and cf. also Caes. *Civ.* 2.9.4, 2.10.6, 3.44.6. For *umectis* cf. the note ad 20.7.13.

The plural *materiae* can denote beams of timber, as in 17.10.9 and 18.2.6 (see the notes ad loc.). Here it is obviously used as a pars pro toto for the *machinae*, as becomes evident in *has admoventes* in the next section, where *has* refers to *materiae*.

aliae unctae alumine diligenter This is another time-worn method to prevent fire-raising; cf. Quad. *hist.* 81, 234. 14-15 Peter about a wooden *turris*: *cum ex omni latere circumplexa igni foret, ardere non quisse, quod alumine ab Archelao oblita fuisset.* In Amm. it occurs only here.

XI. 14 *ne prompta quidem pericula contemnebant* This can hardly be right. At first sight it seems most likely to regard *tamen* as corresponding with *licet*, which results in this shortened paraphrase: 'although the Romans experienced difficulties in defending their *machinae*, nevertheless they did not even disregard the manifest dangers'. One would either expect it being stated that they did not even fear such dangers or that not even the hidden dangers were disregarded. As *prompta* does not seem liable to doubt, emendations aim to present a text which expresses the former alternative. Langen's *contremebant* is not impossible, but one fails to understand how this could have been corrupted to V's *contemneliant*. The same objection can be made to Clark's *continebant*, which in combination with Heraeus' *cupiditatem* results in an acceptable phrase: 'even the manifest dangers did not curb the Romans' desire to capture the town'. Other contributions also fail to present a convincing solution. Baehrens, 1925 is difficult to understand and Češka,

267

1972, 19 suggests an ingenious, but improbable emendation: *non temnebant*. The simplex *temnere* is used a few times in classical poetry and further occurs once in Tac.

If *tamen* does not correspond with *licet* and the latter word only determines *difficile* ('they courageously defended their *machinae*, albeit with some difficulty'), the contrast is different: in that case the sentence beginning with *tamen* expresses that the force used by the Romans to defend their *machinae* did not imply their neglecting even the manifest dangers in their desire to capture the city, the hidden dangers, especially fire, being continuously on their minds. Thus they testified to *consilium*, in contrast to the men who rashly took off their helmets. As can be seen, this explanation is also very unsatisfactory.

All in all it is better to admit the impossibility of the transmitted text and the implausibility of the emendations proposed. A crux should be added to *contemnebant*.

XI. 15 *propugnatores* For Amm.'s use of this word see above the note ad 20.6.2.

iam discussurus turrim oppositam Cf. Liv. 21.12.2 *tribus arietibus aliquantum muri discussit*. The use of *quatere* and its composita is of course to be expected in reports on the action of rams: *arietibus muros quatiebat* (Liv. 38.5.3), *ariete decussi ruebant muri* (33.17.9). The present text, however, provides the only example in Amm. Used as an adi., *oppositus* does not necessarily imply that an object has been placed somewhere purposefully for the occasion: *collis oppositus arcebat* (Liv. 27.48.8), *post montem oppositum* (Verg. *G*. 3.213), *contra oppositum aliud promuntorium* (Amm. 23.6.10).

prominentem eius ferream frontem, quae re vera formam effingit arietis Cf. these phrases in Veg.'s description of the *aries: caput ipsius vestitur ferro et appellatur aries ... habet durissimam frontem qua subruit muros* (Veg.*mil*. 4.14). For *effingere formam*, 'to have assumed the likeness of' with the thing in question itself as a subject cf. Amm. 27.4.5 *eadem loca, formata in cornuti sideris modum, effingunt theatri faciem speciosam*.

arte subtili illaqueatam altrinsecus laciniis retinuere longissimis Such a method to deal with attacking rams is recommended by the experts: Aen. Tact. 32.4 καὶ ὅταν ἢ πύλην ἢ ἄλλο τι τοῦ τείχους διακόπτηι (subj. the ram), χρὴ βρόχωι τὸ προΐσχον ἀναλαμβάνεσθαι, ἵνα μὴ δύνηται προσπίπτειν τὸ μηχάνημα, Veg.*mil*. 4.23 *alii laqueis captos arietes per multitudinem hominum de muro in obliquum trahunt et cum ipsis testudinibus evertunt*. Liv. 36.23.2 implies that the method was often used: *cum ariete quaterentur muri, non laqueis, ut solet, exceptos declinabant ictus.* The expertise needed for this operation is stressed by *arte subtili*, cf. the use of *subtiliter* in the chapter describing the *machinae*: 23.4.2 and 14. The rare word *illaqueare*, which occurs only here in Amm., is used metaphorically elsewhere, e.g. *munera navium / saevos inlaqueant duces* (Hor. *Carm.* 3.16.15/16).

It is not fully clear what is expressed by the adv. *altrinsecus*, which in Amm. always means 'on both sides' (see above the note ad 20.7.11). It might refer to both flanks of the ram, but it is more likely that two different groups of defenders handle the lassoes with considerable skill; cf. Selem's rendering: "con fine arteficio da due parti presero con un laccio la sua prominente fronte di ferro". Instead of the normal term *laqueus* Amm. here uses *laciniae* ('strips of cloth'), as in 31.2.9, where it also concerns a military technique. The perf. *retinuere* deserves attention. After the many instances of the imp., which illustrate the continuity of the operations, it expresses a momentary action: 'they got hold of the ram'.

retrogradiens This very rare word occurs once more in Amm.: 18.8.6.

assultibus densis Cf. the relevant note ad 20.8.10.

contemplabiliter See above the note ad 20.7.9.

ferventissimam picem For the use of pitch by the defenders of a besieged town see above the note ad 20.7.10.

diu promotae machinae stabant As a technical military term *promovere* means 'to move into an attacking position'; some examples: Caes. *Gal.* 7.70.5 *paulum legiones Caesar, quas pro vallo constituerat, promoveri iubet*, Liv. 10.40.12 *promovent et Samnites signa*, Tac. *Ann.* 15.4.3 *cum promovere scalas et machinamenta inciperent.* Amm. also has some instances: *Romana promota sunt signa* (16.12.8), *aptatique arietes aegre promovebantur* (20.7.10), *Valens castra promovit ad Phrygiam* (26.9.7). Wagner's explanation of *stabant* ("inefficaces erant") is correct, although his reference to 19.8.2 *diu cruentum proelium stetit* is not well-judged: in that case *stare* means 'to remain undecided'.

XI. 16 *aggeribus cumulatius excitatis* See ad 20.11.12. The adverb *cumulate* is always used with the meaning "ample", "abunde", according to TLL IV 1384.66 sqq. Here, however, it is rather the equivalent of 'altius'. There are no other instances in Amm. *Excitare* is used of building dams or walls in classical prose. Cf. Caes. *Gal.*3.14.4 *turribus...excitatis* and Liv. 29.18.17 *ad aliquantum iam altitudinis excitata erant moenia*, 38.3.11 *ad aggeres excitandos.*

exitium affore iam sperantes For *adesse* 'to be imminent' cf. 14.7.5 *inediae..metum, quae...affore iam sperabatur*. The verb is found in classical prose with this meaning, e.g. Sal. *Jug.* 9.4 *quom sibi finem vitae adesse intellegeret*, Tac. *Ann.* 14.32.1 *feminae...adesse exitium canebant*. The use of the infin. fut. is caused by *sperare* 'to expect', or even 'to fear', for which see the note ad 14.7.5.

in audaciam ruere praecipitem Bitter 154 n. 484 speaks of a "kaum verständliche Brachylogie" and quotes as a parallel for *ruere in* 17.12.8 *sed ne eos quidem prompta iuvit audacia in discrimina ruentes aperta*. The expression is less bold if *audacia* is interpreted as "audacter factum". Examples of this use of *audacia* are given in TLL II 1242.69 sqq., e.g. Cic. *Cael.* 1 *nullum facinus, nullam audaciam, nullam vim in iudicium vocari*, Tac. *Hist.* 1.55.1 *ceteri silentio proximi cuiusque audaciam exspectantes*, Tac. *Ann.* 1.74.1 *qui formam vitae iniit, quam...celebrem miseriae temporum et audaciae hominum fecerunt*.

repentino decursu portis effusi The first of three sallies, of which the second (§ 18–19) and the third (§ 22–23) are successful. The fighting quality of the garrison of Bezabde has been indicated in 20.7.16.

faces sitellasque ferreas This is the only instance of *sitella* in Amm. Vegetius does not mention the *sitella* at all. In classical prose it is used only of urns from which lots are drawn: Pl. *Cas.* 296, *Rhet. Her.* 1.21, Liv. 25.3.16.

XI. 17 *post ambiguam proelii varietatem* The last two words are Heraeus' conjecture for *proeliam virtutem* V. In itself *proeliantium virtutem* (Walter) is attractive, but *ambigua virtus* seems an odd phrase. *Ambiguus* is found in a military context in 14.10.14 *ut Martis ambigua declinentur*. For *varietas* cf. Cic. *Arch.* 21 *bellum...in multa varietate terra marique versatum* and Tac. *Ann.* 4.33.3 *varietates proeliorum*.

nullo impetrato Seyfarth has accepted this emendation proposed by Haupt and C.F.W. Mueller for *nihil* in VBAG. In view of the practically unanimous transmission of *nihil*, however, it deserves serious consideration. Szantyr 142 mentions it as the earliest instance of the transitive construction of the past passive participle, which is dealt with more fully in Löfstedt, 1911, 290–293, who quotes i.a. Hier. *Tract. in psalm. XV*: *impleto illud quod Paulus ait* and Anon. Vales. 5.18 *quod facto pax ab ambobus firmata est*. The question cannot be decided with certainty, seeing that in 17.5.15 all manuscripts read *legationem nullo impetrato remissam*. Other abl.i abs.i with *nullo* are 14.1.4 *nullo sibi relicto*, 20.8.19 *nullo suppresso*, 28.6.6 *nullo temptato*. For this use of *nullo = nulla re* see the notes ad 14.1.4, 17.5.15 and 20.8.19.

quos erexerant Romani   Clark proposed *erexerunt* on account of the cursus. The pluperfect, however, following *aggeribus...excitatis* in § 16, is perfectly natural. It seems better, therefore, to accept the irregular cursus and to leave the text as it stands.

idem Persae propugnaculis insistentes sagittis incessebantur   The pronoun *idem* is not used anaphorically here, but underlines the reversal in the situation. The Persians, who had attacked the Roman siege-works now come under heavy fire themselves. For *propugnaculum* see the note ad 20.6.4 *Incessere* 'to assail (with missiles)' is found again in 27.1.3 *sagittis aliisque levibus iaculis incessebant*. Cf. Liv. 26.10.7 *lapidibus telisque incessebant*, Tac. *Hist.* 2.22.1 *altiora murorum sagittis aut saxis incessere*.

per tegumenta turrium volitantia   It seems probable that the coverings mentioned here are identical with the *cilicia* of § 9 above. The use of the frequentativum *volitare* suggests a large number of missiles, as in 20.7.6 *sagittarum...nimbi crebrius volitantes* and 29.5.25 *tela reciprocantes volitantia grandinis ritu*.

irrita labebantur   Cf. 20.7.10 *per proclive labentium* (sc. lapidum); Liv. 44.9.9 *tela...testudini iniecta...lubrico fastigio innoxia ad imum labebantur*, Tac. *Hist.* 3.29.1 *cum... superiacta tela testudine laberentur*.

XI. 18   *Cumque pauciores utrubique fierent bellatores*   This is a variation on expressions like *hinc inde multis amissis et vulneratis* (20.6.5) and *caderentque altrinsecus multi* (20.7.11), introducing the final stage of the siege. For *utrubique* see the note ad 20.7.6. *Bellator* is found from Plautus onwards. It probably has a poetic colouring. Vergil has it several times, mostly in apposition (*G.* 2.145, *A.* 9.721, 10.891, 11.89, 11.553, 11.700, 12.614). In Livy it occurs only in the first decade (1.59.9, 5.20.6, 6.23.5, 7.26.13, 8.8.17, 9.1.2). In Tacitus it is altogether rare (*Ger.* 14.2, *Ann* 1.67.3, 4.49.3). Amm. has it no less than seventeen times, four times in combination with *acerrimus* (17.5.1, 19.2.3, 22.8.21, 23.6.80). In other cases, as in the present passage, it is merely an equivalent of *miles*. The word is common in Veg. See the note ad 16.11.12.

et Persae truderentur ad ultima, ni potior ratio succurrisset   But for the use of the subjunctive dependent on *cum*, the sentence follows the pattern of Tac. *Ann.* 1.63.2 *trudebanturque in paludem..., ni Caesar productas legiones instruxisset*. For this "*ni* de rupture", found in Nepos, Livy, Curtius Rufus, Tacitus and Amm., see Chausserie-Laprée, 1969, 636–7. *Trudere* is found with the same meaning in 20.4.18 *trusus ad necessitatem extremam*, where see the note, and 26.10.3.

Potior ratio must mean "a better plan" (Rolfe), sc. than to continue to defend the city as they were doing. For *potior* cf. e.g. Hor. *Epod.* 16.17 *nulla sit hac potior sententia* and Verg. *A.* 4.287 *haec alternanti potior sententia visa est*.

Succurrere combines the notions 'to come to mind' and 'to come to the rescue'. The former is found only here in Amm., for the latter cf. 14.7.13 *succurrens saluti suae quavis ratione*.

impensiore opera procursus temptabatur For *impensiore* see the note ad 17.10.7 *cura...impensiore*. This and similar expressions are found for the first time in Quint. *Inst.* 1.10.35 *impensam huic scientiae operam dederunt* and Gel. 9.14.6 *impensa opera conquisitis veteribus libris*. The ablative of manner indicates the careful preparation of this sally, whereas *procursus* normally has the connotation of hastiness and improvisation, cf. 31.15.15 *quia nullo ordine iam, sed per procursus pugnabatur et globos, quod desperationis erat signum extremae*. Cf. Liv. 22.41.1 *tumultuario proelio ac procursu magis militum quam ex praeparato aut iussu imperatorum orto*. For the imperfect *temptabatur* see the note ad 20.4.17 *iubebatur*.

qui portabant ignes, amplioribus ordinatis The relative clause must be taken substantivally: 'fire-bearers'. This helps to explain both the use of the indicative and the position of the clause within the sentence. Similar instances of abl.i abs.i in which the subject is expressed in a relative clause are discussed by Kühner-Stegmann I 773, Szantyr 141, Flinck-Linkomies, 1929, 223 sqq. and 247 sqq. Cf. Cic. *Ac.* 2.33 *quo...omnia iudicantur, sublato reliqua se negant tollere* and Nep. *Lys.* 1.5 *qui Atheniensium rebus studuissent* (= οἱ ἀττικίζοντες) *eiectis*.

Amplioribus is used predicatively 'in greater numbers', sc. than in the sortie described in the preceding section. With this meaning *amplior* occurs in 15.3.7, 16.2.6 (where see the note) and 19.9.9. *Ampliores copiae* is found in Caes. *Gal.* 5.19.1 and 5.50.2; TLL I 2008.38 sqq.

For *ordinare* see the note ad 20.9.8.

iaciebantur corbes in materias ferreae The word *corbis* is found nowhere else in Amm. and, as Szidat notes, it is never used in a military context. Amm. repeats in different words what he had described in § 16 as *sitellasque ferreas onustas ignibus*. For *materias* referring to the beams of the siege-engines see the note ad 17.10.9.

sarmenta aliaque...aptissima Cf. 21.12.10 *sarmentis ac vario fomite flammarum incessebantur*. Already in Sis. *hist.* 83 we find *partim malleolos partim fasces sarmentorum*. Veg. *mil.* 4.24 speaks of *sarmenta...aliaque fomenta flammarum*.

XI. 19 *classico excitante in pugnam* The abl. abs. is explained by *quia...nubes*. *Excitare* is rarely used in military contexts. The phrase is reminiscent of Hor. *Epod*. 2.5 *neque excitatur classico miles truci*. Caes. *Gal*. 3.10.3 *omnes...Gallos...ad bellum mobiliter celeriterque excitari* is not a real parallel.

legiones procinctae celeri gradu venerunt The meaning of *procinctus* is explained in Fab. Pict. *iur*. 2 *Dialem flaminem...religio est...classem procinctam,...id est exercitum armatum, videre*. For manner expressions with *gradu* see the note ad 20.4.20.

succrescente paulatim ardore bellandi Cf. 21.13.14 *succrescentis rabiem belli*, where the metaphor is continued by *antequam pubescat validius*, 23.5.20 and 28.2.14. The verb is used in a simile in Pl. *Trin*. 30/1: *mores mali/quasi herba inrigua succrevere uberrume*. For *ardor* with a gerund see the note ad 20.6.1.

cum ventum fuisset in manus V reads *in*, EBAG *ad*. Both expressions are found in classical prose as an equivalent of *manus conserere*. Cf. Sal. *Jug*. 89.2 *Iugurtham ob suos tutandos in manus venturum*, Liv. 2.30.12 *ubi ad manum venisset hostis*, 2.46.3 *pugna iam in manus, iam ad gladios...venerat*, Tac. *Hist*. 4.7.5 *ut ventum in manus*, *Ann*. 2.80.4 *ut venere in manus*. The forms of the pluperfect with *fui/fueram* are discussed by Szantyr 320–2 (whose references to Pighi and Hagendahl are misleading).

machinae omnes effusis ignibus urebantur Both § 21 and the immediately following *praeter maiorem* make clear that the rams are meant. For *effusis ignibus* cf. Liv. 30.5.8 *in nocturno effuso tam late incendio* and see TLL V 2.222.80 sqq. The use of the imperfect *urebantur*, where a perfect would have been expected (*repente!*), is discussed in the notes ad 14.2.14 and 20.4.5.

direptis restibus This refers to what has been described in § 15. There is no real parallel for *diripere* in the sense required here 'to break', 'to cut', whereas the instances of *dirumpere* in this sense are numerous (TLL V 1.1264.63 sqq). It seems best, therefore, to accept Bentley's *diruptis*.

semustam The only other instance of *semustus* in Amm. (24.4.30) refers to soldiers smoked out of a tunnel. As the examples in the OLD show, the word occurs mostly, but not exclusively, in poetry.

XI. 20 *non in longum militi quies data* For *in longum* "vi temporali" see TLL VII 2.1642.81 sqq. The phrase is borrowed from Tac. *Hist*. 4.79.1 *nec in longum quies militi data* with only a change in word order to avoid a parrot-like imitation. *Quies* is trisyllabic, cf. 25.6.14 *qúïes dáret*, 29.5.34 *qúïes dédit* and 29.5.49 *qúïes prima*.

refectus...excitus The successive activities are expressed by these unconnected participles. The asyndeton and the closing of the cola by the cursus turn these participial phrases into virtually self-contained sentences. For *rector* with the general sense 'officer' cf. 14.2.15 *rectores militum...armatos omnis celeri eduxere procursu* and 14.6.17 *proeliorum periti rectores*. A specification of rank is added in 16.12.63. See the note ad 20.1.1 *rectore*.

munitiones a muro longe demovit The *munitiones* intended here are specified in 19.5.1. *vineis civitatem pluteisque circumdabat*, where see the note. The construction of the *plutei* and *vineae* and the way in which they were used are described in Veg. *mil.* 4.15, quoted there. Szidat rightly remarks that *munitio* is not found elsewhere with this meaning; TLL VIII 1661.

dimicare succinctius parans per sublimes aggestus Amm. uses *succinctius* in 14.10.13, 15.8.5, 23.6.85 and 28.1.2 with the meaning 'succinctly'. In 19.6.7, where see the note, *Galli...securibus gladiisque succincti*, it means 'equipped', while in 25.3.5 *succinctior armatura* is best taken as "the light-armed forces" (Rolfe). The last parallel suggests that 'unimpeded' is the correct translation here. The removal of the *plutei* and *vineae* leaves more room for the soldiers and the protection offered by them is less needed given the height the *aggestus* have reached by now. For the word *aggestus* see the note ad 19.5.1 *et erigi aggeres coepti* and compare Sen. *Ep.* 84.12 *gradus divitum et magno adgestu suspensa vestibula*. In view of § 23 the following note in the Suda s.v. Ἄγεστα and Ἄκεστα is important: πολεμικὸν μηχάνημα ἐκ λίθων καὶ ξύλων καὶ χοῦ ἐγειρόμενον.

utque facile defensuri moenia pellerentur The reading *defensuri moenia* printed in the Accursiana seems to be a correct inference from *defensori moenia* of V. Moreover, *defensuri* better suits the context, in which the future effect of the Roman measures is envisaged, than the less specific *defensores* would do.

in ipsis ... summitatibus binae sunt locatae ballistae See the note ad 16.10.7 *gemmatisque summitatibus* and for *ballistae* cf. ad 20.7.2.

ne prospicere quidem posse hostium quisquam crederétur As in 20.7.17 *aggredi posset* one may wonder if *posse* + infin. praes. does not serve as a periphrasis of the future infin. Amm. uses *prospicere* with the meaning 'to see in front', as here, e.g. in 19.2.12 *unde longe et late prospici poterat* and 25.1.1

corusci thoraces longe prospecti. More often it means 'to see in the future', e.g. 19.9.4 *accidentia longe ante prospiciens*. In 29.5.46 and 30.10.4 it is linked with *altiore cura*, indicating the careful weighing of the consequences of an action. A third meaning, viz. 'to take measures' can be found e.g. in 16.12.12 *negotiis difficillimis quoque saepe dispositio tempestiva prospexit* and 29.1.6 *quae..., nisi prospectum fuerit, universa confundent*. The *ballistae* do indeed have the effect the Romans expected, as the next section shows: *cum Persas occultari videret*.

XI. 21 *prope ipsum crepusculum* This is the only instance of *crepusculum* in Amm. As TLL IV 1175.39 shows, the instances in which the word refers to evening twilight far outnumber those in which the early morning is meant. Still, Serv. *Aen*. 2.268 writes: *et licet utrique tempori possit iungi, usus tamen ut matutino iungamus obtinuit*. Cf. *Pan*. 3.28 *matutino crepusculo palatium petimus*, Rut. Nam. 277 *roscida puniceo fulsere crepuscula caelo*.

triplex acies...nutans...conabantur The alternation of singular and plural is remarkable, but may possibly be explained by the distance between the collective subject and the main verb. Cf. Blomgren 47, who quotes as a parallel 27.12.8 *iuventus exsiluit velox passibusque insonis expeditis mucronibus repens, cum castra...invasissent, iacentes multos...trucidarunt*.

conisque galearum minacius nutans A reminiscence of Hom. *Il*. 3.337 δεινὸν δὲ λόφος καθύπερθεν ἔνευεν. See Bitter 141 for similar expressions.

scalas Cf. the notes ad 20.6.3 and 20.7.6.

iamque resultantibus armis et tubis In classical Latin *resultare* is used of places echoing sound, not of the source of the sound, as here. Cf. e.g. Verg. *A*. 8.305 *consonat omne nemus strepitu collesque resultant* and Tac. *Ann*. 1.65.1 *cum barbari...truci sonore...resultantis saltus complerent*; Bitter 148 n. 160. For *tubae* see the note ad 20.7.6.

latiusque sese pandente manu Romana The same phrase is used of an encircling manoeuvre in 27.10.13 *barbari...quos latius sese pandens exercitus infusis utrimque cornibus afflictabat*. See TLL X 1.196.2 sqq. This meaning is also found in Livy: *dum se cornua latius pandunt* (2.31.2), *latius pandere aciem non poterat* (28.33.12). *Manu Romana* is an attractive conjecture by Clark on the basis of *romanu* V, corrected to *romana* by Vm2. The construction of the sentence from *latiusque* onward is strained. A plural subject (*Romani*) for the main verb *pulsabant* must be derived from *manus Romana*, which at the same time accounts for the singular *videret*.

cum ligonibus et dolabris et vectibus None of these tools is mentioned elsewhere in Amm. For *ligo* 'mattock' see Tac. *Hist.* 3.27.2 *dum...ligones dolabras et alii falces scalasque convectant*. Its function is, according to Veg. *mil.* 2.25, *ad fossarum opera facienda. Dolabrae* 'picks' are mentioned e.g. in Liv. 9.37.8 *dolabrae calonibus dividuntur ad vallum proruendum fossasque implendas*, 28.3.13 *dolabrisque caedebantur...portae* and Tac. *Ann.* 3.46.3 *miles correptis securibus et dolabris, ut si murum perrumperet*. For *vectis* 'crowbar' cf. Liv. 27.28.10, where it is used to lift a portcullis: *eam...vectibus levant*. Veg. *mil.* 3.4 gives instructions for fighting with these crowbars.

XI. 22 *ictus varii ballistarum tamquam per transennam...decurrentes* The mysterious word *transenna* is found in classical times in Pl. (*Bac.* 792, *Per.* 480, *Rud.* 1236), where it must mean "a trap (for birds) made of netting" (OLD). This is also possible in Sal. *Hist.* 2.70.3 *transenna demissum Victoriae simulacrum*, where it may denote a net used as a container. In their commentary ad Cic. *de Orat.* 1.162 *illam copiam ornamentorum suorum, quam constructam uno in loco quasi per transennam praetereuntes strictim aspeximus* Leeman-Pinkster assume the same basic meaning and explain *transenna* as "covering", "wrapping". The meaning of the word has become problematical in later times. Both Nonius (180.15 M) and Serv. *Aen.* 5.488 explain the passage from Sal. quoted above. According to Nonius it means "per fenestram", Servius interprets *transenna* as "extentus funis". As Rolfe remarks, this tallies with Amm. 25.6.14 *tamquam e transenna simul emissi*, which "refers probably to runners started in a race when the rope is dropped and meaning "all together". In the present passage, according to Rolfe, it refers to the accuracy of the marksmen "as if their missiles slid down a rope stretched from their *ballistae* to the mark at which they aimed" (Seyfarth "schnurgerade"), which suits the context very well. *Structilis* is found only here in Amm. and must mean "manu factus". Its classical meaning 'constructed of concrete' is unacceptable here. There are no parallels for *decurrere* used of shots fired from a high position.

fortunas suas sitas in extremo The phrase may echo Sal. *Cat.* 52.11 *res publica in extremo sita est*.

destinatam ruebant in mortem Amm. writes both *destinare* alqm., e.g. 21.12.3 *Immone...ad hoc destinato*, 28.5.2 *ad mortem destinatae plebi congressus*, or, with a dative, 28.4.15 *destinatum poenae Socraten* and *destinare* alqd., as here and, among many examples, in 17.13.34 *destinatas remearunt ad sedes*, q.v. Cf. Tac. *Ann.* 15.63.1 *sibi quoque destinatam mortem adseverat* and Flor. *Epit.* 1.34.12 (2.18.12) *eo necessitatum compulsi primum ut destinata morte in proelium ruerent* (siege of Numantia); TLL V 1.756.20 sqq. and 60 sqq.

partiti munera dimicandi...valida manus erupit   Strictly speaking the sentence is an anacoluthon. Amm. might have continued with an appositional subdivision like *alii...alii* or *pars...pars*. Instead he inserted the abl. abs. *relictis, qui...tuerentur*, to indicate one of the two groups into which the subject of *partiti* is subdivided, thereby spoiling the balance of the sentence. A similar inconsistency, caused again by the insertion of an abl. abs., is to be seen in 25.1.10 *progressi itaque septuaginta stadia attenuata rerum omnium copia herbis frumentisque crematis ex flammis ipsis raptas fruges et pabula, ut quisque vehere potuit, conservavit*.

inter necessitatis articulos   See ad 14.2.6 and Bitter 152 n. 473, on the use of *necessitas* in Sal., Liv. and Tac. and on *articulus* (καιρός) on p. 78, n. 229. The present phrase is to be compared to 16.12.45 *extremae necessitatis articulo circumventos*, 17.9.6 *inter tot...articulos necessitatum*, 18.2.5 *adigente necessitatum articulo*. See the note ad 16.12.37. It seems best to take these words with *partiti* and to end the colon here, the next colon consisting of the abl. abs. *relictis ... tuerentur*. Both those about to make a sortie and those left behind to defend the walls are in mortal danger.

reserata latenter postica   Another standard element in siege-descriptions, cf. 19.6.7 and 19.8.5 (Amm.'s escape from Amida) and 21.12.13 *qui erumpebant clanculo per posticas* (Aquileia). Cf. for *postica* the note ad 18.6.11.

pone sequentibus aliis   Amm. has *pone* eleven times, both as an adverb and as a preposition. See the note ad 15.10.4 and Szantyr 242.

XI. 23   *qui vehebant foculos*   Cf. *qui portabant ignes* in § 18. Normally, a *foculus* 'brazier' is used in sacrifices. Only here it is found in a military context. In 23.6.34 the Persian *magi* are said to keep the fire from heaven in braziers: *feruntque, si iustum est credi, etiam ignem caelitus lapsum apud se sempiternis foculis custodiri*.

repentes incurvi   For *repere* see the note ad 20.7.13 and cf. 27.12.8 *passibusque insonis...repens*, 29.5.54 *insonis gradibus...manibus repens et pedibus*.

prunas unius aggesti inseruere iuncturis   For these *iuncturae* cf. the Suda s.v. Ἄγεστα, quoted on § 20. In Veg. *mil.* 3.8 we find the following instructions for building a dam: *saepibus ductis vel interpositis stipitibus ramisque arborum, ne terra facile dilabatur, agger erigitur*. Compare the action of the Massiliotae in Caes. *Civ.* 2.14.1/2 *ignem operibus inferunt. hunc sic distulit ventus, uti ... agger plutei testudo turris tormenta flammam conciperent*. Veg. *mil.* 4.28 warns against this danger: *oppidani repente prorumpunt...arietes machinas ipsosque aggeres ignibus concremant.*

ramis...et iunco et manipulis constructi cannarum Instead of the *saepes* prescribed by Veg., the Romans make use of the material ready at hand on the bank of the Tigris.

qui conceptis...nutrimentis iam cremabantur This raises a problem. *Qui* must refer to *rami...iuncus...manipuli*. Then what are the *nutrimenta incendiorum*? One might suppose that the glowing charcoals are meant, set ablaze by the wind. More likely, however, in view of *aridis*, we must think of the *rami* etc. themselves as the fuel that nourishes the flames. Cf. e.g. 18.7.8 *incendiis arida nutrimentorum varietate crescentibus*, 22.13.3 *ignesque aridis nutrimentis erecti*. In that case the subject of *cremabantur* is identical with the subject of the abl. abs. In fact, this is how Seyfarth interprets the sentence: "Das trockene Material fing rasch Feuer und stand schon in Flammen ...". For a similar construction see the note ad 14.11.3, Kühner-Stegmann I 786–788 and Szantyr 139–40, who calls this deviation from the grammatical rule "durchaus vulgär". The construction seems less harsh if one realizes that the *rami* etc. are viewed first as part of the construction of the dam, then as fuel for the flames.

militibus...degressis A good example of 'Satznachtrag'. Blomgren 106–7 gives a number of parallels.

XI. 24 *vespera dedit incedens* Cf. 24.1.6 *vespera incedente* and 31.11.4 *vesperaque incedente*. Amm. has *vespera* eighteen times. The masc. forms he admits are *vesperi* ('in the evening': 14.1.9, 18.8.2, 19.12.14, 22.8.35), *vespero* (31.7.15) and *vesperum* (17.13.8, q.v., 22.8.11, 26.8.13).

imperator in varia sese consilia diducens et versans A Vergilian reminiscence (*A*. 5.720 *in curas animo diducitur omnis*), cherished by Amm. Cf. 21.13.1 *in rationes diducebatur ancipites*, 26.5.9 *curis diducebatur ambiguis*, 31.16.1 *in varias consiliorum vias diducebantur*. In combination with *versari* we find 29.5.7 *sollicitudine diducebatur ancipiti multa cum animo versans*. See also the note ad 20.4.6.

excidio Phaenichae diutius imminere On the mistaken identification of Phaenicha with Bezabde see the note ad 20.7.1. There is no real parallel in Amm. for *imminere* with an abstract dative complement 'to be intent on', but Livy has some comparable expressions both with *in* + acc., e.g. 25.20.5 *in alterius ducis exercitusque opprimendi occasionem imminebat* and with a dative, e.g. 4.25.9 *nequiquam imminentes spei maioris honoris* and 31.47.6 *simul Gallico triumpho imminens*. Tacitus may have provided the model: *Hist.* 3.76.1 *L. Vitellius...excidio Tarracinae imminebat* and *Hist.* 4.15.3 *excidiis castellorum imminebant*.

necessariae rationes 'Compelling reasons'; cf. e.g. Cic. *S. Rosc.* 40 *sine causis multis et magnis et necessariis*, Caes. *Civ.* 1.40.5 *necessaria re coactus*.

quod munimentum...erat obiectum See the note ad 20.7.1 for *munimentum* and for *excursus* ad 20.9.7. Amm. uses *claustra* of mountain passes in 21.13.16 *claustra...occupasse Succorum* and 31.11.3 *claustra patefacta sunt Alpium Iuliarum*. In 25.8.14 he calls Nisibis *orientis firmissimum claustrum*. Livy and Tacitus use *claustra* in the plural in this sense, e.g. Liv. 9.32.1 *ab oppugnando Sutrio, quae urbs...velut claustra Etruriae erat* and 45.11.5 *apparebat claustra Aegypti teneri* (Pelusium). Tac. *Hist*. 1.6.2 *praemissosque ad claustra Caspiarum* and *Hist*. 3.43.1 *Foroiuliensem coloniam, claustra maris*.

Insolubilis is very rare in classical prose. The examples in TLL are all from late Latin prose authors, except Sen. *Ben.* 4.12.1 *beneficium...insolubile* ('that cannot be repaid') and Quint. *Inst.* 5.9.3 *signum insolubile* ('incontestable'). In Amm. we may compare 14.11.26 *necessitatis insolubili retinaculo* and 16.12.20 *velut insolubili muro*, where see the note.

et serum repelleret tempus As Szidat points out, the siege of Bezabde dragged on till mid November. *Serum tempus* for "the lateness of the season" (Rolfe) is unusual, but easily understood on the analogy of 31.15.14 *ad serum usque diem*. Note that *et* has a slightly adversative force here.

alimentis destituendos forsitan cedere existimans Persas As Odelstierna, 1926,9 observes, *destituendos* is the equivalent of *si destituti fuissent*. The future force of the gerundivum, for which see the notes ad 15.5.8, 18.2.3 and 20.2.4, is brought out clearly by 26.9.5 *destituendo iam et casuro*; Szantyr 374. The infin. praes. is used here instead of the infin. fut. *cessuros*, which Amm. avoids altogether. See the note ad 17.12.11 and Szantyr 357-8.

secus atque rebatur evenit Cf. 31.3.6 *verum longe aliter, quam rebatur, evenit*.

11. 25 *cum...remissius pugnaretur* Similarly during the siege of Aquileia (21.12) the attackers changed their tactics after fruitless attempts to storm the city, and tried to starve the defenders into submission: 21.12.15 *quod ubi patrare non poterat...obsideri remissius coepta est*.

umente caelo undantes nubes cum tenebris...minacibus A high-flown description reminiscent of Verg. *A.* 4.351-2 *quotiens umentibus umbris/nox operit terras*. For *umente caelo* cf. Flor. *Epit.* 1.20.2 (2.4.2) *Alpina corpora umenti caelo* ('in a humid climate') *educata*. Tacitus describes similar circumstances in *Hist.* 3.50.1 *ceterum propinqua hieme et umentibus Pado campis*.

immaduerat solum During Julian's expedition the army met with the same difficulties: *quodque liquentibus iam brumae pruinis* (i.e. after the spring) *omne immaduerat solum* (24.8.2).

luti glutinosa mollities The phrase is probably taken from Solinus' description of *bitumen* (1.56): *bitumen in Iudaea...lentum mollitie glutinosa*, cf. 23.6.16 *hic et naphtha gignitur picea specie glutinosa, similis ipsa quoque bitumini*. In 16.12.59 Amm. tells how king Chnodomarius fell from his horse in a marshy region near the Rhine: *calcata mollitie glutinosa equo est evolutus*.

regiones pinguissimi caespitis Amm. speaks about the *praepinguis caespes* of Egypt in 22.15.13 and calls the Persian district of Carmania *caespitisque ubere...fecunda* (23.6.48). Thracia, too, *caespitis est feracissimi* (31.3.8).

et super his...perterrebant This sentence, leading up to the digression about the rainbow, closely resembles the introduction to the excursus on eclipses in 20.3: *intermicabant iugiter stellae; hisque terroribus accedebat...pavidae mentes hominum*. Note the effective 'Klangmalerei' in *iugi fragore tonitrua fulgoraque*.

XI. 26-30 The digression on the rainbow may be analyzed as follows:
§ 26 Cause of the appearance of the rainbow; explanation of its semicircular form;
§ 27 Enumeration of its colours;
§ 28 Explanation of the colours;
§ 29 An alternative theory of its appearance and its colours;
§ 30 The rainbow as an *omen*. Transition to the narrative.

Amm.'s motive to offer this digression is fairly obvious. The rainbow is *indicium permutationis aurae*, as he remarks himself in § 30, which is reminiscent of *remedia permutatae rei* in Julian's first speech as Augustus (20.5.3). Moreover, Iris' role in divine interventions in human affairs is common knowledge. By inserting this excursus here, he gives this book an impressive conclusion. The spectacle of Iris symbolizes and celebrates Julian's succession as sole emperor and provides it with divine sanction.
It has been noticed long ago that Amm.'s digression shows strong

similarities with Aëtius' account of the iris (*Pl.* 3.5.3–9, Diels 372–4). We must suppose that either Aëtius himself or a doxographer working along the same lines furnished the material. The similarities, to which attention will be given in the commentary, are manifest both in the disposition and in the wording of the digression. In Aëtius there is a general discussion of the phenomenon, followed by a number of alternative theories. Amm. reduces the number of alternative doxai to one, namely that of Anaximenes (§ 29), who comes first in Aëtius' account, while his remark on the colours of the rainbow in § 29 is possibly influenced by the doxa of Metrodorus, also quoted in Aëtius. The general explanation follows the reflection theory, of which Arist. gives a precise and detailed version in *Mete.* 3.2–5, 371 b 18 – 377 a 29. According to this theory, the visual rays (ὄψις) emanating from the eyes are reflected by the myriad drops of moisture in a cloud facing the sun (ἀνάκλασις). Each of these drops acts like a tiny mirror, in which, because of its smallness, not the complete form, but only the colour of the sun is reflected. Together these mirrors provide one continuous image, the rainbow. For Aristotle's explanation of the different colours see the comm. on § 28 *quod solis obnoxia claritudini.*

Amm.'s exposition is basically in accordance with this theory, although he does not explicitly mention ἀνάκλασις as the cause of the phenomenon. The notion is, however, implied in expressions like *splendida facta* (§ 26), *intermicante asperginum densitate* (§ 28), and above all, in the term *reciprocatio* (§ 28). The alternative theory given by Amm. in § 29 is virtually identical with Anaximenes' doxa, quoted in the comm. ad loc. Anaximenes distinguished two (groups of) colours, dominated, respectively, by the sun, where its rays penetrate the cloud, or by the darkness of the cloud, where it is stronger than the sun's rays. Cf. Schol. Arat. 940 p. 515f M, quoted by Gilbert, 1907, 606 n. 1: ὅθεν τὸ μὲν πρότερον αὐτοῦ τοῦ ἡλίου φοινικοῦν φαίνεται διακαιόμενον ὑπὸ τῶν ἀκτίνων, τὸ δὲ μέλαν κατακρατούμενον ὑπὸ τῆς ὑγρότητος. This is in complete accordance with the second half of § 29, including the comparison with the colour of the waves of the sea. Since Anaximenes' doxa concerning the colours is not mentioned under his name in Aëtius, Amm. either incorporated the similar theory of Metrodorus, quoted there, into his alternative version or had independent information on this subject.

Another difference between Amm. and Aëtius concerns the number of colours mentioned. It is remarkable that Greek authors distinguish two or three basic colours, whereas in Latin texts, Seneca *Nat.* 1. 3–8 and Amm., the rainbow is analyzed into five or six colours.

It is likely that Amm. knew Seneca's treatise on the rainbow, but he did not follow the text at all closely. He even left out the theory to which Seneca himself subscribed: 1.5.13 *in eadem sententia sum qua Posidonius, ut arcum iudicem fieri nube formata in modum concavi speculi et rotundi, cui forma sit partis e pila secta* ('a segment of a sphere'). This mirror theory implies that the cloud as a whole, not the separate drops, acts as a mirror. The difference in the apparent size between the sun and the rainbow, its semicircular form and the differences in colour are caused by the concave form of this mirror, which distorts the mirrored object. This theory, to which Seneca returns several times, is, pace Szidat, not represented in Amm.'s account of the rainbow.

XI. 26 *accedebant arcus caelestis (-es Seyfarth) conspectus assidui* Both in the text of his Teubner edition and in his bilingual edition Seyfarth prints *arcus caelestes conspectus assidui*, in which *conspectus assidui* must be interpreted as a gen qual., deviating from the reading *caelestis*, which Clark printed without mentioning any varia lectio. The ms. reading (if that is what it is!) *arcus caelestis* can be kept without difficulty. The plural *conspectus* is rare, but attested in Amm.: *ut lucifugae vitantes multitudinis laesae conspectus* (16.7.7) and in late authors like Faust. Rei. (nos) *in die iudicii purissimis angelorum conspectibus offerendi* (*serm.* 12, p. 268.9) and Cassiod. *publicis exhibere conspectibus* (*var.* 9.22.5). Amm. uses both *arcus caelestis* and *iris* in his digression, in conformity with the practice of late Latin authors, who have *iris* as often as *arcus*, or indeed more often, cf. Hier. *in Ezech.* 1.28, p. 31a *arcus similitudinem quae volgo iris dicitur*. Authors of the classical period prefer *arcus*. The adjective *caelestis* is added quite often by Pliny (e.g. *Nat.* 12.110, 17.39, 24.113). *Iris caelestis* is found only in Greg. Tur. *HF* 6.44; TLL II 478.68 sqq. As Szidat points out, the rainy season in Mesopotamia sets in during the second half of November. This, combined with the fact that the rainbow is seen most often after the autumnal equinox (Plin. *Nat.* 2.151 *fiunt autem hieme maxime ab equinoctio autumnali die decrescente*), accounts for *conspectus assidui*.

quae species unde ita figurari est solita Amm. uses *species* for a natural phenomenon again in his digression on comets (25.10.3): *hanc speciem tunc apparere, cum* e.q.s. Cicero in N.D. 3.51 writes *cur autem arqui species non in deorum numero reponatur?* There the connotation of beauty is present, as is shown by the following words *est enim pulchra*.

Unde refers to the physical explanation of the conditions under which the rainbow appears, *ita* to its form. The transition from the first question to the second is formed by *ideo spatioso curvamine sinuosam* below. For *figurari* cf. 26.8.9 *quod machinae genus...ideo figuratur hac specie* and 29.5.41 *aciem rotundo habitu figuratam*.

expositio brevis ostendet The profession of brevity is a standard element in digressions: 19.4.1, 23.4.1 (*breviter*), 27.4.1 (*per brevem excessum*) and see Rosen, 1982, 79-80 with lit.

halitus terrae calidiores et umoris spiramina Cf. Aëtius 3.5.6 (Diels, 1958, 372) δεῖ γὰρ ἐπινοῆσαι τὴν ὑγρὰν ἀναθυμίασιν εἰς νέφος μεταβάλλουσαν, εἶτα ἐκ τούτου κατὰ βραχὺ εἰς μικρὰς ῥανίδας νοτιζούσας. Amm.'s division seems to run parallel to the distinction found in Arist. *Mete.* 1.4, 341 b Θερμαινομένης γὰρ τῆς γῆς ὑπὸ τοῦ ἡλίου τὴν ἀναθυμίασιν ἀναγκαῖον γίγνεσθαι ... διπλῆν, τὴν μὲν ἀτμιδωδεστέραν ('vaporous') τὴν δὲ πνευματωδεστέραν ('like wind'). It is a fundamental distinction in explaining meteorological phenomena. The hot and dry exhalations cause winds, thunder and lightning, the moist vapours produce clouds. Since clouds are a prerequisite for the formation of the rainbow, it is understandable that the moist exhalations are mentioned by Amm. The dry and hot exhalations play no part, and are accordingly left out by Aëtius. Both types of exhalation are mentioned frequently by Latin authors, e.g. Cic. *Div.* 2.44 and N.D. 2.25, where see Pease's notes, Lucr. 6.476 sqq., Sen. *Nat.* 1.7, 2.30, 2.54, Apul. *Mun.* 305: *exhalationes duas physici esse dicunt...harum altera arida est atque fumo consimilis...altera umida et egelida.*

Amm. mentions the *halitus* also in his digressions on Persia, 23.6.17 *hiatus...conspicitur terrae, unde halitus letalis exsurgens* e.q.s. and on comets, 25.10.3 *alii eos arbitrantur ex halitu sicciore terrarum ignescere.* According to Hagendahl, 1921, 36, *spiramen* is a poeticism, which found its way into Latin prose after Arnobius. Amm. uses it for breezes in 17.7.11 *plerumque observatur terra tremente ventorum apud nos spiramina nulla sentiri,* for bodily excretions in 19.4.6 *affirmant etiam aliqui terrarum halitu densiore crassatum aera emittendis corporis spiraminibus resistentem necare nonnullos,* and vapours, as in the present text, *quod et concrescat aer ex umorum spiramine saepe densetus* (22.8.46). For the human breath he prefers *spiramentum* (14.7.15, 28.1.47, 29.1.40). Cf. Szantyr 544-5 and the note ad 17.7.11.

disiecta in aspergines parvas Cf. Aëtius εἰς μικρὰς ῥανίδας νοτιζούσας and Arist. *Mete.* 3.4, 373 b 19 ὅταν ἄρχηται ὕειν καὶ ἤδη μὲν συνιστῆται εἰς ψακάδας ὁ ἐν τοῖς νέφεσιν ἀήρ, μήπω δ'ὕῃ.

Amm. uses *aspergo* in the Persian digression, 23.6.67 on the fabrication of silk *aquarum asperginibus crebris* (cf. Solin. 50.2 *aquarum aspergine inundatis frondibus*), on pearls, 23.6.85 *humores ex lunari aspergine capiunt densius oscitando,* in the Thracian digression, 27.4.14 *perenni viriditate roris asperginibus gelidis corpora constringente* and below § 28 *intermicante asperginum densitate.* Cf. Lucr. 6.524-6:
> *hic ubi sol radiis tempestatem inter opacam*
> *adversa fulsit nimborum aspergine contra*
> *tum color in nigris exsistit nubibus arci.*

radiorum fusione splendida facta Normally, *fusio* is used of liquids. In

Chalcid. *comm.* 248, p. 258.22 Waszink, it is used of light; TLL VI 1655.55 sqq. The expression points to the reflection theory; see the introduction to the digression.

supinantur volubiliter contra ipsum igneum orbem An enigmatical statement. It is a basic fact that the rainbow is formed opposite the sun. Cf. Aëtius 3.5.6 ἀνάγκη πᾶσα Ἶριν ἀντικρὺς ἡλίου φαίνεσθαι, Sen. *Nat.* 1.3.11 *numquam non adversa soli est,* Lucr. 6.525 quoted above and Verg. *A.* 4.701 (Iris) *mille trahens varios adverso sole colores.* But what is the meaning of *supinari*? *Supinus* and its derivatives always indicate a horizontal position, whereas the screen of moisture on which the rainbow is formed is vertical. Possibly Amm. means to say that the *halitus et spiramina,* after their upward movement assume a horizontal position and form the rainbow, the shape of which is determined by the shape of the celestial vault. As an alternative, one may wonder if Amm. does not attribute to *supinari* the meaning of ὑπτιάζεσθαι found in Phlp. *in Mete.* 21.11 (the shadow cast by an object of a size equal to that of the source of light is cylindrical) ὡς μήτε συννεύειν ('converge') προϊούσας (sc. τὰς ἀκτῖνας) μήτε τοὔμπαλιν ὑπτιάζεσθαι ('diverge'). The 'spreading out' of the drops of moisture would follow naturally on *disiecta* as opposed to *conglobata* in the preceding clause. *Volubiliter* probably refers to the swift movement of the raindrops. Cf. Lucr. 3.189–90 *aqua...tantillo momine flutat/quippe volubilibus parvisque creata figuris.* For *igneus orbis* cf. 20.3.3.

ideo spatioso curvamine sinuosam The form of the rainbow is the subject of lengthy discussions in Arist. *Mete* 3.5, 375 b 16 sqq. and Sen. *Nat.* 1.8, in which the authors seek an answer to the question why the rainbow is never greater than a semicircle. Amm. tries to explain why it is a segment of a circle. For *curvamen* cf. 20.3.8 and Ov. *Met.* 11.590 *Iris et arcuato caelum curvamine signans.*

quod in nostro panditur mundo, quem sphaerae dimidiae parti rationes physicae superponunt Amm., or his source, possibly had in mind the opening phrase of the chapter in Arist. *Mete.* on the form of the iris (3.5, 375 b 19): ἡμισφαιρίου γὰρ ὄντος ἐπὶ τοῦ ὁρίζοντος κύκλου e.q.s. Amm. seems to mean that the iris is a semicircle, because it follows the outline of heaven, which is a hemisphere placed over our world. If so, he should have written 'cui sphaerae dimidiae partem ... superponunt'. Alternatively, *sphaerae dimidiae pars* may be taken to mean 'that half of the terrestrial globe on which we live', cf. 20.3.8 *sphaerae inferioris curvamine,* referring to the earth. In that case *in nostro...mundo* means 'in that part of heaven that stretches above our earth (and is visible to us)'. A third possibility would be that *mundus* refers to the surface of the celestial hemisphere, 'the heaven that is placed over the hemisphere'. In any case Amm. connects the semicircular form of the rainbow with the spherical form of the heaven above us, but his terminology is far from clear.

rationes physicae superponunt The reference to the doxographical tradition may be compared with e.g. *geometrica ratio...appellat* in 20.3.2. The daring personification has a parallel in 22.2.3 *Triptolemi curru quem...aeriis serpentibus et pinnigeris fabulosa vetustas imponit* and 31.4.6 *resipiscant tandem memoriae veteres Medicas acies ductantes ad Graeciam.* More examples in Blomgren 83-94 and cf. the note ad 17.4.11.

XI. 27 This section, in which the colours are enumerated, shows strong similarities with Sen. *Nat.* 1.3.12: *Varietas autem non ob aliam causam fit quam quia pars coloris a sole est, pars a nube illa; umor modo caeruleas lineas, modo virides, modo purpurae similes et luteas aut igneas ducit, duobus coloribus hanc varietatem efficientibus, remisso* ('subdued') *et intento* ('intense'). As Szidat remarks, this also helps to explain the order in which the colours are enumerated. They form two groups, of which the first (*lutea, flavescens vel fulva, punicea*) is dominated by the intense colour of the sun, the second (*purpurea, caerulo concreta et viridi*) by the subdued colour of the cloud. Within the first group the colours are given in ascending order of intensity, which is at its strongest in the red band. In the second group the colours are in descending order, the influence of the cloud being at its lowest in the blue and green bands. The spectrum as described by Seneca, and even more by Amm., is already very close to the modern spectrum with its seven colours: red, orange, yellow, green, blue, indigo and violet. See for the development of Greek and Latin colour names Vels Heyn, 1951, 97-102. André, 1949, 13 has a diagram showing that in Greek texts three basic colours are distinguished, viz. violet (πορφυροῦς, ἀλουργής), green-blue (πράσινος, κυανοῦς) and red (φοινικοῦς, ἐρυθρός). Aristotle *Mete.* 3.2, 371 b 33 explicitly calls the rainbow τρίχρως, cf. Gilbert, 1907, 610. Seneca and Amm. differentiate further and distinguish five and six colours, respectively.

quantum mortalis oculus contuetur A similar reservation follows in the next section: *ut terrenae existimant mentes.* There Amm. is dealing with the explanation of the colours, here he speaks about the colours as we see them. We may compare the remark at the end of the digression on eclipses (20.3.12): *ita videri nostris obtutibus.*

prima lutea visitur For the use of ordinalia in the enumeration cf. Aët. 3.5.7-8 τὸ μὲν πρῶτον φοινικοῦν, τὸ δὲ δεύτερον ἀλουργὲς καὶ πορφυροῦν, τὸ δὲ τρίτον κυανοῦν καὶ πράσινον. In the interesting discussion about Greek and Latin names of colours in Gel. 2.26 *luteus* is mentioned, along with *fulvus, flavus* and many others, as a shade of red; compare Vels Heyn, 1951, 98-99. The colours differ from red *aut acuentes eum* (sc. the colour red) *quasi incendentes, aut cum colore viridi miscentes aut nigro infuscantes aut virenti sensim albo illuminantes* (§ 8). It is probable, in view of the etymological connection *luteus – dilutus* alluded to in the next section, which is found in the same chapter of Gel. (*luteus contra rufus color est dilutior* § 15), that Amm. was familiar with this discussion and wanted to present the colours of the first three bands of the rainbow as different shades of red. As André, 1949, 152 points out, the term *luteus* refers to the yellow band. Amm. makes a finer distinction than Seneca in *Nat.* 1.3.12, who mentions only *luteus* in between *viridis* and *igneus* ('red'), whereas Amm. distinguishes *luteus* and *flavescens vel fulva* between green and red.

secunda flavescens vel fulva   See for *flavus*, with its derivatives, and *fulvus* André, 1949, 128-136. As we saw, both are described as shades of red in Gel. 2.26.8, the distinction being that *flavus* is a mixture of green, red and white (§ 12), whereas *fulvus* is *de rufo atque viridi mixtus* (§ 11). Together they indicate the orange band of the rainbow. *Vel* suggests that Amm. does not intend to differentiate between the two colours. Accordingly, in the next section he uses only the term *fulva*.

punicea tertia   André, 1949, 88-90. Gel. 2.26.9 calls it the Latin equivalent of φοῖνιξ, indicating *exuberantiam splendoremque...ruboris*.

quarta purpurea   This is the violet band at the opposite end of the spectrum. For its place in the series it may be compared to Aëtius, who mentions it after φοινικοῦν and before κυανοῦν καὶ πράσινον. André's remark (p. 95) "Ammien Marcellin, xx, 11, 27, place correctement *purpureus* entre le rouge (*puniceus*) et le bleu (*caeruleus*)" is understandable insofar as the colour *purpureus* designates shades ranging from violet to red. It does not, of course, apply to the place of the red band in the rainbow. For *purpureus* and related terms see Gipper, 1964 and Edgeworth, 1979.

postrema caerulo concreta et viridi   Szidat interprets *concretus* as "verdunkelt", "dunkel", as in Cic. *Div.* 1.18 and 1.130, and sees in it a reference to the bipartition of the colours into a lighter and a darker group. This does not seem to be correct. If Amm. had wanted to distinguish between lighter and darker colours, he would have done so probably in connexion with the first and darkest of these colours, viz. violet (*purpurea*). Moreover, in § 28 blue and green are expressly said to be lighter than purple: *qui color, quanto magis diffunditur, concedit in caerulum et virentem*. And finally, if we take *concretus* absolutely, the ablatives *caerulo* and *viridi* are left isolated in the sentence. It is better therefore to interpret the phrase as a description of the blue and green bands in the rainbow, seen as a mixture or combination of these colours, as e.g. in Aët. 3.5.7 τὸ δὲ τρίτον κυανοῦν καὶ πράσινον.

XI. 28 *hac autem mixta pulchritudine temperatur ideo*   Amm. may have had in mind Ov. *Met.* 6.65-67, quoted in Sen. *Nat.* 1.3.4

diversi niteant cum mille colores,
transitus ipse tamen spectantia lumina fallit:
usque adeo quod tangit idem est, tamen ultima distant.

Elsewhere in Amm. *temperare* and its derivatives mean 'to moderate', 'to soften', as e.g. in 18.10.4 *humanitate eum et moribus iam placidis magnitudinem temperasse fortunae.* In 23.6.3 *temperator* means 'a ruler'. With the meaning required in this context ('to mix') only 22.8.46 (Pontus) *irruentium undarum magnitudine temperatur* may be compared.

ut terrenae existimant mentes   Cf. *quantum mortalis oculus contuetur* in § 27 and 14.11.25 (Adrastia) *ius quoddam sublime numinis efficacis humanarum mentium opinione lunari circulo superpositum.*

quod prima eius pars dilutior cernitur aeri concolor circumfuso   For the etymological connection *luteus - dilutus* see ad § 27. *Dilutior* has the same meaning 'lighter', 'less dark' as in 20.3.4. The first three bands are differentiated according to the intensity of their colours. The purple band is the purest (see below), the yellow band is less dark by its contact with the surrounding air, the orange band stands half-way between the two. The contact with the air makes the colour lighter, because the air itself is white, as Aristotle says in the opening sentence of his little treatise *De coloribus*, 791 a 2-3 ἀὴρ μὲν γὰρ καὶ ὕδωρ καθ' ἑαυτὰ τῇ φύσει λευκά, τὸ δὲ πῦρ καὶ ὁ ἥλιος ξανθά.

Szidat sees in *dilutior* a reference to the transparence of the cloud. Indeed, the difference in density between parts of the cloud is mentioned among the reasons for the *varietas arcus* in Sen. *Nat.* 1.3.1, and Amm. seems to allude to this theory in his account of the violet band (*intermicante asperginum densitate* below). Still, it seems preferable to start from *aeri concolor circumfuso*, which Amm. himself gives as an explanation for the lightness of the yellow band.

For *concolor* see Hagendahl, 1921, 52.

sequens fulva, id est paulo excitatior quam lutea   For *excitatus* see TLL V 2.1263.21 sqq. The word is used of sounds, e.g. Cic. *Rep.* 6.18 *acuto et excitato movetur sono*, smells, e.g. Plin. *Nat.* 20.182 *excitatissimi odoris* and only metaphorically of light in Quint. *Inst.* 12.10.49 *haec excitatiora lumina* ("such specially brilliant forms of ornament", Butler). Nowhere else it is found in connection with colour.

quod solis obnoxia claritudini pro reciprocatione spiritus fulgores eius purissime e regione deflorat   According to Aristotle, *Mete.* 3.4, 374 b 10, the colour red is caused by the fusion of the sun's rays with the dark cloud (τὸ λαμπρὸν ἐν τῷ μέλανι ἢ διὰ τοῦ μέλανος χρῶμα ποιεῖ φοινικοῦν). The darker shades of the two other colours distinguished by Arist. are explained by the fact that ἡ ὄψις ἐκτεινομένη ἀσθενεστέρα γίγνεται καὶ ἐλάττων, objects seen at a greater distance seem to be darker. Gilbert, 1907, 609 concludes: "er nimmt also an dass das Rot, die äussere Peripherie des Halbkreises ..., dem Blick näher ist, bzw. dass der Blick sich ihm zuerst zuwendet, während das nach innen folgende πράσινον ferner, oder dem Blick weniger zugänglich ist ... Die dritte, die innere Farbe, τὸ πορφυροῦν, beruht dann auf noch grössere Schwäche des Blickes".

In Aët. 3.5.8 this is formulated as follows: μήποτε ('perhaps') τὸ μὲν φοινικοῦν, ὅτι ἡ λαμπρότης τοῦ ἡλίου προσπεσοῦσα καὶ ἡ ἀκραιφνὴς λαμπηδὼν ἀνακλωμένη ἐρυθρὸν ποιεῖ καὶ φοινικοῦν τὸ χρῶμα. Amm.'s version is closely similar. With προσπεσοῦσα we may compare *solis obnoxia claritudini*, repeated by *e regione*, and with ἡ ἀκραιφνὴς λαμπηδὼν *fulgores eius* and *purissime*. *Pro reciprocatione spiritus* is probably the equivalent of ἀνακλωμένη, *reciprocatio* being the term for a "movement in the reverse direction" (OLD), used of the tidal flow by Pliny (*observata aestus reciprocatione, Nat.* 9.29). Amm.'s use of the verb *reciprocare* is in accordance with this meaning (26.7.15, 29.5.25). Therefore there seems to be no reason to doubt the correctness of *reciprocatio*. The preposition *pro*, however, seems to be otiose. As G. Bakkum has suggested privately, it may have arisen from a supralinear correction *pro* of a corrupt reading *recicatione*, mistaken for the preposition and placed before the noun, which was then 'normalized' into V's *reticatione*. For *spiritus*, where one would expect *aer* as the medium through which the light is reflected, Szidat aptly compares 19.4.8 *concreto spiritu et crassato* as a variation of *crassatum aera* in 19.4.6. The use of the genitive is difficult to explain. In any case it is better understood as a subiectivus than as an obiectivus, as Szidat does. Cf. also Plin. *Nat.* 2.10 quoted ad 20.3.12.

Purissime is Erfurdt's conjecture for V's *purissimem*. In view of Aëtius' ἀκραιφνὴς λαμπηδών *fulgorem eius purissimum* would be an attractive alternative. Note that *fulgor* is always (10 times) used in the singular in Amm., even when the source of the brilliance is plural, as in 25.1.1 *noctem nullo siderum fulgore splendentem*.

The verb *deflorare* is not found before Symmachus. The meaning required here is described in TLL V 1.362.21 as "alqd vel alqm dignitate, honore, splendore privare". The cloud, in reflecting the sun's rays, takes away some of its brilliance.

intermicante asperginum densitate, per quas oritur, radiorum splendorem concipiens Cf. §26 *disiecta in aspergines parvas ac radiorum fusione splendida facta...irimque conformant.* The parallel confirms Madvig's correction *splendorem concipiens* for V's *splendorum conspiciens* and suggests for *per quas oritur* the meaning 'to which it owes its existence'. In Sen. *Nat.* 1.3.8-9 and again in 1.5.4-6 the question is debated how the myriads of drops, each of which mirrors the sun's light, can form one uninterrupted band of colour. Amm., perhaps wisely, sidesteps the issue.

For *intermicare* see Hagendahl, 1921, 64.

aspectum flammeo propriorem In his bilingual edition Seyfarth printed *propiorem* (EBAG). In view of the dative *flammeo* this is distinctly better. Amm. uses *proprius* with the genitive (19.12.18 *quod iudicis lenti...est proprium*) and *propior* with the dative (16.7.2 *ut erat vanidicus et amenti propior*, although here again, and in 26.1.1, V has a form of *proprius*). Cf. also *proximos... albo colores* in the next section. For *flammeus* see the note ad 20.6.3 and André, 1949, 115-6, who describes the colour as "orange vif, très proche du rouge", but also notes that it is used in connection with purple, quoting V. Fl. 5.360-1 *externo iam flammea murice cerno / tegmina* and Stat. *Ach.* 1.297 *illius et roseo flammatur purpura vultu.*

quanto magis diffunditur For *diffundere* in connection with "res caelestes" see TLL V 1.1108.44 sqq. Amm. seems to be of the opinion that the colours, spreading over a wider surface, gradually lose their intensity.

XI. 29 The doxa reported in this section is very close to that of Anaximenes, quoted in Aët. 3.5.10: 'Ἀναξιμένης ἶριν γίγνεσθαι κατ' αὐγασμὸν ἡλίου πρὸς νέφει πυκνῷ καὶ παχεῖ καὶ μέλανι παρὰ τὸ μὴ δύνασθαι τὰς ἀκτῖνας εἰς τὸ πέραν διακόπτειν ἐπισυνισταμένας αὐτῷ .

For the explanation of the colours see the general introduction to this digression.

rebus apparere mundanis This expression stands isolated, but Amm. likes to employ *mundanus* especially in his digressions. Cf. e.g. the phrase *mundani motus et siderum* in 22.16.17, 23.6.33 and 26.1.8. It is found twice in the concluding section on comets, which resembles the present passage both in contents and phraseology (25.10.3): *sedit quorundam opinioni hanc speciem tunc apparere, cum erecta solito celsius nubes aeternorum ignium vicinitate colluceat, vel certe stellas esse quasdam ceteris similes, quarum ortus obitusque...humanis mentibus ignorari. Plura alia de cometis apud peritos mundanae rationis sunt lecta, quae digerere nunc vetat aliorsum oratio properans.*

altius delatae nubi crassae radii solis infusi Cf. 25.10.3 quoted above and 20.3.6 *si erecta solito celsius nubes aeternorum ignium propinquitate collucens* e.q.s. The same phenomenon is adduced to explain three different 'mirabilia', the parhelion, the iris and the comets.

lucem iniecerint liquidam The adjective refers to the brilliance of the light, as in 17.7.5 *aer iam sudus et liquidus.* Cf. Lucr. 5.281 *largus item liquidi fons luminis, aetherius sol*, Sil. 4.103 *liquida, non ullis nubibus aethra* and Suet. *Aug.* 95 *liquido ac puro sereno circulus...solem ambiit.*

in se conglobata nimio splendescit attritu Amm. always uses *conglobatus* of soldiers in close array, except here and in § 26 above. It is the equivalent of Aëtius' ἐπισυνισταμένας. *In se* is Amm.'s own addition; the complement of ἐπισυνισταμένας in the Greek text, αὐτῷ, refers of course to νέφος. Again the digression occasioned by the appearance of the shooting star reported in 25.2.4 is strikingly similar: *scintillas quidam putant ab aetherio candentes vigore parumque porrectius tendere sufficientes exstingui vel certe radiorum flammas iniectas nubibus densis acri scintillare contactu aut, cum lumen aliquod cohaeserit nubi...in aerium solvitur corpus ad substantiam migrans, cuius attritu incaluit nimio* (25.2.6). 'Friction', *attritus*, is the common element in the two phenomena, which in the case of the rainbow causes the sun's rays to glow inside the cloud, and in the case of the shooting star causes the transmutation of the ethereal sparks into the element of *aer*.

proximos...albo colores In conformity with the bipartition of the colours in § 27-8, we must think of *luteus, fulvus* and *puniceus*.

a sole sublimiore decerpit The verb echoes *deflorat* in § 28. The sun stands above the cloud, which explains why in the rainbow red, orange and yellow form the outer bands of the iris.

subvirides...a nubis similitudine superiectae For *subviridis* see André, 1949, 225-6. With this term Amm. indicates green, blue and violet. *Superiectae* does not stand in opposition to *a sole sublimiore*, but refers to *iniecerint*. The cloud 'envelops' the light thrown into it by the sun's rays. Cf. 20.3.10 *(luna) nasci autem putatur, cum...superiectum egerit solem.*

ubi candidae sunt undae The waves breaking on the shore are white, because they are pierced by the sun's rays. At a greater distance, where the sun's rays cannot penetrate the water, their colour is pure (*sine ulla concretione*) blue. A similar observation is used by Lucretius in order to prove that atoms are without colour (2.772-3): *quod si caeruleis constarent aequora ponti / seminibus, nullo possent albescere pacto*. Cf. also Cic. *Ac.* 2.105 *mare...qua a sole collucet, albescit et vibrat dissimileque est proximo et continenti*.

XI. 30 *indicium est permutationis aurae, ut diximus* This has not been said in so many words, but is implied in the description of the start of the rainy season (§ 25). On the rainbow as a meteorological sign see Sen. *Nat.* 1.8.8, Weicker, 1916, 2042.19-28. The most important passages are Hom *Il*.17.547-9, quoted below, and Verg. *G*. 1.380/1 *et bibit ingens / arcus*.

In his digression on eclipses Amm. had left the interpretation of the phenomenon as an *omen* to his readers. Here he is more explicit. *Permutatio* refers the reader to Julian's first speech as Augustus, 20.5.3 *remedia permutatae rei*, where see the note.

a sudo aere...caelum Cf. 17.7.5 *aer iam sudus et liquidus* and Apul. *Met.* 11.7 *caelum...nubilosa caligine disiecta nudo sudoque luminis proprii splendore candebat. Concretus* is here equivalent to *crassatus*, as in 19.4.8. *Mutans in serenam laetitiam caeli* is a daring and vivid phrase, see TLL VII 2.878.75-82 for some, not very close, parallels.

apud poetas legimus For a survey of these passages see Sabbah 550 n. 33 (with lit.), who quotes Servius *Aen*. 5.606 and 9.2, where it is said that Iris always brings discord. This also applies to the present appearance of Iris, but the *permutatio* is no doubt seen as a change for the better by Amm. The most important passage is, of course, Hom. *Il*. 17.547-9

ἠύτε πορφυρέην Ἶριν θνητοῖσι τανύσσῃ
Ζεὺς ἐξ οὐρανόθεν, τέρας ἔμμεναι ἢ πολέμοιο
ἢ καὶ χειμῶνος δυσθαλπέος.

cum praesentium rerum verti necesse sit status Sabbah rightly draws attention to the words *necesse sit*, which once again emphasize that Julian's accession to the throne was not an ordinary usurpation of power, but part of the divine plan, "il (le symbole) situe majestueusement les événements dans le projet divin d'un changement universel".

For *rerum praesentium status* cf. 18.7.10 and 25.9.4, where the inhabitants of Nisibis, who are forced to leave their city, do so *detestantes rerum praesentium statum*. *Necesse est* is found with a different meaning in 17.11.1 ('it was his duty'), where Julian is described as a subservient figure at Constantius' court: *erat enim necesse tamquam apparitorem Caesarem super omnibus gestis ad Augusti referre scientiam*.

suppetunt aliae multae opiniones et variae...festinante We may think e.g. of Posidonius' theory, treated at length by Seneca in *Nat.* 1.5.10–14, and of the doxai of Anaxagoras and Metrodorus reported by Aëtius. Both the *praeteritio* and the insistence on *brevitas* and swiftness are found again at the conclusion of the digression on comets, 25.10.3, quoted ad § 29 *rebus apparere mundanis*. For these formulaic endings see Rosen, 1982, 80, with lit.

XI. 31 The picture of Constantius in § 31 and 32 is one of total confusion. He fears not only surprise attacks from the Persians but even a mutiny of his own soldiers and he is acutely aware of his failure. To this description Amm. adds his personal comment in a series of adjectives that leave no room for doubt about his final judgment of Constantius as a military leader (*vano, aerumnosa, atrocia diuque deflenda*).

His ac talibus imperator inter spem metumque iactabatur Cf. Verg. *A.* 1.218 *spemque metumque inter dubii*, Liv. 8.13.17 *inter spem metumque suspensos animi*. The direct model seems to be Tac. *Hist.* 2.2.1 *his ac talibus inter spem metumque iactatum*. Amm. uses the expression again in 21.13.1 *his ac talibus eo* (Iuliano) *inter spem metumque nova negotia commovente*.

hiemis magnitudine Cf. 25.1.3 *vix toleranda aestuum magnitudine* and Cic. *Planc.* 96 *maritimos cursus praecludebat hiemis magnitudo*.

tumultum exasperati militis Cf. 25.9.4 *quo verbo exasperatus*. In classical prose this meaning is rare, but cf. Liv. 28.25.4 *ad quorum primum adventum exasperati animi, mox...leniti sunt*; TLL V 2.1187.46 sqq. Constantius' fear of a mutiny does not seem to be unjustified. Mutinies were not unprecedented of course (cf. 17.1.2 *petiturus ipse Mogontiacum... refragante vetabatur exercitu*), defects in military discipline were notorious (cf. 22.4.6 sqq.) and during the siege of Bezabde the soldiers had suffered many hardships.

urebat eius anxiam mentem For *urere* cf. ad 20.4.1 *urebant Iuliani virtutes*. There the emperor is consumed by envy, here by the awareness of his failure. "Comparat tacite Constantium Tiberio" (Gronovius), because Suet. *Tib.* 66.1 uses exactly the same phrase to describe Tiberius in the desperate days of his decline.

patefacta ianua...irritus propositi revertetur In § 24 Amm. had called Bezabde *velut insolubile claustrum*. For *irritus* + gen. cf. V. Max. 4.3 ext. 3 *propositi irritum dimisit, irritus consilii* in Vell. 2.63.2 and *inritus legationis* in Tac. *Hist.* 4.32.3. For *revertetur* in stead of *reverteretur* cf 14.11.7 q.v. and see Ehrismann 156–7.

XI. 32 *hiematurus Antiochiae redit in Syriam* Constantius arrived at Antioch (cf. the note ad § 11 for this city) probably very late in the year, for on December 17th he still was in Hierapolis (cf. *Cod Theod.* 7.4.6, correctly dated by Seeck, 1919, 208), some hundred miles away from Antioch.

aerumnosa perpessus vulnera Amm. uses this archaic adjective preferably of losses in battle, cf. 17.13.28 *post aerumnosa dispendia* and 27.1.1 *post aerumnosas iacturas et vulnera* (inflicted on the Alamanni by Julian). See De Jonge ad 15.4.10 *aerumnae*.

quasi fatali constellatione ita regente diversos eventus There are more personal comments of this type on Constantius, e.g. 15.3.3 *Constantius, quasi praescriptum fatorum ordinem convulsurus*, 15.5.18 *hac mole casus inopini icto Constantio quasi fulmine fati* and 16.10.1 *Constantius, quasi cluso* (Heraeus, *quam recluso* V) *Iani templo stratisque hostibus cunctis*. In these remarks Amm. suggests, without explicitly committing himself, that Fate is against Constantius.

Usually *constellatio* means 'horoscope', as in 29.2.27 and HA *Ael.* 4.5, *Gd.* 20.2. This is possible here too, but the more general meaning 'fate as ordained by the stars' seems more appropriate in this context. The combination *fatalis constellatio* is found in August. *civ.* 5.6 and *c. Faust.* 2.5.

ipsum Constantium...fortuna semper sequeretur afflictior In 16.10.2 Amm. writes in the same vein: *nec enim gentem ullam per se superavit*, adding *aut victam fortitudine suorum comperit ducum*. This is somewhat mitigated in the present text, where Amm. reluctantly admits that Constantius' generals were on occasion victorious. In the *elogium* of Constantius (21.16) his successes in establishing internal order are contrasted with his failures in external wars: *in externis bellis...fuit saucius et afflictus*. This may explain *diversos eventus*. In his *Ep. ad Ath.* 271 a Julian maintains that Constantius thought his own cruelty towards his family to be the reason of his failure against the Persians: τά τε ἐς τοὺς πολεμίους τοὺς Πέρσας οὐκ εὐτυχῶς πράττειν ἐκ τούτων ὑπολαμβάνει. For *fortuna afflictior* cf. the ominous sentence in 24.6.4 *tantumque a fortuna sperans* (Iulianus) *nondum afflicta*.

quod aliquotiens meminimus contigisse According to Ruf. Fest. 27, nine major battles were fought during the reign of Constantius. Seven of these were under the direction of Constantius' generals: *Constantius in Persas vario ac magis difficili pugnavit eventu. Praeter leves excubantium in limite congressiones acriori Marte noviens decertatum est, per duces suos septiens, ipse praesens bis adfuit.* Cf. Eadie, 1967, 149–151.

Bibliography

Aalto, P., *Untersuchungen über das lateinische Gerundium und Gerundivum*, Helsinki 1949.
Agozzino, T. and G. Piovene, *Ammiano Marcellino, Giuliano e il paganesimo morente. Antologia delle storie*, Turin 1972.
Alföldi, A., 'Die Ausgestaltung des monarchischen Zeremoniells am römischen Kaiserhofe', *MDAI(R)* 49 (1934) 3-118 = *Die monarchische Repräsentation im römischen Kaiserreiche*, Darmstadt 1980³, 3-118, cited as Alföldi, 1980³.
Alföldi, A., 'Ein spätrömisches Schildzeichen keltischer oder germanischer Herkunft', *Germania* 19 (1935) 324-328.
Alföldi, A., 'Insignien und Tracht der römischen Kaiser', *MDAI(R)* 50 (1935) 3-158 = *Die monarchische Repräsentation im römischen Kaiserreiche*, Darmstadt 1980³, 121-276, cited as Alföldi, 1980³.
Alföldi, A., *Die Kontorniaten. Ein verkanntes Propagandamittel der stadtrömischen heidnischen Aristokratie in ihrem Kampfe gegen das christliche Kaisertum*, Leipzig 1943.
Alföldi, A., 'Cornuti: A Teutonic Contingent in the Service of Constantine the Great and its Decisive Role in the Battle at the Milvian Bridge', *DOP* 13 (1959) 169-179.
André, J., *Étude sur les termes de couleur dans la langue latine*, Paris 1949.
Andreotti, R., 'Problemi del "suffragium" nell' imperatore Giuliano', *Atti 1° Convegno Internazionale Accademia Romanistica Costantiniana*, Perugia 1975, 3-26.
Angliviel de la Beaumelle, L., 'Remarques sur l'attitude d'Ammien Marcellin à l'égard du Christianisme', *Mélanges d'histoire ancienne offerts à William Seston*, Paris 1974, 15-23.
ANRW, *Aufstieg und Niedergang der Römischen Welt. Geschichte und Kultur Roms im Spiegel der neueren Forschung*, H. Temporini (ed.), Berlin 1972 ff.
Asdourian, P., *Die politische Beziehungen zwischen Armenien und Rom von 190 v. Chr. bis 428 n. Chr. Ein Abriss der armenischen Geschichte in dieser Periode*, Venice 1911.
Ashby, T., see S.B. Platner.
Astin, A.E., *Scipio Aemilianus*, Oxford 1967.
Athanassiadi-Fowden, P., *Julian and Hellenism. An Intellectual Biography*, Oxford 1981.
Aujoulat, N., 'Eusébie, Hélène et Julien, I: Le témoignage de Julien', *Byzantion* 53 (1983) 78-103 and 'II: Le témoignage des historiens', *ibid.*, 421-452.
Austin, N.J.E., *Ammianus on Warfare. An Investigation into Ammianus' Military Knowledge*, Brussels 1979.
Avenarius, G., *Lukians Schrift zur Geschichtsschreibung*, Diss. Frankfurt, Meisenheim 1956.
Avery, W.T., 'The *Adoratio Purpurae* and the Importance of the Imperial Purple in the Fourth Century of the Christian Era', *MAAR* 17 (1940) 66-80.

Baehrens, W.A., 'Bericht über die Literatur zu Ammianus Marcellinus 1910-1924', *JAW* 203 (1925) 45-90.
Baldwin, B., 'Some Addenda to the Prosopography of the Later Roman Empire', *Historia* 25 (1976) 118-121.
Baldwin, B., 'Acclamations in the *Historia Augusta*', *Athenaeum* 59 (1981) 138-149.
Barceló, P.A., *Roms auswärtige Beziehungen unter der Constantinischen Dynastie (306-363)*, Regensburg 1981.
Barnes, T.D., 'A Law of Julian', *CPh* 69 (1974) 288-291.
Baumgartner, A., 'Arsakes III', *RE* 2 (1895) 1269.
Baynes, N.H., 'Rome and Armenia in the Fourth Century', *EHR* 25 (1910) 625-643 = *Byzantine Studies and Other Essays*, London 1955, 186-208.
Bechert, T., *Römisches Germanien zwischen Rhein und Maas. Die Provinz Germania Inferior*, Munich 1982.
Behn, F., 'Die Musik im römischen Heere', *MZ* 7 (1912) 36-47.

Béranger, J., 'Le refus du pouvoir. Recherches sur l'aspect idéologique du principat', *MH* 5 (1948) 178-196 = *Principatus. Études de notions et d'histoire politiques dans l'Antiquité gréco-romaine*, F. Paschoud and P. Ducrey (eds.), Geneva 1975, 165-190.
Béranger, J., *Recherches sur l'aspect idéologique du Principat*, Basle 1953.
Béranger, J., 'Remarques sur la "Concordia" dans la propagande monétaire impériale et la nature du principat', *Beiträge zur Alten Geschichte und deren Nachleben, Festschrift für Franz Altheim zum 6.10.1968*, Ruth Stiehl and H.-E. Stier (eds.), Berlin 1969, I, 470-491 = Béranger, *Principatus*, 367-382.
Béranger, J., 'La terminologie impériale. Une application à Ammien Marcellin', *Mélanges d'histoire ancienne et d'archéologie offerts à Paul Collart*, Lausanne 1976, 47-60.
Berger, A., *Encyclopaedic Dictionary of Roman Law*, Philadelphia 1953 (repr. 1968).
BHAC, *Bonner Historia Augusta Colloquia, Antiquitas Reihe 4, Beiträge zur Historia Augusta-Forschung*, A. Alföldi and J.A. Straub (eds.), Bonn 1963 ff.
Bidez, J., *La vie de l'empereur Julien*, Paris 1930 (repr. 1965).
Bitter, N., *Kampfschilderungen bei Ammianus Marcellinus*, Bonn 1976.
Blockley, R.C., 'Constantius Gallus and Julian as Caesars of Constantius II', *Latomus* 31 (1972) 433-468.
Blockley, R.C., 'Tacitean Influence upon Ammianus Marcellinus', *Latomus* 32 (1973) 63-78.
Blockley, R.C., *Ammianus Marcellinus. A Study of his Historiography and Political Thought*, Brussels 1975.
Blockley, R.C., 'Ammianus Marcellinus on the Battle of Strasburg. Art and Analysis in the History', *Phoenix* 31 (1977) 218-231.
Blockley, R.C., 'Constantius II and his Generals', *Studies in Latin Literature and Roman History*, II, C. Deroux (ed.), Brussels 1980, 467-486, cited as Blockley, 1980 (1).
Blockley, R.C., *Ammianus Marcellinus. A Selection, with Introduction, Notes and Commentary*, Bristol 1980, cited as Blockley, 1980 (2).
Blomgren, S., *De sermone Ammiani Marcellini quaestiones variae*, Uppsala 1937.
Boak, A.E.R., 'Imperial Coronation Ceremonies of the Fifth and Sixth Centuries', *HSPh* 30 (1919) 37-47.
Bonanni, S., 'Ammiano Marcellino e i barbari', *RCCM* 23 (1981) 125-142.
Bonfils, G. de, *Il comes et quaestor nell' età della dinastia costantiniana*, Naples 1981.
Bonfils, G. de, 'Consistorium, consilium e consiglieri imperiali in Ammiano Marcellino', *Studi in onore di Arnaldo Biscardi*, III, Milan 1982, 263-275.
Bowersock, G.W., 'Gibbon and Julian', *Gibbon et Rome à la lumière de l'historiographie moderne*, P. Ducrey (ed.), Geneva 1977, 191-213.
Bowersock, G.W., *Julian the Apostate*, Cambridge Mass.-London 1978.
Braun, O., *Ausgewählte Akten Persischer Märtyrer*, Kempten-Munich 1915.
Brightman, F.E., 'Byzantine Imperial Coronations', *JThS* 2 (1901) 359-392.
Brok, M.F.A., 'Demonstratie met een brandpijl', *Hermeneus* 46 (1975) 321-325 (cf. also 48 (1976) 66 for some slight corrections).
Brok, M.F.A., 'Ein spätrömischer Brandpfeil nach Ammianus', *SJ* 35 (1978) 57-60.
Brok, M.F.A., 'Majestätsfrevel durch Missbrauch des Purpurs (Ammianus Marcellinus 16,8,8)', *Latomus* 41 (1982) 356-361.
Brouwer, M., 'Römische *Phalerae* und anderer Lederbeschlag aus dem Rhein', *OMRL* 63 (1982) 145-199.
Browning, R., *The Emperor Julian*, Berkeley-Los Angeles 1976.
Bulla, W.K., *Untersuchungen zu Ammianus Marcellinus*, Munich 1983.
Burian, J., 'Die kaiserliche Akklamation in der Spätantike. Ein Beitrag zur Untersuchung der *Historia Augusta*', *Eirene* 17 (1980) 17-43.
Bury, J.B., 'Magistri scriniorum, ΑΝΤΙΓΡΑΦΗΣ and ΡΕΦΕΡΕΝΔΑΡΙΟΙ', *HSPh* 21 (1910) 23-29.

Calboli, G., 'Ammian und die Geschichtsschreibung seiner Zeit', *Festschrift für Robert Muth*, P. Händel and W. Meid (eds.), Innsbruck 1983, 33-53.

Callu, J.-P., *Genio populi Romani (295–316)*. *Contribution à une histoire numismatique de la tétrarchie*, Paris 1960.
Caltabiano, M., 'La propaganda di Giuliano nella *Lettera agli Ateniesi*', *CISA*, II, *Propaganda e persuasione occulta nell' antichità*, Milan 1974, 123–138.
Caltabiano, M., 'Il comportamento di Giuliano in Gallia verso i suoi funzionari', *Acme* 32 (1979) 417–442.
Cameron, A. and A., 'Christianity and Tradition in the Historiography of the Late Empire', *CQ* n.s. 14 (1964) 316–328.
Camus, P.-M., *Ammien Marcellin. Témoin des courants culturels et religieux à la fin du IVe siècle*, Paris 1967.
Casson, L., *Travel in the Ancient World*, London 1979².
Češka, J., 'Ad Ammiani Marcellini libros XIV–XXI a W. Seyfarth novissime editos adnotationes criticae', *Eirene* 10 (1972) 9–20.
Chastagnol, A., 'Le diocèse civil d'Aquitaine au Bas-Empire', *BSAF* (1970) 272–292.
Chastagnol, A., 'Autour du thème du *princeps clausus*', *BHAC* 17, Bonn 1985, 149–161.
Chastagnol, A., see also A. Piganiol.
Chausserie-Laprée, J.-P., *L'expression narrative chez les historiens latins. Histoire d'un style*, Paris 1969.
Chiabò, M., *Index verborum Ammiani Marcellini*, 2 vols., Hildesheim-Zurich-New York 1983.
Chicca, F. del, '*Purpuratus*', *Sandalion* 5 (1982) 143–167.
Christlein, R., *Die Alamannen. Archäologie eines lebendigen Volkes*, Stuttgart 1979².
Cichocka, H., 'Die Konzeption des Exkurses im Geschichtswerk des Ammianus Marcellinus', *Eos* 63 (1975) 329–340.
Clark, C.U., *Ammiani Marcellini rerum gestarum libri qui supersunt*, Berlin 1910–1915 (repr. 1963).
Clauss, M., *Der magister officiorum in der Spätantike (4.–6. Jahrhundert). Das Amt und sein Einfluss auf die kaiserliche Politik*, Munich 1980.
Collot, C., 'La pratique et l'institution du *suffragium* au Bas-Empire', *RD* 43 (1965) 185–221.
Crook, J.A., *Consilium Principis. Imperial Councils and Counsellors from Augustus to Diocletian*, Cambridge 1955.
Crump, G.A., 'Ammianus and the late Roman Army', *Historia* 22 (1973) 91–103.
Crump, G.A., *Ammianus Marcellinus as a Military Historian*, Wiesbaden 1975.
Cupaiuolo, F., 'Caso, fato e fortuna nel pensiero di alcuni storici latini. Spunti e appunti', *BStudLat* 14 (1984) 3–38.

Dagron, G., *Naissance d'une capitale: Constantinople et ses institutions de 330 à 451*, Paris 1974.
Dauge, Y.A., *Le Barbare. Recherches sur la conception romaine de la barbarie et de la civilisation*, Brussels 1981.
Dellbrueck, R., *Spätantike Kaiserporträts von Constantinus Magnus bis zum Ende des Westreichs*, Berlin-Leipzig 1933.
Delmaire, R., 'La caisse des largesses sacrées et l'armée au Bas-Empire', *Armées et fiscalité dans le monde antique*, A. Chastagnol, C. Nicolet and H. van Effenterre (eds.), Paris 1977, 311–329.
Delmaire, R., 'Le maître de la milice Ursicinus dans le Talmud de Jérusalem', *Mélanges à la mémoire de Marcel-Henri Prévost*, Paris 1982, 273–281.
Demandt, A., *Zeitkritik und Geschichtsbild im Werk Ammians*, Bonn 1965.
Demandt, A., '*Magister militum*', *RE* Suppl. 12 (1970) 553–790.
Demandt, A., 'Verformungstendenzen in der Ueberlieferung antiker Sonnen- und Mondfinsternisse', *Akad.d.Wiss.u. Lit.Mainz, Abh.d.Geistes-u.Sozialw.Kl.*, 7 (1970) 469–527.
Demougeot, E., *La formation de l'Europe et les invasions barbares, II, De l'avènement de Dioclétien (284) à l'occupation germanique de l'empire romain d'Occident (début du VIe siècle)*, Paris 1979.

Demougeot, E., 'Le partage des provinces de l'Illyricum entre la pars Occidentis et la pars Orientis, de la Tétrarchie au règne de Théodoric', *La géographie administrative et politique d'Alexandre à Mahomet*. Actes du colloque de Strasbourg 14–16 juin 1979, Leiden 1981, 229–253.
Dennis, G.T., 'Byzantine Battle Flags', *ByzF* 8 (1982) 51–59.
Devijver, H. and F. van Wonterghem, 'Der "*campus*" der römischen Städte in Italia und im Westen', *ZPE* 54 (1984) 195–206.
Devijver, H. and F. van Wonterghem, 'Neue Belege zum "*campus*" der römischen Städte in Italien und im Westen', *ZPE* 60 (1985) 147–158.
Diels, H., *Doxographi Graeci*, Berlin 1958³.
Dillemann, L., 'Ammien Marcellin et les pays de l'Euphrate et du Tigre', *Syria* 38 (1961) 87–158.
Dillemann, L., *Haute Mésopotamie Orientale et Pays Adjacents. Contribution à la géographie historique de la région, du Ve s. avant l'ère chrétienne au VIe s. de cette ère*, Paris 1962.
Dimaio, M., 'The Antiochene Connection: Zonaras, Ammianus Marcellinus and John of Antioch on the Reigns of the Emperors Constantius II and Julian', *Byzantion* 50 (1980) 158–185.
Dirlmeier, C., G. Gottlieb, W. Kuhoff and K. Sprigade, *Quellen zur Geschichte der Alamannen*, I–VI, Sigmaringen 1976–1984.
Domaszewski, A. von, and B. Dobson, *Die Rangordnung des römischen Heeres*, Cologne-Graz 1967².
Downey, G., *A History of Antioch in Syria from Seleucus to the Arab Conquest*, Princeton 1961.
Drijvers, H.J.W., 'Hatra, Palmyra und Edessa. Die Städte der syrisch-mesopotamischen Wüste in politischer, kulturgeschichtlicher und religionsgeschichtlicher Beleuchtung', *ANRW* 2.8 (1977) 799–906.
Drinkwater, J.F., 'The "Pagan Underground", Constantius II's "Secret Service", and the Survival, and the Usurpation of Julian the Apostate', *Studies in Latin Literature and Roman History*, III, C. Deroux (ed.), Brussels 1983, 348–387.
Dunlap, J.A., *The Office of the Grand Chamberlain in the Later Roman and Byzantine Empires*, New York 1924 (Univ. of Michigan Studies 14, 161–324).

Eadie, J.W., *The Breviarium of Festus. A critical Edition with Historical Commentary*, London 1967.
Eadie, J.W., 'The Development of Roman Mailed Cavalry', *JRS* 57 (1967) 161–173.
Edgeworth, R.J., 'Does "*purpureus*" mean "bright"?', *Glotta* 57 (1979) 281–291.
Ehrismann, H., *De temporum et modorum usu Ammianeo*, Diss. Strasbourg 1886.
Elbern, S., *Usurpationen im spätrömischen Reich*, Bonn 1984.
Eliot, C.W.J., 'New Evidence for the Speed of the Roman Imperial Post', *Phoenix* 9 (1955) 76–80.
Emmet, A., 'Introductions and Conclusions to Digressions in Ammianus Marcellinus', *MPhL* 5 (1981) 15–33.
Ensslin, W., 'Zum Heermeisteramt des spätrömischen Reiches, I. Die Titulatur der *magistri militum* bis auf Theodosius I.', *Klio* 23 (1929) 306–325.
Ensslin, W., 'Zum Heermeisteramt des spätrömischen Reiches, II. Die *magistri militum* des 4. Jahrhunderts', *Klio* 24 (1930) 102–147.
Ensslin, W., 'Zum Heermeisteramt des spätrömischen Reiches, III. Der *magister utriusque militiae et patricius* des 5. Jahrhunderts', *Klio* 24 (1930) 467–502.
Ensslin, W., 'Maurus 2', *RE* 14 (1930) 2396.
Ensslin, W., 'Tiran II', *RE* 6A (1937) 1431.
Ensslin, W., 'Zur Ostpolitik des Kaisers Diokletian', *Sitz.ber. Bayer. Akad.Wiss., Phil.-Hist.Kl.* 1, 1942.
Ensslin, W., 'Zur Torqueskrönung und Schilderhebung bei der Kaiserwahl', *Klio* 35 (1942) 268–298.
Ensslin, W., '*Praefectus praetorio*', *RE* 22 (1954) 2391–2502.
Erfurdt, C.G.A., see J.A. Wagner.

Fesser, H., *Sprachliche Beobachtungen zu Ammianus Marcellinus*, Diss. Breslau 1932.
Fiebiger, H.O., 'Donativum', *RE* 5 (1905) 1542–1545.
Fiebiger, H.O., 'Exploratores', *RE* 6 (1909) 1690–1693.
Fitz, J., *L'administration des provinces pannoniennes sous le Bas-Empire romain*, Brussels 1983.
Fletcher, A., see D.J. Schove.
Fletcher, G.B.A., 'Ammianea', *AJPh* 58 (1937) 392–402.
Fletcher, G.B.A., 'Stylistic Borrowings and Parallels in Ammianus Marcellinus', *RPh* 11 (1937) 377–395, cited as Fletcher, 1937 (2).
Flinck-Linkomies, E., *De ablativo absoluto quaestiones*, Helsingfors 1929.
Flobert, P., *Les verbes déponents latins des origines à Charlemagne*, Paris 1975.
Fontaine, J., *Ammien Marcellin, Histoire, IV (Livres XXIII–XXV)*, 2 vols., Paris 1977.
Forbes, R.J., *Studies in Ancient Technology*, I, Leiden 1964².
Fraenkel, S., 'Bezabde', *RE* 3 (1899) 378–379.
Fraenkel, S., 'Birtha 2', *RE* 3 (1899) 498.
Frank, R.I., *Scholae Palatinae. The Palace Guards of the Later Roman Empire*, Rome 1969.
Frassinetti, P., 'In margine ad Ammiano Marcellino', *Athenaeum* 44 (1966) 298–306.
French, D., 'New Research on the Euphrates Frontier. Supplementary Notes 1 and 2', *Armies and Frontiers in Roman and Byzantine Anatolia*, S. Mitchell (ed.), London 1983, 71–101.
Frere, S.S., *Britannia. A History of Roman Britain*, London 1967.
Frézouls, E., 'La mission du *magister equitum* Ursicin en Gaulle (355–357) d'après Ammien Marcellin', *Hommages à Albert Grenier*, M. Renard (ed.), Brussels 1962, 673–688.
Frézouls, E., 'Les fluctuations de la frontière orientale de l'empire romain', *La géographie administrative et politique d'Alexandre à Mahomet*, Leiden 1981, 177–225.
Frézouls, E., 'Les deux politiques de Rome face aux barbares d'après Ammien Marcellin', *Crise et redressement dans les provinces européennes de l'Empire (milieu du IIIe – milieu du IVe siècle ap. J.-C.)*, E. Frézouls (ed.), Strasbourg 1983, 175–197.

Gabelmann, H., *Antike Audienz- und Tribunalszenen*, Darmstadt 1984.
Garsoïan, N.G., 'Politique ou Orthodoxie? L'Arménie au quatrième siècle', *Revue des Etudes Arméniennes* n.s. 4 (1967) 297–320 (repr. in *Armenia between Byzantium and the Sassanians*, London 1985).
Garsoïan, N.G., 'Armenia in the Fourth Century. An Attempt to Redefine the Concepts "Armenia" and 'Loyalty" ', *Revue des Etudes Arméniennes* n.s. 8 (1971) 341–352 (repr. in *Armenia between Byzantium and the Sassanians*).
Geffcken, J., *Kaiser Julianus*, Leipzig 1914.
Gerth, B., see R. Kühner.
Ghirshman, R., *Iran, Parthes et Sassanides*, Paris 1962.
Gigli, G., 'Forme di reclutamento militari durante il Basso Impero', *RAL* 8.2 (1947) 268–289.
Gilbert, O., *Die meteorologischen Theorien des griechischen Altertums*, Leipzig 1907 (repr. Hildesheim 1967).
Gilliard, F.D., 'The Birth-Date of Julian the Apostate', *CSCA* 4 (1971) 147–151 (cf. 'Das Geburtsdatum von Julian Apostata', *Julian Apostata*, R. Klein (ed.), Darmstadt 1978, 448–454).
Ginzel, F.K., *Spezieller Kanon der Sonnen- und Mondfinsternisse für das Ländergebiet der klassischen Altertumswissenschaften und den Zeitraum von 900 v.Chr. bis 600 n.Chr.*, Berlin 1899.
Gipper, H., 'Purpur. Weg und Leistung eines umstrittenen Farbworts', *Glotta* 42 (1964) 39–69.
Goffart, W., 'Did Julian combat Venal *Suffragium*? A Note on *CTh* 2.29.1', *CPh* 65 (1970) 145–151.

Gottlieb, G., see C. Dirlmeier.
Graves, D.A., *Consistorium Domini. Imperial Councils of State in the Later Roman Empire*, New York 1973.
Grelle, F., *Stipendium vel Tributum. L'imposizione fondiaria nelle dottrine giuridiche del II e III secolo*, Naples 1963.
Grigg, R., 'Inconsistency and Lassitude. The Shield Emblems of the *Notitia Dignitatum*', *JRS* 73 (1983) 132-142.
Grousset, R., *Histoire de l'Arménie des origines à 1071*, Paris 1947.
Günther, R., 'Läten, Föderaten und Gentilen', *Die Römer am Rhein und Donau*, R. Günther and H. Köpstein (eds.), Vienna-Cologne-Graz 1975, 344-352, cited as Günther, 1975 (1).
Günther, R., 'Germanische Laeten, Foederaten und Gentile im nördlichen und nordöstlichen Gallien in der Spätantike', *Römer und Germanen in Mitteleuropa*, H. Gruenert and H.J. Doelle (eds.), Berlin 1975, 225-234, cited as Günther, 1975 (2).
Guilland, R., 'Etudes sur l'histoire administrative de l'empire byzantin. Le questeur, ὁ κοιαίστωρ, quaestor', *Byzantion* 51 (1971) 78-104.
Gutenbrunner, S., 'Die Stammesgliederung der rheinischen Germanen', *Beiträge zur Geschichte der deutschen Sprache und Literatur* 60 (1936) 350-370 (= *Zur germanischen Stammeskunde. Aufsätze zum neuen Forschungsstand*, E. Schwarz (ed.), Darmstadt 1972, 67-86).
Guyot, P., *Eunuchen als Sklaven und Freigelassene in der griechisch-römischen Antike*, Stuttgart 1980.

Haehling, R. von, *Die Religionszugehörigkeit der hohen Amtsträger des Römischen Reiches seit Constantins I. Alleinherrschaft bis zum Ende der Theodosianischen Dynastie (324-450 bzw. 455 n. Chr.)*, Bonn 1978.
Hagendahl, H., *Studia Ammianea*, Diss. Uppsala 1921.
Hagendahl, H., 'Zu Ammianus Marcellinus', *Strena Philologica Upsaliensis (Festschrift Persson)*, Uppsala 1922, 74-90.
Hagendahl, H., 'De abundantia sermonis Ammianei', *Eranos* 22 (1924) 161-216.
Harmon, A.M., *The Clausula in Ammianus Marcellinus*, New Haven 1910 (Trans. Connecticut Acad. Arts and Sc. XVI, 117-245).
Hassenstein, G., *De syntaxi Ammiani Marcellini*, Diss. Königsberg 1877.
Hatt, J.-J., A. Thévenin and H. Vogt, *Histoire de Strasbourg des origines à nos jours, I: Strasbourg des origines à l'invasion des Huns*, Strasburg 1980.
Hazell, P.J., 'The pedite *gladius*', *AntJ* 61 (1981) 73-82.
Heath, T.L., *Greek Astronomy*, London 1932.
Helttula, A., '*Post depositum militiae munus*. Official Phraseology in Ammianus Marcellinus', *Arctos Suppl. II, Studia in honorem Iiro Kajanto*, Helsinki 1985, 41-56.
Hendy, M.F., *Studies in the Byzantine Monetary Economy c. 300-1450*, Cambridge 1985.
Hengst, D. den, *The Prefaces in the Historia Augusta*, Amsterdam 1981.
Hengst, D. den, 'Ammianus Marcellinus on Astronomy (*Res Gestae* 20.3)', *Mnemosyne* 39 (1986) 136-141.
Hertz, M., 'Aulus Gellius und Ammianus Marcellinus', *Hermes* 8 (1874) 257-302.
Heumann, H. and E. Seckel, *Handlexikon zu den Quellen des römischen Rechts*, Jena 1907[9] (repr. Graz 1971).
Heus, W.E., 'Spätrömische *coronae militares*', *Actus. Studies in Honour of H.L.W. Nelson*, Utrecht 1982, 109-113.
Hewsen, R.H., 'The Successors of Tiridates the Great: a Contribution to the History of Armenia in the Fourth Century', *Revue des Etudes Arméniennes* n.s. 13 (1978/79) 99-126.
Hild, F., *Das Byzantinische Strassensystem in Kappadokien*, Vienna 1977.
Hiltbrunner, O., *Latina Graeca. Semasiologische Studien über lateinische Wörter im Hinblick auf ihr Verhältnis zu griechischen Vorbildern*, Bern 1958.

Hind, J.G.F., 'The British "Provinces" of Valentia and Orcades (Tacitean Echoes in Ammianus Marcellinus and Claudian)', *Historia* 24 (1975) 101-111.
Hinz, H., 'Colonia Ulpia Traiana. Die Entwicklung eines römischen Zentralortes am Niederrhein, I, Prinzipat', *ANRW* 2.4, Berlin 1975, 825-869.
Hinz, H., *Xanten zur Römerzeit*, Xanten 1976.
Hoeckmann, O., 'Rheinschiffe aus der Zeit Ammians. Neue Funde in Mainz', *AW* 13.3 (1982) 40-47.
Hoepffner, A., 'Les *magistri militum praesentales* au IVe siècle', *Byzantion* 11 (1936) 483-498.
Hoffmann, D., *Das spätrömische Bewegungsheer und die Notitia Dignitatum*, 2 vols., Düsseldorf 1969.
Hofmann, J.B., *Lateinische Umgangssprache*, Heidelberg 1951[3].
Hofmann, J.B. and A. Szantyr, *Lateinische Syntax und Stilistik*, Munich 1965 (repr. 1972), cited as Szantyr.
Holmberg, E.J., *Zur Geschichte des Cursus Publicus*, Diss. Uppsala 1933.
Hopkins, K., 'Eunuchs in Politics in the Later Roman Empire', *PCPhS* 189 (1963) 62-80 (= *Conquerors and Slaves. Sociological Studies in Roman History*, I, Cambridge 1978, 172-196).
Hosius, C., see M. Schanz.
Humphrey, J.H., *Roman Circuses. Arenas for Chariot Racing*, London 1986.
Hunt, E.D., 'Christians and Christianity in Ammianus Marcellinus', *CQ* 35 (1985) 186-200.

Instinsky, H.U., *'Consensus universorum'*, *Hermes* 75 (1940) 265-278.

Jacob-Karau, L., see W. Seyfarth.
Jacob, L., 'Die Germanen im Urteil Ammians', *Rom und Germanien, dem Wirken Werner Hartkes gewidmet*, J. Herrmann (ed.), Berlin 1982, 77-83.
Johnson, S., 'The Construction of the Saxon Shore Fort at Richborough', *Collectanea Historica. Essays in Memory of Stuart Rigold*, A. Detsicas (ed.), Maidstone 1981, 23-31.
Johnson, S., *Late Roman Fortifications*, London 1983.
Jones, A.H.M., *The Greek City from Alexander to Justinian*, Oxford 1940 (repr. 1979).
Jones, A.H.M., 'The *Dediticii* and the *Constitutio Antoniniana*', *Studies in Roman Government and Law*, Oxford 1960, 127-140 (repr. 1968).
Jones, A.H.M., *The Later Roman Empire 284-602. A. Social Economic and Administrative Survey*, Oxford 1964 (repr. 1986).
Jones, A.H.M., *The Cities of the Eastern Roman Provinces*, Oxford 1971[2].
Jones, A.H.M., see also *PLRE* I.
Jonge, P. de, *Sprachlicher und historischer Kommentar zu Ammianus Marcellinus c.q. Philological and Historical Commentary on Ammianus Marcellinus*, XIV-XIX, Groningen 1935-1982.
Jullian, C., *Histoire de la Gaulle*, VII, Paris 1926 (repr. Brussels 1964).

Kallenberg, H., *Quaestiones grammaticae ammianeae*, Diss. Halle 1868.
Kiechle, F., 'Die Entwicklung der Brandwaffen im Altertum', *Historia* 26 (1977) 253-256.
Kienast, D., *Untersuchungen zu den Kriegsflotten der römischen Kaiserzeit*, Bonn 1966.
Kipp, Th., *'Edictum'*, *RE* 5 (1905) 1940-1948.
Klauser, Th., 'Akklamation', *RAC* 1 (1950) 216-233.
Klein, R., 'Die Kämpfe um die Nachfolge nach dem Tode Constantins des Grossen', *ByzF* 6 (1979) 101-150.
Kloft, H., *Liberalitas Principis. Herkunft und Bedeutung. Studien zur Prinzipatsideologie*, Cologne 1970.
Koestermann, E., ' "Status" als politischer Terminus in der Antike', *RhM* 86 (1937) 225-240.

Kornemann, E., 'Postwesen', *RE* 22 (1954) 988–1014.
Kotula, T., 'Firmus, fils de Nubel. Etait-il usurpateur ou roi des Maures?', *AAntHung* 18 (1970) 137–146.
Krebs, J. Ph. and J.H. Schmalz, *Antibarbarus der lateinischen Sprache*, Basle 1905–1907 (repr. Darmstadt 1984).
Kromayer, J., and G. Veith, *Heerwesen und Kriegführung der Griechen und Römer*, Munich 1928 (repr. 1963).
Krüger, G., see M. Schanz.
Kubitschek, J.W. and O. Seeck, '*Act(u)arius*', *RE* 1 (1894) 301–302.
Kühner, R. and B. Gerth, *Grammatik der griechischen Sprache (Syntax)*, 2 vols., Hannover 1898–1904 (repr. Darmstadt 1966).
Kühner, R. and C. Stegmann, *Ausführliche Grammatik der lateinischen Sprache*, II, Satzlehre, 2 vols., Hannover 1955^4, 1976^5.
Kuhoff, W., *Studien zur zivilen senatorischen Laufbahn im 4. Jahrhundert n. Chr.. Aemter und Amtsinhaber in Clarissimat und Spektabilität*, Frankfurt-Bern 1983.
Kuhoff, W., see also C. Dirlmeier.
Kunkel, W., '*Consilium, Consistorium*. Nachträge zum Reallexikon für Antike und Christentum', *JbAC* 11–12 (1968/69) 230–248.

Lakatos, P., *Quellenbuch zur Geschichte der Heruler*, Szeged 1978.
Lander. J., *Roman Stone Fortifications. Variation and Change from the First Century A.D. to the Fourth*, Oxford 1984.
Lassandro, D., 'I *"cultores barbari"* (*Laeti*) in Gallia da Massimiano alla fine del IV secolo d.C.', *CISA* 6 (1979) 178–188.
Laughton, E., *The Participle in Cicero*, Oxford 1964.
Lausberg, H., *Handbuch der literarischen Rhetorik. Eine Grundlegung der Literaturwissenschaft*, Munich 1960.
Le Boeuffle, A., *Le vocabulaire latin de l'astronomie*, I–III, Paris 1973.
Leedom, J.W., 'Constantius II: Three Revisions', *Byzantion* 48 (1978) 132–145.
Legon, R.P., *Megara. The Political History of a Greek City-State to 336 B.C.*, New York 1981.
Leijenhorst, C.G. van, 'Zu zwei lateinischen Ambtsbezeichnungen', Beiträge aus der Thesaurus-Arbeit XXIII, *MH* 43 (1986) 177–183.
Lesuisse, L., 'Le titre de *Caesar* et son évolution au cours de l'histoire de l'Empire', *LEC* 29 (1961) 271–287.
Leumann, M., *Lateinische Laut- und Formenlehre*, Munich 1977.
Leutsch, E.L. von and F.G. Schneidewin, *Corpus Paroemiographorum Graecorum*, Göttingen 1839.
Liebenam, W., 'Consilium', *RE* 4 (1901) 915–922.
Liebeschuetz, J.H.W.G., *Antioch. City and Imperial Administration in the Later Roman Empire*, Oxford 1972.
Liebs, D., 'Aemterkauf und Aemterpatronage in der Spätantike. Propaganda und Sachzwang bei Julian dem Abtrünnigen', *ZRG* 95 (1978) 158–186.
Lightfoot, C.S., *The Eastern Frontier of the Roman Empire with special Reference to the Reign of Constantius 2nd*, Diss. Oxford 1981.
Lightfoot, C.S., 'The Site of Roman Bezabde', *Armies and Frontiers in Roman and Byzantine Anatolia*, S. Mitchell (ed.), London 1983, 189–204.
Lippold, A., 'Ursicinus 1', *RE* 9A (1961) 1058–1063.
Lippold, A., 'Ursulus 2', *RE Suppl.* 10 (1965) 1148–1149.
Löfstedt, E., *Beiträge zur Kenntnis der späteren Latinität*, Diss. Uppsala 1907.
Löfstedt, E., *Philologischer Kommentar zur Peregrinatio Aetheriae. Untersuchungen zur Geschichte der lateinischen Sprache*, Uppsala 1911.
Löfstedt, E., *Syntactica. Studien und Beiträge zur historischen Syntax des Lateins*, I, Lund 1942^2 (repr. 1956), II, Lund 1933 (repr. 1956).
Löfstedt, E., *Contiectanea. Untersuchungen auf dem Gebiete der antiken und mittelalterlichen Latinität*, I, Uppsala 1950.

Löhken, H., *Ordines Dignitatum. Untersuchungen zur formalen Konstituierung der spätantiken Führungsschicht*, Cologne-Vienna 1982.
Lucien-Brun, X., 'Constance II et le massacre des princes', *BAGB* 32 (1973) 585-602.
Luttwak, E.N., *The Grand Strategy of the Roman Empire. From the First Century A.D. to the Third*, Baltimore-London 1976.

MacCormack, S., 'Roma, Constantinopolis, the Emperor, and his *Genius*', *CQ* 25 (1975) 131-150.
MacMullen, R., *Soldier and Civilian in the Later Roman Empire*, Cambridge Mass. 1967.
Marié, M.-A., *Ammien Marcellin, Histoire, V (Livres XXVI-XXVIII)*, Paris 1984.
Marsden, E.W., *Greek and Roman Artillery*, 2 vols., Oxford 1969 and 1971.
Marsden, P., *Roman London*, London 1980.
Martin, J., *Antike Rhetorik. Technik und Methode*, Munich 1974.
Martin-Kilcher, S. and M. Zaugg, *Augst, Augusta Rauracorum. Porträt einer Römerstadt*, Aare 1982.
Martindale, J.R., 'Prosopography of the Later Roman Empire: Addenda et Corrigenda to Volume I', *Historia* 29 (1980) 474-497.
Martindale, J.R., see also *PLRE* I.
Matthews, J.F., 'Ammianus Marcellinus', *Ancient Writers: Greece and Rome*, II, T.J. Luce (ed.), New York 1982, 1117-1138.
Mau, A., 'Diadema', *RE* 5 (1905) 303-305.
Maxfield, V.A., *The Military Decorations of the Roman Army*, London 1981.
McLeod, W., 'The Range of the Ancient Bow', *Phoenix* 19 (1965) 1-14.
Merrifield, R., *The Roman City of London*, London 1965.
Michael, H., *Die verlorenen Bücher des Ammianus Marcellinus*, Breslau 1880.
Milani, C., 'Lat. *laetus*, etr. lethe', *CISA* 6 (1979) 189-200.
Millar, F., *The Emperor in the Roman World (31 BC-AD 337)*, London 1977.
Mitchell, S., 'Requisitioned Transport in the Roman Empire. A New Inscription from Pisidia', *JRS* 66 (1976) 106-131.
Mitford, T.B., 'Cappadocia and Armenia Minor. Historical Setting of the *limes*', *ANRW* 2.7.2, Berlin 1980, 1169-1228.
Mohrman, Chr., see J. Schrijnen.
Momigliano, A., 'The Lonely Historian Ammianus Marcellinus', *ASNP* ser. III, vol. IV. 4 (1974) 1393-1407 (= *Sesto contributo alla storia degli studi classici e del mondo antico*, I, Rome 1980, 143-157).
Mommsen, Th., *Römisches Staatsrecht*, I, Leipzig 1887³ (repr. Darmstadt 1971).
Mommsen, Th., 'Ammians Geographica', *Hermes* 16 (1881) 602-636 (= *Gesammelte Schriften*, VII, Berlin 1909, 393-425).
Mommsen, Th., 'Das römische Militärwesen seit Diocletian', *Hermes* 24 (1889) 195-279 (= *Gesammelte Schriften*, VI, Berlin 1910, 206-283).
Moreau, J., 'Constans', *JbAC* 2 (1959) 179-184.
Morris, J., see *PLRE* I.
Müller, A., 'Militaria aus Ammianus Marcellinus', *Philologus* 64 (1905) 573-632.
Müller-Seidel, I., 'Die Usurpation Julians des Abtrünnigen im Lichte seiner Germanenpolitik', *HZ* 180 (1955) 225-244.

Naudé, C.P.T., '*Fortuna* in Ammianus Marcellinus', *AClass* 7 (1964) 70-88.
Neri, V., *Costanzo, Giuliano e l'ideale del 'civilis princeps' nelle storie di Ammiano Marcellino*, Rome 1984.
Neri, V., *Ammiano e il Cristianesimo. Religione e politica nelle "Res Gestae" di Ammiano Marcellino*, Bologna 1985.
Nesselhauf, H., *Die spätrömische Verwaltung der gallisch-germanischen Länder*, Berlin 1938 (Abh.d.Preuss.Ak.d.Wiss., Jhrg. 1938, Philosop.-hist. Kl., 2).
Neue, F., *Formenlehre der lateinischen Sprache. Dritte, sehr vermehrte Auflage von C. Wagener*, Leipzig 1892-1905 (repr. Hildesheim 1985).

Neumann, A.R., 'Petulantes', *RE Suppl.* 10 (1965) 531-532.
Neumann, A.R., *'Exploratores'*, *Der kleine Pauly* 2 (1967) 483-484.
Neuscheler, E., 'Ammianus Marcellinus als Quelle für die Alamannengeschichte', *Festgabe für K. Bohnenberger*, Tübingen 1938, 40-52.
Nischer, E. von, 'Das römische Heer und seine Generale nach Ammianus Marcellinus (353-378 n.Chr.)', *Hermes* 63 (1928) 430-456.
Norberg, D., *Beiträge zur spätlateinischen Syntax*, Uppsala 1944.
Norman, A.F., *Libanius. Selected Works, I, The Julianic Orations*, London-Cambridge Mass. 1969.
Nutt, D.C., 'Silvanus and the Emperor Constantius II', *Antichthon* 7 (1973) 80-89.

Oberhummer, E., 'Succi', *RE* 4A (1931) 513-514.
O'Brien, M.B., *Titles of Address in Christian Latin Epistolography to 543 A.D.*, Washington 1930.
Odelstierna, J., *De vi futurali ac finali gerundii et gerundivi latini observationes*, Uppsala 1926.
Ooteghem, J. van, 'Le service postal à Rome', *LEC* 27 (1959) 187-197.
Opelt, I., *Die lateinischen Schimpfwörter und verwandte sprachliche Erscheinungen. Eine Typologie*, Heidelberg 1965.
Ostrogorsky, G., 'Zur Kaisersalbung und Schilderhebung im spätbyzantinischen Krönungszeremoniell', *Historia* 4 (1955) 246-256 (= *Das Byzantinische Herrscherbild*, H. Hunger (ed.), Darmstadt 1975, 94-108).
Otto, A., *Die Sprichwörter und sprichwörtlichen Redensarten der Römer*, Leipzig 1890 (repr. Hildesheim 1962).

Pack, E., *Städte und Steuern in der Politik Julians. Untersuchungen zu den Quellen eines Kaiserbildes*, Brussels 1986.
Painter, K.S., 'The Mildenhall Treasure. A Reconsideration', *BMQ* 37 (1973) 154-180.
Palanque, J.-R., 'La préfecture du prétoire d'Illyricum au IVe siècle', *Byzantion* 21 (1951) 5-14.
Palanque, J.-R., 'Les préfets du prétoire sous les fils de Constantin', *Historia* 4 (1955) 257-263.
Palanque, J.-R., 'Du nouveau sur la préfecture d'Illyricum au IVe siècle', *Hommages à M. Renard*, J. Bibauw (ed.), II, Brussels 1969, 600-606.
Paschoud, F., *Zosime, Histoire Nouvelle, II.1 (Livre III)*, Paris 1979.
Paul, G.M., *'Urbs capta.* Sketch of an Ancient Literary Motif', *Phoenix* 36 (1982) 144-155.
Pauw, D.A., *Karaktertekening bij Ammianus Marcellinus*, Diss. Leiden 1972.
Pelletier, A., *Vienne gallo-romaine au Bas-Empire, 275-478 après J.-C.*, Lyon 1974.
Pelletier, A., *Vienne antique. De la conquête romaine aux invasions Alamanniques (IIe siècle avant - IIIe siècle après J.-C.)*, Roanne 1982.
Périn, P. (ed.), *Lutèce. Paris de César à Clovis*, Paris 1984.
Petit, P., 'Recherches sur la publication et la diffusion des discours de Libanius', *Historia* 5 (1956) 479-509.
Petrikovits, H. von, 'Fortifications in the North-Western Roman Empire from the Third to the Fifth Centuries A.D.', *JRS* 61 (1971) 178-218.
Pflaum, H.-G., *Essai sur le cursus publicus sous le Haut-Empire Romain*, Paris 1940 (*MAI* 14, 89-390).
Philp, B., 'Richborough, Reculver and Lympne. A Reconsideration of three of Kent's Late-Roman Shore-Forts', *Collectanea Historica. Essays in Memory of Stuart Rigold*, A. Detsicas (ed.), Maidstone 1981, 41-49.
Piganiol, A., 'La couronne de Julien César', *Byzantion* 13 (1938) 243-248.
Piganiol, A. and A. Chastagnol, *L'Empire Chrétien (325-395)*, Paris 1972².
Pighi, G.B., *Studia Ammianea. Annotationes criticae et grammaticae in Ammianum Marcellinum*, Milan 1935.

Pighi, G.B., *Nuovi studi Ammianei*, Milan 1936, cited as Pighi, 1936 (1).
Pighi, G.B., *I discorsi nelle storie d'Ammiano Marcellino*, Milan 1936, cited as Pighi, 1936 (2).
Pinkster, H., 'A B & C-coordination in Latin', *Mnemosyne* 22 (1969) 258-267.
Pinkster, H., 'The Development of Future Tense Auxiliaries in Latin', *Glotta* 63 (1985) 186-208.
Piovene, G., see T. Agozzino.
Platner, S.B. and T. Ashby, *A Topographical Dictionary of Ancient Rome*, Oxford 1929 (repr. 1965).
PLRE I, *The Prosopography of the Later Roman Empire, I, A.D. 260-395*, A.H.M. Jones, J.R. Martindale and J. Morris (eds.), Cambridge 1971.
Pugliese Carratelli G., 'La Persia dei Sasanidi nella storiografia romana da Ammiano a Procopio', *Scritti sul mondo antico*, Naples 1976, 35-46.

Ramsay, A.M., 'The Speed of the Roman Imperial Post', *JRS* 15 (1925) 60-74.
Rebuffat, R., '*Propugnacula*', *Latomus* 43 (1984) 3-26.
Reece, R., 'The Roman Coins from Richborough. A Summary', *BIAL* 18 (1981) 49-71.
Regling, K., '*Solidus*', *RE* 3A (1927) 920-926.
Reinhold, M., *History of Purple as a Status Symbol in Antiquity*, Brussels 1970.
Ritter, H.-W., *Diadem und Königsherrschaft. Untersuchungen zu Zeremonien und Rechtsgrundlagen des Herrschaftsantritts bei den Persern, bei Alexander dem Grossen und im Hellenismus*, Munich 1965.
Robinson, H.R., *The Armour of Imperial Rome*, New York-London 1975.
Roes, A., 'Some Gold Torcs found in Holland', *AArch* 18 (1947) 175-187.
Rösger, A., 'Zur Herrscherterminologie der *Historia Augusta*: *princeps* und *purpuratus*', *BHAC* 1977/78, Bonn 1980, 179-201.
Rolfe, J.C., *Ammianus Marcellinus*, with an English translation, 3 vols., London-Cambridge Mass. 1935-1939 (repr. 1971-1972).
Roselle, L.R., *Tacitean Elements in Ammianus Marcellinus*, Ann Arbor 1985.
Rosen, K., *Studien zur Darstellungskunst und Glaubwürdigkeit des Ammianus Marcellinus*, Bonn 1968 (repr. 1970).
Rosen, K., 'Beobachtungen zur Erhebung Julians, 360-361 n. Chr.', *AClass* 12 (1969) 121-149 (= *Julian Apostata*, R. Klein (ed.), Darmstadt 1978, 409-447), cited as Rosen, 1978.
Rosen, K., *Ammianus Marcellinus*, Darmstadt 1982.
Roueché, Ch., 'Acclamations in the Later Roman Empire. New Evidence from Aphrodisias', *JRS* 74 (1984) 181-199.
Rubin, B., 'Die Entstehung der Kataphraktenreiterei im Lichte der chorezmischen Ausgrabungen', *Historia* 4 (1955) 264-283.
Rüger, C.B., *Germania Inferior. Untersuchungen zur Territorial- und Verwaltungsgeschichte Niedergermaniens in der Prinzipatszeit*, Cologne 1968.
Rüger, C.B., 'Die spätrömische Grossfestung in der Colonia Ulpia Traiana', *BJ* 179 (1979) 499-524.
Ryberg, I.S., 'Tacitus' Art of Innuendo', *TAPhA* 73 (1942) 383-404.

Sabbah, G., *La méthode d'Ammien Marcellin. Recherches sur la construction du discours historique dans les Res Gestae*, Paris 1978.
Sabbah, G., 'L'attachement à la "patrie gauloise" au IVe siècle, notamment chez les soldats, d'après le témoignage d'Ammien Marcellin', *La Patrie Gauloise d'Agrippa au VIe siècle*, Actes du Colloque (Lyon 1981), Lyon 1983, 161-180.
Samberger, Ch., 'Die "Kaiserbiographie" in den *Res Gestae* des Ammianus Marcellinus. Eine Untersuchung zur Komposition der ammianeischen Geschichtsschreibung', *Klio* 51 (1969) 349-482.
Schanz, M., C. Hosius and G. Krüger, *Geschichte der römischen Literatur bis zum Gesetzgebungswerk des Kaisers Justinian*, I-IV, Munich 1927[4] ff.

Scheller, P., *De hellenistica historiae conscribendae arte*, Leipzig 1911.
Schilling, R., 'Genius', *RAC* 10 (1978) 52-83.
Schmalz, J.H., see J.Ph. Krebs.
Schmidt, L., *Geschichte der deutschen Stämme bis zum Ausgang der Völkerwanderung, II, Die Westgermanen*, Munich 1940² (repr. 1970).
Schneidewin, F.G., see E.L. von Leutsch.
Schönberger, H., 'The Roman Frontier in Germany: an Archaeological Survey', *JRS* 59 (1969) 144-197.
Schönfeld, M., '*Laeti*', *RE* 12 (1925) 446-448.
Schove, D.J. and A. Fletcher, *Chronology of Eclipses and Comets, A.D. 1-1000*, Woodbridge 1984.
Schrijnen, J. and Chr. Mohrmann, *Studien zur Syntax der Briefe des hl. Cyprian*, 2 vols., Nijmegen 1936 and 1937.
Schuller, W., 'Aemterkauf im römischen Reich', *Der Staat* 19 (1980) 57-71.
Schulten, A., '*Dediticii*', *RE* 4 (1901) 2359-2363.
Seager, R. *Ammianus Marcellinus. Seven Studies in his Language and Thought*, Columbia 1986.
Seckel, E., see H. Heumann.
Seeck, O., 'Agilo', *RE* 1 (1894) 809.
Seeck, O., 'Arbitio 1', *RE* 2 (1896) 411-412.
Seeck, O., 'Barbatio', *RE* 3 (1899) 1-2.
Seeck, O., '*Comes rei militaris*', *RE* 4 (1901) 662-664.
Seeck, O., 'Constans 3', *RE* 4 (1901) 948-952.
Seeck, O., '*Cursus publicus*', *RE* 4 (1901) 1846-1863.
Seeck, O., 'Decentius 2', *RE* 4 (1901) 2269.
Seeck, O., '*Decuriones sacri consistorii* oder *palatii*', *RE* 4 (1901) 2353.
Seeck, O., 'Zur Chronologie und Quellenkritik des Ammianus Marcellinus', *Hermes* 41 (1906) 481-539.
Seeck, O., 'Eusebius 5', *RE* 6 (1909) 1367-1368.
Seeck, O., 'Felix 8', *RE* 6 (1909) 2167.
Seeck, O., 'Florentius 2', *RE* 6 (1909) 2757.
Seeck, O., 'Florentius 3', *RE* 6 (1909) 2757.
Seeck, O., *Regesten der Kaiser und Päpste für die Jahre 311 bis 476 n. Chr.. Vorarbeit zu einer Prosopographie der christlichen Kaiserzeit*, Stuttgart 1919 (repr. 1964).
Seeck, O., 'Sabinianus 7', *RE* 1A (1920) 1585.
Seeck, O., 'Sapor II', *RE* 1A (1920) 2334-2354.
Seeck, O., *Geschichte des Untergangs der antiken Welt*, 6 vols., Stuttgart 1920-1923²⁻⁴.
Seeck, O., '*Scholae palatinae*', *RE* 2A (1921) 621-624.
Seeck, O., '*Silentiarius*', *RE* 3A (1927) 57-58.
Seeck, O., 'Sintula', *RE* 3A (1927) 259.
Seeck, O., 'Lupicinus 1', *RE* 13 (1927) 1844.
Seeck, O., see also J.W. Kubitschek.
Selem, A., 'Considerazioni circa Ammiano ed il Cristianesimo', *RCCM* 6 (1964) 224-261.
Selem, A., 'L'atteggiamento storiografico di Ammiano nei confronti di Giuliano dalla proclamazione di Parigi alla morte di Costanzo', *Athenaeum* 49 (1971) 89-110.
Selem, A., *Le Storie di Ammiano Marcellino. Testo e Traduzione*, Turin 1965 (repr. 1973).
Serbat, G., 'L'ablatif absolu', *REL* 57 (1979) 340-354.
Seston, W., 'Notes critiques sur l'Histoire Auguste, II: Julien et le *cursus publicus*', *REA* 45 (1943) 52-60.
Seston, W., 'Feldzeichen', *RAC* 7 (1969) 689-711 (= *Scripta Varia. Mélanges d'histoire Romaine, de droit, d'épigraphie et d'histoire du Christianisme*, Rome 1980, 263-281).
Seyfarth, W., 'Philologische Probleme um Ammianus Marcellinus', *Klio* 48 (1967) 213-235.

Seyfarth, W., *Ammiani Marcellini rerum gestarum libri qui supersunt*, adiuvantibus L. Jacob-Karau et I. Ulmann, 2 vols., Leipzig 1978.
Seyfarth, W., *Ammianus Marcellinus, Römische Geschichte. Lateinisch und Deutsch und mit einem Kommentar versehen*, II, Berlin 1983[5].
Simpson, C.J., 'Julian and the *laeti*: A Note on Ammianus Marcellinus, XX, 8, 13', *Latomus* 36 (1977) 519-521.
Sittl, C., *Die Gebärden der Griechen und Römer*, Leipzig 1890.
Speidel, M.P., '*Catafractarii clibanarii* and the Rise of the Later Roman Mailed Cavalry. A Gravestone from Claudiopolis in Bithynia', *EA* 4 (1984) 151-156.
Speidel, M.P., 'The Master of the Dragon Standards and the Golden Torc: an Inscription from Prusias and Prudentius' *Peristephanon*', *TAPhA* 115 (1985) 283-287.
Sprigade, K., see C. Dirlmeier.
Stallknecht, B., *Untersuchungen zur römischen Aussenpolitik in der Spätantike (306-395 n. Chr.)*, Bonn 1967.
Starr, Ch. G., *The Roman Imperial Navy, 31 B.C.-A.D. 324*, Cambridge 1960[2].
Ste Croix, G.E.M. de, '*Suffragium*: From Vote to Patronage', *The British Journal of Sociology* 5 (1954) 33-48.
Stegmann, C., see R. Kühner.
Straub, J.A., *Vom Herrscherideal in der Spätantike*, Stuttgart 1939 (repr. 1964).
Straub, J.A., '*Dignatio Caesaris*', *Legio VII Gemina*, Léon 1970, 156-179 (= *Regeneratio imperii. Aufsätze über Roms Kaisertum und Reich im Spiegel der heidnischen und christlichen Publizistik*, Darmstadt 1972, 36-63).
Stroheker, K.F., 'Alamannen im römischen Reichsdienst', *Eranion. Festschrift für Hildebrecht Hommel*, Tübingen 1961, 127-148 = K.F. Stroheker, *Germanentum und Spätantike*, Zurich-Stuttgart 1965, 30-53.
Stroheker, K.F., '*Princeps clausus*. Zu einigen Berührungen der Literatur des fünften Jahrhunderts mit der Historia Augusta', *BHAC* 1968/69, Bonn 1970, 273-283.
Stroheker, K.F., 'Die Alamannen und das spätrömische Reich', *Die Alamannen in der Frühzeit*, W. Hübener (ed.), Bühl/Baden 1974, 9-26 = *Zur Geschichte der Alamannen*, W. Müller (ed.), Darmstadt 1975, 20-48.
Suerbaum, W., *Vom antiken zum frühmittelalterlichen Staatsbegriff. Über Verwendung und Bedeutung von res publica, regnum, imperium und status von Cicero bis Jordanis*, Münster 1977[3].
Svennung, J., *Anredeformen. Vergleichende Forschungen zur indirekten Anrede in der dritten Person und zum Nominativ für den Vokativ*, Lund 1958.
Syme, R., *Tacitus*, 2 vols., Oxford 1958.
Szantyr, A., see J.B. Hofmann.
Szidat, J., *Historischer Kommentar zu Ammianus Marcellinus Buch XX-XXI, Teil I: Die Erhebung Iulians*, Wiesbaden 1977, and *Teil II: Die Verhandlungsphase*, Wiesbaden 1981.

Teitler, H.C., *Notarii and Exceptores. An Inquiry into Role and Significance of Shorthand Writers in the Imperial and Ecclesiastical Bureaucracy of the Roman Empire (from the Early Principate to c. 450 A.D.)*, Amsterdam 1985.
Teitler, H.C., 'De keizer op het schild geheven. Naar aanleiding van Ammianus Marcellinus 20.4.17', *Hermeneus* 59 (1987) 19-29.
Thévenin, A., see J.-J. Hatt.
Thompson, E.A., *The Historical Work of Ammianus Marcellinus*, Cambridge 1947 (repr. Groningen 1969).
Todd, M., *Roman Britain, 55 B.C.-A.D. 400. The Province Beyond the Ocean*, Brighton 1981.
Tomasevic-Buck, T., 'Ein neuentdecktes Gräberfeld in Kaiseraugst', *ArchS* 5 (1982) 141-147.
Tomasevic-Buck, T., 'Ausgrabungen in Augst und Kaiseraugst im Jahre 1976 und im Jahre 1977', *JAK* 2 (1982) 7-41 and 3 (1983) 7-46.
Tomei, M.A., 'La tecnica nel tardo impero romano: le macchine da guerra', *DArch* 4 (1982) no. 1, 63-88.

Treitinger, O., *Die oströmische Kaiser- und Reichsidee nach ihrer Gestaltung im höfischen Zeremoniell*, Darmstadt 1956².
Tumanischvili Bandelli, C., 'Sulla usurpazione di Giuliano l'Apostata', *Atti del II seminario romanistico Gardesano*, Milan 1980, 441-465.

Ulmann, I., see W. Seyfarth.

Vairel-Carron, H., *Exclamation. Ordre et Défense. Analyse de deux systèmes syntaxiques du Latin*, Paris 1975.
Valensi, L., 'Quelques réflexions sur le pouvoir impérial d'après Ammien Marcellin', *BAGB* 4.4 (1957) 62-107.
Veh, O., *Ammianus Marcellinus. Das römische Weltreich vor dem Untergang*, übersetzt von O. Veh, eingeleitet und erläutert von G. Wirth, Zurich-Munich 1974.
Veh, P.-G., *Der Grenzverlauf der römischen Provinz Cappadocia unter Kaiser Trajan und ihrer Nachfolgeprovinzen bis Theodosius I.*, Erlangen 1980.
Veith, G., see J. Kromayer.
Velkov, V., 'La Thrace et la Mésie inférieure pendant l'époque de la basse antiquité (IV-VIe s.)', *Ancient Bulgaria. Papers presented to the international symposium on the ancient history and archaeology of Bulgaria*, A.G. Poulter (ed.), Nottingham 1981, II, 177-193.
Vels Heyn, N., *Kleurnamen en kleurbegrippen bij de Romeinen*, Utrecht 1951.
Vester, E., *Instrument and Manner Expressions in Latin*, Assen 1983.
Veyne, P., 'Clientèle et corruption au service de l'état: la vénalité des offices dans le Bas-Empire Romain', *Annales ESC* 36 (1981) 339-360.
Vogt, H., see J.-J. Hatt.
Vos, L. de, 'L'empereur Julien et le préfet Florentius', *RPh* 34 (1910) 156-166.

Waas, M., *Germanen im Römischen Dienst (im 4. Jn.n.Chr.)*, Bonn 1971².
Wagener, C., see F. Neue.
Wagner, J.A., *Ammiani Marcellini quae supersunt*, cum notis integris Frid. Lindenbrogii, Henr. et Hadr. Valesiorum et Iac. Gronovii, quibus Thom. Reinesii quasdam et suas adiecit, editionem absolvit Car. Gottl. Aug. Erfurdt, 3 vols., Leipzig 1808 (repr. in 2 vols., Hildesheim 1975).
Walter, Ch., 'Raising on a Shield in Byzantine Iconography', *REByz* 33 (1975) 133-175.
Warmington, B.H., 'Objectives and Strategy in the Persian War of Constantius II', *Limes. Akten des XI. Internationalen Limeskongresses*, J. Fitz (ed.), Budapest 1977, 509-520.
Weicker, G., 'Iris 1', *RE* 9 (1916) 2037-2043.
Weiss, P., *Consistorium und Comites Consistoriani. Untersuchungen zur Hofbeamtenschaft des 4. Jahrhunderts n.Chr. auf prosopographischer Grundlage*, Würzburg 1975.
Wickert, L., '*Princeps*', *RE* 22 (1954) 1998-2296.
Wickert, L., 'Neue Forschungen zum römischen Principat', *ANRW* 2.1, Berlin 1974, 3-76.
Widengren, G., 'Iran, der grosse Gegner Roms. Königsgewalt, Feudalismus, Militärwesen', *ANRW* 2.9.1, Berlin 1976, 219-306.
Wiedemann, T.E.J., 'Between Men and Beasts: Barbarians in Ammianus Marcellinus', *Past Perspectives. Studies in Greek and Roman Historical Writing*, I.S. Moxon, J.D. Smart, A.J. Woodman (eds.), Cambridge 1986, 189-201.
Will, Ern., 'Remarques sur la fin de la domination romaine dans le Nord de la Gaulle', *Revue du Nord* 48 (1966) 517-534.
Will, Ern., 'Boulogne et la fin de l'Empire romain d'Occident', *Hommages à M. Renard*, J. Bibauw (ed.), II, Brussels 1969, 820-827.
Willems, W.J.H., *Romans and Batavians. A Regional Study in the Dutch Eastern River Area*, Amsterdam 1986.
Wirth, G., 'Rom, Parther und Sassaniden. Erwägungen zu den Hintergründen eines historischen Wechselverhältnisses', *AncSoc* 11/12 (1980/81) 305-347.
Wirth, G., see also O. Veh.

Wölfflin, E., '*Frustra, nequiquam* und Synonyma', *ALL* 2 (1885) 1–24.
Wölfflin, E., 'Substantiva mit in privativum', *ALL* 4 (1887) 400–412.
Wölfflin, E., 'Das *Breviarium* des Festus, II', *ALL* 13 (1904) 173–180.
Wolff, H., *Die Constitutio Antoniniana und Papyrus Giessensis 40 I*, Diss. Cologne 1976.
Wolfram, H., *Geschichte der Goten. Von den Anfängen bis zur Mitte des sechsten Jahrhunderts. Entwurf einer historischen Ethnographie*, Munich 1979.
Wonterghem, F. van, see H. Devijver.

Zaugg, M., see S. Martin-Kilcher.
Zawadzki, T., '*Dioecesis Thraciarum*, un indice de falsification dans l'Histoire Auguste', *BHAC* 1972–1974, Bonn 1976, 323–330.
Zilliacus, H., 'Anredeformen', *JbAC* 7 (1964)167–182.
Zöllner, E., *Geschichte der Franken bis zur Mitte des 6. Jahrhunderts*, Munich 1970.

INDICES

I LEXICAL (Latin)

abruptus 123
absolvere 225
accidere 15
accire 245
acies 224
adesse 270
ad summam 34
adminiculum 73
admittere 139, 222, 231
adolescere 265
adorea 54
adulari 199
adusque 164
adversus 124
advertere 200
aerumna(e) 163
aeternitas 205
affirmare 207
agere 43, 46
aggestus 274
alacer 258
alioqui 150
aliquotiens 150
altrinsecus 269
altus 116
amarus 253
ambigere 6
ambiguus 270
ambitiosus 115
ambitus 254
ambo 162
amendare 17, 195
amicus 246
angor 84
animam amittere 248
animare 81
annona 66
antequam 227
antistes 163
anxius 183
apertus 38
apparatus 179
apparitor 191
aptare 95, 263
arbitrium 240
arcus caelestis 282
ardor 70, 91, 135
arduus 117
armatus 109
arripere 45

artus 144
asciscere 110, 245
aspergo 283
asportare 147
asserere 225
assignare 191
assultus 197
assurgere 128
attenuare 29
auctoritas 65
audire 16
augere 256
augustus 111
aureus 101
auspicium 95
auxiliari(u)s 61
avidus 160, 201

bellator 271
bellicosus 6
benignitas 205
bitumen 280
bona fide 200

cadere 261
caduceator 159
caerulus 286
callidus 166
calumnia 19
campus 115
canere 259
caries 166
caritas 76
castrum 157
causari 217
caute 244
celsus 55, 221
cessare 85
cilicium 260
circulus 34
circumsaepire 254
circumspicere 184
circumvadere 140
civilis 126
clamores efferre 260
clanculo 213
clare nati 257
clare(sce)re 190
claudere 148
claustra 279

clementia 205
clipeus 259
coactus 37
coagmentum 145
coeptum 128
cohaerenter 159
cohorrescere 195
colligere 118
collustrare 251
columen 117
comitatus 34, 76
commentum 145
commilitium 10
concedere 129, 206
concinere 53, 161
concolor 287
conclamare 91
concordare 133
concrepare 86, 128
concretus 286, 291
condicere 3
confertus 161
confidens 100, 215
confirmare 207
confundere 69
congeries 3
conglobatus 290
congruens 210
congruus 137
conserere 254
consilium 69, 73, 152
consistere 32
conspectus 282
constellatio 293
constringere 101
consultus 129
consumere 265
consurgere 254
contemnere 183
contemplabilis 166
contemplari 77, 116
contemplator 166
contentio 91
conterere 192
contiguus 197, 261
contingere 15
contorquere 159
contrarius 38
contus 254
conus 41
convenire 61
conversio 32
convicium 92
convolare 143
copulare 250

cor 101, 133
corbis 272
corium 267
cornu 6
cornutus 44, 176
corona 94
coronare 96
corrigere 242
corrogare 82
corrumpere 255
coturnus 6
crass(at)us 37, 290
cratis 260
crepusculum 275
crispare 106
cruor 256
culmen 117
cumulate 269
cuneus 254
curiosus 260
currere 190
cur(r)ulis 201
cursare 47
cursus 29, 77
curvamen 41, 284

dare 13
dare litteras 225
decernere 265
declarare 105, 132
decorus 35
deflorare 288
defrustare 18
deinceps 185
deliberare 192
densus 258
deputare 154
desciscere 204
deses 235
destinare 276
destinatio 257
destinatus 87
detorquere 15
diadema 94
dichomenis 44
dictitare 36
diffundere 289
dignitas 103, 127
dilutus 36, 287
dimensio 35
dimidi(at)us 29, 284
dimittere 250
diripere 273
dirumpere 273
discurrere 137

discutere 19
disiunctus 45
disiungere 217
dispalari 108
disparare 38, 84
dispendium 150
dispergere 121
disponere 74
dispositio 129
dissimulare 71
dissolvere 264
distinctio 33
distrahere 4
diutius 28
diuturnitas 123
divellere 217
documentum 15, 191
dolabra 276
domicilium 31
dubietas 66
dudum 185
duplus 256

edicere 83
edictum 229
effectus 190
efferatus 164
effigies 29
effingere 268
effundere 54
egens 194
ego 189
eminere 180
eminus 141
en 253
enim 210
eo usque...ut 197
eous 27
episcopus 165
erigere 64
erumpere 85
evanescere 108
evidens 38
exasperare 292
excandescere 223
excellentia 205
excidere 14
excidium 14, 121
ex(s)cindere 152
excitare 269, 273, 287
exclamare 104
excursus 230
exin(de) 166, 266
exordium 184
expeditio 179

exsertare 260
extimus 40, 239

fabre 263
facies 125
fastigium 124
fateor 195
fatiscere 253
fax 144
felicitas 205
ferre 220
ferre suppetias 53
ferus 2
fervere 142
fervor 255
fidenter 215
fidus 117, 246
figurare 282
finis 33
firmare 207
firmitas, -udo 264
flagitare 117, 237
flammeus 139, 289
flatus 225
flavescens 286
flectere 224
fluctuare 73
foculus 277
formidare 68
fortis 117
fortuna 84, 234
fragor 91, 190
fremere 193
fretum oceani 233
fulgere 111
fundere 266
fusio 283

gens 2
geometrica ratio 32
gestire 132
glacialis 194
glans 145
gracilescere 44
gradus 81, 104, 126, 225

habitus 44, 111
haesitare 109
halitus 283
hebetare 43, 263
hiatus 261
hiems 7, 121
hinc inde 142
horrendus 190

iam inde (ab) 190
idem 46, 64
ignavus 15
(ig)notus 105
illaqueare 269
illidere 128
immensitas 121
imminere 144, 278
immodicus 21
impatiens 193
impendio 154
impensus 272
impetrare 130
implere 192
implicare 3
inaequalis 30
inanis 16
incassum 63, 164
incendiarius 267
incentivum 135
incessere 271
incitamentum 258
in continenti 106
incuria 255
indecorus 89
indigena 148
indigere 209
indurare 257
indutiae 196
inferior spes 262
ingenuus 159
ingruere 124
innocuus 158
innoxius 158
innumerus 121
inopinus 194
inquietus 238
insignia 71
insolubilis 279
insperatus 86
instar 49
instaurare 255
institutor 153
intellegibilis 32
intentare 226
intentus 134, 220
intepescere 235
intercipere 150
interior 141
interiora 262
intermenstruum 30, 46
intermicare 27, 289
internecivus 76
interpretatio 19
interquiescere 116
interstitium 44

intrinsecus 166
intromittere 222
introrsus 160
invidia 215
ira(cundia) 193
irasci 19
iris 282
ita 253
iterare 87
iudex 125
iugis 27
iunctim 35
ius 83

labrum 157
lacinia 268
laetus 234
lanx 28, 40
lar 62
later(culus) 146
latus 206, 258
laxare 259
levis 240
lex 163
libellus 75
liberalitas 83, 246
libramentum 34
licenter 238
ligo 276
limus 223
liniamentum 32
liquidus 290
lituus 116
longe 254
longinquus 207
luctus 164
lunaris 33
luteus 285
lux 115

magnitudo 292
malleolus 144
malum (= monstrum) 144
materia 89
mediocris 154
membrum 147
mens fundata 88
meta noctis 40
militaris 62, 253
minae 138
minutum 32
mirum in modum 196
mobilitas 39
moderator 205
moles 142
mora 73

mordax 12
mortalitas 44
motus 32
movere 80
muliebris 95
mundanus 289
mundus 95, 284
munerare 248
municipium 153
munimentum 153
murus 196
mussare 195

nativus 257
necessitas 100
necessitudo 217
necesse est 291
negotium 240
nigrans 41
niti 91
nomen 107
normalis 45
noscere 16, 119
noster 62, 204
(ig)notus 105
novare 192
nudus 194
numerus 7
nunc...aliquotiens 49
nusquam 80
nutus 163

obequitare 254
obicere 117
obiectus 140
obiurgare 132
obiurgatorius 213
obliquus 152, 221
obscurus 96
observare 7, 132, 233
obsidere 195
obstinatus 69, 162
obtrectator 11
obtutus 48
ocius 8
offerre se 159
olim 132
operire 158
opinio 12
opitulari 18
oppetere 72
opplere 251
opponere 34
opportunus 222
oppositus 268
orbiculatus 143

orbis eous 194
ordinare 231
ordinarius 205
ordo 1, 50, 125, 215
ornare 124
otium 20

pacatus 139
palatium 77, 86
paludamentum 119
pandere 275
paries 140
pars 32, 42
pars...alii 106
parthicus 179
pate(sce)re 146
pauci 147, 266
pectus 196
pellere 138
pellis 149
penitus 43
per flumen 241
percitus 16, 253
perculsus 223
percursare 239
perducere 61
perduellis 218
perfidia 108
perforare 161
permiscere 191
permutare 118
permutatio 291
perpendere 224
perpendiculum 43
perquam 149
perstare 164
perstringere 118
persultare 121
perterrere 103
pertimescere 183
pertinax 15
pervadere 238
petere 126
phalera 95
placere 130
plebs 143
plenilunium 39
plures 148
pluteus 140
pone 277
populus 160
porrigere 44
poscere 117
possessor 240
posthabere 247
potior 62, 64, 126

313

praemonere 246
praestringere 36
praestruere 138
primitus 44
princeps 10, 71, 81
principatus 71
priscus 150
priusquam 227
probabilis 14
probare 14
procedere 102
proceres 82
procinctus 8, 273
procurare 70
profundus 123
proin(de) 266
prolapsio 89
promovere 21, 226
promptus 83
propellere 138
propinquare 237
propior 289
propositum 120
proprius 289
propugnaculum 141
propugnator 117, 137
prosperitas 191
prospicere 274
provincialis 230
prudentia 205, 218
pugnax 68
puniceus 286
purgare 90
purpuratus 119
purpureus 286

quaesitor 13
qualitas 8
quamquam 185
– *que* 263
querela 77
quidam 49, 83
quies 3, 132, 273
quorsum 183

ratio 201, 247
receptus 259
reciprocatio 288
rector 4
regio 33, 45
relatio 68, 255
relatus 185
reluctari 72
remedium 118
remissus 235
reniti 100

renuntiare 93
rependere 193
repentinus 106
replicare 228
repudiare 132
repugnanter 186
res cibaria 251
– *novae* 184
– *publica* 117
reserare 143
residuus 65
respondere 159
resultare 275
retexere 121
retinere 45, 153
retrogradi 269
reverti 51
revocare 31
robur 18
rotundatus 38

sanguis 256
sauciare 160
scire 48
scortum 267
scriptum 69
scruposus 239
scrutari (-tor) 33
secessio 199
secus 198
sedes 90
semenstris 29
semiinteger 121
semustus 273
sensus 187
sententia 188
sequestrare 158
series 1, 213, 215
serius 102
signum 39, 104
singuli 88
solidus 101
solitus 194
sollemnia 186
sollemnis 74, 136
sonus 229
species 118, 282
spectare 13
sperare 198
spes 127
sphaera 41, 284
spiramen 283
spiritus 48
spondere 204
statarius 180
statio 74

stativa 85
status 200
stella 49
stimulare 56
stipator 206
strages 162
stringere 247
structilis 276
struere 145
studium 220
stultus 206
suasor 224
subiectus 260
subito 238
subnectere 12
subserere 40
subtexere 27
suburbanum 80
succurrere 272
sudor 193
super = de 6, 60
supercilium 6
superstare 140
supinare 284
supra modum 19
suscipere 8, 15, 225, 246
suspectus 154
suspicio 232
susurrare 199

taeda 144
tamen 114
temerare 248
temperare 287
tentoria figere 254
tenus 216
terrenus 40
terror 28, 163
textus 76
tormentum 138
torques 98
totus 40
trahere 18
transenna 276
transfretare 222
transmarinus 4

truculentus 134
trudere 100
tum etiam 46
turba 67
turbare (-tor) 53
turbulentus 104
turris 143
tutela 119
tutus 115

ultimus 212
ultra modum 19
ululare 146
umere 280
universi 88
universitas 48
urere 54
usquam 102
usus 123
ut 217
utrubique 162

vagus 106
varietas 102, 270
varius 258
vectis 276
velitaris 7
velox 77
velut 216, 226
venia 192
vereri 4
vergere 154
versabilis 108
versare 65
versus 225
vesania 164
vespera 142, 278
vetustas 255
via 74
vicis 193
vincere 72
vinea 140
violentus 261
viridis 286
volubiliter 284
volucris 107

LEXICAL (Greek)

ἀμφίκυρτος 41, 45
ἀπόκρουσις 46
διχόμηνις 44
διχότομος 41
ἦθος 120

λοξός 223
παρήλιον 22, 37
πνεῦμα 48
προαίρεσις 120
σύνδεσμος 24, 36, 37

II SYNTAX AND STYLE

ablativus absolutus 14, 18, 114, 126, 142
abl. abs. with *nihil* 270
– of duration 141
abstr. pro concreto 44
abundantia sermonis 166, 224, 225
accentuation 5, 45
ad to denote cause 68
adjective with noun in the genitive 123
adoriri + inf. and
– + gerundivum 136
adverbial expression with *in* 106
adverbs in *-im* 118
– ultimate position 100, 134
agere with local adjunct 46
aliquis preceded by *ne* 89
alliteration 70
antequam with coni. 111
apo koinou 63
appositions 7, 28
astronomical terminology 22–51
asyndeton bimembre 21, 142
autem parenthetical 148

cessare with abl. 85
chiasmus 52, 102, 125
comparativus with *solito* 38, 115
– pro positivo 93, 104, 115
comparisons 123
composita of *sedere* 195
concurrere + dative 42
consecutio temporum 138
constructio ad sententiam 275
contingere, absolute use of 15
coordination of participle with abstract verbal substantive 121
– A et B Cque 7
coupling of two verba monendi 246
cum causale with indic. 208
– iterativum 42
– with indic. praes. 65
cumque 65
cursus, influence of 33

dative of the agent 44
daybreak, expressions for 87, 139, 161
deponential conjugation 198
dialysis 261
dies, genitive of 160
digressions, see VI Various Topics
ducere, absolute use of 149
dum with indic. praes. or coni. imperf. 134

enallage 146
– combined with gen. inversus 239

est + infin. 122
et and *-que*, loss of semantic value of 65
– explicativum 74
– *quia* 65

ferrum et ignis 146
frequentativa 36
future, gnomical 45
– imperative, use of 133
– participles, see participles

geminatio 210
genitivus, defining 18
– inversus 38, 142, 146, 153
– partitivus 89
– qualitatis 40, 103
gerundium, abl. of 109
gerundi(v)um construction, use of 135
gerundivum as a part. fut. pass. 18, 194, 216, 279
– with *esse* as a substitute of the inf. fut. pass. 68
Grecisms 43, 164, 242
Greek technical terms 43

haec as nom. pl. fem. 208
hendiadyoin 212
hyperbaton 252

idem, anaphoric use 64
imperativus praes. and fut. 198
imperfect, durative or iterative use 63, 94, 237
– used to sketch a background 91, 143, 147, 148
inconcinnitas 5, 145, 146, 163
indicative in indirect questions 122, 252
– in subordinate clauses of oratio obliqua 82, 225
– in the apodosis of an irrealis 263
indirect questions 7, 122
infin. praes. in AcI with *memini* 240
intensiva 36
is, oblique cases instead of *se* and *sibi* 72

licet 32, 150

metaphors 3, 6, 27, 31, 53, 89
military terminology, inexact use 5, 10, 115

min(it)ari + abl.   106
monere + gen.   81
multiplicativa   2

ne dicam   210
nec = *ne quidem*   124
nec with adversative force   159, 161
neologisms   121
NcI construction   19, 65
ni "de rupture"   271
nullo as abl. of *nihil*   215

obsecrare with coni.   130
oxymoron   15, 95

parenthesis   165, 209
paronomasia   108
participle or neuter adjective with noun in the genitive   123
– coordination with abstract verbal subst.   121
– in apposition   28
– fut. in "Satznachtrag"   164
– fut. in abl. abs.   126
– fut. in a final sense   13
– fut. instead of praes.   159
– praes. and abl. gerundii   109
– praes. with preterite force   110
– praes. instead of missing part. perf. act.   247
– perf. pass. used transitively   270
perfect instead of pluperfect   56, 121, 186, 215
perf. and plup., alternation of   226
perf. pass., tendency to avoid the forms of   63, 94, 149
personification   3, 32, 150, 285
pluperfect instead of perfect   33, 61
– forms with *fui*   273
poeticisms   3, 27, 72, 107, 122, 124, 135, 166

polysyndeton   247
posse with infin. praes. as a periphrasis of the future   274
post with part.   55
praeteritio   121
predicate, position in narrative style   67

quaeso, parenthetical use of   90
quam without *magis* or *potius*   72
quidam preceding an adjective   84
quod-clause instead of AcI   133, 197
quodam modo   122

relative clause used substantivally   272
reluctari with inf. as complement   73

scholarly prose   48
sermocinatio   133
solito, comparative with   38, 115
sonus, declination   88
suadere, constructions with   164
subject-accusative, omission of   164
subjunctive, after *licet*   32
– in virtual oratio obliqua   135, 138
super (= *de*) with gerundium   60
suspicio, quod   232
suus instead of *eius/eorum*   122
synizesis   33, 261
"Synonymenhäufung"   68, 209, 212

tamen   114
tenses   141
transition formulas   38

ut non = *ne*   62
ut, omission of   130

verbal substantive, coordination with participle   121
verba orandi, omission of *ut* after   130

word order   116

III GEOGRAPHICAL NAMES

Amida   9, 251
Antioch   263
Aquitania   236
Argaeus   222
Armenia   246
– minor   246, 250
– I and II   250
Augusta (London)   8
Augusta Rauraca   242

Besantio   243
Bezabde   152, 178, 244
Bononia   7, 233
Bosporus   222
Britain   3, 178, 232, 236
Britannia prima   3
– secunda   3

Caesarea   222, 250

Cappadocia 222, 250
Castrum Rauracense 242
Channel, the 233
Commagene 250
Constantinople 179

Edessa 250
Euphratensis 250
Euphrates 178
Eusebia 222

Flavia Caesariensis 3

Gaul 189, 191, 207, 208, 216, 230
Germania inferior 236
– secunda 236

Illyricum 1

Lacotena 250
London 8
Lutetia 3

Maxima Caesariensis 3
Mazaca 222
Megara 179
Melitene 250
Mesopotamia 18, 178, 223
Mildenhall 232

Nisibis 149, 152, 251

Oceanus 233
Osrhoene 251
Oriens 2

Paris 3, 178, 189, 212, 232
Parisii 3
Persis 147
Phaenicha 152
Pinaka 152
Praefectura Illyrici Italiae et Africae 1

Quinque (septem) provinciae 236

Rutupiae 8

Samosata 250
Singara 137, 178
Spain 201, 236
Strasbourg 122
Succi (pass of) 98

Thrace 182
Tigris 178
Tricensima 237

Vienna 66, 216

Zabdicene 153

IV NAMES OF PERSONS/PEOPLES

Ablabius 249
Aeruli 7
Agilo 20
Alamanni 4, 20, 230
Anatolius 227, 231
Antoninus 135
Antoninus Pius 219
Arbitio 13
Archelaus 222
Arsaces II 245
Arsaces III 245, 248

Barbatio 11, 184
Batavi 7

Canninefates 92
Constans 4
Constantine the Great 10, 21, 225, 231
Constantius II passim
Craugasius 135

Decentius 57, 63, 78, 185, 186
Diocletian 180, 182

(H)eruli 7
Egyptians 233
Eusebius 14
Eutherius 184, 191, 214, 220, 221, 231, 235
Excubitor 107

Felix 227, 231
Florentius (PPO of Gaul) 56, 66, 69, 215, 216, 218, 219, 226
Florentius (magister officiorum) 13
Franci Atthuarii and Salii 238

Galli 207
Gallus 184, 196
Germans 191
Gintonius (see Sintula)
Gomoarius 5, 227

Goths 180

Hannibal 192
Helena (Iul. i uxor) 95

Jovian 232, 246
Julian passim

Leonas 212, 225, 228, 231, 235
Lupicinus 5-6, 66, 73, 178, 227, 232

Magnentius 219
Maurus 96

Nebridius 205, 226

Olympias 249

Palladius 215
Palmatius 202
Parthians 60, 179, 208
Pentadius 184, 214, 220, 221, 231, 235
Persians 52, 221, 223
Petronius 21
Pharandzem 249
Picts 2, 232
Procopius 184, 195, 218, 219, 224

Rauraci 242

Sabinianus 9, 11, 15, 205, 227
Sapor II 134, 152, 158, 178
Scots 2, 232
Scythians 180, 181
Severus 5
Silvanus 218
Sintula 61, 63

Tetraxitae 181
Theodosius 180
Tigranes VII 245
Tiran II 245
Tiridates IV 245

Ursicinus
– accentuation of name 5
– inquiry against 9-21
– downfall of 9, 23
– relationship with Julian 23
– id. with Ammianus 9
Ursulus 252, 253

Valens 181, 191, 196, 199, 211, 232
Valentinian 191, 211
Valentinus 184
Vetranio 227

V MILITARY MATTERS

actuarii 129
adlocutio 113
agger 265
army
　grain supply 66
　field-, created by Constantine 7, 10, 148
　(see also military organisation)
auxilia 7, 58, 148

banners and standards 115

catafracti 156
cavalry 21
Celtae 59
classis Britannica 7
clibanarii 157
cohors 115
cohortes praetoriae 21
comes domesticorum 107
– *rei militaris* 97
cratis 160

decorations 265
dediticii 202-204
dignitates 103
draconarius 96
dux Mesopotamiae 135

excubitores 107
exploratores 53

Gentiles 21
globus 115

hastatus 96
honores 103

indigenous troops 155

laeti 202-204
legio 7
– II Armeniaca 154
– I Flavia Gemina 148
– II Flavia Gemina 154
– I Parthica 148

- II Parthica   154
- XXX Ulpia Victrix   237

machines
  aries   142
  ballista   158
  tormenta   138
magister equitum   10-11
- *in praesenti*   10-11
- *per Gallias*   5, 10
- *militum*   10-11, 103
- *peditum*   10-11
  id. *in praesenti*   10-11
milit. organisation   5-6, 7, 10-11, 52, 58-59, 96-97
militia   20, 103
musical instruments   161

ordo   125

Petulantes   59
proceres   82

promotions   124
protector atque tribunus   103
pseudocomitatenses   155

sagittae   158
scholae palatinae   13, 21, 107
scouts   53
Scutarii   21
sieges   136, 153, 160
standards and banners   115
statio   74
stativa   85
swords   106

terminology, inexact use of   5, 10, 115
testudo   158
titles   13
tribunus   103, 107
- *stabuli*   61

Zabdiceni   155

VI   VARIOUS TOPICS

administrationes   103
agri deserti   240
annona   66
argumentation techniques   162
Arianism   246
astronomy   22-51
"Augustus" in late antiquity   63

barbarians   55

"Caesar" in the late antiquity   63
castrensiani   104
Christian terminology   165
chronology   60, 235, 262
cloak, the imperial   119
coins   101
comes sacrarum largitionum   252
comitatus   76, 111
comites consistoriani   111
commilitium   10
composition of the *Res Gestae*   235
consilium   110
consistorium   111
coronation   92, 96
corrector   103
cubicularii   14
clavularis (cursus)   77

decuriones consistorii   103
- *palatii*   103
diadem (see *insignia*)
dignitates   103
digressions   22-23
  conclusion of –   51
dioecesis Galliarum   68, 236
- *Orientis*   2
- *Viennensis*   66
divinatio   132

earth, place and size of   49
Eastern part of the Roman Empire   52
eclipses   22-38
emphyteuticarius   241
eunuchs   14

formulaic endings of digressions   51, 292

genius   130-131

Hadrian's wall   3
honores   103

insignia principatus   71, 94

landowners, interests of   240
Latin, Amm.'s motives to write in   36
limes   3, 236

magister officiorum 13, 107
militia 20, 103
ministeriales 104
mirror-images 38
moon 22–51

nodes 24–25, 36–37
notarii, tribuni et 57

officia 13
optimates 139

paedagogiani 104
palatium 77, 86
perpetuarius 241
physiognomical data 6
planetarium (*sphaera*) 29, 37
planets 50
postal service 77
praefectura praetorio 56, 66, 70
praefectus praetorio per Gallias 56, 236
praefectus urbi 103
praepositus sacri cubiculi 14
praeses 137
princeps 10, 71, 81
– *clausus* 9

principatus 71
provincial organisation 236

rainbow 280–291
– as an *omen* 280
– form of 284
– colours of 285
– as a weather sign 291
recusatio 88, 91
res privata 252

shooting stars 290
silentiarii 104
sol geminus 22, 37
sphaera (see planetarium)
sphere, celestial 39
stars, movements of the 50
suffragator 126

technical terms (avoidance of) 252
titles 13, 81
tribuni et notarii 57

weeping of emperor 251
whispering 199

VII PASSAGES REFERRED TO (LATIN)

Anonymus Valesianus		Aurelius Victor	
5.18	270	*Caes.* 24.9	200
		33.13	129
Apuleius		39.48	200
Apol. 75.8	194		
92.2	194	*Bellum Africum*	
Fl. 15	263	10.2	14
Met. 3.3.3	88	78.2	258
11.1	43	93.1	162
11.7	291	94.1	265
Mun. 305	283		
Pl. 1.10	33	Boethius	
		Cons. 4, carm. 5.8–9	40
Arnobius			
1.29.6	13	Caesar	
1.64.3	12	*Civ.* 1.40.5	279
		2.9.4	267
Augustinus		2.10.4	145
Civ. 3.25	211	2.10.6	267
5.6	293	3.13.5	149
12.20	266	3.37.3	260
15.7	18	3.44.1	179
c. Faust. 2.5	293	3.105.4	137
gen. ad litt. 4.28	128	*Gal.* 1.5.4	242

1.31.4	182	12.1.1	262
1.38.2	243	12.6a.2	90
1.41.1	196	13.6.3	213
3.14.4	269		
4.1.4	109	*Brut.* 9	212
5.19.1	272	25	207
5.37.3	86, 146	91	116
6.10.5	257	201	210
7.8.2	193		
7.21.1	91	*Cael.* 41	89
7.25.4	137	*Catil.* 1.14	122
7.38.6	91	1.22	185
7.70.5	269	2.5	111
7.82.2	161	4.14	190
7.89.2	159	4.19	190
		4.23	196
Calcidius		*Corn.* 1 fr. 44	228
comm. 33 (p. 83.16W)	32	*Div.* 1.18	286
77 (p. 125.7W)	34	1.130	286
87 (p. 138.17W)	34	2.17	40
124 (p. 167.20W)	34	2.44	283
248 (p. 258.22W)	284	*Dom.* 96	210
267 (p. 272.22W)	199	*Ep. ad. Brut.* 1.15.8	54
302 (p. 304.7W)	33	*Fam.* 1.9.18	256
		4.9.3	90
Cassiodorus		6.12.5	183
in psalm. 148, 276 sqq.	39	8.12.2	223
var. 9.22.5	282	9.5.2	210
		Fin. 3.14	89
Cato		5.33	83
Fil. 1	17	*Inv.* 2.9.28	108
		Lael. 27	211
Catullus		43	190
8.11	69	*Man.* 9	45
40.5	54	32	207
64.62	74	*Mil.* 75	138
		95	184
Censorinus		99	217
8.10	38	*Mur.* 1	93
		50	207
Cicero		*N.D.* 1.4	199
Ac. 1.11	101	2.14	261
2.33	272	2.25	283
2.105	291	2.50	46
		3.51	282
Arch. 13	129	3.87	256
21	270	3.88	191
		Off. 1.66	117
Att. 1.14.6	196	1.90	190
		de Orat. 1.20	187
2.20.5	183	1.162	276
7.3.1	196	1.219	192
7.7.7	34	1.242	192
9.5.2	210	2.347	239
10.16.5	65	*Orat.* 70.1	35
11.17a.3	16	229	237

Part. 70	208	*Codex Iustinianus*	
Phil. 2.17	15	9.44.1	129
2.29	224	*Codex Theodosianus*	
3.32	64, 190	7.1.3	77
Planc. 22	256	7.4.6	293
48	117	7.20.2	230
96	292	8.5.20pr.	129
Q. Rosc. 29	12	8.5.62	77
Rab. Post. 39	194	9.34.10	213
Rep. 1.19	37	11.1.1	248
1.22	30	13.9.5	84
1.25	30, 31, 46	13.11.10	204
2.69	53	15.1.20	255
6.17–18	34, 39	15.10.1	202
6.18	287	16.10.12	131
6.24	28, 31		
Sest. 19	134	*Collectio Avellana*	
125	205	83.298	213
S. Rosc. 40	279	144.5	213
120	66		
Sul. 57	17	Columella	
74	133	2.10.10	46
		11.2.85	39
Tim. 6	48		
17	40	*Concilium Arelatense*	
Top. 71	69	can. 3	71
Tusc. 1.40	49		
1.43	101	*Concilium Carthaginiense a.411*	
1.62	32	1.4.72	229
1.63	30	*Corp. Gloss.* 2.35.51	205
1.108	139	4.51	202
3.28	86	5.188	202
5.12	208		
5.69	32	Curtius Rufus	
Ver. 2.1.31	105	8.2.38	70
2.1.38	206		
2.1.82	86	Cyprianus	
2.5.87	108	*epist.* 50.2	144
3.54	13	55.19.1	259
5.71	117	80.1.2	106
5.120	18		
5.173	14	Donatus	
		Aen. 2.550	38
CIL		Ter. *Eu.* 601	223
3.3726	255		
10629	255	Ennius	
8.22016	255	*Ann.* 131 Sk.	106
22073	255	*Trag.* 72 Joc.	109
10.4524.3–4	40	*var.* 18	54
Claudianus		Eutropius	
In Ruf. 353–4	73	10.15.1	88
Caudianus Mamertus			
anim 1.13	40		

Faustus Reiensis
serm. 12, p. 268.9 — 282

Firmicus Maternus
math. 2.5.1 — 32
4.1.10 — 41

Florus
Epit. 1.20.2 — 280
1.22.19 — 192
1.33.5 — 159
1.34.12 — 276
1.36.10 — 128

Frontinus
Aq. 9.5 — 240

Gaius
1.14 — 202

Gellius
2.2.9 — 116
2.26.8–9 — 286
2.12.3 — 116
7.2.8 — 73
9.14.6 — 272
10.26.1 — 222
19.1.7 — 70

Germanicus
Arat. fr. 2.19–20 — 30

Gregorius Turonensis
HF 6.44 — 282

Hieronymus
adv. Iovin. 1.13 — 4
in Ezech. 1.28 — 282
in Is. 7.10 — 33
epist. 69.9 — 38
tract. in psalm. XV — 270

Historia Augusta
A. 26.4 — 179
43.4 — 9
Ael. 4.5 — 293
AS 21.7 — 81
Car. 18 — 211
Dd. 1.6 — 230
DI 5.3 — 94
Gd 20.2 — 293
23.2 — 37
Max. 3.1 — 76
11.9 — 179
12.5 — 188
OM 1.5 — 118
Q. 9.2 — 230

Horatius
Ars. 272 — 210
Carm. 4.4.40–1 — 54
Ep. 2.1.13–4 — 54
2.1.256 — 68
3.16.15–6 — 269
Epod. 2.5 — 273
16.17 — 272
S. 1.1.12 — 86
2.7.53–4 — 111
Saec. 18–9 — 60

Iohannes Cassianus
Coll. 19.12.3 — 213

Iulius Obsequens
62 — 29

Iulius Valerius
1.35 — 156

Iustinus
5.3.3 — 133
38.4.15 — 123

Iuvenalis
6.131 — 96

Lactantius
inst. 2.5.18 — 29
6.20.7 — 27
mort. pers. 30.4 — 107
32.3 — 6

Livius
pr. 8 — 56
1.29.2 — 146
1.32.3 — 235
1.46.2 — 56
1.47.11 — 184
1.49.4 — 69
1.58.5 — 69
1.58.12 — 91
2.7.1 — 162
2.23.11 — 205
2.30.12 — 273
2.30.14 — 109
2.31.2 — 275
2.45.9 — 135
2.45.10 — 85
2.46.3 — 273
2.47.5 — 134
2.48.2 — 193
2.51.6 — 136
2.65.1 — 185
3.12.5 — 179

3.22.6		7	25.41.6		109
3.27.6		258	26.5.1		153
3.50.5		89	26.10.7		271
4.6.10		207	26.44.9		141
4.25.9		279	27.12.6		201
4.25.11		184	27.13.12		88
5.39.2		239	27.24.3		83
5.49.2		100	27.28.10		276
6.26.5		239	27.40.6		142
6.40.10		192	28.3.5		139
7.25.9		124	28.6.12		184
7.38.6		193	28.15.5		109
7.40.10		259	28.19.18		137
8.1.7		146	28.20.10		199
8.13.17		292	28.25.4		292
8.31.2		18	28.37.7		237
8.38.16		258	29.14.3		190
9.19.8		180	29.17.6		192
9.31.9		95	29.17.16		147
9.32.1		279	29.18.17		269
9.32.5		109	30.5.8		273
9.32.6		161	30.6.3		239
9.37.8		276	30.8.2		18
10.2.12		140	30.11.3		56
10.18.2		182	30.12.22		197
10.40.12		269	30.31.1		187
21.4.8		192	30.38.8		23
21.5.3		1	31.47.6		279
21.6.8		72	32.16.15		154
21.7.7		144	32.17.13		259
21.14.1		192	32.20.2		122
21.16.3		235	33.3.12		64
21.27.8		263	34.3.9		111
21.28.1		146	34.5.4		216
21.28.4		146	34.20.6		121
21.46.4		237	35.12.10		124
21.41.7		56	35.25.3		112
21.58.5		190	35.29.12		18
21.59.10		150	35.48.3		156
21.62.2		86	36.12.7		266
22.7.10		4	36.23.2		268
22.18.3		180	37.7.12		232
22.21.2		238	37.20.12		109
22.41.1		272	37.28.8		109
22.46.6		111	37.53.28		239
22.51.4		192	38.4.2		154
22.52.5		96	38.5.3		268
23.8.4		197	38.7.5		141
23.18.15		149	38.21.7		145
23.42.10		239	40.3.3		43
24.10.10		86	40.15.1		54
24.23.10		139	42.14.3		239
24.39.4		185	42.22.7		197
24.45.4		70	42.39.1		141
25.3.16		270	44.9.9		271
25.20.5		278	44.31.3		258

44.37.5	23	11.590	284
45.11.5	279	12.95–6	41
		13.85–6	266
Lucanus		*Pont.* 1.1.23	70
1.542–3	28	*Rem.* 649	200
6.144	144	*Tr.* 1.1.54	135
		2.563	12
Lucilius			
853 M	73	Pacuvius	
		Trag. 342	132
Lucretius			
2.772–3	291	Panegyrici Latini	
3.189–90	284	3.4.5	55
4.349–50	37	3.22.3	83
5.24–5	261	3.28	275
5.281	290	7.8.4	239
5.466	27	8.21	203
5.687–8	35		
6.476	283	Panegyricus in Messallam	
6.482	27	157	43
6.524–6	283		
		Petronius	
Macrobius		44.10	81
comm. 1.6.55	41		
1.15.10	34	Plautus	
sat. 1.12.10	31	*Am.* 1097	225
1.21.8	48	*As.* 273	132
		Bac. 781	192
Manilius		792	276
1.112	50	*Capt.* 305	184
1.827	43	*Cas.* 296	270
		Cur. 280	105
Martianus Capella		*Per.* 480	276
8.864	29	*Rud.* prol. 10	84
		1236	276
Nepos		*Trin.* 189	69
Han. 5.3	2	*Truc.* 878	70
Lys. 1.5	272		
		Plinius Maior	
Nonius		*Nat.* 2.10	48
180.15 M	276	2.42	42
		2.47	40, 41, 43
Notitia Dignitatum		2.48	31, 32
Occ. 5.160, 161, 205	59	2.51	41
42.33–44	204	2.66	34
Or. 9.26	59	2.80	29, 39
19.11	231	2.151	282
		6.85	196
Ovidius		8.52	223
Am. 1.2.31	149	8.89	144
Ars. 3.481	70	9.29	288
Ep. 7.173	8	11.138	6
Met. 1.377–8	197	12.110	282
2.405–6	179	17.39	282
6.65–7	287	18.14	55
8.788	194	20.182	287

24.113	282	57.1	218
29.61	165	58.21	248
		59.1	259
Plinius Minor		59.5	81
Ep. 4.12.6	196	*Jug.* 9.4	270
5.3.11	148	14.23	248
5.6.46	192	25.5	215
Pan. 1.2	230	61.3	129
15.5	81	89.2	273
26.1	8	68.4	144
		Hist. 2.70.3	276
Porphyrio		4.16	145
		4.64	156
ad Hor. *Carm.* 3.21.18	6		
		Seneca	
Propertius		*Ben.* 2.34.4	201
3.2.6	147	4.12.1	279
		5.6.4	36
Prudentius		*Brev.* 18.6.4	201
c. Symm. 2.370–453	131	*Ep.* 84.12	274
2.386	131	117.5	208
perist. 10.65	72	*Helv.* 6.6	105
		11.6	101
Quadrigarius		*Her.F.* 241	144
hist. 10b, 208.9 P	260	*de ira* 1.6.1	201
81, 234.14–5 P	267	2.21.7	88
		3.9.2	116
Quintillianus		3.25.3	67
Inst. 1.10.29	206	3.34.1	19
1.10.35	272	*Med.* 354	144
5.9.3	279	*Nat.* 1.2.4	37
6.3.55	108	1.3–8	281
7.10.7	12	1.3.4	287
12.2.26	101	1.3.8–9	289
12.10.49	288	1.3.11	284
12.10.59	81	1.5.1	38
		1.5.4–6	289
Rhetorica ad Herennium		1.5.13	281
1.21	270	1.7	283
		1.8	284
Rufinus		1.8.8	291
		1.11.3	38
Adamant. 2.21	71	2.30	283
		2.54	283
Rutilius Namatianus		*Tranq.* 11.10	108
277	275	*Tro.* 626	88
Sallustius		Servius	
Cat. 23.3.	106	*Aen.* 2.333	211
24.1	105	2.268	275
28.1	239	3.50	17
44.5	247	4.242	159
46.2	183	5.488	276
51.9	217	5.606	291
52.11	276	9.2	291
56.4	225	10.677	55

Georg. 1.466–8	28	32.2	122
		33.5	86
Sidonius		40.2	233
epist. 3.3.1	133		
		Ann. 1.25.2	134
Silius Italicus		1.28.1	85
4.103	290	1.51.1	146
4.441	41	1.63.2	271
6.321–2	41	1.65.1	275
		1.68.1	238
Sisenna		1.68.3	161
hist. 83	272	1.71.3	81
103	157	2.21.1	180
		2.40.3	69
Solinus		2.45.2	106
1.56	280	2.45.3	251
1.105	55	2.50.2	99
32.17	29	2.55.1	221
32.22	144	2.55.5	197
50.2	283	2.72.2	234
		2.80.1	199
Statius		2.80.4	273
Ach. 1.297	289	2.82.1	19
Silv. 2.1.67	195	3.15.2	215
2.6.51–2	69	3.34.6	217
5 praef	200	3.46.3	276
Theb. 10.176–7	104	3.52.3	188
11.369–70	162	4.18.1	205
		4.33.3	270
Suetonius		4.40.2	73
Aug. 29.3	36	4.59.1	257
53.3	81	6.8.2	256
95	290	6.9.4	16
Cal. 57.1	264	6.33.2	182
Cl. 42.1	107	11.9.1	121
Dom. 2.3	221	11.23.3	65
Gal. 4.3	131, 132	11.35.2	110
Nero 9	107	12.32.1	256
Tib. 31.3	14	12.50.2	134
37.4	197	12.66.1	142
61.1	85	13.35.3	149
66.1	292	13.39.3	258
Tit. 5.3	232	13.43.1	19
		14.29.2	218
Sulpicius Severus		14.32.1	270
dial. 1.14.4	71	14.33.1	184
		14.37.1	157
Symmachus		14.43.3	200
epist. 4.58	201	15.1.4	234
9.36	71	15.4.3	269
or. 7.5	129	15.5.3	190
rel. 3.8	131	15.6.4	216
13.1	205	15.8.2	239
		15.45.2	216
Tacitus		15.63.1	276
Ag. 25.3	86	16.14.2	150

Dial. 2.6	73	Ulpianus	
3.2	19	*dig.* 50.16.90	230
5.6	190		
32.4	184	Valerius Flaccus	
37.3	136	5.360–1	140, 289
Ger. 11	128	Valerius Maximus	
14.3	193	4.3 ext. 3	292
Hist. 1.6.2	279	Varro	
1.31.3	179	*L.* 5.167	261
1.80.2	105	7.49	218
2.2.1	292	10.46	200
2.10.1	16		
2.17.2	150	Vegetius	
2.21.4	235	*mil.* 1.9	104
2.22.1	271	2.25	276
2.27.2	108	3.3	70
2.32.1	166	3.4	154, 276
2.54.2	125	3.10	119
2.64.1	216	3.14	224
2.68.2	85	3.19	106
3.2.4	143, 224	4.6	260
3.11.2	88	4.14	267, 268
3.14.1	88	4.23	268
3.27.2	276	4.24	272
3.29.1	271	4.28	277
3.43.1	279	4.29	261
3.48.3	190		
3.49.4	18	Velleius Paterculus	
3.68.3	146	2.2.2	120
3.76.1	279	2.59.6	38
3.77.4	142	2.63.2	292
3.82.3	141	2.105.1	238
3.84.5	149		
3.86.3	239	Vergilius	
4.7.1	247	*A.* 1.16	247
4.7.5	273	1.218	292
4.8.5	72	1.313	106
4.15.2	92	2.32	263
4.15.3	279	2.650	164
4.20.4	239	2.735–6	69
4.22.2	134	3.285	194
4.32.3	292	3.425	260
4.46.1	67	3.477	45
4.70.4	144	3.582	27
4.75.1	187	3.651	251
		4.88–9	138
Terentius		4.285–6	65
Eu. 587	154	4.287	272
		4.289	263
Hau. 86	69	4.302	86
		4.351–2	280
Tertullianus		4.561	163
An. 28.5	210	4.701	284
Apol. 23.11	106	5.284	122
Resurr. 24.18	200		

5.442	197	10.464–5	133
5.857	194	10.755–6	164
6.724–6	48	11.108–9	3
7.44	215	11.345	195
7.470	162	11.346	226
7.462–3	224	11.731	81
8.80	95	12.584	143
8.84	210		
8.305	275	*G.* 1.380–1	291
8.509	209	1.466–8	28
9.509–10	259	1.467	96
9.592	266		
10.94–5	128	*Vulgata*	
10.135	95	*Esth.* 5.1	111

PASSAGES REFERRED TO (Greek)

Adamantius		Euclides	
1.1, p. 308 F.	6	*Phaen.* 1.1	49
Aeneas Tacticus		Geminos	
32.4	268	12.23–4	34
		18.4–19	30
Aëtius			
Pl. 3.5.3–9	281	Herodianus	
3.5.6	283	7.10.8	93
3.5.10	289		
		Herodotus	
Alexander Aphrodisiensis		7.208.2	242
Pr. 1.66	45		
		Homerus	
Apollonius Dyscolus		*Il.* 3.337	275
Synt. 3.32 (292.26)	260	17.547–9	291
Aristoteles		Iulianus	
Col. 791 a 2–3	287	*Ep. ad Ath.* 270 c	200
Eth. Nic. 5.1.15 (1129 b 27–8)	199	271 a	293
Mete. 1.4, 341 b	283	277 a	119
3.4, 373 b 19	283	279 b	122
3.4, 374 b 10	288	280 a	241
3.5, 375 b 16	284	280 b	182
Rhet. A 9.1368a 10–1	239	280 d	55, 59
		281 a	232, 233
Athanasius		281 b	200, 219
Hist. Ar. ad Mon. 69	249	282 b	214
		282 c	57
Cleomedes		282 d	58, 61
1.1	49	283 a	71
2.6	37	283 b	59, 75
		283 c	227
Dio Cassius		283 c–d	214
56.29.2–3	23	284 a	79–80
79.30.1	23	284 b	80, 85–87

284 c	87, 114, 131
284 d	87–88, 91, 94, 98, 99, 188
285 b	103, 104, 105
285 c	93, 109
285 d	187
286 a	211
286 c	226
Ep. 26.414 b	234
26.414 c	243
Mis. 340 a-b	202
Or. 263 a-b	60
2.98 d	95

Libanius
Or. 1.164	6
12.58	58, 59
12.59	87, 99
13.34	87, 91, 93
15.16	263
18.90	54, 58
18.96	79
18.98	88
18.99	98, 99
18.102	102, 105
18.104	231
18.105	234, 236
18.106	226
18.169	181

Lucianus
Hist. conscr. 19	22
57	22

Nonnus
D. 4.281	45

Plato
Tim. 42 e 5-6	120

Philoponus
in Mete. 21.11	284

Procopius
Goth. 8.5.6	181

Schol. Arat.
940 p. 515f M	281

Socrates
H.E. 3.1.35	94, 97, 99

Solon
fr. 34.16	223

Sozomenus
HE 5.1	231

Strabo
12.2.7	222
7.292	238

Synesius
De regno 19	181

Theo Smyrnaeus
178.17–179.1	51

Theocritus
20.13	223

Theophanes
Chron. p. 46.33 de B.	99

Thucydides
2.28	27

Xenophon
H.G. 5.1.10	43

Zonaras
13.10.12	92, 197
13.10.14	94, 95, 99
13.10.15	98
13.10.16	193
13.10.16–8	188
13.10.17	200
13.10.18	201
13.10.20	223
13.10.21	226
13.10.21–8	228
13.10.28	212
13.11.1	231

Zosimus
2.54.1	203
3.8.3–4	59
3.9.1	75, 85
3.9.2	91, 93, 98, 99
3.9.3	201
3.9.4	226
3.25.6	181
5.32	225

VIII Passages referred to in Ammianus 14–19 and 21–31

14.1.1	55, 117, 161	14.10.9	93
14.1.2	135	14.10.13	113, 114
14.1.4	215	14.10.14	113, 163
14.1.5	150, 192	14.11.1	245
14.1.8	134	14.11.2	13
14.2.2	49	14.11.3	40
14.2.6	36, 123	14.11.6	150
14.2.8	180	14.11.8	134
14.2.9	7, 63, 164	14.11.10	119
14.2.12	115	14.11.11	133
14.2.14	94	14.11.19	68, 98
14.2.17	128	14.11.26	44
14.2.18	141	14.11.29	121
14.2.20	205	15.1.2	40, 60
14.3.1	18, 108, 135	15.1.3	40
14.5.1	12, 98	15.2.2	12
14.5.4	224	15.2.3	115
14.5.7	3, 130	15.2.4	149, 174
14.5.8	77	15.2.10	14
14.6.1	182	15.3.3	12
14.6.2	122, 164, 211	15.3.5	132
14.6.6	125, 150	15.4.9	226
14.6.8	36	15.4.10	163
14.6.9	194	15.5.3	129, 130
14.6.12	93	15.5.4	98, 221, 231
14.6.15	171	15.5.6	21
14.6.18	229	15.5.8	18
14.6.21	159	15.5.11	238
14.6.23	227	15.5.12	13
14.7.4	248	15.5.13	68
14.7.5	229	15.5.16	44, 97, 115, 119
14.7.6	115	15.5.17	117
14.7.7	196	15.5.18	126
14.7.8	158	15.5.19	64
14.7.9	21, 57, 98, 252	15.5.20	64
14.7.10	36	15.5.24	118, 174
14.7.11	67, 111	15.5.25	239
14.7.12	6, 33	15.5.27	119
14.7.14	133	15.5.29	169
14.7.18	235	15.5.31	106
14.7.19	179	15.5.35	173
14.8.4	27	15.5.36	5
14.8.5	147	15.5.38	199
14.8.7	250	15.6.2	132
14.8.11	43	15.6.3	234
14.9.1	9, 149	15.7.3	191
14.9.6	149	15.7.4	164
14.10.1	134	15.7.5	147, 166
14.10.3	124	15.7.6	163
14.10.4	67	15.7.10	130
14.10.5	14	15.8.4	92
14.10.6	242	15.8.5	113, 114
14.10.8	4, 21	15.8.5–8	113

15.8.6	117	16.12.15	169
15.8.10	120	16.12.17	144
15.8.13	235	16.12.20	125
15.8.15	127, 128	16.12.21	137
15.8.16	62	16.12.23	74
15.8.19	143	16.12.26	139, 181
15.11.1–18	68, 236	16.12.27	161
15.11.3	4	16.12.29	150
15.11.7	236	16.12.35	65
15.11.8	122	16.12.36	74, 136
15.11.11	242, 243	16.12.38	166, 172
16.1.1	125	16.12.41	150
16.2.1	166	16.12.43	123
16.2.2	247	16.12.44	158
16.2.5	157	16.12.49	115
16.2.6	118, 158, 170, 171, 172, 247	16.12.50	117
16.2.7	124, 171	16.12.51	163
16.2.8	46	16.12.58	153
16.2.9	144, 172	16.12.63	123
16.2.13	172	16.12.64	89
16.3.1–2	236	17.1.2	136
16.4.3	53	17.1.4	242
16.5.13	126	17.1.5	27
16.6.1	138	17.1.10	251
16.6.3	126	17.1.12	138
16.7.2	214	17.1.13	148
16.7.4	174	17.1.14	72, 123, 190
16.7.6	245	17.2.1	150, 193, 236
16.7.8	93	17.2.2	87, 183
16.8.1	157	17.2.3	86, 242
16.8.5	64	17.3.1	163, 240
16.8.11	107	17.3.2	57, 175
16.9.4	70	17.3.4	57
16.10.1	132	17.3.5	186, 230
16.10.2	206	17.4.2	153
16.10.4	220	17.4.3	230
16.10.5	125	17.4.5	13
16.10.8	156, 157	17.4.7	118, 174
16.10.9	171	17.4.9	135
16.10.11	150	17.4.14	190
16.10.14	80	17.4.15	27
16.10.16	74, 147	17.5.2	175
16.10.17	82	17.5.3	159
16.11.4	74, 203	17.5.6	18
16.11.6	8, 231	17.5.8	166, 175
16.11.7	11, 185	17.5.11	185
16.12.1	108	17.6.1	105
16.12.3	229	17.7.2	41
16.12.4	6	17.7.3	146
16.12.5	121, 239	17.7.4	94, 196
16.12.7	156	17.7.5	119
16.12.9–12	127	17.7.8	123
16.12.10	129	17.7.9	26
16.12.12	118, 129, 137	17.7.10	44
16.12.13	128	17.8.1	236
16.12.14	57	17.8.2	123

17.8.3	238	18.5.8	179
17.8.4	238	18.6.2	125
17.9.1	190	18.6.5	247
17.9.2	67, 152	18.6.6	124
17.9.3	109	18.6.8	53, 149
17.10.1	196	18.6.12	126
17.10.3	19	18.6.16	226
17.10.5	98	18.6.17	9
17.10.7	179	18.6.18	17
17.10.9	67	18.6.19	2
17.10.10	74	18.6.20	153
17.11.1	119, 132	18.7.1	136
17.11.3	173	18.7.2	110
17.11.4	225	18.7.6	138, 167
17.12.9	68	18.7.7	235
17.12.11	139	18.8.14	170
17.12.15	19	18.9.1	251
17.12.17	231	18.9.3	148, 155
17.12.19	177	18.9.4	159
17.12.21	126	18.10.1	152, 154
17.13.1	236	18.10.1–3	135
17.13.2	207	19.1.2	156
17.13.3	180	19.1.3	103
17.13.5	132	19.1.4–5	156
17.13.6	193, 206	19.1.6	171, 248
17.13.9	44	19.1.7	166
17.13.11	27	19.2.5	168
17.13.16	125	19.2.7	167, 171
17.13.20	45	19.2.8	145
17.13.23	15	19.2.9	137
17.13.24	119	19.2.15	72
17.13.26	113	19.3.1	7
17.13.26–33	113	19.3.1	148
17.13.27	239	19.3.2	100
17.13.28	119	19.4.6	185
17.13.29	158	19.5.1	140
17.13.33	190	19.5.4	174
17.13.34	276	19.5.5	139, 146
18.2.2	149	19.5.6	106
18.2.3	135, 237	19.6.3	185
18.2.3–4	236	19.6.4	108
18.2.4	57, 237	19.6.9	161
18.2.7	5	19.7.2	167
18.2.11	132	19.7.3	160
18.2.12	242	19.7.5	170
18.2.14	160	19.7.6	45
18.2.17	236	19.8.2	91
18.3.2	245	19.8.4	147, 173
18.4.1	135	19.8.5	72
18.4.7	44	19.8.6	159
18.5.1	135	19.8.10	221
18.5.2	76	19.8.12	250
18.5.3	240	19.9.1	160
18.5.4–5	9	19.9.2	14, 149, 152
18.5.5	9, 15	19.9.3–8	135
18.5.7	137, 251	19.9.5	111, 163, 175

19.9.7	218	25.3.15	133
19.9.9	152	25.3.17	120
19.10.1	94, 149	25.4.13	116
19.11.1	108, 239	25.6.10	182
19.11.2	1	25.10.7	129
19.11.4	149	25.10.15	125
19.11.6	3, 130	25.10.17	132
19.11.7	139, 179, 180	26.2.2	92
19.11.13	114	26.2.6–10	113
19.11.17	179	26.2.9	247
19.12.9	60	26.5.15	178
19.12.10	111, 132	26.6.16	127, 128
19.12.17	117	26.8.11	143
19.12.19	246	26.10.4	143
21.1.4	94, 119	27.1.1	239
21.1.7–14	132	27.4.1	181
21.4.6	239	27.6.15	234
21.5.2–8	113, 124, 127	27.6.6–9	113
21.7.1	237	27.7.8	130
21.7.2	235	27.8.6	7
21.8.1	240	27.9.7	239
21.10.8	225	27.12.5	249
21.12.10	168, 170	27.12.8	143
21.13.10–15	113	28.1.3	177
22.8.8	179	28.1.18	101
22.10.1	117	28.1.20	134
22.13.1–5	165	28.6.3	239
23.3.8	149	29.1.6	215
23.4.1–13	138, 143	29.1.24	177
23.4.2	166	29.2.8	246
23.4.4–7	167	29.5.1	178
23.4.11	170	29.5.19	239
23.4.14	144	29.5.20	99
23.5.16	113	29.6.6	239
23.5.18	114, 157, 174	30.1.2	133
23.5.21	247	30.2.6	130
23.6.7	239	30.2.8	239
23.6.15	240	30.5.18	132
23.6.16	145	30.9.3	125
23.6.23	168	31.1.3	132
24.1.1	117	31.5.7	130
24.2.12	154, 168	31.5.17	239
24.3.4	173, 182	31.7.4	239
24.4.10	154	31.9.3	239
24.4.21	140	31.10.21	97, 98
24.4.25	173	31.12.8	130
25.1.13	168	31.14.2	125
25.2.3	130, 133, 149	31.14.6	247
25.3.10	128	31.15.3	235

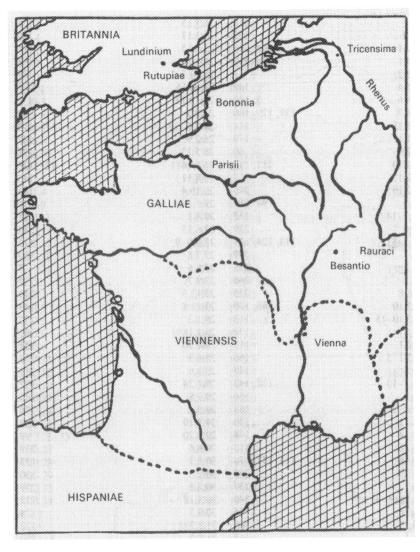

1 The Praetorian Prefecture of Gaul

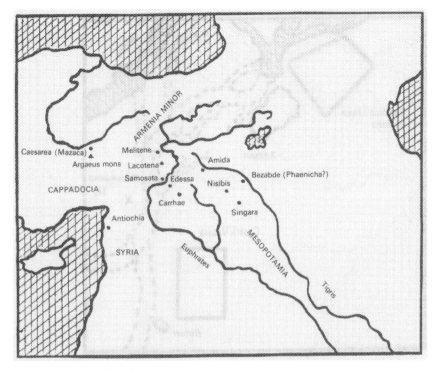

II General map of the East

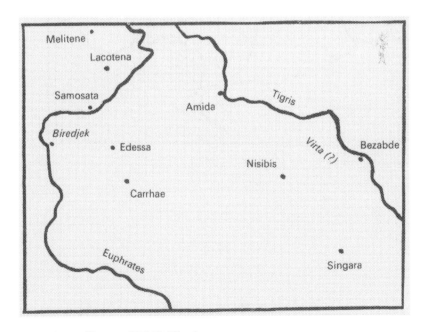

III Map to illustrate 20.7.17 (Virta)

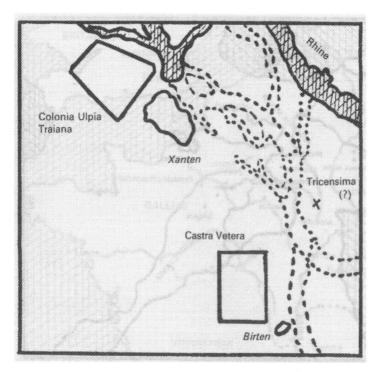

IV The site of Tricensima (20.10.1), after Westermann's Atlas